80386/80286 ASSEMBLY LANGUAGE PROGRAMMING

William H. Murray III
and
Chris H. Pappas

Osborne **McGraw-Hill**
Berkeley, California

Osborne **McGraw-Hill**
2600 Tenth Street
Berkeley, California 94710
U.S.A.

For information on translations and book distributors outside of the U.S.A., please write to Osborne **McGraw-Hill** at the above address.

A complete list of trademarks appears on page 539.

80386/80286 ASSEMBLY
LANGUAGE PROGRAMMING

 234567890   DODO   8987

ISBN 0-07-881217-8

Jon Erickson, Acquisitions Editor
Lyn Cordell, Project Editor
Yashi Okita, Cover Design

Dedicated to our fathers

William H. Murray, Jr.
Christ Pappas

who have quietly, with their faith,
support, and integrity, committed
their lives to our development

CONTENTS

ACKNOWLEDGMENTS

Writing a book can be an arduous job if proper support is not present. That support must come from publishers, software and hardware vendors, and even from the software itself.

In the preparation of this manuscript we have been given the most gratifying support from the people at Osborne/McGraw-Hill. Recognition must go to Mark Haas for his original faith in us as a writing team, and to Phil Robinson and Kevin Shafer for their technical expertise, which supported Mark's vision. Special thanks go to Jon Erickson, Senior Editor, who is our chief contact and friend. Jon Erickson made the difference in this project. Jon was always ready to help with software procurement, search for current literature, and offer suggestions.

Many vendors supplied software for testing. The chief vendors for assembler packages are Speedware (Turbo Editasm), Microsoft (MASM), and IBM (MASM). Intel Corporation, particularly Tim Keating, supplied technical information on the 80286/80287 microprocessors and advanced information on the 80386/80387 before the product was announced. The manuscript was prepared with WordPerfect, version 4.1, from Satellite Software, on two IBM AT computers. All 80286/80287 programs were tested on the same machine, running at 9 MHertz. Program development was done with the NORTON EDITOR and the IBM Professional Editor. A multitasking environment aided testing and manuscript development. DESQview, version 1.2, by Quarterdeck Office Systems, brought many enhanced features to the multitasking environment.

COMPAQ Computer Corporation also supplied a COMPAQ DESKPRO 286 for program testing and editing. A special thanks to Jim Eckhart and Jeff Stives.

A diskette is available containing all of the program listings in this book (.ASM and .MAC files only) with the exception of the program for switching modes. In addition to the listings in the book, several other programs are also included for equivalent graphics work on the EGA (Enhanced Graphics Adapter). To use the diskette, you will need an IBM PC, AT, or equivalent with at least one DSDD disk drive. To edit files, you will need EDLIN or one of the full screen editors recommended in the book. To assemble the programs, you will need one of the macro assemblers recommended in the book. Please make sure your equipment meets the above specifications and those given in the book before ordering the diskette.

Send a bank check, money order, or personal check for $29.95 to the address on the coupon below. Please allow four weeks for personal checks to clear. No purchase orders, please.

Please send me the *80386/80286 Assembly Language Programming* listings on disk. My $29.95 payment is enclosed.

_____ check　　　　_____ money order

Name _____
Address _____
City _____ State _____ ZIP _____

Nineveh National Research, P.O. Box 2943, Binghamton, New York 13902

INTRODUCTION

This book is designed to achieve three goals: (1) to introduce you to the powerful world of assembly language programming, using the 80386/80286 microprocessors and 80387/80287 coprocessors; (2) to teach you how to write both simple and advanced assembly language programs; and (3) to serve as a reference book of both programming instructions and example programs.

The 80386/80286 assembly language is a powerful outgrowth of earlier languages written in 8088/8086 assembly language. Many of the programs presented in this book will also run on the 8088/8086 family of computers. This is due, primarily, to the fact that all members of the 80xxx Intel family are upwardly compatible. Basic instructions and features are common to both the early microprocessors and to this latest series. As future releases of DOS provide access to higher-level programming features such as "protected mode" programming, the gap will widen between earlier and later versions.

Assembly language is a powerful language that gives the programmer absolute control over the computer. High-level compiled languages such as Pascal, Ada, FORTRAN and others leave the programmer at the mercy of the compiler's author. If the writer supports a feature, such as polling the game adapter, okay, but if not, what do you do? In assembly language, you can write your own routine or take advantage of powerful BIOS routines supplied by computer manufacturers. As a matter of fact, a great majority of assembly language programs are patches to high-level languages that add features the original authors overlooked.

This book teaches programming by example—by complete example. Every program listing is complete with all necessary overhead. In other words, if you type the code exactly as it appears, the program will execute. There are no abbreviated examples and no partial listings to save space. Every effort has been made to present, explain, and document each program in a way that will enhance your understanding of individual instructions and programming style, whether you are a novice or an expert programmer.

1

INTRODUCTION TO ASSEMBLY LANGUAGE

A study of assembly language programming can be one of the most personally rewarding and technically challenging tasks a software engineer can undertake. Having the tools and knowledge to expertly blend high-level languages with various hardware configurations makes you the master of your machine. The command and intimate control of peripherals, memory management, speed, code efficiency, data security, and more await the assembly language programmer. Mastery of assembly language programming requires experience and attention to detail.

Unless you are involved in a specialized area of software development, such as dedicated processor design, assembly language will be your most powerful second language. Since it gives the programmer direct access to registers, memory, and the unique world of bit-oriented instructions, assembly language is often the only solution to programming tasks that lie beyond the scope of most high-level languages.

An assembly language program will produce the fastest executable code because it bypasses the language-interpreter step (as with APL and BASIC) and the language-compiler step (as with Pascal, PL/I, C, and Modula-2). This speed advantage does come at a price, however.

Assembler programmers must pay close attention to details. An assembly language program controls the microprocessor in its own language, without the help of compiler checks. As a result of the very basic operations provided by the assembler, which performs simple tasks of data movement, comparisons, and logical operations, one page of assembly language code pales in comparison with the esoteric finesse of one page of high-level language code. For this reason, most large programs are not written in assembly language. (The exception to the rule is a software development project financed by a major corporation that is willing to pay for the many hours required to write an extremely fast and efficient applications program.)

Speaking the machine's language requires understanding many concepts foreign to high-level language programmers. The assembly language programmer must consider the segmenting of memory. When there is direct control of memory access, minute decisions must be made. Where in memory should the program and data be stored? Is a stack needed? If so, in what portion of memory should it reside? Decisions must be made about the size (byte, word, doubleword, quadword, tenbyte) and type (string, BCD, static, dynamic, signed/unsigned, real, floating-point) of each datum. Are these data elements doubly indexed memory variables? Is the 80287/80387 math coprocessor available? Should memory variables be converted to the format required by the 80287 or 80387? Which registers should be used? Which ports access the color monitor, the monochrome monitor, and the printer? Many of these considerations are unique to assembly language programming.

MAJOR ADVANTAGES:
SPEED AND CONTROL

One of the two major advantages of assembly language is the blazing speed at which the code executes. Code that is only one mnemonic (an abbreviated symbolic representation of an actual binary machine instruction) translation away from pure machine code (the language the microprocessor understands) can execute in microseconds.

Language interpreters, such as those used for BASIC and APL, examine the source code and make line-by-line translations into machine code, calling on many built-in subroutines. These subroutines have already been written and are predefined for the microprocessor. Because expressions must be reevaluated and checked for error conditions each time the program is run, they tend to execute very slowly.

Language compilers, such as those used for Pascal, PL/I, and FOR-TRAN, read the source code and convert it into a sequence of op-codes that the microprocessor will execute directly. Compiled programs are faster than interpreted code because the translation is done only once, but there is a disadvantage to compiled programs: compilers must execute a wide variety of commands. This task usually requires considerable code overhead, even for the smallest programs. A compiled BASIC program may take 33K bytes of machine memory and disk storage to print a few characters on a monitor. The same program written in assembly language would take about one-third of that, or roughly 10K bytes.

Now we come to the second major advantage of assembly language programs. Without assembly language, the user is limited to what is offered by canned programs. For example, if someone were writing an application program dealing with highly critical data, and if the user were going to be a moderately trained data-entry person, it might be convenient to have the program inhibit the data-destroying CTRL-ALT-DEL key combination. In most cases, this can be accomplished only at the assembly language level.

Assembly language allows software engineers to interface with the operating system and gives them direct control of input and output operations to monitors, printers, and the important hard/floppy disk storage devices. Applications programmers often have to interface directly with the operating system as well. Such routines are usually written in assembly language.

80286/80386 FAMILY TREE

Many family trees have roots that are centuries old. In microprocessor design, computers are being developed at a phenomenal rate. The microprocessor "family tree" spans only a single decade. If development continues at the current rate, we'll be adding leaves to the tree every other year!

The first IC, or integrated circuit, was developed at the beginning of the 1960s. The IC tremendously reduced the size of capacitors, diodes, and transistors and placed them all on a slice of pure silicon. One decade later, Intel developed its first 8-bit microprocessor chip, the 8008. In 1974 the second-generation microprocessor, the 8080, was developed. It offered the user general-purpose capabilities. At this point the competitors entered the quickly expanding market with such products as the Zilog Z-80.

The third-generation microprocessors followed just four years later. In 1978 Intel developed the 8086. Although this chip contained some upward compatibility with its ancestor, the 8080, it was a much more advanced design, with many new features. Intel also developed the 8088 micro-processor as a variation on the 8086. The 8088 provided a slightly simpler design and included compatibility with current I/O devices. The architecture of the 8088 made it one of the most advanced microprocessors available at that time. It had so many powerful features that IBM based its entire first generation of personal computers on the 8088.

At almost the same time, a cousin of the 8088/8086 appeared: the 8087 real-number math coprocessor chip. This numeric data processor was dedicated to high speed, high precision mathematical computations.

Intel did not rest on its past successes. In mid-1984 the company made another major leap in architecture design with the development of the 80286 microprocessor. This new-generation CPU was designed primarily for applications requiring high performance. Upwardly compatible with the 8088/8086, the 80286 takes advantage of such state-of-the-art features as memory management, protection mechanisms, task management, and virtual-memory support. All of these powerful features are contained on one VLSI chip, an arrangement that provides the microcomputer user with the computational and architectural characteristics of minicomputers.

The 80286 is upwardly compatible with the 8088/8086 because of their common set of addressing modes and basic instructions. The base architecture supports high-level languages like Pascal, PL/M, and C, since the design of the register set is well suited to compiler-generated code.

The 80286 supports several very powerful data types, such as strings, BCD, and floating-point formats. The design also supports efficient addressing of such complex data structures as static/dynamic arrays, records, and arrays within records.

The memory architecture of the 80286 supports modular programming techniques, which enable the software engineer to divide memory into segments. Segmentation of memory provides shorter code, since references within a segment can be shorter. The segmentation scheme lends itself to efficient implementations of sophisticated memory management—for example, virtual memory and memory protection.

The 80286 also provides a large address space, to support today's application requirements. Real memory consists of as many as 16 megabytes (2^{24} bytes) of RAM or ROM. This much space lets the microprocessor keep many large programs and their related data structures simultaneously in memory, enabling high-speed access.

For applications with dynamically changing memory requirements such as multiuser systems, the 80286 supplies each user with as many as 2^{30} bytes (a gigabyte) of virtual address space. The large address space nearly eliminates restrictions on the number or size of programs that can be part of the system.

The Intel 80286 is designed to support multiuser, reprogrammable, and real-time multitasking applications. Microcomputer systems servicing four or five simultaneous users can now be expanded to support more than three times that number, and real-time systems can respond in one-sixth the time (or even less) than was needed before.

The latest entry (at least for now) on Intel's family tree is the 80386. The 80386's 32-bit-wide external data bus is double that of the 80286. The 80386 can address 4 gigabytes of physical memory.

WHAT YOU WILL BE ABLE TO DO ONCE YOU'VE COMPLETED THIS BOOK

After reading the text and trying programs, you will have gained a solid understanding of 80286/80386 and 80287/80387 internal architecture. You will be very familiar with the instruction set and with the internal register structure and usage. After learning assembly language, you will understand how the computer works at its most fundamental level. You will learn the advantages and disadvantages of assembly language programming and know when to incorporate or generate assembly language programs or patches. The in-depth discussions of the three assemblers — IBM, Microsoft, and Speedware — will enable you to select the assembler best suited to your particular applications.

You will learn what a pseudo-op is and when and how to use one. You will also learn how to write your own macros and procedures. This text emphasizes the principles involved in building, incorporating, and maintaining a macro subroutine library.

The many example programs in this book will show you how to access the graphics and file-manipulation features of the your computer. You will understand and be able to use the tremendous speed and precision of the 80287 and 80387 math coprocessor chips.

This text features substantial discussion of interfacing a high-level language with an assembly language patch. Reading the book will also show you how to interface with the operating system through DOS and BIOS routines.

You will learn how to test and use Debug in a program, employing several techniques. These include IBM's DEBUG facility and Microsoft's SYMDEB facility.

WHAT THIS BOOK ASSUMES YOU KNOW

This book assumes that you already know one of the more popular high-level languages, such as BASIC or Pascal. No attempt will be made to teach these languages. Familiarization with the hexadecimal number system is helpful (but not necessary), as is a basic understanding of the logical operations of AND, NAND, OR, NOR, XOR, SHIFT LEFT/RIGHT, ROTATE, COMPLEMENT, and so forth.

NUMBER SYSTEMS

Understanding how a computer stores information is critical to understanding assembly language programming. How is data represented internally? Since the computer is an electrical device, it understands only voltages. In particular, most microprocessors depend on the presence or absence of two reliable voltage levels. We can think of these voltages as being on or off, a 1 or 0. This last pair, which is the smallest unit, is also referred to as a bit.

Humans initially used the decimal numbering system because we have ten fingers. Computers understand only two unique states, represented by the two symbols 0 and 1. Naturally, this leads to a communications problem between people and computers. The development of different symbolic codes was a direct result of this language incompatibility.

ASCII (American Standard Code for Information Interchange) was invented to represent all of the symbols we commonly associate with a typewriter keyboard. Several numeric codes were invented to represent numeric values in a form the computer understands. The two's complement numbering code allows the computer to represent both positive and negative whole numbers. One of the most important numeric codes for assembly language programmers is the hexadecimal code. Hexadecimal improves the readability of information represented in binary form, whether that information is instructions, memory addresses, or data.

BINARY NUMBERS

Our decimal numbering system gets its name from the ten (deci-) unique symbols involved in the code's set: the symbols 0 through 9. Binary code has only two unique symbols: 0 and 1. This may seem like an extremely restrictive set for representing large numbers. You will quickly see that the underlying principle for binary code is something you already know!

First, let's look at a decimal number — say, 1024. We were taught in elementary school that this number has four 1's, two 10's, no 100's, and one 1000. This is a weighted numerical representation. As you move left in the number, each value has an increasing weight, or importance. There is also another way to look at the number 1024. Our decimal, or base 10, number can be thought of in the following manner:

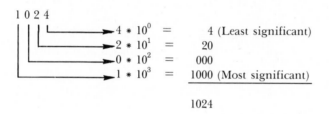

$$
\begin{array}{lll}
4 * 10^0 & = & 4 \text{ (Least significant)} \\
2 * 10^1 & = & 20 \\
0 * 10^2 & = & 000 \\
1 * 10^3 & = & 1000 \text{ (Most significant)}
\end{array}
$$

1024

We made the conversion by multiplying each numeral in the number by the base value raised to the appropriate exponential power. The powers increase as we move from the least-significant position to the most-significant position.

This same principle of conversion will work for any binary number. The binary number 1010, when converted to decimal code, looks like this:

$$
\begin{array}{lll}
0 * 2^0 & = & 0 \text{ (Least-significant bit)} \\
1 * 2^1 & = & 2 \\
0 * 2^2 & = & 0 \\
1 * 2^3 & = & 8 \text{ (Most-significant bit)}
\end{array}
$$

10

In this case, we used base 2 and raised our new base to the appropriate exponential power, starting with the least-significant bit (LSB) and working through to the most-significant bit (MSB). It's easy. To convert from some other base to decimal, use the same procedure described for the decimal representation of 1024 or for the binary representation of 1010. The only difference will be the other base.

We've just seen how easily you can convert a number from binary to decimal. To reverse the process, converting from decimal to binary, simply subtract exponential powers of 2 from the number to be converted. Let's say we want to convert the decimal number 11 to binary. Start by subtracting 2^3 (8) from 11. That leaves a remainder of 3. There is no 2^2 (4) left, but there is $1 - 2^1$ (2). Subtracting 2 leaves a remainder of 1. We finally subtract 2^0 (1) for a remainder of 0. This gives us a conversion of 11 decimal to 1011 binary.

An easier method that will work for larger binary numbers follows. This is a series of repeated divisions, using the base to which you want the number converted as the divisor and the number to be converted as the dividend. Converting the decimal number 50 to binary looks like this:

Dividend	Divisor	Result	Remainder	
50	2	25	0	Answer = 110010
25	2	12	1	
12	2	6	0	
6	2	3	0	
3	2	1	1	
1	2	0	1	

You can use this method to convert any decimal number to any base. To change 428 to hexadecimal, simply substitute 428 for the dividend and 16 for the divisor.

Binary Addition and Subtraction

Binary addition and subtraction are identical to decimal addition and subtraction, except that you are generating a carry or a borrow in some power of 2 rather than in some power of 10. Let's look at two examples:

25
+ 85
─────
110

In this example, when we add the two 5's we generate a carry into the next significant position, or $1 * 10^1$, thereby adding 10 to the next column. We now add 8, 2, and the carry, generate another carry to the 10^2 column, and generate a sum of 10. Bringing the new carry down gives us the result 110.

Now let's look at binary addition:

```
  1010 (10)
+ 0011  (3)
_____
  1101 (12)
```

In this example, the $0 + 1$ gives a sum of 1, with no carry. The $1 + 1$ gives a total of two, which in binary looks like 10. The 1 in the 10 is a carry to the next most-significant bit and represents $1 * 2^1$. This carry is brought down in the 2^2 column, and the 1 in the MSB is also brought down, giving the sum 1101.

The next example illustrates the only other unique possibility to be considered when adding binary numbers:

```
  0011 (3)
+ 0011 (3)
_____
  0110 (6)
```

The first two 1's generate a carry to the 2^1's column. That column already has two 1's and now includes the carry 1, giving that column three 1's. Let's look at this step more closely.

```
  1
  1
+ 1
____
 11
```

$1 + 1$ returns a binary result of 10, and when you add a 1 to 10 in binary, you get 11. You have generated a carry to the next significant bit and returned a result of 1.

Binary subtraction uses the same underlying principles as decimal subtraction. The only difference is that when a borrow is generated from the next significant position, it is the value of 2 raised to some exponential power, instead of 10 raised to some power.

```
  534
- 251
_____
  283
```

There's no difficulty in subtracting a decimal 1 from 4. When we try to subtract 5 from 3, though, we need to generate a borrow from the next significant position, or $1 * 10^2$, enabling us to subtract 50 from 130. Finally, we subtract the 2 from 4 and get the result of 283.

Now let's look at an example of binary subtraction:

```
  1011
- 0110
_____
  0101
```

In the LSB, there's no problem subtracting 0 from 1. Nor is there any difficulty in the next significant bit position, subtracting 1 from 1. We do have a problem subtracting 1 from a 0. This requires a borrow to the next significant bit, which happens to be $1 * 2^3$, or 8, in decimal. We can now subtract the $1 * 2^2$, leaving a difference of $1 * 2^2$. This gives us the 1 in the third column and a final result of 0101.

Bytes

Before we can continue our discussion of different numbering systems, we have to remember that all of our programs and data are stored and executed on a hardware device called a computer. To some degree the computer architecture will determine the format and range for both the code and the data.

Computers do not randomly store varying-length binary numbers or bits. In the 80286 architecture, a hardware memory location is a sequence of eight consecutive bits, known as a byte.

The bit positions are numbered from the LSB (least-significant bit), 0, to the MSB (most-significant bit), 7. Figure 1-1 shows several consecutive memory locations, each holding one byte's worth of information. This information could be a machine instruction, an address to another memory location, or numeric or character data.

Eight bits can generate 256 unique states. This allows one memory location to contain the binary representation for all positive numbers between 0 and 255. It can also hold one ASCII character (see the appendixes for the ASCII character chart). A *word* is the technical way of referring to the number of bits stored in a single memory location. Early computer architectures only had 4-bit memory locations. For this early design, a word represented four bits. Some computers have a memory location capable of storing 64 bits. In such a case, a word would refer to a 64-bit string. With 80286 architecture, a word is 16 bits. An 8-bit byte can be broken down into two 4-bit groupings called nibbles. A nibble can also represent one hexadecimal number.

Characters

The 8 bits in a byte don't always have to represent numeric values. ASCII is a 7-bit code that allows the representation of alphabetic and numeric characters. It assigns an arbitrary binary representation to each letter, digit, and special character associated with what we think of as a standard typewriter keyboard. It also includes representations for special control codes.

The 7-bit code can represent 128 unique symbols and codes. The eighth bit is sometimes used for a data transmission and retrieval error-detection code. Some manufacturers of character ROM chips use this eighth bit to access an extended character set. Adding an additional bit effectively doubles the number of uniquely representable symbols to 256. This allows the representation of special foreign-language symbols, mathematical symbols and, what is very important, graphics symbols.

Signed Numbers

With the 8-bit byte architecture of the 80286 as our hardware template, let's take a closer look at integer data representation. When all 8 bits are used to represent positive whole numbers, then we can represent values from 0 (00000000) to 255 (11111111). Adding 1 to 255 (11111111) brings us full circle, back to 0 (00000000).

Representing positive and negative whole numbers then becomes a compromise, because somehow we have to indicate the sign of the number, using only 8 bits. The only way to do this is to take one of the bit positions to indicate the sign of the value. This leaves 7 bits to represent the numeric value. 2^7 lets us represent values from 0 (0000000) to 127 (1111111). Since we

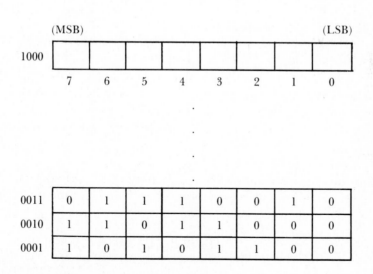

Figure 1-1.

An example of consecutive memory locations

are dealing with binary values, reducing the number of bits by 1 effectively halves the range of unique states.

The sign-magnitude data representation takes the most-significant bit to hold the sign of the value. A 0 in the MSB represents a positive number, and a 1 in the MSB indicates a negative number.

0000 0101	represents a +5
1000 0101	represents a −5

What about the numeric value 0? Theoretically, we could have:

0000 0000	representing a +0
1000 0000	representing a −0

As you might guess, having our 8-bit byte used for this data-storage format will require a new set of rules and arithmetic. The first of these specifies that the numeric value 0 will always be represented as positive: 0000 0000.

Because the number of bits used to represent the value of a number has been reduced to 7, we can talk only about values between 0 and + or − 127.

0000 0000	+0
− 0000 0001	+1
1111 1111	−127

This example did not give us the correct result. To do arithmetic operations on numbers represented in sign-magnitude, we really need 1111 1111 to represent a −1. Another example will show a different way to subtract.

1111 1110	−2
− 0000 0010	+2
1111 1100	−4

If you were to do a binary conversion of 1111 1100, assuming that the MSB is reserved for the sign of the number, then 111 1100 is equivalent to 124. The 1 in the MSB indicates that this is a negative number, −124. Why does the example just shown indicate that the result is −4? Read on.

Two's Complement

For addition and subtraction to work properly on numbers stored in sign-magnitude notation, the numbers must be represented in what is called two's complement form.

The examples just discussed lead to an understanding of the need for representing positive and negative numbers as follows:

0000 0100	+4
0000 0011	+3
0000 0010	+2
0000 0001	+1
0000 0000	0
1111 1111	−1
1111 1110	−2
1111 1101	−3
1111 1100	−4

Note that this format continues to reserve the MSB for the sign of the number. When doing addition and subtraction of two's complement numbers, remember that the result will also be in two's complement form. For example:

	0000 0100	+4	
+	1111 1101	−3	
1)	0000 0001	+1	(The carry generated is ignored)

To generate the negative two's complement representation of a value, you invert each bit and add +1. The following example will show how to change the sign of +5.

	0000 0101	+5
	1111 1010	(Each bit is complemented)
+	0000 0001	(A +1 is added)
	1111 1011	−5

Converting in the opposite direction is just as easy. Let's convert a −4 to its positive counterpart

```
1111 1100   −4

0000 0011   (Each bit is complemented)
+ 0000 0001   (A +1 is added)
──────────
0000 0100   +4
```

One last example:

```
  1111 1001   −7   (Two's complement notation)
+ 1111 1000   −8   (Two's complement notation)
──────────
1) 1111 0001   −15  (Two's complement notation)
```

SIGN EXTENDING

Since the internal data registers on the 80286 are 16 bits wide and one memory location is one byte, it is quite possible that at some point in a program you will need to add numbers of two different sizes. You may want to add an 8-bit-wide two's complement number, represented in sign-magnitude notation, to a 16-bit number stored in the same data format.

```
        0000 0101   +5
+ 1111 1111 1111 1101   −3
```

In this example, we would just append 0000 0000 to the most-significant bits of +5. What if we were dealing with an 8-bit negative number?

```
        1111 1111   −1
+ 0000 0000 0000 0100   +4
```

Since our 8-bit value was negative, we'd append eight 1's: 1111 1111. The general rule in sign extending is to append eight 1's or 0's to the most significant bits, depending upon the sign value of the number. Extending our two 8-bit values would give us:

0000 0000 0000 0101   (16-bit representation of +5)

1111 1111 1111 1111   (16-bit representation of −1)

HEXADECIMAL NUMBERS

The hexadecimal number system gets its name from the 16 unique symbols that define its set. Hexadecimal numbers are useful in reading or writing assembly language code, data, and memory dumps because we can substitute one hexadecimal symbol for each 4-bit binary group.

Hexadecimal numbers contain the symbols 0 through 9, plus, A, B, C, D, E, and F. Table 1-1 shows relationships among the decimal, binary, and hexadecimal codes.

One or two quick examples should prove why hexadecimal numbers are so useful. If a programmer were to dump several consecutive memory locations, the printout might look like this:

10010110
11100011
10101011
00101100

The same information displayed in hexadecimal would look like this:

96
E3
AB
2C

Obviously, the second list would be easier to scan and check. Converting binary to hexadecimal numbers is very straightforward. Starting with the least-significant bit and moving left, group the 1's and 0's into 4-bit nibbles. Convert each nibble to its decimal equivalent and then map to hexadecimal. Figure 1-2 shows this procedure.

Converting from hexadecimal to decimal uses the same underlying principles discussed earlier for converting from binary to decimal. Figure

Decimal	Binary	Hexadecimal
0	0000	0
1	0001	1
2	0010	2
3	0011	3
4	0100	4
5	0101	5
6	0110	6
7	0111	7
8	1000	8
9	1001	9
10	1010	A
11	1011	B
12	1100	C
13	1101	D
14	1110	E
15	1111	F

Table 1-1.

Decimal, Binary, and Hexadecimal Representations of the Same Numbers

10100110

Step 1. Divide the byte into two nibbles.

1010   0110

Step 2. Convert each nibble into its decimal equivalent.

10   6

Step 3. Map to hexadecimal.

A   6

Figure 1-2.

Binary to hexadecimal conversion

1-3 shows how to convert FACE to decimal. Just a reminder: FACE or 64206, represented in binary, would look like this:

1111101011001110

Or it would look like

11111010   11001110

if stored in two memory locations. The above binary number translated into hexadecimal is, FA CE.

BEYOND BYTES:
OTHER BIT GROUPINGS

The eight bits of a byte don't even begin to comfortably handle all assembly language programming problems. Other ways of organizing bits are vital for work on the 80286 and the 80386.

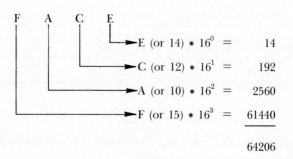

F   A   C   E

$\quad$ E (or 14) $* 16^{0}$ = $\quad$ 14

$\quad$ C (or 12) $* 16^{1}$ = $\quad$ 192

$\quad$ A (or 10) $* 16^{2}$ = $\quad$ 2560

$\quad$ F (or 15) $* 16^{3}$ = $\quad$ 61440

$\qquad\qquad\qquad\qquad$ 64206

Figure 1-3. _____

Hexadecimal to binary conversion

WORDS

Since the 80286 is a 16-bit microprocessor and operates most efficiently on 16-bit values, we'll combine two bytes to form a word, as shown in Figure 1-4. A word will allow us to go beyond the unsigned integer value of 255, or FF in hexadecimal, to 65535, or FFFF. The assembler actually stores and manipulates integers as words. Memory locations of string data and integer variables are kept track of by 16-bit address pointers, from 0000H to FFFFH. This is one K-byte or the multiple of 2 closest to 1000. It is actually 1,024 × 64 or 65,536 (decimal) bits.

When an integer word is stored in memory, the two bytes are stored in reverse order. The least-significant byte (LSB) is stored first, and the most-significant byte (MSB) is stored in the next highest address in memory. Just

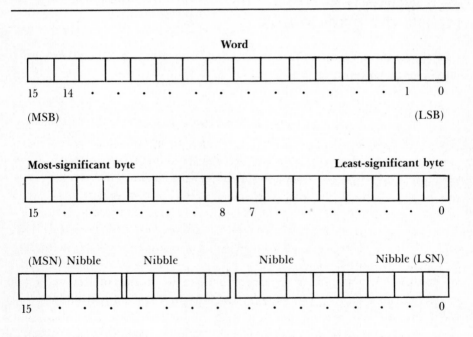

Figure 1-4. _____

The bits, nibbles, and bytes of a word

remember that the lower-order byte is stored at the lower address and the higher-order byte at the higher address. For example, storing the value 3456H in memory would look like this:

Memory Address	Value
0000 0001	34H
0000 0000	56H

Under most circumstances, the assembly language programmer doesn't need to worry about this addressing/storage scheme. All memory instructions understand the storage format and make all of the necessary transfers. The programmer does need to be aware of this storage method in tracing through memory, as in a memory dump. Programs like CodeSmith-86, Trace-86, and DiskLook make this possible. As far as the microprocessor is concerned, it is seeing a 16-bit word, not two 8-bit bytes.

DOUBLEWORDS

A doubleword is exactly what it sounds like: two words. Doublewords are 32 bits wide—as shown in Figure 1-5—and are made up of two consecutively stored adjacent words. This is a very important data format because it is vital to the addressing range of the 80286 and allows it to access more than a million bytes of memory. For this reason, the assembly language programmer will be working with 32-bit doublewords as pointers to data within memory. The 32-bit doubleword also allows arithmetic operations to take advantage of additional precision because of the field width. This 32-bit data can represent very large and small numbers in both the integer and floating-point formats.

Doublewords are stored in an arrangement similar to that used for words. In this case, the lower-order word is stored at the lower address and the higher-order word at the next highest memory location. The 32-bit doubleword is stored as a series of four bytes, starting with the LSB and ending with the MSB. The number 12345678H stored in memory would look like the following.

Memory Address	Value
0000 0011	12 (MSB)
0000 0010	34
0000 0001	56
0000 0000	78 (LSB)

16-bit word (upper)
16-bit word (lower)
Doubleword

QUADWORDS

If a doubleword won't give you the numerical precision you need, then a quadword may solve the problem. A quadword is four words and can be used to store very large numbers or character strings. The storage scheme, as shown in Figure 1-6, is consistent with all previous examples. The least-significant word is stored at the lowest memory location and the most-significant word is stored in the highest consecutive memory address. The number 1234567890ABCDEF stored in memory is shown in Figure 1-6.

TENBYTES

A tenbyte, like a doubleword, is exactly what it sounds like. It is an 80-bit value that can be used to store extremely large numbers or character data. It is the largest defined data type for the 80286 microprocessor. Its storage scheme is identical in structure to that of quadwords and doublewords. The LSB is stored at the lower memory location and the MSB is stored in the highest consecutive memory address.

80386 DATA TYPES

In addition to the data types supported by the 8088, 8086, and 80286, the 80386 architecture supports 32-bit signed and unsigned integers and bit fields from 1 to 32 bits in length. The pointer types supported by the 8088, 8086, and 80286 have also been extended to a 32-bit offset-only pointer and to a 48-bit full pointer. Two new variable types, DBIT (one bit) and DP (48 bits), help support the 80386's data types. These will be discussed in Chapter 6.

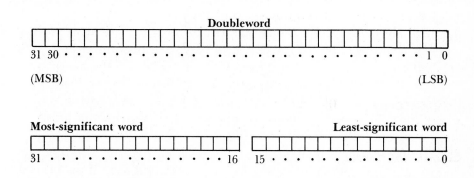

Figure 1-5. _____
The bytes and words of a doubleword

Memory address	Value
0000 0111	12H (MSB)
0000 0110	34H
0000 0101	56H
0000 0100	78H
0000 0011	90H
0000 0010	ABH
0000 0001	CDH
0000 0000	EFH (LSB)

32-bit doubleword

32-bit doubleword

Figure 1-6. _____
A quadword in memory

NONSTANDARD BIT FIELDS

Most of the data an assembly language programmer encounters will fall under one of the previously defined types. There are exceptions. For example, the designers of PC-DOS, not wanting to waste memory utilization, decided to store the date stamp in a unique configuration. By examining the range of values that the year, month, and day fields actually required, they were able to represent a date stamp with only one 16-bit word. The designers dedicated 7 bits to the year field. Theoretically, this arrangement allows the representation of 0 through 127. In actuality, the range is restricted to from 0 to 119, and this value is added to a base of 1980. Since there are only 12 months, 4 bits were allocated to represent this field. The maximum number of days to be considered was 31, and 5 bits generate an ample range of 0 through 32.

Other nonstandard bit divisions involve computer graphic applications. Here, a single bit can represent a dot on the monitor screen. If the bit is 0, the phosphor dot is off. A 1 in the bit indicates that the phosphor is on.

Even this phosphor mapping can vary from system to system. For instance, what if you want to indicate the color of a phosphor if it is on? Allocating 2 bits to a phosphor description enables the phosphor's condition to be described as either off or on, in three different colors.

All of these special nonstandard bit configurations must be considered in storing, accessing, and manipulating binary data. Additional care must be taken in interpreting memory and program dumps.

BINARY OPERATIONS

A close examination of a microprocessor executing even the simplest operations of addition and subtraction will reveal nothing more than a repeated series of bit comparisons. It is true that the CPU includes various "adder circuits," but ultimately even these circuits rely on bit-by-bit comparisons.

These bit-by-bit comparisons involve a very simple process, since there can be only three possible bit-pair combinations. Both of the bits can be a 0, either one of the two bits may be a 1, or both of the bits may be a 1. Whether the operation to be performed is addition, subtraction, multiplication, or division, a simple series of repeated comparisons, based on the above three bit-pair combinations, is applied.

In the case of addition, the following rules are applied, starting from the least-significant bit (LSB):

- Adding two 0 bits sets the Sum flag to 0

- If only one of the bits is a 1, the Sum flag is a 1

• If both bits are a 1, the Sum flag is set to 0 and the Carry flag is set to 1.

This process is repeated on each successive bit, with the operator taking into consideration any previous carries. The CPU keeps track of each individual comparison in an internal storage area, and the result looks to us like binary addition. Actually, this process was nothing more than repeated bit comparisons.

Although the CPU is hardwired to perform these operations of addition, subtraction, multiplication, and division, the assembly language programmer has access to other bit-comparison operations. These operations include logical AND, OR, XOR, SHIFT LEFT, SHIFT RIGHT, ROTATE LEFT, ROTATE RIGHT, and COMPLEMENT. With the logical operations of AND, OR, and COMPLEMENT, it is helpful to see the bit representations as True or False flags, rather than as numeric values.

The logical AND operation compares two bits. If both bits are 1's, the result is a 1. Note that this is different from binary addition, in which the comparison of two 1 bits would result in a Sum flag set to 0 and the Carry flag set to 1.

Logical AND

Bit 0	Bit 1	Result
0	0	0
0	1	0
1	0	0
1	1	1

Very often, the AND operation is used to select out or "mask" certain bit positions. One example of this would be to clear the most-significant four bits of an unpacked decimal number before performing a decimal multiplication or division. This would be accomplished by ANDing the unpacked decimal number to 0000 1111.

```
        1010 0011
AND     0000 1111 (MASK)
       ───────────
        0000 0011
```

The logical OR operation compares two bits and generates a 1 result if either or both bits are a 1. The OR operation is useful for setting specified bit positions.

Logical OR

Bit 0	Bit 1	Result
0	0	0
0	1	1
1	0	1
1	1	1

For example, we can set the most-significant bit (MSB) in an 8-bit number by ORing the number with 1000 0000.

```
        0001 1010
OR      1000 0000
        ─────────
        1001 1010
```

The EXCLUSIVE OR operation compares two bits and returns a result of 1 only when the two bits are complementary. This logical operation can be very useful when it is necessary to complement specified bit positions, as in the case of computer graphics applications.

EXCLUSIVE OR

Bit 0	Bit 1	Result
0	0	0
0	1	1
1	0	1
1	1	0

In the following example, the middle four bits of the 8-bit number will be complemented by EXCLUSIVE ORing them with 0011 1100:

```
          1010 0110
EX. OR    0011 1100
          ─────────
          1001 1010
```

SHIFT LEFT/RIGHT, ROTATE LEFT/RIGHT, and COMPLEMENT operate on single operands. The SHIFT instructions provide an excellent method for efficiently doubling or halving a number. This method requires fewer bytes and fewer machine cycles than an actual multiplication or division instruction would need.

With unsigned numbers, shifting a number one position to the left and filling the LSB with a 0 will double the number's value.

SHL	0100 0001	(65 decimal)
	1000 0010	(130 decimal)

Halving an unsigned number is as simple as shifting the bits one position to the right and filling the MSB position with a 0.

SHR	0000 1010	(10 decimal)
	0000 0101	(5 decimal)

The ROTATE instructions provide the ability to rearrange the bits in a number. Like the SHIFT operations, this one can be done in a LEFT or RIGHT direction. Unlike the SHIFT operations, which lose the bit position that was SHIFTed out left or right, the ROTATE operation moves the bit that falls off one end and rotates it to fill the position vacated on the other end:

ROR	0000 1111	(Rotate right)
	1000 0111	

ROL	0000 1111	(Rotate left)
	0001 1110	

ADDRESSING TECHNIQUES

An 80286/80386 instruction not only contains information about the particular operation to be performed but also includes the specifications for the type of operands to be manipulated, as well as the location of these operands. There are eight major modes of addressing:

1. Immediate addressing
2. Register addressing

3. Direct addressing

4. Register indirect addressing

5. Based addressing

6. Direct indexed addressing

7. Base indexed addressing, with or without displacement

8. 80386 extensions.

IMMEDIATE ADDRESSING

The microprocessor decodes which addressing mode is being referenced by the syntax of the operation. For example, if the instruction is written

```
MOV    AH,00

MOV    AL,04
```

then the operand value is contained within the instruction. Here, the AH register is zeroed out (00) and the AL register is loaded with 0000 0100 in binary. It should be mentioned that the 80386 microprocessor also accepts 32-bit-wide operands. The following example moves a 16-bit-wide source operand (a 0 must precede any hexadecimal letter) into the AX register:

```
MOV    AX,0FFFFH
```

In utilizing the Immediate addressing mode, all operand values are sign-extended as necessary. This means that the most-significant bit of the operand value is replicated to complete the bit width of the destination operand. For example:

```
MOV    AX,302
```

This instruction would take the 10-bit binary equivalent of 302, 0100101110, and extend the value to the 16-bit destination operand width by replicating the '0' sign-bit into the most-significant bit field of the AX register, 0000000100101110.

```
MOV    AL,−40
```

Sign extending also applies to 8-bit source and destination operands. In the above example, the 7-bit representation of −40, 1011000, is extended to eight bits, 11011000.

REGISTER ADDRESSING

With register addressing, the source operand's value has already been stored in one of the 80286/80386's internal storage registers. This can be an 8-bit value, 16-bit value, or, in the case of the 80386, a 32-bit value. The microprocessor interprets the width of the operand by the name of the register. For example:

    MOV   DS,AX

This register addressing mode instructs the microprocessor to take the 16-bit contents of the source operand (AX register) and move them into the 16-bit DS register. This mode can also be employed with 8-bit source and destination registers, as follows:

    MOV   DL,AL

Of the eight major addressing modes, immediate addressing and register addressing take the fewest machine cycles to execute. Since the operand data can be included within the instruction itself and since operand data is already stored internally, all time-consuming external memory or external device accessing is avoided.

The other six addressing modes require more execution time, since the microprocessor must calculate the address of the operand on the basis of segment address, segment offset, and possibly base register or index register contents. This derived operand address is referred to as the operand's effective address, or EA.

DIRECT ADDRESSING

With direct addressing, the segment offset of the operand is contained in the instruction as a 16-bit quantity. This offset is added to the shifted contents of the data segment (DS) register and returns the 20-bit EA, or actual physical address. Usually, the direct addressing operand is a label.

For example, the instruction in Figure 1-7 forces the microprocessor to load the AX register with the contents of the memory location pointed to by the memory address associated with the label MYDATA. Notice how the microprocessor stores the low-order byte at the lower memory address and the high-order byte at the higher memory address.

REGISTER INDIRECT ADDRESSING

With register indirect addressing, instead of the source operand's address being referenced by a label, the operand value is pointed to by an offset address stored in one of the following registers: SI (source index), DI (destination index), BX (base register), or, under some circumstances, the BP (base pointer).

The microprocessor recognizes register indirect addressing by the syntax of the instruction. The source operand's designator is surrounded by square brackets [ ]. The example in Figure 1-8 would have worked only if the BX register had been loaded with the offset address of MYDATA. This could have been accomplished by using the OFFSET operator as follows:

MOV   BX,OFFSET MYDATA

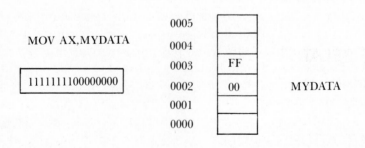

Figure 1-7.
Direct addressing

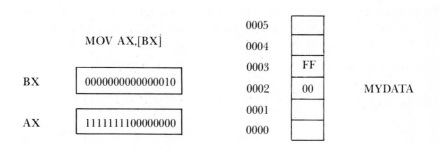

Figure 1-8. _____

Register indirect addressing

Or it could have been done with the LEA (load effective address) instruction:

    LEA   BX,MYDATA

Register indirect addressing can be used for referencing data stored in table format. Thus, accessing individual values becomes more efficient—a cycle of incrementing the base register and accessing the memory location, rather than going through the more time consuming cycle of fetching an address from memory and then accessing the source operand.

BASE RELATIVE ADDRESSING

The effective address of an operand pointed to using base relative addressing is derived by the summation of the displacement and contents of a base register (either BX or BP), relative to the selected segment. Base relative mode is most often used to access complex data structures, such as records. The base register points to the base of the structure, and a particular field is selected by the displacement. Changing the displacement accesses different fields within the record. Accessing the same field within different records is as simple as changing the contents of the base register.

In the partial code of Figure 1-9, MESGE1 contains a character string. The LEA command loads the offset address into the BX register. Referencing the fourth element of MESGE1 is accomplished by adding the base address (BX) of the MESGE1 to the displacement, +4, within the string.

The assembler does recognize the following three methods of indicating base relative addressing:

```
LEA    [BX]+4
LEA    4[BX]
LEA    [BX+4]
```

The first method is the most frequently used syntax, but the displacement may precede the base register or be included within the square brackets [ ]. Moving through MESGE1 would be accomplished by incrementing the displacement, and changing message references would be accomplished by changing the base address (BX), possibly with the following instruction:

```
LEA    BX,MESGE2
```

DIRECT INDEXED ADDRESSING

In direct indexed addressing, the offset address of the operand is calculated by adding the displacement to an index register (SI or DI) within the selected segment. Frequently, direct indexed addressing is used to access elements of a static array. The displacement value locates the beginning of the array, and the value stored in the index register selects a single element within the structure. Unlike records, whose individual field widths can vary in size and data type, array elements are homogeneous. Since the elements are of the same data type and size, moving through the array is a matter of systematically incrementing or decrementing the displacement. For example:

```
MOV    SI,4
MOV    AL,ARAY1[SI]
```

Care must be taken to select an appropriate displacement value relative to the array element's data type. The example just given would load the AL register with the fifth value of ARAY1.

```
MOV    AX,ARAY1[SI]
```

.
.
.

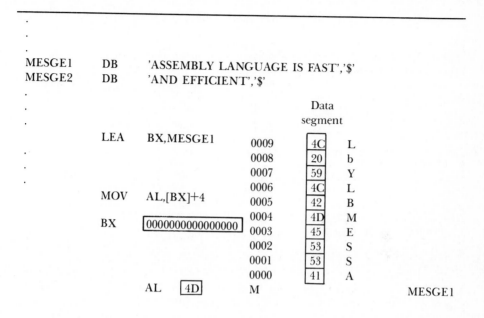

| MESGE1 | DB | 'ASSEMBLY LANGUAGE IS FAST','$' |
| MESGE2 | DB | 'AND EFFICIENT','$' |

Figure 1-9.

Base relative addressing

As shown in Figure 1-10, the same statement could load the AX register with a 16-bit value, depending on the array's data type.

BASE INDEXED ADDRESSING

With base indexed addressing, the operand is located within the selected segment at an offset determined by the sum of the base register's contents, the index register's contents, and, optionally, a displacement. If a displacement is not included, then base indexed addressing is most frequently used to access the elements of a dynamic array (this is an array whose base address can change during the execution of a program). Including a displacement allows the accessing of an individual element of an array, with the array being a field within a structure, such as a record.

In this last case shown in Figure 1-11, the base register would point to the base of the record structure, the displacement (stored in DI) would contain the distance from the beginning of the record to the start of the array

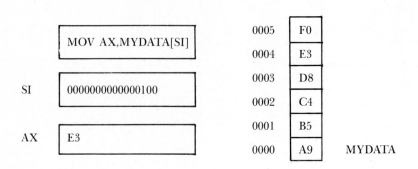

Figure 1-10.

Direct indexed addressing

field, and the element displacement would be contained in the ELEMENT variable. Assume that ELEMENT contains 03.

In the example of Figure 1-11, the base address for the record structure was 0000 and is stored in the BX register. The array field of the third record has a displacement of 0020, stored in DI. The third element of the array field is accessed by the displacement contained in the initialized value of ELEMENT.

80386 EXTENSIONS

The 32-bit addressing modes are extended to allow any register to be used as a base register or index register. The 32-bit modes require that the base and index registers, if used, both hold valid 32-bit values. Any 16-bit mode instructions truncate the contents of a 32-bit register, and therefore the upper 16 bits are ignored.

PROGRAMMING STYLE

An assembly language program is a series of executable statements that tell the assembler what operations it is to perform. This series of statements is often referred to as the source code. Just like any other language, assembly language source code has a predefined syntax.

Each assembly language statement is composed of four fields:

Name field   **Operation field**   **Operand field**   **Comment field**

However, certain assembler instructions do not utilize every field. The

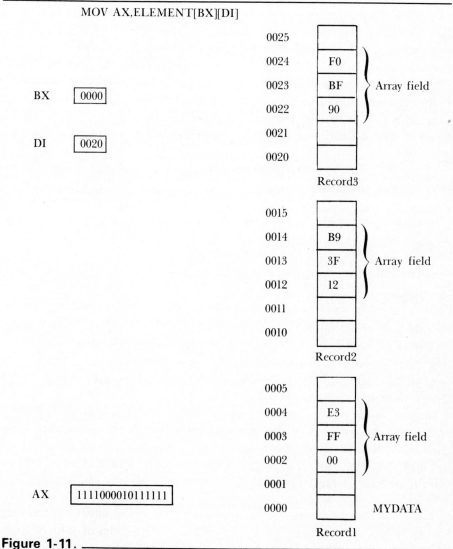

Figure 1-11.

Base indexed addressing

comment field exists for the express purpose of internal programming documentation and is optional.

NAME FIELD

The name field, sometimes called the label field, assigns a symbolic name to the actual beginning memory address of an assembler instruction. This allows the programmer to reference an instruction by name and eliminates the necessity to keep track of instruction addresses. This is especially useful in generating relocatable code. By using a symbolic reference, the programmer allows the linker to select where in memory the assembly language program will be loaded. All instruction references can then automatically vary with code placement. Although any instruction can be given a name, this field is usually reserved for those instructions that will be referenced in data definitions, constants, segments, loops, jumps, and subroutine calls.

A name must begin with an alphabetic character and may contain up to 31 characters, including:

- All letters A through Z
- Numeric digits 0 through 9
- The following special symbols: __ $. ? @ %

Caution must be used in selecting a name. You cannot use a name that is the same as an assembler reserved word or directive. If the name is to include a period (.), then the period must be the first character.

Variables

A variable name represents a memory location that is accessible by a program: and the contents of this memory location can change during program execution. Variable definitions include information about the memory location's address, data type, and size. Variables can be used as operands in simple, indexed, or structured forms.

Labels

Names applied to executable instructions within the applications program are referred to as code-relative. A name, or label in this case, has three attributes: a segment address, segment offset, and a NEAR or FAR accessibility descriptor.

The CPU may address a particular label in two ways. If the label being referenced is within the same code segment, then only the segment offset is necessary to locate the command. In this case, we would say the label type was NEAR. To define a label as NEAR, a colon (:) is placed immediately after the label or the NEAR pseudo-op may be used:

LOOP1:

The colon (:), as shown, tells the assembler this is an instruction referenced within the same code segment.

COUNT LABEL NEAR

In this example, the label is explicitly defined as NEAR by use of the label pseudo-op.

The second method for addressing a label requires both the segment address and offset address. This is the case when the assembler statement to be referenced is not within the same code segment. In this case, the label is defined as being FAR.

MYCODE LABEL FAR

In the example just shown, the label pseudo-op was used with the FAR attribute. FAR attributes can also be used in labeling EQuate and PROcedure, and EXTRNal statements, as seen in the two following examples:

TEN   EQU   FAR   10
PRNTIT   PROC   FAR
EXTRN   RANDM:FAR

Constants

Names can also be given to memory locations that contain initialized values that do not change during program execution. These initialized values are called *constants*. Constants can be of eight types.

Binary   Binary constants contain a series of 0's and 1's and are followed by the letter B. For example:

    EIGHT EQU 00001000B

Decimal   Decimal constants contain a series of digits 0 through 9 and are optionally followed by the letter D. A series of digits is considered to be a decimal number unless the RADIX has been changed. Here is an example of a decimal constant:

    FORTY EQU 40D

Hexadecimal   Hexadecimal constants contain a series of digits 0 through 9 and include the letters A through F, followed by the letter H. The first character must be one of the digits 0 through 9. This tells the compiler that the value is a number and not possibly a label reference or a variable name. If the hexadecimal value begins with one of the letters A through F, then adding a leading 0 will remove this compiler-interpreted ambiguity. A hexadecimal constant declaration would look like this:

    FIFTY   EQU   32H
    HEXNM   EQU   0FFH

In this example, the 0 was appended to the MSD to tell the assembler FFH was a hexadecimal number, not a label or a variable name.

Octal   Octal constants contain the digits 0 through 7, followed by the letter O or Q. For example:

    SIX EQU 6O or 6Q

Character   Character constants may contain any of the ASCII characters enclosed within single or double quotes. If a constant contains more than two characters, the DB (define byte) pseudo-op must be used. If the character string contains only one or two characters, then the DD, DQ, DT, or DW pseudo-op may be used. For example:

    INITL   DD   'B'
    NAME   DB   "J WILLIAMS"

Floating Point   This data type represents values in decimal scientific notation and is not supported by IBM's Small Assembler. For example:

    SINE   DD   0.332E−1

Hexadecimal Real   This is a constant that contains the digits 0 through 9 and the letters A through F, followed by the letter R. Like hexadecimal constants, the first character must be one of the digits 0 through 9. The constant must contain a total number of digits equalling 8, 16, or 20, unless the first digit is a 0. In this case, the total number of digits must be one greater — 9, 17, or 21. This data type is also not supported by IBM's Small Assembler. For example:

    HRNUM   DD   0FAB12345R

Equates   A label in the name field can be assigned to the value of an operand field expression by use of the EQU pseudo-op or by use of the equal (=) sign. Using the EQU pseudo-op assigns the variable a constant that cannot change during program execution. If the = sign pseudo-op is used, the value of the constant can be changed during program execution. For example:

    SCRADD   EQU   [BP+16]
    BASNUM   =   1980

In the first example, SCRADD EQU [BP+16], the name SCRADD can be substituted in place of the index expression [BP+16]. Likewise, - BASNUM - can be substituted in place of the value 1980. In this last case, - BASNUM - could be reassigned a new value while the program was executing.

Segment Names   A segment label is given in the name field of the segment statement. For example:

    MYCODE   SEGMENT   PARA   'CODE'

OPERATION FIELD

The operation field contains a mnemonic for an actual microprocessor instruction. The mnemonic is a two- to six-character "memory aid." Rather than being entered as the binary or hexadecimal value for a machine instruction, the mnemonic is an English-like abbreviation. The operation mnemonic makes code easier to read and understand and is only one internal conversion table away from the actual binary machine code value. An operation, or mnemonic, can represent a machine instruction, macro instruction, or a pseudo-operation. For example:

INITIAL   MOV   AX,0H

INITIAL is the label and MOV is the operation. Following the operation field is the operand field. Each operation not only tells the assembler which instruction to execute but also tells the assembler how many operands are needed and of what type.

An operation may contain a reference to a macro. Such a reference instructs the assembler to process a predefined sequence of code. This causes the assembler to generate source code instructions as if they were in the original part of the program. For example:

DOS_INT   MACRO   SERVICE_ID

This operation flags the assembler and tells it that the code following is part of the MACRO definition. A pseudo-operation, abbreviated pseudo-op, usually does not produce machine code but instead directs the assembler to perform certain operations on data, code listings, branches, and macros.

OPERAND FIELD

The operand field contains the location or locations of the data to be manipulated by the operation instruction. If the instruction requires one or two operands, the operands are separated from the instruction by at least one blank space. If there are two operands, the operands themselves are separated by a comma (,). However, there are operations that require no operands.

When an operation requires two operands, the first operand is called the destination operand and the second operand is called the source operand. Data-transfer, register, immediate, and memory-storage operations are examples of instructions requiring two operands. For example:

MOV   AX,8

This is an example of immediate operand. Here, the data to be manipulated is included as source operand and is moved into the AX register, or destination operand.

COMMENT FIELD

The comment field is the last of the four fields and can be one of the most useful. The comment field is used to internally document the assembler source code. Comments are ignored by the assembler and are useful only in listing the source code. If a comment is included with an operation instruction, then it must be separated from the last field by at least one blank space and begin with a semicolon (;). A comment should be used to describe those lines of source code that aren't immediately understandable. For example:

MOV   AH,45H   ;PARAMETER FOR READING A CHARACTER

As shown, the comment explains why the AH register is being loaded with 45H. In this case, the 45H is used to trigger the appropriate action when an interrupt is called.

ASSEMBLY LANGUAGE'S REWARDS

In the very early days of programming, all code was machine code. The instructions were written in binary or hexadecimal and were decoded by the hardware to perform their intended operations. As programs grew in size and complexity, the sharp rise in software development and debugging time made it apparent that a more productive code development method was necessary.

Assembly language programming was the solution. It was a language that was more immediately and easily understood. It automatically kept track of the many, seemingly infinite, details inherent in machine code. It did not contain all of the overhead of a high-level language, and it generated code that executed very quickly.

AN EXAMPLE ASSEMBLY LANGUAGE PROGRAM

Below is an example of an assembled assembly language program. The right side of the page contains the assembly source code, which is easily read and well documented. Along the left side of the page is the assembled machine-language equivalent. Obviously, to the inexperienced programmer, the machine code will be extremely cryptic.

```
IBM Personal Computer MACRO Assembler    Version 2.00      Page    1-1
                                         09-19-85

1                               page ,132
2                               ;FOR 8088/80386 MACHINES
3                               ;PROGRAM TO ILLUSTRATE A SIMPLE HEXADECIMAL ADDITION WITH
4                               ;IMMEDIATE ADDRESSING
5
6       0000            STACK       SEGMENT     PARA STACK
7       0000    40 [        DB      64 DUP ('MYSTACK ')
8               4D 59 53 54
9               41 43 4B 20
10                              ]
11
12      0200            STACK       ENDS
13
14      0000            MYCODE      SEGMENT     PARA 'CODE'      ;DEFINE CODE SEG. FOR MASM
15      0000            MYPROC      PROC        FAR             ;PROCEDURE IS NAMED MYPROC
16                              ASSUME      CS:MYCODE,SS:STACK
17      0000  1E            PUSH        DS                  ;SAVE LOCATION OF DS REG.
18      0001  2B C0         SUB         AX,AX               ;GET A ZERO IN AX
19      0003  50            PUSH        AX                  ;SAVE ZERO ON STACK, TOO
20
21                      ;ACTUAL ADDITION OF THREE NUMBERS USING IMMEDIATE ADDRESSING
22      0004  B0 23         MOV         AL,23H              ;PUT HEX NUM 23H IN AL REG
23      0006  04 0A         ADD         AL,0AH              ;ADD 0AH TO AL REG
24      0008  04 10         ADD         AL,10H              ;ADD 10H TO AL REG
25                      ;END OF ADDITION EXAMPLE, RESULTS IN AL REGISTER
26
27      000A  CB            RET                             ;RETURN CONTROL TO DOS
28      000B            MYPROC      ENDP                    ;END PROCEDURE NAMED MYPROC
29      000B            MYCODE      ENDS                    ;END CODE SEGMENT NAMED MYCODE
30
31                              END                         ;END WHOLE PROGRAM
```

The first column, numbers 1 through 31, are line numbers inserted by the assembler. The second column contains the actual starting memory location address of where the translated mnemonic operation is stored. These are 16-bit addresses represented in hexadecimal format. The third and fourth columns contain the actual machine code version of the mnemonic operation. These columns vary in their number of entries according to the type of instruction and number of operands required.

The remaining columns follow the programming format for an assembly language source code containing a name field, operation field, operand field, and comment field. Also notice that lines 2 through 4, 21, and 25 contain only comments. In Chapter 5, you will begin learning how to write your own simple assembly language programs.

2

INTRODUCTION
TO ASSEMBLERS

In this chapter we will discuss what an assembler is, why it's needed, and what it does. We will explore the similarities and differences between assemblers and high-level language compilers. Using an example program we will demonstrate how to create, assemble, and execute a simple assembly language program, including all necessary source code overhead.

The SAMPLE.ASM program included in this chapter will be used as a template to demonstrate the necessary components of an assembly language program. For further details regarding the 80286/80386 and 80287/80387 instruction set, refer to Chapters 3 and 4.

An assembler is a computer program written to read a syntactically stylized text file, called *source code*. Source code is written in English-like abbreviations called *mnemonics*. The assembler takes these mnemonics and translates them into the binary 0's and 1's that are the native language of the microprocessor. This translated version is called *machine code*.

Each mnemonic is a meaningful command abbreviation for an actual machine code instruction. Typically, there is a one-to-one correlation between an actual machine code instruction and its English-like mnemonic equivalent. Mnemonics make assembly language source code easy to write, read, and trace. The one-to-one correlation between the two versions makes it easy for the assembler to create a quick, accurate and efficient code translation.

A high-level language compiler performs a similar task in that it too is a computer program written to read a text file and translate this source code into machine code. High-level language source code allows the programmer to concentrate on the programming task rather than minute details, such as which registers, memory locations, and ports are to be used. As a result of this hardware independence, a high-level language program is not as directly tied to a particular microprocessor chip as is its assembly language counterpart.

High-level language source code is wordy and is similar to a structured outline detailing the logic behind a problem solution. There is no one-to-one correlation between high-level language source code and its translated machine code version. The compiled version of a program is usually much larger than a well-written assembly language equivalent. This is not to suggest that compilers are incapable of efficient code generation. In fact, compared to your first attempts at assembly language, you might prefer the streamlined compiled equivalent.

MACHINE CODE VERSUS ASSEMBLY LANGUAGE

The two code segments that follow illustrate the usefulness of an assembler and demonstrate the one-to-one correlation between actual machine code and its assembly language equivalent. Both the machine code and assembly language program fragments are identical in function. They perform some necessary program overhead initializations, load the accumulator with a value stored in the variable NUMONE, and add 3H to the value stored in the accumulator.

```
MACHINE CODE                ASSEMBLY LANGUAGE EQUIVALENT

00011110                    PUSH        DS
00101011                    SUB         AX,AX
11000000
01010000                    PUSH        AX
10111000                    MOV         AX,MYDATA
00000001
11101100
10001110                    MOV         DS,AX
11011000
```

```
10100001                MOV          AX,NUMONE
0000
00000101                ADD          AX,3H
0011
```

The machine code version of the program is also referred to as *object code*. When a program is in object code format, it can be placed directly into memory and immediately executed by setting the appropriate pointers.

Programming in machine code is a very time-consuming, eye-straining, error-prone task at best. As can be seen in the preceding short machine code fragment, it is not immediately apparent what the binary values represent. Are these values instructions, data, or addresses? Not only is writing machine code a programmer's nightmare, but debugging such a program is an ophthalmologist's delight!

Fortunately for us, even though microprocessors are at their best crunching 0's and 1's, we have assemblers to aid in the writing of machine language code. The assembly language version of the preceding program is immediately more understandable. The meaningless numeric instructions have been replaced by comprehensible alphabetic abbreviations, greatly enhancing program walk-throughs and debugging. Note the one-to-one correlation between each assembly language instruction and its machine code counterpart.

This text will discuss three of the most popular assemblers: IBM Macro Assembler, Microsoft Macro Assembler, and Turbo Editasm Assembler. We will see that all three assemblers have many of the same features. Their differences revolve around editing features and compilation options. When it comes to writing and executing actual code, all of the assemblers use the same set, or subset, of instructions. Details regarding each assembler can be found in the appropriate appendix.

While we are on the subject of instruction sets, it is worth noting the philosophy behind Intel's microprocessor developments. Intel has strived to maintain upward compatibility within its microprocessor family, starting with early processors and moving through the 8080, 8088, 8086 series to the current-generation 80386. This means that with each new generation of microprocessors comes a larger instruction set, hardware improvements, speed enhancements, and so on that allow previous applications to be maintained.

Because each new microprocessor contains a superset of the previous generation's commands, older programs will run with no, or few, modifications on the latest-generation microprocessor. This saves the end user from costly software redevelopment.

TYPICAL ASSEMBLY PROCESS

There are several steps involved in creating an assembly language program. This section discusses these steps, stressing those features common to the three assemblers. (A detailed description of elementary programming techniques is presented in Chapter 5.)

Creating an assembly language program is basically a three-step process (see Figure 2-1). In step 1, a text editor is used to create the source code. In step 2, the assembler is used to convert the source code into object code, which, as you have seen, is similar to machine code. Step 3 is linking, which changes the object code into an .EXE file ready for execution.

An alternate assembly method involves the creation of a .COM file. The creation of .COM files is discussed for each assembler in the appropriate appendix.

Since it is unlikely that you will write error-free code, an additional debugging step could be included to round out the assembly language program development cycle.

STEP 1: CREATING SOURCE CODE

To create source code, any text editor that generates text files in ASCII format can be used. The ASCII file format is devoid of any special control codes to add underlining, justification, superscripts, subscripts, boldfacing, and so on. This type of information is superfluous to the assembler.

Included with many microcomputers are simple line editors such as IBM's DOS EDLIN. EDLIN is called a line editor because it handles each line of text separately. This is completely different from a full-screen editor. A full-screen editor allows text modification simply by positioning the cursor any place on the screen and making the appropriate insertions, deletions, and other changes. With EDLIN, only a single line of a text file can be edited at a time.

If you intend to do any serious assembly language programming, you should use a full-screen text editor. All of the program examples in this text were prepared on the full-screen IBM Professional Editor or on a Norton Editor. Many standard word processors can create files in ASCII format simply by selecting the appropriate option. WordPerfect, WordStar, and

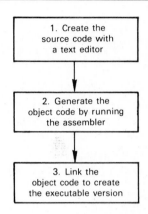

Figure 2-1.

Typical assembly process

EasyWriter are examples of word processors capable of ASCII file creation.

Using a text editor, create the assembly language source code shown in Figure 2-2. Make certain to space each line as shown. Start typing each line in column 1. Since all three of the assemblers we will be discussing expect source code files with an .ASM file extension, make certain you save your file under the name SAMPLE.ASM. (DO NOT include the line numbers when creating your file. The line numbers were inserted for text referencing.)

Now that you've created the source code, take a closer look at what is really going on inside the code and why certain instructions must be included.

The first two lines of the program,

```
1. ;SAMPLE PROGRAM FOR IBM 8088/80286 MACHINES
2. ;PROGRAM TO WRITE A CHARACTER STRING TO THE SCREEN
```

are considered to be comments. Any character string following a semicolon is ignored by the assembler. Here the comment is used to name the program and give a brief description of what the program does.

The following code section contains two statements, SEGMENT (line 3) and ENDS (line 5), which define the beginning and ending of instructions encoded; in this case, the STACK SEGMENT.

```
3. STACK     SEGMENT     PARA 'STACK'
4.           DB    64 DUP ('STACK')
5. STACK     ENDS
```

```
 1. ;SAMPLE PROGRAM FOR IBM 8088/80286 MACHINES
 2. ;PROGRAM TO WRITE A CHARACTER STRING TO THE SCREEN

 3. STACK      SEGMENT PARA 'STACK'
 4.            DB      64 DUP ('STACK')
 5. STACK      ENDS

 6. DATA       SEGMENT     PARA 'DATA'
 7. MESAGE     DB 'NOW ABIDES FAITH, HOPE, LOVE... 1 COR 13:13','$'
 8. DATA       ENDS

 9. CODE       SEGMENT     PARA 'CODE'      ;DEFINE CODE SEG. FOR MASM
10. MAIN       PROC    FAR                  ;NAME THE PROCEDURE MAIN
11.            ASSUME CS:CODE,DS:DATA,ES:DATA,SS:STACK
12.            PUSH    DS                   ;SAVE LOCATION OF DS REG.
13.            SUB     AX,AX                ;GET A ZERO IN AX
14.            PUSH    AX                   ;SAVE ZERO OFFSET ON STACK TOO
15.            MOV     AX,DATA              ;GET DATA LOCATION IN AX
16.            MOV     DS,AX                ;PUT IT IN DS REGISTER
17.            MOV     ES,AX                ;     "     ES     "

18. ;ROUTINE TO PRINT MESAGE STRING TO THE SCREEN
19.                    LEA DX,MESAGE        ;DOS ROUTINE FOR STRING OUTPUT
20.                    MOV AH,09            ;DOS PARAMETER
21.                    INT 21H              ;DOS INTERRUPT

22.            RET                          ;RETURN CONTROL TO DOS
23. MAIN       ENDP                         ;END PROCEDURE NAMED MAIN
24. CODE       ENDS                         ;END CODE SEGMENT NAMED CODE
25.            END                          ;SIGNAL PROGRAM END
```

Figure 2-2. _____

SAMPLE.ASM

The three macro assemblers being discussed here allow up to four concurrently active memory segments: CODE, DATA, STACK, and EXTRA. Segmentation allows for well-structured, modular source code.

Line 3 contains the word STACK in the label field and specifies the name to be assigned to this segment. The operand PARA (line 3) specifies that the segment will begin at a standard paragraph, or 16-byte boundary, in memory. The 'STACK' at the end of the line specifies the name that will be associated with the segment in cross-references.

Line 4 defines the size of the stack, 64 D(efined) B(ytes), and tells the assembler to initialize these locations with the word 'STACK.' The ENDS statement (line 5) contains a matching label and specifies the completion of the segment definition.

The next three lines of code name and define the DATA segment.

```
 6. DATA       SEGMENT     PARA 'DATA'
 7. MESAGE     DB 'NOW ABIDES FAITH, HOPE, LOVE... 1 COR 13:13','$'
 8. DATA       ENDS
```

These also start on a paragraph boundary and will be cross-referenced by the word 'DATA' (line 6). In this very brief data segment only one variable is defined. MESAGE (line 7) is defined to be a D(efined) B(yte) character string variable, initialized to 'NOW ABIDES FAITH, HOPE, LOVE... 1 COR 13:13','$'.

It should be noted that some strongly typed assemblers are very sensitive to the placement of the DATA segment with respect to defining and using variables. All of the examples in this text include the DATA segment at the beginning of the program. DATA segments may be placed below the CODE segment. If the DATA segment is placed at the beginning of your source code and an associated error message is printed, transfer the DATA segment to the end of the program.

Line 9 defines the beginning of the CODE segment, which begins on a paragraph boundary and will be cross-referenced by the word 'CODE.'

```
9. CODE      SEGMENT    PARA 'CODE'    ;DEFINE CODE SEG. FOR MASM
```

Notice that on this line and the several lines that follow, a comment to briefly explain the action of the instruction is included.

The next line of code contains the label name MAIN and the PRO-C(edure) declaration statement.

```
10. MAIN     PROC     FAR             ;NAME THE PROCEDURE MAIN
```

Procedures are sections of code that are executed from various places in a host program by calling them. Each time a procedure is called, the instructions that make up that procedure are executed, and then control is returned to the calling, or host, program.

A PROC(edure) declaration begins and ends with the PROC and ENDP state pair and includes either a NEAR or FAR option. The NEAR or FAR attribute informs the assembler what type of jump or call instruction to generate when going to that particular location.

In most cases the NEAR or FAR attribute also determines the type of return instruction generated for that particular procedure. A CALL to a NEAR procedure leaves only the IP value on the stack, and a CALL to a FAR procedure saves both the CS and IP values.

All of the lines of code, from line 1 through line 10, will vary from program to program. Each program will have its own unique comments and differently dimensioned and initialized STACK and DATA segments. What will not change are the following seven lines of code, lines 11 through 17.

To create a program that properly executes and then returns to the operating system without locking it, certain instructions must be included in all assembly language source code. This necessary section of code is usually referred to as the *program overhead.*

Overhead

The following instruction takes the three defined segments and establishes the means by which the data within them can be addressed:

```
11.              ASSUME CS:CODE,DS:DATA,ES:DATA,SS:STACK
```

The ASSUME statement tells the assembler to associate the C(ode) S(egment) register with the location of CODE, the D(ata) S(egment) and E(xtra) S(egment) registers with the location of DATA, and the S(tack) S(egment) register with the location of STACK.

The next three instructions take care of remembering where the operating system was, so that when the assembly language program terminates, all necessary pointers can be reestablished.

```
12.          PUSH    DS              ;SAVE LOCATION OF DS REG.
13.          SUB     AX,AX           ;GET A ZERO IN AX
14.          PUSH    AX              ;SAVE ZERO OFFSET ON STACK TOO
```

Line 12 pushes the current contents of the D(ata) S(egment) register onto the stack. Line 13 generates a quick zero value offset that is also pushed onto the stack, line 14.

Saving the old contents of the D(ata) S(egment) register is just about as complicated as loading it with a new value. The D(ata) S(egment) register cannot be loaded with a variable's value.

Lines 15 and 16 are the following:

```
15.          MOV AX,DATA             ;GET DATA LOCATION IN AX
16.          MOV DS,AX               ;PUT IT IN DS REGISTER
```

First the location of the DATA segment is loaded into the AX register, line 15, and then it is stored in the DS register by moving it from AX, line 16.

The same principle holds for the E(xtra) S(egment) register.

```
17.          MOV ES,AX               ;    "     ES    "
```

In this example, both segments point to the same location. This is the last line of the program overhead.

The location of lines 18 through 21 is where you would insert the code for your application solution.

```
18. ;ROUTINE TO PRINT MESAGE STRING TO THE SCREEN
19.            LEA DX,MESAGE              ;DOS ROUTINE FOR STRING OUTPUT
20.            MOV AH,09                  ;DOS PARAMETER
21.            INT 21H                    ;DOS INTERRUPT
```

In this case, the four lines of code (lines 18 through 21) set up, initialize, and call a subroutine that prints a character string.

With the brief four-line program (lines 18 through 21) completed, it is necessary to signal the end of the program.

```
22.            RET                        ;RETURN CONTROL TO DOS
23. MAIN       ENDP                       ;END PROCEDURE NAMED MAIN
24. CODE       ENDS                       ;END CODE SEGMENT NAMED CODE
25.            END                        ;SIGNAL PROGRAM END
```

The RET instruction (line 22) pops the return address from the stack and in this case takes you back to the operating system. Line 23 terminates the procedure definition. The CODE segment is ended by the ENDS statement on line 24, and the END instruction (line 25) tells the Assembler that it has reached the end of the source code. With the source code created and saved as SAMPLE.ASM, it is time to go to the second step in the assembly process.

STEP 2: GENERATING OBJECT CODE

At this point, object code will be generated when the assembler is run. There are several options that can be included when any of the three assemblers are run. These are discussed in the appropriate appendixes. The current discussion here describes how to quickly generate an .OBJ file.

With any of the three macro assemblers in drive A, with the SAMPLE.ASM source code in drive B, and with drive B as the default drive, type:

```
B>A:MASM SAMPLE;       ;FOR THE IBM MACRO ASSEMBLER
B>A:MASM/A SAMPLE;     ;FOR THE MICROSOFT ASSEMBLER
```

If you are using Turbo Editasm, use the following instruction sequence:

```
B>A:TASMB SAMPLE;
```

Select the F7 option to generate an .OBJ file. Press the "A" key to initiate the assembly. TASMB will prompt you for the name to give this new .OBJ file. The default name will be SAMPLE.OBJ. You simply type "Y" to accept this name.

Notice that for all three assemblers, it was not necessary to include the .ASM file extension. This is because the assemblers assume this extension for you.

A successful assembly results in the creation of the object file SAMPLE.OBJ. If you request a directory listing of your B disk, you will see the file SAMPLE.OBJ. Even though the file contains all of your program instructions in machine code, it is not in a format that can be loaded into memory by the operating system. It is the .OBJ file that will be used for the third and final step in the assembly process.

STEP 3: LINKING

At this point, it is necessary to use the linker program (LINK) to convert the object file to an execution file. This step also has several options, which are discussed in detail in Appendixes A, B, and C. The current discussion describes how to create a simple .EXE file.

The following instructions assume that the LINK program, supplied with each assembler or with DOS, is in drive A, the SAMPLE.OBJ file is in drive B, and drive B is the default drive. To create the SAMPLE.EXE file type the following:

```
B>A:LINK SAMPLE;        ;FOR THE IBM MACRO ASSEMBLER
B>A:LINK SAMPLE;        ;FOR THE MICROSOFT ASSEMBLER
B>A:LINK SAMPLE;        ;FOR TURBO EDITASM
```

Assuming a successful LINK, you will find the SAMPLE.EXE file created and stored on your B disk. To execute the program, still assuming drive B as the default drive, type:

```
B>SAMPLE
```

After the program prints the brief message on the screen, you automatically return to the DOS B> prompt.

3

ARCHITECTURE: REGISTERS, FLAGS, AND INSTRUCTIONS

80286 MICROPROCESSOR

The 80286 microprocessor has many advanced features designed for high performance and the needs of multiple users and multitasking systems. The 80286 has built-in memory protection for operating systems and task-program and task-data privacy. At 10MHz the 80286 executes tasks up to six times faster than the 5MHz 8086.

The 80286 is upwardly compatible with 8086/8088 software. In real address mode, the 80286 is code compatible with existing 8086/8088 object code. In virtual address mode the 80286 is source-code compatible with 8086/8088 object code, but may require revisions to take advantage of the virtual addresses supported by the 80286, as shown in Figure 3-1.

BASE ARCHITECTURE

The 80286 contains eight 16-bit general-purpose registers—AX, BX, CX, DX, SP, BP, SI, and DI—shown in Figure 3-2. The AX, BX, CX, and DX registers can be used as full 16-bit registers, or each register can be subdivided into two 8-bit registers, providing access to a total of eight 8-bit registers. Registers ending with the letter "X" (for example, BX) use the full

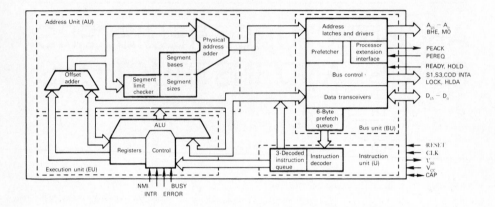

Figure 3-1. _____

80286 internal block diagram

16-bit value. The 8-bit register halves are designated (Reg)L and (Reg)H (for example, AH and AL), with (Reg)L containing the low-order bits, and (Reg)H containing the high-order bits.

The 16-bit SP (stack pointer) and BP (base pointer) register pair are typically used for stack manipulation and contain offsets into the current stack. The SI (source index) and DI (destination index) register pair, called *index registers,* are used as index values that will be incremented or decremented to step through more complex data structures.

Segment Registers

The 80286 supports four simultaneously accessible code modules, called *segments.* These four segments can be addressed by the CS, DS, SS, and ES 16-bit registers, shown in Figure 3-3.

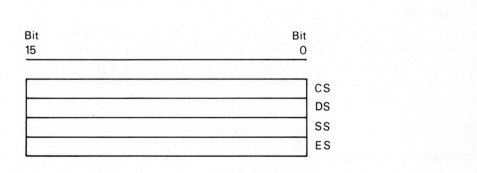

Figure 3-2.
────────────────────────────────
80286 general-purpose registers

Figure 3-2. ─────────────────────────────

80286 general-purpose registers

Bit 15		Bit 0	(for (Reg)X)

| Bit
7 | Bit
0 | Bit
7 | Bit
0 | (for (Reg)H)
(for (Reg)L) |

AH	AL	AX (Accumulator)
BH	BL	BX (Base)
CH	CL	CX (Count)
DH	DL	DX (Data)

SP (Stack pointer)
BP (Base pointer)
SI (Source index)
DI (Destination index)

Figure 3-3. ─────────────────────────────

80286 segment registers

Bit 15	Bit 0

CS
DS
SS
ES

The code of the currently executing program, residing in memory, is addressed by the CS (code segment) register. The base of the currently active data segment is addressed by the DS (data segment) register. Stacks that typically are used for intermediate results and subroutine calls also are given their own segment of memory, and the base address of the currently active stack segment is contained in the SS (stack segment) register. Additionally, the programmer has access to a second concurrently active data segment, called the *extra segment,* which is addressed by the ES register.

Addressing an element within a selected segment is accomplished by first selecting an active segment through one of the four segment registers — CS, DS, SS, or ES — and then providing a 16-bit offset address from the base address. The 16-bit segment address and the 16-bit offset are combined to form the high- and low-order halves of a 32-bit virtual address pointer. Once a segment is selected, only the lower 16-bit offset address need be specified within an instruction.

Segment addresses are interpreted differently, depending upon the mode in which the 80286 is operating. In real address mode the segment registers contain actual physical addresses. In protected mode, the segment registers contain addresses to virtual memory and require translation to convert the logical address into a physical memory address.

Index, Pointer, and Base Registers

As mentioned earlier, the physical address of any given element within a selected segment is obtained by the combination of the segment address and the offset. This offset can be contained in any of the pointer, base, or index registers.

Stack operations are facilitated by the stack segment selector (SS) and the stack pointer (SP) or base pointer (BP) register pair. Offsets into the data segments (DS) and (ES) are obtained from the base register (BX). More complicated data manipulations can be obtained by using the source index (SI) and destination index (DI) in conjunction with the currently active data segment.

Status and Control Registers (Flags)

The 80286 contains a FLAGS register (shown in Figure 3-4) with eleven flag fields. Six of these flags, called *status flags,* are changed by, and provide

BIT
15

BIT
0

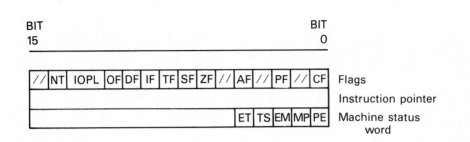

| // | NT | IOPL | OF | DF | IF | TF | SF | ZF | // | AF | // | PF | // | CF | Flags

Instruction pointer

| ET | TS | EM | MP | PE | Machine status word

Figure 3-4. _____

80286 status and control registers

necessary information for, arithmetic and logical control decisions. These are the CF (Carry flag), PF (Parity flag), AF (Auxiliary Carry flag), ZF (Zero flag), SF (Sign flag), and OF (Overflow flag).

- The Carry flag (CF) is set to 1 when a carry or borrow is generated by an arithmetic operation performed on an 8- or 16-bit operand. Otherwise, it is reset to 0. CF is also used in shift and rotate instructions and contains the bit shifted or rotated out of the register.

- The Parity flag (PF) is used primarily for data communications applications and is set to 1 to generate odd parity or reset to 0 to generate even parity.

- The Auxiliary Carry flag (AF) is used in BCD arithmetic to indicate whether there has been a carry out of or borrow into the least-significant 4-bit digit of a BCD value.

- The Zero flag (ZF) indicates when a result is zero by setting itself to 1.

- The Sign flag (SF) is set to 1 for a negative result and reset to 0 for a positive result.

- The Overflow flag indicates whether an operation has generated a carry into the high-order bit of the result, but not a carry out of the high-order bit, or a carry out of the high-order bit without a carry in.

Three of the eleven flags—TF, IF, and DF—are used to direct certain processor operations. The Trap flag (TF), when set, puts the microprocessor into single-step mode and enables the debugging of a program. The Interrupt Enable flag (IF) enables external interrupts when it is set to 1 and disables external interrupts when it is reset to 0. The direction of string operations is controlled by the Direction flag (DF). With DF reset to 0, SI and/or DI are automatically incremented forward. With DF set to 1, SI and/or DI are automatically decremented.

The IOPL and NT flags are two new flags not previously provided and are only used when the microprocessor is in protected mode. The two-bit Input/Output Privilege Level flag (IOPL) is used to guarantee that an instruction performs only those operations it is authorized to perform. The Nested Task flag (NT) is used to indicate whether the execution of the current task is nested within another task. If NT is set to 1, the current nested task has a valid link to the previous task.

Instruction Pointer

The instruction pointer (IP) (refer to Figure 3-4) contains the offset necessary to address the next instruction to be executed within the currently active code segment. This generates a full 32-bit pointer for the next sequential program instruction.

Machine Status Word

The first five bits of the 16-bit machine status word (refer to Figure 3-4) contain the protection enable (PE) bit-0, monitor coprocessor (MP) bit-1, emulate coprocessor (EM) bit-2, task switched (TS) bit-3, and processor extension type (ET) bit-4.

- Protection enable (PE) is used to activate the microprocessor's protected mode. If PE is reset, the processor operates in real address mode. If PE is set, protected mode is activated.

- Monitor coprocessor (MP) is used along with the TS bit to determine whether the WAIT opcode will generate a coprocessor not available fault if TS = 1.

- Emulate coprocessor (EM) is set to cause all coprocessor opcodes to generate a coprocessor not available fault. If EM is reset, all coprocessor opcodes will be executed on an actual 80287 or 80387 coprocessor.

- Task switched (TS) is automatically set whenever a task switch operation is performed. With TS set, a coprocessor opcode will cause a coprocessor not available trap.

80386 MICROPROCESSOR

The 80386 microprocessor is a 32-bit processor designed to support those operating systems optimized for multitasking. With its 32-bit registers and data paths, the 80386 supports 32-bit addresses and data types.

The 80386 microprocessor is capable of addressing up to four gigabytes of physical memory and 64 terabytes 2^{46} of virtual memory. The integrated memory management and protection architecture includes address translation registers, a protection mechanism to support operating systems, and advanced multitasking hardware.

Instruction pipelining (shown in Figure 3-5), a high bus bandwidth, and on-chip address translation significantly shorten the average instruction execution time, yielding high system throughput. These architectural design features enable the 80386 to execute instructions at a rate of 3 to 4 million per second.

Additional features include a self-test, direct access to the page translation cache, and four new breakpoint registers. The 80386 is upwardly object-code compatible with the 8086/8088/80286.

DATA TYPES

The 80386 microprocessor chip supports several data types in addition to those supported by the 8086/80286. The 80386 microprocessor supports 32-bit signed and unsigned integers and bit fields from 1 to 32 bits long. The 80386 microprocessor supports the standard pointer types defined for the 8086/80286 family as well as a 32-bit offset-only pointer and a 48-bit full pointer.

OPERAND ADDRESSING

In addition to the 8- and 16-bit immediate operand sizes supported by the 8086/80286/80386, the 80386 also supports an operand size of 32 bits, with

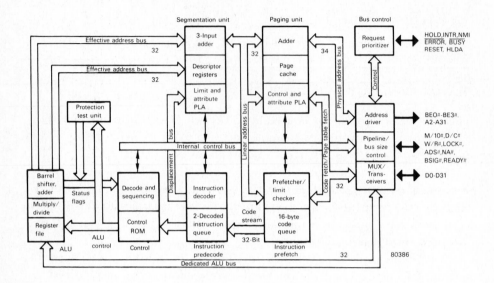

Figure 3-5.

80386 pipelined 32-bit microarchitecture

the general indication that the 16-bit immediate operand field is extended to 32 bits. If a 32-bit operand size is specified, the ENTER and RET instructions take a 16-bit immediate operand of zero extended to 32 bits.

Effective Address Calculation

When accessing a segment larger than 64K, effective addresses can be 32 bits as well as 16 bits. The effective address is formed by adding an optional base register, an optional index register, and an optional displacement. In addition, the 32-bit addressing modes have been expanded to permit use of any general-purpose register as a base or index register.

8086 CODE EXECUTION

The 80386 has two operating modes that are bit compatible with the 8086/80286 instruction set. They are provided for executing 8086 object code. Real mode is provided as it is on the 80286, and is the mode used by the microprocessor after a RESET. The virtual 8086 mode is a subset of the 80386 protected mode, and permits 8086 code to be executed within the protected mode and paged operating environment provided on the 80386.

BASE ARCHITECTURE

The 80386 microprocessor chip provides the programmer with 32 registers. These 32 registers can be divided into seven major categories.

- General-purpose registers
- Segment registers
- Instruction pointer and flags
- Control registers
- System address registers
- Test registers.

These registers are a superset of the 8086 and 80286 registers; therefore, all 16-bit 8086 and 80286 registers are contained within the 32-bit 80386 microprocessor.

General-Purpose Registers

The eight general-purpose registers (shown in Figure 3-6) are used similarly to the eight general-purpose registers associated with the 80286, except that the registers are now 32 bits wide (see the discussion of the 80286 microprocessor earlier in this chapter for descriptions of register uses). The general-purpose registers are capable of supporting data operands of 1, 8, 16, and 32 bits and bit fields of from 1 to 32 bits. These registers also support address operands of 16 and 32 bits. The eight registers are the EAX (accumulator), EBX (base), ECX (count), EDX (data), ESP (stack pointer), EBP (base pointer), ESI (source index), and EDI (destination index).

To access the full 32 bits of a register, all register references must begin with the letter "E." Each of the eight general-purpose registers can be broken down to their 16-bit 8086/80286 equivalents by referencing the registers without using the E prefix.

Segment Registers

The 80386 microprocessor contains six 16-bit segment registers, as shown in Figure 3-7. The six segment registers hold the selector values to the currently addressable memory locations. In real address mode, a segment

Bit 31			Bit 0
Bit 31	Bit 16	Bit 15	Bit 0
	Bit 7	Bit 0	Bit 7	Bit 0

	[AH]	AX	[AL]	EAX
	[BH]	BX	[BL]	EBX
	[CH]	CX	[CL]	ECX
	[DH]	DX	[DL]	EDX

	SP	ESP
	BP	EBP
	SI	ESI
	DI	EDI

Figure 3-6.

80386 general-purpose registers

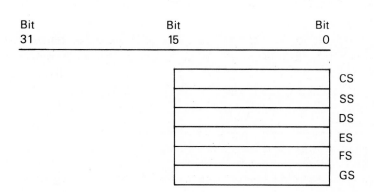

Figure 3-7. _____

80386 segments registers

may vary in size from 1 byte to a maximum segment size of 64K bytes, or 2^{16} bytes. Protected mode addressing enables segment ranges from 1 byte up to the maximum of 4 gigabytes, or 2^{32} bytes.

The six 16-bit segment registers are CS (code segment), DS (data segment), SS (stack segment), ES (extra segment), and FS and GS (the programmer is left to assign an appropriate acronym for the FS and GS registers). The FS and GS registers were added to alleviate the congestion in the ES register and to better match the base and index registers available in the general register set.

Instruction Pointer and EFLAGS

The 80386 microprocessor contains a 32-bit instruction pointer register called EIP (see Figure 3-8). The EIP register holds the offset of the next instruction to be executed. This offset is always relative to the base of the currently active CS (code segment). The lower 16 bits of the EIP may be accessed separately. The lower 16 bits of the EIP are called the IP register and are used in 16-bit addressing.

The EFLAGS register of the 80386 microprocessor, which has also been extended to 32 bits, is shown in Figure 3-9. The EFLAGS register is used to control certain operations and indicate the status of the 80386 itself. The EFLAGS register contains two new flags: VM (virtual 8086 Mode flat) and

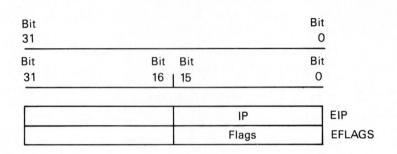

Figure 3-8. _____

80386 instruction pointers and EFLAGS registers

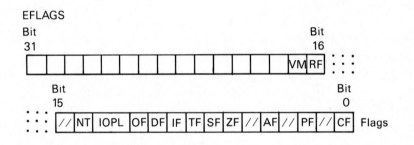

Figure 3-9. _____

Detail of 80386 EFLAGS registers

RF (Resume flag). The lower 16 bits of the EFLAGS register, called the FLAGS register, contain the same operations control and status flags associated with 8086/80286 microprocessors. For more information about the operations control and status flags located in the FLAGS register, refer back to the discussion of flags earlier in this chapter.

The VM flag (Virtual 8086 Mode flag) located in the EFLAGS register enables virtual 8086 mode. If VM is set and 80386 is in protected mode, the microprocessor will switch to virtual 8086 mode operation, causing all segment operations to execute as if they were running on an 8086. While emulating the 8086, the 80386 also will generate exception-13 faults for privileged opcodes.

The RF flag (Resume flag), also located in the EFLAGS register, is used in conjunction with the debug register breakpoints or single steps. When RF is set to 1, all debug faults are ignored in the next instruction. RF will then automatically be reset at the successful completion of each instruction.

Control Registers

The 80386 microprocessor contains three 32-bit control registers—CR0, CR2, and CR3—shown in Figure 3-10. These registers contain information about the non-task-dependent status of the machine. Accessing the control registers is accomplished through load and store instructions.

The CR0 register contains six predefined flags used for microprocessor control and status purposes. Bits 0-15 of the CR0 register are also known as the MSW (machine status word), thus making the 80386 compatible with the 80286 in protected mode. The LMSW and SMSW commands work the same on the 80386 as on the 80286. When accessing CR0, the programmer should use the MOV CR0,Register instruction.

The ET (processor extension type), TS (task switched), EM (emulate coprocessor), MP (monitor coprocessor), and PE (protection enable) bits

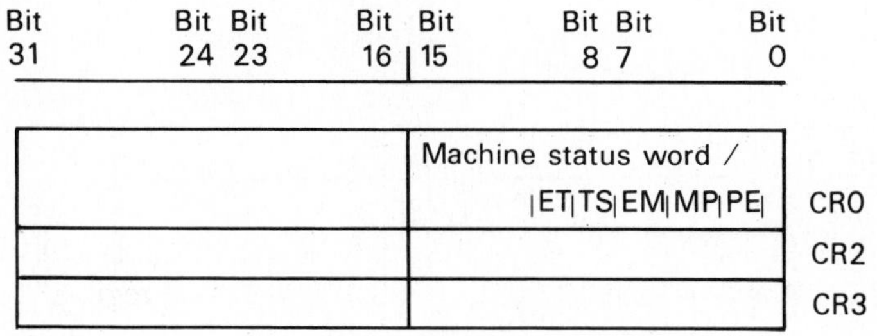

Figure 3-10.
80386 control registers

operate the same as for the 80286 (see "Machine Status Word" earlier in this chapter).

CR1, which is not shown, is reserved for use in future Intel microprocessors. CR2 contains the 32-bit linear address that caused the last page fault detected. CR3 contains the physical base address of the page directory table. Since the 80386 page directory table is always page-aligned, the lowest 12 bits of CR3 are ignored when they are written.

System Address Registers

The 80386 microprocessor contains four special-purpose registers (shown in Figure 3-11) that are used to reference the tables or segments supported by the 80286/80386 protection mode. The GDT (global descriptor table), IDT (interrupt descriptor table), LDT (local descriptor table), and TSS (task state segment table) addresses are stored in these special registers. The system address and system segment registers are named GDTR, IDTR, LDTR, and TR.

The GDTR and IDTR registers are 32-bit registers that hold the 32-bit linear base address and 16-bit limit of the GDT and IDT. The LDTR and TR registers are 16-bit registers that hold the 16-bit selector for the LDT and TSS segments.

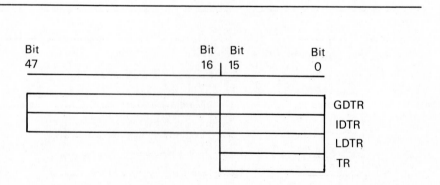

Figure 3-11.
80386 system address registers

Debug and Test Registers

The 80386 microprocessor provides programmer access to six 32-bit debug registers—DR0, DR1, DR2, DR3, DR6, DR7 (see Figure 3-12). DR4 and DR5 are reserved for Intel. Debug control register DR6 is used to set breakpoints. DR7 displays the current state of the breakpoints.

The 80386 microprocessor contains two 32-bit test registers (shown in Figure 3-13) that are used to control the testing of RAM and CAM (content-addressable memories) in the translation lookaside buffer. TR6 is used as the command test register, and TR7 functions as the data register holding the data contained in the translation lookaside buffer test.

Bit 31		Bit 0	
Linear breakpoint address 0			DR0
Linear breakpoint address 1			DR1
Linear breakpoint address 2			DR2
Linear breakpoint address 3			DR3
Reserved for Intel			DR4
Reserved for Intel			DR5
Breakpoint status			DR6
Breakpoint control			DR7

Figure 3-12.
80386 debug registers

Test control	TR6
Test status	TR7

Figure 3-13.
80386 test registers

80286/80386 INSTRUCTION SET

AAA (80286/80386)

ASCII adjust AL after addition

Instruction: AAA

Typical clocks: (80286) 3, (80386) 4

Description: ASCII adjusts AL after addition

Operation: The AAA instruction should only be executed after an ADD instruction that leaves a byte result in the AL register. The AAA instruction converts the contents of AL to an unpacked decimal digit. AAA examines the lower four bits of AL to see if it contains a valid BCD number in the range 0-9. AAA sets the four high-order bits of AL to 0. If there was a decimal carry, the AF (Auxiliary) and CF (Carry) flags are also reset to 0. If the value contained in the lower nibble is greater than 9, or if the AF (Auxiliary Carry flag) is 1, then AAA performs the following actions: the AL register is incremented by 6, AH is incremented by 1, the AF and CF flags are set to 1, and the higher four bits of AL are cleared to 0.

Syntax: AAA (no operands)

Flags affected: AF, CF

Flags undefined: OF, ZF, SF, PF

Protected mode exceptions: None

Real address mode exceptions: None

80386 note: No exceptions

Example: ADD   AL,BL   ;Add the BCD numbers in AL and BL
            AAA   ;Return a result that is in unpacked form

AAD (80286/80386)

ASCII adjust AX before division

Instruction: AAD

Typical clocks: (80286) 14, (80386) 19

Description: ASCII adjusts AX before division

Operation: The AAD instruction takes two unpacked BCD digits, with the least-significant digit in the AL register and the most-significant digit in the AH register, and gets them ready for a division operation that will return an unpacked result. AL is set to AL $+ (10 \times AH)$, and AH is set to 0. The result leaves the AX register equal to the binary equivalent of the original unpacked two-digit number.

Syntax: AAD (no operands)

Flags affected: SF, ZF, PF

Flags undefined: OF, AF, CF

Protected mode exceptions: None

Real address mode exceptions: None

80386 note: No exceptions

Example: AAD   ;Used prior to the division

AAM (80286/80386)

ASCII adjust AX after multiply
Instruction: AAM
Typical clocks: (80286) 16, (80386) 17

Description: ASCII adjusts AX after multiplication

Operation: AAM adjusts the result in the AX register after multiplying two unpacked decimal operands. This instruction should only be executed after a MUL instruction. Because the result is less than 100, it is contained entirely in the AL register. AAM unpacks the AL result by dividing AL by 10 and leaving the most-significant digit (the quotient) in AH and the least-significant digit (the remainder) in the AL register.

Syntax: AAM (no operands)

Flags affected: SF, ZF, PF
Flags undefined: OF, AF, CF
Protected mode exceptions: None
Real address mode exceptions: None
80386 note: No exceptions
Example: AAM   ;Used after a multiplication

AAS (80286/80386)

ASCII adjust AL after subtraction

Instruction: AAS

Typical clocks: (80286) 3, (80386) 4

Description: ASCII adjusts AL after subtraction

Operation: The purpose of the AAS instruction is to correct the result in the AL register after subtracting two unpacked decimal operands. The result is in unpacked decimal format. This is accomplished using the following rules: If the lower four bits of the AL register are greater than 9, or if the AF flag is 1, the AL register is decremented by 6 and the AH register by 1. The CF and AF flags are set to 1. Otherwise, reset CF and AF to 0. The original value of the AL register therefore is replaced by a byte whose upper nibble is all zeroes, and whose lower nibble is a number from 0 to 9.

Syntax: AAX (no operands)

Flags affected: AF, CF

Flags undefined: OF, SF, ZF, PF

Protected mode exceptions: None

Real address mode exceptions: None

80386 note: No exceptions

Example: ASS   ;Used after the subtraction

ADC (80286/80386)

Add with carry

Instruction: ADC

Typical clocks: (80286) 2-7, (80386) 2-7

Description: Adds two operands with a carry

Operation: ADC performs integer addition of two operands. If CF is set, then 1 is added to the sum of the two operands, and the result is returned to the destination.

Syntax: ADC   *destination,source*

Flags affected: OF, SF, ZF, AF, PF, CF

Flags undefined: None

Protected mode exceptions: If the result is in a nonwritable segment, a general protection error is generated. A general protection exception is generated for an illegal memory operand effective address in the CS, DS, or ES segment. If the SS segment contains an illegal address, a stack fault exception is generated.

Real address mode exceptions: INT 13 is generated for a word operand at offset 0FFFFH.

80386 note: Word size is 32 bits.

Example: Add immediate operand with carry to accumulator:

ADC	AL,4
ADC	AX,298
ADC	EBX,22334455H (80386 only)

Add immediate operand with carry to register or memory location:

ADC	CX,341
ADC	BL,10
ADC	TABLE[SI],2
ADC	MEMORY,6293
ADC	NUMBER,12345678 (80386 only)

Add data with carry from: Register to register
                               Register to memory
                               Memory to register

ADC	DL,BL
ADC	MEM—WRD,AX
ADC	SI,MEM—WRD

ADD (80286/80386)

Addition

Instruction: ADD

Typical clocks: (80286) 2-7, (80386) 2-7

Description: Adds two operands

Operation: ADD performs an addition of two operands. The result is stored in the destination operand.

Syntax: ADD   *destination,source*

Flags affected: AF, CF, OF, PF, SF, ZF

Flags undefined: None

Protected mode exceptions: The general protection exception if the result is in a nonwritable segment. If the CS, DS, or ES segment contains an illegal memory operand effective address, a general protection exception is generated. If the SS segment contains an illegal address, a stack fault exception is generated.

Real address mode exceptions: INT 13 is generated for a word operand at offset 0FFFFH.

80386 note: Word size is 32 bits.

Example: Register to register:

        ADD   AX,BX

        ADD   EBX,ECX   (80386 only)

Register to memory:

        ADD   EXTMEM,AX

Memory to register:

        ADD   DX,BUFF

Immediate operand to accumulator:

        ADD   AL,4

        ADD   EAX,98765432H   (80386 only)

Immediate operand to register:

        ADD   CX,1985

Immediate operand to memory:

        ADD   EXTMEM,23

AND (80286/80386)

Logical AND

Instruction: AND

Typical clocks: (80286) 2-7, (80386) 2-7

Description: Finds the logical AND of two operands

Operation: The result contains 1 in those bit positions where both operands contain 1's; all other bit combinations return 0. The OF and CF are reset to 0.

Syntax: AND   *destination,source*

Flags affected: OF = 0, CF = 0, PF, SF, ZF

Flags undefined: AF

Protected mode exceptions: General protected mode exception is generated if the result is in a nonwritable segment. If the CS, DS, or ES segment contains an illegal memory operand effective address, a general protection exception is generated. If the SS segment contains an illegal address, a stack fault exception is generated.

Real address mode exceptions: INT 13 is generated for a word operand at offset 0FFFFH.

80386 note: Word size is 32 bits.

Example: Immediate operand to register:

```
AND     BL,11001110B
AND     EAX,11110000111100001110000011110000B   (80386 only)
```

Immediate operand to memory:

```
AND     EXTMEM,10011100B
AND     NUMBER,0F0F0F0F0H   (80386 only)
```

Immediate operand to accumulator:

```
AND     AX,1001111101010110B
AND     AL,MASK__BYTE
```

Register to register:

```
AND     AX,BX
AND     EAX,ECX   (80386 only)
```

Register to memory:

```
AND     EXTMEM,SI
```

Memory to register:

```
AND     DH,EXTBYTE
```

ARPL (80286/80386)

Adjust RPL field of selector

Instruction: ARPL

Typical clocks: (80286) 10-11, (80386) 20-21

Description: Adjusts RPL of EA word

Operation: The ARPL instruction is designed to prevent operating system software from gaining access to subroutines with a higher priority level. The first of the two operands of ARPL is a 16-bit memory variable, or word register, that contains the value of a selector. The second operand is a word register. If the RPL field (bottom two bits) of the first operand is less than the RPL field of the second operand, then the zero flag is set to 1. The RPL field of the first operand is increased to match the second RPL. Otherwise, the zero flag is reset to 0, with no change being made to the first operand.

Syntax: ARPL (*selector,CS__selector*)

Flags affected: ZF

Flags undefined: None

Protected mode exceptions: If the result is in a nonwritable segment, a general protection error is generated. If the CS, DS, or ES segment contains an illegal memory operand effective address, a general protection exception is generated. If the SS segment contains an illegal address, a stack fault exception is generated.

Real address mode exceptions: INT 6 is generated. ARPL is not recognized in real address mode.

80386 note: No exceptions

Example: ARPL MEM__WRD,BX

BOUND (80286/80386)

Check array index against bounds

Instruction: BOUND

Typical clocks: (80286) 13, (80386) 10

Description: INT 5 occurs if word register not within bounds

Operation: The BOUND operation is used to ensure that a signed array index is within the limits defined by a two-word block of memory. The first operand (a register) must be greater than or equal to the first word in memory and less than or equal to the second word in memory. If these conditions are not met, an interrupt 5 occurs.

Syntax: BOUND *destination,source*

Flags affected: None

Flags undefined: None

Protected mode exceptions: If the bounds test fails, as defined above, INT 5 is generated. A general protected mode exception is generated for an illegal memory operand effective address in the CS, DS, or ES segments. If the SS segment contains an illegal address, a stack fault exception is generated.

Real address mode exceptions: If the bounds test fails, INT 5 is generated. If the second operand is at offset 0FFFDH or higher, INT 13 is generated. When the second operand is a register, INT 6 is generated.

80386 note: Word size is 32 bits.

Example: BOUND   AX,MEM—WORD
BOUND   EBX,NEW—WORD   (80386 only)

CALL (80286/80386)

Call a procedure

Instruction: CALL

Typical clocks: (80286) 7-185, (80386) 3-275

Description: Saves next inst. address, transfers control

Operation: The CALL instruction causes the address of the next instruction to be stored on the stack; then program control is transferred to the parameter operand. When the called procedure is complete, execution of the calling program continues at the instruction that follows the CALL instruction.

Syntax: CALL parameter—operand

Flags affected: None (except when a task switch occurs)

Flags undefined: None

Protected mode exceptions:
FAR CALLS: The general protection exception, descriptor not present exception, stack fault exception, and invalid task state segment are generated.

NEAR direct CALLs: The general protection exception is generated if the procedure location is beyond the code segment limits.

NEAR indirect CALL: The general protection exception is generated for an illegal memory operand effective address in the CS, DS, or ES segments and a stack fault exception for an illegal address in the SS segment. A general protection exception is generated if the indirect offset obtained is beyond the code segment limits.

Real address mode exceptions: INT 13 is generated for a word operand at offset 0FFFFH.

80386 note: Word operands are 32 bits, and pointer operands are 48 bits.

Example: CALL ADDER   ;Inter or Intra segment procedure

80386:

        CALL IMMPTR   ;Pointer operands are 48 bits. Uses
        CALL DISP16   ;32-bit extended instruction pointer.
        CALL register or memory
                     ;Displacement is 32 bits. Word operands
                     ;are 32 bits

CBW (80286/80386)

Convert byte into word

Instruction: CBW

Typical clocks: (80286) 2, (80386) 3

Description: Converts byte into word (AH = top bit of AL)

Operation: The CBW operation converts the signed byte in AL to a signed word in AX. This is accomplished by extending the most-significant bit of AL into all of the bits of AH. See the 80386 note.

Syntax: CBW (no operands)

Flags affected: None

Flags undefined: None

Protected mode exceptions: None

Real address mode exceptions: None

80386 note: Word size is 32 bits. Sign-extended value is in AX; store result in EAX.

Example: CBW

CLC (80286/80386)

Clear Carry flag

Instruction: CLC

Typical clocks: 2

Description: Clears Carry flag

Operation: The CLC operation sets the Carry flag to 0. No other registers or flags are affected.

Syntax: CLC (no operands)

Flags affected: CF = 0

Flags undefined: None

Protected mode exceptions: None

Real address mode exceptions: None

80386 note: No exceptions

Example: CLC

CLD (80286/80386)

Clear Direction flag

Instruction: CLD

Typical clocks: 2

Description: Clears Direction flag, increments SI and DI

Operation: CLD clears the Direction flag. No other registers or flags are affected. After CLD is executed, string operations automatically increment the index registers (SI and/or DI).

Syntax: CLD (no operands)

Flags affected: DF

Flags undefined: None

Protected mode exceptions: None

Real address mode exceptions: None

80386 note: No exceptions

Example: CLD

CLI (80286/80386)

Clear Interrupt flag (disable)

Instruction: CLI

Typical clocks: 3

Description: Clears Interrupt flag, disables interrupts

Operation: The CLI operation clears the Interrupt Enable flag. No other flags are affected. This has the effect of disabling all interrupts, except nonmaskable interrupts, that occur on the NMI line.

Syntax: CLI (no operands)

Flags affected: IF = 0

Flags undefined: None

Protected mode exceptions: When the current privilege level is higher than IOPL in the flags register, a general protection exception is generated. IOPL indicates the least-privileged level at which I/O may be performed.

Real address mode exceptions: None

80386 note: No exceptions

Example: CLI

CLTS (80286/80386)

Clear Task Switched flag

Instruction: CLTS

Typical clocks: (80286) 2, (80386) 5

Description: Clears Task Switched flag

Operation: The CLTS instruction clears the Task Switched flag in the machine status word. It is a privileged instruction that can only be executed at level 0 and is reserved for operating system software. CLTS keeps track of every execution of WAIT or ESC and will be trapped if the MP flag of MSW and the Task Switched flag are set.

Syntax: CLTS (no operands)

Flags affected: TS = 0

Flags undefined: None

Protected mode exceptions: When the current privilege level contains a value other than 0, a general protection error is generated if CLTS is executed.

Real address mode exceptions: None

80386 note: No exceptions

Example: CLTS

CMC (80286/80386)

Complement Carry flag

Instruction: CMC

Typical clocks: 2

Description: Complements Carry flag

Operation: The CMC command flips the bit value of the Carry flag. If the Carry flag is 1, it is reset to 0. If it is 0, it is set to 1.

Syntax: CMC

Flags affected: CF

Flags undefined: None

Protected mode exceptions: None

Real address mode exceptions: None

80386 note: No exceptions

Example: CMC

CMP (80286/80386)

Compare two operands

Instruction: CMP

Typical clocks: (80286) 2-7, (80386) 2-6

Description: Subtracts operands, affects flags

Operation: The CMP operation subtracts the source operand from the destination operand, causing the flags to be altered. It does not alter the operands. The source operand and destination operand must be of the same type, with the exception of CMP in immediate mode. Here, a sign-extended immediate data byte can be compared with a memory word.

Syntax: CMP *destination,source*

Flags affected: OF, SF, ZF, AF, PF, CF

Flags undefined: None

Protected mode exceptions: If the CS, DS cr ES segment contains an illegal memory operand effective address, a general protection exception is generated. If the SS segment contains an illegal address, a stack fault exception is generated.

Real address mode exceptions: When a word operand is at offset 0FFFFH, INT 13 is generated.

80386 note: Word size is 32 bits.

Example: Immediate operand with memory:
```
CMP      EXTMEM,5CAFH
```
Immediate operand with register:
```
CMP      BL,5
CMP      EAX,0FFFF0000H   (80386 only)
```
Immediate operand with accumulator:
```
CMP      AL,7
```
Register with register:
```
CMP      AX,BX
CMP      EDX,EAX   (80386 only)
```
Register with memory:
```
CMP      EXTMEM,DX
```
Memory with register:
```
CMP      CH,EXTMEM
CMP      EBX,VALUE   (80386 only)
```

CMPS/CMPSB/CMPSW (80286/80386)

Compare string operands

Instruction: CMPS/SB/SW

Typical clocks: (80286) 8, (80386) 10

Description: Compares bytes/words ES:[DI] from DS:[SI] or ES:[EDI] from DS:[ESI]

Operation: The CMPS/SB/SW instruction compares the contents of the memory location addressed by the SI (ESI) register with the contents of the memory location addressed by the DI (EDI) register. The CMPS instruction subtracts the contents of the memory location pointed to by the DI (EDI) register from the contents of the memory location pointed to by the SI (ESI) register. The result sets the flags, but does not alter the contents of either memory location. The SI (ESI) and DI (EDI) registers are incremented or decremented according to the value of the DF flag. If DF is reset (0), SI (ESI) and DI (EDI) are incremented. If DF is set (1), SI (ESI) and DI (EDI) are decremented. Either a byte or word comparison may be specified. SI (ESI) and DI (EDI) are incremented by one for byte strings and by two for word strings.

Note: The right argument of CMPS is the operand indexed by the DI register, and this operand is addressed using the ES register. This default cannot be overridden.

Syntax: CMPS *source__string,destination__string*
       CMPSB (no operands)
       CMPSW (no operands)

Flags affected: CF, AF, PF, OF, SF, ZF

Flags undefined: None

Protected mode exceptions: If the CS, DS, or ES segment contains an illegal memory operand effective address, a general protection exception is generated. If the SS segment contains an illegal address, a stack fault exception is generated.

Real address mode exceptions: When a word operand is at offset 0FFFFH, INT 13 is generated.

80386 note: Word operands are 32 bits. Use CDQ instruction.

Example: MOV   SI,OFFSET STRING1

             MOV   DI,OFFSET STRING2

             CMPS   STRING1,STRING2

             CMPS   DS:BYTE PTR[SI],ES:[D1]

             LEA   ESI,STRING1   (80386 only)

             LEA   EDI,STRING2

             CMPS   STRING1,STRING2

CWD (80286/80386)

Convert word to doubleword

Instruction: CWD

Typical clocks: 2

Description: Converts a word to a doubleword

Operation: The CWD instruction converts the signed word in the AX register to a signed doubleword in the DX:AX registers. This is accomplished by extending the most-significant bit of AX into all of the bit positions in DX. See the 80386 note.

Syntax: CWD (no operands)

Flags affected: None

Flags undefined: None

Protected mode exceptions: None

Real address mode exceptions: None

80386 note: Word size is 32 bits. Sign-extended value is in EAX; store results in the EDX:EAX register pair.

Example: CWD

DAA (80286/80386)

Decimal adjust after addition

Instruction: DAA

Typical clocks: (80286) 3, (80386) 4

Description: Decimal adjusts AL after addition

Operation: DAA should only be used after the addition of two packed BCD operands. DAA converts the result in AL into packed decimal form, using the following rules:

If the lower nibble of AL is greater than 9, or if CF is set, AL is incremented by 6, and AF is set; otherwise, AF is reset.

If, as a result of the preceding operation, the result is greater than 9FH, or if CF is set, AL is incremented by 60H, and CF is set; otherwise, CF is reset.

Syntax: DAA (no operands)

Flags affected: AF, CF, SF, ZF, PF

Flags undefined: OF

Protected mode exceptions: None

Real address mode exceptions: None

80386 note: No exceptions

Example: MOV   AL,08
            ADD   AL,03   ;Result in AL is 0BH
            DAA   ;Result in AL is 11H

DAS (80286/80386)

Decimal adjust AL after subtraction

Instruction: DAS

Typical clocks: (80286) 3, (80386) 4

Description: Decimal adjusts AL after subtraction

Operation: The DAS instruction should only be executed after the subtraction of two packed BCD numbers. DAS returns an adjusted BCD result in AL, using the following rules:

If the lower nibble of AL is greater than 9, or if AF is set, then decrement AL by 6 and set the AF flag; otherwise, reset AF.

If, as a result of the preceding operation, AL is greater than 9FH, or if CF is set, then decrement AL by 60H and set CF; otherwise, reset CF.

Syntax: DAS (no operands)

Flags affected: AF, CF, SF, PF, ZF

Flags undefined: OF

Protected mode exceptions: None

Real address mode exceptions: None

80386 note: No exceptions

Example: MOV   AL,12
             SUB   AL,03   ;Result in AL is 0FH
             DAS   ;Result in AL is 09H

DEC (80286/80386)

Decrement by 1

Instruction: DEC

Typical clocks: (80286) 2-7, (80386) 2-6

Description: Decrements EA byte/word register by 1

Operation: The DEC instruction subtracts 1 from the contents (byte or word) of the specified memory location or register.

Syntax: DEC *destination*

Flags affected: SF, OF, ZF, AF, PF

Flags undefined: None

Protected mode exceptions: A general protection exception is generated if the operand is in a nonwritable segment. General protection exception generated for an illegal memory operand effective address in the CS, DS, or ES segment. If the SS segment contains an illegal address, a stack fault exception is generated.

Real address mode exceptions: When a word operand is at offset 0FFFFH, INT 13 is generated.

80386 note: Word size is 32 bits.

Example: DEC   AX
             DEC   EXTMEM
             DEC   TABLE[BX][SI]
             DEC   ECX   (80386 only)

DIV (80286/80386)

Unsigned division

Instruction: DIV

Typical clocks: (80286) 14-25, (80386) 14-41

Description: Performs unsigned divide (byte) of AX
Performs unsigned divide (word) of DX:AX

Operation: The DIV instruction performs an unsigned divide. If a byte source operand is specified, the AX register is divided by the byte operand, with the quotient stored in the AL register and the remainder in the AH register. A word source operand divides DX:AX by the word. The most significant 16 bits of the dividend are stored in the DX, the quotient in AX, and the remainder in DX.

Syntax: DIV *source*

Flags affected: None

Flags undefined: SF, AF, OF, AF, PF, CF

Protected mode exceptions: If the divisor is 0, or if the quotient is too large to fit into the designated register (AX or AL), INT 0 is generated. If the CS, DS, or ES segment contains an illegal memory operand effective address, a general protection exception is generated. If the SS segment contains an illegal address, a stack fault exception is generated.

Real address mode exceptions: If the divisor is 0, or if the quotient is too large to fit into the designated register (AX or AL), INT 0 is generated. If the word operand is at offset 0FFFFH, INT 13 is generated. Double-precision division is accomplished, with a 64-bit dividend in the EDX:EAX register, 32-bit divisor in register or memory, 32-bit quotient in EAX, and 32-bit remainder in EDX.

Example: Dividing a byte by another byte:
```
MOV     AL,NUMER_BTE
DIV     DIVSR_BTE ;Quotient in AL, remainder in AH
```
Dividing a word by a byte:
```
MOV     AX,NUMER_WRD
DIV     DIVSR_BTE ;Quotient in AL, remainder in AH
```

Dividing a doubleword by a word:

```
MOV     DX,NUMER_MSW
MOV     AX,NUMER_LSW
DIV     DIVSR_WRD ;Quotient in AX, remainder in DX
```

80386:

```
MOV     EDX,MSB_NUMBER   ;80386 only
MOV     EAX,LSB_NUMBER
DIV     ECX ;Quotient in EAX, remainder in EDX
```

ENTER (80286/80386)

Make stack frame for procedure parameters

Instruction: ENTER

Typical clocks: (80286) 11-16, (80386) 10-19

Description: Makes stack frame for procedure parameters

Operation: ENTER is used to create the stack frame required by most block-structured high-level languages. The first operand specifies how many bytes of dynamic storage are to be allocated on the stack for the routine being entered. The second operand gives the nesting level of the routine within the high-level language source code. ENTER determines how many stack frame pointers are copied into the new stack frame from the preceding frame. BP (EBP) is used as the current stack frame pointer. If the second operand is 0, ENTER pushes BP (EBP), sets BP (EBP) to SP (ESP), and subtracts the first operand from SP (ESP).

Syntax: ENTER *immediate_word, immediate_byte*

Flags affected: None

Flags undefined: None

Protected mode exceptions: A stack fault exception is generated if SP goes outside the stack limit in any part of the instruction execution.

Real address mode exceptions: None

80386 note: Thirty-two bit EBD and ESP registers are used. A 32-bit display is pushed onto the stack to form a new display. The frame size is extended from 16 bits to 32 bits.

Example: ENTER 12,0

HLT (80286/80386)

Halt

Instruction: HLT

Typical clocks: (80286) 2, (80386) 5

Description: Halts processing

Operation: The HLT instruction causes the program to stop executing. Restarting execution is accomplished only by an external interrupt or a reset. No registers or status flags are affected. If an interrupt is used to resume program execution, the saved CS:IP value will point to the instruction that follows the HLT.

Syntax: HLT (no operands)

Flags affected: None

Flags undefined: None

Protected mode exceptions: HLT is a privileged instruction that generates a general protection exception when the current privilege level is a value other than 0.

Real address mode exceptions: None

80386 note: No exceptions

Example: HLT

IDIV (80286/80386)

Integer division (signed)

Instruction: IDIV

Typical clocks: (80286) 17-28, (80386) 19-43

Description: Performs signed divide (byte) of AX
Performs signed divide (word) of DX:AX

Operation: The IDIV instruction performs a signed divide operation. If a byte source operand is specified, the AX register is divided by the byte operand, with the quotient stored in the AL register and the remainder in the AH register. A word source operand divides DX:AX by the word. The most significant 16 bits of the dividend are stored in DX, the quotient in AX, and the remainder in DX. The remainder has the same sign as the dividend and is always less than the dividend. See the 80386 note.

Syntax: IDIV *source*

Flags affected: None

Flags undefined: SF, AF, OF, AF, PF, CF

Protected mode exceptions: If the divisor is 0, or if the quotient is too large to fit into the designated register (AX or AL), INT 0 is generated. If the CS, DS, or ES segment contains an illegal memory operand effective address, a general protection exception is generated. If the SS segment contains an illegal address, a stack fault exception is generated.

Real address mode exceptions: If the divisor is 0, or if the quotient is too large to fit into the designated register (AX or AL), INT 0 is generated. When a word operand is at offset 0FFFFH, INT 13 is generated.

80386 note: Word size is 32 bits. Double-precision division is accomplished with the dividend in the EDX:EAX register pair. The divisor is a 32-bit value in register/memory. The 32-bit quotient is in EAX and the 32-bit remainder is in EDX.

Example:

```
        Dividing a word by a byte:
        MOV     AX,NUMER__WRD
        IDIV    DIVSR__BTE

        Dividing a word by a word:
        MOV     AX,NUMER__WORD
        CWD             ;Convert the word to a doubleword
        IDIV    DIVSR__WRD

        Dividing a doubleword by a word:
        MOV     DX,NUMER__MSW
        MOV     AX,NUMER__LSW
        IDIV    DIVSR__WRD

        80386:
        MOV     EDX,MSB__NUMBER
        MOV     EAX,LSB__NUMBER
        IDIV    DIVISOR
```

IMUL (80286/80386)

Integer multiply

Instruction: IMUL

Typical clocks: (80286) 13-24, (80386) 9-41

Description: Performs signed multiplication

Operation: The IMUL instruction performs a signed multiplication operation. If the source operand is a single byte, then the source operand is multiplied by the contents of the AL register, and the 16-bit signed result is left in AX. CF and OF are reset to 0 if the AH register is a sign extension of AL; otherwise, CF and OF are set to 1. See the 80386 note.

If the source operand specified in the IMUL instruction is a word, then the source operand is multiplied by the contents of the AX register, and the 32-bit signed result is left in DX:AX. The DX register contains the most-significant 16 bits. CF and OF are reset to 0 if DX is a sign extension of AX (see the 80386 note); otherwise, they are set to 1.

If the IMUL instruction contains three operands, the second operand, which is an effective address word, is multiplied by the third immediate word operand. The 16-bit result is placed in the first word-register operand. CF and OF are set to 0 if the result is a signed word between −32768 and +32768; otherwise, they are set to 1.

Syntax: IMUL *source*

Flags affected: OF, CF

Flags undefined: ZF, SF, AF, PF

Protected mode exceptions: If the CS, DS, or ES segment contains an illegal memory operand effective address, a general protection exception is generated. If the SS segment contains an illegal address, a stack fault exception is generated.

Real address mode exceptions: When a word operand is at offset 0FFFFH, INT 13 is generated.

80386 note: Word size is 32 bits. Double-precision multiplication is performed, and the 64-bit result is placed in the EDX:EAX register pair. This is the result of multiplying EAX times a 32-bit register/memory value.

Example: MOV   AL,NUMBER
          IMUL NUMBER   ;Result in AX

```
MOV      AX,VALUE1
IMUL     VALUE2              ;Result in DX:AX
MOV      EAX,0FCAB1234H  ;80386 only
IMUL     NUMBER             ;Result in EDX:EAX
```

IN (80286/80386)

Input byte or word

Instruction: IN

Typical clocks: (80286) 5, (80386) 5-6

Description: Inputs byte or word

Operation: The IN instruction replaces the contents of the AL or AX register with the contents of the designated port. The transfer data can be a byte or a data word. The programmer can access any port from 0 to 65535 by placing the port number in the DX register. If the port is specified with an inline data byte, fixed access to ports 0 through 255 is allowed.

Intel has reserved I/O port addresses 00F8H to 00FFH; these therefore should not be used.

Syntax: IN *accumulator,port*

Flags affected: None

Flags undefined: None

Protected mode exceptions: When IOPL (found in the flags register) contains a value greater than the current privilege level, a general protection exception is generated.

Real address mode exceptions: None

80386 note: Word size is 32 bits.

Example: IN AL, B_P_ADR   ;Input a byte to AL
IN AX, W_P_ADR   ;Input a word to AX
IN AL,DX   ;Input a byte to AL
IN AX,DX   ;Input a word to AX
IN EAX,PORT8   ;80386 only

INC (80286/80386)

Increment by 1

Instruction: INC

Typical clocks: 2-7

Description: Increments EA byte, word, word reg. by 1

Operation: The INC instruction adds 1 to the operand without altering CF.

Syntax: INC *destination*

Flags affected: SF, OF, ZF, AF, PF

Flags undefined: None

Protected mode exceptions: A general protection exception is generated if the operand is in a nonwritable segment. If the CS, DS, or ES segment contains an illegal memory operand effective address, a general protection exception is generated. If the SS segment contains an illegal address, a stack fault exception is generated.

Real address mode exceptions: INT 13 is generated for a word operand at offset 0FFFFH.

80386 note: Word size is 32 bits.

Example: INC AX
          INC EBX   (80386 only)
          INC MEM — LOC

INS/INSB/INSW (80286/80386)

Input from port to string

Instruction: INS,INSB,INSW

Typical clocks: (80286) 5, (80386) 5-8

Description: Inputs byte, word from port DX to ES:[DI]

Operation: With the DX (EDX) register pointing to an input port, INS transfers a byte or word string element into the memory location at ES:DI. Whether a byte or word is moved is determined by the first operand of the INS instruction. The memory operand must be addressable from the ES register, because there is no provision for a segment override.

The INS instruction does not permit the port number to be specified as an immediate value. The port can only be addressed using the DX register.

After the instruction has been executed, the DI (EDI) register is automatically advanced. If DF is 0 (CLD was executed), DI (EDI) is incremented. If DF is 1 (STD was executed), DI (EDI) is decremented. The increment or decrement is 1 if a byte is moved, and 2 if a word is moved.

Syntax: INS *destination—string,port*
      INSB (no operands)
      INSW (no operands)

Flags affected: None

Flags undefined: None

Protected mode exceptions: When the value of CPL is greater than that of IOPL, a general protection exception is generated. A general protection exception is also generated if the destination is in a nonwritable segment. If the CS, DS, or ES segment contains an illegal memory operand effective address, a general protection exception is generated. If the SS segment contains an illegal address, a stack fault exception is generated.

Real address mode exceptions: When a word operand is at offset 0FFFFH, INT 13 is generated.

80386 note: Word size is 32 bits. Memory addresses are formed from 32-bit effective addresses. The port number is taken from the DX register. The effective address does not affect the I/O port address.

Example: INS   BTE—STRG,DX ;Input a byte
      INS   WRD—STRG,DX ;Input a word   String lengths taken
      INSB   ;Input a byte   from ECS register
      INSW   ;Input a word

INT/INTO (80286/80386)

Interrupt

Instruction: INT

Typical clocks: (80286) 23-167, (80386) 33-287

Description: Generates call to interrupt procedure

Operation: The INT instruction generates a call to an interrupt procedure by means of a software switch. The immediate operand, which contains a value between 0 and 255, inclusive, gives the index number to the interrupt descriptor table of the interrupt procedure being called. In protected mode, the interrupt descriptor table consists of 8-byte descriptors. The descriptor for the interrupt invoked must specify an interrupt gate, a trap gate, or a task gate. In real address mode, the interrupt descriptor table is an array of 4-byte pointers at fixed location 00000H.

The INTO instruction is identical to the INT instruction, with the exception that the interrupt number is implicitly 4. Also, the interrupt is made only when the Overflow flag is set.

In real address mode the INT instruction pushes the flags, CS, and the return IP (EIP) onto the stack, in that order. It then uses the pointer indexed by the interrupt number.

Syntax: INT *interrupt—type*
  INTO (no operands)

Flags affected: All flags are affected if a task switch takes place; otherwise, no flags are affected.

Flags undefined: None

Protected mode exceptions: A general protection exception, descriptor not present exception, stack fault exception, or invalid task state segment may be generated.

Real address mode exceptions: None

80386 note: Operand size has no effect. EIP, ESP, and FLAGS size is taken from the gate.

Example: INT 21H
  INTO

IRET (80286/80386)

Interrupt return

Instruction: IRET

Typical clocks: (80286) 17-169, (80386) 22-275

Description: Interrupts return

Operation: In real address mode, the IRET instruction pops IP (EIP), CS, and FLAGS from the stack and resumes the interrupted code.

In protected mode, the IRET instruction depends on the setting of the Nested Task flag (NT).

If NT = 1, the instruction reverses the operation of the CALL or INT that caused a task switch. The code executing IRET has its updated state saved in its task state segment. This means that if the task is reentered, the instructions following the IRET will be executed.

If NT = 0, IRET returns from an interrupt subroutine without a task switch. The privilege level of the source code returned to must be the same or less than the interrupt routine.

Syntax: IRET (no operands)

Flags affected: The entire flag register is popped from the stack.

Flags undefined: None

Protected mode exceptions: A general protection exception, descriptor not present exception, or stack fault exception may be generated.

Real address mode exceptions: INT 13 is generated if the stack is popped when it has offset 0FFFFH.

80386 note: A 32-bit extended instruction pointer is used. INTER level pops a 48-bit ESP. A 48-bit EIP and a 32-bit FLAG register are popped.

Example: IRET

J(*condition*) (80286/80386)

Jump short if condition met

Instruction		Typical clocks:	Description:
JA	*	7	Jumps if above
JAE	*	7	Jumps if above or equal
JB	*	7	Jumps if below
JBE	*	7-9	Jumps if below or equal

Instruction		Typical clocks:	Description:
JC		7-9	Jumps if carry
JCXZ		8	Jumps if CX register is 0
JE	*	7	Jumps if equal
JG	*	7	Jumps if greater
JGE	*	7	Jumps if greater than or equal
JL	*	7	Jumps if less than
JLE	*	7	Jumps if less than or equal
JNA	*	7	Jumps if not above
JNAE	*	7	Jumps if not above or equal
JNB	*	7	Jumps if not below
JNBE	*	7	Jumps if not below or equal
JNC		7	Jumps if not carry
JNE	*	7	Jumps if not equal
JNG	*	7	Jumps if not greater
JNGE	*	7	Jumps if not greater or equal
JNL	*	7	Jumps if not less
JNO	*	7	Jumps if not less or equal
JNP		7	Jumps if not overflow
JNS	*	7	Jumps if not parity
JNZ	*	7	Jumps if not sign

Instruction		Typical clocks:	Description:
JO	*	7	Jumps if not zero
JP	*	7	Jumps if overflow
JPE	*	7	Jumps if parity
JPO	*	7	Jumps if parity even
JS	*	7	Jumps if parity odd
JZ	*	7	Jumps if sign
		7	Jumps if zero
			Full-size displacement of 16/32 bits for 80386

Operation: The J (followed by a condition from the preceding list) instruction transfers control to the operand specified in the instruction. These are conditional short jumps which test the flags. The test condition operand must be within −128 to +127 bytes of the next instruction. This restriction is necessary for the assembler to construct a 1-byte signed displacement from the end of the current instruction.

Syntax: J(*test_condition*)

Flags affected: None

Flags undefined: None

Protected mode exceptions: When the offset jumped to is beyond the bounds of the code segment, a general protection exception is generated.

Real address mode exceptions: None

80386 note: Uses a 32-bit extended instruction pointer. Displacement is 8 bits, sign extended to 32 bits, unless marked otherwise.

Example: JA   INST_LABEL

JMP (80286/80386)

Jump

Instruction: JMP

Typical clocks: (80286) 7-183, (80386) 7-268

Description: Performs an unconditional jump

Operation: The JMP instruction transfers program control to a different instruction without storing any return information. JMP performs intrasegment direct and indirect jumps and intersegment jumps.

Intrasegment direct jumps use the offset byte following the instruction. Intrasegment indirect jumps use the contents of the location addressed by the bytes that follow the instruction byte. When the instruction is an intrasegment direct jump, the distance from the end of the instruction to the target label is added to IP (EIP).

Intersegment jumps replace the contents of the CS register. For direct jumps, this is accomplished using the second word following the instructions. For indirect jumps, the CS register is replaced with the second word following the indicated data address.

Syntax: JMP *(target)*

Flags affected: All flags are affected if a task switch takes place; otherwise, none are affected.

Flags undefined: None

Protected mode exceptions: If the jump is NEAR, a general protection exception can be generated if the destination offset is beyond the limits of the current code segment. If the jump is FAR, a general protection exception is generated. Other possible exceptions are a descriptor not present exception, a stack fault exception, and an invalid task state segment exception. When the indirect intersegment jump operand is a register, an undefined opcode exception is generated.

Real address mode exceptions: When an indirect intersegment jump operand is a register, an undefined opcode exception is generated.

80386 note: A 32-bit extended instruction pointer is used. Pointer operands are 48 bits and displacements are 32 bits.

Example: Intersegment direct jump:

   JMP   FAR—LABEL

   Intersegment indirect jump:

   JMP   TABLE[BP][DI]
   JMP   TABLE[EBP][EDI]   (80386 only)

   Intrasegment direct jump:

   JMP   NEAR—LABEL

   Intrasegment indirect jump:

   JMP   WORDPTR[BX][DI]

LAHF (80286/80386)

Load AH from flags

Instruction: LAHF

Typical clocks: 2

Description: Loads SF, ZF, AF, PF, CF into selected AH pos.

Operation: The LAHF instruction moves the flag registers SF, ZF, AF, PF, and CF into certain bits of the AH register, as defined here:

SF	ZF	AF	PF	CF

Bit 7   Bit 0

   Bit positions 1, 3, and 5 are undefined.

Syntax: LAHF(no operands)

Flags affected: None

Flags undefined: None

Protected mode exceptions: None

Real address mode exceptions: None

80386 note: No exceptions.

Example: LAHF

LAR (80286/80386)

Load access rights byte

Instruction: LAR

Typical clocks: (80286) 14-16, (80386) 15-16

Description: Loads access rights byte, selector

Operation: The second operand (memory or register word) of the LAR instruction contains a selector. If the associated descriptor is visible at the current privilege level and the selector RPL, then the access rights byte of the descriptor is loaded into the high byte of the first (register) operand, and the low byte is set to 0. The ZF is set if the loading was performed; otherwise, it is reset to 0.

Syntax: LAR (access_rights_byte,selector)

Flags affected: ZF

Flags undefined: None

Protected mode exceptions: If the CS, DS, or ES segment contains an illegal memory operand effective address, a general protection exception is generated. If the SS segment contains an illegal address, a stack fault exception is generated.

Real address mode exceptions: INT 6 is generated. In real address mode, LAR is not recognized.

80386 note: No exceptions.

Example: LAR ARB,SELECTR

LDS/LES (80286/80386)
LSS/LFS/LGS (80386)

Load doubleword pointer

Instruction: LDS/LES

Typical clocks: 7

Description: Loads EA DW into DS/ES and word register

Operation: LDS/LES loads the 4-byte pointer, located at the memory location indicated by the second operand in the instruction, into a segment register and a word register. The first word of the pointer (offset) is loaded into the register indicated by the instruction's first operand. The last word of the pointer is loaded into the DS register (for LDS) or ES register (for LES).

Syntax: LDS *destination,source*

Flags affected: None

Flags undefined: None

Protected mode exceptions: Possible exceptions are a general protection exception and a descriptor not present exception. If the operand lies outside the segment limit, a general protected mode exception or stack fault exception is generated. If the source operand is a register, an undefined opcode exception is generated.

Real address mode exceptions: INT 13 is generated for an operand at offset 0FFFFH or 0FFFFDH. When the source operand is a register, an undefined opcode exception is generated.

80386 note: Word size is 32 bits. Pointer operands are 48 bits. Operation extends to LSS/LFS/LGS.

Example: LDS SI,DOUBLEWORD1
         LES BX,DOUBLEWORD2

LEA (80286/80386)

Load effective address offset

Instruction: LEA

Typical clocks: (80286) 3, (80386) 2

Description: Transfers offset of source to destination

Operation: The first operand of LEA is the target register operand, which is loaded with the offset address of the second operand.

Syntax: LEA *destination,source*

Flags affected: None

Flags undefined: None

Protected mode exceptions: An undefined opcode exception is generated if the second operand is a register.

Real address mode exceptions: An undefined opcode exception is generated if the second operand is a register.

80386 note: Word size is 32 bits. Memory addresses are formed from 32-bit effective addresses.

Example: LEA AX,[BP][DI]
           LEA EBX,MYDATA   (80386 only)

LEAVE (80286/80386)

High-level procedure exit

Instruction: LEAVE

Typical clocks: (80286) 5, (80386) 4

Description: Generates a procedure return for high level language

Operation: The LEAVE instruction performs the opposite operation of the ENTER instruction. LEAVE deallocates all local variables and sets BP to SP, returning the registers to their values immediately after the call to the procedure.

When BP (EBP) is copied into SP (ESP), the stack space used by the procedure is released. The old frame pointer is now popped into BP (EBP), restoring the caller's frame, and a subsequent RET nn instruction follows the back-link and removes any arguments pushed on the stack for the exiting procedure.

Syntax: LEAVE (no operands)

Flags affected: None

Flags undefined: None

Protected mode exceptions: When BP (EBP) does not point to a location within the current stack segment, a stack fault exception is generated.

Real address mode exceptions: When a word operand is at offset 0FFFFH, INT 13 is generated.

80386 note: Word size is 32 bits. EBP and ESP registers are used.

Example: LEAVE

LGDT/LIDT (80286/80386)

Load global/interrupt descriptor table register

Instruction: LGDT/LIDT

Typical clocks: 11-12

Description: Loads mem. into GDT or IDT reg.

Operation: The LGDT or LIDT instruction loads the 6 bytes of memory pointed to by the effective address of the operand into either the global or interrupt descriptor table register. The LIMIT field of the descriptor table register loads from the first word; the next three bytes go to the BASE field of the register; the last byte is ignored. These are operating systems software instructions and are not found in applications programs.

Syntax: LGDT *memory—operand*

Flags affected: None

Flags undefined: None

Protected mode exceptions: A general protection exception is generated if the current privilege level is not 0. If the source operand is a register, an undefined opcode exception is generated. If the CS, DS, or ES segment contains an illegal memory operand effective address, a general protection exception is generated. If the SS segment contains an illegal address, a stack fault exception is generated.

Real address mode exceptions: When a word operand is at offset 0FFFFH, INT 13 is generated.

80386 note: No exceptions.

Example: LGDT MEM—WRD
          LIDT MEM—WRD

LLDT (80286/80386)

Load local descriptor table register

Instruction: LLDT

Typical clocks: (80286) 17-19, (80386) 20

Description: Loads selector into local descriptor table register

Operation: The word operand (memory or register) of LLDT should contain a selector pointing to the global descriptor table. This entry should be a local descriptor table. In this case, the local descriptor table register is loaded from the entry. This is an operating system software instruction and is not found in applications software.

Syntax: LLDT *word___operand*

Flags affected: None

Flags undefined: None

Protected mode exceptions: If the current privilege level is not 0, a general protection exception is generated. A general protection exception is generated if the selector operand does not point to the global descriptor table, or if the entry in GDT is not a local descriptor table. When the LDT descriptor is not present, a descriptor not present exception is generated. If the CS, DS, or ES segment contains an illegal memory operand effective address, a general protection exception is generated. If the SS segment contains an illegal address, a stack fault exception is generated.

Real address mode exceptions: INT 6 is generated. In real address mode, LLDT is not recognized.

80386 note: No exceptions.

Example: LLDT BP

LMSW (80286/80386)

Load machine status word

Instruction: LMSW

Typical clocks: (80286) 3-6, (80386) 10-13

Description: Loads EA word into machine status word

Operation: LMSW is an operating systems software instruction that does not appear in applications programs. LMSW loads the machine status word from the source operand and may be used to switch to protected mode. If protected mode is used, the next instruction must be an intrasegment jump to flush the instruction queue.

Syntax: LMSW *source__operand*

Flags affected: None

Flags undefined: None

Protected mode exceptions: If the current privilege level is not 0, a general protection exception is generated. If the CS, DS, or ES segment contains an illegal memory operand effective address, a general protection exception is generated. If the SS segment contains an illegal address, a stack fault exception is generated.

Real address mode exceptions: When a word operand is at offset 0FFFFH, INT 13 is generated.

Example: LMSW SP

LOCK (80386)

Activate the BUS LOCK signal

Instruction: LOCK

Typical clocks: 0

Description: Activates the BUS LOCK signal

Operation: The LOCK instruction prefix locks the area of memory specified by an instruction's destination operand. This is accomplished by activating the BUS LOCK signal of the 80386 and remains in effect for the duration of the instruction. The memory location remains locked and protected as long as another processor does not execute a nonlocked instruction sharing the same memory area. 80386 instructions that may be preceded by the LOCK prefix are:

BT, BTS, BTR, BTC	memory register/immediate
XCG	register, memory
XCG	memory, register
ADC, SUB, ADC, SBB, OR, XOR, AND	memory, register/immediate
NOT, NEG, INC, DEC	memory

Syntax: LOCK instruction, *operand__type*

Flags affected: None

Flags undefined: None

Protected mode exceptions: A general protection error is generated if the Input/Output privilege level is lower than the current privilege level.

Real address mode exceptions: None

80386 note: The 8086 and 80286 have a superset of the lock function available on the 80386. An application written for the above mentioned processors may not operate properly on the 80386.

Example: LOCK XCG MEM — WORD,AX

LODS/LODSB/LODSW: (80286/80386)

Load byte or word string

Instruction: LODS/LODSB/LODSW

Typical clocks: 5

Description: Loads byte[SI], DS:[SI] into AL

Loads byte[ESI], DS:[ESI] into AL

Operation: The LODS instructions transfer either a byte or word operand from the source operand pointed to by the SI (ESI) register into the accumulator's AL or AX register. SI (ESI) is automatically advanced. If the Direction flag was 0 (CLD was executed), SI (ESI) is incremented. If DF was 1 (STD was executed), SI (ESI) is decremented. The advance is 1 for byte operands and 2 for word operands.

Syntax: LODS *source—string*

LODSB (no operands)

LODSW (no operands)

Flags affected: None

Flags undefined: None

Protected mode exceptions: If the CS, DS, or ES segment contains an illegal memory operand effective address, a general protection exception is generated. If the SS segment contains an illegal address, a stack fault exception is generated.

Real address mode exceptions: When a word operand is at offset 0FFFFH, INT 13 is generated.

80386 note: Word size is 32 bits.

Example: LEA SI,DATA   ;If data is 16 bits, result in AX
          LODS

LOOP (80286/80386)

Loop control with CX counter

Instruction:	Description:*
LOOP	Transfers decrement CX if CX is not zero
LOOPE	Transfers decrement CX if CX $<>$ 0, ZF = 1
LOOPNE	Transfers decrement CX if CX $<>$ 0, ZF = 0
LOOPNZ	Transfers decrement CX if CX $<>$ 0, ZF = 0
LOOPZ	Transfers decrement CX if CX $<>$ 0, ZF = 1

Typical clocks: (80286) 8, (80286) 11

Operation: The LOOP instruction decrements the CX (ECX) register by 1. No flags are affected. Next, the conditions are checked for the LOOPn instruction specified. If the test conditions are met, then an intrasegment transfer is made. The target operand must be in the range from 128 bytes before the instruction to 127 bytes after the instruction.

Syntax: LOOP *short—target*
       LOOPE *short—target*
       LOOPZ *short—target*
       LOOPNZ *short—target*
       LOOPNE *short—target*

Flags affected: None

Flags undefined: None

Protected mode exceptions: A general protection exception is generated if the offset jumped to is beyond the limits of the current code segment.

---

* ECX can be substituted for CX

Real address mode exceptions: None

80386 note: No exceptions.

Example:

	MOV	CL,04H	
AGAIN:	ADD	BX,01H	
	ADD	AL,INFO[BX]	
	DAA		
	LOOP	AGAIN	
	MOV	CX,12H	
Next:	INC	BX	
	CMP	TABLE[BX],0	
	LOOPE	NEXT	
	MOV	ECX,0ABCDEH	(80386 only)
Repeat:	INC	BX	
	MOV	AL,TABLE_A[BX]	
	ADD	AL,TABLE_B[BX]	
	MOV	TOTAL[BX],AL	
	LOOPNZ	REPEAT	

LSL (80286/80386)

Load segment limit

Instruction: LSL

Typical clocks: (80286) 14-16, (80386) 20-26

Description: Loads segment limit, selector

Operation: If the selector in the second (memory or register) operand is visible at CPL, a word that consists of the limit field of the descriptor is loaded into the left operand, which must be a register. The value is the limit field for that segment. The Zero flag is set to 1 if the loading was performed; otherwise, the Zero flag is reset to 0.

Syntax: LSL *seg_limit,selector*

Flags affected: ZF

Flags undefined: None

Protected mode exceptions: If the CS, DS, or ES segment contains an illegal memory operand effective address, a general protection exception is generated. If the SS segment contains an illegal address, a stack fault exception is generated.

Real address mode exceptions: INT 6 is generated. In real address mode, LSL is not recognized.

80386 note: No exceptions.

Example: LSL AX,SELECTR

LTR (80286/80386)

Load task register

Instruction: LTR

Typical clocks: (80286) 17-19, (80386) 23-27

Description: Loads EA word into task register

Operation: The LTR instruction causes the task register to be loaded from the source register or memory location source operand. The loaded TSS is marked busy. This is an operating systems software instruction and does not appear in applications programs.

Syntax: LTR *source__operand*

Flags affected: None

Flags undefined: None

Protected mode exceptions: If the CS, DS, or ES segment contains an illegal memory operand effective address, a general protected mode exception is generated. If the SS segment contains an illegal address, a stack fault exception is generated.

Real address mode exceptions: INT 6 is generated. In real address mode, LTR is not recognized.

80386 note: No exceptions.

Example: LTR MEM__WRD

MOV (80286/80386)

Move

Instruction: Move

Typical clocks: (80286) 2-19, (80386) 2-22

Description: Copies the source to the destination

Operation: There are several MOV instructions, all of which have the same function. They all copy the source operand's contents into the destination operand without destroying the source.

Syntax: MOV *destination,source*

Flags affected: None

Flags undefined: None

Protected mode exceptions: A general protection exception, stack fault exception, or descriptor not present exception may be generated if a segment register is being loaded. A general protection exception also may be generated if the destination is in a nonwritable segment. If the CS, DS, or ES segment contains an illegal memory operand effective address, a general protection exception is generated. If the SS segment contains an illegal address, a stack fault exception is generated.

Real address mode exceptions: When a word operand is at offset 0FFFFH, INT 13 is generated.

80386 note: Word size is 32 bits. Memory addresses are formed using 32-bit effective addresses or 32-bit displacement.

Example: To accumulator from memory:
MOV AX,MEM — WRD
MOV ECX,MYWORD   (80386 only)

To memory from accumulator:
MOV MEM — BYTE,AL

To memory/register from segment register:
MOV BX,ES
MOV TABLE[BX],SS

To segment register from memory/register:
MOV ES,NEXT — WRD[SI]
MOV DS,AX

To register from register:

MOV CX,DI

MOV EAX,ECX   (80386 only)

To register from memory/register:

MOV AX,MEM_VAL

MOV CX,[BP][SI]

To register from immediate data:

MOV DI,513

MOV EAX,12345678H   (80386 only)

To memory/register from immediate data:

MOV TABLE[BP][SI],25

MOV BX,77

MOVS/MOVSB/MOVSW (80286/80386)

Move byte or word string

Instruction: MOVS/SB/SW

Typical clocks: (80286) 5, (80386) 7

Description: Moves byte/word DS:[SI] or ES:[DI]
               Moves byte/word DS:[ESI] or ES:[EDI]

Operation: The MOV instructions copy the byte or word at [SI] ([ESI]) to the byte or word destination operand at ES:[DI] (ES:[EDI]). The destination operand must be addressable from the ES register. Segment overrides are not possible for the destination operand, but the source operand may use a segment override.

After the instruction is executed, both SI (ESI) and DI (EDI) are automatically advanced, based on the following rules. If DF is 0 (CLD was executed), the registers are incremented. If DF is 1 (STD was executed), the registers are decremented. The registers are advanced 1 for byte operands and 2 for word operands.

Syntax: MOVS *destination_string,source_string*

       MOVSB (no operands)

       MOVSW (no operands)

Flags affected: None

Flags undefined: None

Protected mode exceptions: A general protection exception is generated if the destination is in a nonwritable segment. If the CS, DS, or ES segment contains an illegal memory operand effective address, a general protection exception is generated. If the SS segment contains an illegal address, a stack fault exception is generated.

Real address mode exceptions: When a word operand is at offset 0FFFFH, INT 13 is generated.

80386 note: Memory addresses are formed using 32-bit effective addresses. String length (count) is derived from the ECX register.

Example:		LEA	SI,MYSOURCE
		LEA	DI,ES:HERDESTINATION
		MOV	CX,50
	REP	MOVS	HERDESTINATION,MYSOURCE

MOVZX/MOVSX (80386)

Mov reg./mem to sign/zero extension 16/32-bit register

Instruction: MOVZX/MOVSX

Typical clocks: 3-6

Description: Moves source to sign/zero ext. 16 or 32-bit reg.

Operation: The MOVZX and MOVSX instructions are added to move an 8-or 16-bit register or memory value to a register with sign or zero extension to 16 or 32 bits.

Syntax: MOVZX *register,register/memory*
MOVSX *register,register/memory*

Flags affected: None

Flags undefined: None

Protected mode exceptions: A general protection exception is generated if the memory operand violates segment limit or access rights. A stack fault exception is generated for an illegal address in the SS segment.

Real address mode exceptions: INT 13 is generated for a word operand at offset 0FFFFH.

Example: MOVZX EAX,BX
MOVZX CX,AL

```
MOVSX AX,BX        ;Normal move
MOVSX ECX,CL
MOVSX EAX,MYMEMORY
```

MUL (80286/80386)

Multiply, unsigned

Instruction: MUL

Typical clocks: (80286) 13-21, (80386) 9-41

Description: Performs unsigned multiply (AX = AL × specified byte)
Performs unsigned multiply (DX:AX = AX × specified word)

Operation: A byte operand of the MUL instruction causes the byte to be multiplied by the AL register and the result left in the AX register. CF and OF are reset to 0 if AH is 0; otherwise, they are set to 1.

A word operand of the MUL instruction causes the word to be multiplied by the AX register and the result left in DX:AX. DX contains the high-order 16 bits of the result. CF and OF are reset to 0 if DX is 0; otherwise, they are set to 1. See the 80386 note.

Syntax: MUL *source*

Flags affected: OF, CF

Flags undefined: SF, ZF, AF, PF

Protected mode exceptions: If the CS, DS, or ES segment contains an illegal memory operand effective address, a general protection exception is generated. If the SS segment contains an illegal address, a stack fault exception is generated.

Real address mode exceptions: When a word operand is at offset 0FFFFH, INT 13 is generated.

80386 note: Word size is 32 bits. Double precision multiplication is accomplished by multiplying EAX by the 32-bit register/memory location. The 64-bit result is stored in the EDX:EAX register pair.

Example: Multiplying a byte by a word:
```
MOV   AL,MULTP_BTE
CBW                 ;Converts byte in AL to word in AX
MUL   VAL_BTE
```

Multiplying a byte by a byte:

```
MOV   AL,MULTP_BTE
MUL   VAL_BTE
```

Multiplying a word by a word:

```
MOV   AX,MULTP_WRD
MUL   VAL_WRD          ;High bits in DX, low bits in AX
```

80386:

```
MOV   EAX,0FCAB1234H       (80386 only)
MUL   EBX
```

NEG (80286/80386)

Two's complement negation

Instruction: NEG

Typical clocks: (80286) 2-7, (80386) 2-6

Description: Performs two's complement negation of specified byte or word

Operation: This instruction subtracts the operand from 0, adds 1 to it, and returns the result to the operand forming the two's complement. The Carry flag is set to 1, except when the operand is 0; this causes CF to be reset to 0.

Syntax: NEG *destination*

Flags affected: OF, SF, ZF, AF, CF, PF

Flags undefined: None

Protected mode exceptions: A general protected mode exception is generated if the result is in a nonwritable segment. If the CS, DS, or ES segment contains an illegal memory operand effective address, a general protection exception is generated. If the SS segment contains an illegal address, a stack fault exception is generated.

Real address mode exceptions: When a word operand is at offset 0FFFFH, INT 13 is generated.

80386 note: Word size is 32 bits.

Example: NEG AL

```
          NEG EBX       (80386 only)
```

NOP (80286/80386)

No operation

Instruction: NOP

Typical clocks: 3

Description: Performs no operation

Operation: The NOP instruction performs no operation and is a 1-byte instruction that affects only the IP (EIP) register.

Syntax: NOP (no operands)

Flags affected: None

Flags undefined: None

Protected mode exceptions: None

Real address mode exceptions: None

80386 note: No exceptions.

Example: NOP

NOT (80286/80386)

Logical Not

Instruction: NOT

Typical clocks: (80286) 2-7, (80386) 2-6

Description: Reverses each bit of EA byte, word

Operation: The NOT instruction flips each bit in the operand and returns the result to the operand. No flags are affected.

Syntax: NOT *destination*

Flags affected: None

Flags undefined: None

Protected mode exceptions: If the result is in a nonwritable segment, a general protection error is generated. If the CS, DS, or ES segment contains an illegal memory operand effective address, a general protection exception is generated. If the SS segment contains an illegal address, a stack fault exception is generated.

Real address mode exceptions: When a word operand is at offset 0FFFFH, INT 13 is generated.

80386 note: Word size is 32 bits.

Example: NOT AX
NOT EBX   (80386 only)

OR (80286/80386)

Logical inclusive OR

Instruction: OR

Typical clocks: (80286) 2-7, (80386) 2-7

Description: Performs logical inclusive OR operation

Operation: The OR instruction performs an inclusive OR operation on the two operands. Those corresponding bit pairs containing 0's return 0 to the destination operand; otherwise, 1 is returned. The result is stored in the destination operand.

Syntax: OR *destination,source*

Flags affected: CF = 0, OF = 0, SF, ZF, PF

Flags undefined: AF

Protected mode exceptions: If the result is in a nonwritable segment a general protection error is generated. If the CS, DS, or ES segment contains an illegal memory operand effective address, a general protection exception is generated. If the SS segment contains an illegal address, a stack fault exception is generated.

Real address mode exceptions: When a word operand is at offset 0FFFFH, INT 13 is generated.

80386 note: Word size is 32 bits.

Example: OR   CX,DI
OR   EAX,0FFFF0000H   (80386 only)
OR   EBX,ECX   (80386 only)

OUT (80286/80386)

Output byte or word

Instruction: OUT

Typical clocks: (80286) 3, (80386) 3-4

Description: Outputs word, byte to immediate port [DX]

Operation: The contents of the accumulator, AX or AL, are sent to the output port. Any port from 0 to 65535 can be used for output.

Syntax: OUT *port,accumulator*

Flags affected: None

Flags undefined: None

Protected mode exceptions: If IOPL (found in the flags register) contains a higher than the current privilege level, a general protection value specified exception is generated.

Real address mode exceptions: None

80386 note: Word size is 32 bits.

Example: OUT   WRD__PORT,AX
        OUT   BYT__PORT,AL
        OUT   EDX,EAX   (80386 only)

OUTS/OUTSB/OUTSW (80286/80386)

Output string to port

Instruction: OUTS/SB/SW

Typical clocks: (80286) 5, (80386) 7

Description: Outputs byte, word [SI],DS:[SI] to port DX

Operation: The OUT instruction moves a byte or word string from the memory location pointed to by DS:SI to the port pointed to by the address in DX. The second operand of OUT determines which data type, word or byte, is moved.

SI is automatically incremented by 1 if the Direction flag is 0; if DF is set, SI is decremented by 1. The register advance is 1 for byte operands and 2 for word operands.

Syntax: OUTS *port,source___string*
        OUTSB (no operands)
        OUTSW (no operands)

Flags affected: None

Flags undefined: None

Protected mode exceptions: If the value of CPL is greater than or equal to the value of IOPL, a general protection mode exception is generated. This can also happen if the CS, DS, or ES segment contains an illegal memory operand effective address. If the SS segment contains an illegal address, a stack fault exception is generated.

Real address mode exceptions: When a word operand is at offset 0FFFFH, INT 13 is generated.

80386 note: Word size is 32 bits. The memory address is formed from the 32-bit effective address. The 16-bit part number is taken from the DX register. The 32-bit specification does not affect the I/O port address. String length (count) is taken from the ECX register.

Example: OUTS   DX,BYT___STRNG
        OUTS   DX,WRD___STRNG
        OUTSB
        OUTSW

POP (80286/80386)

Pop word off stack to destination

Instruction: POP

Typical clocks: (80286) 5, (80386) 5-7

Description: Pops top of stack into DS, ES, SS, memory, word, register

Operation: The POP instruction takes the word pointed to by the SP pointer and puts it into the destination operand and increments the stack pointer by 2.

Syntax: POP *destination*

Flags affected: None

Flags undefined: None

Protected mode exceptions: A general protection exception, stack fault exception, or descriptor not present exception is generated when a segment register is being loaded. A stack fault exception is generated if the current top of stack is not within the stack segment. A destination address in a nonwritable segment will also generate a general protection exception. If the CS, DS, or ES segment contains an illegal memory operand effective address, a general protection exception is generated. If the SS segment contains an illegal address, a stack fault exception is generated.

Real address mode exceptions: When a word operand is at offset 0FFFFH, INT 13 is generated.

80386 note: Word size is 32 bits. Memory addresses are formed from 32-bit effective addresses.

Example: Register operand:
```
POP    CX
POP    EAX        (80386 only)
```
Segment register:
```
POP    SS
```

POPA (80286/80386)

Pop all general registers

Instruction: POPA

Typical clocks: (80286) 19, (80386) 24

Description: Pops DI, SI, BP, SP, BX, DX, CX, AX (80286)
Pops EDI, ESI, EBP, ESP, EBX, EDX, ECX, EAX (80386)

Operation: The POPA instruction pops all eight general registers listed here, except SP (ESP). The value of SP (ESP) is discarded instead of being loaded into SP (ESP).

POPA reverses a PUSHA instruction, restoring the general registers to their values before the PUSHA was executed. DI (EDI) is the first register popped.

Syntax: POPA (no operands).

Flags affected: None

Flags undefined: None

Protected mode exceptions: When the starting or ending stack address is not within the stack segment, a stack fault exception is generated.

Real address mode exceptions: When a word operand is at offset 0FFFFH, INT 13 is generated.

80386 note: Word size is 32 bits.

Example: POPA

POPF (80286/80386)

Pop flags off stack

Instruction: POPF

Typical clocks: 5

Description: Pops top of stack into flags register

Operation: The POPF instruction uses SS:SP to point to the top of the stack and copies the information into the flags register. SP (ESP) is automatically incremented by 2. The flags are defined from the top bit (bit 15) to the lowest bit (bit 0) as follows: Undefined, Nested Task, I/O Privilege Level (requiring 2 bits), Overflow, Direction, Interrupt Enabled, Trap, Sign, Zero, Undefined, Auxiliary Carry, Undefined, Parity, Undefined, and Carry.

Syntax: POPF (no operands)

Flags affected: The entire flags register is popped from the stack.

Flags undefined: None

Protected mode exceptions: When the top of stack is not within the stack segment, a stack fault exception is generated.

Real address mode exceptions: When a word operand is at offset 0FFFFH, INT 13 is generated.

80386 note: Word size is 32 bits.

Example: POPF

PUSH (80286/80386)

Push word onto stack

Instruction: PUSH

Typical clocks: (80286) 3-5, (80386) 2-5

Description: Pushes ES, CS, SS, DS, reg., mem., immed.

Operation: The PUSH instruction decrements SP (ESP) by 2, and the operand is placed on the new top of the stack. The 80286/80386 PUSH instruction pushes the value of SP (ESP) as it existed before the instruction. This is different from the 8086 PUSH instruction, which pushes the new value (decremented by 2) onto the stack.

Syntax: PUSH *source*

Flags affected: None

Flags undefined: None

Protected mode exceptions: When the new value of SP is outside the stack segment limit, a stack fault exception is generated. If the CS, DS, or ES segment contains an illegal memory operand effective address, a general protection exception is generated. If the SS segment contains an illegal address, a stack fault exception is generated.

Real address mode exceptions: When a word operand is at offset 0FFFFH, INT 13 is generated.

80386 note: Word size is 32 bits. Memory addresses are formed from 32-bit effective addresses.

Example: PUSH AX
             PUSH EBX   (80386 only)
             PUSH CS

PUSHA (80286/80386)

Push all general registers

Instruction: PUSHA

Typical clocks: (80286) 17, (80386) 18

Description: Pushes AX, CX, DX, BX, original SP, BP, SI, DI (80286)
Pushes EAX,ECX,EDX,EBX, original ESP, EBP, ESI, EDI (80386)

Operation: The PUSHA instruction saves the contents of the eight general-purpose registers—(80286) AX, CX, DX, BX, original SP, BP, SI, and DI or (80386) EAX, ECX, EDX, EBX, original ESP, EBP, ESI, EDI—onto the stack. The stack pointer is decremented by 16 to hold the eight word values. The contents of the registers are pushed onto the stack in the order listed here. This causes them to appear in the 16 new stack bytes in reverse order.

Syntax: PUSHA (no operands)

Flags affected: None

Flags undefined: None

Protected mode exceptions: A stack fault exception is generated if the starting or ending address is outside the stack segment limit.

Real address mode exceptions: When a word operand is at offset 0FFFFH, INT 13 is generated.

80386 note: Word size is 32 bits.

Example: PUSHA

PUSHF (80286/80386)

Push flags register onto the stack

Instruction: PUSHF

Typical clocks: (80286) 3, (80386) 4

Description: Pushes flags register

Operation: The PUSHF instruction decrements the SP (ESP) register by 2 and copies all the flag registers into specific bits of the word operand addressed by SP (ESP). The following list defines the flags from the top bit (bit 15) to the lowest bit (bit 0): Undefined, Nested Task, I/O Privilege Level (2 bits required), Overflow, Direction, Interrupt Enabled, Trap, Sign, Zero, Undefined, Auxiliary Carry, Undefined, Parity, Undefined, and Carry.

Syntax: PUSHF (no operands)

Flags affected: None

Flags undefined: None

Protected mode exceptions: When the new value of SP is outside the stack segment limit, a stack fault exception is generated.

Real address mode exceptions: When a word operand is at offset 0FFFFH, INT 13 is generated.

80386 note: Pushes the 32-bit extended flag register.

Example: PUSHF

RCL/RCR/ROL/ROR (80286/80386)

Rotate instructions

Instruction: RC/L/R,RO/L/R

Typical clocks: (80286) 2-5, (80386) 3-10

Description: Rotates instructions

Operation: Each of the rotate instructions shifts the bits of the specified register or memory operand. The ROL (rotate left) instruction shifts all of the bits left by one position, with MSB shifting out and around and becoming LSB. The ROR (rotate right) instruction performs the opposite operation. All bits are shifted to the right by one position, with LSB shifting around and becoming MSB.

The RCL and RCR instructions use the Carry flag as part of the rotated quantity. The RCL instruction shifts the Carry flag into LSB and MSB into the Carry flag. The RCR instruction performs the opposite transition. RCR shifts the Carry flag into MSB and LSB into the Carry flag.

The second operand of the rotate instructions specifies the number of positions to shift the source operand. The Overflow flag is set only for the rotate instructions using a second rotate operand of 1. For RCR, the test for overflow is made before the rotation. For RCL, ROL, and ROR, the check is made after the rotation. The Overflow flag is set based on the following conditions: if the Carry flag equals the high bit of the operand, reset the Overflow flag to 0; if the Carry flag does not equal the high bit of the operand, set the Overflow flag to 1.

Note: The 80286/80386 does not allow rotation counts greater than 31. Only the lower five bits of the rotation count are used if a rotation count greater than 31 is attempted.

Syntax: RCL *destination*,1
RCL *destination*,CL   ;CL determines number of rotations
RCL *destination*,*count*
RCR *destination*,1
RCR *destination*,CL
RCR *destination*,*count*
ROL *destination*,1
ROL *destination*,CL
ROL *destination*,*count*
ROR *destination*,1
ROR *destination*,CL
ROR *destination*,*count*

Flags affected: OF (only for single rotates), CF

Flags undefined: OF for multibit rotates

Protected mode exceptions: If the result is in a nonwritable segment, a general protection error is generated. If the CS, DS, or ES segment contains an illegal memory operand effective address, a general protection exception is generated. If the SS segment contains an illegal address, a stack fault exception is generated.

Real address mode exceptions: When a word operand is at offset 0FFFFH, INT 13 is generated.

80386 note: Word size is 32 bits.

Example: RCL   AH,1
RCL   MEMRY—BTE,REP—VAL
RCL   DH,CL
RCR   BL,1
RCR   MEMRY—BTE,REP—VAL
RCR   TABLE[BX][DI],CL
ROL   CX,1
ROL   MEMRY—BTE,REP—VAL
ROL   AX,CL
ROR   BL,1
ROR   MEMRY—BTE,REP—VAL
ROR   TABLE[BX][DI],CL

REP/REPZ/REPE/REPNE/REPNZ (80286/80386)

Repeat string operation

Instruction: REP/Z/E/NE/NZ

Typical clocks: 5+9*N (N = number of iterations)

Description: Repeats string operation

Operation: REP, REPE, and REPNE are prefix operations that cause the primitive string operation that follows to be done repeatedly, so long as the CX (ECX) register is not zero. For the CMPS and SCAS instructions, if, after any repetition of the primitive operation following the REP instruction, ZF differs from the "z" bit of the repeat prefix, the repetition is ended.

Syntax: REP
REPE
REPNE

Flags affected: None

Flags undefined: None

Protected mode exceptions: None

Real address mode exceptions: None

80386 note: Word size is 32 bits.

Example:

LEA	DI,VALUE1	;Load destination string
LEA	SI,VALUE2	;Load source string
REPE	CMPSB	;Repeat if equal in a byte-by-byte comparison

RET (80286/80386)

Return from procedure

Instruction: RET

Typical clocks: (80286) 15-55, (80386) 10-68

Description: Returns to NEAR or FAR caller

Operation: The RET instruction continues the execution of a program by transferring the control of the program to the return address that was pushed onto the stack. This address is usually placed on the stack by a CALL instruction.

An intrasegment RET moves the top two stack bytes to the instruction pointer. These two bytes provide the offset address of the next instruction to be executed.

An intersegment RET begins the same as an intrasegment RET. Pop the top two bytes of the stack into the instruction pointer. This is the offset address of the next instruction to be executed. Next, pop the next two bytes from the stack into the CS register. These last two bytes contain the code segment address of the next instruction to be executed.

To perform an intrasegment RET and change the stack pointer, pop the top two bytes of the stack into the instruction pointer. Next, pop the next two bytes from the stack into the stack pointer. These last two bytes readjust the stack pointer's past contents, which might have been placed onto the stack prior to the CALL instruction.

To perform an intersegment RET and change the stack pointer, pop the top two bytes of the stack into the instruction pointer. This is the offset address for the next instruction to be executed. Pop the next two stack bytes into the CS register. This is the code segment address of the next instruction to be executed. The next two bytes popped from the stack go into the stack pointer and represent the previous parameters that may have been pushed onto the stack prior to a CALL instruction.

Syntax: RET (no operands)

Flags affected: None

Flags undefined: None

Protected mode exceptions: In certain cases, general protection, descriptor not present, and stack fault exceptions are generated.

Real address mode exceptions: INT 13 is generated if the stack pop wraps around from 0FFFFH to 0.

80386 note: Uses the 32-bit extended instruction pointer. Interlevel pops a 48-bit ESP. A 32-bit EIP is popped off the stack. A 48-bit EIP pointer is popped.

Example: RET

SAHF (80286/80386)

Store AH in flags

Instruction: SAHF

Typical clocks: (80286) 2, (80386) 3

Description: Stores AH in flags SF, ZF, xx, AF, xx, PF, xx, CF

Operation: The values in the AH register are used to load the flags listed here from bits 7, 6, 4, 2, and 0, respectively.

Syntax: SAHF (no operands)

Flags affected: ZF, SF, AF, PF, CF

Flags undefined: None

Protected mode exceptions: None

Real address mode exceptions: None

80386 note: No exceptions.

Example: SAHF

SAL/SAR/SHL/SHR (80286/80386)

Shift instructions

Instruction: SA/L/R,SH/L/R

Typical clocks: (80286) 2-5, (80386) 3-7

Description: Shifts instructions

Operation: The SAL or SHL commands shift the bits of the specified operand to the left. This causes MSB to be shifted into CF and LSB to be reset to 0.

The SAR or SHR instruction shifts the bits of the specified operand to the right. This causes LSB to be shifted into CF. The SAR instruction performs a signed divide, with MSB remaining the same. The SHR instruction performs an unsigned divide, with MSB reset to 0.

The shift is repeated the number of times specified by the second operand. This operand can be either an immediate number or the contents of the CL register.

The 80286/80386 does not allow shifts greater than 31. If a shift greater than 31 is attempted, only the lower five bits of the shift count are used.

OF is set only if a single shift instruction is executed. For left shifts, it is reset to 0 if the MSB of the result is the same as the result Carry flag; otherwise, it is set to 1. For SAR it is reset to 0 for a single shift. The SHR instruction sets OF equal to the MSB of the original operand.

Syntax: SAL *destination,count*
SHL *destination,count*
SAL *destination,*1
SAL *destination,*CL
SAL *destination,count*
SHL *destination,*1
SHL *destination,*CL
SHL *destination,count*

Flags affected: OF (only for single-shift instructions), CF, AF, OF, PF, SF

Flags undefined: AF

Protected mode exceptions: A general protection exception is generated if the operand is in a nonwritable segment. If the CS, DS, or ES segment contains an illegal memory operand effective address, a general protection exception is generated. If the SS segment contains an illegal address, a stack fault exception is generated.

Real address mode exceptions: When a word operand is at offset 0FFFFH, INT 13 is generated.

80386 note: Word size is 32 bits.

Example: SHL   MEMRY__BTE,1
SHL   AX,CL
SHL   TABLE[BX][DI],CL
SAR   BL,1
SAR   MEMRY__BTE,REP__VAL
SAR   DH,CL
SAR   CX,1
SAR   MEMRY__BTE,1
SAR   AX,CL

SBB (80286/80386)

Subtract with borrow
Instruction: SBB
Typical clocks: (80286) 2-3, (80386) 2-7

Description: Performs integer subtraction with borrow

Operation: The SBB instruction adds the second operand to the Carry flag, and this result is subtracted from the first operand. The result is stored in the first operand.

Syntax: SBB *destination,source*

Flags affected: OF, SF, ZF, PF, CF, AF

Flags undefined: None

Protected mode exceptions: A general protection exception is generated if the result is in a nonwritable segment. If the CS, DS, or ES segment contains an illegal memory operand effective address, a general protection exception is generated. If the SS segment contains an illegal address, a stack fault exception is generated.

Real address mode exceptions: When a word operand is at offset 0FFFFH, INT 13 is generated.

80386 note: Word size is 32 bits.

Example:

SBB	AX,BX	
SBB	DX,MEMRY — WRD	
SBB	TABLE[BX][DI],SI	
SBB	AL,3	
SBB	EAX,EBX	(80386 only)
SBB	ECX,0ABCD1234H	(80386 only)

SCAS/SCASB/SCASW (80286/80386)

Compare string data

Instruction: SCAS/B/W

Typical clocks: 7

Description: Compares byte(AL), word(AX) with ES:[DI] or ES:[EDI]

Operation: The SCAS instruction subtracts the memory byte or memory word operand pointed to by ES:DI ([ES:EDI]) from either the AL or AX register. The result is ignored, and the appropriate flags are set.

No segment overrides are permitted. The memory operand must be addressable from the ES segment. After the comparison is made, DI (EDI) is incremented if DF is reset to 0; otherwise, if DF is set to 1, DI (EDI) is decremented. The DI (EDI) advances by 1 if a byte operand was specified and by 2 if a word operand was compared.

Syntax: SCAS *destination—string*
SCASB (no operands)
SCASW (no operands)

Flags affected: OF, SF, ZF, PF, CF, AF

Flags undefined: None

Protected mode exceptions: If the CS, DS, or ES segment contains an illegal memory operand effective address, a general protection exception is generated. If the SS segment contains an illegal address, a stack fault exception is generated.

Real address mode exceptions: When a word operand is at offset 0FFFFH, INT 13 is generated.

80386 note: Word size is 32 bits.

Example:

MOV	CL,10H	;Scan for 16 bytes
LEA	DI,VALUE1	;Location of string
MOV	AL,'S'	;Character to scan
REPNE	SCASB	;Repeat if not equal, scan bytes

SGDT/SIDT (80286/80386)

Store global/interrupt descriptor table register

Instruction: SGDT/SIDT

Typical clocks: (80286) 11, 12, (80386) 9

Description: Stores GDT or SIDT reg. in memory

Operation: Both the SGDT and SIDT instructions load the contents of the descriptor table register into the six bytes of memory pointed to by the destination operand. The LIMIT field of the register goes to the first word at the effective address; the next three bytes get the BASE field of the register; the last byte is undefined.

Syntax: SGDT *destination*
SIDT *destination*

Flags affected: None

Flags undefined: None

Protected mode exceptions: When the destination operand is a register, an undefined opcode exception is generated. A general protection exception is generated if the destination is in a nonwritable segment. If the CS, DS, or ES segment contains an illegal memory operand effective address, a general protection exception is generated. If the SS segment contains an illegal address, a stack fault exception is generated.

Real address mode exceptions: If the destination operand is a register, an undefined opcode exception is generated. When a word operand is at offset 0FFFFH, INT 13 is generated.

Example: SGDT MEM—WRD
        SIDT MEM—WRD

SLDT (80286/80386)

Store local descriptor table register

Instruction: SLDT

Typical clocks: 2

Description: Stores LDT reg. at EA word

Operation: The SLDT instruction uses an effective address operand that points to either a 2-byte register or memory location and stores the local descriptor table register contents.

Syntax: SLDT *destination*

Flags affected: None

Flags undefined: None

Protected mode exceptions: A general protection exception is generated if the destination is in a nonwritable segment. A general protection exception is generated for an illegal memory operand effective address in the CS, DS, or ES segment. A stack fault exception is generated for an illegal address in the SS segment.

Real address mode exceptions: INT 6 is generated. In real address mode, SLDT is not recognized.

Example: SLDT BP

SMSW (80286/80386)

Store machine status word

Instruction: SMSW

Typical clocks: 2

Description: Stores machine status word at EA word

Operation: The destination operand (effective-address, 2-byte register or memory location) receives a copy of the machine status word.

Syntax: SMSW *destination*

Flags affected: None

Flags undefined: None

Protected mode exceptions: A general protection exception is generated if the destination is in a nonwritable segment. If the CS, DS, or ES segment contains an illegal memory operand effective address, a general protection exception is generated. If the SS segment contains an illegal address, a stack fault exception is generated.

Real address mode exceptions: When a word operand is at offset 0FFFH, INT 13 is generated.

Example: SMSW BP

STC (80286/80386)

Set Carry flag

Instruction: STC

Typical clocks: 2

Description: Sets Carry flag

Operation: The STC instruction sets the Carry flag to 1.

Syntax: STC (no operands)

Flags affected: CF = 1

Flags undefined: None

Protected mode exceptions: None

Real address mode exceptions: None

80386 note: No exceptions.

Example: STC

STD (80286/80386)

Set Direction flag

Instruction: STD

Typical clocks: 2

Description: Sets Direction flag

Operation: The STD instruction sets DF to 1. This causes subsequent string instructions to decrement the appropriate SI and/or DI registers.

Syntax: STD (no operands)

Flags affected: DF = 1

Flags undefined: None

Protected mode exceptions: None

Real address mode exceptions: None

80386 note: Word size is 32 bits.

Example: STD

STI (80286/80386)

Set Interrupt Enable flag

Instruction: STI

Typical clocks: (80286) 2, (80386) 3

Description: Sets Interrupt Enable flag

Operation: The STI instruction sets the Interrupt Enable flag to 1. This permits maskable external interrupts to be issued after the execution of the next instruction.

Syntax: STI (no operands)

Flags affected: IF = 1

Flags undefined: None

Protected mode exceptions: When the current privilege level is lower than the I/O privilege level, a general protected mode exception is generated.

Real address mode exceptions: None

80386 note: No exceptions.

Example: STI

STOS/STOSB/STOSW (80286/80386)

Store string data

Instruction: STOS/B/W

Typical clocks: (80286) 3, (80386) 4

Description: Stores AL (byte) or AX (word) at ES:DI or ES:[EDI]

Operation: The STOS instructions transfer the contents of either the AL or AX register to the memory byte or memory word pointed to by ES:DI ([ES:EDI]). The destination operand must be addressable from the ES register, as no segment override is permitted.

DI (EDI) is automatically incremented if DF is reset to 0; DI (EDI) is decremented if DF is set to 1. The increment is 1 for byte moves and 2 for word moves.

Syntax: STS *destination__string*
       STOSB (no operands)
       STOSW (no operands)

Flags affected: None

Flags undefined: None

Protected mode exceptions: A general protection exception is generated if the destination is in a nonwritable segment. If the CS, DS, or ES segment contains an illegal memory operand effective address, a general protection exception is generated. If the SS segment contains an illegal address, a stack fault exception is generated.

Real address mode exceptions: When a word operand is at offset 0FFFFH, INT 13 is generated.

80386 note: Word size is 32 bits.

Example:
```
              MOV     ECX,0FFCCAAH     (80386 only)
              LEA     EDI,VARIABLE
              MOV     AX,'-'
       REP    STOSB
```

STR (80286/80386)

Store task register

Instruction: STR

Typical clocks: (80286) 2, (80386) 23-27

Description: Stores task register at EA word

Operation: This instruction causes the contents of the task register to be copied into the 2-byte register or memory location pointed to by the effective address operand.

Syntax: STR *destination*

Flags affected: None

Flags undefined: None

Protected mode exceptions: A general protection exception is generated if the destination is in a nonwritable segment. If the CS, DS, or ES segment contains an illegal memory operand effective address, a general protection exception is generated. If the SS segment contains an illegal address, a stack fault exception is generated.

Real address mode exceptions: INT 6 is generated. In real address mode, STR is not recognized.

Example: STR BP

SUB (80286/80386)

Subtract

Instruction: SUB

Typical clocks: 2-7

Description: Performs integer subtraction

Operation: The SUB instruction subtracts the source operand from the destination operand. The result is stored in the destination operand.

Syntax: SUB *destination,operand*

Flags affected: OF, SF, ZF, PF, AF, CF

Flags undefined: None

Protected mode exceptions: If the result is in a nonwritable segment, a general protection error is generated. If the CS, DS, or ES segment contains an illegal memory operand effective address, a general protection exception is generated. If the SS segment contains an illegal address, a stack fault exception is generated.

Real address mode exceptions: When a word operand is at offset 0FFFFH, INT 13 is generated.

80386 note: Word size is 32 bits.

Example:	SUB	AX,BX	
	SUB	EAX,EDX	(80386 only)
	SUB	DX,MEMRY＿WRD	
	SUB	MEMRY＿WRD,AX	
	SUB	MEM＿BTE,7	
	SUB	NUMBER,0FC981576H	(80386 only)

TEST (80286/80386)

Test, logical compare

Instruction: TEST

Typical clocks: (80286) 2-6, (80386) 2-5

Description: Performs logical compare operation

Operation: The TEST instruction performs a bit-by-bit logical AND operation on the two operands. Each bit of the result is then set to 1 when the corresponding bits of both operands is 1; otherwise the result bit is reset to 0. The result of the instruction is not used, and only the appropriate flags are modified.

Syntax: TEST *destination,source*

Flags affected: OF = 0, CF = 0, SF, ZF, PF

Flags undefined: AF

Protected mode exceptions: If the CS, DS, or ES segment contains an illegal memory operand effective address, a general protection exception is generated. If the SS segment contains an illegal address, a stack fault exception is generated.

Real address mode exceptions: When a word operand is at offset 0FFFFH, INT 13 is generated.

80386 note: Word size is 32 bits.

Example: TEST AX,BX
           TEST EAX,EBX   (80386 only)
           TEST MEM_BTE,6
           TEST TABLE[BX][DI],CX
           TEST TABLE[BX][DI],ECX   (80386 only)

VERR/VERW (80286/80386)

Verify a segment for reading or writing

Instruction: VERR/VERW

Typical clocks: (80286) 14-16, (80386) 10-16

Description: Sets ZF to 1, if seg. can be written to/read

Operation: The VERR and VERW instructions determine whether the segment pointed to by the 2-byte register or memory operand selector can be reached from the current privilege level. The instruction also determines whether the segment can be read or written to.

If the segment is accessible, ZF is set to 1; otherwise, it is reset to 0.

Syntax: VERR *destination_readable selector*
       VERW *destination_writable selector*

Flags affected: ZF

Flags undefined: None

Protected mode exceptions: If the CS, DS, or ES segment contains an illegal memory operand effective address, a general protected mode exception is generated. If the SS segment contains an illegal address, a stack fault exception is generated.

Real address mode exceptions: INT 6 is generated. In real address mode, VERR/VERW is not recognized.

80386 note: No exceptions

Example: VERR BP
       VERW SELECTR

WAIT (80286/80386)

Wait

Instruction: WAIT

Typical clocks: (80286) 3, (80386) 6 (minimum)

Description: Waits until an external interrupt occurs

Operation: The WAIT instruction causes the 80286/80386 to wait until an external interrupt occurs.

Syntax: WAIT (no operand)

Flags affected: None

Flags undefined: None

Protected mode exceptions: A general protection exception is generated if either operand is in a nonwritable segment. If the CS, DS, or ES segment contains an illegal memory operand effective address, a general protection exception is generated. If the SS segment contains an illegal address, a stack fault exception is generated.

Real address mode exceptions: When a word operand is at offset 0FFFFH, INT 13 is generated.

80386 note: No exceptions.

Example: WAIT

XCHG (80286/80386)

Exchange

Instruction: XCHG

Typical clocks: 3-5

Description: Exchanges bytes or words

Operation: The XCHG instruction exchanges the byte or word source operand with its matching data type destination operand.

Syntax: XCHG *destination,source*

Flags affected: None

Flags undefined: None

Protected mode exceptions: A general protection exception is generated if either operand is in a nonwritable segment. If the CS, DS, or ES segment contains an illegal memory operand effective address, a general protection exception is generated. If the SS segment contains an illegal address, a stack fault exception is generated.

Real address mode exceptions: When a word operand is at offset 0FFFFH, INT 13 is generated.

80386 note: Word size is 32 bits.

Example: XCHG AX,BX
XCHG DH,DATA＿WRD
XCHG AL,DL
XCHG EAX,EBX   (80386 only)

XLAT (80286/80386)

Translate

Instruction: XLAT

Typical clocks: 5

Description: Performs table lookup translation

Operation: The XLAT instruction performs a table lookup byte translation. The AL register is the unsigned index of a table addressed by DS:BX (DS:EBX). The byte indexed by DS:BX (DS:EBX) is copied to AL.

Syntax: XLAT *translation＿table*

Flags affected: None

Flags undefined: None

Protected mode exceptions: If the CS, DS, or ES segment contains an illegal memory operand effective address, a general protection exception is generated. If the SS segment contains an illegal address, a stack fault exception is generated.

Real address mode exceptions: When a word operand is at offset 0FFFFH, INT 13 is generated.

80386 note: Word size is 32 bits.

Example: LEA   BX,MYTABLE   ;Location of table
           MOV   AL,INDEX   ;Offset into table
           XLAT   MYTABLE   ;Value returned in AL

XOR (80286/80386)

Logical exclusive OR

Instruction: XOR

Typical clocks: (80286) 2-3, (80386) 2-7

Description: Peforms logical exclusive OR operation

Operation: The XOR instruction compares each bit of the source and destination operands and performs a bit-wise exclusive OR. The result contains 0's in those positions where the compared operands are both 1 or 0. XOR returns 1 in those corresponding positions where the operands are opposite.

Syntax: XOR *destination,source*

Flags affected: OF = 0, CF = 0, SF, ZF, PF

Flags undefined: AF

Protected mode exceptions: If the result is in a nonwritable segment, a general protection error is generated. If the CS, DS, or ES segment contains an illegal memory operand effective address, a general protection exception is generated. If the SS segment contains an illegal address, a stack fault exception is generated.

Real address mode exceptions: When a word operand is at offset 0FFFFH, INT 13 is generated.

80386 note: Word size is 32 bits.

Example: XOR   AX,MEMRY__WRD
           XOR   AH,BL
           XOR   TABLE[BX][DI],AX
           XOR   EAX,ECX   (80386 only)
           XOR   EDX,0FCAD1579H   (80386 only)

80386 INSTRUCTION SET

BSF/BSR (80386 only)

Scan bit forward/reverse

Instruction: BSF/BSR

Typical clocks: 10+3n

Description: Scans bit forward/reverse

Operation: The BSF and BSR instructions scan the source operand (16 or 32 bits) for the position of the first bit set to 1. The index of the first set bit is placed in the destination register. BSF (scan bit forward) scans from right to left, starting with bit position index 0. BSR (scan bit reverse) scans the source operand from right to left, starting with bit position index 15 for a 16-bit source operand or bit position index 31 for a 32-bit source operand. The Zero flag is set to 1 if the entire word contains only 0's. ZF is reset to 0 if a 1 bit is found. If no 1 bit is found, the destination value is undefined.

Syntax: BSF *destination — reg,source — operand*

   BSR *destination — reg,source — operand*

Flags affected: ZF

Flags undefined: OF, SF, AF, PF, CF

Protected mode exceptions: An exception 13 general protection is generated if the operand cannot be used because of a segment limit violation or an access rights violation.

Real address mode exceptions: An exception 13 general protection is generated if an operand reference that extends beyond the segment limit (0FFFFH) is made.

Example: BSF AX,MEM — WORD

   BSR EAX,ECX

BT/BTS/BTR/BTC (80386 only)

Bit test/set/reset/complement

Instruction: BT/BTS/BTR/BTC

Typical clocks: 3, 13

Description: Performs single-bit memory or register operations

Operation: The BT, BTS, BTR, and BTC instructions operate on one single bit within a memory location or register. If a register is specified, this can be either a 16- or 32-bit string. The selected bit can be specified by an immediate constant in the instruction or by a value in a general-purpose register. This operand is taken modulo the operand size. The range of the immediate bit offset is 0..31 for a 32-bit string and 0..15 for a 16-bit string operand size.

All four instructions first assign the value of the selected bit to the Carry flag. Except for the bit test operation, a new value for the selected bit is assigned according to the instruction chosen.

Syntax: BT   *reg/mem,selector*
BTS   *reg/mem,selector*
BTR   *reg/mem,selector*
BTC   *reg/mem,selector*

Flags affected: CF is set to the value of the selected bit.

Flags undefined: OF, SF, ZF, AF, PF

Protected mode exceptions: An exception 13 general protection is generated if the operand cannot be used because of a segment limit violation or an access rights violation.

Real address mode exceptions: An exception 13 general protection is generated if an operand reference that extends beyond the segment limit (0FFFFH) is made.

Example: BT   AL,BL   ;BL   =offset
BT   MEM_WRD,0BH   ;0BH =immediate offset
BTS   AX,CL   ;CL   =offset
BTS   INFO[BX],7H   ;7H   =immediate offset
BTR   AL,AL   ;AL   =offset
BTR   TABLE[SI],0EH   ;0EH =immediate offset
BTC   BL,AL   ;AL   =offset
BTC   BUFF[BX],2H   ;2H   =immediate offset

IBTS (80386 only)

Insert bit string

Instruction: IBTS

Typical clocks: 12/19

Description: Inserts bits into register or memory location

Operation: The IBTS instruction inserts the low-order bits of a register into another register or memory location without disturbing the bits on either side of the inserted bits.

The IBTS instruction has four operands: the base address of the bit string, the bit offset of the start of the substring to be inserted, the length of the substring, and the register for obtaining the inserted value. The base address can be a register or memory address. The offset is contained in the EAX register (AX for 16-bit operands). The field length is given in the CL register. The last field specifies the general register in which the value is inserted.

Syntax: IBTS *base,offset,length,source*
　　　　　 IBTS *reg/mem*,(E)AX,CL,*reg*

Flags affected: OF, SF, ZF, AF, PF

Flags undefined: CF

Protected mode exceptions: An exception 13 general protection is generated if an operand cannot be used because of a segment limit violation or an access rights violation.

Real address mode exceptions: An exception 13 general protection is generated if an operand reference that extends beyond the segment limit (0FFFFH) is made.

Example: IBTS BX,AX,CL,DX

MOV CRn (80386 only)

Load and store control registers

Instruction: MOV CRn,reg
　　　　　　　　 MOV reg,CRn

Typical clocks: 2-4

Description: Loads CRn register
　　　　　　　　　 Stores CRn in register

Operation: These instructions either load or store values in the control registers (CRn). A 32-bit operand is always used for these instructions, and only CR0, CR2, and CR3 are defined for the 80386.

Syntax: MOV   CRn,*source_operand*
MOV   *destination*,CRn
n = 0, 2, 3

Flags affected: OF, ZF, SF, PF, AF

Flags undefined: CF

Protected mode exceptions: These are privileged instructions. If they are executed at a privilege level other than 0, a protection fault occurs.

Real address mode exceptions: None

Example: MOV   CR2,EAX
MOV   EBX,CR3

MOV DRn (80386 only)

Load and store debug registers

Instruction: MOV Dreg,reg
MOV reg,Dreg

Typical clocks: 2-4

Description: Loads debug register
Stores debug register

Operation: These instructions either load or store 32-bit values in the debug register.

Syntax: MOV D*reg,reg*
MOV *reg*,D*reg*

Flags affected: OF, ZF, SF, AF, PF

Flags undefined: CF

Protected mode exceptions: These are privileged instructions. If they are executed at a privilege level other than 0, a protection fault occurs.

Real address mode exceptions: None

Example: MOV DR4,EAX
MOV EBX,DR5

MOV TRn (80386 only)

Load and store test registers

Instruction: MOV Treg,reg
MOV reg,Treg

Typical clocks: 2-4

Description: Loads test register
Stores test register

Operation: These instructions load and store values in the test registers. Only TR6 and TR7 are defined for the 80386.

Syntax: MOV   T*reg,reg*
MOV   *reg,*T*reg*

Flags affected: None

Flags undefined: None

Protected mode exceptions: These are privileged instructions. If they are executed at a privilege level other than 0, a protection fault occurs.

Real address mode exceptions: None

Example: MOV   TR6,EAX

SETcond. (80386 only)

Byte set on condition

Instruction	Typical Clocks	Description
SETcond.	N/A	Sets/resets byte based on conditional test
SETO	N/A	Overflow
SETNO	N/A	No overflow
SETB	N/A	Below (unsigned)
SETNAE	N/A	Not above or equal
SETNB	N/A	Not below
SETAE	N/A	Above or equal (unsigned)
SETE	N/A	Equal
SETZ	N/A	Zero

Instruction	Typical Clocks	Description
SETNE	N/A	Not equal
SETNZ	N/A	Not zero
SETBE	N/A	Below or equal
SETNA	N/A	Not above
SETNBE	N/A	Not below or equal
SETA	N/A	Above
SETS	N/A	Sign
SETNS	N/A	Not sign
SETP	N/A	Parity
SETPE	N/A	Parity even
SETNP	N/A	Not parity
SETPO	N/A	Parity odd
SETL	N/A	Less than (signed)
SETNGE	N/A	Not greater than or equal
SETNL	N/A	Not less than
SETGE	N/A	Greater or equal
SETLE	N/A	Less than or equal
SETNG	N/A	Not greater than
SETNLE	N/A	Not less than or equal
SETG	N/A	Greater than (signed)

Operation: The SET instructions either set the selected byte to 0 or reset it to 1 based on any of the 16 conditions defined for the 80286. The only operand is a single-byte register or memory destination operand. The following assignments are made: if SET*cond*, then *reg/mem* = 1; else *reg/mem* = 0.

Syntax: SET*cond reg/mem*

Flags affected: None

Flags undefined: None

Protected mode exceptions: An exception 13 general protection is generated if an operand cannot be used because of a segment limit violation or an access rights violation.

Real address mode exceptions: None

Example: SETNO

SHLD/SHRD (80386 only)

Double-shift instructions

Instruction: SHLD/SHRD

Typical clocks: 3-7

Description: Shifts double-precision value left/right

Operation: The SHLD/SHRD instructions shift a double-precision quantity left or right to produce a single-precision value. The register or memory location operand is shifted by the value stored in the count operand. This shift differs from single-precision shifts in that double-precision shifts use the register operand to supply the bits to be shifted in. Single-precision shifts shift only in 0's or 1's. The register or memory location operand specifies the input operand. The register field specifies the bits to be shifted in, and the immediate or CL contains the shift count.

For SHLD, the register or memory operand contains the high-order bits of a double-precision value, and the register field holds the low-order bits. The register or memory operand is shifted left, with the high-order bits from the register operand shifted in on the right (low-order position). The result is stored in the register or memory operand.

FOR SHRD, the register or memory operand contains the low-order part of a double-precision value, and the register operand holds the high-order bits. The register or memory operand is shifted right, with the low-order bits from the register operand shifted in on the left (high-order position). The result is stored in the register or memory operand.

Syntax: SHLD *reg/mem,reg,immediate*
            SHRD *reg/mem,reg,*CL

Flags affected: CF is set to the value of last bit shifted out.
            OF is set if the shifting of the last bit caused overflow.
            SF, ZF, and PF are set according to the result value.

Flags undefined: AF

Protected mode exceptions: None

Real address mode exceptions: None

Example: SHLD AX,BL,0AH   ;0AH = Shift count immediate
            SHRD AL,BL,CL   ;CL = Shift count

XBTS (80386 only)

Extract bit string

Instruction: XBTS

Typical clocks: 6-13

Description: Extracts bit string for reg. right-justify

Operation: The XBTS instruction extracts a bit string, and this substring is stored right-justified and extended, with the high-order bits reset to 0, in the specified register.

The XBTS instruction has four operands; the base address for the bit string, the bit offset of the start of the substring to be extracted, the length of the substring, and the register to which the inserted value is delivered. The base address can be a register or memory address. The offset is contained in the EAX register (AX for 16-bit operands). The field length is given in the CL register. The last field specifies the general register that holds the value extracted.

Syntax: XBTS *dest,base,offset,length*
            XBTS *reg,reg/mem,*(E)AX,CL

Flags affected: OF, SF, ZF, AF, PF

Flags undefined: CF

Protected mode exceptions: An exception 13 general protection is generated if an operand cannot be used because of a segment limit violation or an access rights violation.

Real address mode exceptions: An exception 13 general protection is generated if an operand reference that extends beyond the segment limit (0FFFFH) is made.

Example: XBTS AX,BX,AX,CL

4

80287/80387 MATHEMATICS COPROCESSOR

Chapter 4 discusses those elements of the 80287/80387 mathematics coprocessor that should be of interest to the programmer. These features include a floating point stack; status, control, and tag words; exception pointers; and data types. Included in the chapter is an elementary discussion of the operation of the 80287/80387 chip, its numeric processing capabilities, and its exception handling. A listing of the 80287/80387 instruction set is provided for reference.

80287/80387 OPERATION

The 80287/80387 mathematics coprocessor is designed to work in parallel with the host 80286/80386 microprocessor. The instruction set of the 80287/80387 includes many powerful floating-point operations.

When the 80286/80386 encounters a floating-point instruction, it sends the necessary opcode and memory operand addresses to the 80287/80387. This frees the 80286/80386 to execute the next instruction, while the

80287/80387 simultaneously performs the numeric calculation.

The 80287/80387 can make memory access requests through a dedicated data channel built into the 80286/80386. Such accesses are also checked for protection-rule violation and generate any appropriate error exceptions.

For certain 80286/80386 operations, it is necessary to force the 80286/80386 to wait for the mathematics coprocessor to return its result. This synchronization with the returned result is facilitated using either the WAIT or FWAIT 80286/80386 instruction.

FLOATING-POINT STACK

The 80287/80387 stack consists of eight 80-bit elements (shown in Figure 4-1) divided into fields. These fields correspond to the temporary real data format used in all of the coprocessor's stack calculations.

The individual elements of the floating-point stack can be addressed implicitly or explicitly. Certain floating-point instructions default to certain stack elements; for example:

FSQRT   The FSQRT instruction takes the contents of the current 80287/80387 top-of-stack register, ST(0), and then takes the square root of that value and pushes it onto the stack.

Other instructions permit a programmer-selected stack element, as in the following example:

FST(7)   The FST(7) instruction takes the current value of the top-of-stack register, ST(0), and stores it in element 7 of the floating-point stack.

STATUS WORD

The 80287/80387 status word (Figure 4-2) reflects the overall condition of the coprocessor. The status word is divided into two fields: the Exception flag bit field and the status bit field. The status word can be examined by storing it in a memory location with an 80287/80387 instruction and then examining the individual bits using 80286/80386 code.

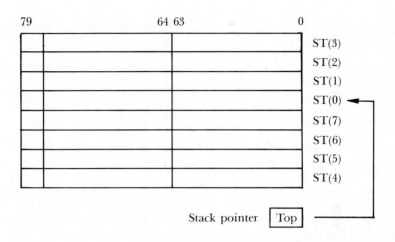

Figure 4-1. _____
80287/80387 stack

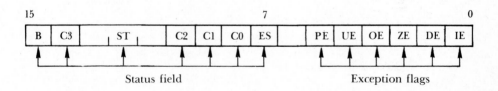

Status field   Exception flags

[B]   This 1-bit field is used to indicate whether the 80287/80387 is currently executing an instruction, or if it is idle.

[ST]   This 3-bit field indicates which of the eight stack elements is currently the top of the stack.

Figure 4-2. _____
80287/80387 status word

ST values:

    000 — Element 0 is stack top

    001 — Element 1 is stack top

    .

    .

    .

    111 — Element 7 is stack top

[C3,C2,C1,C0] These four 1-bit fields are used to obtain additional information about the current top of stack, the results of which are then used to make certain conditional branches. (See FCOM, FCOMP, FCOMPP, FTST, FXAM, and FPREM in the 80287/80387 instruction set for further explanation of C3, C2, C1, and C0.)

[IR] This 1-bit interrupt request field indicates that the 80287/80387 wants to interrupt the 80286/80386.

[PE] The Precision Exception flag is a 1-bit flag that is set if the result must be rounded so they can be represented in floating-point format.

[UE] The Underflow Exception flag is a 1-bit flag that is set when the calculated result is too small to be stored in the designated destination floating-point format without being denormalized.

[OE] This 1-bit flag, the Overflow Exception flag, is set whenever the calculated result is too large to be stored in the designated destination floating-point format.

[ZE] A 1-bit flag called the Zero Divide Exception flag indicates whether the division was by zero and whether the dividend was a nonzero number.

[DE] The Denormalized Operand Exception flag is a 1-bit flag used to indicate whether an instruction has attempted to operate on a denormalized operand.

[IE] The 1-bit Invalid Operation Exception flag indicates whether or not one of several illegal operations, such as an operation on a NAN (not a number) or taking the square root of a negative number, has been performed.

Figure 4-2. _____

80287/80387 status word (*continued*)

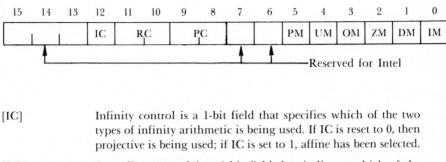

15	14	13	12	11	10	9	8	7	6	5	4	3	2	1	0
			IC	RC		PC				PM	UM	OM	ZM	DM	IM

—Reserved for Intel

[IC]   Infinity control is a 1-bit field that specifies which of the two types of infinity arithmetic is being used. If IC is reset to 0, then projective is being used; if IC is set to 1, affine has been selected.

[RC]   Rounding control is a 1-bit field that indicates which of the four rounding directions has been chosen: unbiased round to the nearest or even value, round toward +, round toward −, or round toward zero.

[PC]   Precision control is a 1-bit field indicating which of three precisions have been chosen: temporary real (64-bit result), long real (53-bit result), or short real (24-bit result).

Figure 4-3. _____

80287/80387 control word

CONTROL WORD

The 80287/80387 control word (Figure 4-3) contains the exception masks, an interrupt enable mask, and several control bits.

Exception Masks

The exception masks in the control word are used to indicate which exceptions should be processed by the standard 80287/80387 corrective actions (this is an example of a masked exception) and which exceptions should cause the 80287/80387 to generate interrupt signals (an unmasked exception). The exception masks are

[PM]   Precision mask
[UM]   Underflow mask
[OM]   Overflow mask
[ZM]   Zero-divide mask
[DM]   Denormalized-operand mask
[IM]   Invalid-operation mask

TAG WORD

The tag word contains tags describing the contents of the associated stack element. The tab values are shown here.

TAG(7)	TAG(6)	TAG(5)	TAG(4)	TAG(3)	TAG(2)	TAG(1)	TAG(0)

Tag values:

00 = Valid (normal or unnormal)

01 = Zero (true)

10 = Special (not a number, infinity, or denormal)

11 = Empty

EXCEPTION POINTERS

Exception pointers are provided so that programmers can write their own exception handlers. When the 80287/80387 executes an instruction, the address of the instruction is stored in the exception pointers. If the executed instruction also referenced a memory operand, the address of the operand is also stored. The programmer can then write an exception handler to store these pointers in memory and obtain information concerning the instruction that caused the error. This information is stored in two formats (shown in Figure 4-4), one for real address mode and the other for protected address mode.

Real address mode

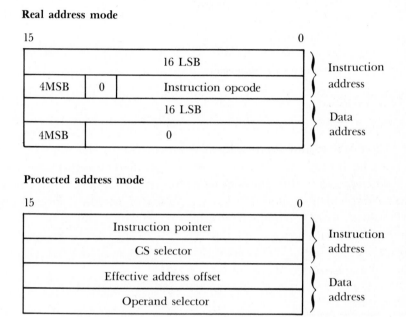

Figure 4-4. _____

80287/80387 instruction and data-pointer formats. The 80387 chip supports a 32-bit data interface with the system bus.

DATA TYPES

The 80287/80387 supports seven different data types. These numeric values are accessed using all of the standard addressing modes supported by the 80286/80386.

For all seven data formats, the sign of the number is always stored in the most significant digit, or left-most digits, of the field.

The following symbols provide additional information:

S	Sign bit (0 = positive, 1 = negative)
d17—d0	Decimal digits stored two per byte
UD	Undefined, have no meaning
^	Position of implicit binary point
[ ]	Integer bit of significand; stores in temporary real, implicit in short and long real.

Binary Integers

The three binary integer data formats are all identical, with the exception of the length field, which governs the range of the number. The left-most bit is interpreted as the number's sign. Negative numbers are represented in two's complement notation. Zero is represented with a positive sign. The 80287/80387 word integer is identical to the 80286/80386 16-bit signed integer data format.

Word integer (range: $-32768 <= X <= +32767$)

15   0

| S | Magnitude |

(Two's complement notation)

Short integer (range: $-2 \times 10^9 <= X <= +2 \times 10^9$)

31   0

| S | Magnitude |

(Two's complement notation)

Long integer (range: $-9 \times 10^{18} <= X <= +9 \times 10^{18}$)

63   0

| S | Magnitude |

(Two's complement notation)

Packed-Decimal Notation

Packed-decimal notation is used to store decimal integers, with two decimal digits being stored, or *packed,* into each byte. The sign bit determines whether the number is positive or negative. The digits must be in the range 0H-9H, inclusive.

Packed decimal (range: $-99\ldots99 <= X <= +99\ldots99$ (18 digits)

79	72			
S	UD	d17	Magnitude (two digits per byte)	d0

Short Real, Long Real, And Temporary Real Formats

Both the short real and long real data formats exist only in memory. When a number stored in one of these formats is loaded onto the floating-point stack, it is automatically converted to the temporary real format.

Short real (range: $0, 1.2 \times 10^{-38} <= X <= 3.4 \times 10^{38}$)

31	↑ [23]	0
S	Biased exponent	Significand

Long real (range: $0, 2.3 \times 10^{-308} <= X <= 1.7 \times 10^{308}$)

63	↑ [52]	0
S	Biased exponent	Significand

Temporary real (range: $0, 3.4 \times 10^{-4932} <= X <= 1.1 \times 10^{4932}$)

79	↑ [64]	63	0
S	Biased exponent	*	Significand

Biased exponent values (normalized):
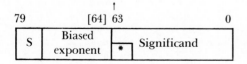
    Short real: 127 (7FH)
    Long real: 1023 (3FFH)
    Temporary real: 16383 (3FFFH)

Special Values

The 80287/80387 mathematics coprocessor includes several special values to increase the flexibility of numeric calculations. These special values include

- Unnormals
- Denormals
- Indefinite values
- NAN values
- $+$ and $-$ infinity representations
- Signed zero.

80287/80387 INSTRUCTIONS

F2XM1 (80287/80387)
2 raised to the X power-1

Instruction
F2XM1

Typical clocks
500 (80287)

Description
Calculates 2 raised to the X power-1

Operation: The F2XM1 instruction calculates the function 2^X-1. The value for X is obtained from the 80287/80387 TOS register ST. The result replaces the original TOS ST value.

Syntax: F2XM1 (no operands)

Exception flags: U, P

Example: F2XM1

FABS (80287/80387)
Absolute value

Instruction
FABS

Typical clocks
14 (80287)

Description
Moves absolute value of 80287/80387 to top of stack

Operation: The FABS instruction takes the element at the top of the 80287/80387 stack and replaces it with the absolute value of the element.

Syntax: FABS (no operands)

Exception flags: I

Example: FABS

FADD (80287/80387)
Add real

Instruction
FADD

Typical clocks
85, 105, 110 (80287)

Description
Adds source and dest. operands

Operation: The FADD instruction takes the source operand and destination operand, adds them together, and stores the result back in the destination operand.

When FADD is executed without any specified operands, the instruction takes the top of the 80287/80387 stack, adds that to the second element on the stack, and returns the result to the new top of stack.

The second form of the FADD instruction permits the source operand to be a real number stored in memory. The implied destination operand is the top of the 80287/80387 stack register. This form of the instruction adds the memory variable to the 80287/80387 top of stack and returns the result to the top of the stack.

The third form of the FADD instruction allows the selection of any of the other registers on the 80287/80387 stack as one of the operands. The second operand remains the 80287/80387 top of stack. The instruction adds the two values and returns the result to the destination operand.

Syntax: FADD (no operands)
FADD *source__operand*
FADD *destination__operand,source__operand*

Exception flags: I, D, U, P, O

Example: FADD
FADD REAL__NUM
FADD ST,ST(1)
FADD ST(7),ST

FADDP (80287/80387)
Add real and pop

Instruction
FADDP

Typical clocks
90 (80287)

Description
Adds operands, stores in dest., pops stack

Operation: The FADDP instruction adds the source and destination operands, returning the sum to the destination operand. The 80287/80387 stack is popped. The source operand is the current 80287/80387 top of stack. The destination operand comes from any one of the other registers on the 80287/80387 stack.

Syntax: FADDP *destination__operand,source__operand*

Exception flags: I, O, U, P, D

Example: FADDP ST(1),ST

FBLD (80287/80387)
Packed decimal (BCD) load

Instruction
FBLD

Typical clocks
300 (80287)

Description
Converts BCD to temp. real, pushes result on stack

Operation: The FBLD instruction converts a packed BCD source operand to a temporary real and pushes the result onto the 80287/80387 stack. The FBLD instruction assumes that the source operand is within the valid BCD range of 0-9H. The instruction performs no error checking on the source operand to validate the BCD value.

Syntax: FBLD *source__operand*

Exception flags: I

Example: FLBD BCD__VALUE

FBSTP (80287/80387)
Packed decimal (BCD) store and pop

Instruction
FBSTP

Typical clocks
530 (80287)

Description
Converts TOS to BCD, stores in dest., pops TOS

Operation: The FBSTP instruction converts the value stored on the top of the 80287/80387 stack to packed decimal integer format, takes the converted result and stores it in the destination operand, and pops the 80287/80387 stack.

Syntax: FBSTP *destination__operand*

Exception flags: I

Example: FBSTP BCD__VALUE

FCHS (80287/80387)
Change sign

Instruction
FCHS

Typical clocks
15 (80287)

Description
Changes the sign of the 80287/80387 TOS

Operation: The FCHS instruction takes the value on the top of the 80287/80387 stack and changes its sign.

Syntax: FCHS (no operands)

Exception flags: I

Example: FCHS

FCLEX (80287/80387)
Clear exceptions

Instruction
FCLEX

Typical clocks
5 (80287)

Description
Clears Exception flags, IRS, and Busy flag

Operation: The FCLEX instruction clears all Exception flags, the Interrupt Request flag, and the Busy flag in the status word.

Syntax: FCLEX (no operands)

Exception flags: None

Example: FCLEX

FCOM (80287/80387)
Compare real

Instruction
FCOM

Typical clocks
45, 65, 70 (80287)

Description
Compares TOS to the source operand

Operation: The FCOM instruction takes the current top of the 80287/80387 stack and compares it with the source operand. If the instruction is executed without a specified source operand, ST(1) is assumed.

The source operand may be a register on the 80287/80387 stack or a short or long real memory operand. The condition codes in the 80287/80387 status word are changed based on the following comparisons:

    if ST > *source_operand*
       then C0 = 0 and C3 = 0
    if ST < *source_operand*
       then C0 = 1 and C3 = 0
    if ST = *source_operand*
       then C0 = 0 and C3 = 1
    if ST < >*source_operand*
       then C0 = 1 and C3 = 1

Syntax: FCOM (no operands)
             FCOM *source_operand*

Exception flags: I, D

Example: FCOM
              FCOM LONG_REAL_VAL
              FCOM SHORT_REAL_VAL

FCOMP (80287/80387)
Compare real and pop

Instruction
FCOMP

Typical clocks
47, 68, 72 (80287)

Description
Compares source and TOS, pops TOS

Operation: The FCOMP takes the current top of the 80287/80387 stack, compares it with the source operand, and then pops the 80287/80387 stack. If the FCOMP instruction is used without a specified source operand, ST(1) is assumed.

The source operand may be a short or long real memory operand or a register on the 80287/80387 stack. The condition codes in the 80287/80387 status word are changed based on the following conditions:

    if ST > *source_operand*
       then C0 = 0 and C3 = 0
    if ST < *source_operand*

        then C0 = 1 and C3 = 0
    if ST = *source—operand*
        then C0 = 0 and C3 = 1
    if ST < > *source—operand*
        then C0 = 1 and C3 = 1

Syntax: FCOMP (no operands)
          FCOMP *source—operand*

Exception flags: I, D

Example: FCOMP
           FCOMP LONG—REAL—VAL
           FCOMP SHORT—REAL—VAL

FCOMPP (80287/80387)

Compare real and pop twice

Instruction
FCOMPP

Typical clocks
50 (80287)

Description
Compares TOS and ST(1), pops stack twice

Operation: The FCOMPP instruction compares the 80287/80387 stack top to the ST(1) register and then pops the 80287/80387 stack twice. The condition codes in the 80287/80387 status word are changed based on the following conditions:

    if ST > *source—operand*
        then C0 = 0 and C3 = 0
    if ST < *source—operand*
        then C0 = 1 and C3 = 0
    if ST = *source—operand*
        then C0 = 0 and C3 = 1
    if ST <> *source—operand*
        then C0 = 1 and C3 = 1

Syntax: FCOMPP (no operands)

Exception flags: I, D

Example: FCOMPP

FCOS (80387)
COSINE

Instruction
FCOS

Typical clocks
N/A

Description
Calculates the COSINE of an angle

Operation: The FCOS instruction computes the COSINE θ of an angle. The angle is taken from the top of the stack, and has no range limit. Upon completion, the cosine value replaces θ on the stack top.

Syntax: FCOS (no operands)

Exception flags: D, IS, I, P

Example: FCOS

FDECSTP (80287/80387)
Decrement 80287/80387 stack pointer

Instruction
FDECSTP

Typical clocks
9 (80287)

Description
Subtracts 1 from the 80287/80387 stack ptr.

Operation: The FDECSTP subtracts 1 from the 80287/80387 (TOP) stack top pointer in the status word.

Syntax: FDECSTP (no operands)

Exception flags: None

Example: FDECSTP

FDISI (80287/80387)
Disable interrupts

Instruction
FDISI

Typical clocks
5 (80287)

Description
Prevents 80287/80387 from issuing int. req.

Operation: The FDISI instruction prevents the 80287/80387 from issuing an interrupt request by setting the interrupt enable mask in the control word.

Syntax: FDISI (no operands)

Exception flags: None

Example: FDISI

FDIV (80287/80387)
Divide real

Instruction
FDIV

Typical clocks
198, 220, 225 (80287)

Description
Divides dest. by source, result to dest.

Operation: The FDIV instruction divides the destination operand by the source operand and returns the quotient to the destination operand.

If the FDIV instruction is used without a source or destination operand, ST(1) and ST, respectively, are assumed. The instruction uses ST for the source operand and ST(1) for the destination operand, pops the stack, and returns the result to ST.

Syntax: FDIV (no operands)
FDIV *source__operand*
FDIV *destination__operand,source__operand*

Exception flags: I, D, O, U, Z, P

Example: FDIV
FDIV ST,ST(7)
FDIV ST(7),ST
FDIV LONG__REAL__VAL
FDIV SHORT__REAL__VAL

FDIVP (80287/80387)
Divide real and pop

Instruction
FDIVP

Typical clocks
202 (80287)

Description
Divides dest. by source, pops stack

Operation: The FDIVP instruction takes ST for the source operand and ST(n) for the destination operand. Next, it pops the 80287/80387 TOS, performs the division, and returns the result to the ST(n) register.

Syntax: FDIVP *destination—operand, source—operand*

Exception flags: I, D, O, U, Z, P

Example: FDIVP ST(7),ST

FDIVR (80287/80387)
Divide real reversed

Instruction
FDIVR

Typical clocks
199, 221, 226 (80287)

Description
Divides source by dest., result to dest.

Operation: The FDIVR instruction performs a reversed division. FDIVR takes the specified source operand and divides it by the destination operand, with the quotient being stored back in the destination operand.

If FDIVR is used without any specified operands, ST(1) and ST, respectively, are assumed.

Syntax: FDIVR (no operands)
　　　　　FDIVR *source—operand*
　　　　　FDIVR *destination—operand,source—operand*

Exception flags: I, D, O, U, P, Z

Example: FDIVR

FDIVR LONG — REAL — VAL

FDIVR SHORT — REAL — VAL

FDIVR ST,ST(7)

FDIVR ST(7),ST

FDIVRP (80287/80387)

Divide real reversed and pop

Instruction
FDIVRP

Typical clocks
203 (80287)

Description
Divides source by dest., result to dest., pops

Operation: The FDIVRP instruction performs a reversed division by dividing the source operand by the destination operand. The quotient is returned to the destination operand, and the 80287/80387 stack is popped.

The source operand is always the ST register, with the destination operand being ST(n).

Syntax: FDIVRP *destination — operand,source — operand*

Exception flags: I, D, O, U, P, Z

Example: FDIVRP ST(7),ST

FDIVRP ST(1),ST

FENI (80287/80387)

Enable interrupts

Instruction
FENI

Typical clocks
5 (80287)

Description

Enables interrupt requests

Operation: The FENI instruction clears the interrupt enable mask in the control word, allowing the microprocessor to generate interrupt requests.

Syntax: FENI (no operands)

Exception flags: None

Example: FENI

FFREE (80287/80387)
Free register

Instruction
FFREE

Typical clocks
11 (80287)

Description
Changes dest. reg. tag to empty

Operation: The FFREE instruction frees the destination register's TAG by changing it to empty without changing the register's contents.

Syntax: FFREE *destination—operand*

Exception flags: None

Example: FFREE ST(1)

FIADD (80287/80387)
Integer add

Instruction
FIADD

Typical clocks
120, 125 (80287)

Description
Adds source and dest., sum returned to dest.

Operation: The FIADD instruction adds the source operand to the destination operand and returns the sum to the destination operand. The implied destination operand is always the 80287/80387 TOS register, ST.

Syntax: FIADD *source—operand*

Exception flags: I, O, P, D

Example: FIADD WORD—INT
          FIADD SHORT—INT

FICOM (80287/80387)
Integer compare

Instruction
FICOM

Typical clocks
80, 85 (80287)

Description
Compares TOS to source operand

Operation: The FICOM instruction converts the source operand to a temporary real and compares the 80287/80387 TOS to it. The status word condition codes are changed based on the following conditions:

> if ST > *source—operand*
>   then C0 = 0 and C3 = 0
> if ST < *source—operand*
>   then C0 = 1 and C3 = 0
> if ST = *source—operand*
>   then C0 = 0 and C3 = 1
> if ST < > *source—operand*
>   then C0 = 1 and C3 = 1

Syntax: FICOM *source—operand*

Exception flags: I, D

Example: FICOM WORD—INT

          FICOM SHORT—INT

FICOMP (80287/80387)
Integer compare and pop

Instruction
FICOMP

Description
Compares TOS and source, pops TOS

Operation: The FICOMP functions the same as the FICOM instruction, with the additional step of popping the 80287/80387 stack top. The status word condition codes of the 80287/80387 are changed based on the following conditions:

if ST > source_operand
  then C0 = 0 and C3 = 0
if ST < source_operand
  then C0 = 1 and C3 = 0
if ST = source_operand
  then C0 = 0 and C3 = 1
if ST < > source_operand
  then C0 = 1 and C3 = 1

Syntax: FICOMP source_operand

Exception flags: I, D

Example: FICOMP WORD_INT
        FICOMP SHORT_INT

FIDIV (80287/80387)
Integer divide

Instruction
FIDIV

Typical clocks
230, 236 (80287)

Description
Divides dest. by source, result to dest.

Operation: The FIDIV instruction divides the destination operand by the source operand and returns the quotient to the destination operand. The implied destination operand is always the 80287/80387 TOS or ST register.

Syntax: FIDIV source_operand

Exception flags: I, D, O, U, P, Z

Example: FDIV WORD_INT
        FDIV SHORT_INT

FIDIVR (80287/80387)

Reversed integer divide

Instruction
FIDIVR

Typical clocks
230, 237 (80287)

Description
Source divided by dest., result to dest.

Operation: The FIDIVR instruction performs a reversed division by dividing the source operand by the implied destination operand ST, returning the quotient to the 80287/80387 TOS, ST.

Syntax: FIDIVR *source—operand*

Exception flags: I, D, O, U, P, Z

Example: FIDIVR WORD—INT
FIDIVR SHORT—INT

FILD (80287/80387)

Integer load

Instruction
FILD

Typical clocks
50, 56, 64 (80287)

Description
Converts source to temp. real, pushes TOS

Operation: The FILD instruction changes the source operand from binary integer format to temporary real format and pushes the result onto the implied destination operand, ST.

Syntax: FILD *source—operand*

Exception flags: I

Example: FILD WORD—INT
FILD LONG—INT
FILD SHORT—INT

FIMUL (80287/80387)
Integer multiply

Instruction

FIMUL

Typical clocks
130, 136 (80287)

Description
Multiplies dest. by source, result to dest.

Operation: The FIMUL instruction multiplies the destination operand by the source operand and returns the result to the implied destination operand, ST.

Syntax: FIMUL *source—operand*

Exception flags: I, D, P, O

Example: FIMUL WORD—INT
        FIMUL SHORT—INT

FINCSTP (80287/80387)
Increment 80287/80387 stack pointer

Instruction
FINCSTP

Typical clocks
9 (80287)

Description
Adds 1 to 80287/80387 TOP

Operation: The FINCSTP instruction adds 1 to the 80287/80387 (TOP) stack top pointer in the status word.

Syntax: FINCSTP (no operands)

Exception flags: None

Example: FINCSTP

FINIT (80287/80387)
Initialize processor

Instruction
FINIT

Typical clocks
5 (80287)

Description
Effective functional 80287/80387 reset

Operation: The FINIT instruction sets the control word to 03FFH, clears Exception flags and busy interrupts, and empties all floating-point 80287/80387 stack elements. This is the functional equivalent of a hardware reset, with the exception that the instruction fetch synchronization of the 80287/80387 is not affected.

Syntax: FINIT (no operands)

Exception flags: None

Example: FINIT

FIST (80287/80387)
Integer store

Instruction
FIST

Typical clocks
86, 88 (80287)

Description
Rounds TOS, result returned to dest.

Operation: The FIST instruction takes the contents of the 80287/80387 TOS, rounds it according to the RC field of the control word, and returns the result to the destination operand.

Syntax: FIST *destination—operand*

Exception flags: I, P

Example: FIST WORD—INT
              FIST SHORT—INT

FISTP (80287/80387)
Integer store and pop

Instruction
FISTP

Typical clocks
88, 90, 100 (80287)

Description
Rounds TOS, result to dest., pop TOS

Operation: The FISTP instruction rounds the contents of the TOS the same way the FIST instruction does, storing the result in the destination operand, and, in addition, pops the 80287/80387 TOS.

Syntax: FISTP *destination—operand*

Exception flags: I, P

Example: FISTP WORD—INT
FISTP LONG—INT
FISTP SHORT—INT

FISUB (80287/80387)
Integer subtract

Instruction
FISUB

Typical clocks
120, 125 (80287)

Description
Subtracts source from dest., result to dest.

Operation: The FISUB instruction subtracts the source operand from the implied destination operand, ST, returning the difference to the 80287/80387 TOS register, ST.

Syntax: FISUB *source—operand*

Exception flags: I, D, P, O

Example: FISUB WORD—INT
FISUB SHORT—INT

FISUBR (80287/80387)
Reversed integer subtraction

Instruction
FISUBR

Typical clocks
120, 125 (80287)

Description
Subtracts dest. from source, result to dest.

Operation: The FISUBR instruction performs a reversed subtraction by subtracting the implied destination operand, ST, from the source operand. The result is pushed back onto the 80287/80387 TOS register, ST.

Syntax: FISUBR *source—operand*

Exception flags: I, D, P, O

Example: FISUBR WORD—INT
          FISUBR SHORT—INT

FLD (80287/80387)
Load real

Instruction
FLD

Typical clocks
20, 43, 46, 57 (80287)

Description
Pushes the source operand onto TOS

Operation: The FLD instruction pushes the source operand onto the 80287/80387 TOS register, ST, by decrementing the 80287/80387 stack pointer by 1 and copying the contents of the source operand to TOS.

Syntax: FLD *source—operand*

Exception flags: I, D

Example: FLD ST(7)
          FLD LONG—REAL
          FLD SHORT—REAL

FLD1 (80287/80387)
Load +1.0 onto 80287/80387 TOS

Instruction
FLD1

Typical clocks
18 (80287)

Description
Pushes +1.0 onto 80287/80387 TOS

Operation: The temporary real 64-bit precision and 19-decimal-place precision, +1.0 constant, is pushed onto the 80287/80387 stack.

Syntax: FLD1 (no operands)

Exception flags: I

Example: FLD1

FLDCW (80287/80387)
Load control word

Instruction
FLDCW

Typical clocks
10 (80287)

Description
Replaces control word with source operand

Operation: The FLDCW instruction changes the current contents of the microprocessor control word with the word defined by the source operand.

Syntax: FLDCW *source—operand*

Exception flags: None

Example: FLDCW MEM—WORD

FLDENV (80287/80387)
Load environment

Instruction
FLDENV

Typical clocks
40 (80287)

Description
Loads environment with source operand

Operation: The FLDENV instruction loads the 80287/80387 environment from the memory area defined by the source operand.

Syntax: FLDENV *source—operand*

Exception flags: None

Example: FLDENV FOURTEEN—BYTES

FLDL2E (80287/80387)

Load $\log_2 e$

Instruction
FLDL2E

Typical clocks
18 (80287)

Description
Pushes $\log_2 e$ onto 80287/80387 stack

Operation: The FLDL2E instruction pushes the temporary real 64-bit precision and 19-decimal-place precision, constant value of $\log_2 e$, onto the 80287/80387 stack.

Syntax: FLDL2E (no operands)

Exception flags: I

Example: FLDL2E

FLDL2T (80287/80387)

Load $\log_2 10$

Instruction
FLDL2T

Typical clocks
19 (80287)

Description
Pushes $\log_2 10$ onto 80287/80387 stack

Operation: The FLDL2T instruction pushes the temporary real 64-bit precision and 19-decimal-place precision, constant value of $\log_2 10$, onto the 80287/80387 stack.

Syntax: FLDL2T (no operands)

Exception flags: I

Example: FLDL2T

FLDLG2 (80287/80387)

Load $\log_{10} 2$

Instruction
FLDLG2

Typical clocks
21 (80287)

Description
Pushes the value of $\log_{10}2$ onto stack

Operation: The FLDLG2 intruction pushes the temporary real 64-bit precision and 19-decimal-place precision, constant value of $\log_{10}2$, onto the top of the floating-point stack.

Syntax: FLDLG2 (no operands)

Exception flags: I

Example: FLDLG2

FLDLN2 (80287/80387)
Load $\log_e 2$

Instruction
FLDLN2

Typical clocks
20 (80287)

Description
Pushes value of $\log_e 2$ onto stack

Operation: The FLDLN2 instruction pushes the temporary real 64-bit precision and 19-decimal-place precision, constant value of $\log_e 2$, onto the top of the floating-point stack.

Syntax: FLDLN2 (no operands)

Exception flags: I

Example: FLDLN2

FLDPI (80287/80387)
Load PI

Instruction
FLDPI

Typical clocks
19 (80287)

Description
Pushes the value of PI onto stack

Operation: The FLDPI instruction pushes the temporary real 64-bit precision and 19-decimal-place precision, constant value of **PI**, onto the top of the floating-point stack.

Syntax: FLDPI (no operands)

Exception flags: I

Example: FLDPI

FLDZ (80287/80387)
Load zero

Instruction
FLDZ

Typical clocks
14 (80287)

Description
Pushes +0.0 onto floating-point stack

Operation: The FLDZ instruction pushes the temporary real 64-bit precision and 19-decimal-place precision, constant value of +0.0, onto the top of the floating-point stack.

Syntax: FLDZ (no operands)

Exception flags: I

Example: FLDZ

FMUL (80287/80387)
Multiply real

Instruction
FMUL

Typical clocks
97, 118, 120, 138, 161 (80287)

Description
Multiply dest. by source, result to dest.

Operation: FMUL instruction multiplies the destination operand by the source operand and stores the result back in the destination operand.

If FMUL is used without any specified operands, ST(1), and ST, respectively, are implied.

Syntax: FMUL (no operands)
    FMUL *source—operand*
    FMUL *destination—operand,source—operand*

Exception flags: I, D, U, P, O

Example: FMUL
    FMUL LONG—REAL
    FMUL SHORT—REAL
    FMUL ST,ST(7)
    FMUL ST(7),ST

FMULP (80287/80387)
Multiply real and pop

Instruction
FMULP

Typical clocks
100, 142 (80287)

Description
Multiplies dest. by source, stores and pops

Operation: The FMULP instruction gets its source operand from the 80287/80387 TOS register ST. The destination operand comes from the ST(n) register. After this, the stack is popped, and the result of the multiplication is stored back in ST(n).

Syntax: FMULP *destination—operand,source—operand*

Exception flags: I, D, U, O, P

Example: FMULP ST(7),ST

FNCLEX (80287/80387)
Clear exceptions

Instruction
FNCLEX

Typical clocks
5 (80287)

Description
Clears Exception flags, Int. req., and Busy

Operation: The FNCLEX instruction clears all the Exception flags, the Busy flag, and the Interrupt Request flag in the status word.

Syntax: FNCLEX (no operands)

Exception flags: None

Example: FNCLEX

FNDISI (80287/80387)
Disable interrupts

Instruction
FNDISI

Typical clocks
N/A

Description
Sets enable mask in control word

Operation: The FNDISI instruction sets the interrupt enable mask in the control word and stops the microprocessor from issuing an interrupt request.

Syntax: FNDISI (no operands)

Exception flags: None

Example: FNDISI

FNENI (80287/80387)
Enable interrupts

Instruction
FNENI

Typical clocks
N/A

Description
Clears interrupt enable mask

Operation: The FNENI instruction clears the interrupt enable mask in the control word and permits the microprocessor to generate interrupt requests.

Syntax: FNENI (no operands)

Exception flags: None

Example: FNENI

FNINIT (80287/80387)
Initialize processor

Instruction
FNINIT

Typical clocks
5 (80287)

Description
Resets microprocessor

Operation: The FNINIT instruction sets the control word to 03FFH, clears Exception flags and busy interrupts, and empties all floating-point 80287/80387 stack elements. This is the functional equivalent of a hardware reset, with the exception that the instruction fetch synchronization of the 80287/80387 is not affected.

Syntax: FNINIT (no operands)

Exception flags: None

Example: FNINIT

FNOP (80287/80387)
No operation

Instruction
FNOP

Typical clocks
13 (80287)

Description
Performs no operation

Operation: The FNOP instruction performs no operation.

Syntax: FNOP (no operands)

Exception flags: None

Example: FNOP

FNSAVE (80287/80387)
Save state

Instruction
FNSAVE

Typical clocks
N/A

Description
Full state storage at memory loc. in dest.

Operation: The FNSAVE instruction saves the full 80287/80387 environment, including the register stack, at the location specified by the destination operand. The 80287/80387 is then initialized.

Syntax: FNSAVE *destination—operand*

Exception flags: None

Example: FNSAVE MEM—LOC

FNSTCW (80287/80387)
Store control word

Instruction
FNSTCW

Typical clocks
15 (80287)

Description
Stores control word in dest. operand

Operation: The FNSTCW instruction stores the current 80287/80387 control word in the memory location specified by the destination operand.

Syntax: FNSTCW (no operands)

Exception flags: None

Example: FNSTCW MEM—LOC

FNSTENV (80287/80387)
Store environment

Instruction
FNSTENV

Typical clocks
45 (80287)

Description
Stores environment in dest. operand

Operation: The FNSTENV instruction stores the current 80287/80387 environment, the exception pointers, tag words, control word, and status word at the memory location specified by the destination operand.

Syntax: FNSTENV *destination___operand*

Exception flags: None

Example: FNSTENV MEM___LOC

FNSTSW (80287/80387)
Store status word

Instruction
FNSTSW

Typical clocks
15 (80287)

Description
Stores status word in dest. operand

Operation: The FNSTSW instruction stores the current contents of the 80287/80387 status word at the memory location specified by the destination operand.

Syntax: FNSTSW *destination___operand*

Exception flags: None

Example: FNSTSW MEM___LOC

FPATAN (80287/80387)
Partial arc tangent

Instruction
FPATAN

Typical clocks
650 (80287)

Description
Calculates ARCTAN of a function

Operation: The FPATAN instruction pops the X value from the current TOS, pops the stack a second time, takes the now-current TOS for the Y value, calculates ARCTAN(Y/X), and returns the result to the TOS register on the 80287/80387, ST. X and Y are assumed to be in the proper range: $0<Y<X<\infty$

Syntax: FPATAN (no operands)

Exception flags: U, P

Example: FPATAN

FPREM (80287/80387)
Partial remainder

Instruction
FPREM

Typical clocks
125 (80287)

Description
Modulo division of ST by ST(1), result to ST

Operation: The FPREM instruction takes the current 80287/80387 TOS register, ST, and divides it by the next element, ST(1), returning the partial remainder to the TOS register, ST.

Syntax: FPREM (no operands)

Exception flags: I, U, D

Example: FPREM

FPTAN (80287/80387)
Partial tangent

Instruction
FPTAN

Typical clocks
450 (80287)

Description
Calculates the TAN of an angle

Operation: The FPTAN instruction computes the $Y/X = TAN(\theta)$ of an angle. θ must be in the range $0 <= \theta < \pi/4$ and is taken from the top of stack. Upon completion, Y replaces θ on the stack, and X is pushed to become the new top of stack. Out-of-range values are not signaled. Values for SIN, COS, and so forth must be derived from this operand. 80387 Note: θ covers the full range of angles. FSIN and FCOS are now available for this coprocessor.

Syntax: FPTAN (no operands)

Exception flags: I, P

Example: FPTAN

FRNDINT (80287/80387)
Round to integer

Instruction
FRNDINT

Typical clocks
45 (80287)

Description
Rounds 80287/80387 stack top to integer

Operation: The FRNDINT instruction rounds the 80287/80387 TOS register's contents to an integer. There are four modes of rounding, based on the RC field of the control word:

RC = 00	Round to the nearest integer. If the value is exactly midpoint, choose the even value.
RC = 01	Round down.
RC = 10	Round up.
RC = 11	Round toward 0.

Syntax: FRNDINT (no operands)

Exception flags: I, P

Example: FRNDINT

FRSTOR (80287/80387)
Restore state

Instruction
FRSTOR

Typical clocks
205 (80287)

Description
Restores state instruction

Operation: The FRSTOR instruction restores the state of the 80287/80387 from the 94-byte memory area referenced by the source operand. For compatibility, this data should have been saved with either the FSAVE or FNSAVE instruction.

Syntax: FRSTOR *source—operand*

Exception flags: None

Example: FRSTOR MEM—LOC

FSAVE (80287/80387)
Save state

Instruction
FSAVE

Typical clocks
205 (80287)

Description
Saves the 80287/80387 state

Operation: The FSAVE instruction stores the entire state of the 80287/80387, including the register stack and the environment. The information is stored at the memory location defined by the destination operand. The 80287/80387 is then initialized.

Syntax: FSAVE *destination—operand*

Exception flags: None

Example: FSAVE MEM—LOC

FSCALE (80287/80387)
Scale

Instruction
FSCALE

Typical clocks
35 (80287)

Description
Multiplies or divides by powers of 2

Operation: The FSCALE instruction takes the value contained in ST(1), interprets this value as an integer, and adds the value to the exponent of the number in ST. The result is ST $* 2^{ST(1)}$.

Syntax: FSCALE (no operands)

Exception flags: I, U, O

Example: FSCALE

FSETPM (80287/80387)
Set protected mode

Instruction
FSETPM

Typical clocks
5 (80287)

Description
Sets protection mode

Operation: The FSETPM instruction puts the 80287/80387 into protected mode. Once the FSETPM instruction has been executed, the 80287/80387 remains in protected mode until the next hardware reset, even after the FRSTOR, FSAVE, or FINIT instructions have been executed.

Syntax: FSETPM (no operands)

Exception flags: None

Example: FSETPM

FSIN (80387)
SINE

Instruction
FSIN

Typical clocks
N/A

Description
Calculates the SINE of an angle

Operation: The FSIN instruction computes the SINE θ of an angle. The angle is taken from the top of stack, and has no range limit. Upon completion, the sine value replaces θ on the stack top.

Syntax: FSIN (no operands)

Exception flags: D, IS, I, P

Example: FSIN

FSINCOS (80387)
SINE/COSINE

Instruction
FSINCOS

Typical clocks
N/A

Description
Calculates the simultaneous SINE and COSINE of an angle

Operation: The FSINCOS instruction computes both the SINE and COSINE θ of an angle. The angle is taken from the top of stack, and has no range limit. Upon completion, the cosine value resides at ST while the sine value is placed at ST(1).

Syntax: FSINCOS (no operands)

Exception flags: D, IS, I, P

Example: FSINCOS

FSQRT (80287/80387)
Square root

Instruction
FSQRT

Typical clocks
183 (80287)

Description
Pushes square root of ST back onto TOS

Operation: The FSQRT instruction takes the contents of the current 80287/80387 TOS register, ST, and takes the square root of that value and pushes it onto the stack.

Syntax: FSQRT (no operands)

Exception flags: I, P, D

Example: FSQRT

FST (80287/80387)
Store real

Instruction
FST

Typical clocks
18, 87, 100 (80287)

Description
Stores value in ST in dest. operand

Operation: The FST instruction takes the value of the 80287/80387 TOS register, ST, and stores it at the memory location specified by the destination operand.

Syntax: FST *destination __ operand*

Exception flags: I, U, O, P

Example: FST ST(7)
                FST LONG __ REAL __ VAL
                FST SHORT __ REAL __ VAL

FSTCW (80287/80387)
Store control word

Instruction
FSTCW

Typical clocks
15 (80287)

Description
Stores control word in dest. operand

Operation: The FSTCW instruction stores the current 80287/80387 control word at the memory location specified by the destination operand.

Syntax: FSTCW *destination __ operand*

Exception flags: None

Example: FSTCW MEM __ LOC

FSTENV (80287/80387)
Store environment

Instruction
FSTENV

Typical clocks
45 (80287)

Description
Stores 80287/80387 status to dest.

Operation: The FSTENV instruction stores the environment, including the status, control, and tag words and exception pointers, at the memory location specified by the destination operand.

Syntax: FSTENV *destination __ operand*

Exception flags: None

Example: FSTENV MEM __ LOC

FSTP (80287/80387)
Store real and pop

Instruction
FSTP

Typical clocks
20, 55, 89, 102 (80287)

Description
Stores ST at memory and pops stack

Operation: The FSTP instruction stores the 80287/80387 TOS register, ST, at the memory location specified by the destination operand, and then the stack is popped.

Syntax: FSTP *destination __ operand*

Exception flags: I, U, O, P

Example: FSTP ST(n)

        FSTP LONG_REAL_VAL

        FSTP SHORT_REAL_VAL

FSTSW (80287/80387)

Store status word

Instruction
FSTSW

Typical clocks
15 (80287)

Description
Stores status word in memory

Operation: The FSTSW instruction stores the current value of the 80287/80387 status word in the memory location specified by the destination operand.

Syntax: FSTSW *destination_operand*

Exception flags: None

Example: FSTSW

FSUB (80287/80387)

Subtract real

Instruction
FSUB

Typical clocks
85, 105, 110 (80287)

Description
Subtracts source from dest., diff. to dest.

Operation: The FSUB instruction subtracts the source operand from the destination operand and returns the result to the destination operand.

If FSUB is used without any operands, ST(1) and ST, respectively, are assumed. If just the source operand is specified, ST is the assumed destination operand.

Syntax: FSUB (no operands)
FSUB *source—operand*
FSUB *destination—operand,source—operand*

Exception flags: I, D, P, O, U

Example: FSUB

FSUB LONG—REAL—VAL
FSUB SHORT—REAL—VAL

FSUB ST,ST(7)
FSUB ST(7),ST

FSUBP (80287/80387)
Subtract real and pop

Instruction
FSUBP

Typical clocks
90

Description
Subtracts source from dest., stores in dest., pops

Operation: The FSUBP instruction subtracts the source operand from the destination operand and returns the difference to the destination operand. The 80287/80387 floating-point stack is popped.

Syntax: FSUBP *destination—operand,source—operand*

Exception flags: I, D, U, O, P

Example: FSUBP ST(7),ST

FSUBR (80287/80387)
Subtract real reversed

Instruction
FSUBR

Typical clocks
87, 105, 110 (80287)

Description
Subracts dest. from source, result to dest.

Operation: The FSUBR instruction performs a reversed subtraction by subtracting the destination operand from the source operand and returning the difference to the destination operand.

If FSUBR is used without any operands, ST(1) and ST, respectively, are assumed. If just the source operand is specified, ST is the assumed destination operand.

Syntax: FSUBR (no operands)

FSUBR *source—operand*

FSUBR *destination—operand,source—operand*

Exception flags: I, O, D, U, P

Example: FSUBR

FSUBR LONG—REAL—VAL
FSUBR SHORT—REAL—VAL

FSUBR ST,ST(7)
FSUBR ST(7),ST

FSUBRP (80287/80387)
Subtract real reversed and pop

Instruction
FSUBRP

Typical clocks
90 (80287)

Description
Subtracts dest. from source, stores and pops

Operation: The FSUBRP instruction performs a reversed subtraction by subtracting the destination operand ST(n) from the source operand ST, the top of stack is popped, and the result is stored back in the destination operand ST(n).

Syntax: FSUBRP *destination—operand,source—operand*

Exception flags: I, O, U, D, P

Example: FSUBRP

FTST (80287/80387)
Test

Instruction
FTST

Typical clocks
42 (80287)

Description
Compares 80287/80387 TOS set condition codes

Operation: The FTST instruction compares the contents of the 80287/80387 TOS register ST with +0.0. The result changes the condition codes in the status word based on the following results:

ST is positive and nonzero	C0 = 0	C3 = 0
ST is negative and nonzero	C0 = 1	C3 = 0
ST is zero	C0 = 0	C3 = 1
ST is not comparable; i.e., NAN	C0 = 1	C3 = 1

Syntax: FIST (no operands)

Exception flags: I, D

Example: FTST

FWAIT (80287/80387)
Wait (CPU instruction)

Instruction
FWAIT

Typical clocks
3+5n (80287)

Description
80286 waits for 80287/80387 to finish

Operation: The FWAIT instruction causes the 80387 to wait until the currently executing 80287/80387 instruction is completed; then the 80286 executes its next instruction. n is number of $\overline{\text{BUSY}}$ examinations before completion of last instruction.

Syntax: FWAIT (no operands)

Exception flags: None

Example: FWAIT

FXAM (80287/80387)

Examine

Instruction
FXAM

Typical clocks
17 (80287)

Description
Sets condition codes of status word on exam

Operation: The FXAM instruction examines the contents of the 80287/80387 TOS register ST and sets the condition codes of the status word based on the following results:

C0	C1	C2	C3	RESULT
0	0	0	0	+Unnormal
0	0	0	1	+NAN
0	0	1	0	−Unnormal
0	0	1	1	−NAN
0	1	0	0	+Normal
0	1	0	1	+00
0	1	1	0	−Normal
0	1	1	1	−00
1	0	0	0	+0
1	0	0	1	Empty
1	0	1	0	−0
1	0	1	1	Empty
1	1	0	0	+Denormal
1	1	0	1	Empty
1	1	1	0	−Denormal
1	1	1	1	Empty

Syntax: FXAM (no operands)

Exception flags: None

Example: FXAM

FXCH (80287/80387)
Exchange registers

Instruction
FXCH

Typical clocks
12 (80287)

Description
Exchanges dest. operand with stack top

Operation: The FXCH instruction exchanges the destination operand with the 80287/80387 TOS register, ST. If the instruction is used without an operand, the default destination operand is ST(1).

Syntax: FXCH (no operands)

    FXCH *destination_operand*

Exception flags: I

Example: FXCH

    FXCH ST(7)

FXTRACT (80287/80387)
Extract exponent and significand

Instruction
FXTRACT

Typical clocks
50 (80287)

Description
Extracts exponent and significand

Operation: The FXTRACT instruction factors the number in the 80287/80387 TOS register, ST, into a significand and an exponent expressed in real numbers. The exponent replaces the original TOS; then the significand is pushed onto the 80287/80387 TOS register, ST.

Syntax: FXTRACT (no operands)

Exception flags: I

Example: FXTRACT

FYL2X (80287/80387)

$Y * \log_2 X$

Instruction
FYL2X

Typical clocks
950 (80287)

Description
Calculates $Y * \log_2 X$

Operation: The FYL2X instruction takes the value for X from the 80287/80387 TOS register, ST, and the value for Y from ST(1). The instruction next pops the stack and stores the calculated result back on TOS or ST.

Syntax: FYL2X (no operands)

Exception flags: P

Example: FYL2X

FYL2XP1 (80287/80387)

$Y * \log_2(X+1)$

Instruction
FYL2XP1

Typical clocks
850 (80287)

Description
Calculates $Y * \log_2(X+1)$

Operation: The FYL2XP1 instruction gets the X value from the 80287/80387 TOS register, ST, the Y value from ST(1), pops the stack, and returns the result of the calculation to the TOS register, ST. This instruction is used when computing the log of a number very close to 1.

Syntax: FYL2XP1 (no operands)

Exception flags: P

Example: FYL2XP1

5

SIMPLE PROGRAMMING TECHNIQUES

The first four chapters of this book have dealt with the fundamentals of assembly language and have introduced the instruction sets for the 80286/80386 microprocessors and 80287/80387 coprocessor chips. In Chapters 3 and 4, a simple example was given for each assembly language processor and coprocessor instruction to illustrate the form and syntax for that instruction. None of those examples were executable programs, however. This chapter will concentrate on program syntax and will teach you how to structure simple programs from top to bottom. Each example has been designed to teach something new about general programming, individual commands, or special techniques. It would be best to start at the beginning of this chapter and work your way through, even if you are not a newcomer to assembly language programming. The examples are generally graded from easier to harder as you progress through the chapter, but again, each program has been carefully designed to present a few new concepts.

All of the necessary program overhead has been included with each example in this chapter, and each example is complete in itself. In other words, if you type in an example and then assemble and link it, the example will run!

Chapter 2 presented and explained the minimum program overhead required when structuring most general assembly language programs. Chapter 2 also described the major differences between COM and EXE files. Almost all of the programs in this book could have been written in one segment (64K) of code and could thus have used the COM structure. However, all of the popular assemblers support EXE files, and EXE files tend to use the more powerful assembler structure. Therefore, all programs in this book, except where noted, are designed for the EXE format. As a reminder, the following listing shows the EXE program overhead. All of the examples in this chapter will use overhead very similar to this.

```
;(descriptive comment describing purpose of program placed here)

STACK     SEGMENT PARA STACK
          DB      64 DUP ('MYSTACK ')
STACK     ENDS

MYDATA    SEGMENT PARA 'DATA'
(actual program data placed here)
MYDATA    ENDS

MYCODE    SEGMENT PARA 'CODE'       ;DEFINE CODE SEG. FOR MASM
MYPROC    PROC    FAR               ;PROCEDURE IS NAMED MYPROC
          ASSUME  CS:MYCODE,DS:MYDATA,SS:STACK
          PUSH    DS                ;SAVE LOCATION OF DS REG.
          SUB     AX,AX             ;GET A ZERO IN AX
          PUSH    AX                ;SAVE ZERO ON STACK, TOO
          MOV     AX,MYDATA         ;GET DATA LOCATION IN AX
          MOV     DS,AX             ;PUT IT IN DS REGISTER

(actual program code inserted here)

          RET                       ;RETURN CONTROL TO DOS
MYPROC    ENDP                      ;END PROCEDURE NAMED MYPROC
MYCODE    ENDS                      ;END CODE SEGMENT NAMED MYCODE

          END                       ;END WHOLE PROGRAM
```

The first fifteen programs in this chapter are general programs that should run on almost any 8088/80386 machine (those based on the 8086 family from 8088 through 80286 to 80386). The remaining programs are much more machine dependent. Some of these programs, designed on the IBM AT computer, use special DOS and BIOS routines that may be unique to the IBM product. If you are using an 80286 (IBM AT) compatible machine, some modifications may be necessary, depending upon the degree of that compatibility. There are also some programs written exclusively for the 80386 microprocessor.

Again, each program in this chapter is a nugget of information—not long, involved, or complicated—intended to teach you elementary programming concepts.

ARITHMETIC PROGRAMS

This section presents and describes nine arithmetic assembly language examples. These include the basic arithmetic operators such as addition, subtraction, multiplication, and division. The section looks at several different programming modes. The last example examines a simple algorithm for determining the square root of a hexadecimal integer. Unless otherwise mentioned, all assembly language arithmetic is done in hexadecimal format. The authors strongly recommend the purchase of a calculator capable of converting numbers from one base (radix) to another.

HEXADECIMAL ADDITION USING IMMEDIATE ADDRESSING

Perhaps the simplest example possible in assembly language is the addition of hexadecimal numbers. This is a straight-line program that requires, in addition to the normal overhead, only three actual lines of code. Figure 5-1 is a diagram of these three steps. This example has a number of features that make it interesting, even though the programming is simple. Refer to the following listing for an implementation of the actual assembly language code.

```
;FOR 8088/80386 MACHINES
;PROGRAM TO ILLUSTRATE A SIMPLE HEXADECIMAL ADDITION WITH
;IMMEDIATE ADDRESSING

STACK     SEGMENT PARA STACK
          DB      64 DUP ('MYSTACK ')
STACK     ENDS

MYCODE    SEGMENT PARA 'CODE'      ;DEFINE CODE SEG. FOR MASM
MYPROC    PROC    FAR              ;PROCEDURE IS NAMED MYPROC
          ASSUME  CS:MYCODE,SS:STACK
          PUSH    DS               ;SAVE LOCATION OF DS REG.
          SUB     AX,AX            ;GET A ZERO IN AX
          PUSH    AX               ;SAVE ZERO ON STACK, TOO

;ACTUAL ADDITION OF THREE NUMBERS USING IMMEDIATE ADDRESSING
          MOV     AL,23H           ;PUT HEX NUM 23H IN AL REG
          ADD     AL,0AH           ;ADD 0AH TO AL REG
          ADD     AL,10H           ;ADD 10H TO AL REG
;END OF ADDITION EXAMPLE, RESULTS IN AL REGISTER

          RET                      ;RETURN CONTROL TO DOS
MYPROC    ENDP                     ;END PROCEDURE NAMED MYPROC
MYCODE    ENDS                     ;END CODE SEGMENT NAMED MYCODE

          END                      ;END WHOLE PROGRAM
```

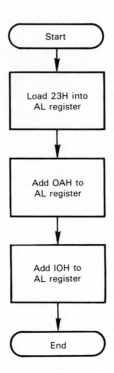

Figure 5-1.

Programming steps for hexadecimal addition

Before talking about the actual code, examine the structure of the program. The program starts with three lines of comments that tell what machines it will run on and then briefly describe what the program hopes to accomplish. Comments at the start of a program not only inform other users of the program's purpose, but will also remind you, five days after the program's creation, what the program does. Recall that comments can be placed in any of the four fields so long as they start with a semicolon. The next code group is the declaration of a stack segment called STACK. The name of the stack segment is arbitrary and could have been anything, even HAYSTACK. By establishing a stack segment and loading it with the word MYSTACK 64 times, you will be able to use software tools, such as debug, to locate programming problems and find solutions to them by examining the computer's memory. The word MYSTACK will serve as a flag so that you can easily find your answers in a section of machine memory.

This example did not use any separately stored data, so the establishment of a data segment was not necessary. The code segment was named MYCODE. Again, this name is arbitrary and could have been composed of any legal assembly language characters. Every code segment must have one procedure. The procedure for this example is titled MYPROC. The remainder of the overhead is standard for assembly language programs and was explained in Chapter 2.

The following lines of code make up the heart of the hexadecimal addition program:

```
MOV    AL,23H    ;PUT HEX NUM 23H IN AL REG
ADD    AL,0AH    ;ADD 0AH TO AL REG
ADD    AL,10H    ;ADD 10H TO AL REG
```

In this example, the hexadecimal number (23H) is MOVed into the AL register. Recall that the AL register is one half of the AX register. The AX register can be broken into two 8-bit parts (AH and AL). Since AL is an 8-bit register, it can hold hexadecimal numbers from 00H to FFH. The MOV command is one of the most frequently encountered commands in 8088/80386 programming, since it gives the programmer the ability to load or save information. The next operation adds the number 0AH to the current contents of the AL register. The AL register will contain 2DH after this operation. The final ADD instruction adds 10H to AL, yielding the final sum of 3DH.

This example has a number of limitations. First, the program does not take into account overflow if the sum in AL exceeds 0FFH. Second, the program does not allow for the addition of numbers greater than 0FFH. Third, the program would be impractically long if there were 1000 numbers to add. Fourth, if the numbers change, the programmer must go back to the code segment and change each program line. Even with these limitations, however, this is not a worthless program. To the contrary, it is a very popular technique for adding several numbers. Remember—to program effectively, you must know the limitations of your program.

HEXADECIMAL SUBTRACTION
USING DIRECT ADDRESSING

Subtraction in assembly language is just as easy as addition. Figure 5-2 is a diagram of the steps necessary to subtract three hexadecimal numbers. In the previous addition example, the immediate addressing mode dictated that the numbers to be added were immediately entered into the individual registers. In this example, the numbers are first assigned variable names in a separate data segment and then subtracted using direct addressing techniques.

In this example 16-bit registers are used instead of 8-bit registers. The 16-bit register is the maximum register size in the 8088/80286 chip family. The 80386 has broken this barrier by allowing 32-bit general registers. The use of 16-bit registers in this example expands the range of numbers from 0000H to 0FFFFH (0 to 65535 decimal). The use of 8-bit registers limited the numbers you could use to a range of 00H to 0FFH (0 to 255 decimal). The following listing shows the complete subtraction program. There are a number of new features introduced with this program that should be noted.

```
;FOR 8088/80386 MACHINES
;PROGRAM TO ILLUSTRATE HEXADECIMAL SUBTRACTION WITH THE USE
;OF DIRECT ADDRESSING

STACK     SEGMENT PARA STACK
          DB      64 DUP ('MYSTACK ')
STACK     ENDS

MYDATA    SEGMENT PARA 'DATA'
NUM1      DW      1234H              ;1st 16 BIT NUMBER
NUM2      DW      24H                ;2nd 16 BIT NUMBER
NUM3      DW      0ABCH              ;3rd 16 BIT NUMBER
ANS       DW      ?                  ;RESERVE STORAGE FOR ANSWER
MYDATA    ENDS

MYCODE    SEGMENT PARA 'CODE'        ;DEFINE CODE SEG. FOR MASM
MYPROC    PROC    FAR                ;PROCEDURE IS NAMED MYPROC
          ASSUME  CS:MYCODE,DS:MYDATA,SS:STACK
          PUSH    DS                 ;SAVE LOCATION OF DS REG.
          SUB     AX,AX              ;GET A ZERO IN AX
          PUSH    AX                 ;SAVE ZERO ON STACK, TOO
          MOV     AX,MYDATA          ;GET DATA LOCATION IN AX
          MOV     DS,AX              ;PUT IT IN DS REGISTER

;ACTUAL SUBTRACTION USING THREE 16 BIT NUMBERS
          MOV     AX,NUM1            ;LOAD NUM1 INTO AX REGISTER
          SUB     AX,NUM2            ;SUBTRACT NUM2 FROM NUM1
          SUB     AX,NUM3            ;SUB NUM3 FROM ABOVE RESULTS
```

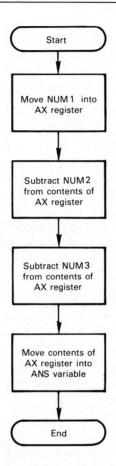

Figure 5-2. _____

Programming steps for hexadecimal subtraction

```
        MOV    ANS,AX           ;STORE RESULT IN ANS
;END OF SUBTRACTION EXAMPLE

        RET                     ;RETURN CONTROL TO DOS
MYPROC  ENDP                    ;END PROCEDURE NAMED MYPROC
MYCODE  ENDS                    ;END CODE SEGMENT NAMED MYCODE

        END                     ;END WHOLE PROGRAM
```

This is the first example program that has used a separate data segment.

```
MYDATA    SEGMENT PARA  'DATA'
NUM1      DW        1234H    ;1st 16 BIT NUMBER
NUM2      DW        24H      ;2nd 16 BIT NUMBER
NUM3      DW        0ABCH    ;3rd 16 BIT NUMBER
ANS       DW        ?        ;RESERVE STORAGE FOR
                             ;ANSWER
MYDATA    ENDS
```

Once again, the name of the data segment is arbitrary. MYDATA could just as well have been called YESTERDAYSDATA, but that is quite a long name to remember and type.

The remainder of the first line of the listing declares that this segment must start on a paragraph boundary in memory and that it will be a data segment. Four variables are declared in this segment. NUM1, NUM2, and NUM3 contain three numbers to be used in the subtraction example. Each variable is declared as a defined word (DW). The numbers 1234H, 24H, and 0ABCH are padded by most 8088/80386 assemblers to 16 bits. The programmer can think of these numbers being stored in memory as 1234H, 0024H, and 0ABCH. The fourth variable, ANS, is declared but not initialized to any value, so the entry is a ? (question mark). The ? reserves 16 bits of storage for the ANSwer. Finally, the last line closes the named data segment with an ENDSegment.

The actual code for subtraction is straightforward.

```
MOV    AX,NUM1    ;LOAD NUM1 INTO AX REGISTER
SUB    AX,NUM2    ;SUBTRACT NUM2 FROM NUM1
SUB    AX,NUM3    ;SUB NUM3 FROM ABOVE RESULTS
MOV    ANS,AX     ;STORE RESULT IN ANS
```

The first number is moved into the AX register. The next two lines of code subtract NUM2 and NUM3 from the contents of the AX register. Finally, the fourth line of code moves the contents of the AX register (754H) into the variable ANS.

At this point, there is no way to view the actual results other than using a register or data-segment dump from memory. The following listing is a dump of the data segment after program execution using IBM's DEBUG program. Can you find each of the numbers in the data segment? Notice, in particular, how 16-bit numbers are broken and stored in 8-bit nuggets.

```
-D DS:0000
1C9D:0000   34 12 24 00 BC 0A 54 07-00 00 00 00 00 00 00 00   4.$...T.........
1C9D:0010   4D 59 53 54 41 43 4B 20-4D 59 53 54 41 43 4B 20   MYSTACK MYSTACK
1C9D:0020   4D 59 53 54 41 43 4B 20-4D 59 53 54 41 43 4B 20   MYSTACK MYSTACK
1C9D:0030   4D 59 53 54 41 43 4B 20-4D 59 53 54 41 43 4B 20   MYSTACK MYSTACK
1C9D:0040   4D 59 53 54 41 43 4B 20-4D 59 53 54 41 43 4B 20   MYSTACK MYSTACK
1C9D:0050   4D 59 53 54 41 43 4B 20-4D 59 53 54 41 43 4B 20   MYSTACK MYSTACK
1C9D:0060   4D 59 53 54 41 43 4B 20-4D 59 53 54 41 43 4B 20   MYSTACK MYSTACK
1C9D:0070   4D 59 53 54 41 43 4B 20-4D 59 53 54 41 43 4B 20   MYSTACK MYSTACK
```

This program, in addition to illustrating hexadecimal subtraction, showed some techniques for overcoming the programming limitations of the previous addition example. First, by using a data segment, the numbers to be subtracted could be changed without having to alter the actual program code. Second, the range of numbers was increased from 8 bits to 16 bits, thus offering greater precision and giving the programmer the option to work with larger numbers.

MULTIPLE-PRECISION ADDITION
USING DIRECT ADDRESSING

The general-purpose registers (AX, BX, CX, and DX) of the 8088/80286 family are limited to 16 bits. If there were not a programming technique for getting around this limitation, programmers would be restricted to working with integers from 0000H to 0FFFFH (0 to 65535 decimal). In the next example a general technique for 32-bit multiple-precision arithmetic is shown. Thirty-two-bit arithmetic allows numbers as large as 0FFFFFFFFH (4294967295 decimal) on 8088/80286 machines. Although the 80386 allows 32-bit arithmetic, the programmer still requires multiple-precision programming for numbers greater than 0FFFFFFFFH. All microprocessors set a Carry flag or Overflow flag when an arithmetic operation dictates. The first two programs have not used this feature. If a carry or borrow operation had occurred, it would have gone unnoticed by the program and produced an incorrect answer. The ADC (add with carry) instruction allows this program to take advantage of any carry information and permits multiple-precision arithmetic. Figure 5-3 shows how multiple-precision addition can be accomplished and Figure 5-4 gives the general program flow.

Recall that the Carry flag is evaluated (set or cleared) after each ADD or ADC operation, but only used by the ADC instruction. In general, the pro-

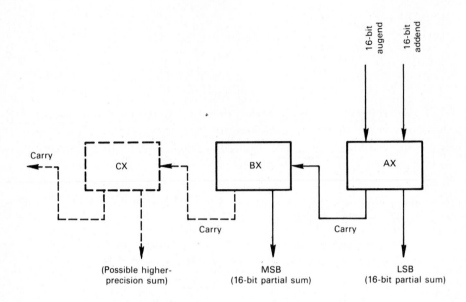

Figure 5-3.

How multiple-precision addition can be accomplished

gram starts with the LSBs (least-significant bits) and works toward the MSBs (most-significant bits). The addition of two 16-bit numbers may or may not produce a carry. Adding 1234H to 1532H does not produce a carry, but adding 0ABCDH to 5600H does. Certainly, if they are LSB numbers, nothing will be passing a carry to them from a previous addition. For that reason, LSB additions are usually done with the ADD command. If the LSB's produce a carry, the Carry flag will be set and used by the ADC instruction when the next-higher 16-bit addition is done. In this example program, only carry information is accumulated in the higher 16 bits, because any given number to be added is limited to (the lower) 16 bits. Thus, ADC operations are done with 0000H in the immediate addressing mode. Figure 5-5 shows the complete program for adding four 16-bit numbers and storing the 32-bit multiple-precision result in two 16-bit variables (LSBANS and MSBANS).

A segment of the total program is shown here.

```
MOV   AX,NUM1      ;PUT FIRST NUMBER IN AX REGISTER
```

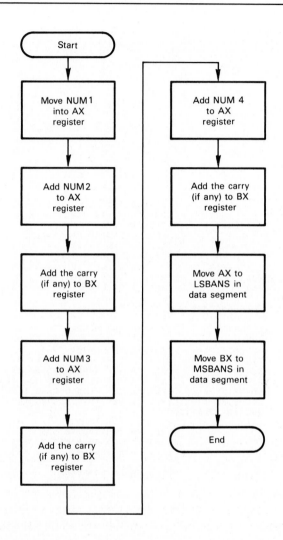

Figure 5-4. _____

Programming steps from multiple-precision addition

```
ADD     AX,NUM2      ;ADD SECOND NUMBER TO FIRST
ADC     BX,00H       ;IF CARRY SET, ADD TO BX REGISTER
ADD     AX,NUM3      ;ADD THIRD NUMBER TO AX REGISTER
ADC     BX,00H       ;IF CARRY SET, ADD TO BX REGISTER
```

```
;FOR 8088/80386 MACHINES
;PROGRAM TO ILLUSTRATE MULTIPLE PRECISION ADDITION
;USING DIRECT ADDRESSING

STACK     SEGMENT PARA STACK
          DB      64 DUP ('MYSTACK ')
STACK     ENDS

MYDATA    SEGMENT PARA 'DATA'
NUM1      DW      0FEEDH
NUM2      DW      1234HH
NUM3      DW      0EFDCH
MUM4      DW      0EA1EH
LSBANS    DW      0
MSBANS    DW      0
MYDATA    ENDS

MYCODE    SEGMENT PARA 'CODE'        ;DEFINE CODE SEG. FOR MASM
MYPROC    PROC    FAR                ;PROCEDURE IS NAMED MYPROC
          ASSUME  CS:MYCODE,DS:MYDATA,SS:STACK
          PUSH    DS                 ;SAVE LOCATION OF DS REG.
          SUB     AX,AX              ;GET A ZERO IN AX
          PUSH    AX                 ;SAVE ZERO ON STACK, TOO
          MOV     AX,MYDATA          ;GET DATA LOCATION IN AX
          MOV     DS,AX              ;PUT IT IN DS REGISTER
          MOV     BX,0               ;SET BX TO ZERO FOR CARRY ACCUMULATION

;ACTUAL START OF PROGRAM CODE FOR ADDITION
          MOV     AX,NUM1            ;PUT FIRST NUMBER IN AX REGISTER
          ADD     AX,NUM2            ;ADD SECOND NUMBER TO FIRST
          ADC     BX,00H             ;IF CARRY SET, ADD TO BX REGISTER
          ADD     AX,NUM3            ;ADD THIRD NUMBER TO AX REGISTER
          ADC     BX,00H             ;IF CARRY SET, ADD TO BX REGISTER
          ADD     AX,NUM4            ;ADD FOURTH NUMBER TO AX REGISTER
          ADC     BX,00H             ;IF CARRY SET, ADD TO BX REGISTER
          MOV     LSBANS,AX          ;PUT AX SUM INTO LSBANS STORAGE
          MOV     MSBANS,BX          ;PUT BX SUM INTO MSBANS STORAGE
;END OF PROGRAM CODE FOR ADDITION

          RET                        ;RETURN CONTROL TO DOS
MYPROC    ENDP                       ;END PROCEDURE NAMED MYPROC
MYCODE    ENDS                       ;END CODE SEGMENT NAMED MYCODE

          END                        ;END WHOLE PROGRAM
```

Figure 5-5. _____

Programming steps for multiple-precision addition using direct addressing

```
ADD    AX,NUM4      ;ADD FOURTH NUMBER TO AX REGISTER
ADC    BX,00H       ;IF CARRY SET, ADD TO BX REGISTER
MOV    LSBANS,AX    ;PUT AX SUM INTO LSBANS STORAGE
MOV    MSBANS,BX    ;PUT BX SUM INTO MSBANS STORAGE
```

NUM1 is added to NUM2 with the simple move/add sequence of the first addition example. If this addition set the Carry flag, then the next line of code (ADC BX,00H) adds the carry to the contents of the BX register. The ADD/ADC sequence is repeated for each number to be added. The final sum is found in two registers. BX contains the MSBs and AX the LSBs of the 32-bit answer. The register contents are moved back to the data segment in two variables, LSBANS and MSBANS. If these two numbers are concatenated, the answer can be read as 0002EB1BH. This technique could be extended to add or accumulate any size number, thus overcoming the register limitations of a particular computer.

There is still one major limitation to the programming techniques described thus far. For each number to be added or subtracted from a register, there is at least one line (sometimes two) of code. For one or two additions this does not cause a problem, but if the number of additions increases even to 20, the code becomes cumbersome and inefficient.

MULTIPLE-PRECISION ADDITION USING INDEXED ADDRESSING

The easiest way to overcome the "one addition, one line of code" restriction of straight-line programming is to use: (1) a storage table for the numbers, (2) program looping over the same code more than once, and (3) indexed addressing to move from one number to another in the storage table.

Many numbers can be stored in a table under one variable name: a new variable name does not need to be used for each entry. The following data segment illustrates this concept:

```
MYDATA   SEGMENT PARA  'DATA'
TABLE    DW        1234H,5678H,9ABCH,0DEF0H,1111H,2222H,3333H
         DW        4444H,5555H,6666H,7777H,8888H,9999H,0AAAAH
         DW        0BBBBH,0CCCCH,0DDDDH,0EEEEH,0FFFFH
LSBANS   DW        ?
MSBANS   DW        ?
MYDATA   ENDS
```

The numbers are stored under the variable TABLE (what else?). TABLE declares each entry to be a defined word (DW). There are 19 entries in this table. Notice, in particular, how one line of TABLE continues to the next line. A program to add several of these numbers needs a technique for entering the TABLE storage location and picking out the correct numbers for an addition. Figure 5-6 shows a diagram of the programming steps for multiple-precision addition using looping and indexed addressing.

When using looping, the program continuously recycles through the code a prescribed number of times. Thus, an add instruction can be used many times from within a loop, eliminating the need for an add instruction for each number. The following listing shows a complete program for adding the first ten 16-bit numbers in TABLE.

```
;FOR 8088/80386 MACHINES
;PROGRAM TO ILLUSTRATE MULTIPLE PRECISION ADDITION USING DATA
;STORED IN A TABLE WITH INDEXED ADDRESSING

STACK    SEGMENT PARA STACK

         DB      64 DUP ('MYSTACK ')
STACK    ENDS

MYDATA   SEGMENT PARA 'DATA'
TABLE    DW      1234H,5678H,9ABCH,0DEF0H,1111H,2222H,3333H
         DW      4444H,5555H,6666H,7777H,8888H,9999H,0AAAAH
         DW      0BBBBH,0CCCCH,0DDDDH,0EEEEH,0FFFFH
LSBANS   DW      ?
MSBANS   DW      ?
MYDATA   ENDS

MYCODE   SEGMENT PARA 'CODE'      ;DEFINE CODE SEG. FOR MASM
MYPROC   PROC    FAR              ;PROCEDURE IS NAMED MYPROC
         ASSUME  CS:MYCODE,DS:MYDATA,SS:STACK
         PUSH    DS               ;SAVE LOCATION OF DS REG.
         SUB     AX,AX            ;GET A ZERO IN AX
         PUSH    AX               ;SAVE ZERO ON STACK, TOO
         MOV     AX,MYDATA        ;GET DATA LOCATION IN AX
         MOV     DS,AX            ;PUT IT IN DS REGISTER

;ACTUAL MUL. PREC. ADDITION OF FIRST TEN NUMBERS IN TABLE
;WITH INDEXED ADDRESSING
         MOV     SI,00H           ;SET INDEX TO ZERO
         MOV     AX,TABLE[SI]     ;GET FIRST NUMBER
         MOV     CX,09H           ;HOW MANY ADDITIONS IN PROGRAM
AGAIN:   ADD     SI,02H           ;INDEX A WORD INTO TABLE
         ADD     AX,TABLE[SI]     ;ADD NEXT NUMBER TO SUM
         ADC     DX,00H           ;IF CARRY SET, ADD TO DX REG
         LOOP    AGAIN            ;IF CX NOT ZERO, ANOTHER NUMBER
         MOV     LSBANS,AX        ;MOVE AX INTO LSBANS
         MOV     MSBANS,DX        ;MOVE DX INTO MSBANS
;END OF MULTIPLE PRECISION ADDITION

         RET                      ;RETURN CONTROL TO DOS
MYPROC   ENDP                     ;END PROCEDURE NAMED MYPROC
MYCODE   ENDS                     ;END CODE SEGMENT NAMED MYCODE

         END                      ;END WHOLE PROGRAM
```

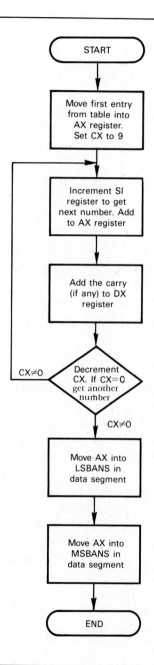

Figure 5-6.

Programming steps for multiple-precision addition using looping and indexed addressing

The critical part of the program is

```
          LEA    BX,TABLE        ;PUT LOCATION OF TABLE INTO
                                 ;BX
          MOV    SI,00H          ;SET INDEX TO ZERO
          MOV    AX,TABLE[SI]    ;GET FIRST NUMBER
          MOV    CX,09H          ;HOW MANY ADDITIONS IN
                                 ;PROGRAM
AGAIN:    ADD    SI,02H          ;INDEX A WORD INTO TABLE
          ADD    AX,TABLE[SI]    ;ADD NEXT NUMBER TO SUM
          ADC    DX,00H          ;IF CARRY SET, ADD TO DX REG
          LOOP   AGAIN           ;IF CX NOT ZERO, ANOTHER
                                 ;NUMBER
```

The index register (SI) serves as the offset into the table and is initialized to zero. The first entry in TABLE (1234H) is moved into the AX register before the program loop is entered. The loop counter (CX) is set to nine. That means a total of ten numbers are added together, because one has already been loaded. The loop exists between the label AGAIN: and the program line LOOP AGAIN. Upon the first entry into the loop, 02H is added to the index register. This moves the pointer to the next number (DW) in TABLE. The microprocessors are byte oriented, so to move to the next word, the programmer must specify moving two bytes (two bytes = one word). The next line of code goes to the location in TABLE, pointed to by the index register (SI), gets the number 5678H, and adds this number to the current contents of the AX register. Any overflow produced by the addition is accumulated in the DX register. If all ten numbers have not been added together, the program loops back to the label AGAIN: and repeats the sequence again. With each pass through the loop, the loop counter is decremented. When the loop counter reaches zero, the program "drops through" the loop and stores the results of DX and AX in the two 16-bit variables. The final result (0003 48BDH) can be viewed in the dump of the data segment in the following listing.

```
-D DS:0000
1CC1:0000   34 12 78 56 BC 9A F0 DE-11 11 22 22 33 33 44 44   4.xV......""33DD
1CC1:0010   55 55 66 66 77 77 88 88-99 99 AA AA BB BB CC CC   UUffww..........
1CC1:0020   DD DD EE EE FF FF BD 48-03 00 00 00 00 00 00 00   .......H........
1CC1:0030   4D 59 53 54 41 43 4B 20-4D 59 53 54 41 43 4B 20   MYSTACK MYSTACK
```

```
1CC1:0040   4D 59 53 54 41 43 4B 20-4D 59 53 54 41 43 4B 20   MYSTACK MYSTACK
1CC1:0050   4D 59 53 54 41 43 4B 20-4D 59 53 54 41 43 4B 20   MYSTACK MYSTACK
1CC1:0060   4D 59 53 54 41 43 4B 20-4D 59 53 54 41 43 4B 20   MYSTACK MYSTACK
1CC1:0070   4D 59 53 54 41 43 4B 20-4D 59 53 54 41 43 4B 20   MYSTACK MYSTACK
```

ADDING DECIMAL NUMBERS USING REGISTER INDIRECT ADDRESSING

Hexadecimal arithmetic is the natural arithmetic mode for assemblers whose microprocessors work in binary. There are, however, times when a programmer might wish to add or subtract decimal numbers and obtain decimal results. It should be repeated that most assemblers allow numeric data to be entered in binary, decimal, hexadecimal, and octal formats. This does not mean that operations are carried out in these different bases. It merely means that the assembler converts these numbers to binary format (instead of forcing you to do so) when it stores the information in memory. Operations in bases other than hexadecimal (binary) require special instructions.

The 8088/80386 microprocessor family features two instructions that allow a limited amount of decimal arithmetic. The individual instructions, DAA and DAS, have already been discussed in their appropriate sections. Figure 5-7 shows the programming steps necessary for decimal addition using register indirect addressing.

When adding many numbers using the DAA command, several points must be remembered. First, the numbers to be added must appear as decimal numbers. For example, the following numbers are valid: 3, 4, 8, 11, 12, 30, 89. The following numbers would not produce valid results: 1AH, 0AH, 1BH. Second, the DAA command only works with the AL register. Third, the DAA instruction must be applied immediately after an ADD or ADC instruction. Review the information listed under the DAA command and notice that DAA does not "convert" anything, in the normal sense of the word. DAA fixes the register contents to appear in decimal format — the computer still thinks it is working with a hexadecimal number. If 6 and 5 are added together to produce the hexadecimal result 0BH, DAA will add 06H to that result and return 11. However, the 11 is really stored as the hexadecimal 11H. The listing for the decimal addition program follows. Notice that the numbers stored in the data segment are all in a form acceptable for decimal addition.

```
;FOR 8088/80386 MACHINES
;PROGRAM TO ILLUSTRATE THE USE OF THE DAA COMMAND IN ADDITION
;USING REGISTER INDIRECT ADDRESSING

STACK     SEGMENT PARA STACK
          DB      64 DUP ('MYSTACK ')
STACK     ENDS
MYDATA    SEGMENT PARA 'DATA'
INFO      DB      1,2,3,4,5,6,7,8,9,10,11,12,13,14,15
ANS       DB      ?
MYDATA    ENDS

MYCODE    SEGMENT PARA 'CODE'        ;DEFINE CODE SEG. FOR MASM
MYPROC    PROC    FAR                ;PROCEDURE IS NAMED MYPROC
          ASSUME  CS:MYCODE,DS:MYDATA,SS:STACK
          PUSH    DS                 ;SAVE LOCATION OF DS REG.
          SUB     AX,AX              ;GET A ZERO IN AX
          PUSH    AX                 ;SAVE ZERO ON STACK, TOO
          MOV     AX,MYDATA          ;GET DATA LOCATION IN AX
          MOV     DS,AX              ;PUT IT IN DS REGISTER

;ADDITION OF FIRST ELEVEN "DECIMAL" NUMBERS IN INFO TABLE
          LEA     BX,INFO            ;GET LOCATION OF INFO
          MOV     CX,10              ;HOW MANY ADDITIONS?
          MOV     AL,INFO            ;GET FIRST NUMBER FROM INFO
AGAIN:    ADD     BX,01H             ;GET NEXT NUMBER
          ADD     AL,[BX]            ;ADD NEW NUMBER TO SUM
          DAA                        ;DECIMAL ADJ. AL REGISTER
          LOOP    AGAIN              ;DONE ALL ELEVEN YET?
          MOV     ANS,AL             ;MOVE DECIMAL RESULT TO ANS
;COMPLETION OF DECIMAL ADDITION EXAMPLE

          RET                        ;RETURN CONTROL TO DOS
MYPROC    ENDP                       ;END PROCEDURE NAMED MYPROC
MYCODE    ENDS                       ;END CODE SEGMENT NAMED MYCODE

          END                        ;END WHOLE PROGRAM
```

The important portion of the code segment is shown here.

```
          LEA   BX,INFO      ;GET LOCATION OF INFO
          MOV   CX,10        ;HOW MANY ADDITIONS?
          MOV   AL,INFO      ;GET FIRST NUMBER FROM INFO
AGAIN:    ADD   ;BX,01H      ;GET NEXT NUMBER
          ADD   AL,[BX]      ;ADD NEW NUMBER TO SUM
          DAA                ;DECIMAL ADJUST AL REGISTER
          LOOP  AGAIN        ;DONE ALL ELEVEN YET?
```

The CX register holds the loop count. This program segment differs from the last in that the index register is not used to increment through the table. Incrementing BX is sufficient to move from one number to another.

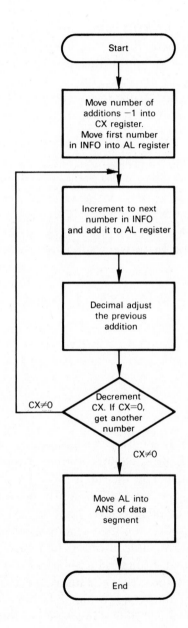

Figure 5-7.
Programming steps for decimal addition using register indirect addressing

BX only needs to be incremented once because the table INFO contains byte-sized numbers. The general concept of the loop is the same as for the previous example, except that the ADD command is immediately followed by the DAA instruction. When the first 11 numbers have been added, the program stores the contents of AL in the variable ANS and exits the program. The following listing shows some interesting results in the data segment after program execution. Remember — every entry in the data segment is in hexadecimal format. Can you find the original numbers? The decimal sum?

```
-D DS:0000
1CE5:0000   01 02 03 04 05 06 07 08-09 0A 0B 0C 0D 0E 0F 66   ................F
1CE5:0010   4D 59 53 54 41 43 4B 20-4D 59 53 54 41 43 4B 20   MYSTACK MYSTACK
1CE5:0020   4D 59 53 54 41 43 4B 20-4D 59 53 54 41 43 4B 20   MYSTACK MYSTACK
1CE5:0030   4D 59 53 54 41 43 4B 20-4D 59 53 54 41 43 4B 20   MYSTACK MYSTACK
1CE5:0040   4D 59 53 54 41 43 4B 20-4D 59 53 54 41 43 4B 20   MYSTACK MYSTACK
1CE5:0050   4D 59 53 54 41 43 4B 20-4D 59 53 54 41 43 4B 20   MYSTACK MYSTACK
1CE5:0060   4D 59 53 54 41 43 4B 20-4D 59 53 54 41 43 4B 20   MYSTACK MYSTACK
1CE5:0070   4D 59 53 54 41 43 4B 20-4D 59 53 54 41 43 4B 20   MYSTACK MYSTACK
```

MULTIPLICATION BY REPEATED ADDITION

Back in the old days of assembly language programming on microprocessors such as the 6800 and 6502, only add and subtract arithmetic operations were provided. The programmer had to search for algorithms to perform multiplication and division. The 8088/80386 family provides both multiplication and division commands. Before looking at these powerful microprocessor operands, examine the next example, which illustrates a simple multiplication algorithm: multiplication by repeated addition.

It is common knowledge that if the product of 5 × 3 is desired, it can be obtained by adding 5 to itself three times. This is the foundation of the multiplication by repeated addition algorithm. The major limitation of this technique is the time consumed in making repeated loops in the addition process. Figure 5-8 is a diagram of the programming steps necessary for multiplying two 8-bit numbers. In this example the multiplier serves as the loop counter. The multiplicand is repeatedly added to itself until the

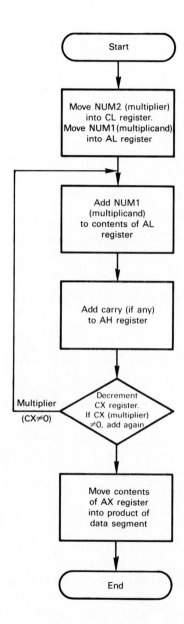

Figure 5-8.

Programming steps for multiplication by repeated addition

number of additions is equal to the original number in the multiplier. The following listing shows the complete program for this multiplication.

```
;FOR 8088/80386 MACHINES
;PROGRAM TO ILLUSTRATE MULTIPLICATION BY REPEATED ADDITION

STACK     SEGMENT PARA STACK
          DB      64 DUP ('MYSTACK ')
STACK     ENDS

MYDATA    SEGMENT PARA 'DATA'
NUM1      DB      2AH
NUM2      DB      78H
PRODUCT   DW      ?
MYDATA    ENDS

MYCODE    SEGMENT PARA 'CODE'          ;DEFINE CODE SEG. FOR MASM
MYPROC    PROC    FAR                  ;PROCEDURE IS NAMED MYPROC
          ASSUME  CS:MYCODE,DS:MYDATA,SS:STACK
          PUSH    DS                   ;SAVE LOCATION OF DS REG.
          SUB     AX,AX                ;GET A ZERO IN AX
          PUSH    AX                   ;SAVE ZERO ON STACK, TOO
          MOV     AX,MYDATA            ;GET DATA LOCATION IN AX
          MOV     DS,AX                ;PUT IT IN DS REGISTER

;ACTUAL CODE FOR MULTIPLICATION BY REPEATED ADDITION
          SUB     AX,AX                ;ZERO OUT AX REGISTER
          SUB     CX,CX                ;ZERO OUT CX REGISTER
          MOV     CL,NUM2              ;PUT MULTIPLIER IN CL
          SUB     CL,01H               ;CORRECT INDEX
          MOV     AL,NUM1              ;PUT MULTIPLICAND IN AL
AGAIN:    ADD     AL,NUM1              ;ADD MULTIPLICAND TO SUM
          ADC     AH,00H               ;ACCUMULATE A 16 BIT TOTAL
          LOOP    AGAIN                ;REPEAT IF MULTIPLIER (CL]0)
          MOV     PRODUCT,AX           ;MOVE FINAL RESULT TO PRODUCT
;END OF MULTIPLICATION EXAMPLE

          RET                          ;RETURN CONTROL TO DOS
MYPROC    ENDP                         ;END PROCEDURE NAMED MYPROC
MYCODE    ENDS                         ;END CODE SEGMENT NAMED MYCODE

          END                          ;END WHOLE PROGRAM
```

The heart of the program code is shown here.

```
          SUB     AX,AX      ;ZERO OUT AX REGISTER
          SUB     CX,CX      ;ZERO OUT CX REGISTER
          MOV     CL,NUM2    ;PUT MULTIPLIER IN CL
          SUB     CL,01H     ;CORRECT INDEX
          MOV     AL,NUM1    ;PUT MULTIPLICAND IN AL
AGAIN:    ADD     AL,NUM1    ;ADD MULTIPLICAND TO SUM
          ADC     AH,00H     ;ACCUMULATE A 16 BIT TOTAL
          LOOP    AGAIN      ;REPEAT IF MULTIPLIER (CL>0)
```

AX and CX are initially set to zero to ensure the proper accumulation of results. AX is the general-purpose register where addition is done, and CL holds the multiplier that controls the number of passes through the program loop. The multiplier is moved into CL and reduced by one, because the multiplicand is moved into AL before the loop is entered. On the first pass through the loop, the multiplicand is added to itself. ADC checks for the Carry flag in order to accumulate a 16-bit answer. The loop is repeated until the multiplier has been automatically decremented to zero. AH held the MSBs and AL the LSBs, so the AX register contains the whole product.

MULTIPLYING, SQUARING, AND CUBING NUMBERS USING THE MULTIPLY COMMAND

The next example contains three program nuggets for multiplying, squaring, and cubing numbers. Figure 5-9 shows the programming steps necessary to achieve the desired results. It should be noted that if it was desired to raise numbers to even higher powers, a power algorithm could be formed similar to the previous one for multiplication. It could raise a number to a power by using "power by repeated multiplication." For finding the square and cube of a number, however, it is hardly worth the bother. The following listing shows the whole program.

```
;FOR 8088/80386 MACHINES
;PROGRAM TO ILLUSTRATE THE USE OF THE MULTIPLY COMMAND IN MULTIPLYING,
;SQUARING AND CUBING NUMBERS.  THE LARGEST NUMBER THAT CAN CUBED WITH
;THIS TECHNIQUE IS 509H.

STACK     SEGMENT PARA STACK
          DB      64 DUP ('MYSTACK ')
STACK     ENDS

MYDATA    SEGMENT PARA 'DATA'
NUM1      DW      1234H
NUM2      DW      00CDH
ANS1      DD      ?
ANS2      DD      ?
ANS3      DD      ?
MYDATA    ENDS

MYCODE    SEGMENT PARA 'CODE'       ;DEFINE CODE SEG. FOR MASM
MYPROC    PROC    FAR               ;PROCEDURE IS NAMED MYPROC
          ASSUME  CS:MYCODE,DS:MYDATA,SS:STACK
          PUSH    DS                ;SAVE LOCATION OF DS REG.
          SUB     AX,AX             ;GET A ZERO IN AX
          PUSH    AX                ;SAVE ZERO ON STACK, TOO
          MOV     AX,MYDATA         ;GET DATA LOCATION IN AX
          MOV     DS,AX             ;PUT IT IN DS REGISTER
```

```
;MULTIPLICATION OF TWO NUMBERS/RESULT STORED IN ONE DD VARIABLE
        SUB     DX,DX           ;ZERO OUT OVERFLOW REGISTER
        MOV     AX,NUM1         ;PUT A NUMBER IN THE AX REGISTER
        MUL     NUM2            ;MULTIPLY IT BY NUM2
        MOV     WORD PTR ANS1,AX ;PUT AX IN LSB OF ANS1
        MOV     WORD PTR ANS1+2,DX ;PUT DX IN MSB OF ANS1
;COMPLETION OF MULTIPLICATION EXAMPLE

;SQUARING A NUMBER BY MULTIPLICATION/RESULT STORED IN ONE VAR.
        SUB     DX,DX           ;ZERO OUT OVERFLOW REGISTER
        MOV     AX,NUM1         ;PUT A NUMBER IN THE AX REGISTER
        MUL     NUM1            ;MULTIPLY BY ITSELF
        MOV     WORD PTR ANS2,AX ;PUT AX IN LSB OF ANS2
        MOV     WORD PTR ANS2+2,DX ;PUT DX IN MSB OF ANS2
;COMPLETION OF SQUARING EXAMPLE

;CUBING A NUMBER BY MULTIPLICATION/RESULT STORED IN ONE VARIABLE
        SUB     DX,DX           ;ZERO OUT OVERFLOW REGISTER
        MOV     AX,NUM2         ;PUT A NUMBER IN AX (7=FFH)
        MUL     NUM2            ;MULTIPLY BY ITSELF
        MUL     NUM2            ;MULTIPLY BY ITSELF
        MOV     WORD PTR ANS3,AX ;PUT AX IN LSB OF ANS3
        MOV     WORD PTR ANS3+2,DX ;PUT DX IN MSB OF ANS3
;COMPLETION OF CUBING EXAMPLE

        RET                     ;RETURN CONTROL TO DOS
MYPROC  ENDP                    ;END PROCEDURE NAMED MYPROC
MYCODE  ENDS                    ;END CODE SEGMENT NAMED MYCODE

        END                     ;END WHOLE PROGRAM
```

The following data segment presents an interesting set of entries:

```
MYDATA    SEGMENT PARA 'DATA'
NUM1      DW      1234H
NUM2      DW      00CDH
ANS1      DD      ?
ANS2      DD      ?
ANS3      DD      ?
MYDATA    ENDS
```

It is clear that there are two numbers, NUM1 and NUM2, each 16 bits long, but what size are the three answers? ANS1, ANS2, and ANS3 are defined doublewords (DD) each 32 bits long. This good news about 32-bit storage on 8088/80286 machines must be tempered with this caution: the largest general purpose register size on 8086/80286 machines is 16 bits. To use 32-bit storage, special programming techniques must be used. The code for simple multiplication is shown here.

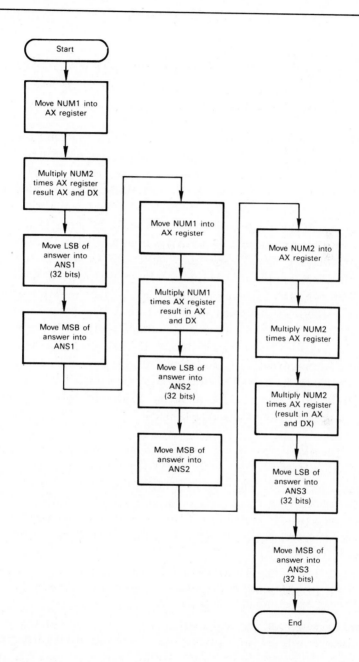

Figure 5-9.

Programming steps for multiplying, squaring, and cubing numbers

```
SUB   DX,DX                    ;ZERO OUT OVERFLOW REGISTER
MOV   AX,NUM1                  ;PUT A NUMBER IN THE AX
                              ;REGISTER
MUL   NUM2                     ;MULTIPLY IT BY NUM2
MOV   WORD PTR ANS1,AX         ;PUT AX IN LSB OF ANS1
MOV   WORD PTR ANS1+2,DX       ;PUT DX IN MSB OF ANS1
```

Recall that the MUL instruction can accumulate a 32-bit result in the DX and AX registers. In this example, NUM1 is placed in the AX register and multiplied by NUM2. Notice that it was not necessary to load NUM2 into a register first. Many arithmetic operations, such as add, subtract, decrement, and increment, can be performed directly on variables in the data segment without having to move them into a general-purpose register first. The results of the multiplication are now located in the DX (000EH) and AX (93A4H) registers. To save the contents of DX and AX in one 32-bit variable, the PTR command is employed. By using the program code MOV WORD PTR ANS1,AX, the contents of the AX register are stored in the first (lower) 16 bits of the ANS1 storage location. The program code MOV WORD PTR ANS1+2,DX stores the contents of the DX register in the upper 16 bits of the ANS1 variable. Notice the use of a two-byte increment. The PTR command removes any ambiguity the assembler might have in placing, for example, a 16-bit result in a 32-bit register.

The following program segment is a simple squaring technique achieved by multiplying a number by itself:

```
SUB   DX,DX                    ;ZERO OUT OVERFLOW REGISTER
MOV   AX,NUM1                  ;PUT A NUMBER IN THE AX
                              ;REGISTER
MUL   NUM1                     ;MULTIPLY BY ITSELF
MOV   WORD PTR ANS2,AX         ;PUT AX IN LSB OF ANS2
MOV   WORD PTR ANS2+2,DX       ;PUT DX IN MSB OF ANS2
```

In this case, the multiplicand and multiplier are the same number. The results in DX (014BH) and AX (5A90H) are returned to the 32-bit variable, ANS2.

The final program segment of this example is the cubing technique. This is done simply by multiplying the number by itself three times.

```
SUB   DX,DX                    ;ZERO OUT OVERFLOW REGISTER
MOV   AX,NUM2                  ;PUT A NUMBER IN AX (>=FFH)
```

```
MUL    NUM2                        ;MULTIPLY BY ITSELF
MUL    NUM2                        ;MULTIPLY BY ITSELF
MOV    WORD PTR ANS3,AX            ;PUT AX IN LSB OF ANS3
MOV    WORD PTR ANS3+2,DX   ;PUT DX IN MSB OF ANS3
```

Check this operation to be sure the answer is not too large for the defined storage location. The number 0FF cubed is 0FD02FF, which fits nicely into a 32-bit register. So long as the number to be cubed does not exceed 0FFH, no overflow problems will occur.

USING THE DIVIDE COMMAND WITH DEFINED DOUBLEWORDS

Figure 5-10 shows the programming steps necessary for a simple divide operation. What cannot be seen in Figure 5-10 is the size of the dividend or the divisor. When the divide instruction was discussed in Chapter 3, it was mentioned that the dividend can occupy two 16-bit registers (DX and AX). In this example the dividend is stored in the data segment as a defined doubleword (DD). The following listing shows the complete program.

```
;FOR 8088/80386 MACHINES
;PROGRAM TO ILLUSTRATE THE USE OF THE DIVIDE COMMAND

STACK     SEGMENT PARA STACK
          DB       64 DUP ('MYSTACK ')
STACK     ENDS

MYDATA    SEGMENT PARA 'DATA'
DIVIDEND DD       02A8B7654H
DIVISOR  DW       5ABCH
QUOTIENT DW       ?
REMAIN   DW       ?
MYDATA    ENDS

MYCODE    SEGMENT PARA 'CODE'        ;DEFINE CODE SEG. FOR MASM
MYPROC    PROC    FAR                ;PROCEDURE IS NAMED MYPROC
          ASSUME  CS:MYCODE,DS:MYDATA,SS:STACK
          PUSH    DS                 ;SAVE LOCATION OF DS REG.
          SUB     AX,AX              ;GET A ZERO IN AX
          PUSH    AX                 ;SAVE ZERO ON STACK, TOO
          MOV     AX,MYDATA          ;GET DATA LOCATION IN AX
          MOV     DS,AX              ;PUT IT IN DS REGISTER

;EXAMPLE DIVIDE OF A 32 BIT DIVIDEND BY A 16 BIT DIVISOR
          MOV     AX,WORD PTR DIVIDEND ;GET LSB AND PUT IN AX
          MOV     DX,WORD PTR DIVIDEND+2 ;GET MSB AND PUT IN DX
          DIV     DIVISOR            ;DIVIDE (DX AX) BY DIVISOR
          MOV     QUOTIENT,AX        ;PUT AX INTO QUOTIENT, AND
          MOV     REMAIN,DX          ;PUT DX INTO REMAIND(ER)
```

```
;DIVISION EXAMPLE COMPLETED

        RET                     ;RETURN CONTROL TO DOS
MYPROC  ENDP                    ;END PROCEDURE NAMED MYPROC
MYCODE  ENDS                    ;END CODE SEGMENT NAMED MYCODE

        END                     ;END WHOLE PROGRAM
```

The data segment shown here contains four variables: DIVIDEND, DIVISOR, QUOTIENT, and REMAIN.

MYDATA	SEGMENT PARA	'DATA'
DIVIDEND	DD	02A8B7654H
DIVISOR	DW	5ABCH
QUOTIENT	DW	?
REMAIN	DW	?
MYDATA	ENDS	

The size of each variable is set prior to program operation. DIVIDEND contains 02A8B7654H (713782868 decimal) and DIVISOR 5ABCH (23228 decimal). The QUOTIENT and the REMAINder cannot be any larger than a defined word (DW), and those memory locations were reserved with the (?) symbol.

The part of this program of real interest is how the 32-bit DIVIDEND is used. A segment of the program is shown here.

MOV	AX,WORD PTR DIVIDEND	;GET LSB AND PUT IN AX
MOV	DX,WORD PTR DIVIDEND+2	;GET MSB AND PUT IN DX
DIV	DIVISOR	;DIVIDE (DX AX) BY DIVISOR
MOV	QUOTIENT,AX	;PUT AX INTO QUOTIENT, ;AND
MOV	REMAIN,DX	;PUT DX INTO REMAIN(DER)

Recall that when the divide instruction is used, AX contains the LSBs and DX the MSBs of the 32-bit number. These requirements are met by using WORD PTR when loading the lower 16 bits of DIVIDEND into AX. Because the chip is byte oriented, WORD PTR DIVIDEND+2 is necessary when loading the upper 16 bits of DIVIDEND into the DX register. For this program, DIVISOR is called directly from the data segment. The quo-

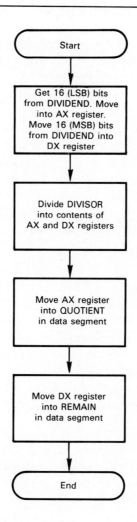

Figure 5-10.

Programming steps for hexadecimal division

tient, 7809H (30729 decimal), is returned in the AX register. The remainder, 25B8H (9656 decimal), is returned in the DX register.

A SQUARE-ROOT ALGORITHM

The first algorithm used in this chapter involved multiplication by repeated addition. That algorithm was not really required, except from the teaching standpoint, because the 8088/80386 family provides a multiply instruction. In this example, an algorithm is necessary, because a square-root instruction is not available.

Figure 5-11 shows the programming steps necessary for finding the square root of a hexadecimal number with a very simple algorithm. The algorithm can be stated as follows: the square root of a number can be approximated by subtracting successively higher odd numbers from the original number until that original number is reduced to zero. The number of subtractions is equal to the approximate square root of the original number. For example, to find the square root of 82 decimal:

$$82 - 1 = 81$$
$$81 - 3 = 78$$
$$78 - 5 = 73$$
$$73 - 7 = 66$$
$$66 - 9 = 57$$
$$57 - 11 = 46$$
$$46 - 13 = 33$$
$$33 - 15 = 18$$
$$18 - 17 = 1 \leftarrow \text{ninth subtraction, before result} < 0$$
$$1 - 19 = -18$$

Thus, the approximate square root of 82 is 9.

The same procedure works in hexadecimal format. The following listing shows an implementation of the square-root algorithm in assembly language.

```
;FOR 8088/80386 MACHINES
;PROGRAM TO ILLUSTRATE A SQUARE ROOT TECHNIQUE

STACK    SEGMENT PARA STACK
         DB      64 DUP ('MYSTACK ')
STACK    ENDS

MYDATA   SEGMENT PARA 'DATA'
NUM      DW      1CE4H
ANS      DW      ?
MYDATA   ENDS

MYCODE   SEGMENT PARA 'CODE'      ;DEFINE CODE SEG. FOR MASM
MYPROC   PROC    FAR              ;PROCEDURE IS NAMED MYPROC
         ASSUME  CS:MYCODE,DS:MYDATA,SS:STACK
```

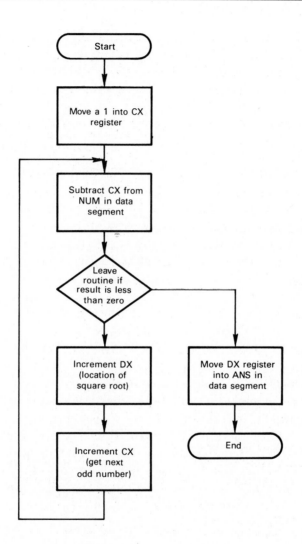

Figure 5-11. _____

Programming steps for extracting a square root from a hexadecimal number

```
PUSH    DS              ;SAVE LOCATION OF DS REG.
SUB     AX,AX           ;GET A ZERO IN AX
PUSH    AX              ;SAVE ZERO ON STACK, TOO
MOV     AX,MYDATA       ;GET DATA LOCATION IN AX
MOV     DS,AX           ;PUT IT IN DS REGISTER
```

```
;SQUARE ROOT ROUTINE
        MOV     DX,0H           ;ZERO ANSWER OUT
        MOV     CX,01H          ;NUMBER TO SUBTRACT
AGAIN:  SUB     NUM,CX          ;SUBTRACT ODD INTEGER
        JL      OUT             ;LEAVE ROUTINE
        INC     DX              ;INCREASE SQ ROOT VALUE
        ADD     CX,02H          ;GET NEXT ODD NUMBER
        JMP     AGAIN           ;DO IT AGAIN
OUT:    MOV     ANS,DX          ;MOVE ANSWER INTO ANS
;END OF SQUARE ROOT ROUTINE

        RET                     ;RETURN CONTROL TO DOS
MYPROC  ENDP                    ;END PROCEDURE NAMED MYPROC
MYCODE  ENDS                    ;END CODE SEGMENT NAMED MYCODE

        END                     ;END WHOLE PROGRAM
```

The actual code is fairly straightforward, using one loop:

```
        MOV     DX,0H       ;ZERO ANSWER OUT
        MOV     CX,01H      ;NUMBER TO SUBTRACT
AGAIN:  SUB     NUM,CX      ;SUBTRACT ODD INTEGER
        JL      OUT         ;LEAVE ROUTINE
        INC     DX          ;INCREASE SQ ROOT VALUE
        ADD     CX,02H      ;GET NEXT ODD NUMBER
        JMP     AGAIN       ;DO IT AGAIN
OUT:    MOV     ANS,DX      ;MOVE ANSWER INTO ANS
```

In this example, DX is initially zeroed out, because it forms the location for the answer (the square root). CX holds the location of the successively higher odd numbers; it is seeded with the first odd number, 1. When the loop is entered, CX is subtracted from the value contained in the variable NUM. If the result of the subtraction is less than zero, the program ends. If the result of the subtraction is greater than or equal to zero, CX is incremented to the next odd number, and the loop is repeated. After the loop is left, the square root is stored in ANS.

LOGIC OPERATIONS

There are many cases in assembly language programming where the logic functions (OR, AND, and XOR) are used as masks in programs. XOR is frequently used in graphing programs to erase a previously plotted dot on the screen, and AND is used to filter only certain bits in a given byte. Both of these applications are discussed later in this book.

SIMULATING LOGIC GATES AND OPERATIONS IN ASSEMBLY LANGUAGE

Another application for the common logic functions is in the simulation of simple hardware logic circuits. Figure 5-12 is a logic diagram using four logic gates. The four inputs, labeled IN1, IN2, IN3, and IN4, represent electrical connections in real hardware gates. The output is labeled F for function. The circuit could be analyzed on paper using a truth table. In this example, the four inputs are supplied with binary data from the data segment. The circuit (program) analyzes the binary input with regard to the individual bits and generates an answer. The operation is carried out bit by bit. If the following input information is supplied, what will the output appear as?

```
IN1   DB    10111010B
IN2   DB    11111100B
IN3   DB    00010100B
IN4   DB    00010011B
ANS   DB    ?
```

First, IN1 is inverted by the logic inverter, which produces 01000101B. This input is fed, along with IN2, into an OR gate. The OR operation produces

01000101B
11111100B
―――――――――
11111101B (output from OR gate)

IN3 and IN4 are directed to the AND gate. They produce the following output:

00010100B
00010011B
―――――――――
00010000B (output from AND gate)

Finally, the output from the OR gate is exclusively ORed (XOR) with the output from the AND gate, producing the following output.

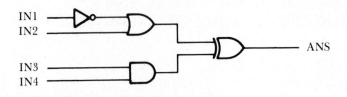

Figure 5-12.
A simple hardware logic circuit for software simulation

11111101B (output from OR gate)
00010000B (output from AND gate)

11101101B (output from XOR gate)
         (0EDH)

Figure 5-13 is a diagram of the programming steps necessary to implement the hardware circuit.

To visually make the program more understandable, the data will be entered in binary format. Even though the numbers appear quite large, they fit into defined byte (DB) storage. If the program is inspected using a debugger, such as IBM's DEBUG, the numbers appear in the data segment in hexadecimal format. The following listing is the complete program for circuit simulation.

```
;FOR 8088/80386 MACHINES
;PROGRAM TO ILLUSTRATE THE LOGIC OPERATIONS: AND/OR/XOR/NOT

STACK     SEGMENT PARA STACK
          DB        64 DUP ('MYSTACK ')
STACK     ENDS

MYDATA    SEGMENT PARA 'DATA'
IN1       DB        10111010B
IN2       DB        11111100B
IN3       DB        00010100B
IN4       DB        00010011B
ANS       DB        ?
MYDATA    ENDS

MYCODE    SEGMENT PARA 'CODE'          ;DEFINE CODE SEG. FOR MASM
MYPROC    PROC     FAR                 ;PROCEDURE IS NAMED MYPROC
          ASSUME   CS:MYCODE,DS:MYDATA,SS:STACK
          PUSH     DS                  ;SAVE LOCATION OF DS REG.
          SUB      AX,AX               ;GET A ZERO IN AX
          PUSH     AX                  ;SAVE ZERO ON STACK, TOO
          MOV      AX,MYDATA           ;GET DATA LOCATION IN AX
          MOV      DS,AX               ;PUT IT IN DS REGISTER

;EXAMPLE OF LOGICAL GATE SYNTHESIS
          MOV      AL,IN1              ;LOAD FIRST INPUT INTO AL
          NOT      AL                  ;INVERT BITS IN AL
```

```
        MOV     AH,IN2          ;LOAD SECOND INPUT INTO AH
        OR      AL,AH           ;OR THE TWO
        MOV     BL,IN3          ;LOAD THIRD INPUT INTO BL
        AND     BL,IN4          ;AND THE TWO
        XOR     AL,BL           ;EX-OR OUTPUTS OF GATES
        MOV     ANS,AL          ;SAVE RESULT IN ANS(WER)
;COMPLETION OF GATE SYNTHESIS EXAMPLE
        RET                     ;RETURN CONTROL TO DOS
MYPROC  ENDP                    ;END PROCEDURE NAMED MYPROC
MYCODE  ENDS                    ;END CODE SEGMENT NAMED MYCODE

        END                     ;END WHOLE PROGRAM
```

In the program segment shown here, the actual program flow is simple. Inputs are read into 8-bit registers, and the required logic operations are performed. The final result is stored in ANS. If the data segment is inspected after this program is run, the binary result will be stored in hexadecimal format.

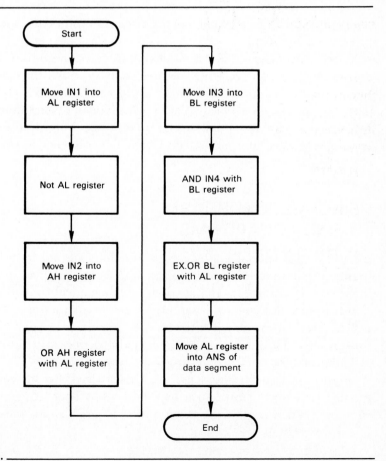

Figure 5-13.

Programming steps to simulate the hardware circuit in Figure 5-12

```
MOV   AL,IN1    ;LOAD FIRST INPUT INTO AL
NOT   AL        ;INVERT BITS IN AL
MOV   AH,IN2    ;LOAD SECOND INPUT INTO AH
OR    AL,AH     ;OR THE TWO
MOV   BL,IN3    ;LOAD THIRD INPUT INTO BL
AND   BL,IN4    ;AND THE TWO
XOR   AL,BL     ;EX-OR OUTPUTS OF GATES
MOV   ANS,AL    ;SAVE RESULT IN ANS(WER)
```

LOOKUP TABLES FOR SPECIAL APPLICATIONS

A lookup table, as the name implies, allows the programmer to look up a value or extract a piece of data from a previously defined table. Lookup tables often form the backbone of high-speed graphics and spelling checker programs. For example, a whole dictionary can be entered into a data segment in the form of a table. By indexing the proper amount into the table, a word can be compared with one previously stored. If the word is found, a message such as "spelled correctly" could be flashed to the screen. Otherwise, "try again" might be displayed. This type of operation is said to use a lookup table. The use of lookup tables is far reaching. In this chapter, two simple examples are presented. Chapter 8 presents a simple spelling checker program that uses a lookup table.

USING A LOOKUP TABLE TO FIND LOGARITHMS

Algorithms for special mathematical functions are not only hard to come by, but also hard to implement in assembly language (perhaps with tongue in cheek it could be said that a special mathematical function is any function that does not have an assembly language instruction). The use of the real number coprocessor is often an easy and effective approach to solving this problem. However, this problem is also perfect for illustrating the use of lookup tables to find hard-to-get mathematical values.

Figure 5-14 shows the steps required to look up the logarithm of a number previously stored in a data table. The data segment shown here shows a TABLE containing the common logarithms for the decimal integers 1 through 10.

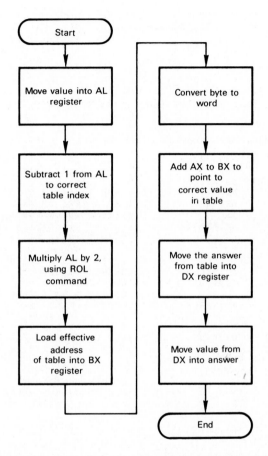

Figure 5-14.

Programming steps for looking up the logarithm of a number

```
TABLE     DW    0,3010,4771,6021,6990,7782,8451,9031,9542,10000
VALUE     DB    7
ANSWER    DW    ?
```

Each number in the table has an implied decimal point. For example, the number 4771 represents the logarithm 0.4771. Also, notice that these numbers are stored in decimal format, so 10000 fits into a defined word

(DW) location. The following listing shows the complete program.

```
;FOR 8088/80386 MACHINES
;PROGRAM TO ILLUSTRATE THE USE OF A LOOKUP TABLE TO FIND LOGS

STACK    SEGMENT PARA STACK
         DB        64 DUP ('MYSTACK ')
STACK    ENDS

MYDATA   SEGMENT PARA 'DATA'
TABLE    DW        0,3010,4771,6021,6990,7782,8451,9031,9542,10000
VALUE    DB        7
ANSWER   DW        ?
MYDATA   ENDS

MYCODE   SEGMENT PARA 'CODE'        ;DEFINE CODE SEG. FOR MASM
MYPROC   PROC      FAR              ;PROCEDURE IS NAMED MYPROC
         ASSUME    CS:MYCODE,DS:MYDATA,SS:STACK
         PUSH.     DS               ;SAVE LOCATION OF DS REG.
         SUB       AX,AX            ;GET A ZERO IN AX
         PUSH      AX               ;SAVE ZERO ON STACK, TOO
         MOV       AX,MYDATA        ;GET DATA LOCATION IN AX
         MOV       DS,AX            ;PUT IT IN DS REGISTER

;EXAMPLE OF USING VALUE GIVEN AS INDEX INTO A LOOKUP TABLE
         MOV       AL,VALUE         ;NUMBER TO LOOKUP
         SUB       AL,1             ;CORRECT INDEX, NO LOG 0
         ROL       AL,1             ;MULTIPLY BY 2, FOR WORD INDEX
         LEA       BX,TABLE         ;FIND START OF TABLE
         CBW                        ;CONVERT AL FROM BYTE TO WORD
         ADD       BX,AX            ;GET INDEX+OFFSET
         MOV       DX,[BX]          ;GET VALUE FROM TABLE
         MOV       ANSWER,DX        ;MOVE VALUE FROM DX TO ANSWER
;COMPLETION OF LOOKUP EXAMPLE

         RET                        ;RETURN CONTROL TO DOS
MYPROC   ENDP                       ;END PROCEDURE NAMED MYPROC
MYCODE   ENDS                       ;END CODE SEGMENT NAMED MYCODE

         END                        ;END WHOLE PROGRAM
```

To keep the program simple, the logarithm to be looked up is contained in the variable VALUE. The answer is returned in a defined word (DW) variable called ANSWER. The segment of this program shown here has some interesting features.

```
MOV    AL,VALUE        ;NUMBER TO LOOKUP
SUB    AL,1            ;CORRECT INDEX, NO LOG 0
ROL    AL,1            ;MULTIPLY BY 2, FOR WORD INDEX
LEA    BX,TABLE        ;FIND START OF TABLE
CBW                    ;CONVERT AL FROM BYTE TO WORD
ADD    BX,AX           ;GET INDEX+OFFSET
MOV    DX,[BX]         ;GET VALUE FROM TABLE
MOV    ANSWER,DX       ;MOVE VALUE FROM DX TO ANSWER
```

The value in AL serves, after some software conditioning, as the index into the lookup table. First, because there is no logarithm for zero, the VALUE in AL must be decreased by one. The program deals with a table using defined words (DW), so this index must be multiplied by two. Instead of using the multiply instruction, a simple rotate left (ROL) command achieves the same result and is faster. The index number is still in byte form, and the table index must be placed in the BX register (a word). To make it possible to use the byte index, the CBW instruction is used to convert the byte to a word. The value in AX is added to the starting location of the TABLE, in BX, to give the total offset into TABLE. The MOV instruction returns the digits 2103 to the DX register, and that value is stored in the variable ANSWER.

Two benefits have been gained by using a lookup table: (1) a relatively easy program and (2) the possibility of high-precision answers in decimal or hexadecimal (or any other) format. The disadvantages might not be as apparent: (1) The results must be previously stored in the data segment, limiting the program's flexibility; for example, in the previous case, if the logarithm of 23 was desired, the program would have to be altered. (2) The precision and accuracy of the answer is controlled by the programmer, not by a mathematical function. Errors do creep into this type of data entry, especially when data tables are many lines long.

PERFORMING CODE CONVERSIONS USING LOOKUP TABLES

The world is full of different types of codes. Bar codes, ZIP codes, and telephone numbers are just a few that are encountered every day. Computer work also has its unique share of special codes. In assembly programming, number bases represent one type of code. Other special codes include ASCII, Gray, Excess-3, and BCD. In assembly language, many times it is necessary to convert from one code to another. Conversion among weighted codes such as different number (radix) bases, is fairly simple; conversion among unweighted codes can be very difficult. The next example, the last lookup table example in this chapter, is a program for converting a hexadecimal number to the Gray code equivalent. The Gray code is an important code when translating rotating shaft speeds to digital numbers. Because the chance of an error increases with each digit change in a binary number, the Gray code was designed to change only one digit between successive readings. In the following data segment, notice the difference between each of the Gray code readings:

GRAY	DB	0000B, 0001B, 0011B, 0010B, 0110B, 0111B, 0101B, 0100B
	DB	1100B, 1101B
VALUE	DB	8H
ANSWER	DB	?

These are the Gray code equivalents for the decimal or hexadecimal digits 0 through 9, stored as binary numbers.

The program is straightforward, as Figure 5-15 shows, and could have been written in a manner similar to the previous example — but then a new instruction could not be introduced. The new instruction is the XLAT instruction. XLAT allows the programmer to index into a BYTE table by the amount specified in the AL register. The answer is then returned in the AL register. With a little programming experience and ingenuity, WORD tables also can be used. The following listing is the complete program for the Hex to Gray code conversion.

```
;FOR 8088/80386 MACHINES
;PROGRAM TO ILLUSTRATE THE USE OF LOOKUP TABLES AND THE XLAT COMMAND
;FOR FINDING THE GRAY CODE EQUIVALENT OF A HEXADECIMAL NUMBER

STACK     SEGMENT PARA STACK
          DB      64 DUP ('MYSTACK ')
STACK     ENDS

MYDATA    SEGMENT PARA 'DATA'
GRAY      DB      0000B, 0001B, 0011B, 0010B, 0110B, 0111B,
          DB      0101B, 0100B, 1100B, 1101B
VALUE     DB      8H
ANSWER    DB      ?
MYDATA    ENDS

MYCODE    SEGMENT PARA 'CODE'     ;DEFINE CODE SEG. FOR MASM
MYPROC    PROC    FAR             ;PROCEDURE IS NAMED MYPROC
          ASSUME  CS:MYCODE,DS:MYDATA,SS:STACK
          PUSH    DS              ;SAVE LOCATION OF DS REG.
          SUB     AX,AX           ;GET A ZERO IN AX
          PUSH    AX              ;SAVE ZERO ON STACK, TOO
          MOV     AX,MYDATA       ;GET DATA LOCATION IN AX
          MOV     DS,AX           ;PUT IT IN DS REGISTER

;EXAMPLE USING THE XLAT INSTRUCTION TO ACCESS BYTE TABLE INFO
          LEA     BX,GRAY         ;GET START OF TABLE
          MOV     AL,VALUE        ;GET LOOKUP VALUE
          XLAT    GRAY            ;LOOKUP VALUE
          MOV     ANSWER,AL       ;MOVE AL TO ANSWER
;COMPLETION OF XLAT EXAMPLE

          RET                     ;RETURN CONTROL TO DOS
MYPROC    ENDP                    ;END PROCEDURE NAMED MYPROC
MYCODE    ENDS                    ;END CODE SEGMENT NAMED MYCODE

          END                     ;END WHOLE PROGRAM
```

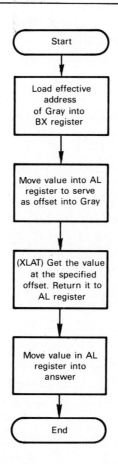

Figure 5-15. _____

Programming steps for conversion from hexadecimal to format Gray code

Notice that the heart of the program is only four lines long. The requirements for LEA are that the start of the byte table be in BX and the index in AL. The syntax is shown in the four lines, repeated here.

```
LEA    BX,GRAY      ;GET START OF TABLE
MOV    AL,VALUE     ;GET LOOKUP VALUE
XLAT   GRAY         ;LOOKUP VALUE
MOV    ANSWER,AL    ;MOVE AL TO ANSWER
```

In this example, the variable VALUE was initialized with the number 08H forming the index. At the completion of the program, ANSWER contains 1110B. If a debugger is used to trace or check the data segment after program execution, this value appears as 0EH.

CONVERSION FROM ASCII NUMBERS TO HEXADECIMAL NUMBERS

The conversion from ASCII numbers to hexadecimal numbers could also be accomplished with the use of a lookup table. In this section, however, the conversion will be done using simple mathematical operations. Almost all information read from keyboards or sent to monitor screens or printers is read or sent using some form of ASCII code. For example, if a 5 is entered from the keyboard, an ASCII 35H might be read into the AL register. If numbers are to be displayed on the screen, they must be in ASCII, not hexadecimal, form. Table 5-1 shows how simple the conversion is.

ASCII	Hexadecimal
30H	0H
31H	1H
32H	2H
33H	3H
34H	4H
35H	5H
36H	6H
37H	7H
38H	8H
39H	9H
41H	0AH
42H	0BH
43H	0CH
44H	0DH
45H	0EH
46H	0FH

Table 5-1.

ASCII-hexadecimal equivalences

For the ASCII digits between 30H and 39H, merely subtract 30H from each number to form the correct hexadecimal result. For digits from 41H to 46H, subtract 37H. Remember to use hexadecimal arithmetic when making the subtractions. Figure 5-16 shows the programming steps necessary for this conversion.

It should be pointed out that there are many ASCII values possible, and that only numeric conversion is being considered in this example. No error checking is performed. In other words, it is assumed that the programmer will enter an ASCII code contained in the listing presented here, or unpredictable results might occur. The following listing shows the complete program.

```
;FOR 8088/80386 MACHINES
;PROGRAM TO ILLUSTRATE CODE CONVERSION FROM ASCII DIGITS TO HEX

STACK     SEGMENT PARA STACK
          DB      64 DUP ('MYSTACK ')
STACK     ENDS

MYDATA    SEGMENT PARA 'DATA'
ASCII     DB      42H               ;ASCII "B"
ANSWER    DB      ?
MYDATA    ENDS

MYCODE    SEGMENT PARA 'CODE'       ;DEFINE CODE SEG. FOR MASM
MYPROC    PROC    FAR               ;PROCEDURE IS NAMED MYPROC
          ASSUME  CS:MYCODE,DS:MYDATA,SS:STACK
          PUSH    DS                ;SAVE LOCATION OF DS REG.
          SUB     AX,AX             ;GET A ZERO IN AX
          PUSH    AX                ;SAVE ZERO ON STACK, TOO
          MOV     AX,MYDATA         ;GET DATA LOCATION IN AX
          MOV     DS,AX             ;PUT IT IN DS REGISTER

;ASCII TO HEXADECIMAL CONVERSION / NO ERROR CHECKING
;ASSUME CORRECT ASCII INPUT FOR 0,1,2,3,4,5,6,7,8,9,A,B,C,D-E,F
          MOV     AL,ASCII          ;ASCII NUMBER TO CONVERT IN AL
          SUB     AL,30H            ;SEE IF IT'S A NUMBER 0-9
          CMP     AL,9
          JG      LETTER            ;IF GREATER THAN 9, IT'S A LETTER
          JMP     END               ;QUIT
LETTER:   SUB     AL,07H            ;SUB 7 TO FINISH LETTER CONVERSION
END:      MOV     ANSWER,AL         ;SAVE RESULT IN ANSWER
;END OF CONVERSION EXAMPLE

          RET                       ;RETURN CONTROL TO DOS
MYPROC    ENDP                      ;END PROCEDURE NAMED MYPROC
MYCODE    ENDS                      ;END CODE SEGMENT NAMED MYCODE

          END                       ;END WHOLE PROGRAM
```

In the program segment that follows, note that 30H is immediately subtracted from the contents of ASCII. This is done because the input is supposed to be in the range 30H to 46H. If the result of the subtraction is a number between 0H and 9H, the program ends. However, if the CMP

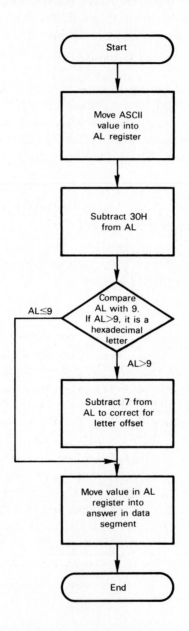

Figure 5-16. _____

Programming steps for conversion from ASCII to hexadecimal format

command finds a number greater than 09H, the character must be a letter. By subtracting 07H (a total of 37H, from ASCII), the letter is placed in the correct range of the hexadecimal digits A through F.

```
        MOV   AL,ASCII    ;ASCII NUMBER TO CONVERT IN
                          ;AL
        SUB   AL,30H      ;SEE IF IT'S A NUMBER 0-9
        CMP   AL,9
        JG    LETTER      ;IF GREATER THAN 9, IT'S A
                          ;LETTER
        JMP   END         ;QUIT
LETTER: SUB   AL,07H      ;SUB 7 TO FINISH LETTER CON-
                          ;VERSION
END:    MOV   ANSWER,AL   ;SAVE RESULT IN ANSWER
```

SIMPLE 32-BIT ARITHMETIC WITH THE 80386 MICROPROCESSOR

In a previous example (Figure 5-5), 32-bit numeric precision was carried out using multiple-precision arithmetic. The 8088/80286 family is limited to 16-bit registers that can directly hold integers up to 0FFFFH (65,535 decimal). The 80386 microprocessor has broken that boundary and allows integers of up to 32 bits. The four general-purpose registers EAX, EBX, ECX, and EDX can hold numbers as large as 0FFFFFFFFH (4,294,967,295 decimal). The 80386 is an extremely fast and powerful microprocessor, partly because of this increased register size. The two examples that follow illustrate how the 80386 performs basic arithmetic operations on very large numbers without resorting to multiple-precision arithmetic.

Figure 5-17 shows the programming steps necessary to add several 32-bit numbers together. Comparing Figure 5-17 with Figure 5-4 also illustrates an increased simplicity in programming, even for this elementary example. The following listing is the complete program for 32-bit addition.

```
;FOR 80386 MACHINES
;PROGRAM TO ILLUSTRATE 32-BIT ADDITION WITH THE 80386 MICROPROCESSOR

STACK   SEGMENT PARA STACK
        DB      64 DUP ('MYSTACK ')
STACK   ENDS
```

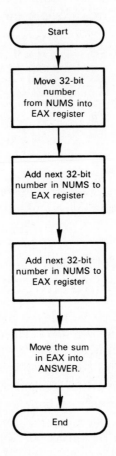

Figure 5-17.

Programming steps for 80386 addition

```
MYDATA    SEGMENT PARA 'DATA'
NUMS      DD 12345678H,9ABCDEF0H,23H,10000000H,0CADH
ANSWER    DD      ?
MYDATA    ENDS

MYCODE    SEGMENT PARA 'CODE'         ;DEFINE CODE SEG. FOR MASM
MYPROC    PROC    FAR                  ;PROCEDURE IS NAMED MYPROC
          ASSUME  CS:MYCODE,DS:MYDATA,SS:STACK
          PUSH    DS                   ;SAVE LOCATION OF DS REG.
          SUB     AX,AX                ;GET A ZERO IN AX
          PUSH    AX                   ;SAVE ZERO ON STACK, TOO
```

```
        MOV     AX,MYDATA           ;GET DATA LOCATION IN AX
        MOV     DS,AX               ;PUT IT IN DS REGISTER

;ACTUAL CODE FOR 32-BIT ADDITION, OF FIRST THREE NUMBERS IN NUMS
        LEA     BX,NUMS             ;GET OFFSET FOR NUMS
        MOV     EAX,[BX]            ;LOAD FIRST 32-BIT NUMBER IN EAX
        ADD     EAX,[BX]+4          ;ADD NEXT 32-BIT NUMBER TO EAX
        ADD     EAX,[BX]+8          ;DITTO
        MOV     ANSWER,EAX          ;STORE 32-BIT RESULT IN ANSWER

        RET                         ;RETURN CONTROL TO DOS
MYPROC  ENDP                        ;END PROCEDURE NAMED MYPROC
MYCODE  ENDS                        ;END CODE SEGMENT NAMED MYCODE

        END                         ;END WHOLE PROGRAM
```

There are several features in this program that will probably be new to programmers who have used only the 8088/80286 instruction set. First, look at the data segment:

```
MYDATA    SEGMENT    PARA    'DATA'
NUMS      DD  12345678H,9ABCDEF0H,23H,10000000H,0CADH
ANSWER    DD          ?
MYDATA    ENDS
```

The numbers to be added (NUMS) are 32 bits each and are stored as defined doublewords. The answer (ANSWER) is limited to 32-bit precision for this example and is also a defined doubleword. In previous examples, these numbers could not be loaded directly into a register because of their size, but look at what can be done now:

```
MOV   EAX,[BX]      ;LOAD FIRST 32-BIT NUMBER IN EAX
ADD   EAX,[BX]+4    ;ADD NEXT 32-BIT NUMBER TO EAX
ADD   EAX,[BX]+8    ;DITTO
MOV   ANSWER,EAX    ;STORE 32-BIT RESULT IN ANSWER
```

The first number (12345678H) is loaded directly into the EAX register with a simple MOVe operation. The second number is added to the contents of the EAX register by using an offset of 4 bytes to accommodate the defined doubleword length. The third number is added in a similar way. Notice that the entire 32-bit contents of EAX are MOVed to ANSWER (0BCF14238H or 3169927736 decimal) with one line of code. Figure 5-18 shows the programming step necessary for multiplying two 32-bit numbers.

The 80386 allows the programmer to accumulate a 64-bit answer in the EDX:EAX registers. A 64-bit answer allows a hexadecimal number as large as 0FFFFFFFFFFFFFFFFH (approximately 1.8446744073709553E19 decimal). A 64-bit answer can be stored in a defined quadword (DQ) register by using the PTR operator. The following listing shows the program for the multiplication of two large integers.

```
;FOR 80386 MACHINES
;PROGRAM TO ILLUSTRATE SIMPLE MULTIPLICATION OF 32-BIT NUMBERS,
;WITH 64-BIT RESULT

STACK    SEGMENT PARA STACK
         DB      64 DUP ('MYSTACK ')
STACK    ENDS

MYDATA   SEGMENT PARA 'DATA'
NUM1     DD      12345678H
NUM2     DD      9ABCDEF0H
ANSWER   DQ      ?
MYDATA   ENDS

MYCODE   SEGMENT PARA 'CODE'         ;DEFINE CODE SEG. FOR MASM
MYPROC   PROC    FAR                 ;PROCEDURE IS NAMED MYPROC
         ASSUME  CS:MYCODE,DS:MYDATA,SS:STACK
         PUSH    DS                  ;SAVE LOCATION OF DS REG.
         SUB     AX,AX               ;GET A ZERO IN AX
         PUSH    AX                  ;SAVE ZERO ON STACK, TOO
         MOV     AX,MYDATA           ;GET DATA LOCATION IN AX
         MOV     DS,AX               ;PUT IT IN DS REGISTER

;ACTUAL CODE FOR MULTIPLICATION OF TWO 32-BIT NUMBERS
         MOV     EAX,NUM1            ;LOAD FIRST 32-BIT NUMBER IN EAX
         MUL     NUM2                ;MULTIPLY NEXT 32-BIT NUMBER X EAX
         MOV     DWORD PTR ANSWER,EAX    ;PUT LOWER 32-BITS IN ANSWER
         MOV     DWORD PTR ANSWER+4,EDX ;PUT UPPER 32-BITS IN ANSWER
;END OF MULTIPLICATION CODE

         RET                         ;RETURN CONTROL TO DOS
MYPROC   ENDP                        ;END PROCEDURE NAMED MYPROC
MYCODE   ENDS                        ;END CODE SEGMENT NAMED MYCODE

         END                         ;END WHOLE PROGRAM
```

The data segment is shown here.

MYDATA	SEGMENT	PARA 'DATA'
NUM1	DD	12345678H
NUM2	DD	9ABCDEF0H
ANSWER	DQ	?
MYDATA	ENDS	

In this example, NUM1 and NUM2 are defined doublewords, each 32 bits long. The ANSWER is stored as a defined quadword 64 bits long.

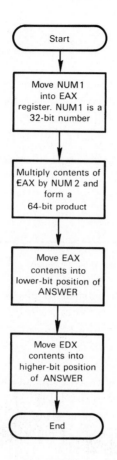

Figure 5-18.

Programming steps for 80386 multiplication

The actual program code is quite simple:

```
MOV     EAX,NUM1        ;LOAD FIRST 32-BIT NUMBER
                        ;IN EAX
MUL     NUM2            ;MULTIPLY NEXT 32-BIT NUMBER X
                        ;EAX
```

```
MOV    DWORD PTR ANSWER,EAX      ;PUT LOWER 32-BITS IN
                                 ;ANSWER
MOV    DWORD PTR ANSWER+4,EDX    ;PUT UPPER 32-BITS IN
                                 ;ANSWER
```

The first number (NUM1) is moved to the 32-bit EAX register. EAX is then multiplied by the contents of NUM2. The results of the multiplication are stored in the EDX and EAX registers. The upper 32 bits are stored in EDX, and the lower 32 bits in EAX. By using DWORD PTR, the 32-bit contents of each register can be properly placed in the defined quadword ANSWER (0B00EA4E242D2080H, or 792891155752493184 decimal).

USING BIOS AND DOS INTERRUPTS

If the microprocessor chip forms the heart of the computer, then certainly the BIOS and DOS routines are the brains of the machine. Every computer is programmed with a certain amount of information before leaving the factory. This information is stored in hardware ROM (read-only memory) chips. Typically, most of the BIOS (basic input/output system) routines are stored here. Anything stored in ROM is permanent. DOS (disk operating system) can be thought of as memory added at a later date. Actually, it is memory that is added every time the computer is turned on or booted with DOS. It is nonpermanent memory, memory that can be updated and changed with each new release of DOS. Typically, DOS operations are stored in RAM (random-access memory) or reside on a disk until they are needed. Together, ROM and RAM control the operation of the computer.

With assembly language, it is possible to tap some of the powerful routines that have been stored in memory, thus making your programs very powerful and reducing programming time. Each machine (8088, 80286, and 80386) has its own set of BIOS and DOS commands; however, many routines are shared. The use of these commands is explained in detail in the *IBM Technical Reference Manual*. The remaining programs in this chapter will run on the specified IBM computers with the proper accessories installed. Most will run on IBM-compatible machines with no alteration; some require alterations based upon the degree of compatibility with the IBM product.

USING BIOS INTERRUPTS TO CLEAR THE SCREEN

There are many times, when programming, that the input or output from the computer needs to be shown on the monitor screen. Often this will just require a simple screen-clear operation; at other times you may want to change screen colors or attributes. Screen control can easily be achieved with BIOS-type 10H interrupts. Table 5-2 is a listing of the programmable variations possible with type 10H interrupts. You can see from this table that a very large degree of screen control can be achieved.

One word of caution: The interrupt call is a hexadecimal number and is entered in a program as INT 10H. The numbers entered into the registers, which control the type of action desired from the interrupt, are almost always entered as decimal numbers: for example MOV AH,13. Also bear in mind that an interrupt call from your program merely points to more code. When you call an interrupt, you are using IBM's code in your program.

Syntax: INT 10H (when the following parameters are set to the required values)

AH Value	Function	Input	Output
		Interface Control of the CRT	
AH = 0	Set the mode of display	AL = 0	40 × 25 B/W
		AL = 1	40 × 25 color
		AL = 2	80 × 25 B/W
		AL = 3	80 × 25 color
		AL = 4	320 × 200 graphics color
		AL = 5	320 × 200 graphics B/W
		AL = 6	640 × 200 graphics B/W
		AL = 10	640 × 350 graphics E.G.A.
AH = 1	Set cursor type	CH =	Bits 4-0 start of line for cursor
		CL =	Bits 4-0 end of line for cursor

Table 5-2. _____

Screen Control With BIOS type-10H Interrupts for the IBM AT (80286) and Close Compatibles. See BIOS listings (August 2, 1984 and later) for E.G.A. specifications.

AH Value	Function	Input	Output
AH = 2	Set cursor position	DH =	Row
		DL =	Column
		BH =	Page number of display
AH = 3	Read cursor position	DH =	Row
	(values upon execution)	DL =	Column
		CH =	Cursor mode
		CL =	Cursor mode
		BH =	Page number of display
AH = 4	Get light pen position	AH = 0	Switch not down/triggered
	(values upon execution)	AH = 1	Valid answers; follow:
		DH =	Row
		DL =	Column
		CH =	Graph line (0-199)
		BX =	Graphic column (0-319/639)
AH = 5	Set active display page	AL =	New page value
			Modes 0 and 1 (0-7)
			Modes 2 and 3 (0-3)
AH = 6	Scroll active page up	AL =	Number of lines; 0 for entire screen
		CH =	Row, upper left corner
		CL =	Column, upper left corner
		DH =	Row, lower right corner
		DL =	Column, lower right corner
		BH =	Attribute to be used
AH = 7	Scroll active page down	AL =	Number of lines; 0 for entire screen
		CH =	Row, upper left corner
		CL =	Column, upper left corner
		DH =	Row, lower right corner
		DL =	Column, lower right corner
		BH =	Attribute to be used

Handling Characters

AH Value	Function	Input	Output
AH = 8	Read attribute/character at cursor position	BH =	Display page
		AL =	Character read
		AH =	Attribute of character
AH = 9	Write attribute/character at cursor position	BH =	Display page

Table 5-2. _____

Screen Control With BIOS type-10H Interrupts for the IBM AT (80286) and Close Compatibles. See BIOS listings (August 2, 1984 and later) for E.G.A. specifications. (*continued*)

AH Value	Function	Input	Output
		CX =	Count of characters to write
		AL =	Character to write
		BL =	Attribute of character
AH = 10	Write character at	BH =	Display page
	cursor position	CX =	Count of characters to write
		AL =	Character to write

Graphics Interface

AH Value	Function	Input	Output
AH = 11	Select color palette	BH =	Palette ID (0-127)
		BL =	Color for palette ID
			0 — Background (0-15)
			1 — Palette
			0 — Green (1), red (2), yellow (3)
			1 — Cyan (1), magenta (2), white (3)
AH = 12	Draw dot on screen	DX =	Row (0-199)
		CX =	Column (0-319/639)
		AL =	Color of dot
AH = 13	Read dot information	DX =	Row (0-199)
		CX =	Column (0-319/639)
		AL =	Value of dot

ASCII Teletype Output

AH Value	Function	Input	Output
AH = 14	Write to active page	AL =	Character to write
		BL =	Foreground color
AH = 15	Video state returned	AL =	Current mode
		AH =	Number of screen columns
		BH =	Current display page
AH = 16	Reserved		
AH = 17	Reserved		
AH = 18	Reserved		
AH = 19	Write string	ES:BP =	Point to string
		CX =	Length of string
		DX =	Cursor position for start
		BH =	Page number

Table 5-2. _____

Screen Control With BIOS type-10H Interrupts for the IBM AT (80286) and Close Compatibles. See BIOS listings (August 2, 1984 and later) for E.G.A. specifications. (*continued*)

AH Value	Function	Input	Output
		AL = 0	BL = attribute (*char,char,char...char*) Cursor not moved
		AL = 1	BL = attribute (*char, char, char...char*) Cursor is moved
		AL = 2	(*char,attr,char,attr...*) Cursor not moved
		AL = 3	(*char,attr,char,attr...*) Cursor is moved

Note: For additional details, see the *IBM Technical Reference Manual* for the AT computer.

Table 5-2. _____

Screen Control With BIOS type-10H Interrupts for the IBM AT (80286) and Close Compatibles. See BIOS listings (August 2, 1984 and later) for E.G.A. specifications. (*continued*)

One of the most frequently desired screen functions is merely one to clear the monitor screen before continuing a program. It is not normally possible to use the DOS CLS (clear screen) command from the assembly language level. Therefore, it is necessary to write a short program to achieve screen-clearing results. This section examines two methods for clearing the screen. One, a type-10H BIOS interrupt, clears the screen by scrolling. The other clears the screen by writing directly to the monitor port.

The following listing shows a complete program for clearing the screen using a type-10H interrupt.

```
;FOR IBM 8088/80286
;PROGRAM TO CLEAR CURRENT SCREEN USING BIOS INTERRUPT

STACK     SEGMENT PARA STACK
          DB      64 DUP ('MYSTACK ')
STACK     ENDS

MYCODE    SEGMENT PARA 'CODE'        ;DEFINE CODE SEG. FOR MASM
MYPROC    PROC    FAR                ;PROCEDURE IS NAMED MYPROC
          ASSUME  CS:MYCODE,SS:STACK
          PUSH    DS                 ;SAVE LOCATION OF DS REG.
          SUB     AX,AX              ;GET A ZERO IN AX
          PUSH    AX                 ;SAVE ZERO ON STACK, TOO
```

```
;ACTUAL CODE TO CLEAR COLOR SCREEN
        MOV     CX,0000          ;ROW,COLUMN UPPER LEFT CORNER
        MOV     DX,2479H         ;ROW,COLUMN LOWER RIGHT CORNER
        MOV     BH,07            ;NORMAL ATTRIBUTE
        MOV     AH,06            ;SCROLL ACTIVE PAGE UP
        MOV     AL,00            ;SCROLL ENTIRE WINDOW
        INT     10H              ;CALL BIOS INTERRUPT
;END OF CLEAR SCREEN ROUTINE

        RET                      ;RETURN CONTROL TO DOS
MYPROC  ENDP                     ;END PROCEDURE NAMED MYPROC
MYCODE  ENDS                     ;END CODE SEGMENT NAMED MYCODE

        END                      ;END WHOLE PROGRAM
```

The actual operation of the interrupt is masked, because the programmer does not see the actual code — written by IBM, in this case. However, for the BIOS routines, IBM has published the actual listings in the *IBM Technical Reference Manual* for each computer. Most of the time, it is sufficient simply to use the interrupt. In the program segment shown here, the registers are initialized to the proper values, as shown in Table 5-2, before the interrupt is called.

```
MOV    CX,0000      ;ROW,COLUMN UPPER LEFT CORNER
MOV    DX,2479H     ;ROW,COLUMN LOWER RIGHT CORNER
MOV    BH,07        ;NORMAL ATTRIBUTE
MOV    AH,06        ;SCROLL ACTIVE PAGE UP
MOV    AL,00        ;SCROLL ENTIRE WINDOW
INT    10H          ;CALL BIOS INTERRUPT
```

AH specifies "Scroll Active Page Up" when it is set to 6. AL blanks the entire window when it is set to 0. BH sets the attribute to normal when it is set to 7 (more about attributes later). CX and DX control the window size. CH and CL control the upper left-hand corner of the window, and DH and DL control the lower right-hand corner. CX is set to 0, which sets CH and CL to 0, or specifies the top left corner of the screen. DX is set to 2479H, which places a 24 in DH and a 79 in DL. This specifies the lower right corner of the screen. When the interrupt is finally called, the entire screen clears. The cursor is returned to the cleared screen as you leave the program and reenter DOS.

The screen can be cleared by blanking out the screen memory directly. The following listing is a program that writes blanks to the memory of the color card.

```
;FOR IBM 8088/80286 WITH RGB MONITORS
;PROGRAM TO CLEAR COLOR SCREEN WITHOUT BIOS INTERRUPT

STACK    SEGMENT PARA STACK
         DB         64 DUP ('MYSTACK ')
STACK    ENDS

MYCODE   SEGMENT PARA 'CODE'         ;DEFINE CODE SEG. FOR MASM
MYPROC   PROC    FAR                 ;PROCEDURE IS NAMED MYPROC
         ASSUME  CS:MYCODE,SS:STACK
         PUSH    DS                  ;SAVE LOCATION OF DS REG.
         SUB     AX,AX               ;GET A ZERO IN AX
         PUSH    AX                  ;SAVE ZERO ON STACK, TOO

;ACTUAL CODE TO CLEAR COLOR SCREEN
         MOV     AX,0B800H           ;POINT OF ENTRY TO COLOR RAM
         MOV     ES,AX               ;MOVE VALUE TO ES
         MOV     DI,00H              ;STARTING ADDRESS
         MOV     AL,00H              ;CHARACTER TO PRINT
         MOV     AH,07H              ;SET NORMAL ATTRIBUTE
         MOV     CX,7D0H             ;WRITE 2000 TIMES
REP      STOSW                       ;DOIT
;END OF CLEAR SCREEN ROUTINE

         RET                         ;RETURN CONTROL TO DOS
MYPROC   ENDP                        ;END PROCEDURE NAMED MYPROC
MYCODE   ENDS                        ;END CODE SEGMENT NAMED MYCODE

         END                         ;END WHOLE PROGRAM
```

This program can only be used with the standard color card. There are several features that you should note in the program segment shown here.

```
     MOV      AX,0B800H   ;POINT OF ENTRY TO COLOR RAM
     MOV      ES,AX       ;MOVE VALUE TO ES
     MOV      DI,00H      ;STARTING ADDRESS
     MOV      AL,00H      ;CHARACTER TO PRINT
     MOV      AH,07H      ;SET NORMAL ATTRIBUTE
     MOV      CX,7D0H     ;WRITE 2000 TIMES
REP  STOSW                ;DO IT
```

The color monitor adapter has on-board memory that can be accessed by placing 0B800H in ES. The monochrome monitor adapter would use 0B000H instead. The ES register cannot be loaded directly, so the value is first placed in AX and then MOVed to ES. The DI register forms the offset in that memory. AH controls the screen attribute, where 7 is normal (white, nonblinking, normal intensity), and AL specifies the character to print—

in this case, a blank. Screen clearing is achieved by writing the blank to each screen position on the 80 × 25 character monitor. These 2000 write operations can be achieved quickly using the REP STOSW (repeat store string word) instruction to place the contents of the AX register in each location.

PRODUCING A SCREEN BANNER PROGRAM USING BIOS INTERRUPTS

By using type-10H interrupts, complete control of the screen can be achieved. The program, shown in the following listing, places a banner on the color monitor screen.

```
;FOR IBM 80286 WITH RGB MONITORS
;PROGRAM TO ILLUSTRATE USE OF (INT 10) WRITE STRING COMMAND

STACK    SEGMENT PARA STACK
         DB      64 DUP ('MYSTACK ')
STACK    ENDS

MYDATA   SEGMENT PARA 'DATA'
BACK     DB      2000 DUP (' ')
LOGO     DB      13 DUP (' '),'                                              ',14 DUP (' ')
         DB      13 DUP (' '),'                                              ',14 DUP (' ')
         DB      13 DUP (' '),'        Programming in Assembly Language      ',14 DUP (' ')
         DB      13 DUP (' '),'                                              ',14 DUP (' ')
         DB      13 DUP (' '),'          with the 80286 / 80386 family       ',14 DUP (' ')
         DB      13 DUP (' '),'                                              ',14 DUP (' ')
         DB      13 DUP (' '),'                                              ',14 DUP (' ')
MYDATA   ENDS

MYCODE   SEGMENT PARA 'CODE'      ;DEFINE CODE SEG. FOR MASM
MYPROC   PROC    FAR              ;PROCEDURE IS NAMED MYPROC
         ASSUME  CS:MYCODE,ES:MYDATA,SS:STACK
         PUSH    DS               ;SAVE LOCATION OF DS REG.
         SUB     AX,AX            ;GET A ZERO IN AX

         PUSH    AX               ;SAVE ZERO ON STACK, TOO
         MOV     AX,MYDATA        ;GET DATA LOCATION IN AX
         MOV     ES,AX            ;PUT IT IN ES REGISTER

;PROGRAM SEGMENT WILL CLEAR THE SCREEN BY WRITING 80x25 BLANKS
;ON SCREEN.  BY WRITING THESE WITH A 40H (01000000B) IN BL
;WE WILL CHANGE THE WHOLE SCREEN TO RED!
         LEA     BP,BACK          ;WRITE A STRING OF BLANKS
         MOV     DX,0000          ;SET CURSOR AT TOP LEFT CORNER
         MOV     AH,19            ;WRITE STRING ATTRIBUTE
         MOV     AL,1             ;PRINT CHARACTERS AND MOVE CURSOR
         MOV     BL,01000000B     ;PRINT A RED BACKGROUND
         MOV     CX,07D0H         ;WRITE 2000 BLANKS
         INT     10H              ;INTERRUPT CALL

;PROGRAM SEGMENT WILL MOVE CURSOR DOWN NINE LINES ON THE SCREEN
;AND PRINT THE LOGO.  BY WRITING WITH A 4EH (01001110B) IN BL
;WE WILL PRINT WITH A RED BACKGROUND AND YELLOW FOREGROUND
         LEA     BP,LOGO          ;GET LOCATION OF ACTUAL LOGO
         MOV     DH,09            ;SET NEW CURSOR POSITION
         MOV     AH,19            ;WRITE STRING ATTRIBUTE
         MOV     AL,1             ;PRINT CHARACTERS AND MOVE CURSOR
         MOV     BL,01001110B     ;SET RED BACK. & YELLOW FOREGND.
         MOV     CX,230H          ;NUMBER OF CHAR. IN LOGO
         INT     10H              ;INTERRUPT CALL

         RET                      ;RETURN CONTROL TO DOS
MYPROC   ENDP                     ;END PROCEDURE NAMED MYPROC
MYCODE   ENDS                     ;END CODE SEGMENT NAMED MYCODE

         END                      ;END WHOLE PROGRAM
```

The banner, shown next, is written on the screen in yellow with a red background.

```
┌─────────────────────────────────────────────────────┐
│ ┌─────────────────────────────────────────────────┐ │
│ │                                                   │ │
│ │        Programming in Assembly Language           │ │
│ │                                                   │ │
│ │        with the 80286/80386 family                │ │
│ │                                                   │ │
│ └─────────────────────────────────────────────────┘ │
└─────────────────────────────────────────────────────┘
```

Naturally, the contents of the message can be changed, but be careful of the overall spacing—assembly language is very unforgiving.

As you can see from the previous listing, the program can be divided into two portions. One portion clears the screen, and the second portion writes the banner. The segment for clearing the screen is shown here.

```
LEA    BP,BACK        ;WRITE A STRING OF BLANKS
MOV    DX,0000        ;SET CURSOR AT TOP LEFT CORNER
MOV    AH,19          ;WRITE STRING ATTRIBUTE
MOV    AL,1           ;PRINT CHARACTERS AND MOVE CURSOR
MOV    BL,01000000B   ;PRINT A RED BACKGROUND
MOV    CX,07D0H       ;WRITE 2000 BLANKS
INT    10H            ;INTERRUPT CALL
```

The BIOS routines for the AT (80286) computer extended the type-10H interrupt to include a Write String option by setting AH to 19. This program uses that option twice: once for clearing the screen and once for writing the banner.

The banner is stored in the ES register, and the effective address of the variable (BACK) is loaded into the BP register, as required by the interrupt. DX starts the cursor at the top left-hand corner of the screen. If AL is set to 1, the interrupt prints a character (in this case a blank) and moves the cursor to the next position.

The BL register allows control of the screen attribute. BL is an 8-bit register. It can be divided as shown next.

BL

7	6	5	4		3	2	1	0

(High bits)   (Low bits)

(Background)   (Foreground)

The background and foreground represent colors selected from the palette in Table 5-3.

In this code segment, the screen is cleared by writing a 4 (red) as the background color and a 0 (no color) as the foreground color. The program enters the values as their binary equivalents, so 40H becomes 01000000B. If a yellow background were desired, 0E0H would be entered, or 11100000B binary. Basically, all this portion of code does is write 2000 blanks (with a red background attribute) to the screen.

The second portion of code writes the banner over a portion of the cleared screen. Therefore, the upper four bits of BL should contain the red background information, and the lower four bits should hold the color for the foreground. In this example, the foreground color is yellow. The banner starts at cursor position 09 (DH) and writes 560 characters (LOGO) to the screen in yellow.

```
LEA     BP,LOGO          ;GET LOCATION OF ACTUAL LOGO
MOV     DH,09            ;SET NEW CURSOR POSITION
MOV     AH,19            ;WRITE STRING ATTRIBUTE
MOV     AL,1             ;PRINT CHARACTERS AND MOVE CURSOR
MOV     BL,01001110B     ;SET RED BACK. & YELLOW FOREGND.
MOV     CX,230H          ;NUMBER OF CHAR. IN LOGO
INT     10H              ;INTERRUPT CALL
```

0 - No color	1 - Blue	2 - Green
3 - Cyan	4 - Red	5 - Magenta
6 - Brown	7 - White	8 - Gray
9 - Lt. blue	10 - Lt. green	11 - Lt. cyan
12 - Lt. red	13 - Lt. magenta	14 - Yellow
15 - Bt. white		

Table 5-3.

IBM PC or AT Color Palette

USING A DOS INTERRUPT TO DISPLAY PROGRAM DATA ON THE SCREEN

The DOS interrupt 21H is a function call interrupt. The specifications and requirements for using this interrupt are shown in Table 5-4. In the next program, this interrupt actually is just an excuse to present a more powerful programming feature. This program allows the programmer to view the contents of a selected variable without resorting to a debugger as in the previous programs. The type-21H DOS interrupt is used to write the results to the screen. The ability to view an answer directly will save you a lot of time when you experiment with various commands, because a separate call to a debugger is not required.

Syntax: INT 21H (when the following parameters are set to the required values)

AH Value	Function	Input	Output
AH = 1	Wait and display keyboard character with CTRL-BREAK check	=	AL — Character entered
AH = 2	Display character with CTRL-BREAK check	DL =	Character to display
AH = 3	Asynchronous character input		AL — Character entered
AH = 4	Asynchronous character output	DL =	Character to send
AH = 5	Character to write	DL =	Character to write
AH = 6	Input keyboard character	DL = 0FFH	Character entered; 0 if none
AH = 7	Wait for keyboard character (no display)		AL — Character entered
AH = 8	Wait for keyboard character (no display — CTRL-BREAK check)		AL — Character entered
AH = 9	String display	DS:DX =	Address of string, Must end with $ sentinel
AH = A	Keyboard string to buf-	DS:DX =	Address of buffer. First byte

Table 5-4. _____

Specifications and Requirements for the DOS 21H Interrupt

Figure 5-19 is a listing of the complete program. To demonstrate the usefulness of the program, a little arithmetic problem is done:

```
MOV    AX,01234H        ;FIRST NUMBER
ADD    AX,02299H        ;SECOND NUMBER
MOV    TMPNUM,AX        ;STORE SUM IN TEMP LOCATION
```

The results of the addition (34CDH) are stored in the variable TMPNUM.
To show the number contained in TMPNUM on the screen, TMPNUM must be converted to an ASCII string. The following section of code accomplishes this:

```
          MOV    CX,04H            ;NUMBER OF DIGITS TO
                                   ;CONVERT
AGAIN:    MOV    AX,TMPNUM         ;GET 16 BITS OF DATA INTO
                                   ;AX
          AND    AX,0FH            ;KEEP ONLY LOWER 4 BITS
          ADD    AL,30H            ;MAKE IT ASCII
          CMP    AL,39H            ;IS IT A LETTER?
          JL     ASCII             ;IF A NUMBER, JUMP TO
                                   ;ASCII
          ADD    AL,07H            ;MAKE LETTER CORRECT
                                   ;ASCII CHAR
ASCII:    MOV    SI,CX             ;SET INDEX EQUAL TO
                                   ;CHARACTER
          MOV    TMPCHAR[SI],AL    ;SAVE CONVERTED NUMBER
                                   ;AS CHARACTER
          ROR    TMPNUM,1          ;ROTATE NEXT DIGIT TO LSB
                                   ;POSITION
          ROR    TMPNUM,1
          ROR    TMPNUM,1
          ROR    TMPNUM,1
          LOOP   AGAIN             ;IF CX>0, THEN ANOTHER
                                   ;DIGIT
```

TMPNUM is a 16-bit register holding four hexadecimal digits. Each digit

```
;FOR IBM 8088/80286 MACHINES
;PROGRAM TO ILLUSTRATE CONVERSION FROM HEX TO ASCII IN ORDER TO
;DISPLAY THE CONTENTS OF A REGISTER ON THE SCREEN

STACK     SEGMENT PARA STACK
          DB      64 DUP ('MYSTACK ')
STACK     ENDS

MYDATA    SEGMENT PARA 'DATA'
TMPNUM    DW      ?                    ;STORAGE FOR REG TO BE DISPLAYED
TMPCHAR   DB      8 DUP(' '),'$'       ;CHARACTER DATA FROM REG
MYDATA    ENDS

MYCODE    SEGMENT PARA 'CODE'          ;DEFINE CODE SEG. FOR MASM
MYPROC    PROC    FAR                  ;PROCEDURE IS NAMED MYPROC
          ASSUME  CS:MYCODE,DS:MYDATA,SS:STACK
          PUSH    DS                   ;SAVE LOCATION OF DS REG.
          SUB     AX,AX                ;GET A ZERO IN AX
          PUSH    AX                   ;SAVE ZERO ON STACK, TOO
          MOV     AX,MYDATA            ;GET DATA LOCATION IN AX
          MOV     DS,AX                ;PUT IT IN DS REGISTER

;A LITTLE ADDITION PROBLEM TO ILLUSTRATE THE USEFULLNESS OF PROGRAM.
;WE CAN VIEW RESULTS OF ADDITION, WITHOUT TRACING OR REGISTER DUMPS!
          MOV     AX,01234H            ;FIRST NUMBER
          ADD     AX,02299H            ;SECOND NUMBER
          MOV     TMPNUM,AX            ;STORE SUM IN TEMP LOCATION

;PROGRAM SEGMENT TO DISPLAY A 16 BIT REGISTER ON THE SCREEN
          MOV     CX,04H               ;NUMBER OF DIGITS TO CONVERT
AGAIN:    MOV     AX,TMPNUM            ;GET 16 BITS OF DATA INTO AX
          AND     AX,0FH               ;KEEP ONLY LOWER 4 BITS
          ADD     AL,30H               ;MAKE IT ASCII
          CMP     AL,39H               ;IS IT A LETTER?
          JL      ASCII                ;IF A NUMBER, JUMP TO ASCII
          ADD     AL,07H               ;MAKE LETTER CORRECT ASCII CHAR
ASCII:    MOV     SI,CX                ;SET INDEX EQUAL TO CHARACTER
          MOV     TMPCHAR[SI],AL       ;SAVE CONVERTED NUMBER AS CHARACTER
          ROR     TMPNUM,1             ;ROTATE NEXT DIGIT TO LSB POSITION
          ROR     TMPNUM,1
          ROR     TMPNUM,1
          ROR     TMPNUM,1
          LOOP    AGAIN                ;IF CX>0, THEN ANOTHER DIGIT

;STRING DISPLAY ROUTINE PRINTS SELECTED STRING AT
;CURRENT CURSOR POSITION
          LEA     DX,TMPCHAR           ;DOS STRING DISPLAY ROUTINE
          MOV     AH,9                 ;DOS PARAMETER
          INT     21H                  ;DOS INTERRUPT

          RET                          ;RETURN CONTROL TO DOS
MYPROC    ENDP                         ;END PROCEDURE NAMED MYPROC
MYCODE    ENDS                         ;END CODE SEGMENT NAMED MYCODE

          END                          ;END WHOLE PROGRAM
```

Figure 5-19. _____

Displaying register contents with a DOS-type 21H interrupt

must be converted separately to its ASCII equivalent. On the first pass through this program, TMPNUM is placed in the AX register and ANDed with 0FH, thus retaining only the lower digit of the number (in this case, 0DH). That digit is ORed with 30H to make it ASCII and then checked to see if it is an ASCII number or letter. In this case, it is a letter, and a jump is made to add another 07H to the contents of the AL register (which now contains 44H, the correct representation for an ASCII "D"). This character is stored in the string variable TMPCHAR at an offset equal to its position value (4, counting left to right) in the original number. TMPNUM is then rotated four bits, or one digit, so that that digit is placed in the LSB position, and the process is repeated until all four digits have been converted.

The code segment shown here is all that is needed to place TMPCHAR on the screen.

```
LEA    DX,TMPCHAR    ;DOS STRING DISPLAY ROUTINE
MOV    AH,9          ;DOS PARAMETER
INT    21H           ;DOS INTERRUPT
```

DOS INT 21H prints data from the data segment until a sentinel is detected. The correct sentinel value is the $ (dollar) sign, which was concatenated with TMPCHAR in storage. If you forget the sentinel, INT 21H will continue to print odd characters to the screen until it finds a sentinel embedded within your code.

USING A DOS INTERRUPT TO READ A KEYBOARD CHARACTER

Often a programmer may want to make a program interactive. Frequently, this interaction requires input from the keyboard in the form of a "Y" (for yes) or "N" (for no) response to a previously asked question. The following listing shows a program that uses a DOS interrupt to intercept keyboard information.

```
;FOR IBM 8088/80286 MACHINES
;PROGRAM TO ILLUSTRATE HOW TO READ AND ECHO PRINT A CHARACTER
;SENT FROM THE KEYBOARD.  IF THE CHARACTER IS A "Y" OR "N" A
;CERTAIN VALUE WILL BE LOADED INTO A VARIABLE CALLED "TEST"

STACK    SEGMENT PARA STACK
         DB      64 DUP ('MYSTACK ')
STACK    ENDS

MYDATA   SEGMENT PARA 'DATA'
```

```
TEST      DW       ?
MYDATA    ENDS

MYCODE    SEGMENT PARA 'CODE'        ;DEFINE CODE SEG. FOR MASM
MYPROC    PROC     FAR               ;PROCEDURE IS NAMED MYPROC
          ASSUME  CS:MYCODE,DS:MYDATA,SS:STACK
          PUSH     DS                ;SAVE LOCATION OF DS REG.
          SUB      AX,AX             ;GET A ZERO IN AX
          PUSH     AX                ;SAVE ZERO ON STACK, TOO
          MOV      AX,MYDATA         ;GET DATA LOCATION IN AX
          MOV      DS,AX             ;PUT IT IN DS REGISTER

;ACTUAL SEGMENT FOR INTERCEPTION AND DISPLAY OF KEYBOARD CHARACTER
          MOV      AH,01H            ;PARAMETER FOR READING A CHARACTER
          INT      21H               ;DISPLAY ONE CHARACTER
          CMP      AL,'Y'            ;IS IT A "Y"
          JNE      HERE              ;IF NOT, JUMP TO "HERE"
          MOV      BX,9999H          ;IF YES, MOVE A 9999H INTO BX
          JMP      ENDO              ;THEN END PROGRAM
HERE:     CMP      AL,'N'            ;IS IT A "N"
          JNE      ENDO              ;IF NOT, JUMP TO "ENDO"
          MOV      BX,5555H          ;IF YES, MOVE A 5555H INTO BX

ENDO:     MOV      TEST,BX           ;SAVE THE VALUE IN TEST

          RET                        ;RETURN CONTROL TO DOS
MYPROC    ENDP                       ;END PROCEDURE NAMED MYPROC
MYCODE    ENDS                       ;END CODE SEGMENT NAMED MYCODE

          END                        ;END WHOLE PROGRAM
```

This program makes a decision based upon whether a "Y" or an "N" is entered from the keyboard. (Note that a lowercase "y" or "n" will not work). A portion of the program code is repeated here.

```
         MOV    AH,01H      ;PARAMETER FOR READING A
                            ;CHARACTER
         INT    21H         ;DISPLAY ONE CHARACTER
         CMP    AL,'Y'      ;IS IT A "Y"
         JNE    HERE        ;IF NOT, JUMP TO "HERE"
         MOV    BX,9999H    ;IF YES, MOVE A 9999H INTO BX
         JMP    ENDO        ;THEN END PROGRAM
HERE:    CMP    AL,'N'      ;IS IT A "N"
         JNE    ENDO        ;IF NOT, JUMP TO "ENDO"
         MOV    BX,5555H    ;IF YES, MOVE A 5555H INTO BX

ENDO:    MOV    TEST,BX     ;SAVE THE VALUE IN TEST
```

Table 5-4 gave the necessary information for DOS type-21H interrupts. When AH is set to 1 and the interrupt is called, the program idles until a key is pressed on the keyboard. The interrupt then echoes the character to the screen and returns the ASCII value for the character in the AL register. If a "Y" is entered, the program stores 9999H in the BX register and eventually in the variable TEST. If an "N" is entered, the program stores 5555H. If any other key is pressed, the contents of BX at the start of the program are stored in the variable TEST.

USING A DOS INTERRUPT TO READ A KEYBOARD STRING

To read a string of keyboard characters into memory, certain decisions need to be made ahead of time, because the same DOS INT 21H will be used. Examine the data segment shown here.

```
BUFF    DB    80 DUP (' '),'$'     ;BUFFER FOR STRING
LINE    DB    0AH,0DH,'$'          ;CARRIAGE RETURN & LINEFEED
```

The variable BUFF accepts and stores an 80-character string. Note that the sentinel value is concatenated to this string. The variable LINE contains two control characters: a carriage return and a line feed to move the location of the cursor. The following listing shows the entire program.

```
;FOR IBM 8088/80286 MACHINES
;PROGRAM TO ILLUSTRATE HOW TO READ AND ECHO PRINT A CHARACTER
;STRING SENT FROM THE KEYBOARD

STACK     SEGMENT PARA STACK
          DB      64 DUP ('MYSTACK ')
STACK     ENDS

MYDATA    SEGMENT PARA 'DATA'
BUFF      DB      80 DUP (' '),'$'   ;BUFFER FOR STRING
LINE      DB      0AH,0DH,'$'        ;CARRIAGE RETURN & LINEFEED
MYDATA    ENDS

MYCODE    SEGMENT PARA 'CODE'        ;DEFINE CODE SEG. FOR MASM
MYPROC    PROC    FAR                ;PROCEDURE IS NAMED MYPROC
          ASSUME  CS:MYCODE,DS:MYDATA,SS:STACK
          PUSH    DS                 ;SAVE LOCATION OF DS REG.
          SUB     AX,AX              ;GET A ZERO IN AX
          PUSH    AX                 ;SAVE ZERO ON STACK, TOO
          MOV     AX,MYDATA          ;GET DATA LOCATION IN AX
          MOV     DS,AX              ;PUT IT IN DS REGISTER
          LEA     BX,BUFF            ;LOCATION OF STORAGE BUFFER

;ACTUAL SEGMENT FOR INTERCEPTION AND DISPLAY OF KEYBOARD CHARACTER
          MOV     AH,01H             ;PARAMETER FOR READING A CHARACTER
          MOV     CX,00H             ;SET COUNTER TO ZERO
HERE:     INT     21H                ;DISPLAY ONE CHARACTER
          CMP     AL,0DH             ;IS IT A CARRIAGE RETURN?
          JE      NOMORE             ;IF SO, LEAVE ROUTINE
```

```
          MOV     BUFF[BX],AL     ;MOVE CHARACTER INTO STORAGE
          CMP     CX,79           ;HAVE WE DONE 80 CHARACTERS YET?
          JE      NOMORE          ;IF SO, LEAVE THIS ROUTINE
          INC     CX              ;INCREMENT LETTER COUNTER
          INC     BX              ;POSITION STORAGE FOR NEXT CHAR.
          JMP     HERE            ;GET ANOTHER CHARACTER
;ROUTINE TO DISPLAY A CHARACTER STRING PREVIOUSLY STORED
NOMORE:
          LEA     DX,LINE         ;PRINT A LINEFEED AND CARRIAGE
          MOV     AH,09           ;RETURN BEFORE PRINTING STRING
          INT     21H             ;DOS INTERRUPT
          LEA     DX,BUFF         ;DISPLAY CHARACTER STRING
          MOV     AH,09
          INT     21H             ;DOS INTERRUPT

          RET                     ;RETURN CONTROL TO DOS
MYPROC    ENDP                    ;END PROCEDURE NAMED MYPROC
MYCODE    ENDS                    ;END CODE SEGMENT NAMED MYCODE

          END                     ;END WHOLE PROGRAM
```

In this program, a counter is used to determine if 80 characters have been entered from the keyboard. The only other way to terminate character input is to enter a carriage return (0DH). Therefore, the string actually can contain from 1 to 80 characters. A portion of code is shown here.

```
          MOV    AH,01H        ;PARAMETER FOR READING A
                                ;CHARACTER
          MOV    CX,00H        ;SET COUNTER TO ZERO
HERE:     INT    21H           ;DISPLAY ONE CHARACTER
          CMP    AL,0DH        ;IS IT A CARRIAGE RETURN?
          JE     NOMORE        ;IF SO, LEAVE ROUTINE
          MOV    BUFF[BX],AL   ;MOVE CHARACTER INTO
                                ;STORAGE
          CMP    CX,79         ;HAVE WE DONE 80 CHARACTERS
                                ;YET?
          JE     NOMORE        ;IF SO, LEAVE THIS ROUTINE
          INC    CX            ;INCREMENT LETTER COUNTER
          INC    BX            ;POSITION STORAGE FOR NEXT
                                ;CHAR.
          JMP    HERE          ;GET ANOTHER CHARACTER
```

In this program segment, the keyboard character is intercepted in a manner similar to the previous example. The contents of AL (the ASCII character) is compared with 0DH to check for a carriage return. If the character is a carriage return, a JE command takes you out of the keyboard loop. If the character is not a carriage return, the character is stored in

BUFF at a location equal to the current **BX** offset. A check is then made to see if 80 characters have been read in, and if not, both **CX** and **BX** are incremented. **CX** keeps a count of the number of letters, and **BX** holds the memory offset to BUFF. The loop is repeated until either a carriage return is detected or the character count reaches 80.

The remaining program segment prints two strings to the screen.

```
LEA    DX,LINE    ;PRINT A LINEFEED AND CARRIAGE
MOV    AH,09      ;RETURN BEFORE PRINTING STRING
INT    21H        ;DOS INTERRUPT
LEA    DX,BUFF    ;DISPLAY CHARACTER STRING
MOV    AH,09
INT    21H        ;DOS INTERRUPT
```

The variable LINE points to the line feed and carriage return string, and BUFF points to the string entered at the keyboard. This program merely prints the string to the screen at the current cursor position.

READING THE CURRENT TIME AND DATE USING A BIOS INTERRUPT

The BIOS interrupt, 1AH, for the IBM AT (80286) computer has been expanded from its 8088 counterpart to allow reading and writing of the current date and time from and to the system clock. Table 5-5 is a listing of the options available with the type-1AH BIOS interrupt. In addition, the alarm function of the 80286 can be set or cleared. The following listing is an 80286 program that allows reading the time and date from the system's clock.

```
;FOR IBM 80286 MACHINES
;PROGRAM TO ILLUSTRATE HOW TO OBTAIN TIME AND DATE FROM BIOS INTERRUPT

STACK    SEGMENT PARA STACK
         DB      64 DUP ('MYSTACK ')
STACK    ENDS

MYDATA   SEGMENT PARA 'DATA'
TIME     DD      OH                 ;STORAGE FOR TIME AS DOUBLE WORD
DATE     DD      OH                 ;STORAGE FOR DATE AS DOUBLE WORD
MYDATA   ENDS

MYCODE   SEGMENT PARA 'CODE'        ;DEFINE CODE SEG. FOR MASM
MYPROC   PROC    FAR                ;PROCEDURE IS NAMED MYPROC
         ASSUME  CS:MYCODE,DS:MYDATA,SS:STACK
         PUSH    DS                 ;SAVE LOCATION OF DS REG.
         SUB     AX,AX              ;GET A ZERO IN AX
```

```
            PUSH    AX                   ;SAVE ZERO ON STACK, TOO
            MOV     AX,MYDATA            ;GET DATA LOCATION IN AX
            MOV     DS,AX                ;PUT IT IN DS REGISTER

;ROUTINE FOR OBTAINING TIME FROM BIOS INTERRUPT
            MOV     AH,02                ;PARAMETER FOR TIME
            INT     1AH                  ;TIME/DATE INTERRUPT
            MOV     BYTE PTR TIME+3,DH ;MOVE SECONDS INTO TIME
            MOV     BYTE PTR TIME+2,CL ;MINUTES INTO TIME
            MOV     BYTE PTR TIME+1,CH ;HOURS INTO TIME

;ROUTINE FOR OBTAINING DATE FROM BIOS INTERRUPT
            MOV     AH,04                ;PARAMETER FOR DATE
            INT     1AH                  ;TIME/DATE INTERRUPT
            MOV     BYTE PTR DATE+3,DL ;MOVE DAY INTO DATE
            MOV     BYTE PTR DATE+2,DH ;MONTH INTO DATE
            MOV     BYTE PTR DATE+1,CL ;YEAR INTO DATE
            MOV     BYTE PTR DATE,CH   ;CENTURY INTO DATE

            RET                          ;RETURN CONTROL TO DOS
MYPROC      ENDP                         ;END PROCEDURE NAMED MYPROC
MYCODE      ENDS                         ;END CODE SEGMENT NAMED MYCODE

            END                          ;END WHOLE PROGRAM
```

As you can see from the listing, the program is divided into two segments. The segment for reading the time is repeated here.

```
MOV   AH,02                  ;PARAMETER FOR TIME
INT   1AH                    ;TIME/DATE INTERRUPT
MOV   BYTE PTR TIME+3,DH     ;MOVE SECONDS INTO TIME
MOV   BYTE PTR TIME+2,CL     ;MINUTES INTO TIME
MOV   BYTE PTR TIME+1,CH     ;HOURS INTO TIME
```

With AH set to 2, interrupt 1AH returns the current time encoded in three 8-bit registers. This program stores the time in a defined doubleword (DD) with the variable name TIME. The program segment illustrates how this is accomplished using the BYTE PTR instruction.

The next program segment reads and decodes the date.

```
MOV   AH,04                  ;PARAMETER FOR DATE
INT   1AH                    ;TIME/DATE INTERRUPT
MOV   BYTE PTR DATE+3,DL     ;MOVE DAY INTO DATE
MOV   BYTE PTR DATE+2,DH     ;MONTH INTO DATE
MOV   BYTE PTR DATE+1,CL     ;YEAR INTO DATE
MOV   BYTE PTR DATE,CH       ;CENTURY INTO DATE
```

To read the date, AH must be set to 4. Four 8-bit registers return the coded date information when interrupt 1AH is called. Again, with the use of the

BYTE PTR instruction, the decoded date information is placed in a defined doubleword (DD) variable called DATE. Both TIME and DATE can be viewed in the data segment after program execution by using IBM's Debug program to dump the memory segment.

Syntax: INT 1AH (when the following parameters are set to the required values)

Function: Allows the system clock to be read or set.

AH Value	Function	Input	Output
AH = 0	Read current clock setting		CX — High bytes of clock DX — Low bytes of clock AL — 0, if timer has not passed 24 hours
AH = 1	Set current clock	CX = DX =	High bytes of clock Low bytes of clock
AH = 2	Read time — real-time clock		CH — BCD hours CL — BCD minutes DH — BCD seconds
AH = 3	Set time — real-time clock	CH = CL = DH = DL =	BCD hours BCD minutes BCD seconds 1 — Daylight savings time 0 — Standard time
AH = 4	Read date — real-time clock		CH — BCD century CL — BCD year CL — BCD year DH — BCD month DL — BCD day
AH = 5	set date — real-time clock	CH = CL = DH = DL =	BCD century BCD year BCD month BCD day
AH = 6	Set alarm (up to 23:59:59)	CH = CL = DH =	BCD hours BCD minutes BCD seconds
AH = 7	Reset alarm		

Table 5-5.

Options Available With the IBM AT (80286) Type-1A BIOS Interrupt

DETERMINING THE SIZE OF THE AT'S MEMORY USING A BIOS INTERRUPT

The amount of installed memory in an AT system can be read using two BIOS interrupts. The following listing shows the program.

```
;FOR IBM 80286 MACHINES
;PROGRAM TO ILLUSTRATE HOW TO DETERMINE THE AMOUNT OF
;MEMORY IN AN IBM AT WITH THE USE OF A BIOS INTERRUPT

STACK     SEGMENT PARA STACK
          DB       64 DUP ('MYSTACK ')
STACK     ENDS

MYDATA    SEGMENT PARA 'DATA'
SYSMEM    DW       ?                  ;MAIN MEMORY (UP TO 640K)
EXTMEM    DW       ?                  ;EXTENDED MEMORY (ABOVE 640K)
MYDATA    ENDS

MYCODE    SEGMENT PARA 'CODE'         ;DEFINE CODE SEG. FOR MASM
MYPROC    PROC    FAR                 ;PROCEDURE IS NAMED MYPROC
          ASSUME  CS:MYCODE,DS:MYDATA,SS:STACK
          PUSH    DS                  ;SAVE LOCATION OF DS REG.
          SUB     AX,AX               ;GET A ZERO IN AX
          PUSH    AX                  ;SAVE ZERO ON STACK, TOO
          MOV     AX,MYDATA           ;GET DATA LOCATION IN AX
          MOV     DS,AX               ;PUT IT IN DS REGISTER

;ROUTINE FOR DETERMINING MAIN MEMORY SIZE
          INT     12H                 ;INTERRUPT CALL FOR MEMORY
          MOV     SYSMEM,AX           ;MOVE VALUE TO MAIN MEMORY VAR

;ROUTINE FOR DETERMINING EXTENDED MEMORY SIZE
          MOV     AH,88H              ;INTERRUPT PARAMETER
          INT     15H                 ;INTERRUPT CALL FOR EXT MEMORY
          MOV     EXTMEM,AX

          RET                         ;RETURN CONTROL TO DOS
MYPROC    ENDP                        ;END PROCEDURE NAMED MYPROC
MYCODE    ENDS                        ;END CODE SEGMENT NAMED MYCODE

          END                         ;END WHOLE PROGRAM
```

Actually, the use of a type-12H interrupt is supported by both the PC (8088) and AT (80286) computers. The type-12H interrupt reads the total amount of contiguous main memory installed in the system.

```
INT   12H            ;INTERRUPT CALL FOR MEMORY
MOV   SYSMEM,AX      ;MOVE VALUE TO MAIN MEMORY VAR
```

The value returned in AX is equal to the number of 1K blocks of installed memory.

The use of the type-15H interrupt in the following program segment is an interesting case of "hide it where you can."

```
MOV    AH,88H          ;INTERRUPT PARAMETER
INT    15H             ;INTERRUPT CALL FOR EXT MEMORY
MOV    EXTMEM,AX
```

The type-15H interrupt in the PC (8088) serviced cassette I/O functions. The AT (80286) does not have a cassette port, so this interrupt has become the dumping ground for various miscellaneous functions. One of those functions is for determining the amount of extended memory. When AX is set to 88H and the interrupt is called, AX returns the amount of extended contiguous memory above 640K in 1K blocks.

DETERMINING OPTIONAL EQUIPMENT INSTALLATION USING A BIOS INTERRUPT

The following listing is a short program that allows the determination of certain pieces of equipment on the PC and AT computers.

```
;FOR IBM 8088/80286 MACHINES
;PROGRAM TO DETERMINE INSTALLED EQUIPMENT ON IBM USING BIOS

STACK     SEGMENT PARA STACK
          DB      64 DUP ('MYSTACK ')
STACK     ENDS

MYDATA    SEGMENT PARA 'DATA'
EQUIP     DW      ?
MYDATA    ENDS

MYCODE    SEGMENT PARA 'CODE'        ;DEFINE CODE SEG. FOR MASM
MYPROC    PROC    FAR                ;PROCEDURE IS NAMED MYPROC
          ASSUME  CS:MYCODE,DS:MYDATA,SS:STACK
          PUSH    DS                 ;SAVE LOCATION OF DS REG.
          SUB     AX,AX              ;GET A ZERO IN AX
          PUSH    AX                 ;SAVE ZERO ON STACK, TOO
          MOV     AX,MYDATA          ;GET DATA LOCATION IN AX
          MOV     DS,AX              ;PUT IT IN DS REGISTER

;ROUTINE FOR EQUIPMENT DETERMINATION
          INT     11H                ;EQUIP. DETERMIN. INTERRUPT
          MOV     EQUIP,AX           ;MOVE INFO INTO EQUIP

          RET                        ;RETURN CONTROL TO DOS
MYPROC    ENDP                       ;END PROCEDURE NAMED MYPROC
MYCODE    ENDS                       ;END CODE SEGMENT NAMED MYCODE

          END                        ;END WHOLE PROGRAM
```

This program was written to work on either the PC or AT, but the results returned in the variable EQUIP have a different meaning for each machine. A segment of the program is shown here.

```
INT    11H            ;EQUIP DETERMIN. INTERRUPT
MOV    EQUIP,AX       ;MOVE INFO INTO EQUIP
```

The value for a particular machine can be viewed by dumping the data segment after program execution or by extending the code and printing the contents of the AX register as shown in Figure 5-19 earlier in this chapter. This hexadecimal value should then be converted into binary format so that each of the 15 bits can be examined. Equipment determination is as shown in Table 5-6.

If 4463H, for example, is returned in the AX register, it can be converted to the binary number:

```
 0  1  0  0  0  1  0  0  0  1  1  0  0  0  1  1   (Binary number)
15 14 13 12 11 10  9  8  7  6  5  4  3  2  1  0   (Bit position)
```

This coding indicates the following equipment, reading from left to right:

Disk drives installed
80287 math coprocessor
80x25 B/W mode using color card
2—Diskette drives
2—RS-232 ports
1—Printer

SENDING A CHARACTER STRING TO THE PRINTER USING A BIOS INTERRUPT

The following listing is a program designed to send a predefined character string to the printer connected to LPT1.

```
;FOR IBM 8088/80286 MACHINES
;PROGRAM TO ILLUSTRATE HOW TO SEND A STRING OF CHARACTERS
;TO THE PRINTER AT LPT1: USING BIOS ROUTINE
;PUSH Ctrl-PrtSc BEFORE RUNNING

STACK    SEGMENT PARA STACK
         DB      64 DUP ('MYSTACK ')
```

```
STACK     ENDS

MYDATA    SEGMENT PARA 'DATA'
MESSGE    DB      'PROGRAMMING IN ASSEMBLY LANGUAGE IS FAST','$'
MYDATA    ENDS

MYCODE    SEGMENT PARA 'CODE'       ;DEFINE CODE SEG. FOR MASM
MYPROC    PROC    FAR               ;PROCEDURE IS NAMED MYPROC
          ASSUME  CS:MYCODE,DS:MYDATA,SS:STACK
          PUSH    DS                ;SAVE LOCATION OF DS REG.
          SUB     AX,AX             ;GET A ZERO IN AX
          PUSH    AX                ;SAVE ZERO ON STACK, TOO
          MOV     AX,MYDATA         ;GET DATA LOCATION IN AX
          MOV     DS,AX             ;PUT IT IN DS REGISTER
          LEA     BX,MESSGE         ;GET THE LOCATION OF MESSGE
```

PC & XT Computers

Bits	Equipment
Bits 15, 14	Number of printers
Bit 13	Not used
Bit 12	Game adapter
Bits 11, 10, 9	Number of RS-232 cards
Bit 8	Not used
Bits 7, 6	Number of floppy drives; if bit 0=1, 00=1, 01=2, 10=3, 11=4
Bits 5, 4	Initial video mode
	01 = 40 × 25 B/W using color card
	10 = 80 × 25 B/W using color card
	11 = 80 × 25 B/W using monochrome card
Bits 3, 2	Planar RAM size
	00 = 16K
	01 = 32K
	10 = 48K
	11 = 64K
Bit 1	Not used
Bit 0	Any diskette drives

AT Computer (same as above, unless indicated)

Bit 12	Not used
Bits 3, 2	Not used
Bit 1	80287 coprocessor

Table 5-6. _____

Meaning of AX Register Bit Position for 11H Interrupt System Determination

```
;ROUTINE TO SEND ONE CHARACTER TO THE PRINTER AT A TIME
        MOV      DX,00H              ;SET FOR ONE PRINTER
        MOV      AH,01H              ;PARAMETER TO INITIALIZE PRINTER

        INT      17H                 ;PRINTER INTERRUPT
AGAIN:  MOV      AL,MESSGE[BX]       ;GET A CHARACTER FROM STRING
        CMP      AL,'$'              ;END OF MESSAGE YET?
        JE       ENDO                ;IF SO, END THE ROUTINE
        MOV      AH,00H              ;PARAMETER FOR PRINT CHARACTER
        INT      17H                 ;PRINTER INTERRUPT
        INC      BX                  ;GET NEXT CHARACTER TO PRINT
        JMP      AGAIN               ;REPEAT
ENDO:

        RET                          ;RETURN CONTROL TO DOS
MYPROC  ENDP                         ;END PROCEDURE NAMED MYPROC
MYCODE  ENDS                         ;END CODE SEGMENT NAMED MYCODE

        END                          ;END WHOLE PROGRAM
```

CTRL-PRTSC must be engaged prior to program execution. Just as in the case where the keyboard was read one character at a time, the printer is sent one character at a time to print. The program segment shown here shows the programming technique required to accomplish this.

```
        MOV    DX,00H          ;SET FOR ONE PRINTER
        MOV    AH,01H          ;PARAMETER TO INITIALIZE
                               ;PRINTER

        INT    17H             ;PRINTER INTERRUPT
AGAIN:  MOV    AL,MESSGE[BX]   ;GET A CHARACTER FROM
                               ;STRING

        CMP    AL,'$'          ;END OF MESSAGE YET?
        JE     ENDO            ;IF SO, END THE ROUTINE
        MOV    AH,00H          ;PARAMETER FOR PRINT
                               ;CHARACTER
        INT    17H             ;PRINTER INTERRUPT
        INC    BX              ;GET NEXT CHARACTER TO
                               ;PRINT
        JMP    AGAIN           ;REPEAT
ENDO:
```

To use the type-17H interrupt, the printer must first be initialized. DX is set to 0, 1, or 2 which corresponds to an actual value in the printer base area (the printer's address). A value of 0 corresponds to LPT1. AH set to 1 initializes the printer port when interrupt 17H is called. As you can see from the program, this only needs to be done once. The program then enters a loop for sending one character at a time. A single character is moved from the variable MESSGE into the AL register. A check is made to see if it is a sentinel value, because the printer port does not have a sentinel built in, as does interrupt 21H. If the character is not a sentinel, a 0 is placed in AH, and interrupt 17H prints the character to the printer. BX is incremented to point to the next character in the string, and the loop is repeated. The loop terminates only when a $ is found, so the string can be quite long.

PLOTTING DOTS ON THE MEDIUM-RESOLUTION COLOR SCREEN USING A BIOS INTERRUPT

The IBM family of personal computers supports two graphics modes on the standard color monitor. One is the medium-resolution mode and the other the high-resolution mode. The medium-resolution mode can plot 320 dots across and 200 dots down, with four colors present on the screen at any given time. The high-resolution mode supports 640 dots across and 200 dots down and two colors (usually black and white). Table 5-2, earlier in this chapter, shows that AH values 11, 12 and 13 form the graphics interface values for BIOS. The following listing is a program designed to plot three tiny dots near the center of the screen.

```
;FOR IBM 8088/80286 MACHINES WITH RGB MONITORS
;PROGRAM TO ILLUSTRATE HOW TO PLOT DOTS ON MEDIUM RESOLUTION
;COLOR GRAPHICS SCREEN USING A BIOS INTERRUPT
;REQUIRES THE USE OF A COLOR GRAPHICS CARD!

STACK    SEGMENT PARA STACK
         DB      64 DUP ('MYSTACK ')
STACK    ENDS

MYCODE   SEGMENT PARA 'CODE'      ;DEFINE CODE SEG. FOR MASM
MYPROC   PROC    FAR              ;PROCEDURE IS NAMED MYPROC
         ASSUME  CS:MYCODE,SS:STACK
         PUSH    DS               ;SAVE LOCATION OF DS REG.
         SUB     AX,AX            ;GET A ZERO IN AX
         PUSH    AX               ;SAVE ZERO ON STACK, TOO

;ROUTINE FOR PLOTTING THREE DOTS NEAR THE CENTER OF THE SCREEN
         MOV     AH,00            ;PREPARE TO SET SCREEN MODE
         MOV     AL,04            ;SET 320x200 COLOR MODE
         INT     10H              ;CALL INTERRUPT

         MOV     AH,11            ;SET COLOR PALETTE
         MOV     BH,00            ;SET BACKGROUND COLOR
         MOV     BL,01            ;SET IT TO BLUE
         INT     10H              ;CALL INTERRUPT

         MOV     AH,11            ;SET COLOR PALETTE
```

```
              MOV        BH,01         ;SELECT FOREGROUND PALETTE
              MOV        BL,00         ;GREEN/RED/YELLOW
              INT        10H           ;CALL INTERRUPT

              MOV        AL,02         ;SET DOT COLOR TO RED
              MOV        AH,12         ;WRITE DOT PARAMETER
              MOV        DX,64H        ;SET FOR 100 ROWS DOWN (VERTICAL)
              MOV        CX,9EH        ;SET FOR 158 COLUMNS OVER (HORIZONTAL)
              INT        10H           ;CALL INTERRUPT
              MOV        AH,12         ;WRITE DOT PARAMETER
              MOV        CX,0A0H       ;PLOT ANOTHER
              INT        10H           ;CALL INTERRUPT
              MOV        AH,12         ;WRITE DOT PARAMETER
              MOV        CX,0A2H       ;PLOT ANOTHER
              INT        10H           ;CALL INTERRUPT

              RET                      ;RETURN CONTROL TO DOS
MYPROC        ENDP                     ;END PROCEDURE NAMED MYPROC
MYCODE        ENDS                     ;END CODE SEGMENT NAMED MYCODE

              END                      ;END WHOLE PROGRAM
```

Before any plotting takes place, it is necessary to initialize the medium-resolution screen, as shown in the following program segment:

```
MOV    AH,00    ;PREPARE TO SET SCREEN MODE
MOV    AL,04    ;SET 320×200 COLOR MODE
INT    10H      ;CALL INTERRUPT
```

If you refer back to Table 5-2, you will see how the values for AH and AL are determined.

Next, it is necessary to set the background and foreground colors:

```
MOV    AH,11    ;SET COLOR PALETTE
MOV    BH,00    ;SET BACKGROUND COLOR
MOV    BL,01    ;SET IT TO BLUE
INT    10H      ;CALL INTERRUPT
```

With BH set to 0, the color selected forms the background color for the screen. The colors range in number from 0 to 15. (See Table 5-3 earlier in this chapter.)

The background color for this example is blue. The foreground palette is selected a little differently:

```
MOV    AH,11    ;SET COLOR PALETTE
MOV    BH,01    ;SELECT FOREGROUND PALETTE
MOV    BL,00    ;GREEN/RED/YELLOW
INT    10H      ;CALL INTERRUPT
```

BH is set to 1 for foreground color selection, and BL selects the green/red/yellow palette. The three steps for initialization only need to be done once, unless a color change is desired for the whole screen.

The remainder of the program uses the write dot command three times:

```
MOV    AL,02       ;SET DOT COLOR TO RED
MOV    AH,12       ;WRITE DOT PARAMETER
MOV    DX,64H      ;SET FOR 100 ROWS DOWN (VERTICAL)
MOV    CX,9EH      ;SET FOR 158 COLUMNS OVER (HORIZONTAL)
INT    10H         ;CALL INTERRUPT
MOV    AH,12       ;WRITE DOT PARAMETER
MOV    CX,0A0H     ;PLOT ANOTHER
INT    10H         ;CALL INTERRUPT
MOV    AH,12       ;WRITE DOT PARAMETER
MOV    CX,0A2H     ;PLOT ANOTHER
INT    10H         ;CALL INTERRUPT
```

When the write dot command is used, the CX register contains the horizontal displacement, and DX contains the vertical displacement. In this case, the dots are plotted in red, by setting AL to 2. CX is moved twice for the remaining dots.

BASIC and Pascal support many graphics commands, but BIOS only supplies write dot and read dot commands. Therefore, to draw a line a program must be written to plot a series of dots in the desired direction. This is usually not a big chore if the line is vertical or horizontal, but it becomes more taxing if the line is anything else. (Circles will not even be mentioned!) This program exits in the medium-resolution color mode.

DRAWING A LINE ON THE HIGH-RESOLUTION SCREEN USING A BIOS INTERRUPT

The example from the previous section will be extended to draw a line on the high-resolution screen. The following listing shows how to accomplish this using a loop.

```
;FOR IBM 8088/80286 MACHINES WITH RGB MONITORS
;PROGRAM TO ILLUSTRATE HOW TO DRAW A LINE ON THE HIGH RESOLUTION
;GRAPHICS SCREEN  BY PLOTTING A SERIES OF DOTS USING BIOS INTERRUPT
;REQUIRES THE USE OF A COLOR GRAPHICS CARD!
```

```
STACK     SEGMENT PARA STACK
          DB      64 DUP ('MYSTACK ')
STACK     ENDS

MYCODE    SEGMENT PARA 'CODE'       ;DEFINE CODE SEG. FOR MASM
MYPROC    PROC    FAR               ;PROCEDURE IS NAMED MYPROC
          ASSUME  CS:MYCODE,SS:STACK
          PUSH    DS                ;SAVE LOCATION OF DS REG.
          SUB     AX,AX             ;GET A ZERO IN AX
          PUSH    AX                ;SAVE ZERO ON STACK, TOO

;ROUTINE FOR DRAWING A LINE BY PLOTTING A SERIES OF DOTS
          MOV     AH,00             ;PREPARE TO SET SCREEN MODE
          MOV     AL,06             ;SET 640x200 GRAPHICS MODE
          INT     10H               ;CALL INTERRUPT

          MOV     AL,01             ;SET DOT COLOR (BLACK OR WHITE)
          MOV     DX,00             ;SET VERTICAL START TO LEFT
          MOV     CX,00             ;SET HORIZONTAL START TO TOP
AGAIN:    MOV     AH,12             ;WRITE DOT PARAMETER
          INT     10H               ;CALL INTERRUPT
          INC     DX                ;INCREMENT VERTICAL POSITION
          INC     CX                ;INCREMENT HORIZONTAL POSITION
          INC     CX
          INC     CX
          CMP     DX,0C8H           ;IS LINE AT SCREEN BOTTOM (200)?
          JE      ENDO              ;IF SO, END PROGRAM
          JMP     AGAIN             ;IF NOT, PLOT ANOTHER DOT
ENDO:

          RET                       ;RETURN CONTROL TO DOS
MYPROC    ENDP                      ;END PROCEDURE NAMED MYPROC
MYCODE    ENDS                      ;END CODE SEGMENT NAMED MYCODE

          END                       ;END WHOLE PROGRAM
```

Because only two colors are used (black and white), and they are the defaults, it is not necessary to set the background and foreground. However, the program segment shown here indicates that the screen must be set for 640×200 graphics by moving 6 into AL.

```
          MOV    AH,00    ;PREPARE TO SET SCREEN MODE
          MOV    AL,06    ;SET 640×200 GRAPHICS MODE
          INT    10H      ;CALL INTERRUPT

          MOV    AL,01    ;SET DOT COLOR (BLACK OR
                          ;WHITE)
          MOV    DX,00    ;SET VERTICAL START TO LEFT
          MOV    CX,00    ;SET HORIZONTAL START TO TOP
AGAIN:    MOV    AH,12    ;WRITE DOT PARAMETER
          INT    10H      ;CALL INTERRUPT
          INC    DX       ;INCREMENT VERTICAL POSITION
          INC    CX       ;INCREMENT HORIZONTAL
                          ;POSITION
```

```
        INC    CX
        INC    CX
        CMP    DX,0C8H   ;IS LINE AT SCREEN BOTTOM (200)?
        JE     ENDO      ;IF SO, END PROGRAM
        JMP    AGAIN     ;IF NOT, PLOT ANOTHER DOT
ENDO:
```

This program plots a diagonal line starting in the upper left corner of the screen (DX=0 and CX=0). The color of the dot is set to white (AL=1), and the first dot is plotted when the loop is entered. The vertical displacement (DX) is increased by one, and the horizontal displacement (CX) increased by three. (Because the screen measures 640 across and 200 down, the horizontal spacing is changed by the ratio 3:1 to give a better diagonal line.) When 200 dots have been plotted vertically (to the bottom of the screen), the program is terminated. This program exits in the high-resolution graphics mode.

USING ADVANCED STRING COMMANDS: SCANNING A STRING FOR A CHARACTER

The string commands presented in this section, along with the associated programs, permit very rapid program execution. The high speed is achieved by the elimination of program loops, which always tend to slow assembly language programs. The first program scans a string looking for a particular character. If this program were written without these special string commands, a loop would be needed to index each character of the string. The second program copies a whole string from one variable location to another, also without using a loop.

The following listing is a program that allows the programmer to search a string for a predetermined character.

```
;FOR IBM 8088/80286 MACHINES
;PROGRAM TO ILLUSTRATE ADVANCED STRING COMMAND FOR SCANNING

STACK    SEGMENT PARA STACK
         DB       64 DUP ('MYSTACK ')
STACK    ENDS

MYDATA   SEGMENT PARA 'DATA'
GROUP1   DB       'FOR IN MUCH WISDOM IS MUCH GRIEF...  ECCL 1:18'
MESS1    DB       'THE LETTER WAS FOUND IN THE STRING$'
MESS2    DB       'THE LETTER WAS NOT FOUND IN THE STRING$'
MYDATA   ENDS
```

```
MYCODE   SEGMENT PARA 'CODE'     ;DEFINE CODE SEG. FOR MASM
MYPROC   PROC    FAR             ;PROCEDURE IS NAMED MYPROC
         ASSUME  CS:MYCODE,DS:MYDATA,ES:MYDATA,SS:STACK
         PUSH    DS              ;SAVE LOCATION OF DS REG.
         SUB     AX,AX           ;GET A ZERO IN AX
         PUSH    AX              ;SAVE ZERO ON STACK, TOO
         MOV     AX,MYDATA       ;GET DATA LOCATION IN AX
         MOV     DS,AX           ;PUT IT IN DS REGISTER
         MOV     ES,AX           ;    "      ES    "

;ROUTINE TO SCAN THE STRING (GROUP1) FOR A CHARACTER
         CLD                     ;SET SCAN DIRECTION LEFT TO RIGHT
         LEA     DI,GROUP1       ;SOURCE OF STRING INFO
         MOV     CX,46           ;MOVE 46 BYTES (LETTERS)
         MOV     AL,'X'          ;SCAN STRING FOR THE LETTER 'X'
REPNE    SCASB                   ;REPEAT SCAN UNLESS AN 'X' IS FOUND
         JCXZ    NONE            ;JUMP TO NONE IF 'X' NOT FOUND
         LEA     DX,MESS1        ;IF FOUND, GET 'FOUND' MESSAGE
         JMP     PRINTIT         ;AND PRINT IT
NONE:    LEA     DX,MESS2        ;IF NOT FOUND, GET 'NOT FOUND' MESSG.

;ROUTINE TO PRINT THE APPROPRIATE STRING TO THE SCREEN
PRINTIT:
         MOV     AH,09           ;DOS PARAMETER
         INT     21H             ;DOS INTERRUPT

         RET                     ;RETURN CONTROL TO DOS
MYPROC   ENDP                    ;END PROCEDURE NAMED MYPROC
MYCODE   ENDS                    ;END CODE SEGMENT NAMED MYCODE

         END                     ;END WHOLE PROGRAM
```

The data segment contains three strings. GROUP1 is a string that will be searched for the occurrence of a particular character. MESS1 and MESS2 report the results to the screen.

```
GROUP1   DB     'FOR IN MUCH WISDOM IS MUCH GRIEF...
                ECCL 1:18'
MESS1    DB     'THE LETTER WAS FOUND IN THE STRING$'
MESS2    DB     'THE LETTER WAS NOT FOUND IN THE
                STRING$'
```

When using the string commands, it is necessary to identify the source and destination of the string information. In small programs such as this one, all data is contained in one segment. The DS and ES registers are both set to the proper segment location. The program code for the actual scan is shown here.

```
CLD                       ;SET SCAN DIRECTION LEFT TO
                          ;RIGHT
LEA     DI,GROUP1         ;SOURCE OF STRING INFO
MOV     CX,46             ;SCAN 46 BYTES (LETTERS)
```

```
                MOV     AL,'X'          ;SCAN STRING FOR THE LETTER
                                        ;'X'
        REPNE   SCASB                   ;REPEAT SCAN UNLESS AN 'X' IS
                                        ;FOUND
                JCXZ    NONE            ;JUMP TO NONE IF 'X' NOT
                                        ;FOUND
                LEA     DX,MESS1        ;IF FOUND, GET 'FOUND'
                                        ;MESSAGE
                JMP     PRINTIT         ;AND PRINT IT
        NONE:   LEA     DX,MESS2        ;IF NOT FOUND, GET 'NOT
                                        ;FOUND' MESSG.
```

CLD sets the direction of the scan from left to right. The location of the string to be scanned is placed in the DI register, and the character to be scanned for is loaded into the AL register. The power and speed of this routine is contained in the REPNE SCASB command. This tells the processor to continue the scan (up to 46 times), unless the character is found. If the character is not found, CX will have been decremented to 0, and JCXZ will print MESS2 to the screen. If the character is found, MESS1 is printed to the screen. This type of scan is used to form the foundation of a spelling checker, as presented in Chapter 8.

USING ADVANCED STRING COMMANDS: MOVING STRINGS WITHIN A SEGMENT

Another string operation is shown in the following listing.

```
;FOR IBM 8088/80286 MACHINES
;PROGRAM TO ILLUSTRATE ADVANCED STRING COMMANDS
STACK     SEGMENT PARA STACK
          DB      64 DUP ('MYSTACK ')
STACK     ENDS

MYDATA    SEGMENT PARA 'DATA'
GROUP1    DB      'FOR IN MUCH WISDOM IS MUCH GRIEF...  ECCL 1:18'
GROUP2    DB      46 DUP (?),'$'
MYDATA    ENDS

MYCODE    SEGMENT PARA 'CODE'        ;DEFINE CODE SEG. FOR MASM
MYPROC    PROC    FAR                ;PROCEDURE IS NAMED MYPROC
          ASSUME  CS:MYCODE,DS:MYDATA,ES:MYDATA,SS:STACK
          PUSH    DS                 ;SAVE LOCATION OF DS REG.
          SUB     AX,AX              ;GET A ZERO IN AX
          PUSH    AX                 ;SAVE ZERO ON STACK, TOO
          MOV     AX,MYDATA          ;GET DATA LOCATION IN AX
```

```
          MOV      DS,AX           ;PUT IT IN DS REGISTER
          MOV      ES,AX           ;    "      ES     "
;ROUTINE TO MOVE GROUP1 STRING TO GROUP2 LOCATION
          LEA      SI,GROUP1       ;SOURCE OF STRING INFO
          LEA      DI,GROUP2       ;DESTINATION OF STRING INFO
          MOV      CX,46           ;MOVE 46 BYTES (LETTERS)
REP       MOVSB                    ;MOV'EM (ALL WORK DONE HERE)

;ROUTINE TO PRINT GROUP2 STRING TO THE SCREEN
          LEA      DX,GROUP2       ;DOS ROUTINE FOR STRING OUTPUT
          MOV      AH,09           ;DOS PARAMETER
          INT      21H             ;DOS INTERRUPT

          RET                      ;RETURN CONTROL TO DOS
MYPROC    ENDP                     ;END PROCEDURE NAMED MYPROC
MYCODE    ENDS                     ;END CODE SEGMENT NAMED MYCODE

          END                      ;END WHOLE PROGRAM
```

This program simply copies a string from one variable to another. This can be accomplished very rapidly with the **REP MOVSB** command, as shown in the following program segment:

```
          LEA      SI,GROUP1       ;SOURCE OF STRING INFO
          LEA      DI,GROUP2       ;DESTINATION OF STRING INFO
          MOV      CX,46           ;MOVE 46 BYTES (LETTERS)
REP       MOVSB                    ;MOV'EM (ALL WORK DONE HERE)
```

The source for the string information (address) is placed in the SI register, and the destination (address) is placed in the DI register. CX is set to move 46 bytes of information when REP MOVSB is called. Once again, the program executes very rapidly. All transfer information is preset in the first three lines of the program segment shown here. All transfer takes place when the **REP MOVSB** instruction is executed.

6

USING ASSEMBLER PSEUDO-OPS

Pseudo-operations are an important part of assembly language programming. A *pseudo-op* is a directive to the assembler to perform a specific operation. Thus, a pseudo-op can be considered an assembly *command* or *operand* rather than an assembly instruction that will be translated to machine code. As a matter of fact, pseudo-ops do not produce an equivalent machine code; they are used only at the time of assembly by the assembler. This fact makes pseudo-ops more assembler dependent than chip dependent.

Previous chapters have discussed the fact that assembly language is very microprocessor dependent. It was no accident that Intel chose to make its microprocessors upwardly compatible. Thus, programs written for an IBM PC (8088) also run on an IBM AT (80286). Because the 80286 instruction set is larger and more powerful than its earlier counterpart, however, the reverse is not always true.

Intel has had a similar effect in the assembly language field. Thus, Intel ASM286 and ASM386 assemblers can assemble code written for the 8088/80386 processors, and upward compatability is achieved with assemblers. All other 8088/80386 assemblers use a subset of Intel's ASM assembler language, which often provides a more workable package for the programmer.

The Microsoft Assembler and the IBM Assembler are almost identical products — after all, they were both written by Microsoft. Both of these products have dominated the 8088/8086 small-computer assembler market in recent years. If any product is to compete with one of these two giants, it will have to be very similar. The only other small-system assembler for the 80286 family that warrants mentioning at this time is TURBO EDITASM from Speedware. TURBO EDITASM supports many of the pseudo-ops created by Microsoft for the Microsoft and IBM products. Thus, there is also a certain amount of product compatibility, even among different software producers. This makes it very easy to switch between assembler products and still understand the program code.

The programs in Chapter 5 were written with a minimum number of pseudo-ops. This allowed a concentrated emphasis on microprocessor opcodes. This chapter concentrates on the pseudo-ops that are popular in the IBM, Microsoft, and Speedware assemblers and offers programming examples of where these pseudo-ops can be effectively used. Pseudo-ops will be used frequently in the remaining chapters of this book, because they make assembly language programming more robust.

PSEUDO-OPERATIONS

Pseudo-ops, just like assembler mnemonics, can be divided into many categories. In this book, pseudo-ops are divided into five categories: conditional, data, listing, macro, and mode. The remainder of this chapter discusses the psuedo-ops in each of these categories. The psuedo-ops are discussed in numeric and alphabetical order.

.186   (Specifies 80186 mode)

Assemblers: Microsoft, Speedware

Description: Enables the assembly of 80186 instructions.

Format: .186 (no operands)

Comments: This instruction can be cancelled with an .8086 pseudo-op. The .186 pseudo-op allows the assembly of all 8086 and 80186 instructions not in protected mode.

Example of use within a program nugget:

```
;PROGRAM WILL RUN ON 80186 MACHINES AND ASSEMBLE INSTRUCTIONS

.186

STACK           SEGMENT PARA STACK
                DB        64 DUP ('MYSTACK')
STACK           ENDS
```

(Remainder of program is placed here.)

.286C   (Specifies 80286 mode)

Assemblers: IBM, Microsoft, and Speedware

Description: The .286C pseudo-op is required by the assemblers to assemble 80286 instructions.

Format: .286C (no operands)

Comment: The 80286 mode, set by .286C, can be terminated with an .8086 pseudo-op. The .286C mode assembles all 8086 and 80286 instructions not in protected mode.

Example of use within a program nugget:

```
;PROGRAM TO ILLUSTRATE THE USE OF A LOOKUP TABLE TO FIND LOGS

.286C

STACK           SEGMENT PARA STACK
DB              64 DUP ('MYSTACK')
STACK           ENDS
```

(Remainder of program is placed here.)

.286P   (Specifies 80286 protect mode)

Assemblers: Microsoft

Description: The .286P pseudo-op is required to assemble 80286 protected mode instructions.

Format: .286P (no operands)

Comment: The 80286 protected mode, set by .286P, can be terminated with a .8086 pseudo-op. The .286P will also assemble all 8086 and 80286 instructions not in protected mode.

Example of use within a program nugget:

```
;PROGRAM TO ILLUSTRATE THE USE OF A LOOKUP TABLE TO FINDS LOGS

.286P

STACK          SEGMENT PARA STACK
               DB          64 DUP ('MYSTACK')
STACK          ENDS
```

(Most of program is placed here.)

```
    CLTS           ;CLEAR TASK SWITCHED FLAGS
```

(Remainder of program placed here.)

.287 (Specifies 80287 mode)

Assemblers: Microsoft

Description: The .287 pseudo-op allows the Microsoft Assembler to assemble additional 80287 instructions.

Format: .287 (no operands)

Comments: The .287 pseudo-op allows the assembly of all 8087 instructions, plus the following:

```
FSETPM                       ;SET PROTECTED MODE
FSTSW          AX            ;STORE STATUS WORD IN AX (WAIT)
FNSTSW         AX            ;STORE STATUS WORD IN AX (NO WAIT)
```

Example of use within a program nugget:

```
;PROGRAM TO SUBTRACT SEVERAL NUMBERS TOGETHER

;SET 80287 MODE

.287

STACK          SEGMENT PARA STACK
DB             64 DUP ('MYSTACK')
STACK          ENDS
```

(Most of program is placed here.)

.8086 (Specifies 8088/8086 mode)

Assemblers: IBM, Microsoft, and Speedware

Description: Essentially, the three assemblers operate in 8088/8086 mode by default. The .8086 pseudo-op is used to reset to a previous mode; for example, .286C.

Format: .8086 (no operands)

Comment: When assemblers operate in this mode, they do not assemble 80286 instructions.

Example of use within a program nugget:

```
;PROGRAM TO ADD SEVERAL NUMBERS TOGETHER

;SET 80286 MODE

.286C

STACK          SEGMENT PARA STACK
               DB        64 DUP ('MYSTACK')
STACK          ENDS
```

(Most of program is placed here.)

```
;RESET BACK TO 8086 MODE
.8086
```

(Remainder of program is placed here.)

.8087   (Specifies 8087/80287 mode)

Assemblers: IBM, Microsoft, and Speedware

Description: The .8087 pseudo-op allows each assembler to assemble 8087/80287 instructions and data.

Format: .8087 (no operands)

Comments: This command has the same effect on the assembler as the /R parameter does when either the IBM or Microsoft assembler is called.

Example of use within a program nugget:

```
;PROGRAM TO ADD REAL NUMBERS

.8087

MYDATA         SEGMENT PARA 'DATA'
NUMBER1        DQ                7123.45678912345      ;REAL NUMBER
NUMBER2        DQ                10.102                ;REAL NUMBER
```

```
THESUM       DQ               ?                    ;REAL ANSWER
MYDATA       ENDS
```

(Remainder of program is placed here.)

&   (& macro operator)

Assemblers: IBM

Description: The and (&) pseudo-op is used in a macro expansion to concatenate text and symbols.

Format: *(text — or — symbol)&(text — or — symbol)*

Comments: A dummy variable or parameter that is in a string or is not preceded by a delimiter must be preceded by & for it to be substituted in the macro expansion.

Example of use within a program nugget:

```
MYLUCK       MACRO        GUESS                  ;PROGRAM MACRO
REP&T:       MOV          DX,01234H
             MOV          AX,'&T'
             ENDM
```

(Most of program is placed here.)

```
             MYLUCK       G                      ;CALL TO MACRO
```

(This code is generated.)

```
REPG:        MOV          DX,01234H
             MOV          AX,'G'
```

=   (= pseudo-op)

Assemblers: IBM, Microsoft, and Speedware

Description: The equal (=) pseudo-op allows definition and redefinition of program constants.

Format: *(label)=(value)*

Comments: The = psuedo-op is limited to numeric expressions. Otherwise, it is very similar to the EQU pseudo-op.

Examples:

VAR1	=	1234H	;CAN BE REDEFINED
VAR2	=	56H	; "
VAR1	=	78H	; "
VAR3	EQU	3456	;CANNOT BE REDEFINED

!

(! macro operator)

Assemblers: IBM

Description: When an exclamation point (!) precedes a character, the literal entry of the character is permitted.

Format: !*(character)*

Comments: !*(character)* is equivalent to <*character*>.

Examples: !* , !@ , !^

%

(% macro operator)

Assemblers: IBM

Description: The symbol following the percent sign (%) is converted to a number in the default number base (radix). During macro expansion, this number replaces the dummy variable.

Format: %*(symbol)*

Comments: The % pseudo-op can only be used in a macro.

Example of use within a program nugget:

```
MYLUCK    MACRO  V
T         =      V−2
          MOV    AX,%T    ;;PUT ANSWER IN AX
          ENDM
```

%OUT

(%OUT pseudo-op)

Assemblers: IBM, Microsoft, and Speedware

Description: The %OUT pseudo-op can be used to display a message to the console as it is encountered during assembly of a program. Typically, %OUT is used to indicate the progress of the assembly.

Format: %OUT(*message*)

Comments: None

Example:
```
%OUT      STARTING ASSEMBLY
```
(Part of program is placed here.)
```
%OUT      BE PATIENT, STILL ASSEMBLING
```
(Remainder of program is placed here.)
```
%OUT      ASSEMBLY COMPLETED
```

;; (;; macro operator)

Assemblers: IBM

Description: When two semicolons (;;) are used before a comment, that comment will not be included in the macro expansion.

Format: ;;(*comment _ string*)

Comments: The use of two semicolons (;;) saves significant memory space in a program when a macro is expanded frequently.

Example of use within a program nugget:
```
MYLUCK      MACRO      GUESS        ;;PROGRAM MACRO
REP&T:      MOV        DX,01234H    ;;LOCATION MOVED
            MOV        AX,'&T'
            ENDM                    ;;END MACRO
```

ASSUME (ASSUME pseudo-op)

Assemblers: IBM, Microsoft, and Speedware

Description: This pseudo-op is directive to the assembler to match a segment with a segment register. ASSUME NOTHING cancels a previous directive.

Format: ASSUME(*segment _ register:segment _ name*)

Comments: CS, DS, ES, and SS are valid segment registers

Example of use within a program nugget:
```
MYCODE      SEGMENT PARA 'CODE'      ;DEFINE CODE SEG. FOR MASM
MYPROC      PROC    FAR              ;PROCEDURE IS NAMED MYPROC
```

```
ASSUME      CS:MYCODE,DS:MYDATA,SS:STACK
PUSH        DS              ;SAVE LOCATION OF DS REG.
SUB         AX,AX           ;GET A ZERO IN AX
PUSH        AX              ;SAVE ZERO ON STACK, TOO
```

COMMENT   (COMMENT pseudo-op)

Assemblers: IBM, Microsoft, and Speedware

Description: This pseudo-op allows commenting a program without semicolons. It is especially useful for multiline comments.

Format: COMMENT(*delimiter*)*text*(*delimiter*)

Comment: The delimiters are the programmer's choice. The length of the comment is not limited.

Example: COMMENT   @The text fits between two like delimiters@

.CREF (.XCREF)   (.CREF pseudo-op)

Assemblers: IBM, Microsoft, and Speedware

Description: .CREF is the default condition that allows cross-reference output when the cross-reference utility is called. .XCREF can be used to toggle the output to off.

Format: .CREF (no operands)

Comments: .XCREF can use an optional operand to prevent named variables from appearing in the cross-reference output.

Example of use within a program nugget:

```
MYDATA      SEGMENT      PARA 'DATA'
INFO        DB           1,2,3,4,5,6,7,8,9,10,11,12,13,14,15
ANS         DB           ?
MYDATA      ENDS
.XCREF ANS
MYCODE      SEGMENT      PARA 'CODE'   ;DEFINE CODE SEG. FOR MASM
```

(Remainder of program is placed here)

DB   (Define Byte pseudo-op)

Assemblers: IBM, Microsoft, and Speedware

Description: Define Byte is used to define a variable or table to initialize a storage location. It sets aside byte-size (8-bit) memory allocations.

Format: (*variable*)DB(*expression*)

Comments: The variable name is optional. The expression can be a constant, a character string, or a table of constants separated by a comma. Two other possibilities are a question mark (?), which only allocates memory, and a duplicate (DUP) command, which produces multiple entries of a value. DB can contain hex numbers from 0 to 0FFH or decimal numbers from 0 to 255.

Examples:

HELLO	DB	23
THERE	DB	0AH
YOU	DB	'G'
LUCKY	DB	'BROOME COMMUNITY COLLEGE'
PERSON	DB	0,1,2,3,4,5,6,7,8,9
HOW	DB	45 DUP ('STACK')
ARE	DB	50 DUP (03CH)
YOU	DB	'YES',34,0FADH

DBIT

(Define Bit pseudo-op)

Assemblers: This pseudo-op is a special 80386 data type, available with the ASM386 assembler.

Description: Define Bit is used to define a single bit or a bit string. A string can have 1 to 32 binary digits and must terminate in a "B."

Format: (*variable*)DBIT(*expression*)

Comments: DBIT initializes a whole byte and usually aligns it on a byte boundary.

Examples:

I	DBIT	100B	;00000100 IN BYTE
AM	DBIT	1B	;00000001 IN BYTE
SMALL	DBIT	3 DUP (1B)	;THREE BYTES OF 00000001

DD

(Define Doubleword pseudo-op)

Assemblers: IBM, Microsoft, and Speedware

Description: Define Doubleword is used to define a variable or table or to initialize a storage location. It sets aside two-word (4-byte or 32-bit) memory allocations.

Format: *(variable)*DD*(expression)*

Comments: The variable name is optional. The expression can be a constant or a table of constants separated by a comma. Two other possibilities are a question mark (?), which only allocates memory, and a duplicate (DUP) command, which produces multiple entries of a value. DD can contain integer hex numbers from 0 to 0FFFFFFFFH or decimal numbers from 0 to 4294967295. If a decimal point or scientific notation is entered, a floating-point number will be generated.

Examples:

HELLO	DD	0FFFFFFFFH
THERE	DD	0H
YOU	DD	1,22,333,4444,55555,666666,7777777,88888888
LUCKY	DD	45H+23H
PERSON	DD	2.17654
HOW	DD	4.567E12
ARE	DD	50 DUP (03CH)
YOU	DD	0.12345E−2

DP   (Define Pointer pseudo-op)

Assemblers: This pseudo-op is a special 80386 data type, available with the ASM386 assembler.

Description: Define Pointer is used to define a 48-bit variable of type PWORD. PWORDS must be of integer type. Constants, segment names, variables, and strings (up to six characters long) are acceptable.

Format: *(variable)*DP*(expression)*

Comments: None

Examples:

AA	DP	'ABCDEF'
BB	DP	?
CC	DP	3 DUP (0A76543H)

DQ   (Define Quadword pseudo-op)

Assemblers: IBM, Microsoft, and Speedware

Description: Define Quadword is used to define a variable, or table or to initialize a storage location. It sets aside four-word (8-byte or 64-bit) memory allocations.

Format: *(variable)*DQ*(expression)*

Comments: The variable name is optional. The expression can be a constant or a table of constants separated by a comma. Two other possibilities are a question mark (?), which only allocates memory, and a duplicate (DUP) command, which produces multiple entries of a value. DQ can contain integer hex numbers from 0 to 0FFFFFFFFFFFFFFFFH or decimal numbers from 0 to 18446744073709551615. If a decimal point or scientific notation is entered, a floating-point number will be generated.

Examples:

THIS	DQ	100,2000,30000,400000,5000000,60000000
	DQ	700000000,8000000000,90000000000
IS	DQ	1000 DUP (45.678)
VERY	DQ	−6.345E−5,+5.0001E45
LARGE	DQ	7989H∗12H

DT
(Define Tenbytes pseudo-op)

Assemblers: IBM, Microsoft, and Speedware

Description: Define Tenbytes is used to define a variable, table or initialize a storage location. It sets aside ten bytes (80 bits) of packed decimal memory allocation, for 80287/80387 numbers.

Format: (*variable*)DT(*expression*)

Comments: The variable name is optional. The expression can be a constant or a table of constants separated by a comma. Two other possibilities are a question mark (?), which only allocates memory, and a duplicate (DUP) command, which produces multiple entries of a value. DT can also contain packed decimal numbers from 0 to 9999999999. If a decimal point or scientific notation is entered, a floating-point number will be generated.

Examples:

THIS	DT	100,2000,30000,400000,5000000,60000000
	DT	700000000
IS	DT	1000 DUP (45.678)
VERY	DT	−6.345E−5,+5.0001E45
LARGE	DT	7989∗12

DW
(Define Word pseudo-op)

Assemblers: IBM, Microsoft, and Speedware

Description: Define Word is used to define a variable or table or to initialize a storage location. It sets aside two-byte (8-bit) memory allocations.

Format: (*variable*)DW(*expression*)

Comments: The variable name is optional. The expression can be a constant or a table of constants separated by a comma. Two other possibilities are a question mark (?), which only allocates memory, and a duplicate (DUP) command, which produces multiple entries of a value. DW can contain hex numbers from 0 to 0FFFFH or decimal numbers from 0 to 65535.

Examples:

TEST1	DW	1234
TEST2	DW	0ABCDH
TEST3	DW	1,22,333,4444
TEST4	DW	23–12
TEST5	DW	23 DUP (100H)
TEST6	DW	50 DUP (?)

ELSE

(ELSE conditional pseudo-op)

Assemblers: IBM, Microsoft, and Speedware

Description: The ELSE pseudo-op allows an alternate operation when it is used in conjunction with any other conditional pseudo-op.

Format: ELSE (no operands)

Comments: Each ELSE must be proceeded by IFxx. These can be nested, and there is no limit on the number of nesting levels.

Example:

```
IFNDEF LIB              ;TRUE IF LIB IS NOT DEFINED
INCLUDE B:MACLIB.MAC    ;THEN LOAD THIS FILE
ELSE                    ;OTHERWISE
INCLUDE B:NEWMAC.LIB    ;LOAD THIS FILE IS LIB
ENDIF                   ;END IFxx
```

END

(END pseudo-op)

Assemblers: IBM, Microsoft, and Speedware

Description: The END pseudo-op is required at the end of a source program. If END uses an optional expression, that expression points to the entry point of the code.

Format: END(*optional_expression*)

Comments: If multiple object modules are to be linked, only one can have an optional expression pointing to the DOS entry point. If no entry point is given, the Linker will identify one on the first object module to be linked.

Example of use within a program nugget:

(All of program precedes this point.)

```
                  RET                        ;RETURN CONTROL TO DOS
       MYPROC     ENDP                       ;END PROCEDURE NAMED MYPROC
       MYCODE     ENDS                       ;END CODE SEGMENT NAMED MYCODE
                  END          MYPROG        ;END WHOLE PROGRAM
```

ENDIF   (ENDIF conditional pseudo-op)

Assemblers: IBM, Microsoft, and Speedware

Description: The ENDIF conditional pseudo-op is used to match each IFxx conditional pseudo-op.

Format: ENDIF (no operands)

Comments: None

Example:
```
       IFNDEF LIB                   ;TRUE IF LIB IS NOT DEFINED
       INCLUDE B:MACLIB.MAC         ;THEN LOAD THIS FILE
       ELSE                         ;OTHERWISE
       INCLUDE B:NEWMAC.LIB         ;LOAD THIS FILE IS LIB
       ENDIF                        ;END IFxx
```

ENDM   (ENDM macro pseudo-op)

Assemblers: IBM, Microsoft, and Speedware

Description: The ENDM pseudo-op is required to terminate each MACRO, REPT, IRP, and IRPC pseudo-op.

Format: ENDM (no operands)

Comment: No name field is associated with this pseudo-op.

Example:
```
       CLEARSCREEN MACRO            ;CLEARS CURRENT SCREEN
       MOV         CX,0
       MOV         DX,2479H
       MOV         BH,7
       MOV         AX,0600H
       INT         10H
       ENDM
```

ENDP   (ENDP pseudo-op)

Assemblers: IBM, Microsoft, and Speedware

Description: The ENDP pseudo-op is required to terminate each procedure.

Format: (*name—of—procedure*)ENDP

Comments: The name field is required.

Example of use within a program nugget:

(All of program precedes this point.)

```
            RET                 ;RETURN CONTROL TO DOS
MYPROC      ENDP                ;END PROCEDURE NAMED MYPROC
MYCODE      ENDS                ;END CODE SEGMENT NAMED MYCODE
            END     MYPROG      ;END WHOLE PROGRAM
```

ENDS   (ENDS pseudo-op)

Assemblers: IBM, Microsoft, and Speedware

Description: The ENDS pseudo-op is required to terminate each SEG-MENT and STRUC.

Format: (*name _ of _ segment _ or _ structure*)ENDS

Comment: The name of the segment or structure is required.

Example: (All of program precedes this point.)

```
            RET                 ;RETURN CONTROL TO DOS
MYPROC      ENDP                ;END PROCEDURE NAMED MYPROC
MYCODE      ENDS                ;END CODE SEGMENT NAMED MYCODE
            END     MYPROG      ;END WHOLE PROGRAM
```

EQU   (EQU pseudo-op)

Assemblers: IBM, Microsoft, and Speedware

Description: The EQU pseudo-op sets a variable to a specific value.

Format: (*variable*)EQU(*value*)

Comment: The EQU pseudo-op, unlike the equal (=) pseudo-op, does not allow redefinition of the variable. EQU cannot be used with the STRUC definition.

Examples:
```
VALUE1      EQU     1234H       ;UP TO 16 BITS
VALUE2      EQU     4.56E5      ;FLOATING POINT
VALUE3      EQU     [SI+6]      ;INDEX
VALUE4      EQU     DAA         ;INSTRUCTION
```

EVEN   (EVEN pseudo-op)

Assemblers: IBM, Microsoft, and Speedware

Description: The EVEN pseudo-op sets the program counter to an even (word) boundary for data alignment.

Format: EVEN (no operands)

Comments: EVEN does nothing if the program counter is at an even boundary. If it is not, EVEN will add a NOP to move the counter to an even boundary.

Example: If the program counter points to 0023H, EVEN causes it to point to 0024H.

If the program counter points to 004AH, EVEN does not change it; it still points to 004AH.

EXITM   (EXITM pseudo-op)

Assemblers: IBM, Microsoft, and Speedware

Description: The EXITM pseudo-op provides an exit from a repetition or macro based upon the results of a pseudo-op test for a particular condition. EXITM can be used with REPT, IRP, IRPC, and MACRO.

Format: EXITM (no operands)

Comments: Nesting of blocks is permitted. EXITM ends only the block in which it is contained.

Example: (Additional code precedes this point.)

```
IFE        VALUE-34H          ;TRUE IF VALUE = 34H
EXITM                         ;EXIT IF TRUE
ELSE                          ;OTHERWISE
INCLUDE B:NEWMAC.LIB          ;LOAD THIS FILE
ENDIF                         ;END IFxx
ENDM
```

EXTRN   (EXTRN pseudo-op)

Assemblers: IBM, Microsoft, and Speedware

Description: The EXTRN pseudo-op identifies symbols or variables used in the current program module whose attributes are defined in another program module.

Format: EXTRN(*name:type*)

Comments: The symbol or variable is declared EXTRN in the current program module. The symbol or variable is declared PUBLIC in the other program module. EXTRN can be placed within the segment containing the program module or outside all segments. The entry type can be BYTE, WORD, DWORD, QWORD, TBYTE, NEAR, FAR, or ABS.

Example of use within a program nugget:

```
MYCODE    SEGMENT PARA 'CODE'              ;DEFINE CODE SEG. FOR MASM
          PUBLIC   VALUE1,VALUE2,ANSWER
MYPROC    PROC     FAR                     ;PROCEDURE IS NAMED MYPROC
          ASSUME   CS:MYCODE,SS:STACK
          PUSH     DS                      ;SAVE LOCATION OF DS REG.
          SUB      AX,AX                   ;GET A ZERO IN AX
          PUSH     AX                      ;SAVE ZERO ON STACK, TOO
```

(Remainder of program is placed here.)

(Another segment:)

```
          EXTRN VALUE1,VALUE2,ANSWER
NUCODE    SEGMENT PARA 'CODE'              ;DEFINE CODE SEG. FOR MASM
```

(Remainder of program is placed here.)

GROUP   (GROUP pseudo-op)

Assemblers: IBM, Microsoft, and Speedware

Description: The GROUP pseudo-op organizes, into one actual 64K segment, all segments identified by one name.

Format: *(name)*GROUP*(name__of__segment)*

Comments: The *name* operand is the identifier under which all segments are to be grouped. This identifier must be unique among all segment labels. The *name__of__segment* operand can be assigned by the SEGMENT pseudo-op or by a SEG variable or label operator.

Example:

```
          MEGA     GROUP                   SMALL1,SMALL2
          SMALL1   SEGMENT                 PARA 'CODE'
                   ASSUME                  CS:MEGA
```

(All code for this segment is placed here.)

```
          SMALL1   ENDS

          SMALL2   SEGMENT                 PARA 'CODE'
                   ASSUME                  CS:MEGA
```

(All code for this segment is placed here.)

```
          SMALL2   ENDS
```

IF, IFE, IF1, IF2, IFDEF, IFNDEF   (IFxxxx conditional pseudo-op)
IFB, IFNB, IFIDN, IFDIF

Assemblers: IBM, Microsoft, and Speedware

Description: A conditional IFxxxx pseudo-op checks for a specified condition before a particular operation is performed. When it is used in conjunction with the ELSE pseudo-op, alternate actions can also be specified.

Format: IFxxxx(*operand*)
            (*additional__code*)
            ENDIF

Comments: All conditional IFxxxx pseudo-ops can be nested to any level. All operands of IFxxxx must be known on pass 1 for each assembler.

Examples:

IF VAR1	;TRUE IF VAR1 IS NOT 0
IFE VAR1	;TRUE IF VAR1 IS 0
IF1 (no operand)	;TRUE IF PASS 1 OF ASSEMBLER
IF2 (no operand)	;TRUE IF PASS 2 OF ASSEMBLER
IFDEF NEWVAL	;TRUE IF A DEFINED SYMBOL OR VARIABLE
IFNDEF OLDVAL	;TRUE IF AN UNDEFINED SYMBOL OR VARIABLE
IFB <OPERAND>	;TRUE IF <operand> IS BLANK
IFNB <OPERAND>	;TRUE IF <operand> IS NOT BLANK
IFIDN <OPERAND1>, <OPERAND2>	;TRUE IF <operand1> IS IDENTICAL TO <operand2>
IFDIF <OPERAND1>, <OPERAND2>	;TRUE IF <operand1> IS NOT IDENTICAL TO <operand2>

INCLUDE   (INCLUDE pseudo-op)

Assemblers: IBM, Microsoft, and Speedware

Description: The INCLUDE pseudo-op couples unassembled source code from another file into the current code.

Format: INCLUDE(*drive/path/filename.ext*)

Comments: This pseudo-op is particularly useful in loading collections (or libraries) of MACROs. The unassembled code is loaded immediately after the INCLUDE pseudo-op. Nesting is permissible, but for DOS 2.0 and later implementations, FILES in the CONFIG.SYS file should be set higher than the default value, 8. If the assembled file is listed, all code from INCLUDE is listed with a "C" in column 30 for easy identification and location of expansions.

Example:
```
IF1
INCLUDE B:MACLIB.MAC
INCLUDE C:REGDIS.MAC
ENDIF
```

IRP   (IRP pseudo-op)

Assemblers: IBM, Microsoft, and Speedware

Description: The IRP pseudo-op is use to repeat the operations between IRP and ENDM. The number of repeats is controlled by the number of operands in *list — of — operands*. For each repeat, the current item in the operand list will be substituted for each *dummy* operand in the block of code.

Format: IRP(*dummy*),<*list — of — operands*>

Comments: The operand list is required. If null (<>) is specified, then the block of code is repeated once.

Example:

```
IRP     VAL,<2,4,6,8>    ;OPERAND LIST OF NUMBERS 2, 4, 6, 8
DW      VAL              ;NEW NUMBER SUB. FOR VAL
ENDM                     ;END BLOCK OF CODE
```

IRPC   (IRPC pseudo-op)

Assemblers: IBM, Microsoft, and Speedware

Description: The IRPC pseudo-op is used to repeat the operations between IRPC and ENDM. The number of repeats is controlled by the number of characters in the *string* operand. For each repeat, the current character in the string will be substituted for each *dummy* operand in the block of code.

Format: IRPC(*dummy*),*string*

Comments: Angle brackets around string are optional.

Example:

```
IRPC    DATA,2468    ;STRING OF CHARACTERS 2, 4, 6, 8
DB      DATA         ;NEW NUMBER ON EACH PASS
DB      DATA*2       ;NEW NUMBER × 2 ON EACH PASS
ENDM                 ;END BLOCK OF CODE
```

LABEL   (LABEL pseudo-op)

Assemblers: IBM, Microsoft, and Speedware

Description: The LABEL pseudo-op permits definition of the attributes of a label name.

Format: (*name*)LABEL(*type*)

Comments: The *name* operand can specify any valid name. The *type* operand can specify any of the following: BYTE, WORD, DWORD, QWORD, or TBYTE.

Example:

```
MYTABLE       LABEL       BYTE
TABLE         DW          1234,5678,1111,4545,6778,4598
(Code is inserted here.)
              MOV         CL,MYTABLE[4]    ;MOVE 11 INTO CL
```

.LALL, .SALL, .XALL   (._ALL listing pseudo-op)

Assemblers: IBM, Microsoft, and Speedware

Description: The pseudo-op controls the listing of program text.

Format: .LALL (no operands)

Comments: .LALL lists the expansions of all MACROS and conditional blocks (if it is used with .TFCOND, .LFCOND, .SFCOND). .SALL cancels the listings of all expanded MACROS. .XALL (the default) lists only the source code that generates actual object code.

Example of use within a program nugget:

```
            .SALL
MYCODE      SEGMENT     PARA 'CODE'          ;DEFINE CODE SEG. FOR MASM
MYPROC      PROC        FAR                  ;PROCEDURE IS NAMED MYPROC
            ASSUME      CS:MYCODE,DS: MYDATA,SS:STACK
            PUSH        DS                   ;SAVE LOCATION OF DS REG.
            SUB         AX,AX                ;GET A ZERO IN AX
            PUSH        AX                   ;SAVE ZERO ON STACK, TOO
```

.LFCOND   (.LFCOND listing pseudo-op)

Assemblers: IBM, Microsoft, and Speedware

Description: The .LFCOND pseudo-op permits the listing of any conditional blocks of code that evaluate as false.

Format: .LFCOND (no operands)

Comments: This condition can be terminated by either .SFCOND or .TFCOND.

Example of use within a program nugget:

```
            .LFCOND
MYCODE      SEGMENT     PARA 'CODE'          ;DEFINE CODE SEG. FOR MASM
MYPROC      PROC        FAR                  ;PROCEDURE IS NAMED MYPROC
            ASSUME      CS:MYCODE, DS:MYDATA,SS:STACK
```

```
        PUSH     DS                        ;SAVE LOCATION OF DS REG.
        SUB      .AX,AX                    ;GET A ZERO IN AX
        PUSH     AX                        ;SAVE ZERO ON STACK, TOO
```

.LIST, .XLIST   (.LIST, .XLIST listing pseudo-ops)

Assemblers: IBM, Microsoft, and Speedware

Description: .LIST and .XLIST are used to control the output to the listing file.

Format: .LIST (no operands)

Comments: .LIST, the default condition, permits a source and object code listing. .XLIST halts the listing

Example of use within a program nugget:

```
            .XLIST
MYCODE      SEGMENT  PARA 'CODE'              ;DEFINE CODE SEG. FOR MASM
MYPROC      PROC     FAR                      ;PROCEDURE IS NAMED MYPROC
            ASSUME   CS:MYCODE,DS:MYDATA,SS:STACK
            PUSH     DS                       ;SAVE LOCATION OF DS REG.
            SUB      AX,AX                    ;GET A ZERO IN AX
            PUSH     AX                       ;SAVE ZERO ON STACK, TOO
```

LOCAL   (LOCAL macro pseudo-op)

Assemblers: IBM, Microsoft, and Speedware

Description: When LOCAL is used, a unique symbol replaces each occurrence of a label within a macro. This permits use of macro expansion more than once in a given segment.

Format: LOCAL(*dummy__list*)

Comments: The LOCAL pseudo-op must be the first statement in a macro. Multiple LOCAL statements are permitted.

Example of use within a macro:

```
DELAY       MACRO                         ;;CREATES A SOFTWARE DELAY
            LOCAL P1,P2                   ;;DECLARES P1 & P2 LOCAL
            MOV      DX,15H               ;;ABOUT 5 SECOND DELAY ON PC & XT
P1:         MOV      CX,0FF00H            ;;LOAD WITH (DECIMAL 65280)
P2:         DEC      CX                   ;;DECREMENT BY ONE
```

```
        JNZ    P2              ;;IS IT ZERO? IF NOT, P2
        DEC    DX              ;;DECREMENT DX
        JNZ    P1              ;;IS IT ZERO? IF NOT, P1
        ENDM
```

MACRO   (MACRO pseudo-op)

Assemblers: IBM, Microsoft, and Speedware

Description: The MACRO pseudo-op, somewhat like a subroutine, allows a single block of code to be called numerous times within a program. MACRO allows different parameters to be used each time the block is called.

Format: *(name—of—macro)*MACRO*(dummy—list)*

Comments: A macro consists of three essential parts: the header, which contains the name of the macro, the MACRO pseudo-op, and an optional dummy list; the body, which contains the macro code; and the end, which consists simply of ENDM and terminates the MACRO pseudo-op. When macros are expanded in a listing, their code is preceded by + to indicate that an expansion has taken place. The position of the elements in the dummy list is important, since substitutions occur entry by entry in the macro code. If extra elements are included in the dummy list, these extra elements are ignored. If too few elements are included, null is substituted for each missing element.

Examples:

```
CLEARSCREEN MACRO           ;;CLEARS CURRENT SCREEN, NO VARIABLES

        MOV  CX,0
        MOV  DX,2479H
        MOV  BH,7
        MOV  AX,0600H
        INT    10H
        ENDM


PRINTCHAR MACRO TEXT        ;;PRINTS STRING PASSED IN "TEXT"

        MOV  DX,OFFSET TEXT ;;STRING IN DATA SEGMENT
        MOV  AH,9           ;;PRINTS UNTIL '$' TERMINATOR.
        INT    21H          ;;PRINTS FROM CURRENT CURSOR
        ENDM                ;;POSITION
```

.MSFLOAT

(.MSFLOAT pseudo-op)

Assemblers: Speedware

Description: All floating-point numbers are converted to Microsoft floating-point number format.

Format: .MSFLOAT (no operands)

Comments: .MSFLOAT can support single- or double-precision floating-point formats. Single-precision numbers occupy four bytes. The first 23 bits are the significand, and the last 8 bits are the exponent. Double-precision numbers occupy eight bytes. The first 55 bits are the significand, and the last 8 bits are the exponent. This yields 6 or 7 significant decimal digits for single-precision numbers and 16 significant decimal digits for double-precision numbers.

Example:

```
.MSFLOAT
          VALUE1    DD        1.234E−23
          VALUE2    DQ        67.65234987432E35
```

NAME

(NAME pseudo-op)

Assemblers: IBM, Microsoft, and Speedware

Description: NAME is used to name a module.

Format: NAME(name—of—module)

Comments: Every module is given a name by the assembler in the following order of preference: (1) NAME pseudo-op, (2) first six characters of a TITLE, or (3) first six characters of a source file name.

Example: NAME BEEPER

```
MYCODE    SEGMENT   PARA 'CODE'              ;DEFINE CODE SEG. FOR MASM
MYPROC    PROC      FAR                      ;PROCEDURE IS NAMED MYPROC
          ASSUME    CS:MYCODE, DS:MYDATA,SS:STACK
          PUSH      DS                       ;SAVE LOCATION OF DS REG.
          SUB       AX,AX                    ;GET A ZERO IN AX
          PUSH      AX                       ;SAVE ZERO ON STACK, TOO
```

ORG

(ORG pseudo-op)

Assemblers: IBM, Microsoft, and Speedware

Description: The ORG pseudo-op is used to set the location counter and thus the starting address of the code involved.

Format: ORG(*value__or__expression*)

Comments: The dollar sign ($) can be used as the current value of the location counter. An expression must be known on pass 1 and must evaluate to a 16-bit absolute number.

Examples:

```
ORG     100H
ORG     $
ORG     $ + 100H
```

PAGE   (PAGE pseudo-op)

Assemblers: IBM, Microsoft, and Speedware

Description: The PAGE pseudo-op, which is placed in the source file, sets the length and width of each listing page.

Format: PAGE(*option__1*)(*option__2*)

Comments: The PAGE pseudo-op without either option causes an advance to the top of the next page. The chapter number is incremented when PAGE + is encountered. Option 1 indicates the number of lines printed per page using a decimal number from 10 to 255. The default value is 58. (Option 2) controls the width of the page using a decimal number from 60 to 132. The default value is 80. (NOTE: The PAGE pseudo-op *does not* initialize the printer. This must be done separately.)

Examples:

```
PAGE              ;ADVANCE TO NEXT PAGE
PAGE ,132         ;CHANGE DEFAULT WIDTH TO 132
PAGE 20,132       ;PAGE LENGTH TO 20, WIDTH TO 132
```

PROC   (PROC pseudo-op)

Assemblers: IBM, Microsoft, and Speedware

Description: PROC identifies a block of source code. Typically, all programs have at least one PROC pseudo-op with the FAR attribute.

Format: (*name__of__procedure*)PROC(*type*)

Comments: A block of code identified as a PROC can be executed inline or called (if an external CALL is used, the PROC name must be PUBLIC). If PROC is the entry point of an .EXE file, or if CS has another value, the type must be FAR. The type can only be NEAR if PROC is called within the same segment. Depending upon the type, the RET will be an intersegment or intrasegment return.

Examples:

```
MYCODE    SEGMENT    PARA 'CODE'      ;DEFINE CODE SEG. FOR MASM
MYPROC    PROC       FAR              ;PROCEDURE IS NAMED MYPROC
          ASSUME     CS:MYCODE, DS:MYDATA, SS:STACK
          PUSH       DS               ;SAVE LOCATION OF DS REG.
          SUB        AX,AX            ;GET A ZERO IN AX
          PUSH       AX               ;SAVE ZERO ON STACK, TOO

          CALL       CURSOR           ;A CALL TO A NEAR PROCEDURE
   (Code continues here.)

CURSOR    PROC       NEAR             ;PROCEDURE WITHIN SAME SEGMENT
          MOV        BX,1             ;SET PARAMETERS
          MOV        AH,2
          INT        10H
          RET                         ;POP RETURN OFFSET FROM STACK
```

PUBLIC   (PUBLIC pseudo-op)

Assemblers: IBM, Microsoft, and Speedware

Description: The PUBLIC pseudo-op permits symbols in the source code to be used by other programs that are to be linked together. The information is passed to the Linker.

Format: PUBLIC(*number,variable — or — label*)

Comments: None

Example:

```
MYCODE    SEGMENT    PARA 'CODE'      ;DEFINE CODE SEG. FOR MASM
          PUBLIC     VALUE1, ANSWER,SUM
MYPROC    PROC       FAR              ;PROCEDURE IS NAMED MYPROC
          ASSUME     CS:MYCODE, DS:MYDATA, SS:STACK
          PUSH       DS               ;SAVE LOCATION OF DS REG.
          SUB        AX,AX            ;GET A ZERO IN AX
          PUSH       AX               ;SAVE ZERO ON STACK, TOO
```

PURGE (PURGE pseudo-op)

Assemblers: IBM and Microsoft

Description: The PURGE pseudo-op deletes the definition of a macro. The space previously occupied by the macro can then be reused.

Format: PURGE(*macro＿name(s)*)

Comments: A macro does not have to be purged before it is redefined.

Example: PURGE CLEARSCREEN

.RADIX (.RADIX pseudo-op)

Assemblers: IBM, Microsoft, and Speedware

Description: The .RADIX pseudo-op allows the radix (number base) to be changed to any value from 2 to 16. The default value is 10.

Format: .RADIX(*value＿specified＿in＿decimal＿format*)

Comments: .RADIX directly affects DB and DW. .RADIX does not affect DD, DQ, or DT. The following must use a suffix to ensure correct results; B-binary, D-decimal, Q or O-octal, H-hexadecimal, R-hexadecimal real.

Examples:

```
.RADIX    16
VALUE     DB     120        ;VALUE IS SET TO 120 HEXADECIMAL

.RADIX    2
NU        DB     10110011   ;NUM IS SET TO 10110011 BINARY

.RADIX    10
ANS       DB     120H       ;ANS IS SET TO 120H, OVERRIDING
                            ;DEFAULT 10 BY .RADIX
```

RECORD (RECORD pseudo-op)

Assemblers: IBM, Microsoft, and Speedware

Description: The RECORD pseudo-op creates a bit pattern to format bytes and words for bit packing. The name of the record becomes a pseudo-op for storage allocation.

Format: (*name＿of＿the＿record*)RECORD(*name＿of＿the＿field :width(=*exp*))

Comments: Both the name of the record and the name of the field are required by the RECORD pseudo-op. Width is a number from 1 to 16 and determines the number of bits defined by the name of the field. Fields are right-justified. The *exp* value contains the value of the default for the field.

Example:

```
MYRECD                    RECORD    H:1,E:2,L:3,P:6
(Yields)
HEEL LLPP PPPP
(Storage is allocated.)
STORE1                    MODULE    <1,2,3,4>
(H=1, E=2, L=3, and P=4)
```

REPT

(REPT pseudo-op)

Assemblers: IBM, Microsoft, and Speedware

Description: The REPT pseudo-op repeats the code between REPT and ENDM the specified number of times.

Format: REPT(*value—or—expression*)

Comments: The block of code does not have to be within a MACRO.

Example: (Other code precedes this code.)

```
VALUE      =        10            ;VALUE SET TO 10
           REPT     3             ;REPT SET TO THREE
           IFE      STORE—VALUE   ;IF STORE = VALUE
           EXITM                  ;EXIT, OTHERWISE REPEAT
           ENDIF                  ;END IF
           ENDM                   ;END REPEAT SECTION
```

SEGMENT

(SEGMENT pseudo-op)

Assemblers: IBM, Microsoft, and Speedware

Description: The SEGMENT pseudo-op is used to contain all code in a program. Typically, several segments are used within the same program.

Format: (*name—of—segment*)SEGMENT(*alignment—type*)(*combination—type*) (*class*)

Comments: The alignment type can be PAGE, PARA, WORD, or BYTE.

A PAGE type starts a segment on a page boundary—an address divisible by 256, in which the two LSBs of the address are equal to 00H. A PARA type starts a segment on a paragraph boundary—an address divisible by 16, in which the LSB of the address equals 0H. A WORD type starts on a word boundary—an even address, in which the LSB of the address is 0H. A BYTE type starts on a byte boundary—which is anywhere. The combination type can be PUBLIC, COMMON, AT(*expression*), STACK, or MEMORY (currently not supported). PUBLIC indicates that the segment will be joined with others when it is linked. COMMON indicates that this segment and others of the same name that are to be linked will begin at the same address. AT(*expression*) indicates that the segment will begin on the paragraph boundary specified by the expression; no code is generated for this segment. STACK specifies that the segment will be part of the run-time stack. STACK is required for .EXE files only.

Example of use within a program nugget:

```
STACK     SEGMENT    PARA STACK
          DB         64 DUP ('MYSTACK ')
STACK     ENDS

MYDATA    SEGMENT    PARA 'DATA'
INFO      DB         1,2,3,4,5,6,7,8,9,10,11,12,13,14,15
ANS       DB         ?
MYDATA    ENDS

MYCODE    SEGMENT    PARA 'CODE'  ;DEFINE CODE SEG. FOR MASM
MYPROC    PROC       FAR          ;PROCEDURE IS NAMED MYPROC
          ASSUME     CS:MYCODE,DS:MYDATA,SS:STACK
          PUSH       DS           ;SAVE LOCATION OF DS REG.
          SUB        AX,AX        ;GET A ZERO IN AX
          PUSH       AX           ;SAVE ZERO ON STACK, TOO
          MOV        AX,MYDATA    ;GET DATA LOCATION IN AX
          MOV        DS,AX        ;PUT IT IN DS REGISTER
```

.SFCOND   (.SFCOND listing peudo-op)

Assemblers: IBM, Microsoft, and Speedware

Description: The .SFCOND pseudo-op is used to halt the listing of conditional blocks of code that are evaluated as false.

Format: .SFCOND (no operands)

Comments: .SFCOND does not list false conditionals. .LFCOND reverses this state.

Example:

```
            .SFCOND
            IF1
                        INCLUDE B:MACLIB.MAC
            ENDIF
MYCODE      SEGMENT     PARA 'CODE'                 ;DEFINE CODE SEG. FOR MASM
            PUBLIC      VALUE1,ANSWER,SUM
MYPROC      PROC        FAR                         ;PROCEDURE IS NAMED MYPROC
            ASSUME      CS:MYCODE,DS:MYDATA,SS:STACK
            PUSH        DS                          ;SAVE LOCATION OF DS REG.
            SUB         AX,AX                       ;GET A ZERO IN AX
            PUSH        AX                          ;SAVE ZERO ON STACK, TOO
```

STRUC   (STRUC pseudo-op)

Assemblers: IBM, Microsoft, and Speedware

Description: The STRUC pseudo-op is similar to RECORD, with the exception that STRUC has a multibyte capability.

Format: *(name_of_structure)*STRUC

Comments: The name of the structure becomes a pseudo-op used to determine storage. One-entry fields can be overridden; fields with more than one entry cannot be overridden. A field that contains a string can be overriden with another string.

Example:

```
            MYSTRUC     STRUC
            AFIELD      DB    8                 ;CAN BE OVERRIDDEN
            BFIELD      DB    1,2,3             ;CANNOT BE OVERRIDDEN
            CFIELD      DB    'Susan McBride' ;CAN BE OVERRIDDEN
            MYSTRUC     ENDS
```
   (Allocation.)
```
            BLUE            MYSTRUC <4,,'Susan Murray '>
```
(Overrides first and third fields.)

SUBTTL   (SUBTTL pseudo-op)

Assemblers: IBM, Microsoft, and Speedware

Description: The SUBTTL pseudo-op allows a subtitle to be listed on the line immediately following the TITLE.

Format: SUBTTL*(string)*

Comments: Sixty characters are allowed in a SUBTTL, and the number of SUBTTL's within a given program is unlimited. A SUBTTL without a string does not cause a skip to the next page.

Example:

```
            TITLE       DISK-FORMATTING
            SUBTTL      CHECK ERROR CODES
            STACK       SEGMENT     PARA STACK
                        DB          64 DUP ('MYSTACK ')
            STACK       ENDS
MYCODE      SEGMENT     PARA 'CODE'  ;DEFINE CODE SEG. FOR MASM
MYPROC      PROC        FAR          ;PROCEDURE IS NAMED MYPROC
            ASSUME      CS:MYCODE,DS:MYDATA,SS:STACK
            PUSH        DS           ;SAVE LOCATION OF DS REG.
            SUB         AX,AX        ;GET A ZERO IN AX
            PUSH        AX           ;SAVE ZERO ON STACK, TOO
```

.TFCOND   (.TFCOND pseudo-op)

Assemblers: IBM and Microsoft

Description: TFCOND toggles the default condition that controls false conditional listings. In effect, it terminates the action of .SFCOND and .LFCOND.

Format: .TFCOND (no operands)

Comments: .TFCOND toggles the current and default conditions to a nondefault condition.

Example: .TFCOND

TITLE   (TITLE pseudo-op)

Assemblers: IBM, Microsoft, and Speedware

Description: The TITLE pseudo-op permits a title to be entered on the second line of each listing page.

Format: TITLE(*string*)

Comments: Only one TITLE is permitted. If a TITLE is not given, a name is created from the source file name. The *string* operand is limited to 60 characters.

Example:

```
            TITLE        DISK-FORMATTING
            SUBTTL       CHECK ERROR CODES
            STACK        SEGMENT     PARA STACK
                         DB          64 DUP ('MYSTACK ')
            STACK        ENDS
MYCODE      SEGMENT      PARA 'CODE'  ;DEFINE CODE SEG. FOR MASM
MYPROC      PROC         FAR          ;PROCEDURE IS NAMED MYPROC
            ASSUME       CS:MYCODE,DS:MYDATA,SS:STACK
            PUSH         DS           ;SAVE LOCATION OF DS REG.
            SUB          AX,AX        ;GET A ZERO IN AX
            PUSH         AX           ;SAVE ZERO ON STACK, TOO
```

MACROS, PROCEDURES, AND LIBRARIES

Macros, procedures, and libraries aid the programmer by making it possible to call and use previously debugged code. This speeds the program-creation process, because the programmer does not have to worry about debugging or "reinventing the wheel" each time a new program is created. Assembly language programmers often develop a bias for one particular technique — some prefer to do everything with macros, and others prefer to use procedures or libraries. Actually, each has its own set of advantages and disadvantages. This chapter is divided into four major sections: "Macros," "Procedures," "Libraries," and "Comparing the Options." In the last section, hints are given to help the programmer select the best method of the three for particular applications.

MACROS

Macros are a versatile option for assembly language programmers. The MACRO syntax was presented in the last chapter, but the real power of the macro will be shown here. A macro is a pseudo-op that allows the establishment of unique assembler operations or the inclusion of frequently called assembly code. Once the operation or code is established in a macro, only the macro name need be called from the body of the program to utilize the code. Each time a macro is named in a program, the assembler copies and pastes the actual MACRO code into the program in place of the macro name. Thus, macros are said to execute *inline* because the program flow is uninterrupted. Macros can be created in the actual program or called from an established macro library. A macro library is simply a file of macros that can be called from the current program at assembly time. The code in a macro or macro library has not been assembled! This is one way in which a library of macros differs from an assembler library, which is only available at link time. Assembler libraries are discussed later in this chapter.

The various assembler packages available for the 8088/80386 chip family have undergone an evolution parallel to that of the new chips that have been added to the original family. Early assemblers did not support 8087/80387 mnemonics, and some current assemblers do not support the 80286/80386 protected virtual mode. Macros can be used at these times to develop the instruction sequences that are not available from the assembler. For example, to establish an increment-stack-pointer operation for the 8087 in an assembler that does not provide 8087 support, the following macro could be used:

```
FINCSTP    MACRO       ;;INCREMENT THE
                       ;;STACK POINTER
           WAIT        ;;SYNC. 8087 & 8088
           ESC 0EH,DI  ;;SEND CORRECT CODE SEQUENCE
           ENDM        ;;END THE MACRO
```

One such macro would be needed for each 8087 instruction. This "roll-your-own" technique is time consuming when numerous operations must be entered and debugged. If you are using the IBM Macro Assembler, Version 2.00, or the Microsoft Assembler, Version 3.00, you will not find support for the 80286/80386 protected control instructions. If you wish this support, it will have to be added with the aid of macro operations. Speedware's Assembler, Version 1.02, does support the 26 protected control instructions.

Macros are more frequently used to hold code that is called many times from within a program. This code could include routines for clearing the screen, cursor control, arithmetic operations, and other frequently called operations.

THE MAKEUP OF A MACRO

In the previous chapter, the syntax for a macro was given. Recall that a macro has three essential parts: a header, a body, and an end (ENDM). The header contains the name of the macro, the pseudo-op MACRO, and optionally, any dummy variables that are to be passed to and from the macro. The body of the macro contains the actual code that will be inserted in any program that calls the macro's name. The end of the macro must include the ENDM statement. For an example of macro use, examine the program given in Figure 7-1. The program is identical in structure to the programs of Chapter 5, except for the inclusion of the DELAY macro. The macro segment is shown here.

```
DELAY     MACRO     TIME
          LOCAL     P1,P2       ;;P1 & P2 ARE LOCAL LABELS
          PUSH      DX          ;;SAVE ORIGINAL DX & CX
                                ;;VALUES

          PUSH      CX
          MOV       DX,TIME     ;;PASS TIME VARIABLE TO DX
P1:       MOV       CX,0FF00H   ;;LOAD CX WITH 00FF00H
                                ;;COUNT
P2:       DEC       CX          ;;WASTE TIME DECREM. CX
          JNZ       P2          ;;IF NOT ZERO, CONTINUE
          DEC       DX          ;;IF CX=0, DECREMENT DX
          JNZ       P1          ;;IF DX NOT ZERO, LOAD CX
                                ;;AGAIN
          POP       CX          ;;IF DX=0, RESTORE CX & DX
                                ;;VALUE
          POP       DX
          ENDM                  ;;LEAVE THE MACRO
```

The name of the macro is DELAY. When the name DELAY is encountered in a program, the assembler copies the body of this macro to that location within the calling program. As this is done, the dummy variable TIME is passed to the DX register. The LOCAL declaration prevents multiple calls, which are not allowed, to the same label by creating a unique label each time DELAY is requested. These unique labels are automatically substituted for P1 and P2. The purpose of this macro is to waste time by decrementing the contents of the DX and CX registers, thus creating a time

```
PAGE ,132
;FOR IBM 8088/80286 WITH RGB MONITORS
;PROGRAM TO ILLUSTRATE USE OF A SIMPLE MACRO

STACK      SEGMENT PARA STACK
           DB         64 DUP ('MYSTACK ')
STACK      ENDS

MYDATA     SEGMENT PARA 'DATA'
BACK       DB         2000 DUP (' ')
MYDATA     ENDS

DELAY      MACRO      TIME
           LOCAL      P1,P2            ;;P1 & P2 ARE LOCAL LABELS
           PUSH       DX               ;;SAVE ORIGINAL DX & CX VALUES
           PUSH       CX
           MOV        DX,TIME          ;;PASS TIME VARIABLE TO DX
P1:        MOV        CX,0FF00H        ;;LOAD CX WITH 00FF00H COUNT
P2:        DEC        CX               ;;WASTE TIME DECREM. CX
           JNZ        P2               ;;IF NOT ZERO, CONTINUE
           DEC        DX               ;;IF CX=0, DECREMENT DX
           JNZ        P1               ;;IF DX NOT ZERO, LOAD CX AGAIN
           POP        CX               ;;IF DX=0, RESTORE CX & DX VALUE
           POP        DX
           ENDM                        ;;LEAVE THE MACRO

MYCODE     SEGMENT PARA 'CODE'         ;DEFINE CODE SEG. FOR MASM
MYPROC     PROC       FAR              ;PROCEDURE IS NAMED MYPROC
           ASSUME     CS:MYCODE,ES:MYDATA,SS:STACK
           PUSH       DS               ;SAVE LOCATION OF DS REG.
           SUB        AX,AX            ;GET A ZERO IN AX
           PUSH       AX               ;SAVE ZERO ON STACK, TOO
           MOV        AX,MYDATA        ;GET DATA LOCATION IN AX
           MOV        ES,AX            ;PUT IT IN ES REGISTER

;PROGRAM SEGMENT WILL CLEAR THE SCREEN BY WRITING 80x25 BLANKS
;ON SCREEN.  BY WRITING THESE WITH A DIFFERENT VALUE IN BL
;WE WILL CHANGE THE COLOR OF THE WHOLE SCREEN!  THE DELAY
;MACRO WILL HOLD THE COLOR FOR A SPECIFIED AMOUNT OF TIME
           MOV        CX,08H           ;REPEAT LOOP 8 TIMES
           MOV        BL,00H           ;SET ORIGINAL BACKGROUND COLOR
AGAIN:     LEA        BP,BACK          ;WRITE A STRING OF BLANKS
           MOV        DX,0000          ;SET CURSOR AT TOP LEFT CORNER
           MOV        AH,19            ;WRITE STRING ATTRIBUTE
           MOV        AL,1             ;PRINT CHARACTERS AND MOVE CURSOR
           PUSH       CX               ;SAVE LOOP COUNTER
           MOV        CX,07D0H         ;WRITE 2000 BLANKS
           INT        10H              ;INTERRUPT CALL
           DELAY      10               ;DELAY 10 UNITS
           ADD        BL,10H           ;CHANGE BACKGROUND COLOR
           POP        CX               ;RESTORE ORIGINAL LOOP COUNTER
           LOOP       AGAIN            ;DO IT 8 TOTAL TIMES

           RET                         ;RETURN CONTROL TO DOS
MYPROC     ENDP                        ;END PROCEDURE NAMED MYPROC
MYCODE     ENDS                        ;END CODE SEGMENT NAMED MYCODE

           END                         ;END WHOLE PROGRAM
```

Figure 7-1. _____

A program illustrating the simple use of macros

delay when the program executes. DX serves as the course control for time, and CX fine tunes the delay. Although hardware delays might be more accurate, this macro serves as a good introduction to macro use.

In Chapter 5, a program was written to change the background color and write a logo on the color screen. The technique for changing the background color has been incorporated within this program. The background color is automatically changed eight times when this program is executed by adding 10H to the BL register each time the program executes the loop. The DELAY macro determines how long each colorful screen is displayed. The value of the dummy variable was determined experimentally for a 9 Mhz IBM AT. If your computer runs at a different speed, adjust this value accordingly. Figure 7-2 is a listing file that shows how the macro was expanded within the program code.

As you view Figure 7-2, notice in particular that the macro is included (along with double semicolon comments) in the source code, but that no machine code is generated at the left. When a macro or macro library is used by a program, it is listed in this manner. Also notice further down the listing that the code appears again. This second occurrence of the code resulted from the macro call DELAY 10 in the program itself. This time, machine code is generated at the left, as shown here.

				DELAY	10
001F	52		+	PUSH	DX
0020	51		+	PUSH	CX
0021	BA	000A	+	MOV	DX,10
0024	B9	FF00	+ ??0000:	MOV	CX,0FF00H
0027	49		+ ??0001:	DEC	CX
0028	75	FD	+	JNZ	??0001
002A	4A		+	DEC	DX
002B	75	F7	+	JNZ	??0000
002D	59		+	POP	CX
002E	5A		+	POP	DX

The (+) signs indicate macro expansion. This sets these lines apart from regular program code and should be an aid in debugging. Since DELAY was only duplicated once within the program, the LOCAL declaration was not actually required. Notice, however, that P1 and P2 were replaced with strange new labels, ??0000 and ??0001, as a result of this local declaration. If DELAY had been duplicated again within the same program, those values would have been changed to ??0002 and ??0003. Making all labels within a macro LOCAL prevents possible future programming accidents.

```
                            PAGE  ,132
                            ;FOR IBM 8088/80286 WITH RGB MONITORS
                            ;PROGRAM TO ILLUSTRATE USE OF A SIMPLE MACRO

0000                        STACK   SEGMENT PARA STACK
0000      40 [                      DB      64 DUP ('MYSTACK ')
          4D 59 53 54
          41 43 4B 20
                     ]

0200                        STACK   ENDS

0000                        MYDATA  SEGMENT PARA 'DATA'
0000      07D0 [            BACK    DB      2000 DUP (' ')
              20
               ]

07D0                        MYDATA  ENDS

                            DELAY   MACRO   TIME
                                    LOCAL   P1,P2           ;;P1 & P2 ARE LOCAL LABELS
                                    PUSH    DX              ;;SAVE ORIGINAL DX & CX VALUES
                                    PUSH    CX
                                    MOV     DX,TIME         ;;PASS TIME VARIABLE TO DX
                            P1:     MOV     CX,0FF00H       ;;LOAD CX WITH 00FF00H COUNT
                            P2:     DEC     CX              ;;WASTE TIME DECREM. CX
                                    JNZ     P2              ;;IF NOT ZERO, CONTINUE
                                    DEC     DX              ;;IF CX=0, DECREMENT DX
                                    JNZ     P1              ;;IF DX NOT ZERO, LOAD CX AGAIN
                                    POP     CX              ;;IF DX=0, RESTORE CX & DX VALUE
                                    POP     DX
                                    ENDM                    ;;LEAVE THE MACRO

0000                        MYCODE  SEGMENT PARA 'CODE'     ;DEFINE CODE SEG. FOR MASM
0000                        MYPROC  PROC    FAR             ;PROCEDURE IS NAMED MYPROC
                                    ASSUME  CS:MYCODE,ES:MYDATA,SS:STACK
0000  1E                            PUSH    DS              ;SAVE LOCATION OF DS REG.
0001  2B C0                         SUB     AX,AX           ;GET A ZERO IN AX
0003  50                            PUSH    AX              ;SAVE ZERO ON STACK, TOO
0004  B8 ---- R                     MOV     AX,MYDATA       ;GET DATA LOCATION IN AX
0007  8E C0                         MOV     ES,AX           ;PUT IT IN ES REGISTER

                            ;PROGRAM SEGMENT WILL CLEAR THE SCREEN BY WRITING 80x25 BLANKS
                            ;ON SCREEN.  BY WRITING THESE WITH A DIFFERENT VALUE IN BL
                            ;WE WILL CHANGE THE COLOR OF THE WHOLE SCREEN!  THE DELAY
                            ;MACRO WILL HOLD THE COLOR FOR A SPECIFIED AMOUNT OF TIME
0009  B9 0008                       MOV     CX,08H          ;REPEAT LOOP 8 TIMES
000C  B3 00                         MOV     BL,00H          ;SET ORIGINAL BACKGROUND COLOR
000E  8D 2E 0000 R          AGAIN:  LEA     BP,BACK         ;WRITE A STRING OF BLANKS
0012  BA 0000                       MOV     DX,0000         ;SET CURSOR AT TOP LEFT CORNER
0015  B4 13                         MOV     AH,19           ;WRITE STRING ATTRIBUTE
0017  B0 01                         MOV     AL,1            ;PRINT CHARACTERS AND MOVE CURSOR
0019  51                            PUSH    CX              ;SAVE LOOP COUNTER
001A  B9 07D0                       MOV     CX,07D0H        ;WRITE 2000 BLANKS
001D  CD 10                         INT     10H             ;INTERRUPT CALL
                                    DELAY   10              ;DELAY 10 UNITS
001F  52                 +          PUSH    DX
0020  51                 +          PUSH    CX
0021  BA 000A            +          MOV     DX,10
0024  B9 FF00            + ??0000:  MOV     CX,0FF00H
0027  49                 + ??0001:  DEC     CX
0028  75 FD              +          JNZ     ??0001
002A  4A                 +          DEC     DX
002B  75 F7              +          JNZ     ??0000
002D  59                 +          POP     CX
002E  5A                 +          POP     DX
002F  80 C3 10                      ADD     BL,10H          ;CHANGE BACKGROUND COLOR
0032  59                            POP     CX              ;RESTORE ORIGINAL LOOP COUNTER
0033  E2 D9                         LOOP    AGAIN           ;DO IT 8 TOTAL TIMES

0035  CB                            RET                     ;RETURN CONTROL TO DOS
0036                        MYPROC  ENDP                    ;END PROCEDURE NAMED MYPROC
0036                        MYCODE  ENDS                    ;END CODE SEGMENT NAMED MYCODE

                                    END                     ;END WHOLE PROGRAM
Macros:

              N a m e               Length

DELAY. . . . . . . . . . . . . .    0007

Segments and Groups:
```

Figure 7-2. _____

A listing file for the program in Figure 7-1 showing macro expansion

```
              N a m e                  Size    Align   Combine  Class

   MYCODE . . . . . . . . . . . . .    0036    PARA    NONE     'CODE'
   MYDATA . . . . . . . . . . . . .    07D0    PARA    NONE     'DATA'
   STACK. . . . . . . . . . . . . .    0200    PARA    STACK

   Symbols:

              N a m e                  Type    Value   Attr

   AGAIN. . . . . . . . . . . . . .    L NEAR  000E    MYCODE
   BACK . . . . . . . . . . . . . .    L BYTE  0000    MYDATA   Length =07D0
   MYPROC . . . . . . . . . . . . .    F PROC  0000    MYCODE   Length =0036
   ??0000 . . . . . . . . . . . . .    L NEAR  0024    MYCODE
   ??0001 . . . . . . . . . . . . .    L NEAR  0027    MYCODE

   49928 Bytes free

   Warning Severe
   Errors  Errors
   0       0
```

Figure 7-2. _____

A listing file for the program in Figure 7-1 showing macro expansion
(*continued*)

A Macro Library

Macros can be entered as in Figure 7-1 and used by a single program or
placed in a macro library that can be included with any program. Many
programmers develop a group of useful, frequently used macros. By placing these in a library, they save time and debugging headaches by simply
calling the library rather than retyping each macro. Figure 7-3 shows a
group of macros saved together and called MACLIB.MAC. As you enter this
code, using an editor, remember that macros are *not* assembled. Simply save
the ASCII file on your disk after you enter each macro.

PUSHA and POPA should be included only for machines using 8088
and 8086 microprocessors. PUSHA and POPA are fully implemented by all
assemblers for 80286/80386 machines. If you are using an 80286 or 80386
machine, be sure to specify the 0.286C or 0.386C pseudo-op at the start of
your program. PUSHA and POPA serve as a convenient means of saving
the current register state of the machine, especially when you are uncertain
how new routines will affect the various individual registers. The DELAY
macro is simply the DELAY macro of Figure 7-1, saved in this library. The
CLEARSCREEN macro was introduced in Chapter 5 as part of a whole
program. Now CLEARSCREEN can be called as frequently as the programmer desires, without having to enter the code. PRINTNUM places a
single-digit ASCII number on the screen. Remember, 05H in the AL register must be converted to an ASCII value before it can be placed on the

```
PUSHA     MACRO                    ;;SAVES SYSTEM'S REGISTERS
          PUSH      AX             ;;NOT NEEDED BY 80286/80386
          PUSH      CX             ;;MACHINES
          PUSH      DX
          PUSH      BX
          PUSH      BP
          PUSH      SI
          PUSH      DI
          ENDM

POPA      MACRO                    ;;RESTORES SYSTEM'S REGISTERS
          POP       DI             ;;NOT NEEDED BY 80286/80386
          POP       SI             ;;MACHINES
          POP       BP
          POP       BX
          POP       DX
          POP       CX
          POP       AX
          ENDM

DELAY     MACRO     TIME           ;;SOFTWARE TIME DELAY CONTROLLED
          LOCAL     P1,P2          ;;BY (TIME) AND SYSTEM CLOCK RATE
          PUSHA                    ;;SAVE REGISTERS
          MOV       DX,TIME        ;;MOVE LARGE UNITS INTO DX
P1:       MOV       CX,0FF00H      ;;SMALL INCREMENTS SET IN CX
P2:       DEC       CX             ;;DECREMENT CX
          JNZ       P2             ;;IF NOT ZERO, P2
          DEC       DX             ;;IF ZERO, DECREMENT DX
          JNZ       P1             ;;IF DX NOT ZERO, P1
          POPA                     ;;RESTORE REGISTERS
          ENDM                     ;;END MACRO

CLEARSCREEN MACRO                  ;;CLEARS COLOR SCREEN
          PUSHA                    ;;SAVE REGISTERS
          MOV       CX,0           ;;SET UPPER CORNER OF WINDOW
          MOV       DX,2479H       ;;SET LOWER CORNER OF WINDOW
          MOV       BH,7           ;;SET SCREEN ATTRIBUTE (NORMAL)
          MOV       AX,0600H       ;;INTERRUPT PARAMETERS
          INT       10H            ;;CALL INTERRUPT
          POPA                     ;;RESTORE REGISTERS
          ENDM                     ;;END MACRO

PRINTNUM MACRO                     ;;PRINTS ASCII NUMBER ON SCREEN
          PUSHA                    ;;SAVE REGISTERS
          PUSH      AX             ;;SAVE AX IT WILL BE DESTROYED
          MOV       AH,15          ;;GET CURRENT SCREEN
          INT       10H            ;;CALL INTERRUPT, SET BX VALUES
          POP       AX             ;;RESTORE AX VALUES
          AND       AL,0FH         ;;KEEP ONLY LOWER 4 BITS
          OR        AL,30H         ;;MAKE IT ASCII
          MOV       AH,10          ;;SET INTERRUPT PARAMETER
          MOV       CX,1           ;;NUMBER OF CHAR. TO WRITE
          INT       10H            ;;CALL THE INTERRUPT
          POPA                     ;;RESTORE THE REGISTERS
          ENDM                     ;;END MACRO
```

Figure 7-3. ———————————————————————————————

A group of useful macros saved together in a file called MACLIB.MAC

```
CURSOR    MACRO    LOCATE             ;;MOVES CURSOR TO (LOCATE)
          PUSHA                       ;;SAVE REGISTERS
          MOV      AH,15              ;;GET CURRENT SCREEN
          INT      10H                ;;CALL INTERRUPT, SET BX VALUES
          MOV      DX,LOCATE          ;;MOVE SCREEN LOCATION TO DX
          MOV      AH,2               ;;SET THE CURSOR PARAMETER
          INT      10H                ;;CALL THE INTERRUPT
          POPA                        ;;RESTORE THE REGISTERS
          ENDM                        ;;END MACRO

PRINTCHAR MACRO TEXT                  ;;PRINTS CHARACTERS FROM DATA
          PUSHA                       ;;SEGMENT.  STRING TO BE PASSED
          LEA      DX,TEXT            ;;IN (TEXT).  PRINTS UNTIL ($),
          MOV      AH,9               ;;IS LOCATED.  PRINTS FROM CURRENT
          INT      21H                ;;CURSOR POSITION.
          POPA                        ;;RESTORE THE REGISTERS
          ENDM                        ;;END MACRO
```

Figure 7-3. _____

A group of useful macros saved together in a file called MACLIB.MAC
(*continued*)

screen. The CURSOR macro uses the value in the dummy variable
LOCATE to obtain the vertical (DH) and horizontal (DL) locations for the
cursor on the 80×25 text screen. The PRINTCHAR macro prints a string
of ASCII characters starting at the current cursor position. The printing
continues until a $ is located in the string. The string is saved in the data
segment.

To illustrate how a library of macros can speed up the program development process and shorten the amount of code that the programmer must
write, examine Figure 7-4. Figure 7-4 is a complete program that uses several macros. The program clears the screen, prints the message "I am a
simple counting program" at the top of the screen, and then continuously
displays a count from 0 to 9 at the center of the screen. The program terminates operation after five complete cycles.

To include a macro library in a program, the IF1 pseudo-op is used.
Use the pseudo-op INCLUDE to specify the drive and the complete name
of the macro library.

Note: The program only displays the lowest digit of the actual count in
the AL register. Therefore, the counter can have 45 in AL and only display
a 5 on the screen.

```
;FOR IBM 8088/80286
;PROGRAM TO ILLUSTRATE USE OF A MACRO LIBRARY

IF1                                 ;NOTICE TO LOAD A PREVIOUSLY
        INCLUDE B:MACLIB.MAC        ;SAVED MACRO LIBRARY FROM B DRIVE
ENDIF

STACK   SEGMENT PARA STACK
        DB      64 DUP ('MYSTACK ')
STACK   ENDS

MYDATA  SEGMENT PARA 'DATA'
MESSAGE DB      'I am a simple counting program$'
MYDATA  ENDS

MYCODE  SEGMENT PARA 'CODE'         ;DEFINE CODE SEG. FOR MASM
MYPROC  PROC    FAR                 ;PROCEDURE IS NAMED MYPROC
        ASSUME  CS:MYCODE,DS:MYDATA,SS:STACK
        PUSH    DS                  ;SAVE LOCATION OF DS REG.
        SUB     AX,AX               ;GET A ZERO IN AX
        PUSH    AX                  ;SAVE ZERO ON STACK, TOO
        MOV     AX,MYDATA           ;GET DATA LOCATION IN AX
        MOV     DS,AX               ;PUT IT IN DS REGISTER

        CLEARSCREEN                 ;CALL CLEARSCREEN MACRO
        CURSOR  0019H               ;CENTER MESSAGE
        PRINTCHAR MESSAGE           ;PRINT THE MESSAGE ABOVE

        MOV     AX,00               ;INITIALIZE COUNT TO ZERO
AGAIN:  CURSOR  0C28H               ;MOVE TO CENTER SCREEN
        PRINTNUM                    ;PRINT NUM. IN AL ON SCREEN
        DELAY   10                  ;WAIT 10 UNITS OF DELAY
        ADD     AL,01               ;ADD A 1 TO AL REGISTER
        DAA                         ;DECIMAL ADJUST RESULTS
        CMP     AL,50H              ;IF FIVE CYCLES, EXIT
        JE      ENDO
        JMP     AGAIN               ;DO IT AGAIN?
ENDO:   CLEARSCREEN                 ;LET'S CLEAR IT AGAIN

        RET                         ;RETURN CONTROL TO DOS
MYPROC  ENDP                        ;END PROCEDURE NAMED MYPROC
MYCODE  ENDS                        ;END CODE SEGMENT NAMED MYCODE

        END                         ;END WHOLE PROGRAM
```

Figure 7-4. _____

Counter program showing the advantage of a macro library

```
IF1                                 ;NOTICE TO LOAD A
                                    ;PREVIOUSLY
        INCLUDE B:MACLIB.MAC        ;SAVED MACRO LIBRARY
                                    ;FROM B DRIVE
ENDIF
```

The first three major lines of code accomplish quite a bit.

```
        CLEARSCREEN              ;CALL CLEARSCREEN MACRO
        CURSOR 0019H             ;CENTER MESSAGE
        PRINTCHAR MESSAGE        ;PRINT THE MESSAGE ABOVE
```

The **CLEARSCREEN** macro clears the monitor screen. CURSOR moves the cursor to the first line and then over 19H (25 spaces) to center the message. The PRINTCHAR macro names the variable MESSAGE as the location for the string to be printed.

The next block of code is responsible for placing the numbers on the screen.

```
        MOV     AX,00      ;INITIALIZE COUNT TO ZERO
AGAIN:  CURSOR  0C28H      ;MOVE TO CENTER SCREEN
        PRINTNUM           ;PRINT NUM. IN AL ON SCREEN
        DELAY   10         ;WAIT 10 UNITS OF DELAY
        ADD     AL,01      ;ADD A 1 TO AL REGISTER
        DAA                ;DECIMAL ADJUST RESULTS
        CMP     AL,50H     ;IF FIVE CYCLES, EXIT
        JE      ENDO
        JMP     AGAIN      ;DO IT AGAIN?
ENDO:   CLEARSCREEN        ;LET'S CLEAR IT AGAIN
```

When PRINTNUM is called, the digit in the lower four bits of AL is converted to an ASCII character and printed to the screen. Decimal numbers are retained by the simple ADD and DAA sequence. Before the program ends, the screen is once again cleared.

If you have the courage, assemble the file and print a copy of the LST file. You will be amazed at just how much code you were saved from repeating when you entered the program.

PROCEDURES

All of the programs that have been written to this point have used only one procedure. Programs, however, can contain many procedures. Procedures can be considered as NEAR (intrasegment) or FAR (intersegment). When routines such as the ones used in the previous macro library are placed in procedures, the procedure behaves more like a subroutine. These (sub) procedures can be CALLed from the (main) procedure and used like the subroutines of Pascal and Fortran. In the following section, both intrasegment and intersegment procedures are examined.

THE MAKEUP OF A PROCEDURE

The structure of most assembly programs is about the same with regard to the placement of stack, data, and code segments. In the segment of code shown here, MYCODE is the name of the segment where the program code will reside. Actually, within the code segment many procedures can be collected.

```
MYCODE    SEGMENT    PARA 'CODE'  ;DEFINE CODE SEG. FOR
                                  ;MASM
MYPROC    PROC       FAR          ;PROCEDURE IS NAMED
                                  ;MYPROC
          ASSUME     CS:MYCODE,DS:MYDATA,SS:STACK
          PUSH       DS           ;SAVE LOCATION OF DS
                                  ;REG.
          SUB        AX,AX        ;GET A ZERO IN AX
          PUSH       AX           ;SAVE ZERO ON STACK, TOO
```

(The body of the procedure is placed here.)

```
          RET                     ;RETURN CONTROL TO
                                  ;DOS
MYPROC    ENDP                    ;END PROCEDURE NAMED
                                  ;MYPROC
MYCODE    ENDS                    ;END CODE SEGMENT
                                  ;NAMED MYCODE

          END                     ;END WHOLE PROGRAM
```

The name of the procedure is MYPROC, and it has a FAR attribute when it is the main procedure. Every procedure is structured in a similar manner with either a NEAR or a FAR attribute. Notice, also, that before the procedure is ended (MYPROC ENDP), a RET must be issued.

The NEAR and FAR attributes for a procedure help the microprocessor determine the type of CALL instruction to generate when that procedure is requested. A path must also be established for the return from the procedure. This path of instructions differs depending upon the NEAR or FAR attribute. If the procedure has the NEAR attribute, the IP (instruction pointer) is saved on the stack; if it has the FAR attribute, both the CS (code segment) and the IP (instruction pointer) are saved on the stack.

Figure 7-5 is similar to the first program in this chapter. Basically, the only difference between the two is that the delay routine has been moved from a macro structure to that of a NEAR procedure. Examine the code of Figure 7-1 to see if you notice what has been added and removed. In the section of code shown here, notice that the original word, DELAY 10, has been replaced with CALL DELAY.

```
           MOV     CX,08H      ;REPEAT LOOP 8 TIMES
           MOV     BL,00H      ;SET ORIGINAL BACK-
                               ;GROUND COLOR
AGAIN:     LEA     BP,BACK     ;WRITE A STRING OF
                               ;BLANKS
           MOV     DX,0000     ;SET CURSOR AT TOP LEFT
                               ;CORNER
           MOV     AH,19       ;WRITE STRING ATTRIBUTE
           MOV     AL,1        ;PRINT CHARACTERS AND
                               ;MOVE CURSOR
           PUSH    CX          ;SAVE LOOP COUNTER
           MOV     CX,07D0H    ;WRITE 2000 BLANKS
           INT     10H         ;INTERRUPT CALL
           CALL    DELAY       ;CALL THE NEAR DELAY
                               ;PROCEDURE
           ADD     BL,10H      ;CHANGE BACKGROUND
                               ;COLOR
           POP     CX          ;RESTORE ORIGINAL LOOP
                               ;COUNTER
           LOOP    AGAIN       ;DO IT 8 TOTAL TIMES

           RET                 ;RETURN CONTROL TO
                               ;DOS
MYPROC     ENDP                ;END PROCEDURE NAMED
                               ;MYPROC
```

Procedures are requested with a CALL. A more subtle change is the removal of the DELAY 10. Parameters and variables cannot be passed to procedures as they were with macros. To get the 10 units of time delay, the 10 was loaded directly in the DELAY procedure. The DELAY procedure

```
PAGE ,132
;FOR IBM 8088/80286 WITH RGB MONITORS
;PROGRAM TO ILLUSTRATE USE OF A NEAR PROCEDURE

STACK     SEGMENT PARA STACK
          DB        64 DUP ('MYSTACK ')
STACK     ENDS

MYDATA    SEGMENT PARA 'DATA'
BACK      DB        2000 DUP (' ')
MYDATA    ENDS


MYCODE    SEGMENT PARA 'CODE'       ;DEFINE CODE SEG. FOR MASM
MYPROC    PROC    FAR               ;PROCEDURE IS NAMED MYPROC
          ASSUME  CS:MYCODE,ES:MYDATA,SS:STACK
          PUSH    DS                ;SAVE LOCATION OF DS REG.
          SUB     AX,AX             ;GET A ZERO IN AX
          PUSH    AX                ;SAVE ZERO ON STACK, TOO
          MOV     AX,MYDATA         ;GET DATA LOCATION IN AX
          MOV     ES,AX             ;PUT IT IN ES REGISTER

;PROGRAM SEGMENT WILL CLEAR THE SCREEN BY WRITING 80x25 BLANKS
;ON SCREEN.  BY WRITING THESE WITH A DIFFERENT VALUE IN BL
;WE WILL CHANGE THE COLOR OF THE WHOLE SCREEN!  THE DELAY
;PROCEDURE WILL HOLD THE COLOR FOR A SPECIFIED AMOUNT OF TIME
          MOV     CX,08H            ;REPEAT LOOP 8 TIMES
          MOV     BL,00H            ;SET ORIGINAL BACKGROUND COLOR
AGAIN:    LEA     BP,BACK           ;WRITE A STRING OF BLANKS
          MOV     DX,0000           ;SET CURSOR AT TOP LEFT CORNER
          MOV     AH,19             ;WRITE STRING ATTRIBUTE
          MOV     AL,1              ;PRINT CHARACTERS AND MOVE CURSOR
          PUSH    CX                ;SAVE LOOP COUNTER
          MOV     CX,07D0H          ;WRITE 2000 BLANKS
          INT     10H               ;INTERRUPT CALL
          CALL    DELAY             ;CALL THE NEAR DELAY PROCEDURE
          ADD     BL,10H            ;CHANGE BACKGROUND COLOR
          POP     CX                ;RESTORE ORIGINAL LOOP COUNTER
          LOOP    AGAIN             ;DO IT 8 TOTAL TIMES

          RET                       ;RETURN CONTROL TO DOS
MYPROC    ENDP                      ;END PROCEDURE NAMED MYPROC

DELAY     PROC    NEAR
          PUSH    DX                ;SAVE ORIGINAL DX & CX VALUES
          PUSH    CX
          MOV     DX,10             ;PASS TIME VARIABLE TO DX
P1:       MOV     CX,0FF00H         ;LOAD CX WITH 00FF00H COUNT
P2:       DEC     CX                ;WASTE TIME DECREM. CX
          JNZ     P2                ;IF NOT ZERO, CONTINUE
          DEC     DX                ;IF CX=0, DECREMENT DX
          JNZ     P1                ;IF DX NOT ZERO, LOAD CX AGAIN
          POP     CX                ;IF DX=0, RESTORE CX & DX VALUE
          POP     DX
          RET                       ;DETERMINE PATH BACK
```

Figure 7-5. _____

Program illustrating how to use a NEAR procedure

```
DELAY   ENDP                    ;END NEAR PROCEDURE
MYCODE  ENDS                    ;END CODE SEGMENT NAMED MYCODE
        END                     ;END WHOLE PROGRAM
```

Figure 7-5.

Program illustrating how to use a NEAR procedure (*continued*)

itself looks like a miniature program:

```
DELAY     PROC    NEAR
          PUSH    DX          ;SAVE ORIGINAL DX & CX
                              ;VALUES
          PUSH    CX
          MOV     DX,10       ;PASS TIME VARIABLE TO
                              ;DX
P1:       MOV     CX,0FF00H   ;LOAD CX WITH 00FF00H
                              ;COUNT
P2:       DEC     CX          ;WASTE TIME DECREM. CX
          JNZ     P2          ;IF NOT ZERO, CONTINUE
          DEC     DX          ;IF CX=0, DECREMENT DX
          JNZ     P1          ;IF DX NOT ZERO, LOAD CX
                              ;AGAIN
          POP     CX          ;IF DX=0, RESTORE CX &
                              ;DX VALUE
          POP     DX
          RET                 ;DETERMINE PATH BACK
DELAY     ENDP                ;END NEAR PROCEDURE
```

At this point, there does not seem to be a major difference between a macro and a NEAR procedure. Actually, the differences are tremendous. Figure 7-6 is the LST file for the program in Figure 7-5. The first thing that might be noticed when comparing this listing to the program in Figure 7-2 is that there are no + characters in the printout. There are no + characters because no macros were expanded. When the DELAY procedure was encountered, it was coded just like any other code. When a macro is used, it is expanded each time it is requested within a program. A procedure like DELAY can be called many times, just by typing CALL DELAY.

```
                                      PAGE ,132
                                      ;FOR IBM 8088/80286 WITH RGB MONITORS
                                      ;PROGRAM TO ILLUSTRATE USE OF A NEAR PROCEDURE
0000                          STACK   SEGMENT PARA STACK
0000      40 [                        DB      64 DUP ('MYSTACK ')
          4D 59 53 54
          41 43 4B 20
                      ]

0200                          STACK   ENDS

0000                          MYDATA  SEGMENT PARA 'DATA'
0000      07D0 [                BACK   DB      2000 DUP (' ')
          20
              ]

07D0                          MYDATA  ENDS

0000                          MYCODE  SEGMENT PARA 'CODE'      ;DEFINE CODE SEG. FOR MASM
0000                          MYPROC  PROC    FAR             ;PROCEDURE IS NAMED MYPROC
                                      ASSUME  CS:MYCODE,ES:MYDATA,SS:STACK
0000   1E                             PUSH    DS              ;SAVE LOCATION OF DS REG.
0001   2B C0                          SUB     AX,AX           ;GET A ZERO IN AX
0003   50                             PUSH    AX              ;SAVE ZERO ON STACK, TOO
0004   B8 ---- R                      MOV     AX,MYDATA       ;GET DATA LOCATION IN AX
0007   8E C0                          MOV     ES,AX           ;PUT IT IN ES REGISTER

                                      ;PROGRAM SEGMENT WILL CLEAR THE SCREEN BY WRITING 80x25 BLANKS
                                      ;ON SCREEN.  BY WRITING THESE WITH A DIFFERENT VALUE IN BL
                                      ;WE WILL CHANGE THE COLOR OF THE WHOLE SCREEN!  THE DELAY
                                      ;PROCEDURE WILL HOLD THE COLOR FOR A SPECIFIED AMOUNT OF TIME
0009   B9 0008                        MOV     CX,08H          ;REPEAT LOOP 8 TIMES
000C   B3 00                          MOV     BL,00H          ;SET ORIGINAL BACKGROUND COLOR
000E   8D 2E 0000 R           AGAIN:  LEA     BP,BACK         ;WRITE A STRING OF BLANKS
0012   BA 0000                        MOV     DX,0000         ;SET CURSOR AT TOP LEFT CORNER
0015   B4 13                          MOV     AH,19           ;WRITE STRING ATTRIBUTE
0017   B0 01                          MOV     AL,1            ;PRINT CHARACTERS AND MOVE CURSOR
0019   51                             PUSH    CX              ;SAVE LOOP COUNTER
001A   B9 07D0                        MOV     CX,07D0H        ;WRITE 2000 BLANKS
001D   CD 10                          INT     10H             ;INTERRUPT CALL
001F   E8 0029 R                      CALL    DELAY           ;CALL THE NEAR DELAY PROCEDURE
0022   80 C3 10                       ADD     BL,10H          ;CHANGE BACKGROUND COLOR
0025   59                             POP     CX              ;RESTORE ORIGINAL LOOP COUNTER
0026   E2 E6                          LOOP    AGAIN           ;DO IT 8 TOTAL TIMES

0028   CB                             RET                     ;RETURN CONTROL TO DOS
0029                          MYPROC  ENDP                    ;END PROCEDURE NAMED MYPROC

0029                          DELAY   PROC    NEAR
0029   52                             PUSH    DX              ;SAVE ORIGINAL DX & CX VALUES
002A   51                             PUSH    CX
002B   BA 000A                        MOV     DX,10           ;PASS TIME VARIABLE TO DX
002E   B9 FF00                P1:     MOV     CX,0FF00H       ;LOAD CX WITH 0OFF00H COUNT
0031   49                    P2:     DEC     CX              ;WASTE TIME DECREM. CX
0032   75 FD                          JNZ     P2              ;IF NOT ZERO, CONTINUE
0034   4A                             DEC     DX              ;IF CX=0, DECREMENT DX
0035   75 F7                          JNZ     P1              ;IF DX NOT ZERO, LOAD CX AGAIN
0037   59                             POP     CX              ;IF DX=0, RESTORE CX & DX VALUE
0038   5A                             POP     DX
0039   C3                             RET                     ;DETERMINE PATH BACK
003A                          DELAY   ENDP                    ;END NEAR PROCEDURE

003A                          MYCODE  ENDS                    ;END CODE SEGMENT NAMED MYCODE

                                      END                     ;END WHOLE PROGRAM

Segments and Groups:

               N a m e                Size    Align   Combine Class

                                      003A    PARA    NONE    'CODE'
MYCODE . . . . . . . . . . . . .      07D0    PARA    NONE    'DATA'
MYDATA . . . . . . . . . . . . .      0200    PARA    STACK
STACK. . . . . . . . . . . . . .

Symbols:
```

Figure 7-6.
A LST file for the program in Figure 7-5

```
                 N a m e              Type   Value   Attr

    AGAIN. . . . . . . . . . . . . .  L NEAR  000E    MYCODE
    BACK . . . . . . . . . . . . . .  L BYTE  0000    MYDATA  Length =07D0
    DELAY. . . . . . . . . . . . . .  N PROC  0029    MYCODE  Length =0011
    MYPROC . . . . . . . . . . . . .  F PROC  0000    MYCODE  Length =0029
    P1 . . . . . . . . . . . . . . .  L NEAR  002E    MYCODE
    P2 . . . . . . . . . . . . . . .  L NEAR  0031    MYCODE

    50092 Bytes free

    Warning  Severe
    Errors   Errors
    0        0
```

Figure 7-6. _____

A LST file for the program in Figure 7-5 (*continued*)

The actual code for DELAY appears only once, regardless of the number of CALLs to the procedure. You might also observe that the actual machine code for a FAR RET is 0CBH, and that of a NEAR RET is 0C3H.

Since procedures are not expanded with each use, programs written with procedures are often more compact. There is a price to be paid for compactness, however. Programs that use procedures as subroutines do not execute inline. Jumping from the main procedure to a subprocedure takes additional time. If the CALL request is within a loop, this difference in time can be quite noticeable.

A LIBRARY OF PROCEDURES

A group of procedures can be collected in a *procedure library* and called by the user's program at link time. These procedures will have a FAR attribute, since they are external to the current code segment. Figure 7-7 shows a program very similar to the one in Figure 7-4. Figure 7-7 uses the EXTRN pseudo-op to establish the names of the external procedures:

```
EXTRN   PUSHA:FAR,POPA:FAR,DELAY:FAR,CLEARSCREEN:FAR
EXTRN   PRINTNUM:FAR,CURSOR:FAR,PRINTCHAR:FAR
```

The name of the file that these procedures are stored under is not critical. It is only required when this file is linked with the main program. Part of the code segment in Figure 7-7 is shown here.

```
        PAGE ,132
        ;FOR IBM 8088/80386
        ;PROGRAM TO ILLUSTRATE USE OF A CALL TO A FAR PROCEDURE

                EXTRN       PUSHA:FAR,POPA:FAR,DELAY:FAR,CLEARSCREEN:FAR
                EXTRN       PRINTNUM:FAR,CURSOR:FAR,PRINTCHAR:FAR

        STACK   SEGMENT PARA STACK
                DB          64 DUP ('MYSTACK ')
        STACK   ENDS

        MYDATA  SEGMENT PARA PUBLIC 'DATA'
        MESSAGE DB          'I am a simple counting program$'
        MYDATA  ENDS

        MYCODE  SEGMENT PARA 'CODE'          ;DEFINE CODE SEG. FOR MASM
        MYPROC  PROC        FAR              ;PROCEDURE IS NAMED MYPROC
                ASSUME  CS:MYCODE,DS:MYDATA,SS:STACK
                PUSH        DS               ;SAVE LOCATION OF DS REG.
                SUB         AX,AX            ;GET A ZERO IN AX
                PUSH        AX               ;SAVE ZERO ON STACK, TOO
                MOV         AX,MYDATA        ;GET DATA LOCATION IN AX
                MOV         DS,AX            ;PUT IT IN DS REGISTER

                CALL        CLEARSCREEN      ;CALL CLEARSCREEN MACRO
                MOV         DX,19H           ;SET LOCATION FOR CURSOR
                CALL        CURSOR           ;CENTER MESSAGE
                LEA         DX,MESSAGE       ;POINT TO TEXT FOR PRINTCHAR
                CALL        PRINTCHAR        ;PRINT THE MESSAGE ABOVE

                MOV         AX,00            ;INITIALIZE COUNT TO ZERO
        AGAIN:  MOV         DX,0C28H         ;SET CURSOR LOCATION
                CALL        CURSOR           ;MOVE TO CENTER SCREEN
                CALL        PRINTNUM         ;PRINT NUM. IN AL ON SCREEN
                MOV         DX,10H           ;PUT IN 10 DELAY UNITS
                CALL        DELAY            ;WAIT 10 UNITS OF DELAY
                ADD         AL,01            ;ADD A 1 TO AL REGISTER
                DAA                          ;DECIMAL ADJUST RESULTS
                CMP         AL,50H           ;IF FIVE CYCLES, EXIT
                JE          ENDO
                JMP         AGAIN            ;DO IT AGAIN?
        ENDO:   CALL        CLEARSCREEN      ;LET'S CLEAR IT AGAIN

                RET                          ;RETURN CONTROL TO DOS
        MYPROC  ENDP                         ;END PROCEDURE NAMED MYPROC
        MYCODE  ENDS                         ;END CODE SEGMENT NAMED MYCODE

                END                          ;END WHOLE PROGRAM
```

Figure 7-7.

Program illustrating CALLS to FAR procedures

```
CALL      CLEARSCREEN      ;CALL CLEARSCREEN MACRO
MOV       DX,19H           ;SET LOCATION FOR CURSOR
```

```
CALL     CURSOR          ;CENTER MESSAGE
LEA      DX,MESSAGE      ;POINT TO TEXT FOR PRINTCHAR
CALL     PRINTCHAR       ;PRINT THE MESSAGE ABOVE
```

Compare this first section of code with that in Figure 7-4. Note that the cursor position is placed in DX before the CURSOR procedure is called. This is also true for PRINTCHAR. The location of MESSAGE is placed in DX before the PRINTCHAR call. This technique solves the problem of passing parameters, by passing them in registers that are global in scope.

Figure 7-8 shows another source file containing all of the external procedures. Compare this figure with Figure 7-3.

The program overhead for external procedures is minimal:

```
MYCODE     SEGMENT
           PUBLIC PUSHA,POPA,DELAY,CLEARSCREEN,
           PRINTNUM,CURSOR,PRINTCHAR

           ASSUME CS:MYCODE
```
(The contents of the procedures are contained here.)

```
MYCODE     ENDS
           END
```

In this case, each procedure is declared public with the PUBLIC pseudo-op. This permits the intersegment exchange of information.

The remainder of the overhead is standard fare. The CLEARSCREEN routine is repeated here and serves as an example of each procedure's structure.

```
CLEARSCREEN PROC FAR      ;CLEARS COLOR SCREEN
        PUSH    AX        ;SAVE REGISTERS
        PUSH    BX
        PUSH    CX
        PUSH    DX
        MOV     CX,0      ;SET UPPER CORNER OF
                          ;WINDOW
        MOV     DX,2479H  ;SET LOWER CORNER OF
                          ;WINDOW
        MOV     BH,7      ;SET SCREEN ATTRIBUTE
                          ;(NORMAL)
```

```
MYCODE   SEGMENT

         PUBLIC PUSHA,POPA,DELAY,CLEARSCREEN,PRINTNUM,CURSOR,PRINTCHAR

         ASSUME CS:MYCODE

PUSHA    PROC    FAR                ;SAVES SYSTEM'S REGISTERS
         PUSH    AX                 ;NOT NEEDED BY 80286/80386
         PUSH    CX                 ;MACHINES
         PUSH    DX
         PUSH    BX
         PUSH    BP
         PUSH    SI
         PUSH    DI
         RET
PUSHA    ENDP

POPA     PROC    FAR                ;RESTORES SYSTEM'S REGISTERS
         POP     DI                 ;NOT NEEDED BY 80286/80386
         POP     SI                 ;MACHINES
         POP     BP
         POP     BX
         POP     DX
         POP     CX
         POP     AX
         RET
POPA     ENDP

DELAY    PROC    FAR                ;SOFTWARE TIME DELAY CONTROLLED
         PUSH    CX                 ;SAVE REGISTERS
         PUSH    DX
P1:      MOV     CX,0FF00H          ;SMALL INCREMENTS SET IN CX
P2:      DEC     CX                 ;DECREMENT CX
         JNZ     P2                 ;IF NOT ZERO, P2
         DEC     DX                 ;IF ZERO, DECREMENT DX
         JNZ     P1                 ;IF DX NOT ZERO, P1
         PQP     DX                 ;RESTORE REGISTERS
         POP     CX
         RET      ;
DELAY    ENDP

CLEARSCREEN PROC FAR                ;CLEARS COLOR SCREEN
         PUSH    AX                 ;SAVE REGISTERS
         PUSH    BX
         PUSH    CX
         PUSH    DX
         MOV     CX,0               ;SET UPPER CORNER OF WINDOW
         MOV     DX,2479H           ;SET LOWER CORNER OF WINDOW
         MOV     BH,7               ;SET SCREEN ATTRIBUTE (NORMAL)
         MOV     AX,0600H           ;INTERRUPT PARAMETERS
         INT     10H                ;CALL INTERRUPT
         POP     DX                 ;RESTORE REGISTERS
         POP     CX
         POP     BX
```

Figure 7-8. _____

A group of procedures that can be called from a user's program

```
            POP      AX
            RET
CLEARSCREEN ENDP

PRINTNUM PROC    FAR                    ;PRINTS ASCII NUMBER ON SCREEN
         PUSH    AX                     ;SAVE REGISTERS
         PUSH    CX
         PUSH    AX                     ;SAVE AX IT WILL BE DESTROYED
         MOV     AH,15                  ;GET CURRENT SCREEN
         INT     10H                    ;CALL INTERRUPT, SET BX VALUES
         POP     AX                     ;RESTORE AX VALUES
         AND     AL,0FH                 ;KEEP ONLY LOWER 4 BITS
         OR      AL,30H                 ;MAKE IT ASCII
         MOV     AH,10                  ;SET INTERRUPT PARAMETER
         MOV     CX,1                   ;NUMBER OF CHAR. TO WRITE
         INT     10H                    ;CALL THE INTERRUPT
         POP     CX                     ;RESTORE THE REGISTERS
         POP     AX
         RET
PRINTNUM ENDP

CURSOR   PROC    FAR                    ;MOVES CURSOR TO (LOCATE)
         PUSH    AX                     ;SAVE REGISTER
         MOV     AH,15                  ;GET CURRENT SCREEN
         INT     10H                    ;CALL INTERRUPT, SET BX VALUES
         MOV     AH,2                   ;SET THE CURSOR PARAMETER
         INT     10H                    ;CALL THE INTERRUPT
         POP     AX                     ;RESTORE THE REGISTER
         RET
CURSOR   ENDP

PRINTCHAR PROC   FAR                    ;PRINTS CHARACTERS FROM DATA
          PUSH   AX                     ;SEGMENT.  STRING TO BE PASSED
          MOV    AH,9                   ;WAS POINTED TO IN MAIN PROCEDURE
          INT    21H                    ;PRINTS FROM CURRENT CURSOR POSITION
          POP    AX                     ;RESTORE THE REGISTER
          RET
PRINTCHAR ENDP

MYCODE   ENDS
         END
```

Figure 7-8. _____

A group of procedures that can be called from a user's program (*continued*)

```
MOV      AX,0600H      ;INTERRUPT PARAMETERS
INT      10H           ;CALL INTERRUPT
POP      DX            ;RESTORE REGISTERS
POP      CX
POP      BX
POP      AX
```

```
        RET
CLEARSCREEN ENDP
```

The procedure has a name, the pseudo-op **PROC**, and a FAR attribute. Each procedure also ends with the **RET** directive followed by the name of the procedure and the **ENDP** pseudo-op. The body of each procedure has only been modified slightly from that of its Figure 7-3 macro counterpart.

At this point, there are two separate programs. One can be considered the main routine and the other as holding the *library* of procedures. Each program must be assembled separately using MASM. Once this is done, the OBJ files for each program can be combined by the LINKer. The IBM and Microsoft DOS manuals give a detailed description of how to do this and also take advantage of various linker options. The following example illustrates one method that assumes that the linker resides in the A drive and the files to be linked are in the B drive:

    B>A:LINK MAINFILE.OBJ+SUBFILE.OBJ

It should be mentioned again that a macro library is a collection of unassembled routines that reside in a source code file, and a library of procedures is a collection of assembled routines residing in an object file. Macros are brought in at the time of assembly (MASM), and the library of procedures is brought in at the time of linking (LINK).

LIBRARIES

How does the library requested by the linker differ from a library of macros or a library of procedures? Not greatly. All three can store debugged code, which can be called by other programs at a future date. The term *library* is most closely associated with the DOS Linker. Recall that when you link a program, the following menu is presented:

```
IBM Personal Computer Linker
Version 2.30 (C) Copyright IBM Corp. 1981, 1985

Object Modules [.OBJ]: B:MYFILE
Run File [MYFILE.EXE]:
List File [NUL.MAP]:
Libraries [.LIB]:
```

The Library option of the DOS Linker is closest to the library of procedures that were used in the last section. Libraries that are called at link time are actually collections of assembled procedures, very much like the library of procedures. Starting with the IBM Assembler (Version 2.0), and the Microsoft Assembler (Version 3.0), a Library Manager is also included to help build and edit library object modules. When a particular library is needed, its name is entered at link time when the Library option is requested. Like its cousins the library of macros and library of procedures, the DOS Link Library can greatly reduce program development because frequently called procedures have already been written and debugged.

Presently, the Library Manager supports the following operations: add object files, delete object files, extract an object module, replace an object module, add additional libraries, list the contents of a library, and change the page size used to store the contents of a library.

To demonstrate how to create a DOS Link Library, the examples in the previous section will be used. Both Figures 7-7 and 7-8 remain unchanged. Figure 7-7 is the main program, and Figure 7-8 contains the library of procedures. Converting the library of procedures to a DOS Link Library can be done using the Library Manager. In the following case, Figure 7-8 will be converted to a library named NEWLIB:

```
IBM personal Computer Library Manager
Version 1.00
(C) Copyright IBM Corp 1984
(C) Copyright Microsoft Corp 1984

Library name:  B:NEWLIB
Library does not exist. Create? Y
Operations:  +FIG7-8
List file:  NEWLIB.LSF
```

Once the library has been created, additional procedures and routines can be added at any time with the use of the Library Manager program. At link time, simply type **NEWLIB** when the prompt asks for the library.

The Library List file (NEWLIB.LSF) contains the following information:

```
CLEARSCREEN...........FIG7-8 CURSOR...........FIG7-8
DELAY.................FIG7-8 POPA.............FIG7-8
PRINTCHAR.............FIG7-8 PRINTNUM.........FIG7-8
PUSHA.................FIG7-8
FIG7-8 Offset: 200H Code and data size: 5E
CLEARSCREEN CURSOR DELAY POPA
PRINTCHAR PRINTNUM PUSHA
```

At first it would appear that the DOS Link Library is not very different from a library of procedures—but it is. First, remember that a library of procedures is coupled with other object modules at link time, at the [.OBJ] option. Second, with the use of the Library Manager program, new procedures can be added or subtracted from the library at any time. This makes a DOS Link Library more dynamic that either of the previous methods.

COMPARING THE OPTIONS

Macros, procedures, and libraries perform many of the same functions. They allow the programmer to write and debug code once and yet use that code in any program they desire. This makes programming more efficient and more modular, promoting a modular programming style. Each type also has its own advantages and disadvantages, as follows:

Macro Advantages

1. Macros are fast because they execute inline within a program.

2. Macros can pass and receive parameters affecting how the macros operate.

3. Macros can be saved in a source code library, which can easily be edited.

4. The programming overhead for using macros is simple; for a macro library, just use IF1....ENDIF.

Macro Disadvantages

1. Macros make the source code longer, since they are expanded each time they are called.

Library of Procedures Advantages

1. Procedures allow source code to remain short, since procedures are not expanded within a program's code.

Library of Procedures Disadvantages

1. Procedures make program execution slower, since with each CALL

the computer must leave the main code and jump to another portion of code.

2. The overhead for procedure use is involved. Procedures must be declared as NEAR or FAR, and any library files must be marked as *external*.

3. Parameters cannot be sent to a procedure to alter how it executes.

DOS Link Library Advantages

1. Same advantages as listed for Library of Procedures.

2. With a Library Manager, routines can be added or deleted from a library.

DOS Link Library Disadvantages

1. Same disadvantages as listed for Library of Procedures.

Which approach is the best? When should you choose a macro over a procedure? When is a DOS Link Library better that a Library of Procedures? Consider the following recommendations:

1. For short routines, choose a macro (operations are faster, with little increase in code length).

2. For routines that are not called frequently within a program, choose a macro (if the routine is not called frequently, code expansion will not affect the program).

3. If you are just creating or experimenting with a program, use a macro (they are easier to create, edit, and call).

4. If the routine is long, choose a procedure (it makes source code shorter).

5. If the routine is called many times within a program, choose a procedure (since procedures are not expanded within a program).

6. If you have found that the same routines are used time and time again in your programs, put them is a DOS Link Library for easy access.

Some assembly language programmers never use macros, and others try to avoid the use of procedures. You should select the technique that best fits your needs.

TOWARD MORE
ADVANCED PROGRAMMING

The example programs of the previous chapters have allowed you to write some interesting assembly language programs. While these programs have been simple, they have allowed you to experiment with assembler instructions and examine the results of those operations. By using BIOS routines and DOS interrupts, simple programs were created to change screen colors, write block messages to the screen, and so forth. The programming techniques in Chapter 5 illustrate and teach just one or two new concepts per program. Those simple concepts form the backbone of the more involved programs in this chapter.

The programs in this chapter may be more complex and initially less interesting to the beginning programmer than the programs of previous chapters. Several examples include menu-driven screens that allow user interaction from the keyboard. Users will not be able to tell that they are running an assembly language program. There are also several programs that allow the reading and writing of data to a diskette. This is usually a topic of interest for more advanced assembly language programmers.

However, it is not the intention of this book to introduce complexity in the programs for the sake of complexity. Again, each of the examples in this chapter have been designed to present the programmer with new ideas, new concepts, and new ways in which to solve programming problems. For example, you may have no interest at all in a program that allows the user to create a file of names and telephone numbers; however, with just minor modifications this program could also be used to store data that a digital to analog (D/A) card can read or that an equation can calculate. As the old programming prospector once said, "Thar's gold in them there programs."

In each of the first five programs in this chapter, you will be confronted with a programming problem. You will then explore various options and methods that might be used to solve the problem. In this way, you will learn how to attack new problems with methods and skills that you have already acquired from previous chapters.

PLOTTING A GRAPH ON THE COLOR SCREEN

Problem 1:   Plot a sine wave on the high-resolution graphics screen.

For engineers, scientists, and mathematicians, one of the most useful features of a small computer system is the ability to draw or plot results of calculations and operations on a graphics screen. As a prelude to bigger and more powerful programs in Chapter 9 involving the 80287/80387 co-processor, this example will plot a sine wave on the 640 × 200 high-resolution graphics screen using lookup tables. Naturally, a color card and monitor are required.

One of the major limitations of programming in assembly language is the lack of powerful mathematical commands. Programmers must write their own routines for square and cube roots, trigonometric functions, integration and differentiation, and statistical analysis. Algorithms for difficult functions are often hard to find and even harder to implement. This is the case for the sine function. Since the sine function (or any other trigonometric function) is not supported by the 80286/80386 processors, the programmer might consider using an algebraic series expansion. But the series expansion for the sine or cosine involves raising numbers to certain powers and dividing them by factorials. Neither job is very pleasant to implement in assembly language. So before continuing your quest for a solution to this graphics problem, consider that when the sine wave is actually plotted, it will fit within the coordinates of the screen, and that every dot that makes up the sine wave has unique X and Y coordinates. These coordinates could be calculated or measured ahead of time and stored in a table. Your program could then merely access the values in the table rather than resort to calculating the actual points of the sine wave. By using this technique, you will avoid fabricating difficult mathematical calculations and also be able to take advantage of a technique presented in a previous chapter. This program will build upon the lookup table concepts presented in Chapter 5. In other words, the values that will be plotted on the screen will have been previously stored in a lookup table (or data table). A section of the program data segment is shown here.

```
SINE      DB      00,02,04,05,07,09,11,12,14,16,17,19,21,23,24,26
          DB      28,29,31,33,34,36,38,39,41,42,44,45,47,49,50
          DB      52,53,55,56,57,59,60,62,63,64,66,67,68,70,71
          DB      72,73,74,76,77,78,79,80,81,82,83,84,85,86,87
          DB      88,88,89,90,91,91,92,93,93,94,95,95,96,96,97
          DB      97,97,98,98,99,99,99,99,100,100,100,100,100,100,100
```

SINE is the name of the lookup table. Where did these values come from? What do they represent? SINE contains 91 values representing the sine of angles from 0 to 90 degrees. The actual sine values have been multiplied by 100 and rounded to two- or three-place accuracy to scale the sine values to the screen resolution. In either the medium- or high-resolution modes, the vertical resolution of the IBM color monitor is 200 pixels. If the sine wave is to have an amplitude of +100, then the sine of 90 degrees (which is 1) must be scaled to 100. A sine wave typically is plotted from 0 to 360 degrees. The SINE table, however, also contains the information for the second through fourth quadrants, since a sine wave is symmetric. The plan of attack will be simple: (1) Look up a value in SINE and use that value for the Y displacement on the screen. (2) The plotting will commence on the left side of the screen and add one horizontal pixel for each vertical point plotted. There are 360 points to plot (360 degrees) and 640 horizontal pixels (dots on the high-resolution screen)—more than enough room. The information in SINE will be enough to plot the data in each of the four quadrants. Figure 8-1 shows the complete program.

This program contains two useful macros named SETSCREEN and WRITEDOT. The SETSCREEN macro is shown here.

```
SETSCREEN MACRO              ;;SET HI-RES SCREEN
          MOV     AH,00      ;;200x640 DOTS BW
          MOV     AL,06
          INT     10H
          ENDM
```

The macro SETSCREEN merely switches to the high-resolution graphics

```
;FOR 8088/80386 MACHINES
;PROGRAM TO ILLUSTRATE THE USE OF A LOOKUP TABLE TO FIND SINE
;OF ANGLES AND DRAW THE RESULTING WAVEFORM USING BIOS INTERRUPTS

SETSCREEN MACRO                          ;;SET HI-RES SCREEN
          MOV      AH,00                 ;;200x640 DOTS BW
          MOV      AL,06
          INT      10H
          ENDM

WRITEDOT MACRO                           ;;MACRO FOR DOT WRITING
          MOV      AH,12
          MOV      AL,01
          MOV      CX,ANGLE
          ADD      CX,140                ;;CENTER DISPLAY
          MOV      DH,00
          MOV      DL,TEMP
          INT      10H
          ENDM

STACK     SEGMENT PARA STACK
          DB       64 DUP ('MYSTACK ')
STACK     ENDS

MYDATA    SEGMENT PARA 'DATA'
SINE      DB       00,02,04,05,07,09,11,12,14,16,17,19,21,23,24,26
          DB       28,29,31,33,34,36,38,39,41,42,44,45,47,49,50
          DB       52,53,55,56,57,59,60,62,63,64,66,67,68,70,71
          DB       72,73,74,76,77,78,79,80,81,82,83,84,85,86,87
          DB       88,88,89,90,91,91,92,93,93,94,95,95,96,96,97
          DB       97,97,98,98,99,99,99,99,100,100,100,100,100,100,100
ANGLE     DW       0
TEMP      DB       0
MYDATA    ENDS

MYCODE    SEGMENT PARA 'CODE'            ;DEFINE CODE SEG. FOR MASM
MYPROC    PROC     FAR                   ;PROCEDURE IS NAMED MYPROC
          ASSUME   CS:MYCODE,DS:MYDATA,SS:STACK
          PUSH     DS                    ;SAVE LOCATION OF DS REG.
          SUB      AX,AX                 ;GET A ZERO IN AX
          PUSH     AX                    ;SAVE ZERO ON STACK, TOO
          MOV      AX,MYDATA             ;GET DATA LOCATION IN AX
          MOV      DS,AX                 ;PUT IT IN DS REGISTER

;EXAMPLE OF USING A LOOK-UP TABLE TO DETERMINE SINEWAVE VALUES
;VALUES OF SINES HAVE BEEN MULTIPLIED BY 100, AND ROUNDED TO
;AN INTEGER VALUE
          SETSCREEN                      ;SET GRAPHICS 200x640 SCREEN
AGAIN:    LEA      BX,SINE               ;FIND START OF TABLE
          MOV      AX,ANGLE              ;MOVE ANGLE VALUE INTO AX REGISTER
          CMP      AX,180                ;IS IT GREATER THAN 180 DEGREES?
          JLE      NEWQUAD               ;IF LESS, ANGLE IN QUAD 1 OR 2
          SUB      AX,180                ;CORRECT ANGLE IF 180 OR GREATER
NEWQUAD:  CMP      AX,90                 ;IS IT GREATER THAN 90 DEGREES?
          JLE      SECQUAD               ;IF GREATER THAN 90, SECOND QUAD
          NEG      AX                    ;SET VALUE TO NEGATIVE
```

Figure 8-1. _____

Sine wave program illustrating the use of a lookup table

```
           ADD      AX,180               ;CORRECT ANGLE IF 90 OR GREATER
SECQUAD: ADD      BX,AX                ;GET OFFSET SUM INTO BX
         MOV      AL,SINE[BX]          ;GET VALUE AND PLACE IN ANS
         CMP      ANGLE,180            ;IF VALUE >180, ADD TO SCREEN DIS.
         JGE      BIGDIS
         NEG      AL                   ;OTHERWISE, GET NEGATIVE OF VALUE
         ADD      AL,100               ;NOW ADD 100 TO VALUE, FOR CORRECT
         JMP      READY                ;SCREEN DISPLACEMENT
BIGDIS: ADD      AL,99
READY:  MOV      TEMP,AL              ;STORE IN TEMP., TRANS TO WRITEDOT
         WRITEDOT                      ;GO TO WRITEDOT MACRO
         ADD      ANGLE,1              ;GET NEXT ANGLE
         CMP      ANGLE,360            ;HAVE WE DONE 360 DEGREES?
         JLE      AGAIN                ;IF NOT DO IT AGAIN
;COMPLETION OF SINEWAVE LOOKUP EXAMPLE

;WAIT FOR A KEY PRESS BEFORE RETURNING & SWITCHING TO TEXT SCREEN
         MOV      AH,07                ;KEYBOARD PARAMETER
         INT      21H                  ;READ KEYBOARD AND LEAVE
         MOV      AH,00                ;SCREEN PARAMETER
         MOV      AL,03                ;25x80 COLOR MODE
         INT      10H                  ;SET SCREEN

         RET                           ;RETURN CONTROL TO DOS
MYPROC  ENDP                          ;END PROCEDURE NAMED MYPROC
MYCODE  ENDS                          ;END CODE SEGMENT NAMED MYCODE

         END                           ;END WHOLE PROGRAM
```

Figure 8-1. _____

Sine wave program illustrating the use of a lookup table (*continued*)

screen when it is called. The various INT 10H options were discussed and listed in Chapter 5.

The WRITEDOT macro is shown here.

```
WRITEDOT MACRO                        ;;MACRO FOR DOT WRITING
         MOV      AH,12
         MOV      AL,01
         MOV      CX,ANGLE
         ADD      CX,140               ;;CENTER DISPLAY
         MOV      DH,00
         MOV      DL,TEMP
         INT      10H
         ENDM
```

The WRITEDOT macro is also a type-10 interrupt. CX contains the horizontal displacement, and DX contains the vertical displacement. Since there are 640 horizontal dots and only 360 degrees (640 − 360 = 280, and 280/2 = 140), an offset of 140 dots from the left will center the sine wave on the screen. The variable TEMP will eventually contain the whole range of vertical values (which range from 0 to 100). When WRITEDOT is called, the values contained in ANGLE and TEMP will determine where on the screen a dot is placed.

The main portion of the plotting code is shown here.

```
           SETSCREEN              ;SET GRAPHICS 200×640 SCREEN
AGAIN:     LEA      BX,SINE       ;FIND START OF TABLE
           MOV      AX,ANGLE      ;MOVE ANGLE VALUE INTO AL REGISTER
           CMP      AX,180        ;IS IT GREATER THAN 180 DEGREES?
           JLE      NEWQUAD       ;IF LESS, ANGLE IN QUAD 1 OR 2
           SUB      AX,180        ;CORRECT ANGLE IF 180 OR GREATER
NEWQUAD:   CMP      AX,90         ;IS IT GREATER THAN 90 DEGREES?
           JGE      SECQUAD       ;IF GREATER THAN 90, SECOND QUAD
           NEG      AX            ;SET VALUE TO NEGATIVE
           ADD      AX,180        ;CORRECT ANGLE IF 90 OR GREATER
```

It is necessary to determine which quadrant the angle is in to obtain the correct sine value from the table. The angle in AX is first compared to 180 (degrees). If the angle is less than or equal to 180, the resulting value will be positive and in the first or second quadrant. If the value is greater than 180, then the result will be negative and in the third or fourth quadrant. In this case, 180 is subtracted before continuing.

Next, it is necessary to determine if the resulting angle is greater than 90 (degrees). If it is greater, the angle will be subtracted from 180. This requires a little thinking, since SUB 180,AX is not permitted—where would the result be placed? Another approach—one that works—is to obtain the complement of AX and add it to 180. The code at label SEC-QUAD determines the proper offset into the table SINE by adding the value in AX to the BX register, as shown here.

```
SECQUAD:   ADD      BX,AX         ;GET OFFSET SUM INTO BX
           MOV      AL,SINE[BX]   ;GET VALUE AND PLACE IN ANS
           CMP      ANGLE,180     ;IF VALUE >180, ADD TO SCREEN DIS.
           JGE      BIGDIS
           NEG      AL            ;OTHERWISE, GET NEGATIVE OF
                                  ;VALUE
           ADD      AL,100        ;NOW ADD 100 TO VALUE, FOR
                                  ;CORRECT
           JMP      READY         ;SCREEN DISPLACEMENT
```

```
BIGDIS:     ADD     AL,99
READY:      MOV     TEMP,AL         ;STORE IN TEMP., TRANS TO
                                    ;WRITEDOT
            WRITEDOT                ;GO TO WRITEDOT MACRO
            ADD     ANGLE,1         ;GET NEXT ANGLE
            CMP     ANGLE,360       ;HAVE WE DONE 360 DEGREES?
            JLE     AGAIN           ;IF NOT DO IT AGAIN
```

The next few lines of code determine how the dots are to be plotted on the screen. The vertical coordinate for the top of the screen is 0, and that of the bottom is 199 (a range of 200 dots). The 0 displacement for the sine wave corresponds to a screen displacement of 100. Once WRITEDOT is called, the ANGLE is incremented and checked to see if all the dots have been plotted. If they have not, the process is repeated. If all of the dots have been plotted, then the program continues to the next section of code.

```
            MOV     AH,07           ;KEYBOARD PARAMETER
            INT     21H             ;READ KEYBOARD AND LEAVE
```

This portion of code is a DOS interrupt (see Chapter 5 for more details) that causes a pause at this spot in the program until a key is pushed. This allows the programmer to view the graphic results before returning to the text screen and erasing the waveform.

```
            MOV     AH,00           ;SCREEN PARAMETER
            MOV     AL,03           ;25×80 COLOR MODE
            INT     10H             ;SET SCREEN
```

Finally, once a key is pushed, the BIOS interrupt returns the user to the 25 × 80 text screen.

This approach — using lookup tables — can be used to plot a wide variety of mathematical functions. The function merely has to be scaled to fit within the available screen coordinates. Once this is done, the values can be placed in a lookup table and recalled at will. This approach is often faster than actually calculating and plotting the points during program execution; however, the values in a lookup table are fixed and thus will always plot exactly the same waveform (except for possible scaling variations), making a program less flexible. For programmers that prefer to actually calculate the data points during program execution, Chapter 9 will revisit this function and use the mathematical abilities of the 80287/80387 coprocessor.

CREATING A PROGRAM THAT ACCURATELY COUNTS ELAPSED TIME IN SECONDS

Problem 2: Create a program that displays elapsed time. Counting should start when the program is run and should produce a count accurate to six digits. Update the count once a second.

This programming problem presents several obstacles: How should the large count (in seconds) be displayed? Where on the screen should the count be displayed? How should the arithmetic be done for the counting process (in ASCII, BCD, or binary form)? How can the accuracy of the count be maintained?

For the problem, the following will be assumed: The program will display a six-digit decimal count, centered on the screen, with accuracy maintained via the computer's hardware. Decimal addition of packed numbers (DAA mnemonic for results) will be used rather than ASCII addition of unpacked numbers (AAA mnemonic for results). The six-digit count will be maintained in three variables: SEC12, SEC34, and SEC56. (A single variable with size DD, or defined doubleword, could have been used and accessed with BYTE PTRs, but that technique would have complicated the situation for this example.)

Figure 8-2 shows the entire program. Notice that the macro library MACLIB.MAC is included with the program. MACLIB.MAC was defined in a previous chapter and must reside on the named disk drive. Two macros are then listed. The macro TD is used to obtain an accurate second count, and the SCREEN macro is used to place the decimal time count on the monitor screen. The macro TD is repeated here.

```
TD      MACRO   AMT         ;;Time Delay (1-60 SEC)
        LOCAL   AGAIN       ;;PASS DELAY IN AMT DUMMY
        PUSH    AX          ;;SAVE REGISTERS
        PUSH    BX
        PUSH    CX
        PUSH    DX
        MOV     AH,2CH      ;;READ CURRENT TIME
        INT     21H
        MOV     BH,DH       ;;ADD DELAY TO CURRENT SECONDS
        ADD     BH,AMT
        CMP     BH,60       ;;ADJUST SO NOT OVER 60
        JL      AGAIN
        SUB     BH,60
```

```
;PROGRAM FOR 8088/80386 MACHINES
;PROGRAM COUNTS SECONDS FROM 0 TO 999999 AND RESETS
;USES MACLIB.MAC WHEN ASSEMBLED WHICH CONTAINS USEFUL MACROS
;
        PAGE ,132                          ;PAGE DIM 66 x 132

        IF1                                ;INCLUDE MACRO LIBRARY
              INCLUDE C:MACLIB.MAC
        ENDIF

TD      MACRO    AMT               ;;Time Delay (1-60 SEC)
        LOCAL    AGAIN             ;;PASS DELAY IN AMT DUMMY
        PUSH     AX                ;;SAVE REGISTERS
        PUSH     BX
        PUSH     CX
        PUSH     DX
        MOV      AH,2CH            ;;READ CURRENT TIME
        INT      21H
        MOV      BH,DH             ;;ADD DELAY TO CURRENT SECONDS
        ADD      BH,AMT
        CMP      BH,60             ;;ADJUST SO NOT OVER 60
        JL       AGAIN
        SUB      BH,60
AGAIN:  MOV      AH,2CH            ;;SAMPLE THE CLOCK AGAIN
        INT      21H
        CMP      BH,DH             ;;IS THE DELAY COMPLETE?
        JNE      AGAIN
        POP      DX                ;;RESTORE REGISTERS
        POP      CX
        POP      BX
        POP      AX
        ENDM

SCREEN  MACRO    TIME,POSITION     ;;DISPLAY MACRO FOR DIGITS
        PUSH     AX
        PUSH     CX
        MOV      AL,TIME           ;;DIGIT TO PRINT
        AND      AL,0FH            ;;MASK AND KEEP LSB
        CURSOR   POSITION          ;;POSITION OF DIGIT ON SCREEN
        PRINTNUM                   ;;PRINT IT
        MOV      AL,TIME           ;;PREPARE SECOND DIGIT
        AND      AL,0F0H           ;;MASK AND KEEP MSB
        MOV      CL,04             ;;ROTATE TO LSB POSITION
        ROR      AL,CL
        CURSOR   POSITION-1        ;;PRINT TO LEFT OF LSB
        PRINTNUM                   ;;PRINT THE DIGIT
        POP      CX
        POP      AX
        ENDM

STACK SEGMENT PARA STACK           ;DEFIN. OF STACK SEGMENT
        DB        64 DUP ('MYSTACK ')
STACK   ENDS                       ;END STACK SEGMENT
```

Figure 8-2. _____

Program to count seconds

```
MYDATA   SEGMENT PARA 'DATA'
SEC12    DB       0
SEC34    DB       0
SEC56    DB       0
MYDATA   ENDS

MYCODE   SEGMENT PARA 'CODE'        ;DEFIN. OF PROG. SEGMENT
MYPROC   PROC FAR
         ASSUME  CS:MYCODE,DS:MYDATA,SS:STACK
         PUSH    DS                 ;SET RETURN SEG TO STACK
         SUB     AX,AX
         PUSH    AX                 ;PUT 0 IN STACK
         MOV     AX,MYDATA          ;GET ADDRESS OF MYDATA
         MOV     DS,AX
         CLEARSCREEN                ;CLEAR SCREEN MACRO
CYCLE:   TD      01                 ;CALL DELAY MACRO (1 SEC)
         MOV     AL,SEC12           ;LOAD DATA
         ADD     AL,1               ;INCRE SEC COUNT
         DAA                        ;DECIMAL ADJUST
         MOV     SEC12,AL           ;STORE RESULTS
         MOV     AL,SEC34           ;LOAD DATA
         ADC     AL,0               ;INC IF CARRY SET
         DAA                        ;DECIMAL ADJUST
         MOV     SEC34,AL           ;STORE RESULTS
         MOV     AL,SEC56           ;LOAD DATA
         ADC     AL,0               ;INC IF CARRY SET
         DAA                        ;DECIMAL ADJUST
         MOV     SEC56,AL           ;STORE RESULTS
         SCREEN  SEC12,0C2BH        ;PRINT SCREEN MACROS
         SCREEN  SEC34,0C29H
         SCREEN  SEC56,0C27H
         CURSOR  1900H              ;CURSOR MACRO
         MOV     AH,06H             ;READ KEYBOARD
         MOV     DL,0FFH
         INT     21H
         CMP     AL,'Q'             ;QUIT IF Q
         JE      ENDO
         CMP     AL,'q'             ;QUIT IF q
         JE      ENDO
         JMP     CYCLE              ;REPEAT CYCLE
ENDO:
         RET                        ;RETURN TO DOS CONTROL
MYPROC   ENDP                       ;END OF PROCEDURE
MYCODE   ENDS                       ;END OF SEGMENT
         END                        ;THE END
```

Figure 8-2. _____

Program to count seconds (*continued*)

```
AGAIN:   MOV     AH,2CH             ;;SAMPLE THE CLOCK AGAIN
         INT     21H
         CMP     BH,DH              ;;IS THE DELAY COMPLETE?
         JNE     AGAIN
```

```
POP     DX              ;;RESTORE REGISTERS
POP     CX
POP     BX
POP     AX
ENDM
```

On the first pass through this macro, a current time sample is taken and passed to the computer using the DH register. The amount of the requested delay is then added to the current time and adjusted so that it is not over 60 seconds. This number is saved in the BH register. The macro next enters into a loop that continuously samples the time and compares it with the number in BH. Only when the two values are equal will the macro terminate. By depending upon hardware interrupts, such as INT 21H, very accurate timing delays can be achieved.

The SCREEN macro, shown here, also has some interesting features.

```
SCREEN  MACRO    TIME,POSITION   ;;DISPLAY MACRO FOR DIGITS
        PUSH     AX
        PUSH     CX
        MOV      AL,TIME         ;;DIGIT TO PRINT
        AND      AL,0FH          ;;MASK AND KEEP LSB
        CURSOR   POSITION        ;;POSITION OF DIGIT ON SCREEN
        PRINTNUM                 ;;PRINT IT
        MOV      AL,TIME         ;;PREPARE SECOND DIGIT
        AND      AL,0F0H         ;;MASK AND KEEP MSB
        MOV      CL,04           ;;ROTATE TO LSB POSITION
        ROR      AL,CL
        CURSOR   POSITION-1      ;;PRINT TO LEFT OF LSB
        PRINTNUM                 ;;PRINT THE DIGIT
        POP      CX
        POP      AX
        ENDM
```

First, the SCREEN macro allows two dummy variables, TIME and POSITION, to be passed to it. Either SEC12, SEC34, or SEC56 is passed to SCREEN through the dummy variable TIME. POSITION accepts the appropriate cursor position for the time digits. TIME contains two packed BCD digits. In displaying them on the screen, each digit is handled separately. TIME is masked with 0FH in order to retain the LSD of the number. When PRINTNUM (from the macro library) is called, this digit will be converted to an ASCII number and sent to the screen at the current cursor position. TIME is then reloaded, but at this instant it is masked with F0H, and thus the MSD of the number is retained. This digit is then displayed in a similar manner. This process is repeated until all six digits (all three variables) are written to the screen.

The main portion of code responsible for the decimal arithmetic is shown here.

```
CYCLE:   TD       01              ;CALL DELAY MACRO (1 SEC)
         MOV      AL,SEC12        ;LOAD DATA
         ADD      AL,1            ;INCRE SEC COUNT
         DAA                      ;DECIMAL ADJUST
         MOV      SEC12,AL        ;STORE RESULTS
         MOV      AL,SEC34        ;LOAD DATA
         ADC      AL,0            ;INC IF CARRY SET
         DAA                      ;DECIMAL ADJUST
         MOV      SEC34,AL        ;STORE RESULTS
         MOV      AL,SEC56        ;LOAD DATA
         ADC      AL,0            ;INC IF CARRY SET
         DAA                      ;DECIMAL ADJUST
         MOV      SEC56,AL        ;STORE RESULTS
         SCREEN   SEC12,0C2BH     ;PRINT SCREEN MACROS
         SCREEN   SEC34,0C29H
         SCREEN   SEC56,0C27H
         CURSOR   1900H           ;CURSOR MACRO
```

This portion of code first requests a one-second time delay by calling the TD (time delay) macro and passing to it the value 1. Once TD accomplishes the requested time delay, the program updates the three variables containing the second count. SEC12 is loaded into the AL register. A 1 is added to AL, and then the results are DAAed (decimal adjusted). Recall that to maintain a decimal-appearing count, the number must be in the AL register. The DAA command must immediately follow the ADD operation. Once the addition is completed for AL, the result is stored in the variable SEC12. If the Carry flag is set as a result of this addition, then the count in SEC34 must be incremented. SEC34 is then loaded into AL, but instead of an ADD command, an ADC command is used. If the Carry flag is set, a 1 will be added to this register. If the Carry flag is not set, nothing will be added — the results will be DAAed and saved. SEC56 is updated in exactly the same way. This process could be continued to obtain any accuracy desired.

If you think that you see an easier or more efficient way of writing this code, give it a try, but beware of the gremlins that are hiding everywhere waiting to thwart your attempts. One final note regarding this code: the call to CURSOR 1900H merely moves the cursor away from the displayed numbers; otherwise, a blinking effect under one or more of the digits will be noticed.

The remaining code checks the keyboard on each pass through the program to see if the user wants to terminate the counter.

```
MOV     AH,06H        ;READ KEYBOARD
MOV     DL,0FFH
INT     21H
CMP     AL,'Q'        ;QUIT IF Q
JE      ENDO
CMP     AL,'q'        ;QUIT IF q
JE      ENDO
JMP     CYCLE         ;REPEAT CYCLE
```

By using DOS INT 21H, a single character can be read from the keyboard. In this case, the program checks for an upper- or lowercase "Q." If a "Q" is entered from the keyboard, the program stops operation.

What has this program illustrated? First, it has shown how to write a very precise time delay routine. Second, it has shown how to perform multiple-precision decimal arithmetic without the use of complicated hexadecimal-to-decimal routines. Third, it has shown how to control the placement of digits on the screen. Fourth, it has shown how to exit gracefully from a program with a continuous loop. It should now be a simple matter to convert this counter to an hour-minute-second counter by placing the appropriate checks (such as **CMP SEC12,59**) in the program code.

CREATING A SIMPLE MENU-DRIVEN PROGRAM

Problem 3:   Create an interactive program that displays some interesting information about a person and that is simple for a computer neophyte to operate.

Interactive menu-driven programs form the heart of all commercial software. Whether a program is a spreadsheet, wordprocessor, assembler, compiler, or game, the programmer has taken special pains to make the program as easy to use as possible. This usually involves the appearance of a *menu* of options on the screen. The program pauses until the user enters the appropriate selection. Commercial programs make extensive use of error checking at these points to ensure that correct responses are registered.

In this simple program, the user will be presented with a menu that will allow him or her to display information about a person for whom data was previously recorded in a file. The options will include the person's name, address, telephone number, social security number, and favorite recipe. The option to leave the program will also be presented. No error checking will be used for user responses except that the program will ignore everything except the letters listed in the menu. This program will also make use of the MACLIB.MAC library of macros presented in an earlier chapter. This program is shown in Figure 8-3.

All information for screen menus is contained in the data segment of the program code. Even for a fairly simple program, this can require extensive code. For large programs, it might even be necessary to use the 64K available in the ES (extra segment) for storage.

By the way, the recipe for the soup was my father's, who was also known as the old fisherman. The soup is delicious and is always considered a special treat around our house.

The DISPLAY macro code is shown here.

```
DISPLAY   MACRO     WHAT        ;;DISPLAY MACRO TO CLEAR SCREEN
          CLEARSCREEN           ;;AND PRINT THE CHARACTER STRING
          CURSOR    0800H       ;;PASSED TO IT. A DELAY IS
          PRINTCHAR WHAT        ;;BUILT IN
          DELAY     45H
          ENDM
```

This macro is responsible for printing to the screen any option that the user selects from the screen menu. DISPLAY (a macro itself) uses four macros that are contained in MACLIB.MAC, the macro library. Whenever a string of information is passed to the dummy variable WHAT, DISPLAY clears the screen, moves the cursor to the fixed position 0800H, prints the information, and leaves the information on the screen for a set amount of time. Note that DELAY is a software delay routine that can easily be used when delay accuracy is not critical. The number passed to DELAY has an indirect correlation to time, since it represents the number of times DELAY will execute a loop. It is easy, however, to adjust the size of the number to obtain a satisfactory viewing period for the responses.

The following code places the main menu on the screen and awaits a keyboard response:

```
KEY:      CLEARSCREEN           ;CALL CLEARSCREEN MACRO
          CURSOR 0200H          ;CALL CURSOR MACRO
          PRINTCHAR MESS        ;CALL PRINTCHAR MACRO
          MOV       AH,1        ;PARAM. FOR KEYBOARD INTER.
          INT       21H         ;INTERRUPT FOR KYBD READ
```

```
;PROGRAM FOR 8088/80386 MACHINES
;PROGRAM ILLUSTRATES HOW TO CREATE A FULLY MENU DRIVEN
;ASSEMBLY LANGUAGE PROGRAM

PAGE ,132                           ;PAGE DIM 66 x 132

IF1                                 ;INCLUDE MACRO LIBRARY
            INCLUDE   C:MACLIB.MAC
ENDIF

DISPLAY MACRO    WHAT               ;;DISPLAY MACRO TO CLEAR SCREEN
            CLEARSCREEN             ;;AND PRINT THE CHARACTER STRING
            CURSOR  0800H           ;;PASSED TO IT.  A DELAY IS
            PRINTCHAR WHAT          ;;BUILT IN
            DELAY   45H
            ENDM

STACK SEGMENT PARA STACK            ;DEFIN. OF STACK SEGMENT
            DB      64 DUP ('MYSTACK ')
STACK     ENDS

MYDATA SEGMENT PARA 'DATA'          ;DEFINE START OF DATA SEGMENT
NAME1     DB      '          THE OLD FISHERMANS$'

ADRES1    DB      '          401 West Summit Avenue',0DH,0AH
          DB      '          Wilmington, Delaware$'

TELE      DB      '          302-994-4297$'

SSNUM     DB      '          005-10-1983$'

REC       DB      'Pop,s Delaware Vegetable Soup',0DH,0AH,0AH
          DB      '1 Soupbone, with lean meat',0DH,0AH
          DB      '3 cups water',0DH,0AH
          DB      '1 large onion, chopped          1 large potato, cubed',0DH,0AH
          DB      '1 cup, corn                     1 cup, chopped celery',0DH,0AH
          DB      '1 cup, lima beans               2 cups tomatoes',0DH,0AH
          DB      '1 cup, green beans              1 cup, barley',0DH,0AH
          DB      '1 cup, peas                     1 tbsp dried parsley',0DH,0AH
          DB      '1 cup, chopped carrots          1/2 tsp thyme',0DH,0AH,0AH
          DB      'Brown Meat, before adding to boiling water and soupbone.',0DH,0AH
          DB      'Simmer for 1 hour, remove bone and add vegetables.',0DH,0AH
          DB      'Cook for an additional 1/2 hour.    Serves 10',0DH,0AH,0AH
          DB      'DUMPLINGS:  1 cup flour, 1 egg, 1/2 cup water.  Drop',0DH,0AH
          DB      '            1 tsp. (size dumpling) mix into soup when cooking'
          DB      '$'
MESS      DB      'Please enter choice by letter to print: ',0DH,0AH,0AH
          DB      'N - Name',0DH,0AH
          DB      'A - Address',0DH,0AH
          DB      'T - Telephone',0DH,0AH
          DB      'S - Social Security Number',0DH,0AH
          DB      'R - Favorite Recipe',0DH,0AH
          DB      'L - To LEAVE program',0DH,0AH
          DB      '$'
MYDATA ENDS

MYCODE    SEGMENT PARA 'CODE'       ;DEFINE CODE SEG. FOR MASM
MYPROC    PROC FAR                  ;PROCEDURE IS NAMED MYPROC
          ASSUME CS:MYCODE,DS:MYDATA,SS:STACK
          PUSH    DS                ;SAVE LOCATION OF DS REG.
          SUB     AX,AX             ;GET A ZERO IN AX
          PUSH    AX                ;SAVE ZERO ON STACK, TOO
          MOV     AX,MYDATA         ;GET DATA LOCATION IN AX
          MOV     DS,AX             ;PUT IT IN DS REGISTER
KEY:      CLEARSCREEN               ;CALL CLEARSCREEN MACRO
          CURSOR 0200H              ;CALL CURSOR MACRO
          PRINTCHAR MESS            ;CALL PRINTCHAR MACRO
          MOV     AH,1              ;PARAM. FOR KEYBOARD INTER.
```

Figure 8-3. _____

Example of a fully menu-driven program

```
          INT     21H            ;INTERRUPT FOR KYBD READ
          CMP     AL,'N'         ;COMPARES N TO AL CONTENTS
          JNE     NOTN           ;JUMPS TO NOTN IF NOT EQUAL
          DISPLAY NAME1          ;OTHERWISE, DISPLAY MACRO
NOTN:     CMP     AL,'A'         ;COMPARES A TO AL CONTENTS
          JNE     NOTA           ;JUMP TO NOTA IF NOT EQUAL
          DISPLAY ADRES1         ;OTHERWISE, DISPLAY MACRO
NOTA:     CMP     AL,'T'         ;COMPARES T TO AL CONTENTS
          JNE     NOTT           ;JUMP TO NOTT IF NOT EQUAL
          DISPLAY TELE           ;OTHERWISE, DISPLAY MACRO
NOTT:     CMP     AL,'S'         ;COMPARES S TO AL CONTENTS
          JNE     NOTS           ;JUMP TO NOTS IF NOT EQUAL
          DISPLAY SSNUM          ;OTHERWISE, DISPLAY MACRO
NOTS:     CMP     AL,'R'         ;COMPARES R TO AL CONTENTS
          JNE     NOTR           ;JUMP TO NOTR IF NOT EQUAL
          DISPLAY REC            ;OTHERWISE, DISPLAY MACRO
NOTR:     CMP     AL,'L'         ;COMPARES L TO AL CONTENTS
          JE      FINISH         ;JUMP IF EQUAL TO FINISH
          JMP     KEY            ;OTHERWISE, REPEAT PROGRAM
FINISH:

          RET                    ;RETURN CONTROL TO DOS
MYPROC    ENDP                   ;END PROCEDURE NAMED MYPROC
MYCODE    ENDS                   ;END CODE SEGMENT NAMED MYCODE

          END                    ;END WHOLE PROGRAM
```

Figure 8-3. _____

Example of a fully menu-driven program (*continued*)

Again, in this section of code, macros from MACLIB.MAC are used. CLEARSCREEN clears the text screen, allowing PRINTCHAR to print the menu at the location set by CURSOR. Users are allowed to view the menu for as long as they wish—no action will be taken until a proper key is struck on the keyboard. The DOS interrupt INT 21H returns the key value in the AL register. The remainder of the program code checks the AL register for a proper key value and then sends DISPLAY the proper item to place on the screen.

Enter and run this program. Notice that the program responds very quickly to user entries. Also note that once the program is in executable form, the user will be unaware that it was written in assembly language. Thus, you can see that assembly language programs can work just as effectively as programs written in high-level languages, and they often execute faster.

CREATING A MORE COMPLICATED MENU-DRIVEN INTERACTIVE PROGRAM

Problem 4: Write a menu-driven program that asks the user to enter two numbers from the keyboard and then adds or multiplies the numbers together. Display the results on the screen.

This programming problem raises some interesting questions: How do you get numbers from the keyboard? What form are those numbers in? How do you perform mathematical operations and display the results on the screen? Fortunately, earlier programs have paved the way for easy answers. The last program illustrated methods for displaying menus and reading keyboard characters. The program in Figure 8-2 showed how numbers can be placed on the screen at locations controlled by the cursor.

To limit the complexity of this problem, certain assumptions will be made about the program. First, only single-digit decimal numbers can be entered from the keyboard. Second, the mathematical operations are limited to addition and multiplication. This means that the largest sum is 18 $(9 + 9)$ and the largest product is 81 (9×9).

Recall that when DOS interrupt INT 21H polls the keyboard, the ASCII equivalent of the key being struck is returned in the AL register. Numbers have ASCII values ranging from 30H to 39H. By limiting responses to single digits, any number intercepted by the program will be in this range. It would be best to leave the numbers in ASCII format, because this is exactly what is required to display them on the monitor screen. However, to do the arithmetic they must be converted to decimal digits by subtracting 30H immediately after they are entered.

Examine the program in Figure 8-4 and notice that two macros are used in addition to the macro library. Also notice that a NEAR procedure is used to place the results on the monitor screen. Since routines can often be placed in macros or procedures, how was the decision made in this program to place ARITH and READKEY in macros and PRINTIT in a procedure? First, READKEY contains only five lines of actual code and is only called three times by the program. It was a natural for a macro. ARITH and PRINTIT are about equal length—which way to go? ARITH is only called once by the program, so its code would have to appear once using either method. The use of a macro for ARITH has a slight edge here, since it would place the code in line and provide faster execution. PRINT-IT is a natural for a NEAR procedure. The code is fairly long, but the deciding factor is that PRINTIT is called three times by the program. This will surely shorten the overall program code. Look at each of these routines (ARITH, READKEY, and PRINTIT) before proceeding with an explanation of the main program.

The code for ARITH is shown here.

```
ARITH    MACRO                    ;;ARITHMETIC MACRO
         PUSH    AX               ;;PUSH AFFECTED REGISTERS
         PUSH    CX
         SUB     AX,AX            ;;PUT A ZERO IN AX
```

```
;FOR 80286/80386 MACHINES
;PROGRAM TO ILLUSTRATE A FULLY MENU DRIVEN INTERACTIVE PROGRAM
;WHICH ADDS OR MULTIPLIES TWO SINGLE DIGIT NUMBERS, ENTERED BY
;THE USER.

        PAGE ,132                       ;SET PAGE DIMENSIONS

        IF1                             ;INCLUDE MARCO LIBRARY
                INCLUDE C:MACLIB.MAC
        ENDIF

ARITH   MACRO                           ;;ARITHMETIC MACRO
        PUSH    AX                      ;;PUSH AFFECTED REGISTERS
        PUSH    CX
        SUB     AX,AX                   ;;PUT A ZERO IN AX
        MOV     AL,NUM1                 ;;PUT FIRST NUMBER IN AL
        CMP     OPER,'A'                ;;IS AN 'ADD' OR 'MUL' DESIRED
        JE      ADDER                   ;;IF ADD, MAKE JUMP
MULTP:  MUL     NUM2                    ;;OTHERWISE, MULTIPLY
        AAM                             ;;ASCII ADJUST RESULT
        JMP     FINISH                  ;;JUMP TO FINISH
ADDER:  ADD     AL,NUM2                 ;;IF NOT MULT, PREPARE TO ADD
        AAA                             ;;ASCII ADJUST RESULT
FINISH: AND     AH,0FH                  ;;KEEP LOWER FOUR BITS OF AH
        MOV     CL,04H                  ;;PREPARE TO SHIFT THEM
        SHL     AH,CL                   ;;SHIFT
        ADD     AL,AH                   ;;NOW AL+AH TO PACK DIGITS
        MOV     ANS,AL                  ;;SAVE SUM/PRODUCT IN ANS
        POP     CX                      ;;RETURN AFFECTED REGISTERS
        POP     AX
        ENDM                            ;;ENDS THE MACRO

READKEY MACRO   THISKEY                 ;;READ A SINGLE KEY
        PUSH    AX                      ;;SAVE AFFECTED REGISTER
        MOV     AH,01H                  ;;SET UP PARAMETERS
        INT     21H                     ;;READ KEY INTERRUPT
        MOV     THISKEY,AL              ;;SAVE KEY RETURNED IN VARIABLE
        POP     AX                      ;;RETURN AFFECTED REGISTER
        ENDM

STACK   SEGMENT PARA STACK      ;DEFINE STACK SEGMENT
        DB      64 DUP ('MYSTACK ')
STACK   ENDS                    ;END STACK SEGMENT

MYDATA SEGMENT PARA 'DATA'
PLUS    DB      '+$'
TIMES   DB      'x$'
EQUAL   DB      '=$'
MENU1   DB      '            CHOOSE OPERATION BY INPUTTING ONE OF THESE CHARACTERS:
        DB      '
        DB      '                  A - ADDS TWO NUMBERS
        DB      '
        DB      '                  M - MULTIPLIES TWO NUMBERS
        DB      '
        DB      '                  E - END THE PROGRAM
        DB      '
        DB      '$'
MENU2   DB      ' Enter first number (0-9):      $'
MENU3   DB      ' Enter second number (0-9):     $'
VALUE   DB      ?
POSTION DW      ?
OPER    DB      ?
NUM1    DB      0
NUM2    DB      0
ANS     DB      0
MYDATA ENDS
MYCODE  SEGMENT PARA 'CODE'     ;DEFIN CODE SEG. FOR MASM
MYPROC  PROC FAR                ;PROCEDURE IS NAMED MYPROC
```

Figure 8-4. _____

Fully menu-driven program to add or multiply two single-digit numbers

```
        ASSUME   CS:MYCODE,DS:MYDATA,SS:STACK
        PUSH     DS              ;SAVE LOCATION OF DS REG.
        SUB      AX,AX           ;GET A ZERO IN AX
        PUSH     AX              ;SAVE ZERO ON STACK, TOO
        MOV      AX,MYDATA       ;GET DATA LOCATION IN AX
        MOV      DS,AX           ;PUT IT IN DS REGISTER

;PRINT MAIN MENU TO SCREEN
MMENU:  CLEARSCREEN              ;CLEAR THE SCREEN
        CURSOR  0C00H            ;CALL CURSOR MACRO
        PRINTCHAR MENU1          ;PRINT MAIN MENU

;READ KEYBOARD FOR CORRECT ARITHMETIC OPERATION
KEY:    READKEY OPER             ;READ KEYBOARD ENTRY
        CMP      OPER,'E'        ;IS PROGRAM TO END?
        JNE      GETNU           ;IF NO, GET FIRST NUMBER
        JMP      END             ;IF YES, END PROGRAM
GETNU:  CLEARSCREEN              ;CLEAR THE MENU
        CURSOR  0C00H            ;MOVE CURSOR
        PRINTCHAR MENU2          ;REQUEST FIRST NUMBER

;READ FIRST SINGLE DIGIT NUMBER
        READKEY NUM1             ;READ KEYBOARD ENTRY
        SUB      NUM1,30H        ;CONDITION NUMBER
        CURSOR  0C00H            ;MOVE CURSOR
        CLEARSCREEN              ;CLEAR THE ENTRY
        PRINTCHAR MENU3          ;PRINTS MENU3

;READ SECOND SINGLE DIGIT NUMBER
        READKEY NUM2             ;READ KEYBOARD ENTRY
        SUB      NUM2,30H        ;CONDITION NUMBER
        CLEARSCREEN              ;CLEAR THE ENTRY

;PROCEED WITH ARITHMETIC
        ARITH                    ;DO ADD OR MULT OPERATION
        MOV      AL,NUM1         ;PREPARE TO PRINT NUM1
        MOV      VALUE,AL
        MOV      POSITION,0C1FH
        CALL     PRINTIT
        CURSOR  0C22H
        CMP      OPER,'A'
        JNE      T
        PRINTCHAR PLUS           ;PRINT + IF ADD OPERATION
        JMP      MORE
T:      PRINTCHAR TIMES          ;PRINT x IF MULT OPERATION
MORE:   MOV      AL,NUM2         ;PREPARE TO PRINT NUM2
        MOV      VALUE,AL
        MOV      POSTION,0C24H
        CALL     PRINTIT
        CURSOR  0C27H
        PRINTCHAR EQUAL          ;PRINT THE = SIGN
        MOV      AL,ANS          ;PREPARE TO PRINT ANS
        MOV      VALUE,AL
        MOV      POSITION,0C29H
        CALL     PRINTIT
        DELAY    25H             ;DELAY OUTPUT FOR READING
        JMP      MMENU           ;JUMP TO MAIN MENU AND REPEAT
END:
        RET                      ;RETURN TO DOS CONTROL
MYPROC  ENDP                     ;END PROCEDURE

PRINTIT PROC     NEAR            ;PROC TO PRINT NUMBERS
        PUSH     AX              ;SAVE AFFECTED REGISTERS
        PUSH     CX
        PUSH     DX
        MOV      AL,VALUE        ;LOAD DATA
        AND      AL,0F0H         ;KEEP ONLY UPPER FOUR BITS
        MOV      CL,4            ;ROTATE TO LOWER FOUR BITS
```

Figure 8-4. _____

Fully menu-driven program to add or multiply two single-digit numbers
(*continued*)

```
          ROR     AL,CL            ;ROTATE
          CURSOR  POSTION          ;CALL CURSOR MACRO
          PRINTNUM                 ;PRINTNUM MACRO
          MOV     AL,VALUE         ;LOAD DATA
          AND     AL,0FH           ;KEEP ONLY LOWER FOUR BITS
          ADD     POSTION,01H      ;PRINT TO LEFT OF FIRST DIGIT
          CURSOR  POSTION          ;CALL CURSOR MACRO
          PRINTNUM                 ;PRINTNUM MACRO
          POP     DX               ;RETURN AFFECTED REGISTERS
          POP     CX
          POP     AX
          RET                      ;END PROCEDURE
PRINTIT   ENDP

MYCODE    ENDS                     ;END CODE SEGMENT
          END                      ;END PROGRAM
```

Figure 8-4. _____

Fully menu-driven program to add or multiply two single-digit numbers
(*continued*)

```
          MOV     AL,NUM1          ;;PUT FIRST NUMBER IN AL
          CMP     OPER,'A'         ;;IS AN 'ADD' OR 'MUL' DESIRED
          JE      ADDER            ;;IF ADD, MAKE JUMP
MULTP:    MUL     NUM2             ;;OTHERWISE, MULTIPLY
          AAM                      ;;ASCII ADJUST RESULT
          JMP     FINISH           ;;JUMP TO FINISH
ADDER:    ADD     AL,NUM2          ;;IF NOT MULT, PREPARE TO ADD
          AAA                      ;;ASCII ADJUST RESULT
FINISH:   AND     AH,0FH           ;;KEEP LOWER FOUR BITS OF AH
          MOV     CL,04H           ;;PREPARE TO SHIFT THEM
          SHL     AH,CL            ;;SHIFT
          ADD     AL,AH            ;;NOW AL+AH TO PACK DIGITS
          MOV     ANS,AL           ;;SAVE SUM/PRODUCT IN ANS
          POP     CX               ;;RETURN AFFECTED REGISTERS
```

The data segment contains, among other items, two variables: NUM1
and NUM2. These are the DB (defined byte) variables that hold the two
single-digit numbers entered by the user. The user also has entered the
letter "A" for add or "M" for multiply. The letter is stored in the variable
OPER. NUM1 is moved into the AL register and then, depending on
whether "A" or "M" is specified, a branch is made to MULTP or ADDER.
Notice that in either case the mathematical operations are done on
unpacked decimal numbers. This requires the use of the AAM instruction
after the MUL operation and the AAA instruction after the ADD operation.
These instructions perform the ASCII adjust operation that was explained
in Chapter 3. Before saving the results, the two decimal digits are isolated
and packed into the AL register. This value is then moved to the variable
ANS.

The READKEY macro is an operation that has been used before.

```
READKEY  MACRO    THISKEY       ;;READ A SINGLE KEY
         PUSH     AX            ;;SAVE AFFECTED REGISTER
         MOV      AH,01H        ;;SET UP PARAMETERS
         INT      21H           ;;READ KEY INTERRUPT
         MOV      THISKEY,AL    ;;SAVE KEY RETURNED IN VARIABLE
         POP      AX            ;;RETURN AFFECTED REGISTER
         ENDM
```

READKEY uses the dummy variable THISKEY to return the keypress information. Notice when this macro is called that one of three variables is placed in the THISKEY position (OPER, NUM1, or NUM2). READKEY returns the ASCII code of the key pressed in the appropriate variable.

The PRINTIT procedure contains code that is almost identical to the display code contained in the program that counted seconds on the screen (shown in Figure 8-2):

```
PRINTIT  PROC     NEAR          ;PROC TO PRINT NUMBERS
         PUSH     AX            ;SAVE AFFECTED REGISTERS
         PUSH     CX
         PUSH     DX
         MOV      AL,VALUE      ;LOAD DATA
         AND      AL,0F0H       ;KEEP ONLY UPPER FOUR BITS
         MOV      CL,4          ;ROTATE TO LOWER FOUR BITS
         ROR      AL,CL         ;ROTATE
         CURSOR   POSTION       ;CALL CURSOR MACRO
         PRINTNUM               ;PRINTNUM MACRO
         MOV      AL,VALUE      ;LOAD DATA
         AND      AL,0FH        ;KEEP ONLY LOWER FOUR BITS
         ADD      POSTION,01H   ;PRINT TO LEFT OF FIRST DIGIT
         CURSOR   POSTION       ;CALL CURSOR MACRO
         PRINTNUM               ;PRINTNUM MACRO
         POP      DX            ;RETURN AFFECTED REGISTERS
         POP      CX
         POP      AX
         RET                    ;END PROCEDURE
PRINTIT  ENDP
```

The PRINTIT procedure is responsible for printing the original two single-digit numbers to the screen as well as the two-digit answer. Since procedures do not permit the use of dummy variables, the number to be printed will be passed to the procedure through the variable VALUE. This procedure prints the upper digit of the number and then moves the cursor and prints the lower digit. The routine expects a packed decimal number to be passed in the VALUE variable. This procedure uses two macros from the MACLIB.MAC library. CURSOR uses the variable POSTION to determine where on the screen printing will occur. PRINTNUM merely takes the unpacked decimal digit and converts it to ASCII in order to display it on the screen.

Why have numbers been unpacked, packed, and then unpacked? This is a function of the available routines. First, the add and multiply routines required unpacked numbers. Second, the results of AAA and AAM place the results in the registers in slightly different forms. AAA leaves the answer in AL, and AAM places the answer in both AH and AL. The decision was made to pack the answer, since a routine (PRINTIT) was already available for displaying a packed two-digit BCD number.

The program, when executed, displays the menu shown here in the program's data segment. The user can decide to add, multiply, or end the program at this level.

```
;PRINT MAIN MENU TO SCREEN
MMENU:   CLEARSCREEN                  ;CLEAR THE SCREEN
         CURSOR 0C00H                 ;CALL CURSOR MACRO
         PRINTCHAR MENU1              ;PRINT MAIN MENU

;READ KEYBOARD FOR CORRECT ARITHMETIC OPERATION
KEY:     READKEY    OPER              ;READ KEYBOARD ENTRY
         CMP        OPER,'E'          ;IS PROGRAM TO END?
         JNE        GETNU             ;IF NO, GET FIRST NUMBER
         JMP        END               ;IF YES, END PROGRAM
GETNU:   CLEARSCREEN                  ;CLEAR THE MENU
         CURSOR     0C00H             ;MOVE CURSOR
         PRINTCHAR  MENU2             ;REQUEST FIRST NUMBER
```

The first three lines of code clear the screen, set the cursor position, and display the main menu. The next section calls for a keyboard entry. If the entry is not "E" (for end), the program will continue and request a number from the user.

```
;READ FIRST SINGLE DIGIT NUMBER
         READKEY    NUM1              ;READ KEYBOARD ENTRY
         SUB        NUM1,30H          ;CONDITION NUMBER
         CURSOR     0C00H             ;MOVE CURSOR
         CLEARSCREEN                  ;CLEAR THE ENTRY
```

The second number is requested in a similar manner:

```
;READ SECOND SINGLE DIGIT NUMBER
         READKEY    NUM2              ;READ KEYBOARD ENTRY
         SUB        NUM2,30H          ;CONDITION NUMBER
         CLEARSCREEN                  ;CLEAR THE ENTRY
```

Once this information is entered, the main routine does the arithmetic and prepares the screen for the output:

```
;PROCEED WITH ARITHMETIC
            ARITH                       ;DO ADD OR MULT OPERATION
```

The main routine makes a call to the ARITH macro. NUM1 and NUM2 supplies ARITH with the two single-digit numbers. ARITH returns its packed two-digit BCD number in ANS:

```
            MOV       AL,NUM1         ;PREPARE TO PRINT NUM1
            MOV       VALUE,AL
            MOV       POSTION,0C1FH
            CALL      PRINTIT
```

The preceding section of code passes the number in NUM1 to the PRINT-IT procedure. The cursor position is set to 0C1FH. These four lines print the first number entered by the user slightly to the left of the center of the screen. Moving from left to right, the proper symbol for addition or multiplication is now printed:

```
            CURSOR    0C22H
            CMP       OPER,'A'
            JNE       T
            PRINTCHAR PLUS            ;PRINT + IF ADD OPERATION
            JMP       MORE
    T:      PRINTCHAR TIMES           ;PRINT × IF MULT OPERATION
```

The symbol for add (+) was saved as character data in the data segment under the variable name PLUS. A small multiplication sign (×) was saved in TIMES to represent multiplication. Since both are character data, the PRINTCHAR macro is used to place them on the screen at the current cursor position.

```
    MORE:   MOV       AL,NUM2         ;PREPARE TO PRINT NUM2
            MOV       VALUE,AL
            MOV       POSITION,0C24H
            CALL      PRINTIT
```

The second number is then printed by PRINTIT, and preparation is made to print the equal sign. The equal sign (=) was saved as character data in the variable EQUAL.

```
CURSOR     0C27H
PRINTCHAR  EQUAL            ;PRINT THE = SIGN
```

Finally, the answer is printed to the right of the equal sign:

```
MOV    AL,ANS          ;PREPARE TO PRINT ANS
MOV    VALUE,AL
MOV    POSTION,0C29H
CALL   PRINTIT
```

The answer is displayed for a predetermined amount of time before the user is returned to the main menu.

```
DELAY  25H             ;DELAY OUTPUT FOR READING
JMP    MMENU           ;JUMP TO MAIN MENU AND REPEAT
```

In this program, the simpler software delay routine is used because timing considerations are not critical.

This program can be the foundation for more complex programs. It can be expanded to include all four basic arithmetic operations (addition, multiplication, subtraction, and division) that provide integer results. It can also be altered to allow the user to enter an answer for the arithmetic problem. This answer can then be compared to the computer's answer, and the user could be awarded points based upon the number of correct answers given. Finally, the program could be modified to accept two-digit numbers for each entry (see the square-wave program in Chapter 9). Be aware, though, that this is not a simple expansion. Writing the routine to accept two digits is a bit of a challenge, but it is nothing compared to the manipulation required to do the addition and multiplication of a two-bit number and return the results to the screen.

USING ADVANCED STRING COMMANDS

Problem 5:   Create a menu-driven program that allows the user to check the spelling of a word entered from the keyboard.

This program is quite different from previous menu-driven programs. The difference is not in the creation of the menu, but in how data is entered from the keyboard and then used within the program.

Several programming problems must be solved: How are words entered from the keyboard and saved by the program? How, if at all, does word length affect data input? Where is the dictionary that is used to compare the user's entry? Several interesting options are open to you.

Out of necessity, this will be a fairly simple spelling checker. No sorting will be done with the dictionary. A linear search will be made of each entry in the dictionary until a match with the user's word is found, or the dictionary is exhausted. The dictionary will be limited to eight words that start with the letter "X." Feel free to expand the number of words in the dictionary. The dictionary is only limited by the size of the data segment and the patience of the person entering the words. Figure 8-5 shows the complete program. The data segment is repeated here:

```
MYDATA   SEGMENT   PARA 'DATA'      ;DATA AREA OF PROGRAM
NAME1    DB        11,11 DUP(' '),'$'
MAIN     DB        'Type in a word for a spelling check', 0DH,0AH,'$'
MESS1    DB        0DH,0AH,'NOT IN DICTIONARY$'
MESS2    DB        0DH,0AH,'SPELLED CORRECTLY$'
DICTION  DB        'XANTHIC    ','XANTHIN   ','XENIS     '
         DB        'XENON      ','XYLEM     ','XYLIC     '
         DB        'XYLOTOMOUS ','XYSTER    '
MYDATA   ENDS
```

The variable NAME1 is reserved for user input from the keyboard. Each of the words in the dictionary is limited to ten characters (this number could be enlarged in an expanded dictionary). When the user's word is checked with the dictionary, one of two responses is returned: NOT IN DICTIONARY or SPELLED CORRECTLY. Naturally, it would be possible to spell a word correctly and still have it flagged if the word is not included in the dictionary. The menu consists of a single line message: Type in a word for a spelling check.

The program is divided into three main sections: data entry, word comparison, and message output. The data entry section of the program takes on the characteristic appearance of the programs that appeared in Chapter 5:

```
;PROGRAM SEGMENT ALLOWS WORD ENTRY FROM KEYBOARD
        LEA     DX,NAME1      ;WHERE TO STORE STRING
        MOV     AH,0AH        ;KEYBOARD READ PARAMETER
        INT     21H           ;READ KEYBOARD
```

```
;FOR 80286/80386 MACHINES
;PROGRAM TO ILLUSTRATE HOW TO BUILD A SIMPLE SPELLING CHECKER
;USING ADVANCED STRING COMMANDS
;
PAGE ,132                              ;SET PAGE DIMENSIONS

IF1
          INCLUDE C:MACLIB.MAC      ;INCLUDE EXTERNAL FILE
ENDIF                                ;OF USEFUL FUNCTIONS

MYDATA   SEGMENT PARA 'DATA'      ;DATA AREA OF PROGRAM
NAME1    DB      11,11 DUP(' '),'$'
MAIN     DB      'Type in a word for a spelling check',0DH,0AH,'$'
MESS1    DB      0DH,0AH,'NOT IN DICTIONARY$'
MESS2    DB      0DH,0AH,'SPELLED CORRECTLY$'
DICTION  DB      'XANTHIC   ','XANTHIN   ','XENIS     '
         DB      'XENON     ','XYLEM     ','XYLIC     '
         DB      'XYLOTOMOUS','XYSTER    '
MYDATA   ENDS

STACK    SEGMENT PARA STACK       ;STACK SEGMENT OF PROGRAM
         DB      64 DUP('MYSTACK ')
STACK    ENDS

MYCODE   SEGMENT PARA 'CODE'      ;DEFINE CODE SEG. FOR MASM
MYPROC   PROC    FAR              ;PROCEDURE IS NAMED MYPROC
         ASSUME  CS:MYCODE,DS:MYDATA,SS:STACK,ES:MYDATA
         PUSH    DS               ;SAVE LOCATION OF DS REG.
         SUB     AX,AX            ;GET A ZERO IN AX
         PUSH    AX               ;SAVE ZERO ON STACK, TOO
         MOV     AX,MYDATA        ;GET DATA LOCATION IN AX
         MOV     DS,AX            ;PUT IT IN DS REGISTER
         MOV     ES,AX            ;PUT IT IN ES ALSO

;MAIN MENU OF SPELLING CHECKER
         CLEARSCREEN              ;CLEAR THE SCREEN
         PRINTCHAR MAIN           ;PRINT MAIN MENU MESSAGE

;PROGRAM SEGMENT ALLOWS WORD ENTRY FROM KEYBOARD
         LEA     DX,NAME1         ;WHERE TO STORE STRING
         MOV     AH,0AH           ;KEYBOARD READ PARAMETER
         INT     21H              ;READ KEYBOARD

;PROGRAM SEGMENT REMOVES CARRIAGE RETURN FOR WORDS WITH LESS
;THAN 10 CHARACTERS
         MOV     AL,NAME1+1       ;GET CHARACTER COUNT IN STRING
         ADD     AL,2             ;OFFSET BY TWO
         CBW                      ;CONVERT TO A WORD
         MOV     BX,AX            ;MOVE TO BX REGISTER
         MOV     NAME1[BX],' '    ;REPLACE CR WITH A BLANK

;COMPARE KEYBOARD ENTRY WITH DICTIONARY LIST
         CLD                      ;SET DIRECTION FLAG
```

Figure 8-5. _____

Building a simple spelling checker using advanced string commands

```
          MOV     BX,00H              ;SET BX FOR INDEX DISPLACEMENT
          MOV     AX,00H              ;SET NUMBER OF WORDS INIT TO 0
NXTWRD:   MOV     CL,0AH              ;SET SIZE OF EACH WORD IN BYTES
          LEA     DI,NAME1+2          ;LOAD EFFECTIVE ADDRESS OF DATA
          LEA     SI,DICTION[BX]      ;LOAD DIC. WITH BX OFFSET
          REPE    CMPSB               ;COMPARE 10 BYTES FROM DICTIONARY
          JE      CONGRD              ;DO ALL 10 BYTES MATCH?
          ADD     BX,0AH              ;IF NO, SET OFFSET FOR NEXT WORD
          ADD     AX,01H              ;INCREMENT WORD COUNTER
          CMP     AX,08H              ;HAVE WE DONE ALL THE WORDS YET?
          JNE     NXTWRD              ;IF NO, CONTINUE
;PRINT APPROPRIATE MESSAGE TO MONITOR
          PRINTCHAR MESS1             ;WORD NOT IN DICTIONARY
          JMP     OUT
CONGRD:   PRINTCHAR MESS2             ;WORD IN DICTIONARY
OUT:

          RET                         ;RETURN CONTROL TO DOS
MYPROC    ENDP                        ;END PROCEDURE NAMED MYPROC
MYCODE    ENDS                        ;END CODE SEGMENT NAMED MYCODE

          END                         ;END WHOLE PROGRAM
```

Figure 8-5. _____

Building a simple spelling checker using advanced string commands
(*continued*)

DOS interrupt 21H allows keyboard entry into NAME1. The number of
letters entered depends entirely upon the size to which NAME1 was initialized. Eleven blanks were used to pad NAME1 to accept up to ten letters
because INT 21H with AH set to 0AH returns the character count for the
entered word in the first position. You must also deal with the problem of a
carriage return being entered with the string when the number of letters in
the word is less than the maximum. Since the words in the dictionary do
not have a carriage return included in their strings, carriage returns must be
removed from the words entered by the user. This is done as follows:

```
;PROGRAM SEGMENT REMOVES CARRIAGE RETURN FOR WORDS WITH LESS
;THAN 10 CHARACTERS
          MOV     AL,NAME1+1          ;GET CHARACTER COUNT IN STRING
          ADD     AL,2                ;OFFSET BY TWO
          CBW                         ;CONVERT TO A WORD
          MOV     BX,AX               ;MOVE TO BX REGISTER
          MOV     NAME1[BX],' '       ;REPLACE CR WITH A BLANK
```

The first "11" under the NAME1 definition represents the maximum number of characters that NAME1 can accept, the second "11" (11 DUP...) merely pads NAME1 with 11 blanks. The $ sign is the sentinel value for a DOS print call. Therefore, NAME1 contains the maximum number of characters, 11 blanks, and $.

To determine how many characters were actually entered by the user, NAME1+1 must be used to obtain this value from the string. An offset of 2 is required by this routine to move the cursor to the position one byte past the last letter in the word (the position of the carriage return). Why two instead of one? The program had to skip that first 11, too. The index into NAME1 is done using the BX register, so the value in AL is converted to a word size by using the CBW instruction. In the final step, the carriage return is replaced with a blank.

The actual comparison of the user's word with the words in the dictionary is achieved with the following code:

```
;COMPARE KEYBOARD ENTRY WITH DICTIONARY LIST
        CLD                         ;SET DIRECTION FLAG
        MOV     BX,00H              ;SET BX FOR INDEX DISPLACEMENT
        MOV     AX,00H              ;SET NUMBER OF WORDS INIT TO 0
NXTWRD: MOV     CL,0AH              ;SET SIZE OF EACH WORD IN BYTES
        LEA     DI,NAME1+2          ;LOAD EFFECTIVE ADDRESS OF DATA
        LEA     SI,DICTION[BX]      ;LOAD DIC. WITH BX OFFSET
        REPE    CMPSB               ;COMPARE 10 BYTES FROM DICTIONARY
        JE      CONGRD              ;DO ALL 10 BYTES MATCH?
        ADD     BX,0AH              ;IF NO, SET OFFSET FOR NEXT WORD
        ADD     AX,01H              ;INCREMENT WORD COUNTER
        CMP     AX,08H              ;HAVE WE DONE ALL THE WORDS YET?
        JNE     NXTWRD              ;IF NO, CONTINUE
```

The strategy for the search is to use CMPSB to compare the string byte of the user's word with a word in the dictionary. If a complete match is not achieved, the program will advance to the next word in the dictionary. This process continues until a match is found, or until the dictionary is exhausted.

The BX register holds the offset into the dictionary. To move from one word to another requires that BX be incremented by the length of the words contained in the dictionary. All words are ten characters long—remember, the padded blanks count too. The AX register keeps a count of how many words have actually been compared and compares that number with the total words in the dictionary (eight, for this dictionary). CL holds the count for the number of bytes to compare in each word (ten in this case). The effective address for NAME1 is NAME1+2 in order to avoid the maximum number of letters and the actual number of letters stored at the beginning of the variable. Using REPE CMPSB, the program exits immediately upon finding a match. If a match is found, this section of code terminates and the message indicating a match is printed. If no match is found, BX is incremented by 10 (0AH), and the ten letters of the next word in the dictionary are compared. If the dictionary is exhausted without a match, the message indicating this is printed.

The dictionary, in this simple form, suffers from two major flaws. First, since no sorting is provided, each word in the dictionary will be checked if any entry is spelled incorrectly or does not appear in the dictionary, and each word in the dictionary may be checked even if the word is spelled correctly if the word is the last entry in the dictionary. An efficient sorting algorithm would greatly improve the speed of operation. Second, each entry in the dictionary is padded to the same number of characters. Initially, it might seem easy not to pad individual words and just check letters. Why not set the number of comparisons equal to the number of letters entered from the keyboard? The problem with this approach, if all else remains the same, is that if the user enters the letters *xyle*, for example, this "word" might be flagged as correct, even though it is not in the dictionary, because the word *xylem* is in the dictionary. If only the first four letters were checked, the program would have found a match. The problem could arise in many ways, since the letter combinations could be imbedded within a dictionary word in different means. Thus, there is room for improvement, but proceed with caution.

CREATING AND USING
DISKETTE FILES

The previous five programming examples emphasized problem-solving techniques using the tools developed in Chapters 5, 6, and 7. These five programs required the user to be more creative and ingenious with the tools already at hand. The remaining programs of this chapter will emphasize concepts that are usually considered more advanced—concepts for which no tools have yet been developed.

The next three programs involve file manipulation, a topic which many introductory assembly language books skip or only mention briefly. However, being able to read and write to a file is a fundamental task in any language.

DOS 2.0 marked a significant change in how files could be handled by assembly language programs. It is true that files can also be handled at the BIOS level, but is not the preferred method. DOS interrupts offer more complete services and are expected to have a longer supported lifetime than BIOS routines (at least in the file handling areas). DOS versions 1.0 to 1.1 and some in-house variations required the use of the FCB (file control block) when accessing files with INT 21H (AH=0FH to 29H). The FCB contained information about the file — drive number, file name, file name extension, current block number, record size, file size, date, record number, and relative record number. Detailed information about FCB can be found in DOS manuals up to DOS version 3.0. Starting with DOS 3.0, this information was removed from the DOS manual and placed in a separate DOS technical manual. FCB gave the programmer great control over the individual files, but it was at best a very messy solution that had to be applied each time a file was accessed. Current versions of DOS still support these interrupt possibilities, but their use is not recommended.

The enhancements that were included in DOS 2.0 and expanded in DOS 3.0 later enabled the programmer to access files without the use of FCB. The new DOS services for files still use INT 21H, but use AH=39H to 46H. Refer to the DOS 21H table listing in Chapter 5 for more details regarding these commands.

When a file is created with the use of these enhanced DOS commands, DOS creates a *file handle* for that file, which is returned to the program any time the file is opened for reading or writing. The file handle is returned to the AX register when the file is opened (see the OPENFIL MACRO in Figure 8-7). The file handle automatically performs all of the housekeeping functions that were once done by FCB, but with a lot less programmer intervention. Of course, the price paid is loss of control over FCB.

As with other extended DOS functions, error codes are returned to the AX register when creating, opening, reading, writing, or closing a file is not permitted. The original 18 error messages in DOS 2.0 have been expanded to 39 in DOS 3.0 and later versions. For example, AX=1 indicates an invalid function number, AX=2 indicates file not found, and AX=1FH indicates a general failure. More details about these numbers can be found in the *DOS Technical Manual* or in books such as Peter Norton's *Programmer's Guide to the IBM PC*. It is good programming practice to test for returned error codes and signal the programmer when they occur.

The next three programming problems illustrate different aspects of file manipulation. In Problem 6 you will create a diskette file; in Problem 7 you will enable the programmer to open, write to, and close the file; and in

Problem 8 you will enable the user to read the file.

Problem 6: Create a disk file.

Before using a file for the first time, the file must be created using AH=3CH. Figure 8-6 illustrates just how easy this is with the extended DOS commands. The main body of the program, shown here, simply calls the CRETFIL macro, and the job is done.

```
CRETFIL   MACRO                         ;;MACRO TO CREATE A FILE
          MOV      AH,3CH               ;;DOS 21H PARAMETER TO CREATE FILE
          MOV      CX,OOH               ;;NORMAL FILE ATTRIBUTE
```

```
;FOR 80286/80386 MACHINES
;PROGRAM TO ILLUSTRATE HOW TO CREATE A FILE USING
;EXTENDED DOS SERVICES
;FOR LATER READ/WRITE OPERATIONS

PAGE ,132                           ;SET PAGE DIMENSIONS

CRETFIL MACRO                       ;;MACRO TO CREATE A FILE
        MOV      AH,3CH              ;;DOS 21H PARAMETER TO CREATE FILE
        MOV      CX,OOH              ;;NORMAL FILE ATTRIBUTE
        LEA      DX,FILENAM          ;;DISK/NAME/EXT OF FILE TO CREATE
        INT      21H                 ;;CREATE
        ENDM

STACK   SEGMENT PARA STACK
        DB       64 DUP ('MYSTACK ')
STACK   ENDS

MYDATA  SEGMENT PARA 'DATA'
FILENAM DB       'B:NUMBERS.DAT',O ;NAME OF FILE TO BE CREATED
MYDATA  ENDS

MYCODE  SEGMENT PARA 'CODE'        ;DEFINE CODE SEG. FOR MASM
MYPROC  PROC     FAR               ;PROCEDURE IS NAMED MYPROC
        ASSUME   CS:MYCODE,DS:MYDATA,SS:STACK
        PUSH     DS                ;SAVE LOCATION OF DS REG.
        SUB      AX,AX             ;GET A ZERO IN AX
        PUSH     AX                ;SAVE ZERO ON STACK, TOO
        MOV      AX,MYDATA         ;GET DATA LOCATION IN AX
        MOV      DS,AX             ;PUT IT IN DS REGISTER
        CRETFIL                    ;CREATE A FILE
        RET                        ;RETURN DOS CONTROL
MYPROC  ENDP                       ;END PROCEDURE
MYCODE  ENDS                       ;END CODE SEGMENT NAMED MYCODE
        END                        ;END WHOLE PROGRAM
```

Figure 8-6. _____

Creating a file using extended DOS services

```
    LEA       DX,FILENAM      ;;DISK/NAME/EXT OF FILE TO CREATE
    INT       21H             ;;CREATE
    ENDM
```

CRETFIL (create file) sets the parameters for opening or creating a file using the DOS type-21H interrupt. The value in CX determines the file's attribute.

OH	Normal file
1H	Read only file
2H	Hidden file
4H	System file
8H	Volume label
10H	Subdirectory
20H	Archive file

The FILENAM points to an ASCIIZ string in the data segment that contains the disk drive, path name, file name, and file extension.

```
MYDATA    SEGMENT PARA 'DATA'
FILENAM   DB         'B:NUMBERS.DAT',0 ;NAME OF FILE TO BE CREATED
MYDATA    ENDS
```

The program in the next problem (see Figure 8-7) allows the user to enter names and telephone numbers in a file called NUMBERS.DAT, which resides on the disk in drive B. The zero after the file extension is a delimiter to mark the end of the string. CRETFIL, using AH=3CH, opens or creates a file and sets the length of the file to 0. Therefore, it should only be used to create a new file or erase an existing file. The file handle, if it is needed, is returned to the AX register. It should be an easy exercise, using your knowledge from previous programs, to allow the user to enter the information into FILENAM directly from the keyboard.

Problem 7: Open, Write to, and Close a disk file.

Four macros, similar to the one used in Figure 8-6, are used by the next program to open, index to the end of the file, write to, and close a file. Figure 8-7 is a complete listing of a program that allows access to the previously created file.

To read or write to a file, the file must first be opened. If AH=3CH is used to open a file, the file length is set to zero, indicating an empty file. This only needs to be done upon file creation—from that point on,

```
;FOR 80286/80386  IBM MACHINES
;PROGRAM TO ILLUSTRATE HOW TO OPEN, WRITE TO AND CLOSE
;A PREVIOUSLY CREATED FILE

PAGE ,132                               ;SET PAGE DIMENSIONS

IF1
          INCLUDE C:MACLIB.MAC          ;INCLUDE EXTERNAL FILE
ENDIF                                   ;OF USEFUL FUNCTIONS

OPENFIL MACRO                           ;;MACRO TO OPEN A PREV. CREATED FILE
        MOV       AL,01H                ;;OPEN FILE FOR WRITE ONLY
        MOV       AH,3DH                ;;PARAMETER TO OPEN
        LEA       DX,FILENAM            ;;DISK/NAME/EXT OF FILE TO OPEN
        INT       21H                   ;;OPEN
        MOV       FHAND,AX              ;;SAVE FILE HANDLE, JUST RETURNED
        ENDM

INDEXNUM MACRO                          ;;MACRO FOR FINDING END OF FILE
        MOV       AL,02H                ;;PARAMETERS FOR DOS 21H CALL
        MOV       AH,42H
        MOV       BX,FHAND
        MOV       CX,OH
        MOV       DX,OH
        INT       21H                   ;;GET INDEX
        ENDM

WRITFIL MACRO                           ;;MACRO TO WRITE AN ENTRY TO FILE
        MOV       AH,40H                ;;PREPARE TO WRITE TO FILE
        MOV       BX,FHAND              ;;PLACE FILE HANDLE IN BX
        MOV       CX,80                 ;;NUMBER OF BYTES TO WRITE
        LEA       DX,NAMEFLD            ;;POINT TO CHARACTERS TO WRITE
        INT       21H                   ;;WRITE
        ENDM

CLOSFIL MACRO                           ;;MACRO TO CLOSE A FILE
        MOV       AH,3EH                ;;PREPARE TO CLOSE FILE
        MOV       BX,FHAND              ;;PUT FILE HANDLE IN BX
        INT       21H                   ;;CLOSE
        ENDM

STACK    SEGMENT PARA STACK
         DB      64 DUP ('MYSTACK ')
STACK    ENDS

MYDATA   SEGMENT PARA 'DATA'
NAMEPAR  LABEL   BYTE
MAXLEN   DB      81                     ;MAXIMUM LENGTH OF INFO + 1
ACTLEN   DB      ?                      ;ACTUAL LENGTH OF INFO
NAMEFLD  DB      80 DUP(' '),'$'        ;INFO TO BE PLACED ON DISK
FILENAM  DB      'B:NUMBERS.DAT',0 ;NAME OF FILE TO BE WRITTEN TO
FHAND    DW      ?                      ;STORAGE FOR FILE HANDLE
PROMPT   DB      'NAME                                  TELEPHONES'
MYDATA   ENDS

MYCODE   SEGMENT PARA 'CODE'            ;DEFINE CODE SEG. FOR MASM
```

Figure 8-7. _____

Program to open, write to, and close a previously created file

```
MYPROC    PROC      FAR            ;PROCEDURE IS NAMED MYPROC
          ASSUME    CS:MYCODE,DS:MYDATA,SS:STACK,ES:MYDATA
          PUSH      DS             ;SAVE LOCATION OF DS REG.
          SUB       AX,AX          ;GET A ZERO IN AX
          PUSH      AX             ;SAVE ZERO ON STACK, TOO
          MOV       AX,MYDATA      ;GET DATA LOCATION IN AX
          MOV       DS,AX          ;PUT IT IN DS REGISTER
          MOV       ES,AX          ;PUT IT IN ES REGISTER

          CLEARSCREEN              ;CLEAR THE SCREEN
          OPENFIL                  ;OPEN THE FILE
          INDEXNUM
AGAIN:
          CALL      PASINFO        ;PASS KEYBOARD INFORMATION
          CMP       ACTLEN,00      ;IF NO INPUT, END PROGRAM
          JNE       AGAIN          ;OTHERWISE, GET MORE INPUT
          CLOSFIL                  ;CLOSE THE FILE
          RET
MYPROC    ENDP

PASINFO   PROC      NEAR           ;PASS INFO TO DISK FILE
          CURSOR    0000H          ;SET CURSOR FOR TOP OF PAGE
          PRINTCHAR PROMPT         ;REQUEST FOR USER INPUT
          CURSOR    0100H          ;MOVE CURSOR DOWN, FOR WRITE
          MOV       AH,0AH         ;PARAMETER FOR STRING INPUT
          LEA       DX,NAMEPAR     ;STRING IN 'NAMEPAR'
          INT       21H            ;READ KEYBOARD INPUT
          CLEARSCREEN              ;CLEARS SCREEN OF LAST NAME
          CMP       ACTLEN,00      ;IS INPUT NOTHING?
          JE        ENDO           ;IF YES, END THIS PROGRAM
          MOV       BH,00          ;PUT STRING LENGTH IN BX
          MOV       BL,ACTLEN
          MOV       NAMEFLD[BX],' ' ;PREPARE TO MOVE STRING TO DISK
          WRITFIL                  ;WRITE TO DISK FILE

          CLD                      ;SET DIRECTION OF STRING OPT
          LEA       DI,NAMEFLD     ;PREPARE TO STORE BLANKS
          MOV       CX,80          ;IN NAMEFLD VARIABLE
          MOV       AL,20H         ;BLANK (20H) VALUE
          REP       STOSB          ;REPEAT/STORE 80 TIMES
ENDO:
          RET
PASINFO   ENDP                     ;END PROCEDURE

MYCODE    ENDS                     ;END CODE SEGMENT NAMED MYCODE
          END                      ;END WHOLE PROGRAM
```

Figure 8-7. ─────────────────────────────────────

Program to open, write to, and close a previously created file (*continued*)

AH=3DH will be used to open a previously created file.

```
OPENFIL MACRO                    ;;MACRO TO OPEN A PREV. CREATED
                                 ;;FILE
        MOV       AL,01H         ;;OPEN FILE FOR WRITE ONLY
```

```
MOV     AH,3DH          ;;PARAMETER TO OPEN
LEA     DX,FILENAM      ;;DISK/NAME/EXT OF FILE TO OPEN
INT     21H             ;;OPEN
MOV     FHAND,AX        ;;SAVE FILE HANDLE, JUST RETURNED
ENDM
```

In the OPENFIL (open file) macro, AL determines whether the file is a read only or write only file or both. If AL=0, the file permits read-only access, AL=1 signals write-only access, and AL=2 signals read and write access. This information occupies the lower three bits of the AL byte. The upper five bits, in DOS 3.0 and later versions, support file sharing information. FILENAM must meet the same requirements as it did when the file was created (disk drive, path name, file name, file extension, and a one-byte delimiter). Typically, FILENAM is an ASCIIZ string located in the data segment. The file handle returned in the AX register is saved in the variable FHAND, also located in the data segment, for future program calls.

Before writing to this file, it is necessary to determine where the end-of-file (EOF) is, or the program will overwrite previously stored information when the file is opened and written to. The macro INDEXNUM (index number) provides this service.

```
INDEXNUM MACRO                  ;;MACRO FOR FINDING END OF FILE
        MOV     AL,02H          ;;PARAMETERS FOR DOS 21H CALL
        MOV     AH,42H
        MOV     BX,FHAND
        MOV     CX,0H
        MOV     DX,0H
        INT     21H             ;;GET INDEX
        ENDM
```

When AH=42H, DOS provides the user with the ability to move the file pointer. Before calling this interrupt, BX must be loaded with the previously saved file handle, and AL must contain the pointer's starting location. If AL=0, the offset is measured from the starting point of the file. If AL=1, the offset is measured from the current location. If AL=2, the offset is taken from the end-of-file. The offset value is contained in the CX:DX pair. CX is typically 0, unless the file is larger than 64K. When AL=2 the program is searching for the offset (or file size), so CX and DX traditionally are set to 0. When interrupt 21H is called, the returned offset is placed in the DX:AX register pair. In this code, it was only necessary to move the pointer to the end-of-file.

When you write to an opened file using the extended DOS services, the WRITFIL (write file) macro sets up the necessary DOS parameters.

```
WRITFIL MACRO                       ;;MACRO TO WRITE AN ENTRY TO FILE
        MOV     AH,40H              ;;PREPARE TO WRITE TO FILE
        MOV     BX,FHAND            ;;PLACE FILE HANDLE IN BX
        MOV     CX,80               ;;NUMBER OF BYTES TO WRITE
        LEA     DX,NAMEFLD          ;;POINT TO CHARACTERS TO WRITE
        INT     21H                 ;;WRITE
        ENDM
```

AH=40H is the DOS write-to-file parameter. BX, again, is loaded with the previously saved file handle. CX contains the count of the total number of bytes to write (this program writes a whole line of text each time it is called). The address of the bytes that are to be written is pointed to by the DS:DX register pair. In this case, NAMEFLD is saved in the data segment. It initially contains 80 blanks and the "$" sentinel, as shown here.

```
MYDATA      SEGMENT   PARA 'DATA'
NAMEPAR     LABEL     BYTE
MAXLEN      DB        81              ;MAXIMUM LENGTH OF INFO + 1
ACTLEN      DB        ?               ;ACTUAL LENGTH OF INFO
NAMEFLD     DB        80 DUP(' '),'$' ;INFO TO BE PLACED ON DISK
FILENAM     DB        'B:NUMBERS.DAT',0  ;NAME OF FILE TO BE CREATED
FHAND       DW        ?               ;STORAGE FOR FILE HANDLE
PROMPT      DB        'NAME           ;TELEPHONE$'
MYDATA      ENDS
```

When the program has entered all of its data into the file, any opened files should be closed. This is done with the CLOSFIL (close file) macro by using AH=3EH.

```
CLOSFIL MACRO                       ;;MACRO TO CLOSE A FILE
        MOV     AH,3EH              ;;PREPARE TO CLOSE FILE
        MOV     BX,FHAND            ;;PUT FILE HANDLE IN BX
        INT     21H                 ;;CLOSE
        ENDM
```

Notice again that it is necessary to specify the file handle, but not the FILENAM information. In other words, BX should contain the file handle of the last opened file.

A careful look at the overhead in the code segment reveals that this program uses advanced string commands. Notice that Figure 8-7 does contain REP STOSB. The actual program code of the main procedure is fairly short:

```
            CLEARSCREEN                 ;CLEAR THE SCREEN
```

```
            OPENFIL                    ;OPEN THE FILE
            INDEXNUM
AGAIN:
            CALL      PASINFO          ;PASS KEYBOARD INFORMATION
            CMP       ACTLEN,00        ;IF NO INPUT, END PROGRAM
            JNE       AGAIN            ;OTHERWISE, GET MORE INPUT
            CLOSFIL                    ;CLOSE THE FILE
            RET
MYPROC      ENDP
```

The screen is initially cleared with the **CLEARSCREEN** macro from the MACLIB.MAC library. The file B:NUMBERS.DAT is opened (it was created by running the program in Figure 8-6), and the file pointer is set to the end-of-file by **INDEXNUM**. The file is now ready to have additional information added to it. The **NEAR** procedure PASINFO allows the user to enter character text from the keyboard, save it to NAMEFLD, and write it to the file. If the information entered from the keyboard contains nothing more than a carriage return, the program will terminate and execute the **CLOSFIL** macro.

Examination of the PASINFO (pass information) procedure reveals a lot of activity.

```
PASINFO  PROC      NEAR              ;PASS INFO TO DISK FILE
         CURSOR    0000H             ;SET CURSOR FOR TOP OF PAGE
         PRINTCHAR PROMPT            ;REQUEST FOR USER INPUT
         CURSOR    0100H             ;MOVE CURSOR DOWN, FOR WRITE
```

In the first few lines of code, the cursor is positioned with the **CURSOR** macro from the MACLIB.MAC library to the upper left corner of the text screen. The **PRINTCHAR** macro, from the same library, then prints the prompt to the user at the top of the screen. Note in the data segment that the prompt requests a name and telephone number. Actually, users can enter any information they wish, up to 80 bytes. The cursor is then moved to the beginning of the next line in order to accept and echo keyboard input.

```
         MOV        AH,0AH           ;PARAMETER FOR STRING INPUT
         LEA        DX,NAMEPAR       ;STRING IN 'NAMEPAR'
         INT        21H              ;READ KEYBOARD INPUT
         CLEARSCREEN                 ;CLEARS SCREEN OF LAST NAME
         CMP        ACTLEN,00        ;IS INPUT NOTHING?
         JE         ENDO             ;IF YES, END THIS PROGRAM
         MOV        BH,00            ;PUT STRING LENGTH IN BX
         MOV        BL,ACTLEN
```

```
MOV        NAMEFLD[BX],' '   ;PREPARE TO MOVE STRING TO DISK
WRITFIL                      ;WRITE TO DISK FILE
```

The NAMEPAR LABEL BYTE definition in the data segment allows up to 80 characters of keyboard input to be saved in NAMEFLD. Recall that this interrupt returns the length of the string in the first byte; thus, 81 bytes were saved in MAXLEN. Once this string is entered and saved to NAMEFLD, the screen is cleared in preparation for further data entry. A check is made of ACTLEN to see if information was entered into the string, or if a program termination was requested by a carriage return. The actual string length is moved to the BX register, and the carriage return is over-written with a space (' '). WRITFIL transfers the text information to the disk, and the file pointer is automatically indexed to the end-of-file.

Before calling for more entries from the keyboard, a little cleanup is required:

```
CLD                          ;SET DIRECTION OF STRING OPT
LEA        DI,NAMEFLD        ;PREPARE TO STORE BLANKS
MOV        CX,80             ;IN NAMEFLD VARIABLE
MOV        AL,20H            ;BLANK (20H) VALUE
REP        STOSB             ;REPEAT/STORE 80 TIMES
```

NAMEFLD still contains the previous entry. If the first entry is not blanked out and if the next entry is shorter, a portion of the first entry will be saved along with the second entry. To ensure that this does not occur, 80 blanks (' '), or 20H, are written to NAMEFLD using the REP STOSB operation.

The PASINFO loop is called over and over again, until a carriage return is entered without text. The program then terminates, and the file is closed. This file can now be typed at the DOS level by entering the following:

A> TYPE B:NUMBERS.DAT

The next program looks at a method of reading a file from the assembly language level using a DOS type-21H interrupt.

Problem 8:   Open, Read, and Close a disk file.

In the last two programs a data file was created, and the user was allowed to write information to this file. In this program, the previously created file will be opened and read. Figure 8-8 shows a program that allows access to this data.

This program makes use of three macros and one NEAR procedure. The macros, named OPENFIL (open file), READFIL (read file), and CLOSFIL (close file), are listed here.

```
OPENFIL  MACRO                      ;;MACRO TO OPEN A PREV. CREATED
                                    ;;FILE
         MOV    AL,00H              ;;OPEN FILE FOR READ ONLY
         MOV    AH,3DH              ;;PARAMETER TO OPEN
         LEA    DX,FILENAM          ;;DISK/NAME/EXT OF FILE TO OPEN
         INT    21H                 ;;OPEN
         MOV    FHAND,AX            ;;SAVE FILE HANDLE, JUST RETURNED
         ENDM

READFIL  MACRO                      ;;MACRO TO READ AN ENTRY FROM A
                                    ;;FILE
         MOV    AH,3FH              ;;PREPARE TO READ FILE
         MOV    BX,FHAND            ;;PLACE FILE HANDLE IN BX
         MOV    CX,80               ;;NUMBER OF BYTES TO READ
         LEA    DX,NAMEFLD          ;;POINT TO CHARACTERS TO READ
         INT    21H                 ;;READ
         ENDM

CLOSFIL  MACRO                      ;;MACRO TO CLOSE A FILE
         MOV    AH,3EH              ;;PREPARE TO CLOSE FILE
         MOV    BX,FHAND            ;;PUT FILE HANDLE IN BX
         INT    21H                 ;;CLOSE
         ENDM
```

A close inspection of OPENFIL and CLOSEFIL reveal that these are exactly the same macros that were used in the previous program to open, write to, and close a file. READFIL, using AH=3FH, permits the user to read the file specified by the information contained in the file handle and moved into the BX register. CX, as usual, specifies the number of bytes to be read, and the effective address of NAMEFLD is moved to DX. The DS register points to the address of the data segment. NAMEFLD has reserved for it, in the data segment, enough memory to accommodate the number of bytes requested in CX. When DOS interrupt 21H is performed, AX will be returned with the actual number of bytes read. If AX is 0, the end-of-file has been encountered.

The data segment for this program looks more or less like the data segment of Figure 8-7. This is not a surprise, since the information being read from the file appears in the same format as it was entered.

```
;FOR 80286/80386 MACHINES
;PROGRAM TO ILLUSTRATE HOW TO READ A PREVIOUSLY SAVED FILE

PAGE ,132                              ;SET PAGE DIMENSIONS

IF1
            INCLUDE C:MACLIB.MAC       ;INCLUDE EXTERNAL FILE
ENDIF                                  ;OF USEFUL FUNCTIONS

OPENFIL MACRO                          ;;MACRO TO OPEN A PREV. CREATED FILE
        MOV     AL,00H                 ;;OPEN FILE FOR READ ONLY
        MOV     AH,3DH                 ;;PARAMETER TO OPEN
        LEA     DX,FILENAM             ;;DISK/NAME/EXT OF FILE TO OPEN
        INT     21H                    ;;OPEN
        MOV     FHAND,AX               ;;SAVE FILE HANDLE, JUST RETURNED
        ENDM

READFIL MACRO                          ;;MACRO TO READ AN ENTRY FROM A FILE
        MOV     AH,3FH                 ;;PREPARE TO READ FILE
        MOV     BX,FHAND               ;;PLACE FILE HANDLE IN BX
        MOV     CX,80                  ;;NUMBER OF BYTES TO READ
        LEA     DX,NAMEFLD             ;;POINT TO CHARACTERS TO READ
        INT     21H                    ;;READ
        ENDM

CLOSFIL MACRO                          ;;MACRO TO CLOSE A FILE
        MOV     AH,3EH                 ;;PREPARE TO CLOSE FILE
        MOV     BX,FHAND               ;;PUT FILE HANDLE IN BX
        INT     21H                    ;;CLOSE
        ENDM

STACK   SEGMENT PARA STACK
        DB      64 DUP ('MYSTACK ')
STACK   ENDS

MYDATA  SEGMENT PARA 'DATA'
NAMEPAR LABEL   BYTE
MAXLEN  DB      81                     ;MAXIMUM LENGTH OF INFO + 1
ACTLEN  DB      ?                      ;ACTUAL LENGTH OF INFO
NAMEFLD DB      80 DUP(' '),'$' ;INFO TO BE PLACED ON DISK

FILENAM DB      'B:NUMBERS.DAT',0 ;NAME OF FILE TO BE OPENED
FHAND   DW      ?                      ;STORAGE FOR FILE HANDLE
PROMPT  DB      'NAME                              TELEPHONE$'
POSITION DW     0100H
MYDATA  ENDS

MYCODE  SEGMENT PARA 'CODE'    ;DEFINE CODE SEG. FOR MASM
MYPROC  PROC    FAR            ;PROCEDURE IS NAMED MYPROC
        ASSUME  CS:MYCODE,DS:MYDATA,SS:STACK
        PUSH    DS             ;SAVE LOCATION OF DS REG.
        SUB     AX,AX          ;GET A ZERO IN AX
        PUSH    AX             ;SAVE ZERO ON STACK, TOO
        MOV     AX,MYDATA      ;GET DATA LOCATION IN AX
        MOV     DS,AX          ;PUT IT IN DS REGISTER

        CLEARSCREEN            ;CLEAR THE SCREEN
        OPENFIL               ;OPEN THE FILE
```

Figure 8-8. _____

Reading a previously saved file

```
AGAIN:
           CALL      PASINFO         ;REQUEST DISK READ
           CMP       ACTLEN,00       ;IF NO INFO, END PROGRAM
           JNE       AGAIN           ;OTHERWISE, GET MORE INFO
           CLOSFIL                   ;CLOSE THE FILE
           RET
MYPROC     ENDP

PASINFO PROC      NEAR              ;READ INFO FROM DISK FILE
           CURSOR    0000H           ;SET CURSOR TO TOP OF SCREEN
           PRINTCHAR PROMPT          ;PRINT 'SEND INFO' PROMPT
REPTN:     CURSOR    POSITION        ;MOVE CURSOR DOWN, FOR WRITE
           READFIL                   ;READ THE FILE
           MOV       ACTLEN,AL
           CMP       ACTLEN,00       ;IS INPUT NOTHING?
           JE        ENDO            ;IF YES, END THIS PROGRAM
           PRINTCHAR NAMEPAR+2
           ADD       POSITION,0100H
           JMP       REPTN
ENDO:
           RET
PASINFO ENDP                        ;END PROCEDURE

MYCODE     ENDS                     ;END CODE SEGMENT NAMED MYCODE
           END                      ;END WHOLE PROGRAM
```

Figure 8-8. _____

Reading a previously saved file (*continued*)


```
MYDATA     SEGMENT   PARA 'DATA'
NAMEPAR    LABEL     BYTE
MAXLEN     DB        81               ;MAXIMUM LENGTH OF INFO + 1
ACTLEN     DB        ?                ;ACTUAL LENGTH OF INFO
NAMEFLD    DB        80 DUP(' '),'$'  ;INFO TO BE PLACED ON DISK

FILENAM    DB        'B:NUMBERS.DAT',0 ;NAME OF FILE TO BE OPENED
FHAND      DW        ?                ;STORAGE FOR FILE HANDLE
PROMPT     DB        'NAME                         TELEPHONE$'
POSITION   DW        0100H
MYDATA     ENDS
```

Recall that FILENAM has an attached byte that serves as a sentinel for the end of the name of the file to be opened. The PROMPT is identical to the one that requested information from the user in the last program.

The actual code contained in the main procedure is short and straightforward:

```
           CLEARSCREEN               ;CLEAR THE SCREEN
```

```
              OPENFIL                       ;OPEN THE FILE
      AGAIN:
              CALL       PASINFO            ;REQUEST DISK READ
              CMP        ACTLEN,00          ;IF NO INFO, END PROGRAM
              JNE        AGAIN              ;OTHERWISE, GET MORE INFO
              CLOSFIL                       ;CLOSE THE FILE
```

CLEARSCREEN, a macro from the MACLIB.MAC library, clears the screen before the file is opened with the OPENFIL macro.

If opening the file is successful, a call to the PASINFO (NEAR) procedure will return information from the file to the user. If PASINFO returns nothing from the file, ACTLEN will equal 0, and the program will terminate with the CLOSEFIL macro operation. The PASINFO procedure is repeated here.

```
PASINFO   PROC       NEAR            ;READ INFO FROM DISK FILE
          CURSOR     0000H           ;SET CURSOR TO TOP OF SCREEN
          PRINTCHAR PROMPT           ;PRINT 'SEND INFO' PROMPT
REPTN:    CURSOR     POSITION        ;MOVE CURSOR DOWN, FOR WRITE
          READFIL                    ;READ THE FILE
          MOV        ACTLEN,AL
          CMP        ACTLEN,00       ;IS INPUT NOTHING?
          JE         ENDO            ;IF YES, END THIS PROGRAM
          PRINTCHAR NAMEPAR+2
          ADD        POSITION,0100H
          JMP        REPTN
ENDO:
```

The PASINFO procedure uses several macros from the MACLIB.MAC library. The CURSOR macro moves the cursor to the upper left portion of the text screen. PRINTCHAR then proceeds to print the PROMPT contained in the data segment beginning at that cursor position. The cursor position is then updated to a position specified by the variable POSITION. POSITION is changed each time the loop is repeated in order to put each piece of information on a separate line. READFIL, as explained earlier, secures the requested information and places it in the NAMEPAR structure. A check is made for an end-of-file to determine whether to continue in the loop. The PRINTCHAR macro from the MACLIB.MAC library prints the information in the NAMEPAR structure, starting two bytes into memory. Recall that the first byte contains the maximum length, and the second byte contains the actual length of the string. POSITION is then incremented to the next line, and the program continues.

If the list of telephone numbers is long, the list will be printed until the last line of the screen is used. From that point on, no other names in the list will be shown. What alterations would be necessary in the program to allow a list of any size to be scrolled down the screen?

You, as a programmer, are now in a position to write a menu-driven program that performs the functions of the last three examples. The menu could be designed to give the user the following options:

1. Create a file

2. Write to a file

3. Read a file

4. Exit.

If the user selected options 1, 2 or 3, the program would then prompt for the disk drive, file name, and file name extension. In this manner, files could be created, written to, and read without the use of individual programs.

REAL MODE AND PROTECTED VIRTUAL MODE PROGRAMMING: AN EXAMPLE

The ability to program in the real or virtual addressing mode was introduced with Intel's 80286 microprocessor. Previous processors, such as the 8086, could only operate in the real addressing mode. In the real addressing mode, there is an actual physical address for any address reference in a program. When the 80286 operates in the real addressing mode, it can access 16,777,216 (0FFFFFFH + 1) memory locations, because its address bus is 24 lines wide. When the 80286 operates in the virtual addressing mode, it can access one gigabyte of virtual memory.

What is virtual mode addressing? Virtual mode addressing can be best defined as a method of swapping blocks of code or data between real memory and a secondary storage location, such as a hard disk. This operation must be independent of and invisible to the current application program. This memory management is currently handled directly by the 80286/80386 microprocessor. If you thought the 80286 chip could access a large quantity of memory, consider this: The 80386 has a 32-bit address bus, capable of accessing 4,294,967,296 (0FFFFFFFFH + 1) physical memory locations, or four gigabytes of physical memory. The 80386 chip can also access 64 terabytes of virtual memory. We have come a long way from 64K machines!

The access to this large range of memory has put a strain on disk operating systems, which were more or less designed around 640K machines. In fact, it was not possible to access memory beyond 640K, except for use by a virtual disk drive, all the way through DOS 3.2. This limitation put a road block in front of programs such as IBM's Topview, which needed to access large amounts of memory — and the memory we are talking about is physical memory, not virtual memory. Virtual memory access is another challenge to DOS designers.

At present, it is not an easy task to move into and out of protected virtual memory. Even at the assembler level, the operation is not directly supported. Details regarding virtual memory access are given in such Intel books as *iAPX 286 Operating Systems Writer's Guide* (121960-001), Chapter 9; and *iAPX 386 High-Performance Microprocessor with Integrated Memory Management* (231630-001), Chapter 4. It is beyond the scope of this book to go into the detail necessary to explain virtual memory control.

In the August 1985 issue of the *PC Tech Journal*, Guy Quedens and Gary Webb published an article titled "Switching Modes," which allows the programmer a peek at how to move from real mode addressing to virtual mode addressing. Their program, written in 80286 assembly language, switches from real mode to virtual mode, changes the screen attribute to reverse video, and then switches back to real addressing mode. Figure 8-9 presents that program, slightly modified to work with the standard color graphics adapter and monitor.

In their article, Quedens and Webb explain the difficult job of physically switching modes on the IBM AT computer. Their program is a testimony to good, tight assembly language programming.

```
;FOR 80286/80386 MACHINES ONLY
;PROGRAM TO ILLUSTRATE HOW TO ENTER AND LEAVE PROTECTED MODE

COMMENT *
Reprinted from PC TECH JOURNAL, August 1985, Copyright 1985 by
Ziff-Davis Publishing Company.  Original Program by Guy Quedens
and Gary Webb
```

Figure 8-9. _____

Program illustrating how to enter and leave protected mode (Adapted from Guy Quedens and Gary Webb, "Switching Modes," *PC Tech* [Aug. 1985]. Used with permission.)

```
This program switches into Protected Virtual Mode, changes
the display attribute to reverse video, and returns to Real
Mode to exit to DOS.  Modified for color monitor and card.

--------> Assemble as a COM file <-----------

WARNING: This program will "kill" a PC.  It should only
be run on an AT.*


PAGE      ,132

bios_data_seg SEGMENT at 0040h
              ORG       0067h
io_rom_init   dw ?           ; dword variable in BIOS data segment
io_rom_seg    dw ?           ;  used to store a dword address
bios_data_seg ENDS

descriptor    STRUC
seg_limit     dw 0           ; segment limit (1-65536 bytes)
base_lo_word  dw 0           ; 24 bit physical address
base_hi_byte  db 0           ; (0 - (16M-1))
access_rights db 0           ; access rights byte
              dw 0           ; reserved_386
descriptor    ENDS

cmos_port         equ 070h
code_seg_access   equ 10011011b ;access rights byte for code seg
data_seg_access   equ 10010011b ;access rights byte for data seg
disable_bit20     equ 11011101b ;8042 function code to de-gate A20
enable_bit20      equ 11011111b ;8042 function code to gate A20
inta01            equ 021h      ;8259 Int Controller #1
intb01            equ 0A1h      ;8259 Int Controller #2
port_a            equ 060h      ;8042 port A
shut_cmd          equ 0FEh      ;cmd to 8042: shut down AT
shut_down         equ 00Fh      ;CMOS shut down byte index
status_port       equ 064h      ;8042 status port
virtual_enable    equ 0001h     ;LSB=1: Protected Virtual Mode

;*****************************************************************
;MACROS NEEDED IF NOT SUPPORTED BY ASSEMBLER (IBM MASM 2.0 DOES NOT
;SUPPORT.  SPEEDWARE TURBO ASSEMBLER DOES SUPPORT!

lgdt    MACRO   lgdt1     ;;load global descriptor table
        LOCAL   lgdt2,lgdt3
        db      00FH

lgdt2   label   byte
        mov     dx,word ptr lgdt1
lgdt3   label   byte
        org     offset lgdt2
        db      001h
        org     offset lgdt3
        ENDM

lmsw    MACRO   lmsw1              ;;load machine status word
        LOCAL   lmsw2,lmsw3
        db      00FH
```

Figure 8-9. _____

Program illustrating how to enter and leave protected mode (*continued*)

```
lmsw2    label    byte
         mov      si,ax
lmsw3    label    byte
         org      offset lmsw2
         db       001h
         org      offset lmsw3
         ENDM
;**********************************************************

jumpfar MACRO    jumpfar1,jumpfar2
         db       0EAh
         dw       (offset jumpfar1)
         dw       jumpfar2
         ENDM


cseg     SEGMENT para public 'code'
         ASSUME   cs:cseg
         ORG      100h
start:   jmp      short main
EVEN
gdt      LABEL    word
gdt_desc     EQU  (($-gdt)/8)*8 + 0000000000000000b
gdt1         descriptor  <gdt_leng,,,data_seg_access,>
cs_code      EQU  (($-gdt)/8)*8 + 0000000000000000b
gdt2         descriptor  <cseg_leng,,,code_seg_access,>
cs_data      EQU  (($-gdt)/8)*8 + 0000000000000000b
gdt3         descriptor  <cseg_leng,,,data_seg_access,>
ss_desc      EQU  (($-gdt)/8)*8 + 0000000000000000b
gdt4         descriptor  <0FFFFh,,,data_seg_access,>
ds_desc      equ  (($-gdt)/8)*8 + 0000000000000000b
gdt5         descriptor  <0FFFFh,,,data_seg_access,>
es_desc      equ  (($-gdt)/8)*8 + 0000000000000000b
gdt6         descriptor  <0FFFFh,,,data_seg_access,>
gdt_leng     EQU  $-gdt
PAGE
```

```
;-----------------------------------------------------------:
; Format of the Segment Selector Component:                 :
;                                                           :
; +--+--+--+--+--+--+--+--+--+--+--+--+--+--+--+--+          :
; |          INDEX                  +TI+ RPL +              :
; +--+--+--+--+--+--+--+--+--+--+--+--+--+--+--+--+          :
;                                                           :
; TI = Table Indicator (0=GDT, 1=LDT)                       :
; RPL = Requested Privelege Level (00 = highest; 11 = Lowest) :
;-----------------------------------------------------------:
; Format of the Global Descriptor Table                     :
;                      .------------+           +---> TI    :
;                      V            |           |++-> RPL   :
;     GDT ==> +----------------+    |           |||         :
;            |   GDT_DESC      | --+  0000000000000000b     :
;            +----------------+                             :
;            |   CS_CODE       |      0000000000001000b     :
;            +----------------+                             :
;            |   CS_DATA       |      0000000000010000b     :
;            +----------------+                             :
;            |   SS_DESC       |      0000000000011000b     :
```

Figure 8-9. _____

Program illustrating how to enter and leave protected mode (*continued*)

```
;                       +----------------+
;                       |    DS_DESC     |        0000000000100000b        :
;                       +----------------+                                 :
;                       |    ES_DESC     |        0000000000101000b        :
;                       +----------------+                                 :
;----------------------------------------------------------------------- :

i8259_1  db       ?            ; store for status of 8259 #1
i8259_2  db       ?            ; store for status of 8259 #2

;----------------------------------------------------------------------- :
; MAIN                                                                    :
;----------------------------------------------------------------------- :

         ASSUME   ds:cseg
main     PROC                          ;ES=DS=CS
         cld                           ;forward
         mov      dx,cs                ;form 24bit address out of
         mov      cx,offset gdt        ; CS:GDT
         call     form_24bit_address
         mov      gdt1.base_lo_word,dx   ;DESC now points to gdt
         mov      gdt1.base_hi_byte,cl
         mov      dx,cs                ;form 24bit address out of
         xor      cx,cx                ; CS:0000
         call     form_24bit_address
         mov      gdt2.base_lo_word,dx   ;CS_CODE now points to
         mov      gdt2.base_hi_byte,cl   ; CSEG as a code segment
         mov      gdt3.base_lo_word,dx   ;CS_DATA now points to
         mov      gdt3.base_hi_byte,cl   ; CSEG as a data segment
         mov      dx,ss                ;form 24bit address out of
         xor      cx,cx                ; SS:0000
         call     form_24bit_address
         mov      gdt4.base_lo_word,dx   ;SS_DESC now points to
         mov      gdt4.base_hi_byte,cl   ; stack segment
         lgdt     gdt                  ;Load the GDTR
         mov      ah,enable_bit20      ;gate address bit 20 on
         call     gate_a20
         or       al,al                ; was the command accepted?
         jz       m_10                 ; go if yes
         mov      dx,offset gate_failure  ;print error msg
         mov      ah,9                           ; and terminate
         int      21h
         int      20h
gate_failure      db    "Address line A20 failed to Gate open$"
m_10:    cli                           ;No interrupts
         in       al,inta01            ;get status of Int Controller #1
         mov      i8259_1,al
         in       al,intb01            ;get status of Int Controller #2
         mov      i8259_2,al
         ASSUME   ds:bios_data_seg
         mov      dx,bios_data_seg     ;Real Mode Return address
         mov      ds,dx
         mov      io_rom_seg,cs
         mov      io_rom_init,offset real
         mov      al,shut_down         ;Set shutdown byte
         out      cmos_port,al         ; to shut down x05.
         jmp      short $+2            ;I/O delay
         mov      al,5
```

Figure 8-9. _____

Program illustrating how to enter and leave protected mode (*continued*)

```
          out       cmos_port+1,al
          mov       ax,virtual_enable ;machine status word needed to
          lmsw      ax                ;switch to virtual mode
          jumpfar   m_20,cs_code      ;Must purge prefetch queue
m_20:     ASSUME    ds:cseg           ;IN VIRTUAL MODE ...
          mov       ax,ss_desc        ;stack segment selector
          mov       ss,ax             ;user's ss+sp is not a descriptor
          mov       ax,cs_data
          mov       ds,ax             ;DS = CSEG as data
          mov       gdt5.base_lo_word,8000h  ;use 0000 for MONO MONITOR
          mov       gdt5.base_hi_byte,0Bh
          mov       gdt6.base_lo_word,8000h  ;use 0000 for MONO MONITOR
          mov       gdt6.base_hi_byte,0Bh
          mov       ax,ds_desc
          mov       ds,ax
          mov       ax,es_desc
          mov       es,ax
          mov       cx,80*25
          xor       si,si
          xor       di,di
m_30:     lodsw
          mov       ah,70h            ;attribute reverse video
          stosw
          loop      m_30
          mov       al,shut_cmd       ;shutdown cmd
          out       status_port,al    ;get back into REAL mode
m_40:     hlt
          jmp       short m_40

;------------------------------------------------------------:
; GATE_A20                                                    :
; This routine controls a signal which gates address bit 20.  :
; The gate A20 signal is an output of the 8042 slave processor.:
; Address bit 20 should be gated on before entering protected  :
; mode.  It should be gated off after entering real mode from  :
; protected mode.                                             :
; Input:  (AH)=0DDh addr bit 20 gated off (A20 always 0)      :
;         (AH)=0DFh addr bit 20 gated on  (286 controls A20)  :
; Output: (AL)=0 operation successful.  8042 has accepted cmd :
;                                                             :
;         (AL)=2 Failure -- 8042 unable to accept command.    :
;------------------------------------------------------------:

gate_a20  PROC
          cli                         ;disable ints while using 8042
          call      empty_8042        ;insure 8042 input buffer empty
          jnz       gate_a20_01       ;ret if 8042 unable to accept cmd
          mov       al,0D1h           ;8042 command to write output port
          out       status_port,al    ;output cmd to 8042
          call      empty_8042        ;wait for 8042 to accept command
          jnz       gate_a20_01       ;ret if 8042 unable to accept cmd
          mov       al,ah             ;8042 port data
          out       port_a,al         ;output port data to 8042
          call      empty_8042        ;wait for 8042 to port data
gate_a20_01:
          ret
gate_a20  ENDP
```

Figure 8-9. _____

Program illustrating how to enter and leave protected mode (*continued*)

```
;-----------------------------------------------------------;
; EMPTY_8042                                                 :
; This routine waits for the 8042 buffer to empty           :
; Input:  None                                              :
; Output: (AL)=0 8042 input buffer empty (ZF=1)             :
;         (AL)=2 Time out, 8042 buffer full (ZF=0)          :
;-----------------------------------------------------------;

empty_8042  PROC
        push    cx              ;save CX
        sub     cx,cx           ;CX=0 will be the time out value
empty_8042_01:
        in      al,status_port  ;read 8042 status port
        and     al,00000010b    ;test input buffer full flag (D1)
        loopnz  empty_8042_01   ;loop until input buffer empty
        pop     cx              ;restore CX
        ret
empty_8042  ENDP

;-----------------------------------------------------------;
; FORM_24BIT_ADDRESS                                         :
;   Input:  DX has some segment                              :
;           CX has some offset                               :
;   Output: DX has base_lo_word                              :
;           CL has base_hi_byte                              :
;-----------------------------------------------------------;

form_24bit_address  PROC
        push    ax
        rol     dx,4
        mov     ax,dx
        and     dl,0F0h
        and     ax,0Fh
        add     dx,cx       ;form_24bit_address
        mov     cx,ax       ;get base_hi_byte in CL
        adc     cl,ch       ;carry in (CH=0)
        pop     ax

        ret
form_24bit_address ENDP

        ASSUME ds:cseg              ;IN REAL MODE ...
real:   mov     dx,cs
        mov     ds,dx               ;DS = CS
        mov     ah,disable_bit20    ;gate address bit 20 on
        call    gate_a20
        mov     al,i8259_1
        out     inta01,al           ;set status of Int Controller #1
        mov     al,i8259_2
        out     intb01,al           ;set status of Int Controller #2
        sti                         ;turn the interrupts on
        int     20h                 ;back to DOS
main        ENDP
cseg_leng   EQU $
cseg        ENDS
            END  start
```

Figure 8-9. ⎯⎯⎯⎯⎯⎯⎯⎯⎯⎯⎯⎯⎯⎯⎯⎯⎯⎯⎯⎯⎯⎯⎯⎯⎯⎯⎯⎯⎯⎯⎯⎯

Program illustrating how to enter and leave protected mode (*continued*)

PROGRAMMING WITH THE 80287/80387 COPROCESSOR

The Intel 8087/80387 microprocessor family works in conjunction with the appropriate 8088/80386 microprocessor chip. The 8088/80386 is considered a general-purpose microprocessor, while the 8087/80387 is dedicated to real-number arithmetic. The 8087/80387 is always used with the appropriate 8088/80386 microprocessor and hence is called a *coprocessor*. The 80286 chip supports the operation of the 80287 coprocessor, and the 80386 chip supports the 80287 or 80387 coprocessor.

All of the assembly language programming you have done to this point has involved the use of integer arithmetic. The 80286/80386 can perform integer arithmetic operations without the aid of special software conversion routines for real numbers. Software conversion routines have been available for a long time and are used by all high-level languages, such as BASIC, APL, Fortran, and Pascal. The job of the software conversion routine, in simplified terms, is to take a real number, such as 3.14159, 100.3456, or −4.565E12, and convert it to a series of digits that will look like an integer to the 80286/80386. Once it is in this form, the number is processed by another set of routines and converted back to a real number by yet another software routine. Converting back and forth, of course, consumes considerable CPU time—so much, in fact, that an early microcomputer offered two forms of BASIC: one that could only perform integer arithmetic, and another that could perform integer and real-number arithmetic. The integer BASIC was significantly faster and often was used for computer games.

The challenge to design a hardware chip that could handle real-number arithmetic with speed and precision went to Intel. At about the same time, the Institute of Electrical and Electronic Engineers (IEEE) was setting a standard by which real numbers were to be represented. Intel adopted the IEEE format for real-number representation, which since that time has become accepted as a standard for small systems.

Today, two real-number formats are most often referred to: the Microsoft Real-Number Format, which is used by most high-level languages that do not support coprocessors, and the Intel or IEEE format used by the 80287/80387 coprocessor. This is one of the reasons that merely plugging a 80287/80387 chip into a small system will not, in itself, change the system from a software to a hardware real-number processing system.

In assembly language, by using the .8087 directive, a program can be directed to store real numbers in IEEE format. Without this directive, real numbers are stored in Microsoft format, but cannot be used by coprocessors. Converting numbers to real-number format is done at assembly time. There is, however, no equivalent process for answers returned by coprocessors when programs are executed. Returning an answer to the user in a form that can be easily understood is yet another programming problem. Answers are returned from coprocessors in coded real-number format.

CHIP SPECIFICATIONS

The 8087 coprocessor was introduced in 1979 as the companion for the 8088/8086 microprocessor. In 1982, Intel introduced the 80287 coprocessor and three years later it announced the 80387. Both the 80287 and the 80387 use 80-bit internal architecture; implement the IEEE floating-point format; include seven data types (32-bit single real, 64-bit double real, 80-bit extended real, 16-bit word integer, 32-bit short integer, 64-bit long integer, and 18-digit BCD integer); and directly extend the 80286/80386 instruction set to include trigonometric, logarithmic, exponential, and arithmetic instructions for all types of data. In addition, the 80387 coprocessor supports full 32-bit interfacing with the 80386 data bus; provides all tangent, sine, and cosine trigonometric functions (the 80287 only supports the tangent function from 0 to 45 degrees); and uses CHMOS III chip technology. The 80287 chip is provided on a standard 40-pin ceramic DIP package, and the 80387 chip is fabricated on a 68-pin ceramic grid array (similar to that used by the 80286/80386). The clock speed of the 80287 can be 5, 8, 10, or 12 MHz, and that of the 80387 can be 12 or 16 MHz.

While the coprocessors support seven data types, they hold all data in extended real format. Load instructions, which place data on the coprocessor's stack, automatically convert the data from one of the seven supported

Operation	Operation		
Integer ADD	Square root		
Integer SUBTRACT	Scale (div./mult. by power of 2)		
Integer MULTIPLY	Partial remainder		
Integer DIVIDE	Round to integer		
Integer COMPARE	Extract exponent and significand		
Real ADD	Absolute value		
Real SUBTRACT	Change sign		
Real MULTIPLY	Test for zero		
Real DIVIDE	Examine top of stack		
Real COMPARE			
Load zero			
Load one			
Load pi			
Load $\log_2 10$			
Load $\log_2 e$			
Load $\log_{10} 2$			
Load ln 2			
	80287:	**80387:**	
Tangent	0 to pi/4 radians	Full range of values	
Arctangent	Full range of values	Full range of values	
Sine	N.A.	Full range of values	
Cosine	N.A.	Full range of values	
Simul. sine and cosine	N.A.	Full range of values	
2x − 1	0 <= x <= .5	0 <= x <= .5	
y ($\log_2$ x)	Full range of values	Full range of values	
y ($\log_2$ (x + 1))	Full range of values	Full range of values	

Table 9-1. _____

80287/80387 Operations

data types to extended real format. Store instructions, which return the data from the coprocessor's stack to memory, perform the conversion process in reverse. The 80287/80387 operations are shown in Table 9-1.

As already mentioned, the coprocessors are stack oriented microprocessors. The stack can be imagined in the form shown in Figure 9.1. The ST (stack top) is pointed to with three bits in the environment register. Numbers can be pushed onto the stack with *load* commands and pulled from the stack with *pop* commands.

INTEGER ARITHMETIC AND THE INTEL COPROCESSORS

It is true that both the 80286/80386 and the 80287/80387 perform integer arithmetic. Why the duplication of arithmetic functions? Isn't the coprocessor supposed to be a real-number chip? There are three good reasons for including integer arithmetic capabilities in the coprocessors: (1) It is often necessary to multiply real numbers by integers, (2) high-precision integer operations can be performed accurately and often more quickly than real-number work, and (3) it is possible to do real-number arithmetic on the coprocessor and return a rounded integer result to storage (this will aid you in several graphics examples). In terms of formatting, the integers are passed to and from the coprocessor in the form you have become accustomed to seeing. What better way to be introduced to this new programming mode? Two simple programming examples follow, both using integer arithmetic.

ST(0)   ST (stack top) upon initialization
ST(1)
ST(2)
ST(3)
ST(4)
ST(5)
ST(6)
ST(7)

Figure 9-1.
The 80287/80387 stack

Adding Two Integers

Look at the program shown in the following listing. It looks very much like the programming you've done in previous chapters.

```
;FOR COMPUTERS WITH 80287\80387 MATH COPROCESSOR
;PROGRAM TO ILLUSTRATE SIMPLE INTEGER ADDITION WITH THE 80287\80387
;COPROCESSOR.  RESULTS WILL BE VIEWED WITH THE USE OF DEBUG

PAGE ,132                        ;SET PAGE DIMENSIONS

  .8087                          ;PSEUDO-OP FOR COPROC. ASSEMBLY

STACK     SEGMENT PARA STACK
          DB      64 DUP ('MYSTACK ')
STACK     ENDS

MYDATA    SEGMENT PARA 'DATA'
NUM1      DQ      123456789ABCDEF0H
NUM2      DD      12345678H
ANS       DQ      ?
MYDATA    ENDS

MYCODE    SEGMENT PARA 'CODE'      ;DEFINE CODE SEG. FOR MASM
MYPROC    PROC    FAR              ;PROCEDURE IS NAMED MYPROC
          ASSUME  CS:MYCODE,DS:MYDATA,SS:STACK
          PUSH    DS               ;SAVE LOCATION OF DS REG.
          SUB     AX,AX            ;GET A ZERO IN AX
          PUSH    AX               ;SAVE ZERO ON STACK, TOO
          MOV     AX,MYDATA        ;GET DATA LOCATION IN AX
          MOV     DS,AX            ;PUT IT IN DS REGISTER

          FINIT                    ;INITIALIZE COPROCESSOR
          FILD    NUM1             ;LOAD NUM1 ON COPROC. STACK TOP
          FIADD   NUM2             ;ADD TO NUM1, RESULT ON STACK TOP
          FISTP   ANS              ;POP COPROC. STACK AND STORE
          FWAIT                    ;SYNCHRONIZE

          RET                      ;RETURN CONTROL TO DOS
MYPROC    ENDP                     ;END PROCEDURE NAMED MYPROC
MYCODE    ENDS                     ;END CODE SEGMENT NAMED MYCODE

          END                      ;END WHOLE PROGRAM
```

Notice that this program includes a directive (.8087) to the assembler. This directive accomplishes two purposes: (1) It allows the assembly of all co-processor instructions, and (2) it converts all real numbers that appear after it into IEEE format instead of Microsoft format. The stack and the data segments appear normal, except for some very large integer values that are stored in the variables NUM1 and NUM2. The code segment is normal except for the following five lines of code:

```
FINIT                    ;INITIALIZE COPROCESSOR
FILD    NUM1             ;LOAD NUM1 ON COPROC. STACK TOP
FIADD   NUM2             ;ADD TO NUM1, RESULT ON STACK TOP
FISTP   ANS              ;POP COPROC. STACK AND STORE
FWAIT                    ;SYNCHRONIZE
```

Notice that each mnemonic begins with the letter "F." Think of the letter "F" as standing for *fast*. All coprocessor mnemonics, and only coprocessor mnemonics, begin with the letter "F." When the 80286/80386 encounters the machine code for these mnemonics, control is shifted to the coprocessor for processing. While the coprocessor is handling a particular instruction, the processor (80286/80386) is fetching the next instruction. In this manner, true coprocessing takes place.

FINIT performs the functional equivalent of a hardware reset on the 80287/80387 chip. In effect, all stack elements are emptied, and all busy interrupts and exception flags are cleared. FILD is the mnemonic for an integer load operation. The operand (NUM1), called the *source memory operand*, is taken from the specified memory location and converted from binary integer format to temporary real format (80 bits) as the number is loaded onto the coprocessor's stack top (ST), which in this case is ST(0). This operand can be one of three integer types: short (32 bits, as in DD), word (16 bits, as in DW), or long (64 bits, as in DQ). The FIADD instruction adds the source operand (NUM2) to the current contents of the stack top (ST) and returns the sum to the ST. FIADD supports two integer types: word (DW) and short (DD). Again, remember that once a number is on the coprocessor's stack, it is held in 80-bit temporary real-number format. FISTP is the integer mnemonic for popping and storing the current contents of the stack top (ST) to the specified destination (ANS). In so doing, the coprocessor rounds the temporary real number to an integer according to the RC field of the control word (more concerning the control word later). Finally, the FWAIT instruction synchronizes the coprocessor to the 80286/80386 processor. This instruction is generally used before returning to 80286/80386 assembler mnemonics. A dump of the data segment after this program is executed is shown here.

```
85B0:0100  1E 2B C0 50 B8 C2 85 8E-D8 9B DF 2E 00 00 9B DA   .+@P8B...X._.....Z
85B0:0110  06 08 00 9B DF 3E 0C 00-9B CB 00 00 00 00 00 00   .....>...K......
85B0:0120  F0 DE BC 9A 78 56 34 12-78 56 34 12 68 35 F1 AC   p^<.xV4.xV4.h5q.
85B0:0130  78 56 34 12 00 00 00 00-00 00 00 00 00 00 00 00   xV4.............
85B0:0140  4D 59 53 54 41 43 4B 20-4D 59 53 54 41 43 4B 20   MYSTACK MYSTACK
85B0:0150  4D 59 53 54 41 43 4B 20-4D 59 53 54 41 43 4B 20   MYSTACK MYSTACK
85B0:0160  4D 59 53 54 41 43 4B 20-4D 59 53 54 41 43 4B 20   MYSTACK MYSTACK
85B0:0170  4D 59 53 54 41 43 4B 20-4D 59 53 54 41 43 4B 20   MYSTACK MYSTACK
```

A portion of that dump is repeated here.

```
1E  2B  C0  50  B8  C2  85  8E-D8  9B  DF  2E  00  00  9B  DA
06  08  00  9B  DF  3E  0C  00-9B  CB  00  00  00  00  00  00
F0  DE  BC  9A  78  56  34  12-78  56  34  12  68  35  F1  AC
78  56  34  12  00  00  00  00-00  00  00  00  00  00  00  00
```

The line F0 DE BC 9A 78 56 34 12 represents the value for NUM1, displayed in bytes, with the most-significant byte at the lowest memory location and the least-significant byte at the highest memory location. The bytes 78 56 34 12 represent NUM2, and 68 35 F1 AC 78 56 34 12 represent the hexadecimal sum 12345678ACF13568.

How many lines of code would it have taken with the 80286/80386 to achieve the same degree of precision? How long would it have taken to execute the program?

The coprocessors are called stack-oriented microprocessors, since all operations occur on the chip's internal hardware stack. In contrast, the 80286/80386 is a memory or register oriented microprocessor, with all operations being performed in or on a register, and information moved in and out of memory.

Adding a Table of Integers

In the next example, the program we just discussed will be expanded to allow the sum of a series of numbers to be calculated. The numbers will be contained in a table within the data segment. A portion of the data segment is repeated here.

```
NUMS
    DD    11111111H,22222222H,33333333H,44444444H,55555555H
    DD    66666666H,77777777H,88888888H,99999999H,0AAAAAAAAH
    DD    0BBBBBBBBH,0CCCCCCCCH,0DDDDDDDDH,0EEEEEEEEH
    DD    0FFFFFFFFH,12345678H,9ABCDEF0H
```

Notice that all of the numbers contained under the variable NUMS are defined doublewords (DD), or 32 bits. Recall that the largest number the FIADD command can handle directly is the short integer, which is 32 bits long.

The program, shown here, performs the addition with the aid of a simple loop.

```
;FOR COMPUTERS WITH 80287\80387 MATH COPROCESSOR
;PROGRAM WILL ILLUSTRATE HOW TO ADD A TABLE OF LARGE INTEGER
;VALUES WITH THE USE OF THE MATH COPROCESSOR.  RESULT WILL BE
;VIEWED WITH THE USE OF DEBUG

PAGE ,132                          ;SET PAGE DIMENSIONS

 .8087                             ;PSEUDO-OP FOR COPROC. ASSEMBLY

STACK    SEGMENT PARA STACK
         DB      64 DUP ('MYSTACK ')
```

```
STACK      ENDS

MYDATA     SEGMENT PARA 'DATA'
NUMS       DD      11111111H,22222222H,33333333H,44444444H,55555555H
           DD      66666666H,77777777H,88888888H,99999999H,0AAAAAAAAH
           DD      0BBBBBBBBH,0CCCCCCCCH,0DDDDDDDDH,0EEEEEEEEH
           DD      0FFFFFFFFH,12345678H,9ABCDEF0H
ANS        DQ      ?
MYDATA     ENDS

MYCODE     SEGMENT PARA 'CODE'          ;DEFINE CODE SEG. FOR MASM
MYPROC     PROC    FAR                  ;PROCEDURE IS NAMED MYPROC
           ASSUME  CS:MYCODE,DS:MYDATA,SS:STACK
           PUSH    DS                   ;SAVE LOCATION OF DS REG.
           SUB     AX,AX                ;GET A ZERO IN AX
           PUSH    AX                   ;SAVE ZERO ON STACK, TOO
           MOV     AX,MYDATA            ;GET DATA LOCATION IN AX
           MOV     DS,AX                ;PUT IT IN DS REGISTER

           MOV     CX,14                ;ADD FIRST 15 NUMBERS IN NUMS
           LEA     BX,NUMS
           FINIT                        ;INITIALIZE COPROCESSOR
           FILD    NUMS[BX]             ;GET FIRST NUMBER FROM NUMS
AGAIN:     ADD     BX,04H               ;MOVE TO NEXT DD NUMBER
           FIADD   NUMS[BX]             ;ADD TO TOP OF STACK
           LOOP    AGAIN
           FISTP   ANS                  ;SAVE RESULT FROM TOP OF STACK
           FWAIT                        ;SYNCHRONIZE

           RET                          ;RETURN CONTROL TO DOS
MYPROC     ENDP                         ;END PROCEDURE NAMED MYPROC
MYCODE     ENDS                         ;END CODE SEGMENT NAMED MYCODE

           END                          ;END WHOLE PROGRAM
```

A portion of the code segment is shown here:

```
           MOV    CX,14          ;ADD FIRST 15 NUMBERS IN NUMS
           LEA    BX,NUMS
           FINIT                 ;INITIALIZE COPROCESSOR
           FILD   NUMS[BX]       ;GET FIRST NUMBER FROM NUMS
AGAIN:     ADD    BX,04H         ;MOVE TO NEXT DD NUMBER
           FIADD  NUMS[BX]       ;ADD TO TOP OF STACK
           LOOP   AGAIN
           FISTP  ANS            ;SAVE RESULT FROM TOP OF STACK
           FWAIT                 ;SYNCHRONIZE
```

In this example, only the first 15 integer values are added together. A loop is created to perform the addition, with the value in the CX register serving as the loop's counter. The value is set to one less than the number of additions, since one number is loaded from the table before the loop is entered for the first time. The BX register contains the offset address of the data within the table (NUMS), and therefore the address of the first element is placed in the BX register with the LEA (load effective address). FINIT initializes (resets) the coprocessor, and FILD loads the first integer (in temporary real format) onto the stack top (ST) of the coprocessor. As the program enters the loop, a 4 is added to the BX register in order to point to the next (DD) number. FIADD NUMS[BX] adds this number to the current stack top (ST) and replaces the stack top with the new sum. This process is repeated until 15 numbers have been added together.

During this entire operation, the sum has remained within the coprocessor. When all of the additions have been performed, and only then, the sum is popped off the stack top and stored in memory under the variable name ANS. In terms of precision, it is a very important programming practice to leave the numbers on the coprocessor's stack until it is absolutely necessary to place them in storage. This way, rounding errors are kept to a minimum. The program terminates with the synchronization command, FWAIT.

Now use DEBUG to examine the data segment after program execution, and then locate the answer. A portion of the data segment is shown here.

```
7EAC:0100   1E 2B C0 50 B8 BF 7E 8E-D8 B9 0E 00 8D 1E 00 00   .+@P8?~.X9......
7EAC:0110   9B DB 87 00 00 83 C3 04-9B DA 87 00 00 E2 F6 9B   [....C..Z...bv.
7EAC:0120   DF 3E 44 00 9B CB 00 00-00 00 00 00 00 00 00 00   _>D..K..........
7EAC:0130   11 11 11 11 22 22 22 22-33 33 33 33 44 44 44 44   ...."""""3333DDDD
7EAC:0140   55 55 55 55 66 66 66 66-77 77 77 77 88 88 88 88   UUUUffffwwww....
7EAC:0150   99 99 99 99 AA AA AA AA-BB BB BB BB CC CC CC CC   ....****;:::LLLL
7EAC:0160   DD DD DD DD EE EE EE EE-FF FF FF FF 78 56 34 12   JJJJnnnn....xV4.
7EAC:0170   F0 DE BC 9A F8 FF FF FF-FF FF FF FF 00 00 00 00   p^<.x...........
```

The answer should be located immediately after the last number in NUMS, which was 9ABCDEF0. Can you find it? In the debug dump, it's listed as F0 DE BC 9A. That means that the entry F8 FF FF FF FF FF FF FF must be the answer. Rearranging the bytes produces the following hexadecimal result: FFFFFFFFFFFFFF8. With a pencil and paper, the results are calculated to be 7FFFFFF8—what went wrong? Actually, nothing went wrong. The coprocessor performs signed arithmetic on integer numbers. For short integers (32 bits), any number equal to or less than 7FFFFFFF is considered positive, and any number equal to or greater than 80000000 is considered negative. This same concept can be extended to the other integer sizes. In the previous addition, the last eight numbers added to the sum were negative values. The result obtained was the algebraic sum of all the numbers. (Hint: If you're making this calculation by hand, remember that any accumulated sum over 7FFFFFFF is considered negative also.)

VIEWING INTEGERS WITH THE HELP
OF A MACRO

In previous chapters macros were created to help clear the screen, set the cursor, and print the text. The macro shown here permits a program to write a quadword (DQ) directly to the screen, at the cursor position pointed to by the DX register.

```
COMMENT /This macro will print DQ (Quad word) number to the screen
         starting at cursor position set in DX register.
         By moving cursor and BX pointer, many values can be
         printed directly to the screen.
         This program will eliminate the need for DEBUG
         when testing 80287/80387 programs.

         FORMAT:    LEA        BX,VARIABLE          ;VARIABLE LOCATION
                    MOV        DX,0100H             ;CURSOR LOCATION
                    QUADIS                          ;CALL TO MACRO    /

QUADIS   MACRO                                ;;MAIN ROUTINE
         LOCAL     MORE, FINISH
         PUSH      DX
         PUSH      CX
         PUSH      BX
         PUSH      AX
         MOV       SI,07H               ;;SET INDEX REGISTER COUNT
MORE:    MOV       AL,BYTE PTR [BX+SI]  ;;TAKE A BYTE OF THE QUAD
         MOV       CL,04H               ;;SET CL FOR ROTATE
         ROR       AL,CL                ;;ROTATE BYTE 4 PLACES
         AND       AL,0FH               ;;KEEP LOWER 4 BITS
         SETPXY                         ;;MOVE CURSOR
         DISPXY                         ;;DISPLAY THE 4 BITS
         MOV       AL,BYTE PTR [BX+SI]  ;;TAKE SAME BYTE AGAIN
         AND       AL,0FH               ;;MASK AGAIN
         INC       DX                   ;;DECREMENT CURSOR POSITION
         SETPXY                         ;;MOVE CURSOR
         DISPXY                         ;;DISPLAY THOSE 4 BITS
         INC       DX                   ;;DECREMENT CURSOR
         DEC       SI                   ;;PREPARE TO GET NEXT BYTE
         CMP       SI,00H               ;;DONE ALL 8 BYTES YET?
         JL        FINISH               ;;IF YES, GOTO FINISH
         JMP       MORE                 ;;IF NO, GOTO MORE
FINISH:  POP       AX
         POP       BX
         POP       CX
         POP       DX
         ENDM                           ;;END MAIN MACRO

SETPXY   MACRO                          ;;MACRO TO SET CURSOR
         PUSH      BX                   ;;FOR PRINTING ONLY
         PUSH      AX                   ;;LOCATION IN DX REG.
         MOV       BX,01H               ;;INPUT PARAMTERES
         MOV       AH,02H
         INT       10H
         POP       AX
         POP       BX
         ENDM

DISPXY   MACRO                          ;;MACRO TO DISPLAY NUMBERS
         LOCAL     ADJUST               ;;AND HEX LETTERS ON SCREEN
         PUSH      CX                   ;;VALUE PASSED IN AL REGISTER
         PUSH      BX
         PUSH      AX
         MOV       AH,10                ;;PARAMETERS FOR CHARACTER PRINT
         MOV       BX,01H
```

```
            MOV     CX,01H
            AND     AL,0FH
            CMP     AL,09H
            JLE     ADJUST          ;;IF NUMBER, NOT LETTER
            ADD     AL,07H          ;;ADD 7 TO CHARACTER VALUE
ADJUST:     ADD     AL,30H          ;;CONVERT TO ASCII
            INT     10H             ;;CALL INTERRUPT
            POP     AX
            POP     BX
            POP     CX
            ENDM
```

This macro should be created and saved on the current disk. It should not be assembled or linked—that will come as it is integrated into the user's program. The syntax for using QUADIS is quite simple. The location of the quadword to be displayed is moved into the BX register using the LEA command. The desired cursor position is set in the DX register. DH sets the vertical position and DL the horizontal position on the text screen. As an example, assume a program's data segment contains the quadword, VARIABLE. To display VARIABLE on the screen one line down and against the left edge, the following code is required:

```
LEA         BX,VARIABLE
MOV         DX,0100H
QUADIS
```

MULTIPLICATION OF LARGE POSITIVE INTEGERS

The data segment shown here contains three positive integers: 1234H, 5678H, and 12345678H. These numbers will be multiplied together, and the result will be stored in the (DQ) variable ANS. That answer will be printed to the screen with the aid of QUADIS.

```
;FOR COMPUTERS WITH 80287\80387 MATH COPROCESSOR
;PROGRAM TO ILLUSTRATE MULTIPLICATION OF SEVERAL LARGE INTEGER
;NUMBERS.  RESULT WILL BE DISPLAYED TO THE SCREEN WITH QUADIS.MAC
;MACRO


PAGE ,132                       ;SET PAGE DIMENSIONS

.8087                           ;PSEUDO-OP FOR COPROC. ASSEMBLY

IF1
        INCLUDE C:MACLIB.MAC    ;LOCATION OF MACLIB.MAC LIBRARY
        INCLUDE C:QUADIS.MAC    ;LOCATION OF QUADIS.MAC MACRO
ENDIF                           ;FOR DISPLAY OF QUADWORDS ON SCREEN

STACK   SEGMENT PARA STACK
        DB      64 DUP ('MYSTACK ')
STACK   ENDS
```

```
MYDATA    SEGMENT PARA 'DATA'
NUMS      DD      1234H,5678H,12345678H
ANS       DQ      ?
MYDATA    ENDS

MYCODE    SEGMENT PARA 'CODE'          ;DEFINE CODE SEG. FOR MASM
MYPROC    PROC    FAR                  ;PROCEDURE IS NAMED MYPROC
          ASSUME  CS:MYCODE,DS:MYDATA,SS:STACK
          PUSH    DS                   ;SAVE LOCATION OF DS REG.
          SUB     AX,AX                ;GET A ZERO IN AX
          PUSH    AX                   ;SAVE ZERO ON STACK, TOO
          MOV     AX,MYDATA            ;GET DATA LOCATION IN AX
          MOV     DS,AX                ;PUT IT IN DS REGISTER

          MOV     CX,2                 ;MULTIPLY FIRST THREE NUMBERS
          LEA     BX,NUMS              ;ADDRESS OF NUMS
          FINIT                        ;INITIALIZE COPROCESSOR
          FILD    NUMS[BX]             ;GET FIRST NUMBER FROM NUMS
MORE:     ADD     BX,04H               ;GET NEXT NUMBER IN NUMS
          FIMUL   NUMS[BX]             ;MULTIPLY/PRODUCT ON STACK TOP
          LOOP    MORE
          FISTP   ANS                  ;POP OFF COPROC AND SAVE TO VARIABLE
          FWAIT                        ;SYNCHRONIZE

          CLEARSCREEN                  ;CLEAR THE SCREEN FOR OUTPUT
          MOV     DX,0100H             ;DISPLAY ANSWER ON LINE #2
          LEA     BX,ANS               ;GET LOCATION OF ANS IN BX
          QUADIS

          RET                          ;RETURN CONTROL TO DOS
MYPROC    ENDP                         ;END PROCEDURE NAMED MYPROC
MYCODE    ENDS                         ;END CODE SEGMENT NAMED MYCODE

          END                          ;END WHOLE PROGRAM
```

Notice that two external macro libraries are identified with the IF1 pseudo-op.

```
IF1
          INCLUDE C:MACLIB.MAC     ;LOCATION OF MACLIB.MAC LIBRARY
          INCLUDE C:QUADIS.MAC     ;LOCATION OF QUADIS.MAC MACRO
ENDIF                             ;FOR DISPLAY OF QUADWORDS ON SCREEN
```

In the data segment, MACLIB.MAC clears the screen, and QUADIS.MAC prints the variable ANS.

The actual coprocessor code is simple and similar in structure to the previous addition example:

```
          MOV     CX,2          ;MULTIPLY FIRST THREE NUMBERS
          LEA     BX,NUMS       ;ADDRESS OF NUMS
          FINIT                 ;INITIALIZE COPROCESSOR
          FILD    NUMS[BX]      ;GET FIRST NUMBER FROM NUMS
MORE:     ADD     BX,04H        ;GET NEXT NUMBER IN NUMS
          FIMUL   NUMS[BX]      ;MULTIPLY/PRODUCT ON STACK TOP
          LOOP    MORE
          FISTP   ANS           ;POP OFF COPROC AND SAVE TO VARIABLE
FWAIT                           ;SYNCHRONIZE
```

FIMUL has the same size restriction that FIADD had with respect to the source operand. The source operand must be a short integer (32 bits) or a word integer (16 bits). In this program CX is again set to one less than the total number of numbers to be multiplied, since one number is loaded onto the stack top before the loop is entered.

The code required to print the answer to the screen is shown here:

```
CLEARSCREEN                 ;CLEAR THE SCREEN FOR OUTPUT
MOV        DX,0100H         ;DISPLAY ANSWER ON LINE #2
LEA        BX,ANS           ;GET LOCATION OF ANS IN BX
QUADIS
```

Upon execution, the following result is printed to the cleared screen:

006FEDD279706D00

This is the correct hexadecimal product for the three numbers.

PRINTING A GROUP OF INTEGERS TO THE SCREEN

The QUADIS macro can be used to display a series of numbers by simply making repetitive calls to the macro. The next example, which obtains the square roots of integers 1 to 20, illustrates how this is done. Here is a listing of the complete program.

```
;FOR COMPUTERS WITH 80287\80387 MATH COPROCESSOR
;PROGRAM TO ILLUSTRATE SIMPLE REAL NUMBER ARTIHMETIC WITH FINAL
;ANSWERS PRINTED IN INTEGER FORMAT.
;PROGRAM WILL OBTAIN THE SQ. ROOT OF INTEGERS FROM 1 TO 20, AND
;PRINT THEM TO SCREEN BY MULTIPLE CALLS TO QUADIS.  ANSWERS WILL
;BE IN HEXADECIMAL

PAGE ,132                          ;SET PAGE DIMENSIONS

 .8087                             ;PSEUDO-OP FOR COPROC. ASSEMBLY

IF1
        INCLUDE C:MACLIB.MAC       ;LOCATION OF MACLIB.MAC LIBRARY
        INCLUDE C:QUADIS.MAC       ;LOCATION OF QUADIS.MAC MACRO
ENDIF                             ;FOR DISPLAY OF QUADWORDS ON SCREEN

STACK    SEGMENT PARA STACK
         DB        64 DUP ('MYSTACK ')
STACK    ENDS

MYDATA   SEGMENT PARA 'DATA'
NUM      DD        1
CONST    DQ        100000000
ANS      DQ        ?
MYDATA   ENDS
```

```
MYCODE   SEGMENT PARA 'CODE'          ;DEFINE CODE SEG. FOR MASM
MYPROC   PROC    FAR                  ;PROCEDURE IS NAMED MYPROC
         ASSUME  CS:MYCODE,DS:MYDATA,SS:STACK
         PUSH    DS                   ;SAVE LOCATION OF DS REG.
         SUB     AX,AX                ;GET A ZERO IN AX
         PUSH    AX                   ;SAVE ZERO ON STACK, TOO
         MOV     AX,MYDATA            ;GET DATA LOCATION IN AX
         MOV     DS,AX                ;PUT IT IN DS REGISTER

         CLEARSCREEN                  ;CLEAR THE SCREEN FOR OUTPUT
         MOV     DX,0000H             ;CURSOR LOCATION FOR FIRST ANSWER
         FINIT                        ;INITIALIZE COPROCESSOR
MORE:    FILD    NUM                  ;GET NUMBER FROM NUM
         FSQRT                        ;OBTAIN SQUARE ROOT OF NUMBER
         FILD    CONST                ;MULTIPLY RESULT TIMES CONSTANT
         FMUL                         ;MULTIPLY/PRODUCT ON STACK TOP
         FISTP   ANS                  ;POP OFF COPROC AND SAVE TO VARIABLE
         FWAIT                        ;SYNCHRONIZE

         LEA     BX,ANS               ;GET LOCATION OF ANS IN BX
         QUADIS
         INC     DH                   ;MOVE CURSOR DOWN A LINE
         INC     BYTE PTR NUM         ;ADD A 1 TO NUM
         CMP     BYTE PTR NUM,21      ;SEE IF ALL 20 ARE DONE
         JE      ENDO                 ;IF YES, END PROGRAM
         JMP     MORE                 ;IF NO, CONTINUE
ENDO:
         RET                          ;RETURN CONTROL TO DOS
MYPROC   ENDP                         ;END PROCEDURE NAMED MYPROC
MYCODE   ENDS                         ;END CODE SEGMENT NAMED MYCODE

         END                          ;END WHOLE PROGRAM
```

Recall that when integers are loaded on the coprocessor's stack, they are loaded as 80-bit temporary real numbers. In fact, all numbers, integer or real, are held on the stack in this format. Commands such as FIADD or FIMUL merely convert integer format to 80-bit real format as the numbers are used. In this program, an integer number will be loaded onto the co-processor stack. The square root will be extracted and at this point will contain a fractional result (for instance, the square root of 2 is 1.4142...). If the FISTP command is used, only the 1 will be returned to ANS. To obtain a more precise answer without real-number conversion routines, the square root will be multiplied by 100,000,000 and then popped from the stack. In this manner, a very precise square root can be returned as an integer. The format of QUADIS requires the user to insert the decimal point at the appropriate location. Actually, it would not be difficult to print a period that could serve as a decimal point using the routines presented in Chapter 5. The data segment must also contain the constants needed by the pro-gram, since it is not possible to pass immediate values to a coprocessor mnemonic as operands.

```
NUM     DD   1
CONST   DQ   100000000
ANS     DQ   ?
```

The first portion of assembly code is shown here:

```
          CLEARSCREEN              ;CLEAR THE SCREEN FOR OUTPUT
          MOV      DX,0000H        ;CURSOR LOCATION FOR FIRST ANSWER
          FINIT                    ;INITIALIZE COPROCESSOR
MORE:     FILD     NUM             ;GET NUMBER FROM NUM
          FSQRT                    ;OBTAIN SQUARE ROOT OF NUMBER
          FILD     CONST           ;MULTIPLY RESULT TIMES CONSTANT
          FMUL                     ;MULTIPLY/PRODUCT ON STACK TOP
          FISTP    ANS             ;POP OFF COPROC AND SAVE TO VARIABLE
          FWAIT                    ;SYNCHRONIZE
```

The CLEARSCREEN macro is called in preparation for the screen output of the square-root values. The DX register contains the position to which the answers will be printed on the screen. DH points to the vertical position (0 to 24), and DL points to the horizontal position (0 to 64). In this program DL remains fixed at 0, thus printing the answers in a column at the left edge of the screen.

The integer NUM is placed on the stack top (ST) of the coprocessor with the FILD mnemonic. Remember, once on the stack, this number will be in 80-bit real-number format. The square root is extracted, and the result is placed on the stack top, overwriting the original (ST) number. The multiplier CONST is loaded onto the stack top (ST), pushing the square root one position deeper in the coprocessor's stack. The square root now resides at ST(1). FMUL used in this manner defaults to ST as the destination and ST(1) as the source. If this arrangement is not desired, any of the other eight stack positions can be specified with the following syntax:

```
FMUL    ST,ST(6)
```

The real number on the stack top is then popped and converted to integer format as it is returned to the variable ANS.

The remaining code, shown here, allows you to properly format the output.

```
LEA     BX,ANS               ;GET LOCATION OF ANS IN BX
QUADIS
INC     DH                   ;MOVE CURSOR DOWN A LINE
INC     BYTE PTR NUM         ;ADD A 1 TO NUM
CMP     BYTE PTR NUM,21      ;SEE IF ALL 20 ARE DONE
JE      ENDO                 ;IF YES, END PROGRAM
JMP     MORE                 ;IF NO, CONTINUE
```

Recall that the location of ANS must be in the BX register—thus the need for the LEA mnemonic. QUADIS prints the integer at the current cursor position. DH is indexed to move the next number down one line on the screen. The integer in NUM is increased by one and compared with 21 to see if 20 values have been printed to the screen. If they have not, the whole process is repeated again. A copy of the data printed to the screen is shown here.

```
000000005F5E100
00000000086DEB2C
00000000A52E659
000000000BEBC200
00000000D53F80E
00000000E999FEE
00000000FC5189B
0000000010DBD658
0000000011E1A300
0000000012D940B6
0000000013C4C48F
0000000014A5CCB2
00000000157DA278
00000000164D50EB
000000001715B41F
0000000017D78400
0000000018935C23
0000000019 49C185
0000000019FB26E6
000000001AA7F01B
```

Surprise! The results are in hexadecimal format—of course. If the last entry (000000001AA7F01B) is converted to decimal format, the following number results: 447213595. Dividing this number by 100,000,000 produces the square root of 20: 4.47213595. Much greater accuracy could be obtained for the answer by increasing the size of the constant, CONST.

REAL-NUMBER ARITHMETIC AND THE INTEL COPROCESSORS

In the previous examples in this chapter, numbers were entered in integer format and printed in integer format. Why? The answer involves how real numbers are coded for the coprocessor. Consider the listing here (the complete program appears later in this chapter).

```
PAGE ,132                              ;SET PAGE DIMENSIONS

.8087                                  ;PSEUDO-OP FOR COPROC. ASSEMBLY

STACK        SEGMENT PARA STACK
             DB        64 DUP ('MYSTACK ')
STACK        ENDS

MYDATA       SEGMENT PARA 'DATA'
RADIUS       DQ        8.567
AREA         DQ        ?
MDATA        ENDS
```

If the .8087 directive were not included, the real number 8.567 for RADIUS would be coded in Microsoft format—the format used by languages that do not support the coprocessor. With the .8087 directive given, 8.567 will be encoded in the IEEE floating-point format. Intel coprocessors require the IEEE format. To move and store real numbers using the 80286/80386 processor, the numbers must be made to appear as integers. These numbers are automatically coded in the specified format when the program is assembled (you will see how how this is done later). Unfortunately, there is no decoding process for numbers that are returned by the coprocessor, because there is no process comparable to assembly when a program is executed. That means that real results will have to be decoded by the user to make sense. Now for some good and bad news: (1) Microsoft provides, in its symbolic debugger, an option for displaying data in real-number format. If you have the Microsoft Assembler, you're all set. Of course, you will always have to display real answers with the use of the symbolic debugger. (2) IBM provides, in its assembler package, several conversion routines in a utility library named IBMUTIL.LIB. With the use of IBMUTIL.LIB, numbers can be decoded into a format understood by humans. If you have the IBM Assembler, you're all set. Of course, you will always be tied to IBMUTIL, but you will see that that is not so bad. If neither of these options appeals to you, you can write your own conversion routine—that's the bad news.

IEEE REAL-NUMBER FORMATS

There are a number of ways in which a real number can be coded and formed using hexadecimal digits. Fortunately, the IEEE set a floating-point standard, to which Intel engineers carefully shaped the 80287/80387 coprocessors. Although the coprocessors hold data in temporary real format (80 bits), it is the short real (32 bits) and long real (64 bits) formats that interest us most here. In variables in a data segment, the short real number corresponds to the defined doubleword (DD), and the long real number corresponds to the defined quadword (DQ).

The short real number is returned to memory as a 32-bit encoded number. The MSB is used to decode the sign, the next 8 bits the exponent, and the remaining 23 bits the significand. For the long real number, a

64-bit encoded number is returned. The MSB is used to decode the sign, the next 11 bits the exponent, and the remaining 52 bits the significand. The general equation for conversion is fairly simple:

$$real\ number = (-1)^{sign} \times (significand) \times 2^{\,exponent}$$

Look at an example for a long real number. Assume that a program was executed, and the following information was taken from a dump of the data segment:

82   ED   FC   79   51   D2   6C   40

Arranging the bits in proper order yields the following coded hexadecimal real number:

406CD25179FCED82

Converting this number to binary format yields the following:

0100000001101100110100100101000101111001111111001110110110110000010

Separating the number according to sign, exponent, and significand yields

0 10000000110 1100110100100101000101111001111111001110110110110000010

Using the general equation, the following results are obtained: The MSB = 0, so −1 raised to the 0th power is 1, and the sign is positive. The number 10000000110 converted to decimal format is 1030. For long real numbers, the exponent is biased by 1023. The actual exponent thus is 7. The significand is a base-2 number formed from the remaining digits, with the first digit before the decimal point assumed to be 1:

1.1100110100100101000101111001111111001110110110110000010

Converting this binary number to decimal involves working with fractional weights. Unfortunately, base-change calculators do not perform the conversion of fractional numbers. You will proceed cautiously. The first place to the right of the decimal point represents 1/2, the second 1/4, the third 1/8, and so forth. At every location where there is a 1, you will add the weight of that digit.

    1.0
    .5
    .25
    .03125
    .015625
    .00390625
    .00048828125
    .00006103515625
    _____

    1.80133056640625

This only accounts for the first eight 1s. Your calculator probably can't keep up with the required precision, but you have done enough to get the idea.

Now, back to the formula:

real number $= +1.80133056640625 \times 2^7$
$= +1.80133056640625 \times 128$
$= +230.5703124$

The answer is 230.5724458637233.

Conversions of short real numbers are done in a similar manner, except that the significand is 23 bits long, and the exponent bias is 127. Here is another example.

Assume that the following short real number was returned to a data segment after program execution:

    00   00   58   BE

Rearranging the terms yields

    BE580000

Converting this number to binary format yields

    10111110010110000000000000000000

Separating the sign exponent and significand yields

    1 01111100 10110000000000000000000

The sign bit is 1; (-1) raised to the 1 power makes the answer negative.

The exponent 01111100, converted to decimal format, is 124. The actual exponent is $124 - 127$, or -3. The significand becomes

    1.10110000000000000000000

Converting this number to decimal format yields

1.0
.5
.125
.0625
———
1.6875

Returning to the formula, we have

$$real\ number = -1.6875 \times 2^{-3}$$
$$= -1.6875 \times (.125)$$
$$= -.2109375$$

In the following examples, you will use the various conversion routines provided in the Microsoft and IBM assembler packages instead of hand conversion.

A SIMPLE PROGRAM USING REAL-NUMBER ARITHMETIC

This example will use the Microsoft Symbolic Debug program to view the answer. The following is the listing for a program that calculates the area of a circle using the equation $A = PI \times R^2$. The radius and answer will be returned as real numbers (64-bit precision).

```
;FOR COMPUTERS WITH 80287\80387 MATH COPROCESSOR
;PROGRAM TO ILLUSTRATE SIMPLE REAL NUMBER ARITHMETIC WITH FINAL
;REAL ANSWER VIEWED WITH MICROSOFT SYMBOLIC DEBUGGER
;PROGRAM WILL CALCULATE THE AREA OF A CIRCLE

        PAGE ,132                       ;SET PAGE DIMENSIONS

        .8087                           ;PSEUDO-OP FOR COPROC. ASSEMBLY

STACK   SEGMENT PARA STACK
        DB      64 DUP ('MYSTACK ')
STACK   ENDS

MYDATA  SEGMENT PARA 'DATA'
RADIUS  DQ      8.567
AREA    DQ      ?
MYDATA  ENDS

MYCODE  SEGMENT PARA 'CODE'     ;DEFINE CODE SEG. FOR MASM
MYPROC  PROC    FAR             ;PROCEDURE IS NAMED MYPROC
        ASSUME  CS:MYCODE,DS:MYDATA,SS:STACK
        PUSH    DS              ;SAVE LOCATION OF DS REG.
        SUB     AX,AX           ;GET A ZERO IN AX
        PUSH    AX              ;SAVE ZERO ON STACK, TOO
        MOV     AX,MYDATA       ;GET DATA LOCATION IN AX
        MOV     DS,AX           ;PUT IT IN DS REGISTER

        FINIT                   ;INITIALIZE COPROCESSOR
        FLD     RADIUS          ;PUT RADIUS ON STACK TOP
        FMUL    RADIUS          ;OBTAIN SQUARE ON STACK TOP
        FLDPI                   ;PUT PI ON STACK TOP
        FMUL                    ;PI x RADIUS SQUARED
        FSTP    AREA            ;POP OFF COPROC AND SAVE TO VARIABLE
        FWAIT                   ;SYNCHRONIZE
```

```
          RET                    ;RETURN CONTROL TO DOS
MYPROC    ENDP                   ;END PROCEDURE NAMED MYPROC
MYCODE    ENDS                   ;END CODE SEGMENT NAMED MYCODE

          END                    ;END WHOLE PROGRAM
```

Real numbers can be entered in the data segment with DD and DQ data types. The defined doubleword (DD) is used for 32-bit real numbers, and the defined quadword (DQ) is used for 64-bit double real numbers. Real numbers can be entered in the following formats:

$$8.567$$
$$+12.345$$
$$-234.9$$
$$-12.4E2$$
$$1.234E-10$$

A portion of the code segment is repeated here.

```
FINIT                   ;INITIALIZE COPROCESSOR
FLD        RADIUS       ;PUT RADIUS ON STACK TOP
FMUL       RADIUS       ;OBTAIN SQUARE ON STACK TOP
FLDPI                   ;PUT PI ON STACK TOP
FMUL                    ;PI × RADIUS SQUARED
FSTP       AREA         ;POP OFF COPROC AND SAVE TO VARIABLE
FWAIT                   ;SYNCHRONIZE
```

FLD is used to load the real number from system memory onto the coprocessor's stack top. FMUL performs multiplication with the number on the stack top and the number RADIUS, which is, again, in real-number format. The multiplication leaves the squared radius on the stack top. FLDPI loads the value of PI on the stack top, pushing R^2 to ST(1). FMUL multiplies ST and ST(1) together, leaving the product on the stack top, ST. The final command, FSTP, transfers the answer, in real-number format, to the variable AREA.

Microsoft's Symbolic Debug program is now used to examine the data segment. Two different reports for the same portion of memory are shown here.

```
-D DS:0100  014F
85B0:0100   1E 2B C0 50 B8 C2 85 8E-D8 9B DD 06 00 00 9B DC   .+@P8B..X.]....\
85B0:0110   0E 00 00 9B D9 EB 9B DE-C9 9B DD 1E 08 00 9B CB   ....Yk.^I.]....K
85B0:0120   FC A9 F1 D2 4D 22 21 40-82 ED FC 79 51 D2 6C 40   !)aRM"!@.m!yQRl@
85B0:0130   4D 59 53 54 41 43 4B 20-4D 59 53 54 41 43 4B 20   MYSTACK MYSTACK
85B0:0140   4D 59 53 54 41 43 4B 20-4D 59 53 54 41 43 4B 20   MYSTACK MYSTACK

-DL DS:0100  014F
85B0:0100   1E 2B C0 50 B8 C2 85 8E    -0.1044298876043245E+65299
85B0:0108   D8 9B DD 06 00 00 9B DC    -0.1255977334619014E-65397
85B0:0110   0E 00 00 9B D9 EB 9B DE    -0.5578447610515987E-65388
85B0:0118   C9 9B DD 1E 08 00 9B CB    -0.1655102779799069E+57
85B0:0120   FC A9 F1 D2 4D 22 21 40    +0.8567E+1
85B0:0128   82 ED FC 79 51 D2 6C 40    +0.2305724458637233E+3
85B0:0130   4D 59 53 54 41 43 4B 20    +0.4066692443677049E+65384
85B0:0138   4D 59 53 54 41 43 4B 20    +0.4066692443677049E+65384
85B0:0140   4D 59 53 54 41 43 4B 20    +0.4066692443677049E+65384
```

The first section of output, from 85B0:0100 to 85B0:014F, is reported in normal form. IBM's Debug program would produce identical results. The second portion of code, shown here, is called with the DL option.

```
-DL DS:0100 014F
```

Here, DL stands for dump long. The real numbers are then created from groups of eight bytes. Naturally, as in all dumps, some of these numbers are meaningless. The pair of numbers you are interested in are

```
85B0:0120  FC A9 F1 D2 4D 22 21 40  +0.8567E+1
85B0:0128  82 ED FC 79 51 D2 6C 40  +0.2305724458637233E+3
```

The first number (8.567) is the radius, and the second number (230.5724458637233) is the calculated area of the circle (without regard to significant digits).

THE IBM MACRO ASSEMBLER DATA CONVERSION ROUTINE

Included with the IBM Macro Assembler, version 2.0 and later implementations, are a group of data conversion routines. These routines allow the programmer to convert from ASCII strings to 80287/80387 floating-point format, from long real floating-point format to ASCII strings, and from Microsoft format to 80287/80387 format (using several different methods) and back. The various options are as follows:

$I8_INPUT	ASCII strings to 80287/80387
$I8_OUTPUT	Long real 80287/80387 to ASCII string
$I4_M4	Microsoft single to 80287/80387 short real
$I8_M8	Microsoft double to 80287/80387 long real
$M4_I4	80287/80387 short real to Microsoft single
$M8_I8	80287/80387 long real to Microsoft double
$I4_I8	80287/80387 long real to 80287/80387 short real
$I8_I4	80287/80387 short real to 80287/80387 long real

These conversion routines are particularly useful if you are interfacing assembler code with a high-level language that does not support the coprocessors. In fact, the library of conversion routines, which contains all of these options, is linked to the host program using the IBM Linker. The library is called IBMUTIL.

For the example here, only one of these conversion routines is needed. We need a method for converting 80287/80387 real numbers into scientific or floating-point notation. The $I8__OUTPUT routine will take the coded real format and convert it to an ASCII character string that can then be directly printed to the screen.

The following requirements (not options) are assumed when the $I8__ OUTPUT conversion routine is used:

1. The code segment is declared exactly as shown:

```
MATHCODE    SEGMENT    BYTE    PUBLIC    'CODE'
            EXTRN      $I8__OUTPUT:NEAR
```

(Contents of code segment here)

```
MATHCODE    ENDS
```

2. The data segment is declared exactly as shown:

```
DATA        SEGMENT    WORD    PUBLIC    'DATA'
```

(Contents of data segment here.)

```
DATA        ENDS
DGROUP      GROUP      DATA
```

3. All routines are near procedures.

4. The DS and ES registers are equal.

5. All nonsegment registers (except SP) are destroyed.

6. SI:DS points to the (offset) address of the long real number before the routine is called.

7. SI:DS points to the (offset) address of LSTRING. This is a 17-byte memory location with the length of the ASCII string in the first byte. The decimal point is assumed to be on the left.

8. AX is 1 if the original number is used, and the number 0 if it was indefinite.

9. BL contains a blank for a positive number and a dash for a negative number.

10. DX contains the exponent of the number in base-10 format.

The procedure might sound complicated at this point, but you will see in the next example that the requirements are easy to implement. The output from this routine will not be in polished form, but the program contains a method for putting the output in scientific notation.

Before continuing, however, look at Figure 9-2, which shows a typical assembly and link operation when the library is used. The IBM Assembler and Linker are in the C drive when assembly begins, and the program is in the B drive.

Assembly proceeds in the normal fashion. It is not until LINK time that any changes are noted. In this case, C:IBMUTIL, specifies the name of the external library that is to be linked with your program. This library then becomes permanently bonded to your program in .EXE form.

A PROGRAMMING EXAMPLE USING THE IBM UTILITY LIBRARY

Recall from the last section that IBM's routine for real-number conversion, $I8$__OUTPUT, converts a double-precision (DQ) floating-point real number

```
B>C:MASM PROGNAME;
IBM Personal Computer MACRO Assembler    Version 2.00
(C)Copyright IBM Corp 1981, 1984
(C)Copyright Microsoft Corp 1981, 1983, 1984

48774 Bytes free

Warning Severe
Errors  Errors
0       0

B>C:LINK PROGNAME,PROGNAME,NUL,C:IBMUTIL;

IBM Personal Computer Linker



Version 2.30 (C) Copyright IBM Corp. 1981, 1985

B>
```

Figure 9-2. _____

Typical assembly and link using the library

into an ASCII string. The BL register will contain the sign character, and DX the information for the base-10 exponent. This information is not immediately in the form of a formatted output. In the following listing, additional programming will be required to completely format the number in scientific notation.

```
;FOR COMPUTERS WITH 80287\80387 MATH COPROCESSOR
;PROGRAM TO ILLUSTRATE SIMPLE REAL NUMBER ARITHMETIC WITH FINAL
;REAL ANSWER VIEWED WITH USE OF IBM'S DATA CONVERSION ROUTINE
;IBMUTIL.LIB MUST BE LINKED TO PROGRAM AT RUN TIME
;PROGRAM WILL CALCULATE THE VOLUME OF A SPHERE

        PAGE ,132                       ;SET PAGE DIMENSIONS

        .8087                           ;PSEUDO-OP FOR COPROC. ASSEMBLY

        IF1
                INCLUDE C:MACLIB.MAC
        ENDIF

STACK     SEGMENT PARA STACK
          DB      64 DUP ('MYSTACK ')
STACK     ENDS

MYDATA    SEGMENT PARA 'DATA'           ;DATA SEGMENT MUST BE PUBLIC
CONT1     DD      4.0                   ;NUMERIC CONSTANT
CONT2     DD      3.0                   ;NUMERIC CONSTANT
RADIUS    DD      123.45E2              ;RADIUS OF SPHERE
VOLUME    DQ      ?                     ;VOLUME/INTEL REAL NUM FORMAT
PADDER    DB      20 DUP (' ')          ;BREATHING ROOM FOR IBM ROUTINE
ANSWER    DB      17 DUP (?),'$'        ;CHARACTER ANSWER FROM IBM ROUTINE
FIRDIG    DB      ' ','$'               ;FUTURE LOCATION OF FIRST DIGIT
POWER     DW      ?                     ;EXPONENT STORAGE
TBUFF     DB      4 DUP(' ')            ;4 BYTES FOR EXPONENT CHARACTERS
SIGN      DB      '-'                   ;NEGATIVE SIGN
POINT     DB      '.$'                  ;DECIMAL POINT
EXP       DB      ' E $'                ;EXPONENT SYMBOL
MYDATA    ENDS

MATHCODE SEGMENT BYTE PUBLIC 'CODE' ;DEFINE CODE SEG. FOR IBM ROUTINE
          EXTRN   $I8_OUTPUT:NEAR  ;ROUTINE IN EXTERNAL LIBRARY
MYPROC    PROC    FAR              ;PROCEDURE IS NAMED MYPROC
          ASSUME  CS:MATHCODE,DS:MYDATA,SS:STACK,ES:MYDATA
          PUSH    DS               ;SAVE LOCATION OF DS REG.
          SUB     AX,AX            ;GET A ZERO IN AX
          PUSH    AX               ;SAVE ZERO ON STACK, TOO
          MOV     AX,MYDATA        ;GET DATA LOCATION IN AX
          MOV     DS,AX            ;PUT IT IN DS REGISTER
          MOV     ES,AX            ;ALSO IN ES REGISTER

          LEA     SI,VOLUME        ;VOLUME IS SOURCE INDEX FOR STRING

          FINIT                    ;INITIALIZE COPROCESSOR
          FLD     RADIUS           ;PUT RADIUS ON STACK TOP
          FMUL    RADIUS           ;OBTAIN SQUARE ON STACK TOP
          FMUL    RADIUS           ;OBTAIN CUBE ON STACK TOP
          FLDPI                    ;PUT PI ON STACK TOP
          FMUL                     ;PI x RADIUS SQUARED
          FMUL    CONT1            ;MULTIPLY BY 4.0
          FDIV    CONT2            ;DIVIDE BY 3.0
          FSTP    QWORD PTR [SI]   ;POP OFF COPROC AND SAVE TO VARIABLE
          FWAIT                    ;SYNCHRONIZE
```

```
        CALL    $I8_OUTPUT          ;RETURNED BY PROCEDURE
        CALL    FORMAT              ;MAKE OUTPUT SCIENTIFIC NOTATION

        RET                         ;RETURN CONTROL TO DOS
MYPROC  ENDP                        ;END PROCEDURE NAMED MYPROC

COMMENT /The following near procedure is used to format the output
         of $I8_OUTPUT into a number expressed in scientific not-
         ation.  Example:  -3.5678912345 E -123                    /

FORMAT  PROC    NEAR
        SUB     DX,01H              ;REDUCE EXP BY 1
        MOV     POWER,DX            ;DX IS CORRECTED EXPONENT OF ANS
        CMP     BL,'-'              ;DETERMINE IF ANSWER IS + OR -
        JNE     NONEG
        LEA     DX,SIGN             ;IF NEGATIVE, PRINT CHAR TO SCREEN
        MOV     AH,09
        INT     21H
NONEG:
        CLD                         ;PREPARE TO TRANSFER STRING TO ANS
        MOV     CL,17               ;STRING IS 17 BYTES LONG (16 DIGITS)
        LEA     DI,ANSWER           ;DESTINATION OF MOVE, SI PTS TO SOURCE
REP     MOVSB                       ;MOVE'EM
        MOV     CL,1                ;MOVE FIRST CHAR OF ANSWER TO FIRDIG
        LEA     SI,ANSWER[1]
        LEA     DI,FIRDIG
REP     MOVSB
        LEA     DX,FIRDIG           ;PRINT FIRST DIGIT TO SCREEN
        MOV     AH,09
        INT     21H
        LEA     DX,POINT            ;PRINT A DECIMAL POINT
        MOV     AH,09
        INT     21H
        LEA     DX,ANSWER[2]        ;PRINT REMAINING DIGITS OF ANSWER
        MOV     AH,09
        INT     21H
        LEA     DX,EXP              ;PRINT " E " FOR EXPONENT AFTER
        MOV     AH,09               ;CHARACTER STRING
        INT     21H
        MOV     DX,POWER            ;CONVERT NUMBER IN DX TO A STRING
        CMP     DX,8000H            ;IS IT POS OR NEG?
        JB      POSIT               ;IF POSITIVE, GO TO POSIT
        LEA     DX,SIGN             ;IF NEG, PRINT A NEGATIVE SIGN FIRST
        MOV     AH,09
        INT     21H
        MOV     DX,POWER            ;CORRECT HEX VALUE, FOR A NEGATIVE
        XOR     DX,0FFFFH
        ADD     DX,01
POSIT:  MOV     CX,0
        LEA     DI,TBUFF            ;TBUFF WILL SERVE AS A FOUR BYTE
POWER1: PUSH    CX                  ;CHARACTER STORAGE AS THE HEX NUMS
        MOV     AX,DX               ;IN DX ARE CONVERTED TO DECIMAL
        MOV     DX,0                ;ASCII VALUES FOR SCREEN PRINTING
        MOV     CX,10
        DIV     CX
        XCHG    AX,DX
        ADD     AL,30H              ;MAKE NUMBER AN ASCII DIGIT
        MOV     [DI],AL             ;SAVE IT IN TBUFF
        INC     DI                  ;POINT TO NEW LOCATION IN TBUFF
        POP     CX
        INC     CX                  ;CX CONTAINS THE NUMBER OF DIGITS
        CMP     DX,0
        JNZ     POWER1
PRIT:   DEC     DI                  ;PREPARE TO PRINT VALUES TO SCREEN
        MOV     AL,[DI]             ;GET DIGIT FROM TBUFF
        PUSH    DX                  ;PROTECT ORIGINAL DX VALUE
        MOV     DL,AL               ;MOVE DIGIT FOR PRINTING
        MOV     AH,2                ;PARAMETER FOR DOS PRINT
```

```
          INT     21H              ;PRINT POWER TO SCREEN
          POP     DX               ;RETURN ORIGINAL DX VALUE
          LOOP    PRIT             ;CONTINUE TILL ALL DONE
          RET
FORMAT    ENDP
MATHCODE ENDS                      ;END CODE SEGMENT NAMED MYCODE

          END                      ;END WHOLE PROGRAM
```

This particular program calculates the volume of a sphere, using the equation $V = 4/3 \times PI \times R^3$, and prints the formatted answer to the screen. The data contained in the data segment can be divided into two categories: data used for the calculation, and data used for formatting the answer. The data for the calculation is shown here.

```
CONT1    DD    4.0              ;NUMERIC CONSTANT
CONT2    DD    3.0              ;NUMERIC CONSTANT
RADIUS   DD    123.45E2         ;RADIUS OF SPHERE
VOLUME   DQ    ?                ;VOLUME/INTEL REAL NUM FORMAT
```

Since operands for the coprocessors must be called from memory, all necessary constants must be saved ahead of time. CONT1 and CONT2 are the numbers 4 and 3 that will be divided in the equation. It would have been just as easy to save them as integers and just as correct to use them in that form. The RADIUS for this particular sphere is saved as 12345 in mixed notation. VOLUME must be returned as a defined quadword in order for the conversion routine to be used.

The remainder of the data segment is for formatting the ANSWER.

```
PADDER   DB    20 DUP ('  ')     ;BREATHING ROOM FOR IBM ROUTINE
ANSWER   DB    17 DUP (?),'$'    ;CHARACTER ANSWER FROM IBM ROUTINE
FIRDIG   DB    ' ','$'           ;FUTURE LOCATION OF FIRST DIGIT
POWER    DW    ?                 ;EXPONENT STORAGE
TBUFF    DB    4 DUP('  ')       ;4 BYTES FOR EXPONENT CHARACTERS
SIGN     DB    '—$'              ;NEGATIVE SIGN
POINT    DB    '.$'              ;DECIMAL POINT
EXP      DB    ' E $'            ;EXPONENT SYMBOL
```

When $I8_OUTPUT is called from the program, the value pointed to by the SI register (in this case, VOLUME) is converted to a string. That string is returned to the location pointed to by the SI register. A buffer—in this case, several empty spaces—is needed between this string and any remaining data in the data segment; PADDER forms that buffer. ANSWER eventually will hold the 17-byte string. The $ sign indicates that an interrupt 21H will probably be used to print the results to the screen. FIRDIG will eventually hold the first digit of the answer. This program formats results in correct scientific notation, so the first digit will be printed, a decimal point, and then all remaining digits. POWER will hold the exponent of the answer that is returned in the DX register after \$I8—OUTPUT is called. TBUFF will be used in the conversion of DX's exponent number into ASCII character data. Finally, SIGN, POINT, and EXP hold the characters for, respectively, the minus, decimal point, and exponent symbols.

The code segment of this program is different from that of previous programs because it conforms to the specifications set by \$I8—OUTPUT.

```
MATHCODE SEGMENT BYTE PUBLIC 'CODE'          ;DEFINE CODE SEG. FOR IBM
                                             ;ROUTINE
          EXTRN     $I8—OUTPUT:NEAR          ;ROUTINE IN EXTERNAL
                                             ;LIBRARY
MYPROC         PROC        FAR               ;PROCEDURE IS NAMED MYPROC
               ASSUME      CS:MATHCODE,DS:MYDATA,SS:STACK,ES:MYDATA
```

MATHCODE must be the name of the code segment, and it must be declared PUBLIC in order for information to be exchanged with the IBM Utility Library, IBMUTIL.LIB. An external declaration, EXTRN, is made for \$I8—OUTPUT in order to share information between the two routines (there are other routines provided in the library). Except for linking IBMUTIL.LIB at link time, this is all that is required to tie into the library.

The coprocessor code, shown here, is probably the smallest part of the whole program:

```
FLD     RADIUS     ;PUT RADIUS ON STACK TOP
FMUL    RADIUS     ;OBTAIN SQUARE ON STACK TOP
FMUL    RADIUS     ;OBTAIN CUBE ON STACK TOP
```

The radius is first cubed. The cubed value remains on the stack top.

```
FLDPI              ;PUT PI ON STACK TOP
FMUL               ;PI × RADIUS SQUARED
```

FLDPI loads the value of PI on the stack top, pushing the cubed value to ST(1). FMUL multiplies the value at ST(1) by ST and leaves the product at ST, the stack top.

```
FMUL    CONT1      ;MULTIPLY BY 4.0
FDIV    CONT2      ;DIVIDE BY 3.0
FSTP    QWORD PTR [SI]     ;POP OFF COPROC AND SAVE TO VARIABLE
```

The result on the stack top is then multiplied by 4 and divided by 3. FSTP returns the answer, in real-number format, to VOLUME.

```
CALL      $I8_OUTPUT         ;RETURNED BY PROCEDURE
CALL      FORMAT             ;MAKE OUTPUT SCIENTIFIC NOTATION
```

A CALL to $I8_OUTPUT converts the DQ value pointed to by SI (in this case, VOLUME) and returns the converted string to the same location. A CALL to FORMAT takes the information returned by IBM's routine and formats it in scientific notation.

The FORMAT procedure prints the answer starting at the current cursor position. All output is in the form of ASCII characters, not numeric information. The formatting process can be divided into the following categories:

1. Print a negative sign?

2. Print the first digit of the result.

3. Print a decimal point.

4. Print the remaining digits of the answer.

5. Print the exponent symbol "E."

6. Print a negative sign for the exponent?

7. Print the exponent.

The following code determines if a negative sign is to be printed:

```
FORMAT    PROC    NEAR
          SUB     DX,01H      ;REDUCE EXP BY 1
          MOV     POWER,DX    ;DX IS CORRECTED EXPONENT OF ANS
          CMP     BL,'-'      ;DETERMINE IF ANSWER IS + OR -
          JNE     NONEG
          LEA     DX,SIGN     ;IF NEGATIVE, PRINT CHAR TO SCREEN
          MOV     AH,09
          INT     21H
NONEG:
```

The code SUB DX,01H and MOV POWER,DX merely saves the exponent information for a future operation. The test for a negative sign is made with respect to the BL register. If BL contains the negative character (−), the SIGN character will be printed to the screen. If it contains any other character (a plus sign), nothing will be printed to the screen.

The 17 ASCII digits in VOLUME are now copied to ANSWER using the following code:

```
        CLD                      ;PREPARE TO TRANSFER STRING TO ANS
        MOV     CL,17            ;STRING IS 17 BYTES LONG (16 DIGITS)
        LEA     DI,ANSWER        ;DESTINATION OF MOVE, SI PTS TO SOURCE
REP     MOVSB                    ;MOVE'EM
```

Remember that SI (the source index) is already pointing to VOLUME.

The first digit of the answer is now copied from ANSWER to FIRDIG.

```
        MOV     CL,1             ;MOVE FIRST CHAR OF ANSWER TO FIRDIG
        LEA     SI,ANSWER[1]
        LEA     DI,FIRDIG
REP     MOVSB
```

The CL register is set to 1, since only one character is to be copied. The character is located at ANSWER[1], not ANSWER[0]. ANSWER[0] contains the count of characters in the string.

The following code prints the first digit (FIRDIG), a decimal point, and the remaining ASCII string characters to the screen:

```
LEA     DX,FIRDIG        ;PRINT FIRST DIGIT TO SCREEN
MOV     AH,09
INT     21H
LEA     DX,POINT         ;PRINT A DECIMAL POINT
MOV     AH,09
INT     21H
LEA     DX,ANSWER[2]     ;PRINT REMAINING DIGITS OF ANSWER
MOV     AH,09
INT     21H
```

This is a straightforward application of the techniques for printing character information to the screen presented in Chapter 5.

The next task is to print the exponent information to the screen. The exponent symbol is easy:

```
LEA     DX,EXP    ;PRINT "E" FOR EXPONENT AFTER
MOV     AH,09     ;CHARACTER STRING
INT     21H
```

Before the exponent is printed, it must be converted to ASCII character format. The sign of the exponent must also be determined.

```
        MOV    DX,POWER      ;CONVERT NUMBER IN DX TO A STRING
        CMP    DX,8000H      ;IS IT POS OR NEG?
        JB     POSIT         ;IF POSITIVE, GO TO POSIT
        LEA    DX,SIGN       ;IF NEG, PRINT A NEGATIVE SIGN FIRST
        MOV    AH,09
        INT    21H
        MOV    DX,POWER      ;CORRECT HEX VALUE, FOR A NEGATIVE
        XOR    DX,0FFFFH
        ADD    DX,01
POSIT:  MOV    CX,0
```

POWER is the variable that contains the exponent information in the form of decimal digits. If POWER is less than 8000H, the exponent will be positive, and a jump will be made to POSIT. If POWER is equal to or greater than 8000H, the number is negative, and a minus sign will be printed to the screen. The two's complement of the negative number is then calculated to convert the information into a positive exponent.

The individual digits of POWER are now converted.

```
POSIT:   MOV    CX,0
         LEA    DI,TBUFF      ;TBUFF WILL SERVE AS A FOUR BYTE
POWER1:  PUSH   CX            ;CHARACTER STORAGE AS THE HEX NUMS
         MOV    AX,DX         ;IN DX ARE CONVERTED TO DECIMAL
         MOV    DX,0          ;ASCII VALUES FOR SCREEN PRINTING
         MOV    CX,10
         DIV    CX
         XCHG   AX,DX
         ADD    AL,30H        ;MAKE NUMBER AN ASCII DIGIT
         MOV    [DI],AL       ;SAVE IT IN TBUFF
         INC    DI            ;POINT TO NEW LOCATION IN TBUFF
         POP    CX
         INC    CX            ;CX CONTAINS THE NUMBER OF DIGITS
         CMP    DX,0
         JNZ    POWER1
```

The exponent contained in POWER can be a four-digit number. To see how this conversion routine works, assume that the exponent is 34. The MOV AX,DX operation places 34 in the AX register. Zero is then placed in DX. CX contains 10 and will act as the divisor in the following divide operation. After DIV CX, AX will contain 3, and DX 4. XCHG reverses this order. AX will then contain 4, and DX 3. Actually, AL contains the 4. When 30H is added to AL, the contents are converted to the correct ASCII format and stored as the MSD in TBUFF. The process is repeated, and this time the 3 is saved in the next location of TBUFF as an ASCII character. The process is not repeated again, since DX contains 0 when the last DIV and XCHG operation is complete. Note that the digits in TBUFF are in reverse order. This will not cause any problems.

The next job is to print this character exponent to the screen.

```
PRIT:   DEC    DI        ;PREPARE TO PRINT VALUES TO SCREEN
        MOV    AL,[DI]   ;GET DIGIT FROM TBUFF
        PUSH   DX        ;PROTECT ORIGINAL DX VALUE
        MOV    DL,AL     ;MOVE DIGIT FOR PRINTING
        MOV    AH,2      ;PARAMETER FOR DOS PRINT
        INT    21H       ;PRINT POWER TO SCREEN
        POP    DX        ;RETURN ORIGINAL DX VALUE
        LOOP   PRIT      ;CONTINUE TILL ALL DONE
```

Since the character data was saved in reverse order, it will be read back in decreasing order as it is printed to the screen. The number of digits printed is controlled by CX, which was calculated in the previous operation.

This is the code required to print a number to the screen in scientific format. If you find this procedure handy and you are using the IBM Macro Assembler, you might want to add it to the IBMUTIL.LIB.

FINDING THE TANGENT OF A REAL ANGLE

The Intel coprocessors support the tangent function. The 80287 returns correct results when the argument is between 0 and PI/4 radians. The 80387 supports the tangent over the full range of values. As a prelude to more involved work with trigonometric functions, the following listing calculates the tangent of a selected real angle (from the range 0 to PI/4) and returns the real result to the screen with the aid of the IBM Utility Library. The angle will be specified in degrees and the then converted to radians by the program.

```
;FOR COMPUTERS WITH 80287\80387 MATH COPROCESSOR
;PROGRAM TO ILLUSTRATE SIMPLE REAL NUMBER ARITHMETIC WITH FINAL
;REAL ANSWER VIEWED WITH USE OF IBM'S DATA CONVERSION ROUTINE
;IBMUTIL.LIB MUST BE LINKED TO PROGRAM AT RUN TIME
;PROGRAM WILL CALCULATE THE TANGENT OF AN ANGLE
;THE ANGLE MUST BE BETWEEN 0 AND 45 DEGREES!

PAGE ,132                        ;SET PAGE DIMENSIONS

 .8087                           ;PSEUDO-OP FOR COPROC. ASSEMBLY

IF1
        INCLUDE C:MACLIB.MAC
ENDIF
```

```
STACK     SEGMENT PARA STACK
          DB      64 DUP ('MYSTACK ')
STACK     ENDS

MYDATA    SEGMENT PARA 'DATA'      ;DATA SEGMENT MUST BE PUBLIC
ANGLE     DD      25.5             ;ANGLE IN DEGREES
CONST     DD      180.0            ;NUMERIC CONSTANT
TANGENT   DQ      ?                ;TANGENT IN REAL NUMBER FORMAT
PADDER    DB      20 DUP (' ')     ;BREATHING ROOM FOR IBM ROUTINE
ANSWER    DB      17 DUP (?),'$'   ;CHARACTER ANSWER FROM IBM ROUTINE
FIRDIG    DB      ' ','$'          ;FUTURE LOCATION OF FIRST DIGIT
POWER     DW      ?                ;EXPONENT STORAGE
TBUFF     DB      4 DUP(' ')       ;4 BYTES FOR EXPONENT CHARACTERS
SIGN      DB      '-$'             ;NEGATIVE SIGN
POINT     DB      '.$'             ;DECIMAL POINT
EXP       DB      ' E $'           ;EXPONENT SYMBOL
MYDATA    ENDS

MATHCODE SEGMENT BYTE PUBLIC 'CODE' ;DEFINE CODE SEG. FOR IBM ROUTINE
         EXTRN   $I8_OUTPUT:NEAR    ;ROUTINE IN EXTERNAL LIBRARY
MYPROC   PROC    FAR                ;PROCEDURE IS NAMED MYPROC
         ASSUME  CS:MATHCODE,DS:MYDATA,SS:STACK,ES:MYDATA
         PUSH    DS                 ;SAVE LOCATION OF DS REG.
         SUB     AX,AX              ;GET A ZERO IN AX
         PUSH    AX                 ;SAVE ZERO ON STACK, TOO
         MOV     AX,MYDATA          ;GET DATA LOCATION IN AX
         MOV     DS,AX              ;PUT IT IN DS REGISTER
         MOV     ES,AX              ;ALSO IN ES REGISTER

         LEA     SI,TANGENT         ;TANGENT IS SOURCE INDEX FOR STRING

         FINIT                      ;INITIALIZE COPROCESSOR
         FLDPI                      ;LOAD PI ON STACK
         FLD     CONST              ;LOAD CONSTANT ON STACK
         FDIV                       ;DIVIDE CONSTANT BY PI
         FLD     ANGLE              ;LOAD ANGLE ON STACK
         FMUL                       ;MULTIPLY PREV. RESULT x ANGLE
         FPTAN                      ;TAKE TANGENT OF ABOVE PRODUCT
         FDIV                       ;DIVIDE ST/ST(1) TO GET DECIMAL
         FSTP    QWORD PTR [SI]     ;POP OFF COPROC AND SAVE TO VARIABLE
         FWAIT                      ;SYNCHRONIZE

         CALL    $I8_OUTPUT         ;RETURNED BY PROCEDURE
         CALL    FORMAT             ;MAKE OUTPUT SCIENTIFIC NOTATION

         RET                        ;RETURN CONTROL TO DOS
MYPROC   ENDP                       ;END PROCEDURE NAMED MYPROC

COMMENT /The following near procedure is used to format the output
        of $I8_OUTPUT into a number expressed in scientific not-
        ation.  Example:  -3.5678912345 E -123                    /

FORMAT   PROC    NEAR
         SUB     DX,01H             ;REDUCE EXP BY 1
         MOV     POWER,DX           ;DX IS CORRECTED EXPONENT OF ANS
         CMP     BL,'-'             ;DETERMINE IF ANSWER IS + OR -
         JNE     NONEG
         LEA     DX,SIGN            ;IF NEGATIVE, PRINT CHAR TO SCREEN
         MOV     AH,09
         INT     21H
NONEG:
         CLD                        ;PREPARE TO TRANSFER STRING TO ANS
         MOV     CL,17              ;STRING IS 17 BYTES LONG (16 DIGITS)
         LEA     DI,ANSWER          ;DESTINATION OF MOVE, SI PTS TO SOURCE
REP      MOVSB                      ;MOVE'EM
         MOV     CL,1               ;MOVE FIRST CHAR OF ANSWER TO FIRDIG
         LEA     SI,ANSWER[1]
         LEA     DI,FIRDIG
```

```
REP       MOVSB
          LEA     DX,FIRDIG        ;PRINT FIRST DIGIT TO SCREEN
          MOV     AH,09
          INT     21H
          LEA     DX,POINT         ;PRINT A DECIMAL POINT
          MOV     AH,09
          INT     21H
          LEA     DX,ANSWER[2]     ;PRINT REMAINING DIGITS OF ANSWER
          MOV     AH,09
          INT     21H
          LEA     DX,EXP           ;PRINT " E " FOR EXPONENT AFTER
          MOV     AH,09            ;CHARACTER STRING
          INT     21H
          MOV     DX,POWER         ;CONVERT NUMBER IN DX TO A STRING
          CMP     DX,8000H         ;IS IT POS OR NEG?
          JB      POSIT            ;IF POSITIVE, GO TO POSIT
          LEA     DX,SIGN          ;IF NEG, PRINT A NEGATIVE SIGN FIRST
          MOV     AH,09
          INT     21H
          MOV     DX,POWER         ;CORRECT HEX VALUE, FOR A NEGATIVE
          XOR     DX,0FFFFH
          ADD     DX,01
POSIT:    MOV     CX,0
          LEA     DI,TBUFF         ;TBUFF WILL SERVE AS A FOUR BYTE
POWER1:   PUSH    CX               ;CHARACTER STORAGE AS THE HEX NUMS
          MOV     AX,DX            ;IN DX ARE CONVERTED TO DECIMAL
          MOV     DX,0             ;ASCII VALUES FOR SCREEN PRINTING
          MOV     CX,10
          DIV     CX
          XCHG    AX,DX
          ADD     AL,30H           ;MAKE NUMBER AN ASCII DIGIT
          MOV     [DI],AL          ;SAVE IT IN TBUFF
          INC     DI               ;POINT TO NEW LOCATION IN TBUFF
          POP     CX
          INC     CX               ;CX CONTAINS THE NUMBER OF DIGITS
          CMP     DX,0
          JNZ     POWER1
PRIT:     DEC     DI               ;PREPARE TO PRINT VALUES TO SCREEN
          MOV     AL,[DI]          ;GET DIGIT FROM TBUFF
          PUSH    DX               ;PROTECT ORIGINAL DX VALUE
          MOV     DL,AL            ;MOVE DIGIT FOR PRINTING
          MOV     AH,2             ;PARAMETER FOR DOS PRINT
          INT     21H              ;PRINT POWER TO SCREEN
          POP     DX               ;RETURN ORIGINAL DX VALUE
          LOOP    PRIT             ;CONTINUE TILL ALL DONE
          RET
FORMAT    ENDP
MATHCODE ENDS                      ;END CODE SEGMENT NAMED MYCODE

          END                      ;END WHOLE PROGRAM
```

The data segment contains two real numbers. ANGLE holds the number of degrees—in this case, 25.5. CONST will be used to convert the angle to radians. The structure of the program is similar to that of the previous program. The code used to calculate the tangent of the angle is shown here.

```
FINIT                   ;INITIALIZE COPROCESSOR
FLDPI                   ;LOAD PI ON STACK
FLD       CONST         ;LOAD CONSTANT ON STACK
```

```
FDIV                                ;DIVIDE CONSTANT BY PI
FLD         ANGLE                   ;LOAD ANGLE ON STACK
FMUL                                ;MULTIPLY PREV. RESULT × ANGLE
FPTAN                               ;TAKE TANGENT OF ABOVE PRODUCT
FDIV                                ;DIVIDE ST/ST(1) TO GET DECIMAL
FSTP        QWORD PTR [SI]          ;POP OFF COPROC AND SAVE TO
                                    ;VARIABLE
FWAIT                               ;SYNCHRONIZE
```

PI is loaded on the stack top and then pushed to ST(1) when CONST is placed in ST(0). FDIV divides PI by 180 and leaves the result on the stack top. FLD loads ANGLE on the stack top, pushing the result of the previous division one level deeper on the stack. FMUL multiplies ST by ST(1) and leaves the result on the stack top. This result is the equivalent angle in radians. Evoking FPTAN returns the tangent as the ratio of two numbers: Y and X. Y is placed at ST and then pushed one level deeper on the stack as X is pushed to ST. FDIV divides Y by X and puts the quotient on the stack top. FSTP returns the real answer to TANGENT, and the IBM utility routine converts it to real-number format.

A ROUTINE FOR FINDING THE SINE OF AN ANGLE

If your computer uses an 80287 coprocessor, the sine and cosine functions are not supported. Indeed, angles greater than 45 degrees (PI/4) are not supported by the tangent function. With the use of a little trigonometry, however, sines and cosines can be derived from the tangent function for this coprocessor. If your computer uses an 80387 coprocessor, the tangent, sine, and cosine functions are fully supported. The following listing shows the complete code for this program.

```
;FOR COMPUTERS WITH 80287\80387 MATH COPROCESSOR
;PROGRAM TO ILLUSTRATE SIMPLE REAL NUMBER ARTIHMETIC WITH FINAL
;REAL ANSWER VIEWED WITH MICROSOFT SYMBOLIC DEBUGGER
;PROGRAM WILL CALCULATE THE SINE OF A SPECIFIED INTEGER ANGLE,
;BETWEEN 0 & 90 DEGREES

PAGE ,132                           ;SET PAGE DIMENSIONS

    .8087                           ;PSEUDO-OP FOR COPROC. ASSEMBLY

STACK       SEGMENT PARA STACK
            DB      64 DUP ('MYSTACK ')
STACK       ENDS

MYDATA      SEGMENT PARA 'DATA'
ANGLE       DW      65
```

```
TEMP      DW       ?
CONST     DD       180.0
SINE      DQ       ?
MYDATA    ENDS

MYCODE    SEGMENT PARA 'CODE'     ;DEFINE CODE SEG. FOR MASM
MYPROC    PROC    FAR             ;PROCEDURE IS NAMED MYPROC
          ASSUME  CS:MYCODE,DS:MYDATA,SS:STACK
          PUSH    DS              ;SAVE LOCATION OF DS REG.
          SUB     AX,AX           ;GET A ZERO IN AX
          PUSH    AX              ;SAVE ZERO ON STACK, TOO
          MOV     AX,MYDATA       ;GET DATA LOCATION IN AX
          MOV     DS,AX           ;PUT IT IN DS REGISTER
{*************************************************************}
          MOV     AX,ANGLE        ;LET'S LOOK AT ANGLE
          CMP     AX,45           ;45 IS BOUNDARY CONDITION
          JG      FIXIT           ;IF LARGER, MAKE JUMP
          JMP     CONT            ;IF NOT, CONTINUE
FIXIT:    NEG     AX              ;SUB 90-AX
          ADD     AX,90           ;RESULT IN AX REGISTER
CONT:     MOV     TEMP,AX         ;SAVE RESULT IN TEMP

          FINIT                   ;INITIALIZE COPROCESSOR
          FLDPI                   ;PUT PI ON STACK
          FLD     CONST           ;PUT CONSTANT ON STACK
          FDIV                    ;DIVIDE CONSTANT BY PI
          FILD    TEMP            ;LOAD ADJ INTEGER ANGLE
          FMUL                    ;MULTIPLY BY PREVIOUS RESULT
          FPTAN                   ;TAKE THE TANGENT OF THE PRODUCT
          FWAIT

          MOV     AX,ANGLE        ;CHECK ANGLE SIZE
          CMP     AX,45           ;IF 45 OR LESS, USE SINE
          JG      COSIN           ;IF GREATER, USE COSINE
          JMP     SININ

COSIN:    FXCH    ST(1)           ;EXCHANGE STACK IF COSIN IS NEEDED
SININ:    FMUL    ST(0),ST        ;NO STACK EXCHANGE FOR SINE
          FXCH    ST(1)           ;
          FLD     ST(0)           ;TRIG IDENITY FOR SINE OR COSINE
          FMUL    ST(0),ST        ;X OR Y DIVIDED BY HYPOT.
          FADD    ST(0),ST(2)     ;
          FSQRT                   ;
          FDIVP   ST(1),ST        ;
          FSTP    SINE            ;POP RESULT INTO STORAGE
          FWAIT                   ;SYNCHRONIZE
{*************************************************************}
          RET                     ;RETURN CONTROL TO DOS
MYPROC    ENDP                    ;END PROCEDURE NAMED MYPROC
MYCODE    ENDS                    ;END CODE SEGMENT NAMED MYCODE

          END                     ;END WHOLE PROGRAM
```

If you are using an 80387 coprocessor, all of the code between the two lines of asterisks can be replaced with the following simplified program:

```
FINIT
FLDPI
FLD       CONST
FDIV
FILD      ANGLE
FMUL
FSIN
FSTP      SINE
FWAIT
```

It is fortunate that between 0 and PI/2 radians (0 to 90 degrees), the sine of an angle yields the same result as cosine of PI/2 minus the angle:

SINE(X) = COSINE(PI/2 − X)

You might recall that at PI/4 radians (45 degrees), the sine and cosine both yield the value .707. We will take advantage of these relationships in the program.

The program in this example has three main parts: one to convert the original angle to radians and reduce it to PI/4 or less, one to find the tangent of the reduced angle, and, one to convert the result using cosine conversion if the original angle was greater than PI/4, and sine conversion if the original angle was less than PI/4.

The code for adjusting the angle to a size between 0 and PI/4 is shown here.

```
            MOV     AX,ANGLE     ;LET'S LOOK AT ANGLE
            CMP     AX,45        ;45 IS BOUNDARY CONDITION
            JG      FIXIT        ;IF LARGER, MAKE JUMP
            JMP     CONT         ;IF NOT, CONTINUE
FIXIT:      NEG     AX           ;SUB 90−AX
            ADD     AX,90        ;RESULT IN AX REGISTER
CONT:       MOV     TEMP,AX      ;SAVE RESULT IN TEMP
```

ANGLE is a defined word (DW) integer that contains the original angle in degrees. If this angle is greater than 45 degrees, a branch is made to FIXIT; otherwise, a JMP is made to CONT. FIXIT complements AX and adds it to 90 degrees, effectively subtracting the angle from 90 degrees. The result is placed in the variable TEMP and will be used by the tangent function during the next stage.

```
FINIT                        ;INITIALIZE COPROCESSOR
FLDPI                        ;PUT PI ON STACK
FLD         CONST            ;PUT CONSTANT ON STACK
FDIV                         ;DIVIDE CONSTANT BY PI
FILD        TEMP             ;LOAD ADJ INTEGER ANGLE
FMUL                         ;MULTIPLY BY PREVIOUS RESULT
FPTAN                        ;TAKE THE TANGENT OF THE PRODUCT
FWAIT
```

This code is similar to that of the previous example, with the exception that TEMP is an integer value. When FPTAN is executed, the X and Y values that form the ratio are placed so that X is at the stack top (ST), and Y is one location deeper than the stack top.

Refer to the right triangle in Figure 9.3 as you review the code necessary to obtain the sine of the angle.

Since Y and X have been returned to the coprocessor stack as a result of the previous operation, it is only necessary to calculate R to obtain either the sine or cosine function.

```
(1) COSIN:   FXCH    ST(1)        ;EXCHANGE STACK IF COSIN IS NEEDED
(2) SININ:   FMUL    ST(0),ST     ;NO STACK EXCHANGE FOR SINE
(3)          FXCH    ST(1)        ;
(4)          FLD     ST(0)        ;TRIG IDENTITY FOR SINE OR COSINE
(5)          FMUL    ST(0),ST     ;X OR Y DIVIDED BY HYPOT.
(6)          FADD    ST(0),ST(2)  ;
(7)          FSQRT                ;
(8)          FDIVP   ST(1),ST     ;
(9)          FSTP    SINE         ;POP RESULT INTO STORAGE
(10)         FWAIT                ;SYNCHRONIZE
```

Examine Table 9-2 to see what is happening to the stack of the coprocessor as this section of code is executed.

If the original angle was PI/4 (45 degrees) or less, the SINE PATH will be taken. If the original angle is greater than PI/4 (and less than or equal to PI/2 − 90 degrees), the COSINE PATH will be taken, since cosine 30 = sine 60. Thus, angles greater than PI/4 can be used to obtain the sine of the angle. At step 2, either X^2 or Y^2 is on the stack top. Following the sequence in Table 9-2, $R = (Y^2 + X^2)^{.5}$ is eventually placed on the stack top. Step 8 divides R into either Y (for sine) or X (for cosine) and returns the quotient to ST(1), the new ST. However, before completion of the step, the stack top is popped, moving the quotient to ST(0). When step 9 is executed, the real result is transferred to the variable SINE. The result placed here will be correct for any angle between 0 and PI/2 degrees.

This program was designed to be used with the Microsoft Symbolic Debug program. Here are a few lines from a data segment dump:

```
46FB:0158   F9 9B DD 1E 08 00 9B CB   −0.1655102779799079E+57
46FB:0160   41 00 19 00 00 00 34 43   +0.5629499535851585E+16
46FB:0168   67 D7 2D 30 79 00 ED 3F   +0.9063077870366499E+0
46FB:0170   4D 59 53 54 41 43 4B 20   +0.4066692443677049E−152
```

The sine of 65 degrees is +0.9063077870366499E+0. What precision!

While this is a rather neat application of trigonometry and algebra, think how much easier the program was to implement with the enhanced 80387 instructions.

```
        SUB     AX,AX           ;GET A ZERO IN AX
        PUSH    AX              ;SAVE ZERO ON STACK, TOO
        MOV     AX,MYDATA       ;GET DATA LOCATION IN AX
        MOV     DS,AX           ;PUT IT IN DS REGISTER

        LEA     BX,SINE
AGAIN:  MOV     AX,ANGLE        ;LET'S LOOK AT ANGLE
        CMP     AX,45           ;45 IS BOUNDARY CONDITION
        JG      FIXIT           ;IF LARGER, MAKE JUMP
        JMP     CONT            ;IF NOT, CONTINUE
FIXIT:  NEG     AX              ;SUB 90-AX
        ADD     AX,90           ;RESULT IN AX REGISTER
CONT:   MOV     TEMP,AX         ;SAVE RESULT IN TEMP

        FINIT                   ;INITIALIZE COPROCESSOR
        FLDPI                   ;PUT PI ON STACK
        FLD     CONST           ;PUT CONSTANT ON STACK
        FDIV                    ;DIVIDE CONSTANT BY PI
        FILD    TEMP            ;LOAD ADJ INTEGER ANGLE
        FMUL                    ;MULTIPLY BY PREVIOUS RESULT
        FPTAN                   ;TAKE THE TANGENT OF THE PRODUCT
        FWAIT                   ;SYNCHRONIZE

        MOV     AX,ANGLE        ;CHECK ANGLE SIZE
        CMP     AX,45           ;IF 45 OR LESS, USE SINE
        JG      COSIN           ;IF GREATER. USE COSINE
        JMP     SININ
COSIN:  FXCH    ST(1)           ;EXCHANGE STACK IF COSINE IS NEEDED
SININ:  FMUL    ST(0),ST        ;NO STACK EXCHANGE FOR SINE
        FXCH    ST(1)           ;
        FLD     ST(0)           ;TRIG IDENITY FOR SINE OR COSINE
        FMUL    ST(0),ST        ;X OR Y DIVIDED BY HYPOT.
        FADD    ST(0),ST(2)     ;
        FSQRT                   ;
        FDIVP   ST(1),ST        ;
        FSTP    SINE[BX]        ;POP RESULT INTO STORAGE
        FWAIT                   ;SYNCHRONIZE

        ADD     BX,08H          ;POINT TO NEXT SINE LOCATION
        ADD     ANGLE,1         ;INCREMENT ANGLE
        CMP     ANGLE,90        ;DO FOR 0 TO 90 DEGREES
        JLE     AGAIN           ;IF NOT 91, DO AGAIN

        RET                     ;RETURN CONTROL TO DOS
MYPROC  ENDP                    ;END PROCEDURE NAMED MYPROC
MYCODE  ENDS                    ;END CODE SEGMENT NAMED MYCODE

        END                     ;END WHOLE PROGRAM
```

Notice that only the following section of code has been altered:

```
FSTP    SINE[BX]        ;POP RESULT INTO STORAGE
FWAIT                   ;SYNCHRONIZE

ADD     BX,08H          ;POINT TO NEXT SINE LOCATION
ADD     ANGLE,1         ;INCREMENT ANGLE
CMP     ANGLE,90        ;DO FOR 0 TO 90 DEGREES
JLE     AGAIN           ;IF NOT 91, DO AGAIN
```

In the data segment, the SINE variable has been declared as a table capable of storing all 91 DQ (defined quadword) answers. As each answer is calculated, BX is incremented eight bytes to point to the next storage location. ANGLE is compared with 90 (90 degrees), and the decision is made to continue or terminate. Table 9-3 is the sine table produced by this program.

PLOTTING A SINE WAVE

The program in the previous example calculated the sine of angles between 0 and 90 degrees and returned the real answer to SINE[BX]. To plot these answers on the screen, several modifications must be made in the original program: The real answers must be converted to integers so they can be plotted on the screen, the answers must be scaled to fit the coordinates of the plotting screen, and values for the other three coordinates (91 to 360 degrees) must be obtained.

The change in steps necessary to convert a real number to integer format is as simple as changing the command FSTP SINE to FISTP SINE. However, this would not work if the answers had not already been scaled for the screen. The high-resolution screen of the IBM PC/AT plots 200 pixels vertically and 640 pixels horizontally. A sine wave varies between $+1.00$ and -1.00. Therefore, a scaling factor of 100 will permit the plotted waveform to vary between $+100$ and -100 (a total of 200) vertical pixels. If one horizontal pixel position is used for every degree, then only 360 horizontal pixels out of 640 are needed. To center the waveform, an offset of 140 pixels from the left-hand edge will be used ($640-360 = 280$, and $280/2 = 140$). The piece of code that performs steps 1 and 2 is

```
FIMUL    MULTIP
FISTP    SINE[SI]       ;POP RESULT INTO STORAGE
```

where MULTIP has been defined in the data segment as 100. The SI register is used to index the integer storage table SINE. Note the extreme loss of precision in the answers. At most, the values are accurate only to three significant digits, but this problem is caused by the resolution of the screen and not the computer.

Obtaining the results for angles between 91 and 360 degrees, step 3, is a bit more of a challenge. There are actually two paths that can be taken: the algorithm can be changed, and all 361 points can be calculated; or the 0 to 90 degree pattern can be used four times.

Recall that the second path was used in Chapter 8, when a sine wave was plotted from values stored in a lookup table. The major difference

+0.0E+0
+0.1745240643728351E)−1
+0.3489949670250097E)−1
+0.5233595624294383E)−1
+0.697564737441253E)−1
+0.8715574274765818E)1
+0.1045284632676535E+0
+0.1218693434051475E+0
+0.1391731009600654E+0
+0.1564344650402309E+0
+0.1736481776669304E+0
+0.1908089953765448E+0
+0.2079116908177593E+0
+0.224951054343865E+0
+0.2419218955996677E+0
+0.2588190451025207E+0
+0.2756373558169992E+0
+0.2923717047227367E+0
+0.3090169943749475E+0
+0.3255681544571566E+0
+0.3420201433256687E+0
+0.3583679495453003E+0
+0.374606593415912E+0
+0.3907311284892738E+0
+0.4067366430758002E+0
+0.4226182617406994E+0
+0.4383711467890774E+0
+0.4539904997395468E+0
+0.4694715627858908E+0
+0.484809620246337E+0
+0.5E+0
+0.5150380749100542E+0
+0.5299192642332049E+0
+0.5446390350150271E+0
+0.5591929034707468E+0
+0.573576436351046E+0
+0.5877852522924731E+0
+0.6018150231520483E+0
+0.6156614753256583E+0
+0.6293203910498375E+0
+0.6427876096865394E+0
+0.6560590289905073E+0
+0.6691306063588582E+0

Table 9-3. _____

Very Precise Sine Values for Angles 0 to 90 Degrees

+0.6819983600624985E+0
+0.6946583704589973E+0
+0.7071067811865476E+0
+0.7193398003386512E+0
+0.7313537016191705E+0
+0.7431448254773942E+0
+0.754709580222772E+0
+0.766044443118978E+0
+0.7771459614569709E+0
+0.7880107536067219E+0
+0.7986355100472928E+0
+0.8090169943749475E+0
+0.8191520442889918E+0
+0.8290375725550417E+0
+0.8386705679454241E+0
+0.848048096156426E+0
+0.8571673007021123E+0
+0.8660254037844386E+0
+0.8746197071393959E+0
+0.882947592858927E+0
+0.8910065241883679E+0
+0.898794046299167E+0
+0.9063077870366499E+0
+0.9135454576426009E+0
+0.9205048534524404E+0
+0.9271838545667874E+0
+0.9335804264972017E+0
+0.9396926207859084E+0
+0.9455185755993168E+0
+0.9510565162951535E+0
+0.9563047559630354E+0
+0.9612616959383189E+0
+0.9659258262890683E+0
+0.9702957262759965E+0
+0.9743700647852352E+0
+0.9781476007338057E+0
+0.981627183447664E+0
+0.984807753012208E+0
+0.9876883405951378E+0
+0.9902680687415704E+0
+0.992546151641322E+0
+0.9945218953682733E+0

Table 9-3. _____

Very Precise Sine Values for Angles 0 to 90 Degrees (*continued*)

+0.9961946980917455E+0
+0.9975640502598242E+0
+0.9986295347545738E+0
+0.9993908270190958E+0
+0.9998476951563913E+0
+0.1E+1

Table 9-3. _____

Very Precise Sine Values for Angles 0 to 90 Degrees (*continued*)

between that program and this one is that in this program the values are actually being calculated as they are being placed in a table. This is the program that was promised in Chapter 8—it is a composite of Figure 8-1 and the last two programs of this chapter. Examine the code in the following listing and notice that it is indeed composed of previous examples.

```
;FOR COMPUTERS WITH 80287\80387 MATH COPROCESSOR
;PROGRAM TO ILLUSTRATE SIMPLE REAL NUMBER ARTIHMETIC WITH FINAL
;ANSWERS SCALED AND CONVERTED TO INTEGERS.
;PROGRAM WILL CALCULATE THE SINE OF INTEGER ANGLES FROM 0 TO 90 DEGREES
;AND PLOT THE SINE WAVE (0 TO 360 DEGREES) ON THE GRAPHICS SCREEN

      PAGE ,132                        ;SET PAGE DIMENSIONS

       .8087                           ;PSEUDO-OP FOR COPROC. ASSEMBLY

      SETSCREEN MACRO                  ;;SET HI-RES SCREEN
                MOV     AH,00          ;;200x640 DOTS BW
                MOV     AL,06
                INT     10H
                ENDM

      WRITEDOT MACRO                   ;;MACRO FOR DOT WRITING
                MOV     AH,12
                MOV     AL,01
                MOV     CX,POS
                ADD     CX,140         ;;CENTER DISPLAY
                MOV     DH,00
                MOV     DL,INDEP
                INT     10H
                ENDM

      STACK     SEGMENT PARA STACK
                DB      64 DUP ('MYSTACK ')
      STACK     ENDS

      MYDATA    SEGMENT PARA 'DATA'
      ANGLE     DW      0              ;STARTING ANGLE
      TEMP      DW      ?              ;TEMP STORAGE LOCATION
      CONST     DD      180.0          ;CONSTANT FOR CONVERSION
      MULTIP    DW      100            ;CONVERT SINE 0 TO 100
      POS       DW      0
      INDEP     DB      0
      SINE      DW      91 DUP (?)     ;STORAGE FOR ANSWERS
      MYDATA    ENDS
```

```
MYCODE  SEGMENT PARA 'CODE'        ;DEFINE CODE SEG. FOR MASM
MYPROC  PROC    FAR               ;PROCEDURE IS NAMED MYPROC
        ASSUME  CS:MYCODE,DS:MYDATA,SS:STACK
        PUSH    DS                ;SAVE LOCATION OF DS REG.
        SUB     AX,AX             ;GET A ZERO IN AX
        PUSH    AX                ;SAVE ZERO ON STACK, TOO
        MOV     AX,MYDATA         ;GET DATA LOCATION IN AX
        MOV     DS,AX             ;PUT IT IN DS REGISTER
        MOV     SI,0              ;SI WILL INDEX INTO SINE
AGAIN:  MOV     AX,ANGLE          ;LET'S LOOK AT ANGLE
        CMP     AX,45             ;45 IS BOUNDARY CONDITION
        JG      FIXIT             ;IF LARGER, MAKE JUMP
        JMP     CONT              ;IF NOT, CONTINUE
FIXIT:  NEG     AX                ;SUB 90-AX
        ADD     AX,90             ;RESULT IN AX REGISTER
CONT:   MOV     TEMP,AX           ;SAVE RESULT IN TEMP

        FINIT                     ;INITIALIZE COPROCESSOR
        FLDPI                     ;PUT PI ON STACK
        FLD     CONST             ;PUT CONSTANT ON STACK
        FDIV                      ;DIVIDE CONSTANT BY PI
        FILD    TEMP              ;LOAD ADJ INTEGER ANGLE
        FMUL                      ;MULTIPLY BY PREVIOUS RESULT
        FPTAN                     ;TAKE THE TANGENT OF THE PRODUCT
        FWAIT                     ;SYNCHRONIZE

        MOV     AX,ANGLE          ;CHECK ANGLE SIZE
        CMP     AX,45             ;IF 45 OR LESS, USE SINE
        JG      COSIN             ;IF GREATER. USE COSINE
        JMP     SININ

COSIN:  FXCH    ST(1)             ;EXCHANGE STACK IF COSINE IS NEEDED
SININ:  FMUL    ST(0),ST          ;NO STACK EXCHANGE FOR SINE
        FXCH    ST(1)             ;
        FLD     ST(0)             ;TRIG IDENITY FOR SINE OR COSINE
        FMUL    ST(0),ST          ;X OR Y DIVIDED BY HYPOT.
        FADD    ST(0),ST(2)       ;
        FSQRT                     ;
        FDIVP   ST(1),ST          ;
        FIMUL   MULTIP
        FISTP   SINE[SI]          ;POP RESULT INTO STORAGE
        FWAIT                     ;SYNCHRONIZE

        ADD     SI,02H            ;POINT TO NEXT SINE LOCATION
        ADD     ANGLE,1           ;INCREMENT ANGLE
        CMP     ANGLE,90          ;DO FOR 0 TO 90 DEGREES
        JLE     AGAIN             ;IF NOT 91, DO AGAIN

;ROUTINE SIMILAR TO FIGURE 8.1 FOR PLOTTING CALCULATED POINTS
;TO HI-RES GRAPHICS SCREEN

        SETSCREEN                 ;SET GRAPHICS 200x640 SCREEN
REPT:   MOV     SI,0              ;FIND START OF TABLE
        MOV     AX,POS            ;MOVE ANGLE VALUE INTO AL REGISTER
        CMP     AX,180            ;IS IT GREATER THAN 180 DEGREES?
        JLE     NEWQUAD           ;IF LESS, ANGLE IN QUAD 1 OR 2
        SUB     AX,180            ;CORRECT ANGLE IF 180 OR GREATER
NEWQUAD: CMP    AX,90             ;IS IT GREATER THAN 90 DEGREES?
        JLE     SECQUAD           ;IF GREATER THAN 90, SECOND QUAD
        NEG     AX                ;SET VALUE TO NEGATIVE
        ADD     AX,180            ;CORRECT ANGLE IF 90 OR GREATER
SECQUAD: ADD    SI,AX             ;GET OFFSET SUM INTO BX
        SHL     SI,1              ;FIX TO WORD INDEX (x2)
        MOV     AL,BYTE PTR SINE[SI] ;GET VALUE AND PLACE IN ANS
        CMP     POS,180           ;IF VALUE >180, ADD TO SCREEN DIS.
```

```
            JGE       BIGDIS
            NEG       AL                ;OTHERWISE, GET NEGATIVE OF VALUE
            ADD       AL,100            ;NOW ADD 100 TO VALUE, FOR CORRECT
            JMP       READY             ;SCREEN DISPLACEMENT
BIGDIS:     ADD       AL,99
READY:      MOV       INDEP,AL          ;STORE IN TEMP., TRANS TO WRITEDOT
            WRITEDOT                    ;GO TO WRITEDOT MACRO
            ADD       POS,1             ;GET NEXT ANGLE
            CMP       POS,360           ;HAVE WE DONE 360 DEGREES?
            JLE       REPT              ;IF NOT DO IT AGAIN
;COMPLETION OF SINEWAVE LOOKUP EXAMPLE

;WAIT FOR A KEY PRESS BEFORE RETURNING & SWITCHING TO TEXT SCREEN
            MOV       AH,07             ;KEYBOARD PARAMETER
            INT       21H               ;READ KEYBOARD AND LEAVE
            MOV       AH,00             ;SCREEN PARAMETER
            MOV       AL,03             ;25x80 COLOR MODE
            INT       10H               ;SET SCREEN

            RET                         ;RETURN CONTROL TO DOS
MYPROC      ENDP                        ;END PROCEDURE NAMED MYPROC
MYCODE      ENDS                        ;END CODE SEGMENT NAMED MYCODE

            END                         ;END WHOLE PROGRAM
```

Figure 9-4 is a screen dump of the sine wave. The coprocessor allows the data points to be calculated and plotted very fast. You will examine a program in the next example that allows you to compare the plotting speed of assembly graphics with that of popular high-level languages.

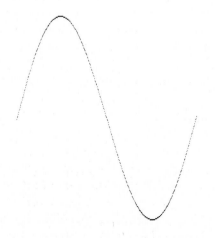

Figure 9-4.

Plot of sine wave

IMPLEMENTING A FOURIER SERIES TO PRODUCE GRAPHICS

The following graphics program shows the speed and precision that can be obtained with the 80286/80386 in conjunction with the Intel coprocessor. This example was written and executed on a 9 MHz 80286 IBM AT computer, with an 80287 running at standard speed. If an 80386 machine is used along with an 80387 coprocessor, hang onto your socks — the 80386/80387 pair has redefined the meaning of fast. Time reductions as great as a factor of ten can be anticipated.

It was observed by mathematician Jean Baptiste Fourier (1768-1830) that almost any periodic waveform can be constructed by simply adding the correct combinations of sine wave harmonics together. (For a more detailed treatment of this subject, refer to almost any college-level physics or electrical engineering textbook.) Fourier's formal equation is usually expressed as

$$y = A + A1(SIN\ \omega t) + A2(SIN\ 2\omega t) + A3(SIN\ 3\omega t) + A4(SIN\ 4\omega t)...$$

For some waveforms, only odd or even harmonics are included, while for others all terms are included. For some waveforms, the signs of adjacent terms alternate between + and −.

In this example, you are going to construct a square wave by adding the harmonic terms in a Fourier Series. The more terms you use in the series, the more the final result will approach a precise square wave. For a square wave, the general Fourier Series equation is this exact equation:

$$y = (SIN\ \omega t) + (1/3)(SIN\ 3\omega t) + (1/5)(SIN\ 5\omega t) + (1/7)(SIN\ 7\omega t)...$$

Thus, only odd harmonics contribute to the final result. Notice in the equation that if only one harmonic is chosen, the result will be a sine wave. Also notice that each successive term uses a fractional multiplier — in other words, each successively higher harmonic affects the waveform less and less.

To fully appreciate what this program can accomplish, remember that each term in a Fourier Series is calculated separately by the program, with the sum of these individual terms being continuously updated. Therefore, if you ask for 500 harmonics, 500 separate sine values will be scaled, calculated, and added together to form a single point on the screen, and this must be repeated for each point that is to be plotted on the screen. This requires 500 calculations × 360 points, or 180,000 calculations! How long would it take you to make these calculations with a calculator? How long would it take a BASIC, Pascal, or APL program to make them? If it takes, for example, 5 minutes to calculate 50 terms on a calculator, it will take 50 minutes to calculate 500 terms. Fifty minutes $\times$ 360 points = 18,000 minutes or 12.5 days nonstop. How long would it take BASIC, Pascal, or APL? We will run a benchmark later to see how they compare.

The following program is the complete listing for the Fourier Series program.

```
;FOR COMPUTERS WITH 80287/80387 MATH COPROCESSOR
;PROGRAM WILL GENERATE A SQUARE WAVE BY ADDING APPROPRIATE
;TERMS OF A FOURIER SERIES TOGETHER.  THE RESULTING WAVEFORM
;IS DRAWN TO THE HI-RESOLUTION SCREEN
;500 HARMONICS REQUIRES APPROX. 1.8 MINUTES

        PAGE ,132                       ;SET PAGE DIMENSIONS

        .8087                           ;PSEUDO-OP FOR COPROC. ASSEMBLY

HARMONIC  MACRO                         ;;INPUT 4 DIGIT DECIMAL NUMBER
          LOCAL MOREIN,DONE             ;;FROM KEYBOARD
          PUSH    AX                    ;;PROTECT REGISTER VALUES
          PUSH    BX
          PUSH    CX
          PUSH    DX
          MOV     DX,0                  ;;PAD DX WITH ZEROS
          MOV     CX,4                  ;;LIMIT TO FOUR DIGIT INPUT MAX
MOREIN:   MOV     AH,1                  ;;DOS INTERRUPT CALL PARAMETER
          INT     21H                   ;;GET ASCII CHARACTER FROM KEYBOARD
          CMP     AL,30H                ;;NUMBER TO LOW?
          JL      DONE                  ;;IF YES, THEN DATA ENTRY IS DONE
          CMP     AL,39H                ;;NUMBER TO HIGH?
          JG      DONE                  ;;IF YES, THEN DATA ENTRY IS DONE
          AND     AX,000FH              ;;PRESERVE LOWER FOUR BITS (HEX DIGIT)
          PUSH    AX                    ;;SAVE ON STACK
          MOV     AX,DX                 ;;PUT ACCUMULATED NUM IN AX
          MOV     BX,10                 ;;MULTIPLY IT BY 10
          MUL     BX
          MOV     DX,AX                 ;;RETURN IT TO DX
          POP     AX
          ADD     DX,AX                 ;;ADD TO IT THE LAST ENTERED DIGIT
          LOOP    MOREIN
DONE:     MOV     HARM,DX               ;;SAVE ENTRY AS NUMBER OF HARMONICS
          POP     DX                    ;;RESTORE PROTECTED REGISTERS
          POP     CX
          POP     BX
          POP     AX
          ENDM

SETSCREEN MACRO                         ;;SET HI-RES SCREEN
          PUSH    AX                    ;;SAVE VALUE IN AX
          MOV     AH,00                 ;;200x640 DOTS BW
          MOV     AL,06
          INT     10H
          POP     AX                    ;;RETURN VALUE IN AX
          ENDM

WRITEDOT  MACRO                         ;;MACRO FOR DOT WRITING
          PUSH    AX
          MOV     AH,12                 ;;SAVE VALUE IN AX
          MOV     AL,01
```

```
                MOV      CX,ANGLE            ;;HORZ DOT POSITION
                ADD      CX,140             ;;CENTER DISPLAY (HORZ OFFSET)
                MOV      DH,00
                INT      10H
                POP      AX                 ;;RETURN VALUE IN AX
                ENDM

STACK     SEGMENT PARA STACK
          DB        64 DUP ('MYSTACK ')
STACK     ENDS

MYDATA    SEGMENT PARA 'DATA'
ANGLE     DW        0                  ;STARTING ANGLE (0 THRU 360)
FOUR      DW        4                  ;A CONSTANT
MULTIP    DW        50                 ;CONVERT SINE 0 TO 100
RADIAN    DW        180                ;A CONSTANT
REDUCE    DW        360                ;A CONSTANT
TEMP1     DW        ?
TEMP2     DW        ?
TEMP3     DW        ?
STATWD    DW        ?                  ;80287 STATUS WORD
SINE      DD        361 DUP (0)        ;STORAGE FOR REAL ANSWERS
ISINE     DW        361 DUP (0)        ;STORAGE FOR INTEGER RESULTS
MESSG1    DB        'ENTER THE NUMBER OF HARMONICS TO BE ADDED, (0 TO 9999): $',13H
MESSG2    DB        'CALCULATING $'
HARM      DW        ?                  ;USER ENTERED - No. OF HARMONICS
MYDATA    ENDS

MYCODE    SEGMENT PARA 'CODE'          ;DEFINE CODE SEG. FOR MASM
MYPROC    PROC      FAR                ;PROCEDURE IS NAMED MYPROC
          ASSUME    CS:MYCODE,DS:MYDATA,SS:STACK
          PUSH      DS                 ;SAVE LOCATION OF DS REG.
          SUB       AX,AX              ;GET A ZERO IN AX
          PUSH      AX                 ;SAVE ZERO ON STACK, TOO
          MOV       AX,MYDATA          ;GET DATA LOCATION IN AX
          MOV       DS,AX              ;PUT IT IN DS REGISTER

          SETSCREEN                    ;CLEAR SCREEN
          LEA       DX,MESSG1          ;PRINT MESSAGE FOR INPUT
          MOV       AH,9
          INT       21H
          HARMONIC                     ;ACCEPT DATA ENTRY
          SETSCREEN                    ;CLEAR SCREEN AND WAIT
          LEA       DX,MESSG2          ;PRINT "CALCULATING" MESSAGE
          MOV       AH,9
          INT       21H


          MOV       SI,0               ;SI WILL INDEX INTO SINE
NXTPT:    MOV       TEMP1,01H          ;LET'S LOOK AT ANGLE
ADMORE:   MOV       AX,ANGLE           ;MOVE CURRENT ANGLE INTO AX
          MOV       DX,TEMP1           ;CURRENT FOURIER HARMONIC IN CAL
          SHL       DX,1               ;MULTIPLY IT BY 2
          SUB       DX,1               ;SUBTRACT 1
          MOV       TEMP2,DX           ;SAVE FACTOR FOR LATER
          MUL       TEMP2              ;MULTIPLY ANGLE BY FACTOR
          DIV       REDUCE             ;DIVIDE ANGLE BY 360
          MOV       TEMP3,DX           ;KEEP REMAINING DEGREES IN TEMP3

          FINIT                        ;INITIALIZE COPROCESSOR
          FILD      RADIAN             ;PREPARE TO CONVERT DEGREES TO RADIANS
          FLDPI                        ;LOAD PI ON STACK
          FDIV      ST(0),ST(1)        ;DIVIDE TO GET .0174.....+
          FILD      TEMP3              ;PUT THE ANGLE ON STACK (IN DEGREES)
          FMUL                         ;MULTIPLY TO GET ANGLE IN RADIANS

COMMENT / IF USING A 80387 WITH EXTENDED TRIG FUNCTIONS, THE FOLLOWING
          CODE BETWEEN THE MARKERS CAN BE REPLACED WITH -->   FSIN     /
```

```
;*************************************************************************
        FLDPI                       ;LOAD PI ON STACK TOP              *
        FIDIV     FOUR              ;DIVIDE BY FOUR, RESULT ON STACK TOP *
        FXCH                        ;EXCHANGE POSITION OF ANGLE        *
        FPREM                       ;REDUCE TO 0 TO PI/4 RANGE FOR TAN *
        FSTSW     STATWD            ;PUT CURRENT STATUS WORD IN VARIABLE *
        FWAIT                       ;SYNCHRONIZE                       *
        MOV       AX,STATWD         ;GET STATWD IN AX REGISTER         *
        TEST      AH,00000010B      ;TEST BIT, IF ZERO ANGLE<46 DEGREES *
        JZ        CALTAN            ;PROCEED FOR STACK SWITCH          *
        FSUBP     ST(1),ST(0)       ;IF MATCH, SUB FROM 45 DEGREES     *
CALTAN:
        FPTAN                       ;GET TANGENT OF ANGLE              *
        TEST      AH,01000010B      ;+- SIN (PI/4 - HYP)               *
        JPE       TST2              ;IF YES, MAKE ANOTHER TEST         *
        JMP       FIXIT             ;OTHERWISE, EXCHANGE ST AND ST1    *
TST2:   TEST      AH,00000000B      ;+- SIN (HYP)                      *
        JPE       CALSIN            ;IF TEST BOTH ZERO OR BOTH ONE     *
FIXIT:  FXCH                        ;EXCHANGE UTILIZE COSINE FUNCTION  *
CALSIN:                             ;OTHERWISE, USE SINE FUNCTION      *
        FMUL      ST(0),ST          ;USE TRIG FUNCTION TO CONVERT      *
        FXCH      ST(1)             ;TANGENT ANSWER INTO PROPER SINE   *
        FLD       ST(0)             ;VALUE                             *
        FMUL      ST(0),ST          ;                                  *
        FADD      ST(0),ST(2)       ;                                  *
        FSQRT                       ;                                  *
        FDIVP     ST(1),ST          ;                                  *
        TEST      AH,00000001B      ;A ZERO MEANS A POSITIVE RESULT    *
        JZ        POSSIG            ;                                  *
        FCHS                        ;OTHERWISE, CHANGE SIGN OF ANSWER  *

;*************************************************************************

POSSIG: FIMUL     MULTIP            ;MULTIPLY RESULT BY SCREEN FACTOR
        FIDIV     TEMP2             ;DIVIDE BY HARMONIC FACTOR
        FADD      SINE[SI]          ;ADD ANS IN STORAGE TO NEW VALUE
        FSTP      SINE[SI]          ;SAVE NEW REAL SUM BACK IN MEMORY
        FWAIT                       ;SYNCHRONIZE

        INC       TEMP1             ;PREPARE FOR NEXT HIGHER HARMONIC
        MOV       CX,HARM           ;MAX NUMBER OF HARMONICS IN CX
        CMP       TEMP1,CX          ;COMPARE PRESENT WITH MAXIMUM
        JG        IDXPOS            ;IF GREATER, END AND DO NEXT ANGLE
        JMP       ADMORE            ;CONTINUE ACCUMULATING HARMONIC VALUES

IDXPOS: ADD       SI,04H            ;POINT TO NEXT SINE LOCATION
        INC       ANGLE             ;INCREASE TO NEXT ANGLE
        CMP       ANGLE,360         ;DO FOR 0 TO 360 DEGREES
        JG        TRANS             ;IF DONE, TRANSFER DATA
        JMP       NXTPT             ;IF NOT 361, DO AGAIN

;COPY 361 REAL NUMBERS FROM SINE INTO ISINE BY CONVERTING THEM
;TO INTEGER VALUES THAT RANGE FROM +- 100
TRANS:  MOV       SI,00             ;SET INDEX REGISTERS TO ZERO
        MOV       DI,00
        LEA       BX,SINE           ;LOAD ADDRESSES OF TWO TABLES
        LEA       BP,ISINE
        MOV       CX,361            ;PREPARE TO TRANSFER 361 VALUES
TFMOR:  FLD       SINE [SI]         ;LOAD REAL NUMBER ON STACK
        FISTP     ISINE [DI]        ;POP AND STORE INTEGER NUMBER
        ADD       SI,04             ;INCREMENT NEXT REAL LOCATION
        ADD       DI,02             ;INCREMENT NEXT INTEGER LOCATION
        LOOP      TFMOR

;PLOT THE INTEGER POINTS ON THE SCREEN
PLOTP:  SETSCREEN                   ;SET GRAPHICS 200x640 SCREEN
        LEA       BP,ISINE          ;LOAD EFFECTIVE ADDRESS OF ISINE
```

```
              MOV      SI,0                   ;FIND START OF INTEGER TABLE
              MOV      ANGLE,0                ;ANGLE TO BE PLOTTED
    DOALL:    MOV      DL,BYTE PTR ISINE[SI]  ;GET VALUE AND PLACE IN AL
              NEG      DL                     ;SUBTRACT VALUE FROM 100
              ADD      DL,100                 ;THIS IS VERTICAL SCREEN COORD.
              WRITEDOT                        ;GO TO WRITEDOT MACRO
              ADD      SI,02                  ;POINT TO NEXT WORD LOCATION
              ADD      ANGLE,1                ;GET NEXT ANGLE
              CMP      ANGLE,360              ;HAVE WE DONE 360 DEGREES?
              JLE      DOALL                  ;IF NOT DO IT AGAIN

    ;WAIT FOR A KEY PRESS BEFORE RETURNING & SWITCHING TO TEXT SCREEN
              MOV      AH,07                  ;KEYBOARD PARAMETER
              INT      21H                    ;READ KEYBOARD AND LEAVE
              MOV      AH,00                  ;SCREEN PARAMETER
              MOV      AL,03                  ;25x80 COLOR MODE
              INT      10H                    ;SET SCREEN

              RET                             ;RETURN CONTROL TO DOS
    MYPROC    ENDP                            ;END PROCEDURE NAMED MYPROC
    MYCODE    ENDS                            ;END CODE SEGMENT NAMED MYCODE

              END                             ;END WHOLE PROGRAM
```

While initially it may appear very complicated, this program actually uses parts of other programs.

There are three macros in this program: HARMONIC, SETSCREEN, and WRITEDOT. SETSCREEN and WRITEDOT can be dispensed with immediately — they are the same macros for setting the graphics screen and plotting a dot that were used in the last program. HARMONIC, on the other hand, is a very exciting macro. To make the program as flexible as possible, the user should be able to enter the number of harmonics to be used by the program each time the program is run. This means that a method for entering a multiple-digit number from the keyboard must be created. There are many approaches to this goal, but the technique used here was chosen because it is both straightforward and easy to understand.

The heart of the macro, shown here, allows a four-digit decimal number to be entered from the keyboard. This number is accumulated in the DX register.

```
              MOV      DX,0          ;;PAD DX WITH ZEROS
              MOV      CX,4          ;;LIMIT TO FOUR DIGIT INPUT MAX
    MOREIN:   MOV      AH,1          ;;DOS INTERRUPT CALL PARAMETER
              INT      21H           ;;GET ASCII CHARACTER FROM KEYBOARD
              CMP      AL,30H        ;;NUMBER TO LOW?
              JL       DONE          ;;IF YES, THEN DATA ENTRY IS DONE
              CMP      AL,39H        ;;NUMBER TO HIGH?
              JG       DONE          ;;IF YES, THEN DATA ENTRY IS DONE
              AND      AX,000FH      ;;PRESERVE LOWER FOUR BITS (HEX DIGIT)
              PUSH     AX            ;;SAVE ON STACK
              MOV      AX,DX         ;;PUT ACCUMULATED NUM IN AX
              MOV      BX,10         ;;MULTIPLY IT BY 10
              MUL      BX
```

```
            MOV     DX,AX       ;;RETURN IT TO DX
            POP     AX
            ADD     DX,AX       ;;ADD TO IT THE LAST ENTERED DIGIT
            LOOP    MOREIN
DONE:       MOV     HARM,DX     ;;SAVE ENTRY AS NUMBER OF HARMONICS
```

The DX register is zeroed out to ensure that all digits initially are zero. CX controls the loop counter. During each pass through the loop, it is possible to accumulate another digit. A 4 in CX limits the user to four digits. A 1 in the AH register allows a keyboard read when INT 21H is encountered. Naturally, this value will be in ASCII format. The macro then checks to make sure the value received is truly a decimal number (ASCII 30H to 39H). If it is not a true decimal number, the routine is exited. By ANDing the contents of AX with 000F, only the decimal portion of the ASCII number is saved. Notice that a quick switch to the AX register was made in that step. This means that the AX register now holds a number from 0 to 9. The value in AX is now pushed to the stack, and the value in DX is placed in the AX register. A 10 is placed in BX and will serve as a multiplier. Whatever number was in DX and then moved into AX is now multiplied by 10. The product is returned in AX (at least the part you are interested in here) and moved back to DX. The AX register is popped from the stack and added to DX, forming the correct decimal number. If an incorrect digit is entered, or if four digits are accumulated, the macro is terminated.

Now look at an actual example. If 9 had been entered by a previous operation, DX would contain the digit 9. Assume that the program is passing through the loop the second time. A 5 is entered from the keyboard. The ASCII value 35 is received, found to be a good digit, ANDed with 000F, and pushed onto the stack. DX (the 9 previously entered) is returned to the AX register and multiplied by 10, leaving the equivalent of 90 in the AX register. This value is then transferred to the DX register, and the AX register is popped from the stack. DX and AX are added together, yielding 95 in the DX register. If a carriage return (an invalid character) is entered, the value 95 will be transferred to the variable HARM (harmonic), and the macro will be exited.

Before examining the program itself, take a look at the values in the data segment.

```
ANGLE       DW      0       ;STARTING ANGLE (0 THRU 360)
FOUR        DW      4       ;A CONSTANT
MULTIP      DW      50      ;CONVERT SINE 0 TO 100
RADIAN      DW      180     ;A CONSTANT
REDUCE      DW      360     ;A CONSTANT
TEMP1       DW      ?
```

```
TEMP2      DW     ?
TEMP3      DW     ?
STATWD     DW     ?
SINE       DD     361 DUP (0)   ;STORAGE FOR REAL ANSWERS
ISINE      DW     361 DUP (0)   ;STORAGE FOR INTEGER RESULTS
MESSG1     DB     'ENTER THE NUMBER OF HARMONICS TO BE ADDED, (0 TO
           DB     9999): $',13H
MESSG2     DB     'CALCULATING $'
HARM       DW     ?                      ;USER ENTERED—No. OF HARMONICS
```

ANGLE actually represents the horizontal position on the screen. As in the previous example, this program plots 361 horizontal points or pixels. FOUR, MULTIP, RADIAN, and REDUCE are constants that are used by the program at various stages. TEMP1 through TEMP3 serve as storage locations for intermediate values. STATWD holds the status word of the coprocessor and helps determine which of the four quadrants the angle is in. SINE is a table that holds the 361 real sums (each sum is formed by adding the appropriate Fourier Series together). The sum is accumulated as a group of real numbers in one table and converted to integer storage in another to preserve the accuracy of the answer. ISINE holds the integer value of magnitude for each point on the screen. MESSG1 signals the user that the number of harmonics can be entered. MESSG2 informs the user that calculations are being performed. Nothing will be printed to the screen until all points have been calculated. For 500 harmonics, the calculations could take as long as 1.8 minutes on a 9 MHz machine.

The first section of code requests input from the user:

```
SETSCREEN                      ;CLEAR SCREEN
LEA          DX,MESSG1         ;PRINT MESSAGE FOR INPUT
MOV          AH,9
INT          21H
HARMONIC                       ;ACCEPT DATA ENTRY
SETSCREEN                      ;CLEAR SCREEN AND WAIT
LEA          DX,MESSG2         ;PRINT "CALCULATING" MESSAGE
MOV          AH,9
INT          21H
```

SETSCREEN transfers screen output to the high-resolution graphics screen. In so doing, the screen is cleared. MESSG1 is printed, requesting the number of harmonics for the program. HARMONIC then intercepts the user's input. Numbers from 0 to 9,999 are permitted. (You will see in later figures that 500 harmonics produce a very good square wave.) MESSG2 informs the user that the input has been accepted and that calculations are underway.

The programming philosophy of this program is different from that of the previous examples. In the last program in particular, only values from 0 to 90 were calculated. The program then took advantage of the waveform's symmetry to plot the shape from 91 to 360 degrees. That same approach could have been used here, except for the fact that not all Fourier waveforms are symmetric in all quadrants. A more general approach to the programming problem allows easier modification by the user should other waveforms be desired. In this example, each of the 361 points will be calculated, stored, and plotted. That means that all harmonic angles must be reduced to the range $0 <= ANGLE <= 360$. Another note of interest is that as the harmonic number increases, so does the multiplier for the angle. Look now at some very important code.

```
                MOV     SI,0            ;SI WILL INDEX INTO SINE
NXTPT:          MOV     TEMP1,01H       ;LET'S LOOK AT ANGLE
ADMORE:         MOV     AX,ANGLE        ;MOVE CURRENT ANGLE INTO AX
                MOV     DX,TEMP1        ;CURRENT FOURIER HARMONIC IN CAL
                SHL     DX,1            ;MULTIPLY IT BY 2
                SUB     DX,1            ;SUBTRACT 1
                MOV     TEMP2,DX        ;SAVE FACTOR FOR LATER
                MUL     TEMP2           ;MULTIPLY ANGLE BY FACTOR
                DIV     REDUCE          ;DIVIDE ANGLE BY 360
                MOV     TEMP3,DX        ;KEEP REMAINING DEGREES IN TEMP3
```

This code contains the "real action" of this program. SI is set to 0, which hereafter forms the offset into SINE. A 1 is moved into TEMP1. This is a seed value for the start of each angle. TEMP1 keeps track of the particular Fourier harmonic being calculated in the loop (it varies between 1 and HARM for every ANGLE calculated). ANGLE contains the current horizontal position (ANGLE varies from 0 to 360 degrees) being calculated. TEMP1 now helps calculate the Fourier factor for the particular harmonic being calculated — recall that for a square wave these are successively higher odd numbers. TEMP1 is moved into DX, shifted left (SHL effectively multiplies this number by 2), and then reduced by one. DX now contains an odd number, which is saved in TEMP2 for future use. The value ANGLE in AX is now multiplied by this factor. The 32-bit product in the AX/DX register pair is divided by REDUCE (360) to scale the angle to a value between 0 and 360 degrees. Only the remainder of the division operation is saved in the DX register. The integer values in the AX register are of no use, since they just represent multiples of 360 degrees — since this is a periodic waveform, it repeats every 360 degrees anyway. The remainder is saved in TEMP3.

At this point, TEMP3 is an angle between 0 and 360 degrees. The following code converts the angle from degrees to radians:

```
FINIT                      ;INITIALIZE COPROCESSOR
FILD        RADIAN         ;PREPARE TO CONVERT DEGREES TO RADIANS
FLDPI                      ;LOAD PI ON STACK
FDIV        ST(0),ST(1)    ;DIVIDE TO GET .0174...+
FILD        TEMP3          ;PUT THE ANGLE ON STACK (IN DEGREES)
FMUL                       ;MULTIPLY TO GET ANGLE IN RADIANS
```

When completed, the angle will be on the stack top of the coprocessor. The code contained between the stars will calculate the sine of any angle from 0 to 2 PI radians (0 to 360 degrees). If you are using the 80387 coprocessor, all of this code can be replaced with the code FSIN. Otherwise, dig in for some heavy-duty programming.

Recall that all angles were reduced to the range 0 to 360 degrees by an earlier operation. It will be necessary to reduce (or scale) any angle from 0 to 2 PI that is currently on the stack top to a value between 0 to PI/4 (0 to 45 degrees) for the tangent function to operate properly. In a previous program you saw that it was possible to find the sine of any angle from 0 to 90 degrees with the use of simple trigonometric functions. In this portion of code, a slightly different approach is used.

THE STATUS WORD

The status word register of the 80287 contains a 16-bit register that describes the current standing of the coprocessor. Each of the exception conditions for the coprocessor is shown here.

bit 0	IE	Invalid Operation
bit 1	DE	Denormalized Operation
bit 2	ZE	Zero Divide
bit 3	OE	Overflow
bit 4	UE	Underflow
bit 5	PE	Precision
bit 6		(reserved)
bit 7	IR	Interrupt Request
bit 8	C0	Condition Code Bit
bit 9	C1	Condition Code Bit

bit 10	C2	Condition Code Bit
bit 11	ST	Stack Top Pointer Bit
bit 12	ST	Stack Top Pointer Bit
bit 13	ST	Stack Top Pointer Bit
bit 14	C3	Condition Code Bit
bit 15	B	Busy

The status word conditions can be used in making decisions in program code. Look at another section of code for the current example:

```
FLDPI                       ;LOAD PI ON STACK TOP
FIDIV       FOUR            ;DIVIDE BY FOUR, RESULT ON STACK TOP
FXCH                        ;EXCHANGE POSITION OF ABOVE AND ANGLE
FPREM                       ;REDUCE TO 0 TO PI/4 RANGE FOR TAN
FSTSW       STATWD          ;PUT CURRENT STATUS WORD IN VARIABLE
FWAIT                       ;SYNCHRONIZE
MOV         AX,STATWD       ;GET STATWD IN AX REGISTER
TEST        AH,00000010B    ;TEST BIT, IF ZERO ANGLE<46 DEGREES
JZ          CALTAN          ;PROCEED FOR STACK SWITCH
FSUBP       ST(1),ST(0)     ;IF MATCH, SUB FROM 45 DEGREES
```

In this code, PI is first loaded onto the stack top, pushing the previously stored angle one level deeper. The stack top (PI) is divided by FOUR, a constant, and the result is placed on the stack top. At this point, the stack top contains PI/4, and ST(1) contains the angle from the previous operations. ST and ST(1) are exchanged, and FPREM is executed. FPREM performs a modulo divide of the stack top — ST is divided by ST(1). That means that the angle on the stack top is divided by PI/4. Assume, for example, that the angle is 4.88692 radians. If you divide this number by PI/4, you obtain 6.22222. The partial remainder is .22222, or about 12.73 degrees. This scaled-down angle actually corresponds to a real angle of 282.73 degrees. Sin(282.73) degrees = −sin(90 − 12.73) degrees. But how do you know that the sign of the angle is negative and that it must be subtracted from 90 degrees (PI/2)? By using a scaling factor of PI/4 on an angle that can range from 0 to 2 PI (0 to 360 degrees), you effectively are dividing the range of angles into octants. Choose an angle in each octant to see if any unique features can be observed (see Table 9-4).

One unique feature is obvious — there is a linear relationship between the octant and the quotient! Therefore, the quotient could be used to determine the octant of the angle. Once you know the octant, you can determine the proper trigonometric function to be applied.

At this point, it would be possible to use FDIV instead of FPREM for

Octant	Angle (in radians)	Angle/(PI/4)	Quotient	Remainder
1	0.1745	0.22222	0	.22222
2	1.3963	1.77778	1	.77778
3	1.7453	2.22222	2	.22222
4	2.9671	3.77778	3	.77778
5	3.3161	4.22222	4	.22222
6	4.5379	5.77778	5	.77778
7	4.8869	6.22222	6	.22222
8	6.1087	7.77778	7	.77778

Table 9-4.

Experimental Results for Octant Determination in Sine Program

the division. If that choice were made, the integer (the quotient) would have indicated the octant and the remainder used by the tangent function to obtain the sine of the angle. However, exactly the same information is stored in the status word after FPREM is executed, as shown in Table 9-5.

The first test that is performed is on C1. The status word STATWD is moved into the AX register. The binary number 00000010B (2H) is tested with AH. If the C1 bit is also a one, the test is true, and no jump occurs. The remainder, ST(0), is subtracted from PI/4, ST(1), and the stack is popped. This leaves the new angle on the stack top.

```
CALTAN:
            FPTAN                        ;GET TANGENT OF ANGLE
            TEST     AH,01000010B        ;+- SIN (PI/4 - HYP)
            JPE      TST2                ;IF YES, MAKE ANOTHER TEST
            JMP      FIXIT               ;OTHERWISE, EXCHANGE ST AND ST1
TST2:       TEST     AH,00000000B        ;+- SIN (HYP)
            JPE      CALSIN              ;IF TEST BOTH ZERO OR BOTH ONE
FIXIT:      FXCH                         ;EXCHANGE FOR COSINE FUNCTION
```

The tangent is then taken of the angle. Two different tests are now performed. If C3 and C1 are both 0s or both 1s, the trigonometric function for a sine will be performed; otherwise, a cosine function will be performed by exchanging ST with ST(1). This is similar to the sine wave plotting program.

```
CALSIN:                                  ;OTHERWISE, USE SINE FUNCTION
            FMUL     ST(0),ST            ;USE TRIG FUNCTION TO CONVERT
```

Octant	Quotient	C0	C3	C1	Function
1	0	0	0	0	Sin(angle)
2	1	0	0	1	Cos(PI/4−angle)
3	2	0	1	0	Cos(angle)
4	3	0	1	1	Sin(PI/4−angle)
5	4	1	0	0	−Sin(angle)
6	5	1	0	1	−Cos(PI/4−angle)
7	6	1	1	0	−Cos(angle)
8	7	1	1	1	−Sin(PI/4−angle)

Table 9-5.

Final Octant Test for Sine Program

```
FXCH     ST(1)          ;TANGENT ANSWER INTO PROPER SINE
FLD      ST(0)          ;VALUE
FMUL     ST(0),ST       ;
FADD     ST(0),ST(2)    ;
FSQRT                   ;
FDIVP    ST(1),ST       ;
```

After FDIVP is executed, the stack top will have the correct sine magnitude value for the original angle, with the exception of the sign information. The sign of the angle can be determined by examining C0. C0 is 1 for negative results and 0 for positive results.

```
TEST     AH,00000001B   ;A ZERO MEANS A POSITIVE RESULT
JZ       POSSIG         ;
FCHS                    ;OTHERWISE, CHANGE SIGN OF ANSWER
```

The result on the stack top must now be scaled and accumulated with the results from previous harmonic calculations:

```
POSSIG:  FIMUL    MULTIP     ;MULTIPLY RESULT BY SCREEN FACTOR
         FIDIV    TEMP2      ;DIVIDE BY HARMONIC FACTOR
         FADD     SINE[SI]   ;ADD ANS IN STORAGE TO NEW VALUE
         FSTP     SINE[SI]   ;SAVE NEW REAL SUM BACK IN MEMORY
         FWAIT               ;SYNCHRONIZE
```

Remember that TEMP2 was the harmonic multiplication factor saved near the start of the program. For square waves this factor serves as a multiplier for the angle and a divisor for the amplitude of each harmonic. The FADD command adds any previously accumulated total to the stack top and then stores the new results in the same location.

If 50 harmonics are to be considered, then 50 separate values will be added together before SI is incremented to the next horizontal position. The number of iterations is controlled by TEMP1.

```
INC     TEMP1       ;PREPARE FOR NEXT HIGHER HARMONIC
MOV     CX,HARM     ;MAX NUMBER OF HARMONICS IN CX
CMP     TEMP1,CX    ;COMPARE PRESENT WITH MAXIMUM
JG      IDXPOS      ;IF GREATER, END AND DO NEXT ANGLE
JMP     ADMORE      ;CONTINUE ACCUMULATING HARMONIC VALUES
```

HARM contains the total number of harmonics.

A simple test is made to determine whether more harmonic values are left to be calculated. If there are, a jump is made to ADMORE; otherwise, the program is ready to index the next horizontal position and start the harmonic calculation all over again.

```
IDXPOS:  ADD     SI,04H      ;POINT TO NEXT SINE LOCATION
         INC     ANGLE       ;INCREASE TO NEXT ANGLE
         CMP     ANGLE,360   ;DO FOR 0 TO 360 DEGREES
         JG      TRANS       ;IF DONE, TRANSFER DATA
         JMP     NXTPT       ;IF NOT 361, DO AGAIN
```

SINE is a defined doubleword table, so SI is moved four bytes to point to the next storage location. ANGLE represents the horizontal position from 0 to 360 degrees. Once all harmonics are calculated for a particular position, the ANGLE is incremented, and the process continues until all 361 positions have been calculated.

Because the values in SINE must be accumulated as precisely as possible, real number results were stored. Before the results are plotted on the screen, these numbers will be converted to integers:

```
TRANS:   MOV     SI,00       ;SET INDEX REGISTERS TO ZERO
         MOV     DI,00
         LEA     BX,SINE     ;LOAD ADDRESSES OF TWO TABLES
         LEA     BP,ISINE
         MOV     CX,361      ;PREPARE TO TRANSFER 361 VALUES
TFMOR:   FLD     SINE [SI]   ;LOAD REAL NUMBER ON STACK
         FISTP   ISINE [DI]  ;POP AND STORE INTEGER NUMBER
         ADD     SI,04       ;INCREMENT NEXT REAL LOCATION
         ADD     DI,02       ;INCREMENT NEXT INTEGER LOCATION
         LOOP    TFMOR
```

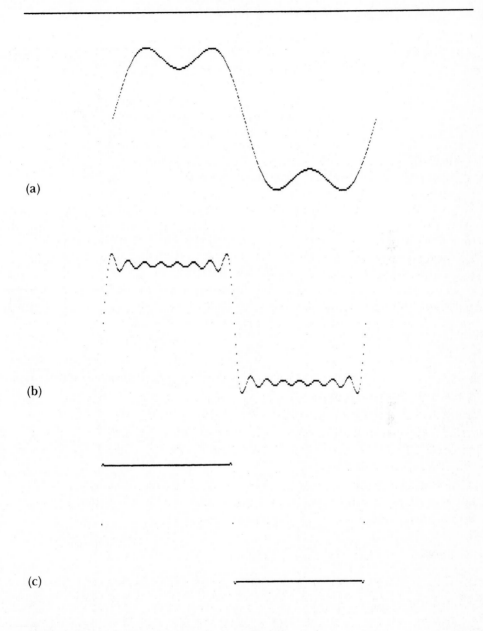

Figure 9-5.

Plots of Fourier Series program:
(a) 2 harmonics, (b) 8 harmonics, (c) 500 harmonics

Square-wave routines 500 harmonics (9 MHertz IBM AT computer)			
BASICA	(noncompiled)	69.75	minutes
APL	(noncompiled)	19.58	minutes
BASIC	(compiled)	10.66	minutes
PASCAL	(compiled)	3.21	minutes
ASSEMBLY	(assembled)	1.80	minutes

Table 9-6.

Execution Times for Fourier Square-Wave Routine

The final results in SINE (real numbers) are loaded back into the coprocessor, one at a time. They are then popped and saved, in integer format, in the ISINE table. ISINE is a defined word (DW) table.

The values in ISINE need only be offset properly for the screen coordinates and plotted. The remaining code for the program accomplishes that operation and waits for a keypress before erasing the screen.

Figure 9-5 shows a screen dump when this program is executed using three different values: (a) 2 harmonics, (b) 8 harmonics, and (c) 500 harmonics. The execution of the program is very fast, even when 500 harmonics are requested.

Similar programs written in BASIC, Pascal, and APL were also tested. Their plotting times are shown in Table 9-6. None of the routines were fine tuned for maximum speed, but the chart does indicate relative values.

It certainly is worth writing code in assembly language!

10

INTERFACING WITH
HIGH-LEVEL LANGUAGES

Many programmers first turn to assembly language programming because they need to perform a job or function that is not supported by the high-level languages that they usually use. Programmers who use APL, BASIC, C, FORTRAN, and Pascal, for instance, are limited by the design of the compilers used on their systems. A programmer using a high-level language can only take advantage of the features that another programmer included in the compiler package.

Consider, for example, that IBM's first Pascal compiler did not support graphics. The only immediate solution was to write an assembly language patch for the Pascal compiler. Situations like this one are common. Whether it be graphics, a game adapter, a parallel port, a serial port, or some other interface support that was not included with the original compiler, all eyes turn to assembly language for the solution. Often patches to existing software are very simple to implement.

In most cases when a high-level language and assembly language must interface, the programmer is confronted with the problem of actually connecting the two programs and passing variables from one program to the other. In the following examples, detailed explanations of how to create patches for numerous languages are given with the hope that these will save you hours of experimenting.

The following examples illustrate how to patch an assembly language program that polls the game adapter of an IBM AT computer. This patch will permit the user to pass a value from the host program that determines whether the push buttons or potentiometers of the game adapter will be sampled. The results of the sampling will be returned to the high-level calling program. As you study this example, you will see how to send and receive variables.

A portion of the game adapter assembly code is generic to all high-level programs. This code is shown here:

```
;CODE FOR SAMPLING THE FOUR PUSHBUTTONS
        MOV     AH,84H          ;JOYSTICK INTERFACE
        MOV     DX,0            ;DX=0 FOR PUSHBUTTON INFO
        INT     15H             ;DO IT
        MOV     CL,04           ;ROTATE FOUR BITS
        ROR     AL,CL           ;7-4 TO 3-0 BIT POSITIONS
        AND     AX,0FH          ;KEEP ONLY LOWER 4 BIT INFORMATION
        JMP     SEND            ;RETURN INFORMATION

;CODE FOR SAMPLING THE FOUR GAME POTS (A(X), A(Y), B(X), & B(Y))
POTS:   MOV     AH,84H          ;JOYSTICK INTERFACE
        MOV     DX,01H          ;READ POTS
        INT     15H             ;DO IT
```

The joystick interface for the IBM AT computer is done with INT 15H. AH is set to 84H. If DX is 0, data regarding the status of the four push buttons will be returned in the AL register. If DX=1, the values of the four game potentiometers (two for each joystick) will be returned in the AX, BX, CX, and DX registers. In this program segment, the DX information has already been passed by a previous operation. A decision, based on the value of DX, is made. If DX=0, the button information is returned to bits 7 through 4 of the AL register. This program will rotate the information to the lower four bits (0 to 3) of the AL register and then exit (the jump is made to SEND). However, if DX=1, a jump is made to POTS. When the interrupt is called, the potentiometer values (integers in the range of 0 to 270, depending on the particular joystick used) are returned to the four general registers.

Interfacing examples will be given for STSC's APL, Borland's Turbo Pascal, Microsoft's compiled BASIC and C, and IBM's FORTRAN and Pascal. If you examine the assembly language program for each high-level language example, you will note many similarities and many subtle differences in the support code. For this reason, complete programs are given for each example.

STSC'S APL

APL often has been called the best-kept secret in programming languages. This is an unfortunate situation, because APL is a language rich in features, with considerable computational power. One of the finest implementations of the APL language for the IBM computer family is produced by STSC, Inc., in Rockville, Maryland. This implementation of APL is a deluxe version, offering full-screen editing and full graphics and file-handling routines along with standard APL features. All other implementations of APL are measured against this one.

APL is an interpreted language, somewhat like the BASIC supplied with many computer systems. That is where the similarity ends, however. Since an interpreted program must be handled differently than a compiled language (because you never leave the interpreter to return to the system level), this example will diverge most from the other examples in this chapter.

STSC APL permits a □CALL to machine language routines that is very simple to implement. The syntax for this operation is as follows:

```
result ←              □CALL routine
result ←   registers □CALL routine
```

The *result* is the explicit result returned by the routine. The *registers* are a singleton or vector of 0 to 7 integers for registers AX, BX, CX, DX, BP, SI, and DI. The *routine* is a nonempty array containing the routine to be executed. The routine that you are about to enter must conform to the following requirements: (1) it must be terminated with a far return (0CBH), (2) the SS and SP registers must be returned intact, (3) it cannot use more than 498 bytes of stack depth, (4) it must be relocatable, and (5) an offset of 10 bytes at the beginning of the code is required if any addresses are based on the offset. To obtain the code required for this routine, the program shown in Figure 10-1 is entered and assembled. During the assembly process a .LST file is requested. The .LST file is shown in Figure 10-2.

The numbers in the extreme left portion of the .LST file represent line numbers, while those just to the right represent the machine language equivalent of the assembler mnemonics. We are interested here in the code between the (CMP DX,0) instruction and the second (INT 15H) instruc-

```
;FOR 80286/80386
;PROGRAM REQUESTS BUTTON OR POT VALUES FROM JOYSTICKS A & B, WITH BIOS
;INTERRUPT RETURNS VALUES TO HIGH LEVEL LANGUAGE HOST PROGRAM

            PUBLIC  GAME
MYCODE      SEGMENT 'CODE'
            ASSUME  CS:MYCODE
GAME        PROC    FAR              ;PROCEDURE IS NAMED GAME
            PUSH    BP               ;SAVE LOCATION OF BP REG.
            MOV     BP,SP            ;MOVE STACK POINTER TO BP REGISTER

            MOV     SI,[BP]+22       ;INPUT OPERATION INFORMATION FROM HOST
            MOV     DX,[SI]          ;SAVE INFO IN DX REGISTER
            CMP     DX,0             ;IF ZERO, CONTINUE AND READ BUTTONS
            JNE     POTS             ;IF NOT, MAKE JUMP AND READ POTS

;CODE FOR SAMPLING THE FOUR PUSHBUTTONS
            MOV     AH,84H           ;JOYSTICK INTERFACE
            MOV     DX,0             ;DX=0 FOR PUSHBUTTON INFO
            INT     15H              ;DO IT
            MOV     CL,04            ;ROTATE FOUR BITS
            ROR     AL,CL            ;7-4 TO 3-0 BIT POSITIONS
            AND     AX,0FH           ;KEEP ONLY LOWER 4 BIT INFORMATION
            JMP     SEND             ;RETURN INFORMATION

;CODE FOR SAMPLING THE FOUR GAME POTS (A(X), A(Y), B(X), & B(Y))
POTS:       MOV     AH,84H           ;JOYSTICK INTERFACE
            MOV     DX,01H           ;READ POTS (VALUES RETURNED IN AX, BX, CX, DX)
            INT     15H              ;DO IT

;CODE FOR RETURNING AX, BX, CX, & DX REGISTER VALUES
SEND:       MOV     DI,[BP]+18       ;PREPARE TO SEND A(X) POT VALUE
            MOV     [DI],AX
            MOV     DI,[BP]+14       ;PREPARE TO SEND A(Y) POT VALUE
            MOV     [DI],BX
            MOV     DI,[BP]+10       ;PREPARE TO SEND B(X) POT VALUE
            MOV     [DI],CX
            MOV     DI,[BP]+6        ;PREPARE TO SEND B(Y) POT VALUE
            MOV     [DI],DX

            MOV     SP,BP            ;RETURN PARAMETERS
            POP     BP
            RET     10

GAME        ENDP                     ;END PROCEDURE NAMED GAME
MYCODE      ENDS                     ;END CODE SEGMENT NAMED MYCODE

            END                      ;END WHOLE PROGRAM
```

Figure 10-1. _____

Assembly language code for interfacing game adapter with APL host program

tion. No additional support code is required, since the APL □CALL instruction will handle the necessary overhead. The machine code is shown in hexadecimal and decimal form in Table 10-1.

```
                              ;FOR 80286/80386
                              ;PROGRAM REQUESTS BUTTON OR POT VALUES FROM JOYSTICKS A & B, WITH BIOS
                              ;INTERRUPT RETURNS VALUES TO HIGH LEVEL LANGUAGE HOST PROGRAM
                                      PUBLIC  GAME
0000                          MYCODE  SEGMENT 'CODE'
                                      ASSUME  CS:MYCODE
0000                          GAME    PROC    FAR              ;PROCEDURE IS NAMED GAME
0000  55                              PUSH    BP               ;SAVE LOCATION OF BP REG.
0001  8B EC                           MOV     BP,SP            ;MOVE STACK POINTER TO BP REGISTER

0003  8B 76 16                        MOV     SI,[BP]+22       ;INPUT OPERATION INFORMATION FROM HOST
0006  8B 14                           MOV     DX,[SI]          ;SAVE INFO IN DX REGISTER
0008  83 FA 00                        CMP     DX,0             ;IF ZERO, CONTINUE AND READ BUTTONS
000B  75 11                           JNE     POTS             ;IF NOT, MAKE JUMP AND READ POTS

                              ;CODE FOR SAMPLING THE FOUR PUSHBUTTONS
000D  B4 84                           MOV     AH,84H           ;JOYSTICK INTERFACE
000F  BA 0000                         MOV     DX,0             ;DX=0 FOR PUSHBUTTON INFO
0012  CD 15                           INT     15H              ;DO IT
0014  B1 04                           MOV     CL,04            ;ROTATE FOUR BITS
0016  D2 C8                           ROR     AL,CL            ;7-4 TO 3-0 BIT POSITIONS
0018  25 000F                         AND     AX,0FH           ;KEEP ONLY LOWER 4 BIT INFORMATION
001B  EB 08 90                        JMP     SEND             ;RETURN INFORMATION

                              ;CODE FOR SAMPLING THE FOUR GAME POTS (A(X), A(Y), B(X), & B(Y)
001E  B4 84                 POTS:     MOV     AH,84H           ;JOYSTICK INTERFACE
0020  BA 0001                         MOV     DX,01H           ;READ POTS (VALUES RETURNED IN AX, BX, CX, DX)
0023  CD 15                           INT     15H              ;DO IT

                              ;CODE FOR RETURNING AX, BX, CX, & DX REGISTER VALUES
0025  8B 7E 12              SEND:     MOV     DI,[BP]+18       ;PREPARE TO SEND A(X) POT VALUE
0028  89 05                           MOV     [DI],AX
002A  8B 7E 0E                        MOV     DI,[BP]+14       ;PREPARE TO SEND A(Y) POT VALUE
002D  89 1D                           MOV     [DI],BX
002F  8B 7E 0A                        MOV     DI,[BP]+10       ;PREPARE TO SEND B(X) POT VALUE
0032  89 0D                           MOV     [DI],CX
0034  8B 7E 06                        MOV     DI,[BP]+6        ;PREPARE TO SEND B(Y) POT VALUE
0037  89 15                           MOV     [DI],DX

0039  8B E5                           MOV     SP,BP            ;RETURN PARAMETERS
003B  5D                              POP     BP
003C  CA 000A                         RET     10

003F                          GAME    ENDP                     ;END PROCEDURE NAMED GAME
003F                          MYCODE  ENDS                     ;END CODE SEGMENT NAMED MYCODE

                                      END                      ;END WHOLE PROGRAM
```

Figure 10-2.

The .LST listing for the STSC APL assembly code

Figure 10-3 illustrates how this assembly language code is entered in an APL function called LOADGAME. This very simple function simply saves the decimal equivalent of the machine language code in an array called CODE. To execute the program, another APL function must be built. Figure 10-4 is an APL function named READGAME. READGAME can be called numerous times once LOADGAME has been loaded into CODE.

Hexadecimal	Decimal	
83	131	
FA	250	
00	0	
75	117	
11	17	
B4	180	
84	132	
BA	186	
0000	0	
	0	
CD	205	
15	21	
B1	177	
04	4	
D2	210	
C8	200	
25	37	
000F	15	(lower byte first)
	0	
EB	235	
08	8	
90	144	
B4	180	
84	132	
BA	186	
0001	1	(lower byte first)
	0	
CD	205	
15	21	
(CB)	203	(added and required)

Table 10-1. _____

Machine Code Translation of APL Game Adapter Program

In this example, 1 is passed to the DX register to request the potentiometer readings using the following code:

```
REPEAT:R←0 0 0 1 □CALL CODE
```

The four values are then returned from the array (R) into the variables AX, BX, CX, and DX. If push-button data had been desired, this code would

```
        ∇LOADGAME[□]∇
[0]   LOADGAME;A;B;C;□IO
[1]   □IO←1
[2]   ⍝ MACHINE LANGUAGE PROGRAM FOR READING GAME ADAPTER PORT
[3]   A← 131 250 0 117 17 180 132 186 0 0 205 21 177 4
[4]   B← 210 200 37 15 0 235 8 144 180 132 186 1 0 205 21 203
[5]   C←A,B
[6]   CODE←□AV[□IO+C]
```

Figure 10-3. _____

APL program function LOADGAME

```
        ∇READGAME[□]∇
[0]   READGAME;□IO
[1]   □IO←1
[2]   LOADGAME
[3]   ⍝ EXECUTE THE PROGRAM STORED IN SYSTEM MEMORY
[4]   ⍝ TO READ POTS, SET VECTOR TO 0 0 0 1
[5]   ⍝ TO READ PUSHBUTTONS (RETURNED IN AX ONLY) SET VECTOR TO 0 0 0 0
[6]   REPEAT:R← 0 0 0 1 □CALL CODE
[7]   AX←R[1]
[8]   AY←R[2]
[9]   BX←R[3]
[10]  BY←R[4]
[11]  ⍝ SHOW A CONTINUOUS READING FOR PUSHBUTTONS OR JOYSTICK A AND B
[12]  □←AX,AY,BX,BY
[13]  →REPEAT
```

Figure 10-4. _____

APL program READGAME

have been changed to the following:

```
REPEAT:R←0 0 0 0 □CALL CODE
```

When this APL function is executed, a continuous sampling of all four joystick resistors is printed to the screen. To halt execution, simply type Ctrl/Exit from the APL environment.

Additional information about machine language interfacing can be found in the STSC APL manual under the heading "System Functions."

BORLAND'S TURBO PASCAL

Pascal is the most commonly used teaching language on college and university campuses today. Borland's lean, clean interpretation of Pascal is shipped complete with a full-screen editor and is available with optional 80287 and BCD math support. The speed of the compiler makes programming in Turbo Pascal almost like programming in an interpreted language. Turbo Pascal is the best computer language bargain available to programmers.

In the example here, we'll simply poll the game adapter repeatedly until a key is pressed. The assembly language program will contain support code to aid in receiving and sending variable information. Figure 10-5 is a complete listing of the assembly language code. A portion of the support code is shown here.

```
;FOR 80286/80386
;PROGRAM REQUESTS BUTTON OR POT VALUES FROM JOYSTICKS A & B, WITH BIOS
;INTERRUPT RETURNS VALUES TO HIGH LEVEL LANGUAGE HOST PROGRAM

MYCODE   SEGMENT
         ASSUME   CS:MYCODE
GAME     PROC     NEAR              ;PROCEDURE IS NAMED GAME
         PUSH     BP                ;SAVE LOCATION OF BP REG.
         MOV      BP,SP             ;MOVE STACK POINTER TO BP REGISTER

         MOV      SI,[BP]+20        ;INPUT OPERATION INFORMATION FROM HOST
         MOV      DX,[SI]           ;SAVE INFO IN DX REGISTER

(-->game adapter code removed from this section<--)

;CODE FOR RETURNING AX, BX, CX, & DX REGISTER VALUES
SEND:    MOV      DI,[BP]+16        ;PREPARE TO SEND A(X) POT VALUE
         MOV      [DI],AX
         MOV      DI,[BP]+12        ;PREPARE TO SEND A(Y) POT VALUE
         MOV      [DI],BX
         MOV      DI,[BP]+8         ;PREPARE TO SEND B(X) POT VALUE
         MOV      [DI],CX
         MOV      DI,[BP]+4         ;PREPARE TO SEND B(Y) POT VALUE
         MOV      [DI],DX

         MOV      SP,BP             ;RETURN PARAMETERS
         POP      BP
         RET      10
```

The assembly language routine will eventually be assembled, linked, and converted to a .COM file. For that reason, Turbo Pascal programs can have only one segment. The procedure (GAME) is declared as a NEAR procedure. The BP (base pointer) is pushed onto the stack so that the value in the SP (stack pointer) register can be transferred to BP. In most interfacing, values are passed back and forth using the stack. Variables can be

```
;FOR 80286/80386
;PROGRAM REQUESTS BUTTON OR POT VALUES FROM JOYSTICKS A & B, WITH BIOS
;INTERRUPT RETURNS VALUES TO HIGH LEVEL LANGUAGE HOST PROGRAM

MYCODE    SEGMENT
          ASSUME    CS:MYCODE
GAME      PROC      NEAR              ;PROCEDURE IS NAMED GAME
          PUSH      BP                ;SAVE LOCATION OF BP REG.
          MOV       BP,SP             ;MOVE STACK POINTER TO BP REGISTER

          MOV       SI,[BP]+20        ;INPUT OPERATION INFORMATION FROM HOST
          MOV       DX,[SI]           ;SAVE INFO IN DX REGISTER
          CMP       DX,0              ;IF ZERO, CONTINUE AND READ BUTTONS
          JNE       POTS              ;IF NOT, MAKE JUMP AND READ POTS

;CODE FOR SAMPLING THE FOUR PUSHBUTTONS
          MOV       AH,84H            ;JOYSTICK INTERFACE
          MOV       DX,0              ;DX=0 FOR PUSHBUTTON INFO
          INT       15H               ;DO IT
          MOV       CL,04             ;ROTATE FOUR BITS
          ROR       AL,CL             ;7-4 TO 3-0 BIT POSITIONS
          AND       AX,0FH            ;KEEP ONLY LOWER 4 BIT INFORMATION
          JMP       SEND              ;RETURN INFORMATION

;CODE FOR SAMPLING THE FOUR GAME POTS (A(X), A(Y), B(X), & B(Y)
POTS:     MOV       AH,84H            ;JOYSTICK INTERFACE
          MOV       DX,01H            ;READ POTS (VALUES RETURNED IN AX, BX, CX, DX)
          INT       15H               ;DO IT

;CODE FOR RETURNING AX, BX, CX, & DX REGISTER VALUES
SEND:     MOV       DI,[BP]+16        ;PREPARE TO SEND A(X) POT VALUE
          MOV       [DI],AX
          MOV       DI,[BP]+12        ;PREPARE TO SEND A(Y) POT VALUE
          MOV       [DI],BX
          MOV       DI,[BP]+8         ;PREPARE TO SEND B(X) POT VALUE
          MOV       [DI],CX
          MOV       DI,[BP]+4         ;PREPARE TO SEND B(Y) POT VALUE
          MOV       [DI],DX

          MOV       SP,BP             ;RETURN PARAMTERES
          POP       BP
          RET       10

GAME      ENDP                        ;END PROCEDURE NAMED GAME
MYCODE    ENDS                        ;END CODE SEGMENT NAMED MYCODE

          END                         ;END WHOLE PROGRAM
```

Figure 10-5._____

Assembly language code for interfacing game adapter with Turbo Pascal host program

transferred from the host program to the assembly language program via the SI (source index) register. Values can be transferred from the assembly language program to the host program via the DI (destination index) register. In this program, five word (DW) variables will be moved back and forth. Since this is a NEAR procedure, the return address occupies the first four bytes of the stack. The address of the host variable (BY) is [BP]+4.

This address is moved into the DI register. The integer value contained in the DX register is then moved into that address with the MOV [DI],DX statement. Four bytes away is the location of the next variable, and so on. In this manner, four integer values are returned to the host program. These four values represent the joystick potentiometer readings, assuming that DX initially was set to 1. If DX was set to 0, only the value returned to the AX register has any meaning; AX will contain the coded information about the push buttons.

The variable at address [BP]+20 transfers a variable from the host program to the assembly language program. In this manner, the DX register can be set to 1 (to read the potentiometer) or 0 (to read the push buttons) from the host calling program. The address at [BP]+20 is moved into the SI register. The integer contents of the SI location are then moved into the DX register. Using the same techniques, any number of variables can be transferred back and forth.

Before leaving this routine, the BP register is restored, and a RET (return) is issued. This is a NEAR return. The 10 in the operand column cleans the stack of the five words (ten bytes) that were passed onto the stack.

Figure 10-6 shows the host Turbo Pascal program. Notice that the assembly language program is called using an external procedure. The name of the assembly language program is TGAME.COM, and this program is located in the B drive. The other point of interest in this host program is the order in which the variables are passed. OPER, AX, AY, BX, and BY are declared as integers. OPER passes 1 or 0 to the DX register in the assembly language program. OPER's address is [BP]+20. The values for AX, AY, BX, and BY are passed back from the assembly language program. Notice that BY's address is [BP]+4.

The assembly language program must be written, assembled, linked, and converted to a .COM file using the EXE2BIN utility. The actual screen output is shown here.

```
B>C:MASM TGAME;
IBM Personal Computer MACRO Assembler    Version 2.00
(C)Copyright IBM Corp 1981, 1984
(C)Copyright Microsoft Corp 1981, 1983, 1984

50096 Bytes free

Warning Severe
Errors  Errors
0       0


B>C:LINK TGAME,TGAME,NUL,;
IBM Personal Computer Linker
Version 2.30 (C) Copyright IBM Corp. 1981, 1985
```

```
Warning: no stack segment

B:

B>C:EXE2BIN TGAME TGAME.COM
```

The next step is to use the Turbo editor to create the host program shown in Figure 10-6. Upon exiting the editor, choose the (O)ptions category and request a .COM file for the host program.

All that's left now is to exit Turbo Pascal and execute the program. Since the compiler creates a .COM file, the program itself actually is very small. One note of caution: Both the Pascal and assembly language files must be available at run time. These files have not been linked together (as many Microsoft programs are linked) to form a single operational program.

MICROSOFT'S BASIC COMPILER

Microsoft's QuickBASIC compiler is one of the most affordable BASIC compilers on the market today. QuickBASIC offers support for almost all

```
PROGRAM TPGAME;

VAR
  OPER,AX,AY,BX,BY:INTEGER;

PROCEDURE REP(VAR OPER,AX,AY,BX,BY:INTEGER); EXTERNAL 'B:TGAME.COM';

PROCEDURE INFORM;
BEGIN
  OPER:=1;
  REP(OPER,AX,AY,BX,BY);
  WRITELN(AX,'        ',AY,'        ',BX,'        ',BY,'        ')
END;

BEGIN {MAIN PROCEDURE}
WHILE NOT KEYPRESSED DO
    INFORM
END.
```

Figure 10-6.————————————————————————————————
Turbo Pascal host program that calls assembly language program to sample game adapter port

of interpreted BASIC's commands, including graphics. QuickBASIC is the ideal BASIC compiler for the casual user and in many ways rivals much more expensive compilers. The interface techniques presented in this section will work with most BASIC compilers for the IBM PC family.

To make this next example as simple as possible, the BASIC program will poll the assembly language program repeatedly. To stop the output, a Ctrl/Alt/Del operation must be performed. The assembly language program contains support code to aid in receiving and sending variable information. Figure 10-7 shows a complete listing of the assembly language code. A portion of the support code is shown here.

```
            PUBLIC   BGAME
MYCODE      SEGMENT  'CODE'
            ASSUME   CS:MYCODE
BGAME       PROC     FAR                    ;PROCEDURE IS NAMED BGAME
            PUSH     DS
            PUSH     BP                     ;SAVE LOCATION OF BP REG.
            MOV      BP,SP                  ;MOVE STACK POINTER TO BP REGISTER

            MOV      SI,[BP]+16             ;INPUT OPERATION INFORMATION FROM HOST
            MOV      DX,[SI]                ;SAVE INFO IN DX REGISTER
            CMP      DX,0                   ;IF ZERO, CONTINUE AND READ BUTTONS
            JNE      POTS                   ;IF NOT, MAKE JUMP AND READ POTS

     (-->game adapter code removed from this section<--)

SEND:       MOV      DI,[BP]+14             ;PREPARE TO SEND A(X) POT VALUE
            MOV      [DI],AX
            MOV      DI,[BP]+12             ;PREPARE TO SEND A(Y) POT VALUE
            MOV      [DI],BX
            MOV      DI,[BP]+10             ;PREPARE TO SEND B(X) POT VALUE
            MOV      [DI],CX
            MOV      DI,[BP]+8              ;PREPARE TO SEND B(Y) POT VALUE
            MOV      [DI],DX

            MOV      SP,BP                  ;RETURN PARAMETERS
            POP      BP
            POP      DS
            RET      10
```

This assembly language routine will eventually be assembled and linked with the compiled BASIC program. Assembly language routines that are linked with BASIC programs can have more than one segment. The procedure that will be called from the BASIC routine must be declared public in order for it to pass variables between itself and the host program. The procedure BGAME must be declared as a FAR procedure and will require a FAR RET when completed. The BP (base pointer) is pushed onto the stack so that the value in SP (stack pointer) can be placed in BP. In most interfacing, values are passed to and from programs using the stack. Variables can be transferred from the host program to the assembly language program via the SI (source index) register. Values can be transferred

```
;FOR 80286/80386
;PROGRAM REQUESTS BUTTON OR POT VALUES FROM JOYSTICKS A & B, WITH BIOS
;INTERRUPT RETURNS VALUES TO HIGH LEVEL LANGUAGE HOST PROGRAM

          PUBLIC   BGAME
MYCODE    SEGMENT  'CODE'
          ASSUME   CS:MYCODE
BGAME     PROC     FAR              ;PROCEDURE IS NAMED BGAME
          PUSH     DS
          PUSH     BP               ;SAVE LOCATION OF BP REG.
          MOV      BP,SP            ;MOVE STACK POINTER TO BP REGISTER

          MOV      SI,[BP]+16       ;INPUT OPERATION INFORMATION FROM HOST
          MOV      DX,[SI]          ;SAVE INFO IN DX REGISTER
          CMP      DX,0             ;IF ZERO, CONTINUE AND READ BUTTONS
          JNE      POTS             ;IF NOT, MAKE JUMP AND READ POTS

;CODE FOR SAMPLING THE FOUR PUSHBUTTONS
          MOV      AH,84H           ;JOYSTICK INTERFACE
          MOV      DX,0             ;DX=0 FOR PUSHBUTTON INFO
          INT      15H              ;DO IT
          MOV      CL,04            ;ROTATE FOUR BITS
          ROR      AL,CL            ;7-4 TO 3-0 BIT POSITIONS
          AND      AX,0FH           ;KEEP ONLY LOWER 4 BIT INFORMATION
          JMP      SEND             ;RETURN INFORMATION

;CODE FOR SAMPLING THE FOUR GAME POTS (A(X), A(Y), B(X), & B(Y)
POTS:     MOV      AH,84H           ;JOYSTICK INTERFACE
          MOV      DX,01H           ;READ POTS (VALUES RETURNED IN AX, BX, CX, DX)
          INT      15H              ;DO IT

;CODE FOR RETURNING AX, BX, CX, & DX REGISTER VALUES
SEND:     MOV      DI,[BP]+14       ;PREPARE TO SEND A(X) POT VALUE
          MOV      [DI],AX
          MOV      DI,[BP]+12       ;PREPARE TO SEND A(Y) POT VALUE
          MOV      [DI],BX
          MOV      DI,[BP]+10       ;PREPARE TO SEND B(X) POT VALUE
          MOV      [DI],CX
          MOV      DI,[BP]+8        ;PREPARE TO SEND B(Y) POT VALUE
          MOV      [DI],DX

          MOV      SP,BP            ;RETURN PARAMETERS
          POP      BP
          POP      DS
          RET      10

BGAME     ENDP                      ;END PROCEDURE NAMED BGAME
MYCODE    ENDS                      ;END CODE SEGMENT NAMED MYCODE

          END                       ;END WHOLE PROGRAM
```

Figure 10-7. _____

Assembly language code for interfacing game adapter with QuickBASIC host program

from the assembly language program to the host program via the DI (destination index) register. In this program, five word (DW) variables will be moved back and forth. The information required to return to the host program occupies the first eight bytes of the stack. The address of the host variable (BY) is [BP]+8. This address is moved into the DI register. The integer value in the DX register is then moved to that address with the command MOV [DI],DX. Two bytes (one word) away is the memory location of the next variable, and so on. In this manner, four integer values are returned to the host program. These four values represent the joystick potentiometer readings, assuming that DX initially was set to 1. If DX was set to 0, only the value returned in the AX register has any meaning; AX will contain the coded information about the push buttons.

The variable at address [BP]+16 transfers a variable from the host program to the assembly language program. In this manner, the DX register can be set to 1 (to read the potentiometer) or 0 (to read the push buttons) from the host calling program. The address at [BP]+16 is moved into the SI register. The integer contents of the SI location are then moved into the DX register. Using the same techniques, any number of variables can be transferred back and forth.

Before leaving this routine, the BP and DS registers are restored, and a RET (return) is issued. This is a FAR return. The 10 in the operand column cleans the stack of the five words (ten bytes) that were passed onto the stack.

Figure 10-8 shows the host BASIC program. Notice that the assembly language program is called using a call to the external procedure. The name of the assembly language program is BGAME.ASM, and this program is located in the B drive along with the assembled .OBJ file. The other point of interest in this host program is the order in which the variables are passed. OPER%, AX%, AY%, BX%, and BY% are declared as integers. OPER% passes 1 or 0 to the DX register in the assembly language program. OPER%'s address is [BP]+16. The values for AX%, AY%, BX%, and BY% are passed back from the assembly language program. Notice that BY's address is [BP]+8.

```
LET OPER%=1
FOR I=1 TO 200
   CALL BGAME(OPER%,AX%,BX%,CX%,DX%)
   PRINT AX%,BX%,CX%,DX%
NEXT I
END
```

Figure 10-8.‾‾

QuickBASIC program that calls assembly language program to sample game adapter port

The assembly language program must be written and assembled. The actual screen output is shown here.

```
B>C:MASM BGAME.ASM;
IBM Personal Computer MACRO Assembler    Version 2.00
(C)Copyright IBM Corp 1981, 1984
(C)Copyright Microsoft Corp 1981, 1983, 1984


50096 Bytes free

Warning Severe
Errors  Errors
0       0
```

The next procedure is to enter the BASIC program in a program editor, such as Peter Norton's full-screen editor. Once this task is completed, the BASIC program is compiled using the following commands:

```
C:BASCOM B:MSBGAME/O,B:,,;
Microsoft Quick BASIC Compiler
Version 1.00
(C) Copyright Microsoft Corp. 1982, 1983, 1984, 1985


49158 Bytes Available
48704 Bytes Free

    0 Warning Error(s)
    0 Severe  Error(s)
```

The /O switch was used here so that the final program will operate without need of the BASRUN file.

Finally, the host program and the assembly language program are linked together using these system linker commands (for the IBM Personal Computer Linker, version 2.30; ©copyright IBM Corp., 1981, 1985).

```
C:LINK B:MSBGAME+B:BGAME,B:,,C:;
```

The BASIC host program MSBGAME.OBJ has been compiled, and it resides on the B disk. The assembly language program BGAME.OBJ also resides on the B disk. These programs are linked together with the (+) option of the linker. Once the assembly language program is linked to the host program, the assembly language program is no longer needed on the disk. The host program MSBGAME.EXE is now a complete working program.

MICROSOFT'S C COMPILER

The C programming language has been called by many the general-purpose programming language of the century. C originally found its greatest use in computer operating systems. It has evolved into a language for writing programs ranging from database applications to assemblers. C is considered to fit somewhere between the high-level languages and assembler code. Because C is a single-threaded language without the attached enhancements of high-level languages, C compilers are small and simple.

Microsoft's C compiler, starting with version 3.0, is a standard for small systems. Microsoft's C compiler also is repackaged and sold under the IBM name.

Microsoft used its C language to completely rework its Macro Assembler for the IBM family. Macro Assembler 4.0 and later implementations run up to three times faster than version 3.0 of the Microsoft Macro Assembler and version 2.0 of the IBM Macro Assembler. This is testimony to the speed and compactness of well-written C code. Usually nothing beats assembly language for speed.

In the interfacing example here, we'll again simply poll the game adapter repeatedly until a Ctrl/Alt/Del procedure is executed. The C program will print the results to the screen. The assembly language program will contain support code to aid in receiving and sending variable information. Figure 10-9 shows the complete assembly code. A portion of the support code is shown here.

```
            public _cgame                ;NECESSARY "C" DECLARATIONS
   _text    segment byte public 'code'
            assume cs:_text
   _cgame   PROC    NEAR                 ;PROCEDURE IS NAMED _CGAME
            push    bp                   ;SAVE LOCATION OF BP REG.
            mov     bp,sp                ;MOVE STACK POINTER TO BP REGISTER
            push    di                   ;SAVE ORIGINAL DI & SI VALUES
            push    si

            mov     si,[bp+4]            ;INPUT OPERATION INFORMATION FROM HOST
            mov     dx,[si]              ;SAVE INFO IN DX REGISTER
            cmp     dx,0                 ;IF ZERO, CONTINUE AND READ BUTTONS
            jne     pots                 ;IF NOT, MAKE JUMP AND READ POTS

   (-->game adapter code removed from this section<--)

   send:    mov     di,[bp+6]            ;PREPARE TO SEND A(X) POT VALUE
            mov     [di],ax
            mov     di,[bp+8]            ;PREPARE TO SEND A(Y) POT VALUE
            mov     [di],bx
            mov     di,[bp+10]           ;PREPARE TO SEND B(X) POT VALUE
            mov     [di],cx
```

```
        mov     di,[bp+12]          ;PREPARE TO SEND B(Y) POT VALUE
        mov     [di],dx

        pop     si                  ;RETURN PARAMETERS
        pop     di
        mov     sp,bp
        pop     bp
        ret
```

```
;FOR 80286/80386
;PROGRAM REQUESTS BUTTON OR POT VALUES FROM JOYSTICKS A & B, WITH BIOS
;INTERRUPT RETURNS VALUES TO HIGH LEVEL LANGUAGE HOST PROGRAM

        public  _cgame              ;NECESSARY "C" DECLARATIONS
_text   segment byte public 'code'
        assume  cs:_text
_cgame  PROC    NEAR                ;PROCEDURE IS NAMED _CGAME
        push    bp                  ;SAVE LOCATION OF BP REG
        mov     bp,sp               ;MOVE STACK POINTER TO BP REGISTER
        push    di                  ;SAVE ORIGINAL DI & SI VALUES
        push    si

        mov     si,[bp+4]           ;INPUT OPERATION INFORMATION FROM HOST
        mov     dx,[si]             ;SAVE INFO IN DX REGISTER
        cmp     dx,0                ;IF ZERO, CONTINUE AND READ BUTTONS
        jne     pots                ;IF NOT, MAKE JUMP AND READ POTS

;CODE FOR SAMPLING THE FOUR PUSHBUTTONS
        mov     ah,84H              ;JOYSTICK INTERFACE
        mov     dx,0                ;DX=0 FOR PUSHBUTTON INFO
        int     15h                 ;DO IT
        mov     cl,04               ;ROTATE FOUR BITS
        ror     al,cl               ;7-4 TO 3-0 BIT POSITIONS
        and     ax,0fH              ;KEEP ONLY LOWER 4 BIT INFORMATION
        jmp     send                ;RETURN INFORMATION

;CODE FOR SAMPLING THE FOUR GAME POTS A(X), B(X), C(X), & D(X)
pots:   mov     ah,84H              ;JOYSTICK INTERFACE
        mov     dx,01H              ;READ POTS (VALUES RETURNED IN AX, BX, CX, DX)
        int     15H                 ;DO IT

;CODE FOR RETURNING AX, BX, CX, & DX REGISTER VALUES
send:   mov     di,[bp+6]           ;PREPARE TO SEND A(X) POT VALUE
        mov     [di],ax
        mov     di,[bp+8]           ;PREPARE TO SEND A(Y) POT VALUE
        mov     [di],bx
        mov     di,[bp+10]          ;PREPARE TO SEND B(X) POT VALUE
        mov     [di],cx
        mov     di,[bp+12]          ;PREPARE TO SEND B(Y) POT VALUE
        mov     [di],dx

        pop     si                  ;RETURN PARAMETERS
        pop     di
        mov     sp,bp
        pop     bp
        ret

_cgame  endp                        ;END PROCEDURE NAMED _CGAME
_text   ends                        ;END CODE SEGMENT NAMED MYCODE

        end                         ;END WHOLE PROGRAM
```

Figure 10-9. _____

Assembly language code for interfacing game adapter with C host program

The assembler language code will eventually be assembled and linked to the compiled C code. Notice the interesting features of this assembly language program. First, it is written in lowercase letters in case the particular C compiler that you are using is case sensitive. Second, the segment and procedure start with the underline character. This is a requirement for any interface program. The procedure cgame is declared both public and NEAR. The cgame procedure will require a NEAR RET when completed. The BP (base pointer) is pushed onto the stack so that the value in SP (stack pointer) can be placed in BP. In most interfacing, values are passed to and from programs using the stack. Variables can be transferred from the host program to the assembly language program via the SI (source index) register. Values can be transferred from the assembly language program to the host program via the DI (destination index) register. If SI and DI are to be used by the assembly language program, the original values must be preserved on the stack as they were in this program. In this example, five word (DW) variables are moved back and forth. The information required to return to the host program occupies the first four bytes of the stack. The address of the host variable (&oper) is [BP]+4. This address is moved into the SI register. The integer value at the [SI] address is then moved to the dx register using the command mov dx,[si]. Two bytes (one word) away is the memory location of the next variable (&ax), and so on. In this manner, one variable is sent from the host program to the assembly program, and four integer values are returned to the host program. These four integer values represent the joystick potentiometer readings, assuming that DX initially was set to 1. If DX was set to 0, only the value returned in the AX register has any meaning; AX will contain the coded information about the push buttons. Using the same techniques, any number of variables can be transferred back and forth.

Before leaving this routine, the SI, DI and BP registers are restored, and a RET (return) is issued. This is a NEAR return.

Figure 10-10 shows the host C program. Notice that the assembly language program is called using a call to the external procedure. Also notice that the call is made without the underscore character in front of CGAME. The name of the assembly language program is CGAME.ASM, and the program is located in the B drive along with the assembled .OBJ file. The other point of interest in this host program is the order in which the variables are passed: oper%, ax%, ay%, bx%, and by% are declared as integers. The variable oper% passes 1 or 0 to the dx register in the assembly language program. The address of oper% is [BP]+4. The values for ax%, ay%, bx%, and by% are passed back from the assembly language program. Notice that by's address is [BP]+12.

The procedure for creating the C interfacing example is fairly straight-forward. First, the assembly language program is written with an editor such as the Norton full-screen editor. Next, the program is assembled as shown here.

```
B>C:MASM CGAME.ASM;
IBM Personal Computer MACRO Assembler    Version 2.00
(C)Copyright IBM Corp 1981, 1984
(C)Copyright Microsoft Corp 1981, 1983, 1984


50096 Bytes free

Warning Severe
Errors  Errors
0       0
```

This process creates an .OBJ file on the B diskette.

Next, the C program is created with the same editor and compiled with the C compiler to produce an .OBJ file. The small model was created by entering the command shown here (for Microsoft C Compiler, version 3.0; ©copyright Microsoft Corp., 1984, 1985).

```
C>MSC B:MSCGAME,B:,/G2/FPc87;
```

The final step in the process is to link the two .OBJ files together with the system linker using the command shown here (for Microsoft 8086

```
int oper, ax, ay, bx, by;

main()
{
        extern cgame();
        oper = 1;
repeat: cgame(&oper,&ax,&ay,&bx,&by);
        printf("%d %d %d %d\n", ax, ay, bx, by);
        goto repeat;
}
```

Figure 10-10. _____

C program that calls assembly language program to sample game adapter port

Object Linker, version 3.01; © copyright Microsoft Corp., 1983, 1984, 1985).

```
C>LINK B:MSCGAME+B:CGAME,B:,,C:;
```

In this example, the C host program MSCGAME.OBJ has been compiled, and it resides on the B disk. The assembly language program CGAME.OBJ also resides on the B disk. These programs are linked together using the (+) option of the linker. Once the assembly language program is linked to the host program, the assembly language program is no longer needed on the disk. The host program MSCGAME.EXE is now a complete working program.

IBM'S FORTRAN COMPILER

FORTRAN is the workhorse of the scientific and engineering community. It is possibly the first language you learned on a mainframe computer. Although today its position as a good programming language is being severely challenged by Ada, Pascal, and C, FORTRAN will continue to be a popular language for many people. IBM'S FORTRAN Compiler is considered the standard for small-system FORTRAN compilers.

To make the example here as simple as possible, the FORTRAN program will poll the assembly language program repeatedly. To stop the output, a Ctrl/Alt/Del procedure must be performed. The assembly language program will contain support code to aid in receiving and sending variable information. Figure 10-11 shows a complete listing for the assembly language code. A portion of the support code is shown here.

```
          PUBLIC   FGAME
MYCODE    SEGMENT  'CODE'
          ASSUME   CS:MYCODE
FGAME     PROC     FAR            ;PROCEDURE IS NAMED FGAME
          PUSH     BP             ;SAVE LOCATION OF BP REG.
          MOV      BP,SP          ;MOVE STACK POINTER TO BP REGISTER

          MOV      SI,[BP]+22     ;INPUT OPERATION INFORMATION FROM HOST
          MOV      DX,[SI]        ;SAVE INFO IN DX REGISTER
          CMP      DX,0           ;IF ZERO, CONTINUE AND READ BUTTONS
          JNE      POTS           ;IF NOT, MAKE JUMP AND READ POTS

     (-->game adapter code removed from this section<--)

SEND:     MOV      DI,[BP]+18     ;PREPARE TO SEND A(X) POT VALUE
          MOV      [DI],AX
          MOV      DI,[BP]+14     ;PREPARE TO SEND A(Y) POT VALUE
```

```
      MOV     [DI],BX
      MOV     DI,[BP]+10        ;PREPARE TO SEND B(X) POT VALUE
      MOV     [DI],CX
      MOV     DI,[BP]+6         ;PREPARE TO SEND B(Y) POT VALUE
      MOV     [DI],DX

      MOV     SP,BP             ;RETURN PARAMETERS
      POP     BP
      RET     10
```

The assembler language code will eventually be assembled and linked to the compiled FORTRAN code. The procedure FGAME is declared both public and FAR. FGAME will require a FAR RET when completed. The BP (base pointer) is pushed onto the stack so that the value in SP (stack pointer) can be placed in BP. In most interfacing, values are passed to and from programs using the stack. Variables can be transferred from the host program to the assembly language program via the SI (source index) register. Values can be transferred from the assembly language program to the host program via the DI (destination index) register. In this example, five word (DW) variables are moved back and forth. The information required to return to the host program occupies the first six bytes of the stack. The address of the host variable (BY) is [BP]+6. This address is moved into the DI register. The integer value in DX is moved into the address [DI] using the command MOV [DI],DX. Four bytes away, at memory location [BP]+10, is the memory location of the next variable (BX). In this manner, one variable is sent from the host program to the assembly program, and four integer values are returned to the host program. These four integer values represent the joystick potentiometer readings, assuming that DX initially was set to 1. If DX was set to 0, only the value returned in the AX register has any meaning; AX will contain the coded information about the push buttons. Using the same techniques, any number of variables can be transferred back and forth.

Before leaving this routine, the BP register is restored, and a RET (return) is issued. This is a FAR return. The 10 (next to RET) is required to remove the variables from the stack.

Figure 10-12 shows the host FORTRAN program. Notice that the assembly language program is called using a call to the external procedure. The name of the assembly language program is FGAME.ASM, and it is located on the B drive along with the assembled .OBJ file. The other point of interest in this host program is the order in which the variables are passed: OPER, AX, AY, BX, and BY are declared as integers. The variable OPER passes 1 or 0 to the DX register in the assembly language program. The address of OPER is [BP]+22. The values for AX, AY, BX, and BY are

```
;FOR 80286/80386
;PROGRAM REQUESTS BUTTON OR POT VALUES FROM JOYSTICKS A & B, WITH BIOS
;INTERRUPT RETURNS VALUES TO HIGH LEVEL LANGUAGE HOST PROGRAM

          PUBLIC   FGAME
MYCODE    SEGMENT  'CODE'
          ASSUME   CS:MYCODE
FGAME     PROC     FAR            ;PROCEDURE IS NAMED FGAME
          PUSH     BP             ;SAVE LOCATION OF BP REG.
          MOV      BP,SP          ;MOVE STACK POINTER TO BP REGISTER

          MOV      SI,[BP]+22     ;INPUT OPERATION INFORMATION FROM HOST
          MOV      DX,[SI]        ;SAVE INFO IN DX REGISTER
          CMP      DX,0           ;IF ZERO, CONTINUE AND READ BUTTONS
          JNE      POTS           ;IF NOT, MAKE JUMP AND READ POTS

;CODE FOR SAMPLING THE FOUR PUSHBUTTONS
          MOV      AH,84H         ;JOYSTICK INTERFACE
          MOV      DX,0           ;DX=0 FOR PUSHBUTTON INFO
          INT      15H            ;DO IT
          MOV      CL,04          ;ROTATE FOUR BITS
          ROR      AL,CL          ;7-4 TO 3-0 BIT POSITIONS
          AND      AX,0FH         ;KEEP ONLY LOWER 4 BIT INFORMATION
          JMP      SEND           ;RETURN INFORMATION

;CODE FOR SAMPLING THE FOUR GAME POTS (A(X), A(Y), B(X), & B(Y))
POTS:     MOV      AH,84H         ;JOYSTICK INTERFACE
          MOV      DX,01H         ;READ POTS (VALUES RETURNED IN AX, BX, CX, DX)
          INT      15H            ;DO IT

;CODE FOR RETURNING AX, BX, CX, & DX REGISTER VALUES
SEND:     MOV      DI,[BP]+18     ;PREPARE TO SEND A(X) POT VALUE
          MOV      [DI],AX
          MOV      DI,[BP]+14     ;PREPARE TO SEND A(Y) POT VALUE
          MOV      [DI],BX
          MOV      DI,[BP]+10     ;PREPARE TO SEND B(X) POT VALUE
          MOV      [DI],CX
          MOV      DI,[BP]+6      ;PREPARE TO SEND B(Y) POT VALUE
          MOV      [DI],DX

          MOV      SP,BP          ;RETURN PARAMETERS
          POP      BP
          RET      10

FGAME     ENDP                    ;END PROCEDURE NAMED FGAME
MYCODE    ENDS                    ;END CODE SEGMENT NAMED MYCODE

          END                     ;END WHOLE PROGRAM
```

Figure 10-11. _____

Assembly language code for interfacing game adapter with FORTRAN host
program

passed back from the assembly language program. Notice that BY's address
is [BP]+6.

The procedure for creating the FORTRAN interfacing example is fairly
straightforward. First, the assembly language program is written with an
editor, such as the Norton full-screen editor. Next, the program is
assembled as shown next.

```
B>C:MASM FGAME;
IBM Personal Computer MACRO Assembler    Version 2.00
(C)Copyright IBM Corp 1981, 1984
(C)Copyright Microsoft Corp 1981, 1983, 1984


50096 Bytes free

Warning Severe
Errors  Errors
0       0
```

Using the same editor, the FORTRAN program is created. The FOR-
TRAN compiler is then used to compile this program and create an .OBJ
file, as shown here.

```
A>FOR1 B:MSFGAME,B:MSFGAME,NUL,NUL;

IBM Personal Computer FORTRAN Compiler
Version 2.00
(C)Copyright IBM Corp 1982, 1984
(C)Copyright Microsoft Corp 1982, 1984

 Pass One    No Errors Detected
              8 Source Lines

A>FOR2

 Code Area Size = #00D1  (  209)
 Cons Area Size = #000C  (   12)
 Data Area Size = #0021  (   33)

 Pass Two    No Errors Detected.
```

When the two-step compiling process is complete, the .OBJ file for the
FORTRAN program will reside on the B diskette. A final step is needed to

---

```
              INTEGER OPER,AX,AY,BX,BY
              OPER=1
              DO 3 I=1,500
        1     CALL FGAME(OPER,AX,AY,BX,BY)
              WRITE(*,2)AX,AY,BX,BY
        2     FORMAT (4I5)
        3     CONTINUE
              END
```

Figure 10-12. _____

FORTRAN program that calls assembly language program to sample game
adapter port

link the two .OBJ files together using the following command (for IBM Personal Computer Linker, version 2.30; ©copyright IBM Corp., 1981, 1985).

```
A>LINK B:MSFGAME+B:FGAME,B:,,A:;
```

In this example, the FORTRAN host program MSFGAME.OBJ has been compiled, and it resides on the B disk. The assembly language program FGAME.OBJ also resides on the B disk. These programs are linked together with the (+) option of the linker. Once the assembly language program is linked to the host program, the assembly language program is no longer needed on the disk. The host program MSFGAME.EXE is now a complete working program.

IBM'S PASCAL COMPILER

IBM's Pascal compiler does not offer many of the enhancements that Borland's Turbo Pascal compiler offers. It is a much more expensive compiler, it does not have an editor, and it is noted for the very long compilation time required to produce final code. IBM's Pascal Compiler, however, might be the choice of the serious Pascal programmer. The latest version supports the 80287 coprocessor. The IBM Pascal Compiler also creates .OBJ files that can be linked to multisegment assembler programs. This is a feat not possible with the Borland product.

In the example here, we'll simply poll the game adapter repeatedly until a key is pressed. The assembly language program will contain support code to aid in receiving and sending variable information. Figure 10-13 shows a complete listing for the assembly language code. A portion of the support code is shown here.

```
        PUBLIC  PGAME
MYCODE  SEGMENT 'CODE'
        ASSUME  CS:MYCODE
PGAME   PROC    FAR             ;PROCEDURE IS NAMED PGAME
        PUSH    BP              ;SAVE LOCATION OF BP REG.
        MOV     BP,SP           ;MOVE STACK POINTER TO BP REGISTER

        MOV     SI,[BP]+14      ;INPUT OPERATION INFORMATION FROM HOST
        MOV     DX,[SI]         ;SAVE INFO IN DX REGISTER
        CMP     DX,0            ;IF ZERO, CONTINUE AND READ BUTTONS
        JNE     POTS            ;IF NOT, MAKE JUMP AND READ POTS

(-->game adapter code removed from this section<--)

SEND:   MOV     DI,[BP]+12      ;PREPARE TO SEND A(X) POT VALUE
```

```
        MOV     [DI],AX
        MOV     DI,[BP]+10      ;PREPARE TO SEND A(Y) POT VALUE
        MOV     [DI],BX
        MOV     DI,[BP]+8       ;PREPARE TO SEND B(X) POT VALUE
        MOV     [DI],CX
        MOV     DI,[BP]+6       ;PREPARE TO SEND B(Y) POT VALUE
        MOV     [DI],DX

        MOV     SP,BP           ;RETURN PARAMETERS
        POP     BP
        RET     10
```

```
;FOR 80286/80386
;PROGRAM REQUESTS BUTTON OR POT VALUES FROM JOYSTICKS A & B, WITH BIOS
;INTERRUPT RETURNS VALUES TO HIGH LEVEL LANGUAGE HOST PROGRAM

        PUBLIC  PGAME
MYCODE  SEGMENT 'CODE'
        ASSUME  CS:MYCODE
PGAME   PROC    FAR             ;PROCEDURE IS NAMED PGAME
        PUSH    BP              ;SAVE LOCATION OF BP REG.
        MOV     BP,SP           ;MOVE STACK POINTER TO BP REGISTER

        MOV     SI,[BP]+14      ;INPUT OPERATION INFORMATION FROM HOST
        MOV     DX,[SI]         ;SAVE INFO IN DX REGISTER
        CMP     DX,0            ;IF ZERO, CONTINUE AND READ BUTTONS
        JNE     POTS            ;IF NOT, MAKE JUMP AND READ POTS

;CODE FOR SAMPLING THE FOUR PUSHBUTTONS
        MOV     AH,84H          ;JOYSTICK INTERFACE
        MOV     DX,0            ;DX=0 FOR PUSHBUTTON INFO
        INT     15H             ;DO IT
        MOV     CL,04           ;ROTATE FOUR BITS
        ROR     AL,CL           ;7-4 TO 3-0 BIT POSITIONS
        AND     AX,0FH          ;KEEP ONLY LOWER 4 BIT INFORMATION
        JMP     SEND            ;RETURN INFORMATION

;CODE FOR SAMPLING THE FOUR GAME POTS (A(X), A(Y), B(X), & B(Y)
POTS:   MOV     AH,84H          ;JOYSTICK INTERFACE
        MOV     DX,01H          ;READ POTS (VALUES RETURNED IN AX, BX, CX, DX)
        INT     15H             ;DO IT

;CODE FOR RETURNING AX, BX, CX, & DX REGISTER VALUES
SEND:   MOV     DI,[BP]+12      ;PREPARE TO SEND A(X) POT VALUE
        MOV     [DI],AX
        MOV     DI,[BP]+10      ;PREPARE TO SEND A(Y) POT VALUE
        MOV     [DI],BX
        MOV     DI,[BP]+8       ;PREPARE TO SEND B(X) POT VALUE
        MOV     [DI],CX
        MOV     DI,[BP]+6       ;PREPARE TO SEND B(Y) POT VALUE
        MOV     [DI],DX

        MOV     SP,BP           ;RETURN PARAMETERS
        POP     BP
        RET     10

PGAME   ENDP                    ;END PROCEDURE NAMED PGAME
MYCODE  ENDS                    ;END CODE SEGMENT NAMED MYCODE

        END                     ;END WHOLE PROGRAM
```

Figure 10-13. _____

Assembly language code for interfacing game adapter with IBM Pascal host program

The assembler language code will eventually be assembled and linked to the compiled Pascal code. The procedure PGAME is declared both public and FAR. PGAME will require a FAR RET when completed. The BP (base pointer) is pushed onto the stack so that the value in SP (stack pointer) can be placed in BP. In most interfacing, values are passed to and from programs using the stack. Variables can be transferred from the host program to the assembly language program via the SI (source index) register. Values can be transferred from the assembly language program to the host program via the DI (destination index) register. In this example, five word (DW) variables are moved back and forth. The information required to return to the host program occupies the first six bytes of the stack. The address of the host variable (BY) is [BP]+6. This address is moved into the DI register. The integer value in DX is moved into the address [DI] using the command MOV [DI],DX. Two bytes away, at memory location [BP]+8, is the memory location of the next variable (BX). In this manner, one variable is sent from the host program to the assembly program, and four integer values are returned to the host program. These four integer values represent the joystick potentiometer readings, assuming that DX initially was set to 1. If DX was set to 0, only the value returned in the AX register has any meaning; AX will contain the coded information about the push buttons. Using the same techniques, any number of variables can be transferred back and forth.

Before leaving this routine, the BP register is restored, and a RET (return) is issued. This is a FAR return. A 10 is issued with the RET command to clear the stack of the variables (5 variables × 2).

Figure 10-14 shows the host Pascal program. Notice that the assembly language program is called using a call to the external procedure. The name of the assembly language program is PGAME.ASM, and this program is located in the B drive along with the assembled .OBJ file. The other point of interest in this host program is the order in which the variables are passed: OPER, AX, AY, BX, and BY are declared as integers. The variable OPER passes 1 or 0 to the DX register in the assembly language program. The address of OPER is [BP]+14. The values for AX, AY, BX, and BY are passed back from the assembly language program. Notice that BY's address is [BP]+6.

The procedure for creating the Pascal interfacing example is fairly straightforward. First, the assembly language program is written with an editor, such as the Norton full-screen editor. Next, the program is assembled as shown here.

```
B>C:MASM PGAME;
IBM Personal Computer MACRO Assembler     Version 2.00
(C)Copyright IBM Corp 1981, 1984
```

```
PROGRAM MSPGAME(INPUT,OUTPUT);

VAR
  OPER,AX,AY,BX,BY:INTEGER;
  CH:CHAR;

PROCEDURE PGAME(VAR OPER,AX,AY,BX,BY:INTEGER);
  EXTERNAL;

PROCEDURE INFORM;
BEGIN
  OPER:=1;
  PGAME(OPER,AX,AY,BX,BY);
  WRITELN(AX,'  ',AY,'  ',BX,'  ',BY)
END;

BEGIN {MAIN PROCEDURE}
  REPEAT
    INFORM;
  UNTIL CH='Q'
END.
```

Figure 10-14. _____

IBM Pascal program that calls assembly language program to sample game
adapter port

```
(C)Copyright Microsoft Corp 1981, 1983, 1984


50096 Bytes free

Warning Severe
Errors  Errors
0       0
```

The Pascal program is then created with the same editor and compiled
with the IBM Pascal Compiler, as shown here.

```
A>PAS1 B:MSPGAME,B:,,;

IBM Personal Computer Pascal Compiler
Version 2.00
(C)Copyright IBM Corp 1981, 1984
(C)Copyright Microsoft Corp 1981, 1984

 Pass One    No Errors Detected.

A>PAS2

 Code Area Size = #00DB  (  219)
 Cons Area Size = #000D  (   13)
 Data Area Size = #0024  (   36)

 Pass Two    No Errors Detected.
```

The last step in the interfacing procedure is to link the two .OBJ files together with the system linker using the command shown here (for IBM Personal Computer Linker version 2.30; ©copyright IBM Corp., 1981, 1985).

```
A>LINK B:MSBGAME+B:PGAME,B:,,A:;
```

In this example, the Pascal host program MSPGAME.OBJ has been compiled, and it resides on the B disk. The assembly language program PGAME.OBJ also resides on the B disk. These programs are linked together using the (+) option of the linker. Once the assembly language program is linked to the host program, the assembly language program is no longer needed on the disk. The host program MSPGAME.EXE is now a complete working program.

THE IBM MACRO ASSEMBLER

This appendix is designed to give you a greater understanding of how to use the various features and utilities supplied with your IBM Macro Assembler. Using an example program, you will learn how to create, assemble, and link an assembly language program (see Figure A-1).

Once you have created the source code, you will take a closer look at how the assembler uses the source code to create an .OBJ file and what a listing and cross reference file are and why they are needed. After learning how to create the .OBJ file, you will see how the linker converts the .OBJ files into .EXE files. You will explore one of the options available at this step, the creation of a .MAP file, and see why this file can be so useful.

Included in this appendix is an explanation of the differences between an .EXE file and a .COM file. You will learn how to use the EXE2BIN.EXE program supplied with DOS to convert .EXE files to .COM files.

GENERAL INFORMATION

The IBM Macro Assembler is delivered with both a small assembler and a large (macro) assembler. Although the small assembler requires less memory, it does not support all of the functions and options provided by

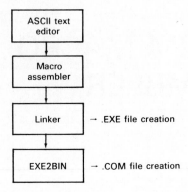

Figure A-1. _____

Steps for creating an assembly language program

the macro assembler. For this reason we will concentrate our discussion on the macro assembler.

The macro assembler will operate with a minimum of 128K of memory under DOS 2.0 or later implementation. During the assembly process, the macro assembler can use up to 192K of memory, if this much memory is available.

CREATING ASSEMBLER SOURCE CODE

The assembly language application development cycle begins with the definition of a problem that needs to be solved at machine level. For example, you might want to read the resistive (pot) values of the game adapter connected to your computer.

Before attempting a programming solution, some research into how the computer accesses this game adapter information is required. This information is contained in the BIOS listings of the *IBM Technical Reference Manual*.

Knowing this information permits creation of the source code. As discussed in Chapter 2, source code uses mnemonics to represent actual machine-code instructions. Source code must follow the grammatical rules, or syntax, of the assembler in order for it to be interpreted properly. Source code can be written on any text processor with a line or full-screen editor, such as the Norton Editor or IBM Professional Editor, that generates an output file in ASCII format.

Using an ASCII text editor, create the following source code and give it the file name **GAME.ASM**. The .ASM extension designates this as an assembly language source code file.

```
;FOR 80286/80386 MACHINES
;PROGRAM WILL SAMPLE GAME ADAPTER, IF ONE IS CONNECTED, RETURNING
;POT VALUES TO THE INDICATED REGISTERS.


PAGE ,132                         ;SET PAGE DIMENSIONS

MYCODE  SEGMENT PARA 'CODE'       ;DEFINE CODE SEG. FOR MASM
MYPROC  PROC    FAR               ;PROCEDURE IS NAMED MYPROC
        ASSUME  CS:MYCODE
        PUSH    DS                ;SAVE LOCATION OF DS REG.
        SUB     AX,AX             ;GET A ZERO IN AX
        PUSH    AX                ;SAVE ZERO ON STACK, TOO

;SAMPLE GAME ADAPTER POTS. AX=A(X), BX=A(Y), CX=B(X), DX=B(Y)
;AFTER INTERRUPT
        MOV     AH,84H            ;SAMPLE JOYSTICK
        MOV     DX,01H            ;SAMPLE POTS
        INT     15H               ;DO IT

        RET                       ;RETURN CONTROL TO DOS
MYPROC  ENDP                      ;END PROCEDURE NAMED MYPROC
MYCODE  ENDS                      ;END CODE SEGMENT NAMED MYCODE

        END                       ;END WHOLE PROGRAM
```

Having created the source code, you now are ready for the next phase in the application development cycle. You will have to use the macro assembler to translate the English-like source code into a form the microprocessor can understand.

USING THE MACRO ASSEMBLER

The IBM Macro Assembler takes source code, or .ASM files, and generates the machine code equivalent, or .OBJ files. This is accomplished by passing over the source code twice.

Pass 1 defines what the relative offset is for each line of source code by building a symbol table; it does not generate any object code (see the discussion of the /D parameter in Table A-1). Pass 2 takes the values defined in pass 1 and generates an .OBJ file.

PHASE ERRORS

Pass 2 may generate *phase errors*. A phase error indicates that the assembler found a different value for a variable, label, or procedure during pass 2

Option	Description
/A	This parameter causes the assembler to list the segments of the source code in alphabetical order. It is the default setting for the assembler.
/D	When a phase error has been generated, it is due to a discrepancy between the values generated by pass 1 and pass 2 in the assembly process. To help pinpoint this inconsistency, the assembler can be forced to generate a listing for pass 1 by using the /D parameter. This additional listing can then be compared to the one automatically generated by pass 2.
/E	This parameter assembles the source code for the 80287/80387 and generates floating-point constants in the form expected by the coprocessor. It operates the same way as the /R parameter.
/N	This parameter stops the assembler from generating a symbol table at the end of listings.
/O	This parameter causes the assembler to generate octal equivalents for the machine language translation.
/R	This parameter assembles the source code for the 80287/80387, generating numeric values in the form expected by the coprocessor. Machine code generated by this option will not run properly on systems not containing the coprocessor.
/S	This parameter overrides the /A default for the assembler and leaves the segments listed in the same order as they appear in the source code.

Table A-1. _____

IBM Macro Assembler Parameters

than was stored in the pass 1 symbol table. Such an error can be caused by forward referencing of a register or by an instruction that violates the assembler's assumptions.

The instructions that follow assume that your GAME.ASM source code is in drive B, the IBM Macro Assembler is in drive A, and drive B is the default drive. The B> prompt should be on your screen.

To invoke the assembler, type the following:

```
B>A:MASM
```

You will see the following lines of text printed:

```
IBM Personal Computer MACRO Assembler    Version 2.00
(C)Copyright IBM Corp 1981, 1984
(C)Copyright Microsoft Corp 1981, 1983, 1984

Source filename [.ASM]:
```

The assembler requests the name of the source code to be translated. Any contents within square brackets [ ] are the assembler's default value. In this case, the default file extension for the source code is .ASM. Since the GAME source code was saved with the .ASM extension, simply type **GAME** and press ENTER in response to this first prompt.

Note that the IBM Macro Assembler Version 2.0 allows the specification of path names should you wish to perform these operations on fixed disks. In this case, the responses to the prompts may include drive and subdirectory designations.

After pressing ENTER, you will see the second prompt:

```
Object filename [GAME.OBJ]:
```

The assembler is indicating that unless specified otherwise, the .OBJ file created will be named GAME.OBJ. Press ENTER to accept this logical naming convention. You will now see the third prompt:

```
Source listing  [NUL.LST]:
```

A file with the .LST extension is a translated version of the original source code. The source code has been modified to include line numbers, machine-code equivalents for each instruction, and a symbol table. The assembler does not generate this file by default, as indicated by the NUL mnemonic in the listing.

We do want to see this useful option, so to override NUL, type **GAME** and press ENTER. It isn't necessary to type .LST, as the assembler will supply the extension automatically.

After pressing ENTER, you will see the fourth and final assembler prompt:

```
Cross reference [NUL.CRF]:
```

Files with the .CRF extension are created by the assembler as an intermediate step toward generating a cross-reference listing. The file is called CREF.EXE.

Again, the default setting is NUL, which means that no .CRF file will be generated. To override this default value, type **GAME** and press ENTER. This will generate the file GAME.CRF, which you will use later.

The assembler now performs the specified operations on the source file GAME.ASM and produces .OBJ, .LST, and .CRF files. Take a moment to generate a directory listing of drive B to make certain these steps were accomplished. The following files should be listed:

```
GAME      ASM       758   12-27-85    6:47p
GAME      OBJ        57   12-29-85    2:55p
GAME      LST      1656   12-29-85    2:55p
GAME      CRF        69   12-29-85    2:55p
```

You already know that the file GAME.ASM contains the ASCII code for the program and that the file GAME.OBJ cannot be listed, since it is the machine-code representation of your program. Also, GAME.CRF cannot be listed since it is the intermediate step necessary in creating a cross-reference table. The file that can be listed is GAME.LST.

As previously mentioned, files with the .LST extension contain the source code translated to include line numbers, machine-code instruction equivalents, and a symbol table. This file usually is used as a hard-copy reference and is printed once. There are many ways to get a hard copy of this file, but the simplest is to turn the printer on, type **TYPE GAME.LST**, press CTRL-PRTSC, and press ENTER. You should see something similar to the following listing:

```
IBM Personal Computer MACRO Assembler    Version 2.00       Page     1-1
                                            12-29-85
    1                       ;FOR 80286/80386 MACHINES
    2                       ;PROGRAM WILL SAMPLE GAME ADAPTER, IF ONE IS CONNECTED, RETURNING
    3                       ;POP VALUES TO THE INDICATED REGISTERS.
    4
    5
    6               PAGE ,132              ;SET PAGE DIMENSIONS
    7
```

```
8     0000                    MYCODE    SEGMENT    PARA 'CODE'    ;DEFINE CODE SEG. FOR MASM
9     0000                    MYPROC    PROC       FAR            ;PROCEDURE IS NAMED MYPROC
10                                      ASSUME     CS:MYCODE
11    0000  1E                          PUSH       DS             ;SAVE LOCATION OF DS REG.
12    0001  2B C0                       SUB        AX,AX          ;GET A ZERO IN AX
13    0003  50                          PUSH       AX             ;SAVE ZERO ON STACK, TOO
14
15                            ;SAMPLE GAME ADAPTER POTS. AX=A(X), BX=A(Y), CX=B(X), DX=B(Y)
16                            ;AFTER INTERRUPT
17    0004  B4 84                       MOV        AH,84H         ;SAMPLE JOYSTICK
18    0006  BA 0001                     MOV        DX,01H         ;SAMPLE POTS
19    0009  CD 15                       INT        15H            ;DO IT
20
21    000B  CB                          RET                       ;RETURN CONTROL TO DOS
22    000C                    MYPROC    ENDP                      ;END PROCEDURE NAMED MYPROC
23    000C                    MYCODE    ENDS                      ;END CODE SEGMENT NAMED MYCODE
24
25                                      END                       ;END WHOLE PROGRAM


IBM Personal Computer MACRO Assembler    Version 2.00       Page      Symbols-1
                                            12-29-85


Segments and Groups:

            N a m e                    Size     Align     Combine    Class

MYCODE . . . . . . . . . . . . . .     000C     PARA      NONE       'CODE'

Symbols:

            N a m e                    Type     Value     Attr

MYPROC . . . . . . . . . . . . .       F PROC   0000      MYCODE     Length =000C

50096 Bytes free

Warning Severe
Errors    Errors
0     0
```

PARAMETERS

The IBM Macro Assembler provides many options to the user assembling a program. The options, or parameters are specified on the command line and begin with a slash (/). They are listed alphabetically in Table A-1. (For further details, see the *IBM Macro Assembler Reference Manual.*)

COMMAND ABBREVIATIONS

There are several shortcuts to invoking the assembler. The seasoned programmer will find these useful.

As discussed in Chapter 2, when

```
B>A:MASM GAME;
```

is typed, the assembler immediately generates the .OBJ file without any file name prompts; however, it does not generate the .LST or .CRF files.

The following command abbreviations will accept the default naming convention for each of the .LST and .CRF files, which allows the programmer to avoid the time-consuming process of responding to each of the assembler's prompts.

```
B>A:MASM GAME,,,;
```

Each comma (,) inhibits the assembler prompt and automatically supplies the default file name for that particular option. The command NUL may be substituted for a comma to inhibit any particular option.

Optional parameters are included on the command line as follows:

```
B>CREF
```

This example stops the assembler from generating a symbol table at the end of the listing.

CROSS-REFERENCE LISTINGS: CREF.EXE

The cross-reference listing is most useful in debugging programs. It supplies the programmer with an alphabetical listing of data, variables, labels, constants, and other code symbols. The listing includes the line number on which the symbol was defined and all of the succeeding lines on which the symbol is used.

To generate a cross-reference listing you must select the fourth assembler option, which generates the *filename*.CRF intermediate file. This file will be used by CREF.EXE to create the actual cross-reference list.

To create the cross-reference listing, simply type

```
B>A:MASM GAME/N;
```

and press ENTER. You will see something similar to the following:

```
The IBM Personal Computer CREF, Version 2.00
(C)Copyright IBM Corp 1981, 1984
(C)Copyright Microsoft Corp 1981, 1983, 1984

Cref filename [.CRF]:
```

The CREF.EXE utility is seeking the name of the *filename*.CRF file to use. In the example here, your response will be to type **GAME** and press ENTER. Remember that it is not necessary to add the file extension .CRF, as the utility will automatically supply it.

After performing the preceding step, you will see the following prompt:

```
List filename [GAME.REF]:
```

The default file name, as supplied by the CREF.EXE utility, is GAME.REF. This can be overridden by the user, and a different drive designation can be used, if necessary. To accept this meaningful default naming convention, press ENTER.

CREF.EXE COMMAND ABBREVIATION

As for the macro assembler, there is an abbreviated command to invoke the cross-reference utility. Typing

```
B>CREF GAME;
```

will cause the CREF.EXE program to automatically look for the file GAME.CRF and then generate an .REF file with the same name. In the example here, the file would be named GAME.REF.

If the file was created without any errors, all you will see printed on your screen is the default drive designation. Generate a directory listing of drive B to make certain the file was created. You should see a file by the name of GAME.REF. Type **TYPE GAME.REF**, and you will see the cross-reference listing. It will look like the following:

```
B>TYPE GAME.REF


 Symbol Cross Reference              (# is definition)
 Cref-1

 CODE . . . . . . . . . . . . . .    8

 MYCODE . . . . . . . . . . . . .    8#    10    23
 MYPROC . . . . . . . . . . . . .    9#    22

 3 Symbols

 63048 Bytes Free
```

From this listing you can determine the number of segments in the program. In this case, there is only one: the CODE segment. You can also see the declarations of MYCODE and MYPROC. The # symbol following a line number indicates that the symbol was defined on this line. The line numbers that follow indicate the other lines on which the symbol was used.

Even in this brief example, you can use the cross-reference listing to make certain that each of your code sections have matching end statements, as do MYCODE on line 23 and MYPROC on line 22. As the size of the assembly language program increases, so does the usefulness of this cross-reference listing for debugging.

You can obtain a hard copy of this file simply by turning the printer on and typing (**TYPE**) followed by the name of the file, as follows:

```
B>TYPE GAME.REF
```

Then press CTRL-PRTSC and then ENTER. Remember to press CTRL-PRTSC again after the listing is completed to avoid printing everything typed to the monitor.

Whether or not you generated a cross-reference listing, you must perform the next step in the assembly language application development cycle: The .OBJ file must be linked. This is accomplished by running the LINK. EXE program supplied with your assembler.

LINKING: LINK.EXE

The LINK.EXE utility generates what is called a *relocatable program*. By adding additional overhead to the .OBJ file, the linker enables the operating system to place the assembly language program anywhere in available memory.

This is an advantage, since it allows more than one program to be loaded into memory at one time and executed. The alternative is to assemble a program and fix it to certain memory locations. For instance, the program may start at 0100H, with the value for the user-defined variable RESULT stored in memory location 4F3AH. If another program needs the same memory locations, conflict will occur. A relocatable program, however, would simply be inserted higher or lower in available memory, with all necessary addresses modified by the linker overhead.

The linker also performs several other extremely useful operations. It can combine separately assembled .OBJ files. This is very helpful when you are writing large assembly language programs that have been broken into small modules. The linker also can search libraries for source-code-referenced subroutines.

To invoke the linker, simply type **LINK**. You will see the prompt that follows on the next page.

```
IBM Personal Computer Linker
Version 2.20 (C)Copyright IBM Corp 1981, 1982, 1983, 1984
Object Modules [.OBJ]:
```

The linker is requesting the name of the .OBJ file to be linked.

For the example here, type **GAME**. Again, it is not necessary to supply the file extension .OBJ — the linker will do that for you. You will then see the following prompt:

```
Run File [GAME.EXE]:
```

By default, the linker supplies the name of the executable version of your program. You may override the file name, but the linker will always supply a file extension of .EXE.

Press ENTER to accept this file name. You will now see the following prompt:

```
List File [NUL.MAP]:
```

A file with the .MAP extension contains a listing for each segment in the source code and shows the offset address in the run file. This can also be a very useful tool for debugging.

By default, the linker does not generate this file, as indicated by the NUL in square brackets in the listing. To generate the .MAP file for the example program, give it the name **GAME** and then press ENTER. You will now see the fourth and final prompt:

```
Libraries [.LIB]:
```

The linker is now asking for the names of any libraries containing sub-routines referenced by the source code. In this example, no user-defined libraries are being used. Pressing ENTER will skip this step.

The following messages now appear:

```
Warning: No STACK segment
There was 1 error detected.
```

These messages are valid because the example source code does not contain a defined STACK segment. In this case, this message can be ignored because of the type of file you are creating. The example GAME.ASM program was written to be converted into an extremely compact file called a *.COM file*.

Now generate a directory listing of drive B. You should see something similar to the following listing if you have followed each step in the application development cycle.

```
GAME     ASM      758   12-27-85   6:47p
GAME     OBJ       57    1-02-86   6:36p
GAME     LST     1656    1-02-86   6:36p
GAME     CRF       69    1-02-86   6:36p
GAME     REF      268    1-02-86   6:36p
GAME     MAP      154    1-02-86   7:13p
GAME     EXE      524    1-02-86   7:13p
        7 File(s)    4159488 bytes free
```

If you wanted to, you could run the GAME.EXE file, which is the relocatable, executable version of the GAME program.

Before converting this file to a .COM file, look at some of the linker options and command abbreviations.

LINKER PARAMETERS AND COMMAND ABBREVIATIONS

The optional parameters listed in Table A-2 may be included on the linker command line simply by typing a slash (/), followed by the option.

As with the macro assembler, there are abbreviated command instructions that can be used to invoke the linker. Some of these are listed in Table A-3.

.EXE VERSUS .COM

The advantages of .EXE files are two-fold. First, the file is relocatable. This enables more than one program to be loaded into memory by using all available space. Second, .EXE files allow the use of up to four segments: STACK, DATA, CODE, and EXTRA. This enables good program modularity and also permits the creation of large programs. The disadvantage of .EXE files is the size of the overhead added by the linker to make relocation possible. In the example here, the size of the GAME.EXE program file is 524 bytes.

In contrast, a .COM file can only contain one segment. This one segment includes the STACK, DATA, and CODE information. When an assembly language program is not large, a .COM file is more than sufficient to include all of the data, instructions, and stack manipulations. Unlike the .EXE file, the .COM file is not relocatable and must begin at

0100H. The advantage of a .COM file over an .EXE file is that the .COM file will significantly reduce the size of the executable file. To create a .COM file, use the EXE2BIN.EXE utility supplied with DOS.

CREATING .COM FILES

Running the EXE2BIN.EXE utility creates a .COM file from an .EXE file. To use this utility, type the following:

```
B>A:EXE2BIN GAME GAME.COM
```

Option	Description
/DS ALLOCATION	This parameter, which can be abbreviated /DS, directs the linker to load all of the data defined in the data group at the high end of that group. By default, the data is loaded at the low end of the group, starting at offset 0.
/HIGH	Abbreviated /H, this parameter directs the linker to load the run file as high as possible in memory without interfering with the transient portion of COMMAND.COM.
/LINE	/L directs the linker to include line numbers and addresses for each of the source statements of input modules in the list file.
/NODEFAULT LIBRARY SEARCH	This parameter can be abbreviated to /NOD. It tells the linker not to perform its usual search for default libraries.
/NOGROUP ASSOCIATION	Abbreviated /NOG, this parameter directs LINK to correct long external addresses, even if the symbol was defined in a segment within a defined group.
/PAUSE	/P instructs LINK to print a message requesting the insertion of a diskette to contain the run file.
/STACK:*size*	/S followed by a decimal value greater than 0 and up to 65,536 allows the programmer to specify the size of the STACK segment. Values greater than 0 and less than 512 assign the minimum stack size of 512 bytes.

Table A-2.
LINK Parameters

and then press ENTER. Assuming that the EXE2BIN.EXE program is on the disk in drive A, A:EXE2BIN invokes the program. The .EXE file to be converted is GAME (note that it was not necessary to specify .EXE), and the name of the .COM file to be created is GAME.COM. It is important to remember to add the file extension in this case. If .COM is not included, EXE2BIN will automatically append a .BIN file extension. This is not a recognizable, executable file extension and would have to be changed with the rename command.

Now compare the byte sizes of GAME.EXE and GAME.COM. They should be similar to the following:

```
GAME    EXE    524    1-02-86    7:45p
GAME    COM     12    1-02-86    7:45p
```

Notice the dramatic reduction in size for the .COM file version.

Table A-4 contains a review of each of the utilities supplied with the IBM Macro Assembler, the files they expect, and the files each creates.

Command	Description
LINK *filename*;	This command abbreviation invokes the linker, uses the file *filename*.OBJ for input, and automatically names the output file *filename*.EXE.
LINK *filename*,,;	This abbreviated command causes the linker to look for the file *filename*.OBJ for input and to generate the output files *filename*.EXE and *filename*.MAP.

Note: Each comma (,) inhibits the linker prompt and automatically supplies the default file name for that particular option. The command NUL may be substituted for a comma to inhibit any particular option.

Table A-3. _____

LINK Command Abbreviations

Utility	Description
MASM	Input file expected: MYFILE.ASM (ASCII text file)
	Output file created: MYFILE.OBJ (Machine-language code)
	MYFILE.LST (Listing-file option)
	MYFILE.CRF (Symbol file used by CREF)
CREF	
	Input file expected: MYFILE.CRF (Symbol file used by CREF)
	Output file created: MYFILE.REF (Cross-reference file)
LINK	
	Input file expected: MYFILE.OBJ (Machine-language code)
	MYLIB.LIB (User-defined library)
	Output file created: MYFILE.EXE (Executable file)
	MYFILE.MAP (Memory-map file)
EXE2BIN	
	Input file expected: MYFILE.EXE (One-segment code)
	Output file created: MYFILE.COM (Executable file)

Table A-4.

Utility Input/Output File Requirements

THE MICROSOFT MACRO ASSEMBLER

This appendix is designed to give you a greater understanding of how to use the various features and utilities supplied with your Microsoft Macro Assembler. Using an example program, you will learn how to create, assemble, and link an assembly language program.

Once you have created the source code, you will take a closer look at how the assembler uses the source code to create an .OBJ file and what a listing and cross-reference file are and why they are needed. After learning how to create the .OBJ file, you will see how the linker converts .OBJ files into .EXE files. One of the options available at this step is the creation of a .MAP file. The example program will show how this file is generated, and why it can be so useful.

Included in this appendix is an explanation of the differences between an .EXE file and a .COM file. You will learn how to use the EXE2BIN. EXE program supplied with DOS to convert .EXE files to .COM files.

GENERAL INFORMATION

The Microsoft Macro Assembler is capable of assembling programs to run on the 8086, 80186, 80286 microprocessors and for systems using the 8087 and 80287 math coprocessors. The Microsoft Macro Assembler requires DOS Version 2.0 or a later implementation and a minimum of 128K of memory.

CREATING ASSEMBLER SOURCE CODE

The assembly language application development cycle begins with the definition of a problem that needs to be solved at machine level. For example, you might want to read the resistive (pot) values of the game adapter connected to your computer.

Before attempting a programming solution, some research into how the computer accesses this game adapter information is required. This information is contained in the BIOS listings of the *IBM Technical Reference Manual.*

Knowing this information, you can begin to create the source code. As discussed in Chapter 2, source code uses mnemonics to represent actual machine-code instructions. Source code must follow the grammatical rules, or syntax, of the assembler in order for it to be interpreted properly. Source code can be created on any text processor with a line or full-screen editor that generates an output file in ASCII format.

Using any ASCII text editor (such as the Norton Editor), create the following source code and give it the file name **GAME.ASM**. The .ASM extension designates this as an assembly language source code file.

```
;FOR 80286/80386 MACHINES
;PROGRAM WILL SAMPLE GAME ADAPTER, IF ONE IS CONNECTED, RETURNING
;POT VALUES TO THE INDICATED REGISTERS.


PAGE ,132                         ;SET PAGE DIMENSIONS

MYCODE   SEGMENT PARA 'CODE'      ;DEFINE CODE SEG. FOR MASM
MYPROC   PROC    FAR              ;PROCEDURE IS NAMED MYPROC
         ASSUME  CS:MYCODE
         PUSH    DS               ;SAVE LOCATION OF DS REG.
         SUB     AX,AX            ;GET A ZERO IN AX
         PUSH    AX               ;SAVE ZERO ON STACK, TOO

;SAMPLE GAME ADAPTER POTS.  AX=A(X), BX=A(Y), CX=B(X), DX=B(Y)
;AFTER INTERRUPT
         MOV     AH,84H           ;SAMPLE JOYSTICK
         MOV     DX,01H           ;SAMPLE POTS
         INT     15H              ;DO IT

         RET                      ;RETURN CONTROL TO DOS
```

```
MYPROC   ENDP              ;END PROCEDURE NAMED MYPROC
MYCODE   ENDS              ;END CODE SEGMENT NAMED MYCODE

         END               ;END WHOLE PROGRAM
```

Having created the source code, you now are ready for the next phase in the application development cycle. The macro assembler will be used to translate the English-like source code into a form the microprocessor can understand.

USING THE MACRO ASSEMBLER

The Microsoft Macro Assembler takes source code, or .ASM files, and generates the machine code equivalent, or .OBJ files. This is accomplished by passing over the source code twice.

Pass 1 defines what the relative offset is for each line of source code by building a symbol table; it does not generate any object code (see the discussion of the /D parameter in Table B-1). Pass 2 takes the values defined in pass 1 and generates an .OBJ file.

PHASE ERRORS

Pass 2 may generate phase errors. A phase error indicates that the assembler found a different value for a variable, label, or procedure on pass 2 than was stored in the pass 1 symbol table. Such an error can be caused by forward referencing of a register or by an instruction that violates the assembler's assumptions.

The instructions that follow assume that your GAME.ASM source code is in drive B, the Microsoft Macro Assembler is in drive A, and drive B is the default drive. The B> prompt should be on your screen.

To invoke the assembler, type the following:

```
B>A:MASM/A
```

You will see the following lines of text printed:

```
Microsoft (R) Macro Assembler  Version 4.00
Copyright (C) Microsoft Corp 1981, 1983, 1984, 1985.  All rights
reserved.

Source filename [.ASM]:
```

Option	Description
/A	This parameter causes the assembler to list the segments of the source code in alphabetical order. It is the default setting for the assembler.
/B	This parameter sets the file size buffer for the source code. This is defined in K-bytes, with 32K bytes being the default value. The file buffer size may be increased to a maximum of 63K (not 64K).
/C	This parameter instructs MASM to generate a cross-reference file.
/D	When a phase error has been generated, it is due to a discrepancy between the values generated by pass 1 and pass 2 in the assembly process. To help pinpoint this inconsistency, the assembler can be forced to generate a listing for pass 1 by using the /D parameter. This additional listing can then be compared to the one automatically generated by pass 2.
/E	This parameter assembles the source code for the 80287/80387 and generates floating-point constants in the form expected by the coprocessor. It operates the same way as the /R parameter.
/I	This option sets the search paths to be used for any include files. Up to 10 search paths may be defined by using this option for each path.
/ML	This parameter tells MASM to view variables spelled the same way but using different cases as two separate variables. With this option, for example, MEM_WORD and Mem_Word are two different variables.
/MU	This default setting instructs MASM to convert all lowercase letters to uppercase in public and external names.
/MX	This parameter instructs MASM to preserve case sensitivity for all public and external names. With this option, for example, the variables MEM_WORD and Mem_Word would be written to the object module exactly as shown.
/N	This parameter stops the assembler from generating a symbol table at the end of listings.
/P	This option tells MASM to check for unacceptable 80286 protected-mode exceptions. This option is only active under 80286/80386 microprocessor control.
/R	This parameter assembles the source code for the 80287/80387, generating numeric values in the form expected by the coprocessor. Machine code generated by this option will not run properly on systems not containing the coprocessor.
/S	This parameter overrides the /A default for the assembler and leaves the segments listed in the same order as they appear in the source code.
/T	This parameter inhibits the printing of the successful assembly message.

Table B-1. _____

Microsoft Macro Assembler Parameters

Option	Description
/V	This parameter, an abbreviation for *verbose*, instructs the assembler to provide additional statistics during assembly. This includes the number of lines and symbols processed.
/X	This option tells the assembler to send to the listing file a copy of those statements forming the body of an IF directive that evaluates to false.
/Z	This very useful option instructs MASM to display on the screen those lines of code containing errors.

Table B-1. _____

Microsoft Macro Assembler Parameters (*continued*)

The assembler wants you to supply the name of the source code to be translated. The information within square brackets, [ ], is what the assembler is assuming. In this case, the default file extension for the source code is .ASM. Because you saved your GAME source code with the .ASM extension, simply type **GAME** and press ENTER in response to this first prompt.

Note that the Microsoft Macro Assembler allows the specification of path names should you wish to perform these operations on fixed disks. In this case, the responses to the prompts may include drive and subdirectory designations.

After pressing ENTER, the second prompt will appear.

```
Object filename [GAME.OBJ]:
```

The assembler is indicating that unless specified otherwise, the .OBJ file created will be named GAME.OBJ. Press ENTER to accept this logical naming convention. The third prompt appears.

```
Source listing  [NUL.LST]:
```

A file with the .LST extension is a translated version of the original source code. The source code has been modified to include line numbers, machine-code equivalents for each instruction, and a symbol table. The assembler does not generate this file by default, as indicated by the NUL mnemonic in the listing.

We do want to see this useful option, so to override NUL, type **GAME** and press ENTER. It isn't necessary to type .LST, as the assembler will supply the extension automatically.

After pressing ENTER, the fourth and final assembler prompt appears.

```
Cross reference [NUL.CRF]:
```

Files with the .CRF extension are created by the assembler as an intermediate step toward generating what is known as a cross-reference listing. The .CRF files are used by another utility and are discussed later in this appendix.

Again, the default setting is NUL, which means that no .CRF file will be generated. To override this default value, type **GAME**, and press ENTER. This will generate the file GAME.CRF, which will be used later on.

The assembler now performs the specified operations on the source file GAME.ASM and produces .OBJ, .LST, and .CRF files. Take a moment to generate a directory listing of drive B to make certain these steps were accomplished. The list of files should look similar to this:

```
GAME    ASM     758   12-27-85   6:47p
GAME    OBJ      57   12-29-85   2:55p
GAME    LST    1656   12-29-85   2:55p
GAME    CRF      69   12-29-85   2:55p
```

You already know that the file GAME.ASM contains the ASCII code for the program, and that the file GAME.OBJ cannot be listed, since it is the machine-code representation of your program. Also, GAME.CRF cannot be listed, since it is the intermediate step necessary in creating a cross-reference table. The file that can be listed is GAME.LST.

As previously mentioned, files with the .LST extension contain the source code translated to include line numbers, machine-code instruction equivalents, and a symbol table. This file usually is used as a hard-copy reference and is printed once. There are many ways to get a hard copy of this file, but the simplest is to turn the printer on, type **TYPE GAME.LST**, press CTRL-PRTSC, and press ENTER. The following listing should appear on the monitor's screen:

```
Microsoft (R) Macro Assembler   Version 4.00        12/29/85 02:55:37

                                                    Page    1-1

       1                                 ;FOR 80286/80386 MACHINES
       2                                 ;PROGRAM WILL SAMPLE GAME ADAPTER, IF ONE IS CONNECTED, RETURNING
       3                                 ;POT VALUES TO THE INDICATED REGISTERS.
       4
       5
       6                         PAGE ,132                    ;SET PAGE DIMENSIONS
       7
       8 0000                   MYCODE  SEGMENT PARA 'CODE'   ;DEFINE CODE SEG. FOR MASM
       9 0000                   MYPROC  PROC    FAR           ;PROCEDURE IS NAMED MYPROC
      10                                 ASSUME  CS:MYCODE
      11 0000  1E                        PUSH    DS            ;SAVE LOCATION OF DS REG.
      12 0001  2B C0                     SUB     AX,AX         ;GET A ZERO IN AX
```

```
13 0003 50                               PUSH    AX              ;SAVE ZERO ON STACK, TOO
14
15                              ;SAMPLE GAME ADAPTER POTS.  AX=A(X), BX=A(Y), CX=B(X), DX=B(Y)
16                              ;AFTER INTERRUPT
17 0004 B4 84                            MOV     AH,84H          ;SAMPLE JOYSTICK
18 0006 BA 0001                          MOV     DX,01H          ;SAMPLE POTS
19 0009 CD 15                            INT     15H             ;DO IT
20
21 000B CB                               RET                     ;RETURN CONTROL TO DOS
22                              MYPROC   ENDP                    ;END PROCEDURE NAMED MYPROC
23 000C                         MYCODE   ENDS                    ;END CODE SEGMENT NAMED MYCODE
24
25                                       END                     ;END WHOLE PROGRAM


Microsoft (R) Macro Assembler   Version 4.00               12/29/86 02:55:37

                                                              Symbols-1


Segments and Groups:

                  N a m e               Size    Align   Combine Class

MYCODE . . . . . . . . . . . .          000C    PARA    NONE      'CODE'

Symbols:

                  N a m e               Type    Value   Attr

MYPROC . . . . . . . . . . . .          F PROC  0000    MYCODE    Length = 000C


      25 Source  Lines
      25 Total   Lines
      24 Symbols

   24832 Bytes symbol space free

       0 Warning Errors
       0 Severe  Errors
```

PARAMETERS

The Microsoft Macro Assembler provides many options to the user assembling a program. The options, or parameters, are specified on the command line and begin with a slash (/). They are listed alphabetically in Table B-1. (For further details, see the *Microsoft Macro Assembler Reference Manual.*)

COMMAND ABBREVIATIONS

There are several shortcuts to invoking the assembler. The seasoned programmer will find these useful.

As discussed in Chapter 2, when

```
B>A:MASM/A GAME;
```

is typed, the assembler immediately generates the .OBJ file without any file name prompts; however, it does not generate the .LST or .CRF files.

The following command abbreviations will accept the default naming convention for each of the .LST and .CRF files, which allows the programmer to avoid the time-consuming process of responding to each of the assembler's prompts.

```
B>MASM/A GAME,,,;
```

Each comma (,) inhibits the assembler prompt and automatically supplies the default file name for that particular option. The command NUL may be substituted for a comma to inhibit any particular option.

Optional parameters are included on the command line as follows:

```
B>A:MASM/A GAME/N;
```

This example stops the assembler from generating a symbol table at the end of the listing.

CROSS-REFERENCE LISTING:
CREF.EXE

The cross-reference listing is most useful in debugging programs. It supplies the programmer with an alphabetical listing of data, variables, labels, constants, and other code symbols. The listing includes the line number on which the symbol was defined and all of the succeeding lines on which the symbol is used.

To generate a cross-reference listing you must select the fourth assembler option, which generates *filename*.CRF intermediate file. This file will be used by **CREF.EXE** to create the actual cross-reference list.

To create the cross-reference listing, simply type

```
B>CREF
```

and press ENTER. You will see something similar to the following:

```
Microsoft (R) Cross-Reference Utility  Version 4.00
     Copyright (C) Microsoft Corp 1981, 1983, 1984, 1985.  All rights
     reserved.

     Cross-reference [.CRF]:
```

The CREF.EXE utility is asking for the name of the *filename*.CRF file to use. In the example here, your response will be to type **GAME**, and press ENTER.

Remember that it is not necessary to add the file extension .CRF, as the utility will automatically supply it.

After performing the preceding step, you will see the following prompt:

```
List filename [GAME.REF]:
```

The default file name, as supplied by the CREF.EXE utility, is GAME.REF. This can be overridden by the user, and a different drive designation can be used, if necessary. To accept this meaningful default naming convention, press ENTER.

CREF.EXE COMMAND ABBREVIATION

As for the Macro Assembler, there is an abbreviated command to invoke the cross-reference utility. Typing

```
B>CREF GAME;
```

will cause the CREF.EXE program to automatically look for the file GAME.CRF and then generate an .REF file with the same name. In the example here, the file would be named GAME.REF.

If the file was created without any errors, the default drive designation will be printed on your screen. Generate a directory listing of drive B to make certain the file was created. There should be a file named GAME.REF. Type **TYPE GAME.REF**, and you will see the cross-reference listing. It will look like the following:

```
        B>TYPE GAME.REF

    Microsoft Cross-Reference   Version 4.00               Mon Dec 02
    02:35:00 1985

      Symbol Cross-Reference          (# is definition)
    Cref-1

    CODE . . . . . . . . . . . . .    8

    MYCODE . . . . . . . . . . . .    8     8#     10     23
    MYPROC . . . . . . . . . . . .    9     9#

     3 Symbols

      Symbol Cross Reference                   (# is definition)
    Cref-1

    CODE . . . . . . . . . . . . .    8

    MYCODE . . . . . . . . . . . .    8#    10     23
    MYPROC . . . . . . . . . . . .    9#    22
```

```
3 Symbols

63048 Bytes Free
```

From this listing you can determine the number of segments in the program. In this case, there is only one, the CODE segment. You can also see the declarations for MYCODE and MYPROC. The # symbol following a line number indicates that the symbol was defined on this line. The line numbers that follow indicate the other lines on which the symbol was used.

Even in this brief example, the cross-reference listing can be used to make certain that each of the code sections have matching end statements, as do MYCODE on line 23 and MYPROC on line 22. As the size of the assembly language program increases, so does the usefulness of this cross-reference listing for debugging.

You can obtain a hard copy of this file simply by turning the printer on and typing **TYPE** followed by the name of the file, as follows:

```
B>TYPE GAME.REF
```

Then press CTRL-PRTSC and then ENTER. Remember to press CTRL-PRTSC again after the listing is completed to avoid printing everything typed to the monitor.

Whether or not the optional cross-reference listing was generated, the next step in the assembly language application development cycle is required: The .OBJ file must be linked. This is accomplished by running the LINK.EXE program supplied with your assembler.

LINKING: LINK.EXE

The LINK.EXE utility generates what is called a *relocatable program*. By adding additional overhead to the .OBJ file, the linker enables the operating system to place the assembly language program anywhere in available memory.

This is an advantage, since it allows more than one program to be loaded into memory at one time and executed. The alternative is to assemble a program and fix it to certain memory locations. For instance, the program may start at 0100H, with the value for the user-defined variable RESULT being stored in memory location 4F3AH. If another program needs the same memory locations, a conflict will occur. A relocatable program, however, would simply be inserted higher or lower in available memory, with all necessary addresses modified by the linker overhead.

The linker also performs several other extremely useful operations. It can combine separately assembled .OBJ files. This is very helpful when you are writing large assembly language programs that have been broken into small modules. The linker also can search libraries for source-code-referenced subroutines.

To invoke the linker, simply type **LINK**. The following message will appear:

```
Microsoft (R) 8086 Object Linker   Version 3.05
Copyright (C) Microsoft Corp 1983, 1984, 1985.  All rights
reserved.

Object Modules [.OBJ]:
```

The linker is asking for the name of the .OBJ file to be linked.

For the example here, type **GAME**. Again, it is not necessary to supply the file extension .OBJ—the linker will do that for you. The linker responds with the following prompt:

```
Run File [GAME.EXE]:
```

By default, the linker supplies the name for the executable version of your program. You may override the file name, but the linker will always supply a file extension of .EXE.

Press ENTER to accept this file name. The linker responds with the following prompt:

```
List File [NUL.MAP]:
```

A file with the .MAP extension contains a listing for each segment in the source code and shows the offset address in the run file. This can also be a very useful tool for debugging.

By default, the linker does not generate this file, as indicated by the NUL in square brackets in the listing. To generate the .MAP file for the example program, give it the name **GAME** and then press ENTER. You will now see the fourth and final prompt:

```
Libraries [.LIB]:
```

The linker is now asking for the names of any libraries containing subroutines referenced by the source code. In this example, no user-defined libraries are being used. Pressing ENTER will skip this step.

The following message now appears:

`Warning: No STACK segment.`

This message is valid because the example source code does not contain a defined STACK segment. In this case, this message can be ignored because of the type of file you are creating. The example GAME.ASM program was written to be converted into an extremely compact file called a *.COM file*.

Now generate a directory listing of drive B. You should see something similar to the following listing if you have followed each step in the application development cycle.

```
GAME     ASM      758   12-27-85   6:47p
GAME     OBJ       57    1-02-86   6:36p
GAME     LST     1656    1-02-86   6:36p
GAME     CRF       69    1-02-86   6:36p
GAME     REF      268    1-02-86   6:36p
GAME     MAP      154    1-02-86   7:13p
GAME     EXE      524    1-02-86   7:13p
        7 File(s)   4159488 bytes free
```

It is possible to run the GAME.EXE file, which is the relocatable, executable version of the GAME program.

Before converting this file to a .COM file, look at some of the linker parameters and command abbreviations.

LINKER PARAMETERS AND COMMAND ABBREVIATIONS

The optional parameters listed in Table B-2 may be included on the linker command line simply by typing a slash (/), followed by the option.

As with the macro assembler, there are abbreviated command instructions that can be used to invoke the linker. Some of these are listed in Table B-3.

.EXE VERSUS .COM

The advantages of .EXE files are twofold. First, the file is relocatable. This enables more than one program to be loaded into memory by using all available space. Second, .EXE files allow the use of up to four segments: STACK, DATA, CODE, and EXTRA. This enables good program

Parameter	Description
/HELP	Abbreviated /HE, this option instructs the linker to print a list of available options to the screen.
/DSALLOCATION	This parameter, which can be abbreviated /DS, directs the linker to load all of the data defined in the data group at the high end of that group. By default, the data is loaded at the low end of the group, starting at offset 0.
/EXEPACK	Abbreviated /E, this parameter forces LINK to remove sequences of repeated bytes to minimize the size of the loadtime relocation table. However, this option can actually increase the file size. This option is best used on source code containing many sections of repeated characters.
/HIGH	Abbreviated /H, this parameter directs the linker to load the run file as high as possible in memory without interfering with the transient portion of COMMAND.COM.
/LINENUMBERS	/L or /LINE directs the linker to include line numbers and addresses for each of the source statements of input modules in the list file.
/MAP	The /M parameter causes LINK to generate a listing of all public symbols in the source code.
/NOIGNORECASE	This parameter, abbreviated /NOI, forces LINK to be sensitive to the use of uppercase and lowercase letters. This option can be combined with the /ML or /MX option to make public variables in MASM case sensitive.
/NODEFAULT LIBRARYSEARCH	This parameter can be abbreviated /NOD. It tells the linker not to perform its usual search for default libraries.
/NOGROUP ASSOCIATION	Abbreviated /NOG, this parameter directs LINK to correct long external addresses, even if the symbol was defined in a segment within a defined group.
/PAUSE	/P instructs LINK to print a message requesting the insertion of a diskette to contain the run file.
/STACK:size	/S followed by a decimal value greater than 0 and up to 65,536 allows the programmer to specify the size of the STACK segment. Values greater than 0 and less than 512 assign the minimum stack size of 512 bytes.
/CPARMAXALLOC	This parameter, abbreviated /C, sets the maximum number of 16-byte paragraphs needed by a program when it is loaded into memory.

Table B-2.
LINK Parameters

Instruction	Description
LINK *filename*;	This command abbreviation invokes the linker, uses the file *filename*.OBJ for input, and automatically names the output file *filename*.EXE.
LINK *filename*,,,;	This abbreviated command causes the linker to look for the file *filename*.OBJ for input and to generate the output files *filename*.EXE and *filename*.MAP.

Note: Each comma (,) inhibits the linker prompt and automatically supplies the default file name for that particular option. The command NUL may be substituted for a comma to inhibit any particular option.

Table B-3.
LINK Command Abbreviations

modularity and also permits the creation of large programs. Each segment in an .EXE file can be as large as 64K bytes. The disadvantage of .EXE files is the size of the overhead added by the linker to make relocation possible. In the example here, the size of the GAME.EXE program file is 524 bytes.

In contrast, a .COM file can only contain one 64K byte segment. This one segment includes the STACK, DATA, and CODE information. When an assembly language program is not large, 64K is more than sufficient to include all of the data, instructions, and stack manipulations. Unlike the .EXE file, the .COM file is not relocatable and must begin at 0100H. The advantage of a .COM file over an .EXE file is the .COM file's significantly reduced size. To create a .COM file, use the EXE2BIN.EXE utility supplied with DOS.

CREATING .COM FILES

Running the EXE2BIN.EXE utility creates a .COM file from an .EXE file. To use this utility, type the following:

```
B>A:EXE2BIN GAME GAME.COM
```

then press ENTER. Assuming that the EXE2BIN.EXE program is on the disk in drive A, A:EXE2BIN invokes the program. The .EXE file to be converted is GAME (note that it was not necessary to specify .EXE), and the name of the .COM file to be created is GAME.COM. It is important to remember to add the file extension in this case. If .COM is not included, EXE2BIN will automatically append a .BIN file extension. This is not a recognizable, executable file extension and would have to be changed with the rename command.

Now compare the byte sizes of GAME.EXE and GAME.COM. They should be similar to the following:

```
GAME      EXE      524    1-02-86    7:45p
GAME      COM       12    1-02-86    7:45p
```

Notice the dramatic reduction in size for the .COM file version.

TURBO EDITASM

Appendix C is designed to help you immediately take advantage of the special features found in Turbo Editasm. An example program will be used to guide you through the various assembly language steps, including source-code generation and assembling the program into executable .COM files or into an .EXE file using the linker. Figure C-1 illustrates the two possible assembly language development paths.

GENERAL INFORMATION

Turbo Editasm has a coresident full-screen editor. Unlike the IBM and Microsoft Macro Assemblers, which require a separate ASCII file text editor, Turbo Editasm incorporates the ASCII text editor into the assembler. With this feature, you can instantaneously return during assembly to a line of code generating an error message. Turbo Editasm also incorporates many other useful features, such as a built-in cross-reference utility, line-by-line assembly, and a last-assembly symbol table, stored in memory.

Turbo Editasm includes a full set of instructions to support the 80286 microprocessor running in both real and protected modes. Also supported are the instructions for the 8087 and 80287 math coprocessors, including five floating-point data types, BCD and long integers, and the ability to include both Microsoft and 8087 data types in the same source file.

513

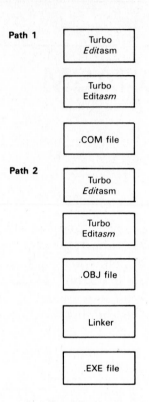

Path 1

Turbo *Edit*asm

Turbo Edit*asm*

.COM file

Path 2

Turbo *Edit*asm

Turbo Edit*asm*

.OBJ file

Linker

.EXE file

Figure C-1. —————————————————————

Two assembly language development paths

Appendix C will use Turbo Editasm TASMB, which is the version allowing both .COM file and .EXE file generation and using the coresident full-screen editor.

Note that if problems arise with the placement of the data segment ahead of the code segment during program assembly, moving the data segment to a position after the code segment may help, since Turbo Editasm is more strongly typed than the IBM Macro Assembler.

CREATING ASSEMBLER SOURCE CODE

The assembly language application development cycle begins with the definition of a problem that needs to be solved at machine level. For example, you might want to print a message to the monitor.

Before attempting a programming solution, some research into how the computer processes character strings is required. For this application, you can make use of the DOS interrupt, introduced earlier in this book.

Knowing this information permits the creation of the source code. As discussed in Chapter 2, source code uses mnemonics to represent actual machine-code instructions. Source code must follow the grammatical rules, or syntax, of the assembler in order for it to be interpreted properly.

To create source code using Turbo Editasm, place Turbo Editasm, hereafter referred to as TASMB, in drive A and your work disk in drive B. With drive A as the default drive, type

```
TASMB
```

You will see the following screen:

```
------------------------------------
TURBO EDITASM          Ver 1.03B
                       PC-DOS

    Copyright (C) 1984,1985 by SPEEDWARE
------------------------------------

    Assem Source  Edit Source  Get Source    Write Source

    Run Codefile  Hexdump File  Kill File    List File

    Symbol List   Xrefer List   Directory    New Drive - Directory

    Asm Options   Value         Quit

    65278 Byte(s) Available.
        0 Byte(s) Used.

    (A)
```

The highlighted letters represent the command instruction abbreviation for each of TASMB's various options. At the bottom of the screen, the (A) is a prompt from TASMB. At this prompt, you can enter any of TASMB's commands.

Press the letter **E** (for **E**dit Source). You will see a blank screen with the following information on the upper right-hand side, indicating that you are in edit mode.

```
Line 1    Col 1    Insert
```

Enter the following code exactly as it appears here.

```
                                    ;SET PAGE DIMENSIONS
      PAGE ,132
                SEGMENT     PARA 'DATA'
      MYDATA    DB      'The 80286/80386 are powerful microprocessors'
      BLOCK     DB      '$'
                ENDS
      MYDATA
                SEGMENT     PARA 'CODE'     ;DEFINE CODE SEG. FOR MASM
      MYCODE    PROC        FAR             ;PROCEDURE IS NAMED MYPROC
      MYPROC    ASSUME      CS:MYCODE,DS:MYDATA
                PUSH        DS              ;SAVE LOCATION OF DS REG.
                SUB         AX,AX           ;GET A ZERO IN AX
                PUSH        AX              ;SAVE ZERO ON STACK, TOO
                MOV         AX,MYDATA       ;GET DATA LOCATION IN AX
                MOV         DS,AX           ;PUT IT IN DS REGISTER
                LEA         DX,BLOCK        ;GET LOCATION OF MESSAGE
                MOV         AH,9H           ;SET UP PARAMETERS
                INT         21H             ;PRINT MESSAGE

                RET                         ;RETURN CONTROL TO DOS
      MYPROC    ENDP                        ;END PROCEDURE MYPROC
      MYCODE    ENDS                        ;END CODE SEGMENT MYCODE

                END                         ;END WHOLE PROGRAM
```

TASMB's editor commands are similar to those of the well-known word processor WordStar. You can use the cursor movement keys and the INS and DEL keys to edit what you type.

Save the source code you have created on a disk. Pressing the F2 key will invoke the following upper left-hand screen prompt from TASMB:

```
Write Source File:
```

Respond with

```
B:PROGEXE
```

and press the ENTER key. TASMB will automatically append the .ASM file extension.

To assemble the program, quit the editor by typing CTRL-K-D. TASMB will respond with (**A**). Type the letter A to **A**ssemble the program. You will see the following prompt:

```
Use File: B:PROGEXE.OBJ (Y/N) ?
```

Press Y to create an .OBJ file with the same name. TASMB is a two-pass assembler. It indicates which pass is currently being executed by printing the following prompts:

```
Assembling
Pass One

Pass Two
```

Assuming there were no editing errors, you should now see something similar to the following lines:

```
25 Source Line(s), No Assembly Error(s).
12 Object Byte(s),54716 Byte(s) Free.
Assembly Time: 1 second(s)


(A)
```

ASSEMBLY OPTIONS

TASMB provides very easy-to-use assembly options. By typing an O (for **O**ptions) from the main menu, you can select from such options as hard-copy listings, cross-reference and symbol table generation, screen display, and disk writing. For the example here (assuming you are still in TASMB), type an O to display the list of options. You will see the following information (some of your ON/OFF options may be different).

```
* Editasm Options *

F1 - Screen   (ON)
F2 - Printer  (OFF)
F3 - Symbols  (OFF)
F4 - Xrefer.  (OFF)
F5 - Memory   (OFF)
F6 - ErrWait  (OFF)
```

```
F7 - OBJ File (OFF)
F8 - COM File (OFF)
F9 - LST File (OFF)
F10- Undefd.  (OFF)

Select option or <CR> to Exit.
```

CREATING .OBJ FILES

The creation of the .OBJ file is an intermediate step necessary to prepare the source code for final linking. Linking an .OBJ file creates an executable .EXE file. An .EXE file contains additional code overhead that allows the code to be relocated anywhere there is available memory.

To create the .OBJ file, select the **O** option from TASMB's main menu and then activate the .OBJ option by pressing the F7 key. Pressing the ENTER key will return you to the main menu, where you can press the A key to assemble the code. TASMB will prompt you with the file name to use, as follows:

```
B:\PROGEXE.OBJ (Y/N)?
```

Press the letter **Y** to accept this default name.

You have generated the .OBJ file. To verify this, from TASMB's main menu press the **D** option to get a **D**irectory listing of your files. You should see

```
PROGEXE.ASM
PROGEXE.OBJ
```

The next step is to link the .OBJ file using the linker supplied with your disk operating system (see "Creating .EXE Files" later in this appendix).

CREATING A LISTING FILE

To facilitate code walkthrough and debugging, it is often useful to have an assembled listing. To create a listing, select Asm Options from TASMB's main menu and turn option F9 on (see Table C-1 at the end of this appendix for further details). Leave the Asm Options menu by pressing the ENTER key. Now when you press the **A** option to assemble the program,

TASMB will prompt twice: once for the assembled file name

```
Use Object File: B:\PROGEXE.OBJ (Y/N)?
```

and a second time for the name to be used for the listing file, which, for the example here, would be

```
Use File: B:\PROGEXE.LST (Y/N)?
```

To see the file you could use the TASMB editor or type the file using the DOS TYPE command. If you want a hard copy, then before creating the listing, turn the F2 option on. This will send the assembled listing directly to the printer. Alternatively, the assembled listing can be sent to the screen by turning on the F1 option.

For the example file **PROGEXE.ASM**, the assembled listing would look similar to this:

```
TURBO ASSEMBLER       March 2,1986      02:41:57 p.m.          Page 1


     1                             PAGE ,132                        ;SET PAGE DIMENSIONS
     2
     3  0000                       MYDATA  SEGMENT PARA 'DATA'
     4  0000 54 68 65 20 38 30     BLOCK   DB      'The 80286/80386 are powerful microprocessors'
          32 38 36 2F 38 30
          33 38 36 20 61 72
          65 20 70 6F 77 65
          72 66 75 6C 20 6D
          69 63 72 6F 70 72
          6F 63 65 73 73 6F
          72 73
     5  002C 24                            DB      '$'
     6  002D                       MYDATA  ENDS
     7
     8  0000                       MYCODE  SEGMENT PARA 'CODE'      ;DEFINE CODE SEG. FOR MASM
     9  0000                       MYPROC  PROC    FAR              ;PROCEDURE IS NAMED MYPROC
    10                                     ASSUME  CS:MYCODE,DS:MYDATA
    11  0000 1E                            PUSH    DS               ;SAVE LOCATION OF DS REG.
    12  0001 29 C0                         SUB     AX,AX            ;GET A ZERO IN AX
    13  0003 50                            PUSH    AX               ;SAVE ZERO ON STACK, TOO
    14  0004 B8 ----                       MOV     AX,MYDATA        ;GET DATA LOCATION IN AX
    15  0007 8E D8                         MOV     DS,AX            ;PUT IT IN DS REGISTER
    16
    17  0009 8D 16 0000                    LEA     DX,BLOCK         ;GET LOCATION OF MESSAGE
    18  000D B4 09                         MOV     AH,9H            ;SET UP PARAMETERS
    19  000F CD 21                         INT     21H              ;PRINT MESSAGE
    20
    21  0011 CB                            RET                      ;RETURN CONTROL TO DOS
    22  0012                       MYPROC  ENDP                     ;END PROCEDURE NAMED MYPROC
    23  0012                       MYCODE  ENDS                     ;END CODE SEGMENT NAMED MYCODE
    24
    25                                     END                      ;END WHOLE PROGRAM


 25 Source Line(s), No Assembly Error(s).
 63 Object Byte(s),54619 Byte(s) Free.
 Assembly Time: 1 Second(s)
```

CREATING SYMBOL TABLES
AND CROSS-REFERENCE LISTINGS

As you may have noticed, the TASMB Asm Options can easily be reconfigured to give you those options you need for the moment. A symbol table and cross-reference listing can be very useful in debugging a program. They list each symbol used in the source code and the line on which each of the symbols was used. Creating these useful listings is as simple as activating the correct Asm Option. Option F3 creates the symbol table, and F4 the cross-reference listing. The symbol table for **PROGEXE.ASM** will look similar to the following listing.

```
Assembling
Pass One
Pass Two                                              02:51:39
p.m.


Segs & Groups:

             N a m e        Size    Align    Line   Combine  Class

MYCODE . . . . . . *        0012    PARA     8      NONE     'CODE'
MYDATA . . . . . .          002D    PARA     3      NONE     'DATA'


Symbols:

             N a m e        Type    Value    Line   Attr

BLOCK. . . . . . .          Byte    0000     4      MYDA
MYPROC . . . . . . *        F Proc  0000     9      MYCO     Length = 0012

25 Source Line(s), No Assembly Error(s).
63 Object Byte(s),54575 Byte(s) Free.
Assembly Time:


(A)
```

To see the cross-reference listing, from TASMB's main menu select the **X**refer List option by pressing the letter **X**. For the example here, the listing will look similar to this:

```
             N a m e            Cross Reference(s):

BLOCK. . . . . . .      4,17
MYCODE . . . . . .      8,23
MYDATA . . . . . .      3,6,14
MYPROC . . . . . .      9,22
```

```
    6 Symbol(s) Used.
28672 Byte(s) for Symbols.
28671 Byte(s) for Workarea.
```

CREATING .EXE FILES

Any Microsoft-compatible linker can be used to convert an .OBJ file into its executable .EXE version. The linker will add the necessary code to enable the system to relocate the program anywhere there is available memory.

To use the linker, you must quit TASMB by pressing the letter **Q** from the main menu and insert the disk containing the linker into drive A. With your .OBJ file in drive B and drive A your default drive, type

```
A>LINK
```

The linker will respond with

```
IBM Personal Computer Linker
Version 2.30 (C) Copyright IBM Corp. 1981, 1985

Object Modules [.OBJ]:
```

Enter the name of the .OBJ file you want linked. For the example here, type **B:PROGEXE.** It is not necessary to include the .OBJ extension. The linker will now respond with three prompts.

```
Run File [B:PROGEXE.EXE]:
List File [NUL.MAP]:
Libraries [.LIB]:
```

Simply press ENTER to accept the default parameters. (See Appendixes A and B for further discussion on how the IBM and Microsoft linkers work.)

You will now see this error message:

```
Warning: no stack segment
```

This is merely a warning indicating that a stack segment has not been defined. For this application, the stack segment was not needed.

At this point you have created an executable .EXE file. A directory listing of drive B should look similar to the following:

```
PROGEXE.ASM
PROGEXE.OBJ
PROGEXE.EXE
```

To run the .EXE file created on drive B, type the name of the program. For the example here, type

```
A>B:PROGEXE
```

You will see the message "The 80286/80386 are powerful microprocessors" printed on the screen.

CREATING .COM FILES

Before you can assemble a .COM file, your source code must be in the correct format. Take a moment to look at the code used to create the .EXE file PROGEXE.ASM. Notice that two separate code segments, one for data and the other for the main procedure, called the code segment, are used. By segmenting a program you can go beyond the 64K byte restriction for .COM files on 80286 machines.

The source code in the following listing can be translated into a .COM file for either the 80286 or 80386 microprocessor, because it uses only one segment. A .COM file will execute faster than its equivalent .EXE version for two reasons: Since there is only one segment, there are no time-consuming multiple-segment address calculations to be performed, and the .COM file version is not relocatable. Not including the overhead necessary to make the code relocatable also reduces the code size and contributes to the increased execution speed.

The following source code, PROGCOM.ASM, incorporates the .COM file-creation restrictions. Using TASMB's full-screen editor as previously described (CTRSYOMH assembler source code), enter PROGCOM.ASM exactly as shown here.

```
        LEA     DX,BLOCK        ;GET LOCATION OF MESSAGE
        MOV     AH,9H           ;SET UP PARAMETERS
        INT     21H             ;PRINT MESSAGE

        INT     20H             ;RETURN TO DOS CONTROL

BLOCK   DB      'The 80286/80386 are powerful microprocessors'
        DB      '$'

        END                     ;END WHOLE PROGRAM
```

There are fewer lines of code in PROGCOM.ASM than there are in the PROGEXE.ASM version because segment declarations are unnecessary for a .COM file.

To create an executable .COM file from an appropriately structured source file, select the **O** option from TASMB's assembler options.

```
* Editasm Options *

F1  - Screen    (ON)
F2  - Printer   (OFF)
F3  - Symbols   (OFF)
F4  - Xrefer.   (OFF)
F5  - Memory    (OFF)
F6  - ErrWait   (OFF)
F7  - OBJ File  (OFF)
F8  - COM File  (ON)
F9  - LST File  (OFF)
F10- Undefd.    (OFF)

Select option or <CR> to Exit.
```

Activate the .COM File option by pressing F8 and then pressing ENTER. Make certain that option F7 is turned off, as PROGCOM.ASM is not in proper form to generate an .EXE file. Now, press the **A** option to activate the assembler. You will see the following message:

```
Use File: B:PROGCOM.COM (Y/N) ? Y
```

Type a **Y** to accept this default output file name. You will now see the following:

```
Assembling
Pass One

Pass Two


11 Source Line(s), No Assembly Error(s).
55 Object Byte(s),54783 Byte(s) Free.
Assembly Time: 1 second(s)
```

Generate a directory listing of disk B. You should see something similar to this:

```
PROGCOM.ASM
PROGCOM.COM
```

To execute a .COM file, simply type the name of the program. Make certain that you have quit TASMB. For the example here, to execute PROGCOM.-COM, type **PROGCOM**. You will see the following message printed at the current cursor position: **The 80286/80386 are powerful microprocessors.**

OTHER TASMB ASSEMBLER OPTIONS

From the preceding examples, you already know that the TASMB Asm Option's list contains several options. To see the list of options available, select Asm Options by pressing the letter **O**. The list will look similar to the following (some of the ON/OFF settings may be different).

```
* Editasm Options *

F1 - Screen    (ON)
F2 - Printer   (OFF)
F3 - Symbols   (OFF)
F4 - Xrefer.   (OFF)
F5 - Memory    (OFF)
F6 - ErrWait   (OFF)
F7 - OBJ File  (OFF)
F8 - COM File  (OFF)
F9 - LST File  (OFF)
F10- Undefd.   (OFF)

Select option or <CR> to Exit.
```

Table C-1 lists each Asm Option and explains when and why to use each option.

Function Key	Option Description
F1	SCREEN — Activating the F1 option will cause the assembled listing to be printed to the screen. If F1 is in the off position, only the errors found during the assembly process will be printed to the screen. In the off mode, the assembler will run much faster, because it will not have to pause to write each assembled line to the screen.
F2	PRINTER — When this option is turned on, a listing of the assembled code will be sent only to the printer. TASMB will not simultaneously print the assembled listing to the screen and the printer.
F3	SYMBOLS — This option instructs the assembler to include a symbol table at the end of the assembly source listing. The table will be printed to the selected output device as defined by F1 and F2.

Table C-1.

Asm Options

Function Key	Option Description
F4	XREF — Activating the F4 option forces the assembler to generate a cross-reference listing of each symbol used followed by the line or lines within the source code where each symbol was referenced. This listing will go to the default output device as selected by the F1 and F2 options.
F5	MEMORY — With F5 in the on position, TASMB is instructed to send the machine-code version of the program directly into memory, where it can be executed by the RUN command from TASMB's main menu. (Note: For this option to work, INT20h must be inserted into your source code at the point where you would like to return to TASMB.)
F6	ERRWAIT — A very useful option for long listings, this option instructs the assembler to pause for each error found in the source listing. At the pause, the programmer can either jump to the line of code causing the error and correct it (by pressing the ESC key) or continue assembling by pressing the ENTER key.
F7	OBJ FILE — This option creates an .OBJ file (as described above in the section "CREATING .OBJ FILES").
F8	COM FILE — This option creates .COM files (as described in the section "CREATING .COM FILES").
F9	LST FILE — This option determines whether a listing file is created and whether or the not the listing will include a symbol table and/or a cross-reference listing. When F9 is in the on position, TASMB prompts for the name of the listing file. For example, for the program PROGEXE.ASM, TASMB prompts with: **Use File: PROGEXE.LST (Y/N)?** If the F3 (symbol table option) is in the on position, the listing will be followed by the symbol table. Similarly, if the F4 option has been selected, a cross-reference listing will be appended.
F10	Not currently used.

Table C-1. _____

Asm Options (*continued*)

ASCII CHARACTERS

Table D-1 lists the ASCII codes for characters.

DEC	OCTAL	HEX	ASCII	DEC	OCTAL	HEX	ASCII
0	000	00	NUL	17	021	11	DC1
1	001	01	SOH	18	022	12	DC2
2	002	02	STX	19	023	13	DC3
3	003	03	ETX	20	024	14	DC4
4	004	04	EOT	21	025	15	NAK
5	005	05	ENQ	22	026	16	SYN
6	006	06	ACK	23	027	17	ETB
7	007	07	BEL	24	030	18	CAN
8	010	08	BS	25	031	19	EM
9	011	09	HT	26	032	1A	SUB
10	012	0A	LF	27	033	1B	ESC
11	013	0B	VT	28	034	1C	FS
12	014	0C	FF	29	035	1D	GS
13	015	0D	CR	30	036	1E	RS
14	016	0E	SO	31	037	1F	US
15	017	0F	SI	32	040	20	SPACE
16	020	10	DLE	33	041	21	!

Table D-1.

ASCII Character Codes

DEC	OCTAL	HEX	ASCII	DEC	OCTAL	HEX	ASCII
34	042	22	"	76	114	4C	L
35	043	23	#	77	115	4D	M
36	044	24	$	78	116	4E	N
37	045	25	%	79	117	4F	O
38	046	26	&	80	120	50	P
39	047	27	'	81	121	51	Q
40	050	28	(	82	122	52	R
41	051	29	)	83	123	53	S
42	052	2A	*	84	124	54	T
43	053	2B	+	85	125	55	U
44	054	2C	,	86	126	56	V
45	055	2D	—	87	127	57	W
46	056	2E	.	88	130	58	X
47	057	2F	/	89	131	59	Y
48	060	30	0	90	132	5A	Z
49	061	31	1	91	133	5B	[
50	062	32	2	92	134	5C	\
51	063	33	3	93	135	5D	]
52	064	34	4	94	136	5E	^
53	065	35	5	95	137	5F	—
54	066	36	6	96	140	60	'
55	067	37	7	97	141	61	a
56	070	38	8	98	142	62	b
57	071	39	9	99	143	63	c
58	072	3A	:	100	144	64	d
59	073	3B	;	101	145	65	e
60	074	3C	<	102	146	66	f
61	075	3D	=	103	147	67	g
62	076	3E	>	104	150	68	h
63	077	3F	?	105	151	69	i
64	100	40	@	106	152	6A	j
65	101	41	A	107	153	6B	k
66	102	42	B	108	154	6C	l
67	103	43	C	109	155	6D	m
68	104	44	D	110	156	6E	n
69	105	45	E	111	157	6F	o
70	106	46	F	112	160	70	p
71	107	47	G	113	161	71	q
72	110	48	H	114	162	72	r
73	111	49	I	115	163	73	s
74	112	4A	J	116	164	74	t
75	113	4B	K	117	165	75	u

Table D-1.

ASCII Character Codes (*continued*)

DEC	OCTAL	HEX	ASCII	DEC	OCTAL	HEX	ASCII
118	166	76	v	123	173	7B	{
119	167	77	w	124	174	7C	|
120	170	78	x	125	175	7D	}
121	171	79	y	126	176	7E	~
122	172	7A	z	127	177	7F	DEL

Table D-1.

ASCII Character Codes (*continued*)

APPENDING A LIBRARY USING A LIBRARY MANAGER

IBM's Macro Assembler (version 2.0 and later implementations) and Microsoft's Macro Assembler (version 3.0 and later implementations) each contain a library manager to aid in the construction and maintenance of manufacturer- or user-created libraries. This appendix uses a dynamic example to illustrate how to add a procedure to an existing library. In Chapter 7, several simple features of library maintenance were presented. It might be profitable to review Chapter 7 before proceeding.

LOW-OVERHEAD FORMATTING

In Chapter 9, the IBM Utility Library IBMUTIL.LIB was used to help format the output from the 80287 coprocessor. This library contains many conversion routines, one of which ($I8__OUTPUT) was used by the examples in that chapter. Since $I8__OUTPUT did not return the answer in the required format, additional coding was necessary in the program starting on page 415. This program code was over 60 lines long. Its length inhibited its continuous use from program to program. However, since this conversion routine is quite handy, it is a prime candidate for inclusion in a utility library.

In this appendix, this code will be appended to the IBM Utility Library using the library manager. One special note: While both IBM and Microsoft contain a library manager, only IBM supplies the IBMUTIL.LIB on its MASM diskette.

SPECIFIC PROGRAM INFORMATION

The program starting on page 415 is quite long, and yet most of the program is concerned with formatting the answer rather than obtaining it. Figures E-1 and E-2 are very similar. Figure E-1 is a program that calculates the sum of two real numbers using the 80287 coprocessor. Figure E-2 converts the answer of Figure E-1 into the proper format. The earlier program included the equivalent of both E-1 and E-2 in one program. In this example you will see how to save the formatting portion of the code in the utility library. Once this is done, programs can call the utility library any time an 80287 answer needs to be formatted in scientific notation.

Many important details regarding the use of the IBM Utility Library are discussed in Chapter 9 and in the IBM Macro Assembler manual. You may wish to review this material before proceeding. Give special attention to the necessary PUBLIC declarations for variables, data segments, and code segments.

USING THE LIBRARY MANAGER

The code of both Figures E-1 and E-2 must be assembled with the appropriate MASM diskette. Once successful assembly has been achieved, Figure E-2 is ready to be appended to the IBM Utility Library.

The library manager, included on the MASM diskette, allows five prompts to be defined when the manager is entered from DOS: Library File, Page Size, Operations, List File, and New Library. The syntax for this operation is

LIB *lib__file[page__size][operations],[list__file],[new__lib]...[;]*

Details regarding each prompt are given in the IBM MASM manual. For

```
COMMENT    /THIS PROGRAM ILLUSTRATES THE USE OF THE 80287 CO-PROCESSOR
            TO ADD REAL NUMBERS. THERE IS A MINIMUM AMOUNT OF OVER-
            HEAD NECEESSARY FOR DISPLAYING ANSWERS IN REAL NUMBER
            FORMAT. THE 8087 PSEUDO-OP ENCODES THE REAL NUMBERS IN
            THE DATA SEGMENT FOR 8087 & 80287 PROCESSING. IN ORDER TO
            VIEW AN ANSWER, IN REAL NUMBER FORMAT, THE LINKER MUST CALL
            A CONVERSION ROUTINE AT THE LIBRARY PROMPT CALLED "IBMUTIL".
            THE ACTUAL CONVERSION USES PRTREAL. THIS ROUTINE CONVERTS
            AN 80287 FORMATTED NUMBER INTO A CHARACTER STRING. FORMATS THE
            OUTPUT AND PRINTS THE RESULTS AT THE CURRENT CURSOR POSITION./

        PAGE ,132                               ;SIGNALS FOR CO-PROC ASSEMBLY
        .8087
        COMMENT /REAL NUMBERS CAN BE OF THE FORM:
                        123.4567      0.000048976
                        1.3E20       -4.5789E-3       /

                PUBLIC RESULT                   ;VAR CALLED BY LIBRARY
        MYDATA  SEGMENT PARA PUBLIC 'DATA'      ;MUST BE PUBLIC
        NUMBER1 DQ          1.2345E21           ;REAL NUMBER
        NUMBER2 DQ          -13.456789E20       ;REAL NUMBER
        RESULT  DQ          ?                   ;ANSWER IN 80287 FORMAT
        MYDATA  ENDS

        CODEGRP GROUP MATHCODE                  ;REQUIRED NAME OF CODE SEG
        MATHCODE SEGMENT BYTE PUBLIC 'CODE'     ;DEFINE CODE SEG FOR MASM
        MYPROC  PROC    FAR                     ;PROCEDURE IS NAMED MYPROC
                ASSUME  CS:MATHCODE,DS:MYDATA,ES ;MYDATA
                EXTRN   PRTREAL:NEAR            ;SETUP FOR EXTERNAL LIBRARY
                PUSH    DS                      ;SAVE LOCATION OF DS REG
                SUB     AX,AX                   ;GET A ZERO IN AX
                PUSH    AX                      ;SAVE ZERO ON STACK, TOO
                MOV     AX,MYDATA               ;GET LOCATION OF MYDATA
                MOV     DS,AX                   ;PUT INTO DS & ES SEG REG
                MOV     ES,AX

                LEA     SI,RESULT               ;GET LOCATION OF VARIABLE
                FLD     NUMBER1                 ;LOAD REAL ONTO 80287 STACK
                FADD    NUMBER2                 ;ADD A NUMBER TO IT
                FSTP    QWORD PTR [SI]          ;POP AND STORE RESULT
                FWAIT                           ;SYNCH WITH 80286

                CALL    PRTREAL                 ;CALL PRTREAL TO FORMAT RESULT

                RET                             ;RETURN CONTROL TO DOS
        MYPROC  ENDP                            ;END PROCEDURE NAMED MYPROC
        MATHCODE ENDS                           ;END CODE SEGMENT NAMED MATHCODE

                END                             ;END WHOLE PROGRAM
```

Figure E-1. _____

Program that calculates the sum of two real numbers

the example here, the library already exists — it was provided by IBM on the MASM diskette under the name IBMUTIL.LIB. Let's use the library manager to determine the contents of IBMUTIL.LIB.

If your IBM MASM program is on drive C, type **LIB** from the C prompt as follows:

```
C>LIB

IBM Personal Computer Library Manager
Version 1.00
(C)Copyright IBM Corp 1984
```

```
                    PUBLIC PRTREAL
MYDATA      SEGMENT    PARA PUBLIC 'DATA'       ;DATA SEGMENT MUST BE PUBLIC
            EXTRN      RESULT:QWORD             ;VARIABLE TO PASS
PADDER      DB         20 DUP (' ')             ;BREATHING ROOM FOR IBM ROUTINE
ANSWER      DB         17 DUP (?),'$'           ;CHARACTER ANSWER FROM IBM ROUTINE
FIGDIG      DB         ' ','$'                  ;FUTURE LOCATION OF FIRST DIGIT
POWER       DW         ?                        ;EXPONENT STORAGE
TBUFF       DB         4 DUP(' ')               ;4 BYTES FOR EXPONENT CHARACTERS
SIGN        DB         '-$'                     ;NEGATIVE SIGN
POINT       DB         '.$'                     ;DECIMAL POINT
EXP         DB         ' E $'                   ;EXPONENT SYMBOL
MYDATA      ENDS

CODEGRP     GROPU      LIBSEG
LIBSEG      SEGMENT    BYTE PUBLIC 'CODE'
            ASSUME CS:CODEGRP,DS:MYDATA
            EXTRN      $I8_OUTPUT:NEAR
PRTREAL     PROC       NEAR
            CALL       $I8_OUTPUT
            SUB        CX,01H                   ;REDUCE EXP BY 1
            MOV        POWER,DX                 ;DX IS CORRECTED EXPONENT OF ANS
            CMP        BL,'-'                   ;DETERMINE IF ANSWER IS + OR -
            JNE        NONEG
            LEA        DX,SIGN                  ;IF NEGATIVE, PRINT CHAR TO SCREEN
            MOV        AH,09
            INT        21H
NONEG:
            CLD                                 ;PREPARE TO TRANSFER STRING TO ANS
            MOV        CL,17                    ;STRING IS 17 BYTES LONG
            LEA        DI,ANSWER[1]             ;DESTINATION OF MOVE
REP         MOVSB                               ;MOVE 'EM
            MOV        CL,1                     ;MOVE 1ST CHAR OF ANSWER TO FIRDIG
            LEA        SI,ANSWER[1]
            LEA        DI,FIRDIG
REP         MOVSB
            LEA        DX,FIRDIG                ;PRINT 1ST DIGIT TO SCREEN
            MOV        AH,09
            INT        21H
            LEA        DX,POINT                 ;PRINT A DECIMAL POINT
            MOV        AH,09
            INT        21H
            LEA        DX,ANSWER[2]             ;PRINT REMAINING DIGITS
            MOV        AH,09
            LEA        DX,EXP                   ;PRINT "E" FOR EXPONENT AFTER
            MOV        AH,09                    ;CHARACTER STRING
            INT        21H
            MOV        DX,POWER                 ;CONVERT NUMBER IN DX TO A STRING
            CMP        DX,8000H                 ;IS IT POS OR NEG?
            JB         POSIT                    ;IF POSITIVE, GO TO POSIT
            LEA        DX,SIGN                  ;IF NEG, PRINT A NEG SIGN FIRST
            MOV        AH,09
            INT        21H
            MOV        DX,POWER                 ;CORRECT HEX VALUE
            XOR        DX,0FFFFH
            ADD        DX,01
POSIT:      MOV        CX,0
            LEA        DI,TBUFF                 ;TBUFF WILL SERVE AS A 4 BYTE
POWER1:     PUSH       CX                       ;CHARACTER STORAGE AS THE HEX NUMS
            MOV        AX,DX                    ;IN DX ARE CONVERTED TO DECIMAL
            MOV        DX,0                     ;ASCII VALUES FOR SCREEN PRINTING
            MOV        CX,10
            DIV        CX
            XCHG       AX,DX
            ADD        AL,30H                   ;MAKE NUMBER AN ASCII DIGIT
            MOV        [DI],AL                  ;SAVE IT IN TBUFF
```

Figure E-2. _____

Program to format output

```
           INC     DI                      ;POINT TO NEW LOCATION IN TBUFF
           POP     CX
           INC     CX                      ;CX CONTAINS THE NUMBER OF DIGITS
           DMP     DX,0
           JNZ     POWER1
PRIT:      DEC     DI                      ;PREPARE TO PRINT VALUES TO SCREEN
           MOV     AL,[DI]                 ;GET DIGIT FROM TBUFF
           PUSH    DX                      ;PROTECT ORIGINAL DX VALUE
           MOV     DL,AL                   ;MOVE DIGIT FOR PRINTING
           MOV     AH,2                    ;PARAMETER FOR DOS PRINT
           INT     21H                     ;PRINT POWER TO SCREEN
           POP     DX                      ;RETURN ORIGINAL DX VALUE
           LOOP    PRIT                    ;CONTINUE TILL ALL DONE
           RET
PRTREAL    ENDP                            ;END PRTREAL PROCEDURE
LIBSEG     ENDS                            ;END CODE SEGMENT NAMED LIBSEG

           END                             ;END WHOLE PROGRAM
```

Figure E-2. _____

Program to format output (*continued*)

```
(C)Copyright Microsoft Corp 1984

Library name: IBMUTIL
Operations:
List file: C:CONTENTS
```

In this operation the library manager will read the contents of IBMUTIL, which exists on the default drive, and create a listing file named CONTENTS on the same drive. The listing file is an ASCII file that can be printed as shown here.

```
$I4_I8............ifconv        $I4_M4............bfconv
$I8_I4............ifconv        $I8_INPUT.........i8fin
$I8_M8............bfconv        $I8_OUTPUT........i8fout
$I8_TMUL..........i8tmul        $I8_TPWR10........i8tmul
$M4_I4............bfconv        $M8_I8............bfconv


bfconv                Offset: 200H  Code and data size: F0
   $I4_M4                $I8_M8             $M4_I4                $M8_I8

ifconv                Offset: 400H  Code and data size: C0
   $I4_I8                $I8_I4

i8fin                 Offset: 600H  Code and data size: 2FD
   $I8_INPUT

i8fout                Offset: C00H  Code and data size: 1A2
   $I8_OUTPUT

i8tmul                Offset: 1000H Code and data size: 1EA
   $I8_TMUL              $I8_TPWR10
```

The library manager can now be used to add the code of Figure E-2 to the IBM Utility Library. The name of the program listing in Figure E-2 is PRTREAL. Only .OBJ files can be appended to libraries, which is why the previous assembly of this program was needed.

The syntax for appending the routine is shown here.

```
C>LIB IBMUTIL.LIB + PRTREAL.OBJ
```

That's all there is to it! Check the listing file and see if the operation was successful.

```
C>LIB

IBM Personal Computer Library Manager
Version 1.00
(C)Copyright IBM Corp 1984
(C)Copyright Microsoft Corp 1984

Library name: IBMUTIL
Operations:
List file: C:NEWINFO
```

The listing file was stored in NEWINFO on the C drive. Printing NEWINFO to the screen yields

```
$I4_I8............ifconv          $I4_M4............bfconv
$I8_I4............ifconv          $I8_INPUT.........i8fin
$I8_M8............bfconv          $I8_OUTPUT........i8fout
$I8_TMUL..........i8tmul          $I8_TPWR10........i8tmul
$M4_I4............bfconv          $M8_I8............bfconv
PRTREAL...........PRTREAL

bfconv            Offset: 200H  Code and data size: F0
   $I4_M4            $I8_M8            $M4_I4            $M8_I8

ifconv            Offset: 400H  Code and data size: C0
   $I4_I8            $I8_I4
   $I8_INPUT

i8fout            Offset: C00H  Code and data size: 1A2
   $I8_OUTPUT

i8tmul            Offset: 1000H  Code and data size: 1EA
   $I8_TMUL          $I8_TPWR10

PRTREAL           Offset: 1400H  Code and data size: DB
   PRTREAL
```

With the successful attachment of PRTREAL to the IBM Utility Library, it will only be necessary to specify IBMUTIL as the LIBRARY at link time.

```
C>LINK

IBM Personal Computer Linker
Version 2.30 (C) Copyright IBM Corp. 1981, 1985

Object Modules [.OBJ]: ADDER
Run File [ADDER.EXE]:
List File [NUL.MAP]:
Libraries [.LIB]: IBMUTIL
```

Many of the routines developed in this book can be added to your own library, created with the library manager. The library manager facilitates effective programming management.

TRADEMARKS

The following names are trademarked products of the corresponding companies.

ASM286/ASM387™	Intel
COMPAQ DESKPRO 286®	COMPAQ Computer Corporation
DESQview™	Quarterdeck Office Systems
EDLIN™	International Business Machines Corporation
IBM AT®	International Business Machines Corporation
IBM Macro Assembler™	International Business Machines Corporation
IBM Professional Editor™	International Business Machines Corporation
Microsoft Basic®	Microsoft Corporation
Microsoft C®	Microsoft Corporation
Microsoft Macro Assembler™	Microsoft Corporation

INDEX

Program Listings

Other related Osborne/McGraw-Hill titles include:

8080A/8085 Assembly Language Programming

by Lance A. Leventhal

"...an excellent encyclopedia of assembly language programming." (Byte)

More quality programming examples and instruction sets than can be found in any other book on the subject. Information on assemblers, program loops, code conversion and more.

$19.95 p
0-07-931010-9, 448 pp., 6½ x 9¼

8080A/8085 Assembly Language Subroutines

by Lance A. Leventhal
and Winthrop Saville

"The text is beautifully designed with many, many examples complete with source code. The routines included can actually be used to save hours of tedious development time. Whether you program in assembly for fun or profit check this one out. You'll be impressed!" (Lifelines/The Software Magazine)

$19.95 p
0-07-931058-3, 500 pp., 7½ x 9¼

The 8086 Book

by Russell Rector and George Alexy

"...is far superior to any other book about the 8086." (Dr. Dobbs Journal)

Anyone using, designing, or simply interested in an 8086-based system will be delighted by this book's scope and authority. As the 16-bit microprocessor gains wider inclusion in small computers, this book becomes invaluable as a reference tool which covers the timing, architecture and design of the 8086, as well as optimal programming techniques, interfacing, special features and more.

$18.95 p
0-07-931029-X, 624 pp., 6½ x 9¼

65816/65802 Assembly Language Programming

by Michael Fischer

This addition to the Osborne/McGraw-Hill ALP series is a complete handbook to assembly language programming with the 65816 and 65802 microprocessors. Serious programmers will find complete coverage of the 65816 and 65802 chip series. Assemblers, instruction sets, arithmetic operations, loops, and code conversion are presented. You'll also learn about sorting and searching, subroutines, I/O and interrupts, debugging and testing. Michael Fischer, a columnist for Bay Area Computer Currents, provides you with concise, comprehensive information. 65816/65802

Assembly Language Programming is both a tutorial and a lasting reference.

$19.95 p
0-07-881235-6, 425 pp., 6⅜ x 9¼

68000 Assembly Language Programming, Second Edition, Includes 68010 & 68020

by Lance A. Leventhal, Doug Hawkins,
Gerry Kane,
and William D. Cramer

This classic on assembly language programming for the 68000 microprocessor has been revised to provide complete coverage of the entire 68000 family, including the 68010 and 68020 chips. Every instruction you need to program in assembly language is thoroughly described. Fully debugged, practical programming examples with solutions in both object code and source code are used throughout the text to illustrate techniques. The authors also discuss assembler conventions, I/O device programming, and interfacing methods. If you're designing software for the Macintosh,™ Commodore Amiga,™ Atari® ST,™ Altos® 3068, Tandy® 6000, or other 68000-based computers, you'll find essential information in this lasting reference. (Part of the Osborne/McGraw-Hill Assembly Language Programming series.)

$19.95 p
0-07-881232-1, 625 pp., 6⅜ x 9¼

68000 Microprocessor Handbook, Second Edition

by William Cramer and Gerry Kane

For serious programmers and hardware designers, this is a complete handbook to the 68000 microprocessor family. In this revised, expanded edition, all of the 68000 chips, including the 68008, 68010, 68012, and 68020, are examined. You'll find in-depth coverage of addressing modes, signal conventions, instruction sets, exception processing logic, as well as timing and bus operations. If you're designing software for the Macintosh,™ Atari® ST, Commodore Amiga,™ Tandy® 6000, AT&T UNIX™ PC, or other 68000 computers, this handbook is an invaluable resource for all your programming queries.

$14.95 p
0-07-881205-4, 176 pp., 7⅜ x 9¼

Modula-2 Made Easy

by Herbert Schildt

Herbert Schildt, author of C Made Easy, has written a new "Made Easy" tutorial on the Modula-2 programming language. Modula-2's modular structure allows teams of programmers to write segments that can be easily linked together. In many ways, Modula-2 is more suited to today's competitive programming environment than are C and Pascal. With *Modula-2 Made Easy*, beginning programmers can quickly learn Modula-2 techniques through step-by-step, hands-on exercises. Start with the fundamentals — basic structure, variables, constants, and program control statements — and you'll soon be handling more advanced procedures — pointers, arrays, modules, and co-routines. By the time you finish *Modula-2 Made Easy*, you'll be writing and debugging effective, full-scale applications programs.

$18.95p
0-07-881241-0, 375 pp., 7³/₈ x 9¹/₄

Using Turbo Pascal™
by Steve Wood

Maximize your advanced programming skills with *Using Turbo Pascal™* by Steve Wood. Wood, a programmer for Precision Logic Systems, thoroughly covers Turbo Pascal, including version 3.0, for the experienced programmer. The book discusses program design and Pascal's syntax requirements, develops a useful application of the program, and gives an overview of some of the advanced utilities and features available with Turbo Pascal.

$19.95p
0-07-881148-1, 350 pp., 6¹/₂ x 9¹/₄

Advanced Turbo Pascal®: Programming & Techniques
by Herbert Schildt

For instruction and reference, *Advanced Turbo Pascal®* is an invaluable resource. This guide benefits experienced Turbo Pascal® users who want to build their programming skills. Every stand-alone chapter presents a complete programming topic: sorting and searching; stacks, queues, linked lists, and binary trees; dynamic allocation using pointers; and operating-system interfacing. You'll also examine statistics, encryption and compressed data formats, random

numbers and simulations, expression parsers, converting C and BASIC to Pascal, efficiency, porting and debugging.

$18.95p
0-07-881220-8, 350 pp., 7³/₈ x 9¹/₄

Turbo Pascal® Programmer's Library
by Kris Jamsa and Steven Nameroff

This library of programming tools enables Turbo Pascal® users to write more effective programs that take full advantage of Borland's best-selling compiler. In this varied collection there are utility routines for Pascal macros as well as routines for string and array manipulation, records, pointers, and pipes. You'll also find I/O routines and a discussion of sorting that covers bubble, shell, and quick-sort algorithms. In addition, the authors provide routines for the Turbo Toolbox® and the Turbo Graphix® package. *Turbo Pascal® Library* complements two other Osborne books, *Using Turbo Pascal®* and *Advanced Turbo Pascal®,* and provides programmers with an excellent resource of practical tools.

$18.95p
0-07-881238-0, 300 pp., 7³/₈ x 9¹/₄

C Made Easy
by Herbert Schildt

With Osborne/McGraw-Hill's popular "Made Easy" format, you can learn C programming in no time. Start with the fundamentals and work through the text at your own speed. Schildt begins with general concepts, then introduces functions, libraries, and disk input/output, and finally advanced concepts affecting the C programming environment and UNIX™ operating system. Each chapter covers commands that you can learn to use immediately in the hands-on exercises that follow. If you already know BASIC, you'll find that Schildt's C equivalents will shorten your learning time. *C Made Easy* is a step-by-step tutorial for all beginning C programmers.

$18.95p
0-07-881178-3, 350 pp., 7³/₈ x 9¹/₄

Available at fine bookstores and computer stores everywhere.

For a complimentary catalog of all our current publications contact: Osborne/McGraw-Hill, 2600 Tenth Street, Berkeley, CA 94710

Phone inquiries may be made using our toll-free number. Call 800-227-0900 or 800-772-2531 (in California). TWX 910-366-7277.

Prices subject to change without notice.